ISBN-O-87747-075-8

TABLE OF CONTENTS.

VOLUME II.

CHAPTER I

THE YEAR EIGHTEEN HUNDRED AND THIRTY-FOUR—AFFAIRS IN ZION
AND KIRTLAND.

CHAPTER II.

ORGANIZATION OF THE HIGH COUNCIL—FIRST CASES BEFORE THE
COUNCIL.

IV   CONTENTS.

CONTENTS.

CHAPTER VI.

ZION'S CAMP IN MISSOURI—LETTERS OF GOVERNOR DUNKLIN AND
OTHERS.

CHAPTER VII.

ZION'S CAMP IN MISSOURI—EFFORTS AT ARBITRATION—THE WORD
OF THE LORD.

CHAPTER VIII.

ZION'S CAMP DISBANDED—AN APPEAL.

CHAPTER IX.

RETURN OF THE PROPHET TO KIRTLAND—SUNDRY EVENTS IN MISSOURI.

CHAPTER X.

CHARGES AGAINST THE PROPHET ON HIS RETURN FROM ZION'S CAMP EXPEDITION—TRIAL OF ELDER SYLVESTER SMITH.

CHAPTER XI.

A MOMENT'S PEACE—COUNCIL MEETINGS IN OHIO AND MISSOURI.

VIII CONTENTS.

CHAPTER XII.

CHANGE IN CHURCH PERIODICALS—THE COVENANT OF TITHING—CLOSE
OF THE YEAR 1834.

CHAPTER XIII—1.*

THE LECTURES ON FAITH—TWELVE APOSTLES CHOSEN AND ORDAINED.

CHAPTER XIII—2.*

THE ORGANIZATION OF THE SEVENTIES—BLESSING OF THE FAITHFUL
ELDERS AND SAINTS.

* By typographical error there are two chapters numbered xiii.

CHAPTER XIV.

THE GREAT REVELATION ON PRIESTHOOD.

CHAPTER XV.

THE FIRST MISSION OF THE TWELVE.

CHAPTER XVI.

PROGRESS OF AFFAIRS AT KIRTLAND—DISCOVERY OF THE BOOK OF ABRAHAM.

CHAPTER XVII.

SUNDRY COUNCIL MEETINGS IN VERMONT, OHIO AND NEW YORK.

CHAPTER XXII.

THE MINISTRY OF THE PROPHET IN KIRTLAND.

CHAPTER XXIII.

THE MINISTRY OF THE PROPHET IN KIRTLAND.

CHAPTER XXIV.

MISCELLANEOUS LABORS OF THE PROPHET IN KIRTLAND.

CHAPTER XXV.

THE TROUBLES OF ORSON HYDE AND WILLIAM SMITH—THE BOOK OF ABRAHAM—CLOSE OF THE YEAR.

CHAPTER XXVI.

OPENING OF THE YEAR 1836—THE AMERICAN INDIANS—SPECIAL COUNCIL MEETING IN KIRTLAND.

CHAPTER XXVII.

RECONCILIATION OF THE FIRST PRESIDENCY AND TWELVE APOSTLES— PENTECOSTAL TIMES IN KIRTLAND.

CHAPTER XXVIII.

THE PROPHET'S MINISTRY AND STUDIES IN KIRTLAND.

CHAPTER XXIX.

DEDICATION OF THE KIRTLAND TEMPLE—SPIRITUAL MANIFESTATIONS.

CHAPTER XXX.

THE ORDINANCE OF WASHING OF FEET—VISIONS IN THE KIRTLAND
TEMPLE—THE PROPHET ON ABOLITION.

CHAPTER XXXI.

PREDICTION OF THE PROPHET'S GRANDPARENTS—AGITATION FOR THE
REMOVAL OF THE SAINTS FROM CLAY COUNTY, MISSOURI.

CHAPTER XXXII.

THE PROPHET'S MISSION—LABORS IN MASSACHUSETTS—THE ORGANIZATION OF THE KIRTLAND SAFETY SOCIETY.

CONTENTS.

CHAPTER XXXIII.

MEETINGS OF THE QUORUMS OF PRIESTHOOD IN THE KIRTLAND TEMPLE—
THE PROPHET'S INSTRUCTIONS ON PRIESTHOOD.

CHAPTER XXXIV.

AFFAIRS IN ZION—APOSTASY AT KIRTLAND—APPOINTMENT OF THE
BRITISH MISSION—ITS DEPARTURE FOR ENGLAND.

CHAPTER XXXV.

FINANCIAL CONDITIONS IN VARIOUS NATIONS—PROGRESS OF THE BRITISH
MISSION—CONFERENCES AT FAR WEST AND KIRTLAND.

CHAPTER XXXVI.

THE GATHERING SAINTS—INCREASE IN THE NUMBER OF STAKES CONTEMPLATED—COUNCILS IN ZION AND KIRTLAND—CLOSE OF THE VOLUME.

INTRODUCTION TO VOLUME II.

Summary Review of Volume One.

THE events which make up the first volume of the History of the Church moved forward from the back ground of successive dispensations of the Gospel which preceded the Dispensation of the Fullnes of Times. That volume covered the period from the birth of the Prophet Joseph Smith, 1805, to the close of the year 1833, and included as its chief events: the birth of the Prophet: his first vision of the Father aud the Son; the coming forth of the Book of Mormon; the organization of the Church, April 6th, 1830; the mission to the Lamanites; the gathering of the people from the state of New York, first to Kirtland, Ohio, and subsequently the gathering of many of them to Jackson county, Missouri; the location of the site of the future city of Zion and its temple; the introduction of the doctrine of consecration and stewardship; the experience of the Elders of Israel in their movements back and forth between Kirtland and Zion; the spread of the work throughout the states of the American Union and Canada; the Prophet's own mission to the latter place; the founding of the first Church periodical, *The Evening and Morning Star;* the selection of a number of the revelations of God for publication under the title, "The Book of Commandments;" the establishment of the Mercantile and Literary firms of Zion and Kirtland; the laying of the corner stones of the Kirtland Temple; the planting of a number of settlements in Jackson county, Missouri; the awakening jealousy of the old settlers against the more progressive Saints; the fanning of these flames of jealousy by sectarian priests; the rise of that religio-political persecution which culminated in the terrible suffering of the Saints—the destruction of their printing establishment, the burning of their homes, their final expulsion from Jackson county; also the negotiations between the Saints and the civil authorities of the state of Missouri for reinstatement of the exiles upon their lands. The first volume closed with the narration of these circumstances of discouragement which befell the Saints in their efforts to establish Zion in Missouri.

Summary of Volume Two.

In this second volume is recorded the arrival of a delegation from the exiled Saints in Missouri, seeking advice and the word of the Lord from the Prophet; the organization of Zion's Camp for the deliverance of Zion; its march from Kirtland to Missouri; its rich educational experiences; its disbandment and the return of many of the brethren to Ohio; the establishment of a school for the Elders at Kirtland, the first educational movement in the Church; the discovery of the Book of Abraham; the organization of the first, or Kirtland High Council; the organization of the quorums of the foreign ministry; the Twelve and the Seventy; the publication of the Doctrine and Covenants; the completion and dedication of the Kirtland Temple; the purification and spiritual endowment of the Elders of the Church; the appearance of Messiah in the Temple declaring His acceptance of it; the appearance of Moses, Elias and Elijah, on the same occasion, delivering the keys of their respective dispensations to the Prophet of the Dispensation of the Fullness of Times; the commencement of the ministry of the Twelve among the branches of the Church in the eastern States of the American Union; the misunderstandings that arose between them and the Presidency of the Church; the revelations of God which came in consequence of their misunderstandings, more clearly defining the rights, powers, and relations of the respective quorums of the Priesthood; the peaceful exodus of the Saints from Clay county, Missouri, and the founding of Far West; the opening of the first foreign mission by sending two of the Twelve and several Elders to England; the attempt to mass the several industrial pursuits and temporal interests of the Saints under one general concern, the "Kirtland Safety Society Company;" the failure of that concern in the general financial maelstrom that swept over the country in 1837, hastened also— sad to relate—by the unwise management and dishonesty of some of the incorporators and directors; the manifestation of excessive pride and worldliness on the part of some of the Saints at Kirtland; the disaffection of many hitherto leading Elders of the Church against the Prophet Joseph; the extensive apostasy of many Elders and Saints in Kirtland; with the account of which calamitous events this volume closes.

The Expedition of Zion's Camp.

The time covered by this volume may properly be called the Kirtland period of the Church History, since that city is the chief center of activity. The four years which comprise the period are marked, on the one hand, by rapid doctrinal development, institutional growth, outward enlargement and internal spiritual progress; and, on the other hand, are marked by internal dissensions, abundant manifestations of human weakness and wickedness, resulting in bitterness and apostasy. The period is one in which the Church is manifestly militant, and not always, from surface appearances, triumphant. Yet removed from that period by well nigh three-quarters of a century, one may see now that it was a glorious period, notwithstanding sombre shadows are now and then cast athwart the pathway of the Church's progress. Who can rightly estimate the value of the experiences of that movement for the redemption of Zion, called Zion's Camp? Nothing so completely reveals the worth or worthlessness of human character as expeditions of this description. Men are thrown into such relations with each other that all that is in them, good or bad, comes to the surface. As opportunities in time of war reveal noble or debased natures, so in expeditions such as Zion's Camp the base or exalted phases of human nature are forced to the surface, and are known and read of men. God, it appears, was about to choose His foreign ministry, His Especial Witnesses to the world, the Twelve and the Seventy. After the expedition of Zion's Camp He could choose them from among men who had offered their all in sacrifice—even to life itself—for the work's sake. Are not such manifestly fitter witnesses than those who are untried? Will it be argued that to the All-knowing the untried are as well known as the tried, and that God needed no such demonstration of fidelity as was afforded by the expedition of Zion's Camp in order to guide Him in the choice of His Witnesses to the nations of the earth? If so, my answer would be an acquiescence—God needs no such expedition in order to reveal to Him the worthiness of those who shall be His special Witnesses. But what of the world—what of men? Do not they need some such evidence back of those who shall testify of a new dispensation of the Gospel? Will not men have more regard for the testimony of Witnesses who have offered their all in sacrifice for any given work, than for the testimony of witnesses who have made no such sacrifice? Undoubtedly. Not for God's guidance, then, but for the qualification of the Witnesses in the eyes of men was the expedition of Zion's Camp in part conceived and executed. Also that those men who, under God— the Prophet Joseph Smith and the Three Witness to the Book of Mormon—were to make choice of especial Witnesses might know whom to select because of actually demonstrated fitness and worthiness.

Moreover there were men in that expedition who later will be called upon to conduct larger expeditions much of the same character—an exodus of thousands from Missouri; an exodus of tens of thousands from the confines of the United States, a thousand miles into the wilderness of the Rocky Mountains. May not the Lord have designed in part this expedition of Zion's Camp for their instruction, for their training? The leaders of these later movements are all there—Brigham Young, Heber C. Kimball, Orson Pratt, Parley P. Pratt, Charles C Rich, George A. Smith, Wilford Woodruff and many more. It is significant, too, that Brigham Young at least sensed the true importance of the Zion's Camp expedition. That expedition for the redemption of Zion was regarded by many weak-faithed Saints as a sad failure, a humiliation of a presumptuous prophet. One of these attempted to ridicule it in the presence of Brigham Young, as a case of marching men up a hill to march them down again. "Well," said the scoffer, "what did you gain on this useless journey to Missouri with Joseph Smith?" "All we went for," promptly replied Brigham Young. "I would not exchange the *experience* gained in that expedition for all the wealth of Geauga county." A remark which proves that Brigham Young had a keen insight into the purpose of the Zion's Camp movement.

First Educational Movement of the Church.

The value of the educational movement in the Church by the establishment of a school for the Elders in Kirtland, cannot be fully appreciated even yet. It stands as a direct contradiction to the oft-repeated charges that Mormonism seeks to thrive through the ignorance of its devotees. "Seek ye diligently, and teach one another words of wisdom," was an admonition the Church in the Kirtland period of its history sought earnestly to carry into effect. "Yea, seek ye out of the best books words of wisdom: seek learning even by study, and also by faith." To the sphere of their learning there were no limitations set. "Teach ye diligently," said the Lord, "and my grace shall attend you, that you may be instructed more perfectly in theory, in principle, in doctrine, in the law of the Gospel, in all things that pertain unto the kingdom of God, that are expedient for you to understand; of things both in heaven and in the earth, and under the earth; things which have been, things which are, things which must shortly come to pass; things which are at home, things which are abroad; the wars and the perplexities of the nations, and the judgments which are on the land, and a knowledge also of countries and of kingdoms." I know of nothing that lies outside this boundless field of research into which the Elders of the Church especially were invited—nay, commanded, to enter. It comprehends the whole possible sphere of human investigation; and furnishes all necessary contradiction to the theory that the Church at any time contemplated an ignorant ministry. By intelligence, not stupidity; by knowledge, not ignorance, has the Church from the very beginning hoped to succeed in her mission.

The Organization of the Foreign Ministry.

It is during the Kirtland period of her history also that the Church raised her eyes and for the first time gazed out upon the world-wide sphere of her future activities. Until now she had confined her missions and labors to the United States and Canada. But lo! a foreign minis try had been organized, a quorum of Twelve Apostles and two quorums of Seventy had been called into existence and ordained. Was that without significance? Do ordinations count for nothing, or is there virtue in divine appointment? Undoubtedly there is power in ordinances, in divine appointments: "Joshua the son of Nun was full of the spirit of wisdom; for Moses had laid his hands upon him and the children of Israel hearkened unto him and did as the Lord commanded Moses." While Timothy, the young Christian evangelist, was admonished by Paul to stir up the gift of God which was in him by the putting on of the Apostle's hands. Since, then, there is virtue in ordinations of divine appointing, it is but to be expected that the Church of Christ in this last dispensation would be influenced by the appointment and ordination of her foreign ministry. It was but a proper sequence of the appointment of this ministry that Apostles and their associates should be sent to England. The Church of Jesus Christ of Latter-day Saints was never intended to be merely an American sect of religion. It is a new and the last dispensation of the Christian religion—the Dispensation of the Fullness of Times, the dispensation into which will be gathered all former dispensations of the Gospel of Christ; all keys of authority, all powers, all gifts, all graces essential to the welfare and salvation of man—all that is essential to the completion of the mission of the Christian religion. The mission of the Church in such a dispensation is general not local, world-embracing. Had it been less than one of the world's great movements, Mormonism had been inadequate to the world's needs—less than sufficient for a world's redemption. There was marked, therefore, a mighty bound forward in the progress of the work when the foreign ministry of the Church was organized, and a mission appointed to England. The work would have perished had it not taken this step forward. The Church had reached that stage of its development when there must be a forward movement. Things do not stand inert in this world. Inertia is death. In progress only is there life. The thing that does not grow dies. The very rocks increase or decay. For the time being the elements on which the Church lived were exhausted in the land where it came forth. The material which had been gathered into it was passing through tne crucible. There was need of an enlargement of action, a necessity for new elements being brought into the body religious. That enlargement of action was found in opening the British mission. The new elements essential to the preservation of the work were found in the English people; for among them were given the evidences of the existence of the spiritual light and life which had characterized the work at its coming forth: and as that mission had been directly appointed by the Prophet Joseph Smith, it supplied the proofs that God was still with him, honored the authority which had been given him, and still directed his movements in the administration of the affairs of the Church; for it was the prompting of the Spirit of God in the Prophet, that led to the appointment of this first foreign mission. These considerations made the opening of the British mission an epoch in the history of the Church.

The Restoration of the Keys for the Gathering of Israel.

The work of God was also greatly enlarged during this Kirtland period, by the appearance of Moses and Elias and Elijah, and bestowing upon the Prophet the keys of their respective dispensations. Let us contemplate the event. "Moses appeared before us," says the Prophet, "and committed unto us the keys of the gathering of Israel, from the four parts of the earth, and the leading of the ten tribes from the land of the north." Who, at the time comprehended the full import of this incident? Who comprehends it now? From the beginning of the great Latter-day work men had their attention directed to the gathering of Israel and the establishment of Zion and Jerusalem as a part of the purposes of God to be accomplished in the work. The angel Moroni on the occasion of his first visit to the Prophet Joseph, quoted a number of Old Testament scriptures referring to the Lord's promises concerning the redemption of Judah and Jerusalem;[*] also concerning the gathering of Israel from all the lands whither they had been driven.[†] Numerous are the prophecies relating to the return of Israel from the land of the north, and other parts of the earth, into which they were driven in the day of their rebellion and apostasy;[‡] but it occurred to no one that before these prophecies could be fulfilled Israel's great prophet, Moses, who held the keys of the dispensation pertaining to the gathering of Israel, must come and give to men the authority to proceed with that work. The moment he appears, however, and gives such authority, the propriety of it, the fitnes of it is apparent. The appearance of Moses was also in proper sequence of events in the development of the great Latter-day work. Although, as already stated, the gathering of Israel in the last days had been made a prominent feature in the communication of Moroni to the Prophet Joseph, and the subject also of some other early revelations to the Church § not until the foreign ministry had been organized—the Twelve and the Seventy—the quorums of Priesthood on which rests the re-

* See Mal. iii: 1-7.

† Isaiah xi: 11-16; also History of the Church, vol. I, pp. 12, 13.

‡ Following are a few of the most prominent of these prophecies: Deut. xxx: 1-6; Isaiah ii: 1-4; Jeremiah iii, 12-18. Also xvi: 4-18; xxiii: 1-8, and xxxi: 7-14.

§ See Doc. & Cov. sec. xlv: 15-71, this revelation was given in 1831; also Doc. & Cov. sec. cxxxiii. This is the revelation called the appendix and was given November 3, 1831.

sponsibility to travel in all the world and preach the Gospel and gather Israel—not until this ministry was organized did Moses appear and commit the keys of the gathering of Israel from the four parts of the earth. What order is here? The organization of the foreign ministry to go into all the nations of earth, and then the coming of Moses to commit the keys of the gathering of Israel from the four parts of the earth, and the leading of the ten tribes from the land of the north. In this incident as in a thousand others in the great work of God in the last days, the evidence of a divine wisdom having regard for the eternal fitness of things, for the proper sequence in the order of events in the development of the Lord's purposes, is apparent. Note, too, the spiritual effect opon the Saints of the restoration of these keys of the gathering of Israel. Before the mission for England under Elders Kimball and Hyde departed, the prophet enjoined them to adhere strictly to the first principles of the Gospel, and say nothing for the present in relation to the gathering; this, doubtless on account of the unsettled condition of the Church at the time. Similar instructions, and for the same reason, were given to the Twelve Apostles in 1839 when they went on their mission to England. But the Saints could not be kept in ignorance of these matters. No sooner were the people baptized than they were seized with a desire to gather with the main body of the Church. "I find it is difficult to keep anything from the Saints," writes Elder Taylor in his journal of this period, "for the Spirit of God reveals it to them.   *   *   *   *   Some time ago Sister Mitchell dreamed that she, her husband and a number of others were on board a vessel, and that there were other vessels, loaded with Saints, going somewhere. She felt very happy and was rejoicing in the Lord." Another sister, Elder Taylor informs us, had a similar dream, and was informed that all the Saints were going. Neither of these sisters nor any of the Saints at that time, knew anything about the principle of gathering, yet all were anxious to leave their homes, their kindred and the associations of a lifetime, to join the main body of the Church in a distant land, the members of which were total strangers to them.* The same spirit has rested upon the people in every nation where the Gospel has been received. There has been little need of preaching the gathering, the people as a rule have had to be restrained rather than encouraged in the matter of gathering to Zion and her stakes.

The Spirit of Gathering on the Jews.

During the last ten years the world has witnessed a remarkable change of spirit come over the Jewish race. We hear of Jewish aspirations for national existence; for the perpetuation of the Jewish customs

* Life of John Taylor, p. 96.

and Jewish ideals. After saying so long, "May we celebrate the next Passover in Jerusalem," the thought at last seems to have occurred to some Jewish minds that if that expressed wish is ever realized, some practical steps must be taken looking to the actual achievement of that possibility—which has given rise among the Jews to what is called the "Zionite Movement." The keynotes of that movement are heard in the following utterances of some of the leaders in explanation of it: "We want to resume the broken thread of our national existence; we want to show to the world the moral strength, the intellectual power of the Jewish people. We want a place where the race can be centralized."* "It is for these Jews [of Russia, Roumania and Galicia] that the name of their country [Palestine] spells 'Hope.' I should not be a man if I did not realize that for these persecuted Jews, Jerusalem spells reason, justice, manhood and integrity"† "Jewish nationalism on a modern basis in Palestine, the old home of the people."‡ "Palestine needs a people, Israel needs a country. Give the country without a people, to the people without a country."§ In a word, it is the purpose of "Zionism" to redeem Palestine and give it back to Jewish control—create, in fact, a Jewish state in the land promised to their fathers.

Of course, for hundreds of years there has been talk of the Jews returning to Jerusalem, and from time to time societies have been formed to keep alive that hope, and keep the Jew's face turned toward the chief city and land of his forefathers; but little was achieved by those societies, however, except to foster the hope of Israel's return in the heart of a widely dispersed, persecuted and discouraged race, who have waited long for the realization of the promises made to their fathers. I say but "little" was accomplished by the various Jewish societies existing before the Zionite movement began beyond fostering the hope of Israel based on the predictions of their prophets; but that "little" was much. It was nourishing in secret and through ages of darkness that spark of fire which when touched with the breath of God should burst forth into a flame that not all the world could stay. They made possible this larger movement, now attracting the attention of the world, and known as the "Zionite Movement;" which, in reality, is but the federation of all Jewish societies which have had for their purpose the realization of the hopes of scattered Israel.

"Zionism" is considered to have grown out of the persecution of the Jews during the last eighteen years in such European countries as Russia, France, Germany, and Roumania. It held its first general confer-

* Leon Zeltekoff
† Rabbi Emil G. Hirsch.
‡ Max Nordau.
§ Israel Zangwill.

ence in August, 1897, in Basle, Switzerland; and since then has continued to hold annual conferences that have steadily increased both in interest and the number of delegates representing various Jewish societies, until now it takes on the appearance of one of the world's great movements. It is not so much a religious movement as a racial one: for prominent Jews of all shades of both political and religious opinions have participated in it under the statesmanlike leadership of Doctor Herzel of Austria.   Not to persecution alone, however, is due this strange awakening desire on the part of the Jews to return to the city and the land of their fathers; but to the fact of the restoration of the keys of the gathering of Israel by Moses to the Prophet of the Dispensation of the Fullness of Times.   Under the divine authority restored by Moses, Joseph Smith sent an Apostle of the Lord Jesus Christ to the land of Palestine to bless it and dedicate it once more to the Lord for the return of His people.   This Apostle was Orson Hyde, and he performed his mission in 1840-2.   In 1872 an Apostolic delegation consisting of the late Presidents George A. Smith and Lorenzo Snow were sent to Palestine.   The purpose of their mission, in part, is thus stated in President Young's letter of appointment to George A. Smith: "When you get to the land of Palestine, we wish you to dedicate and consecrate that land to the Lord, that it may be blessed with fruitfulness, preparatory to the return of the Jews, in fulfillment of prophecy and the accomplishment of the purposes of our heavenly Father."*

Acting, then, under the divine authority restored to earth by the Prophet Moses, this Apostolic delegation—as well as the Apostle first sent—from the summit of Mount Olivet blessed the land, and again dedicated it for the return of the Jews.   It is not strange, therefore, to those who look upon such a movement as Zionism in connection with faith in God's great latter-day work, to see this spirit now moving upon the minds of the Jewish people prompting their return to the land of their fathers. It is but the breath of God upon their souls turning their hearts to the promises made to the fathers.   It is but the fulfillment in part of one of the many prophecies of the Book of Mormon relating to the gathering of Israel, viz: "It shall come to pass that the Lord God shall commence His work among all nations, kindreds, tongues, and people, to bring about the restoration of His people upon the earth." The spirit attendant upon the restoration of the keys of authority to gather Israel from the four quarters of the earth, and the exercise of that divine authority, though unrecognized as yet by the world, is the real cause of this movement Palestine-ward by the Jews.

Elijah's Mission.

The work accomplished by Elijah in giving to the Prophet Joseph the particular dispensation of the Priesthood which should plant in the

* Biography of Lorenzo Snow, p. 496.

hearts of the children the promises made to the fathers—lest the whole earth should be utterly wasted at His coming*—is attended by evidences of virtue and power of God no less palpable than those which bear witness to the virtue and power of God in the work accomplished by Moses in giving to the Prophet the keys of authority for the gathering of Israel. The work done by Elijah was to open the door of salvation for the dead. From that event comes the knowledge of the principles by which the saving power of the Gospel may be applied to men who have died without receiving its benefits in this life. From of old men had read in the scriptures that Messiah would bring out the prisoners from the prison, and them that sit in darkness out of the prison house;† that in addition to being given as a restorer of the tribes of Jacob and a light to the gentiles, the Messiah should have power to say to the prisoners, "Go forth; to them that sit in darkness, show yourselves;"‡ "to proclaim liberty to the captives, and the opening of the prison to them that are bound."§ From the beginning of Christianity men had read in the New Testament how Jesus had once suffered for sins, the just for the unjust; and how that being put to death in the flesh He was quickened by the Spirit by which He went and preached to the spirits in prison which were disobedient when the long suffering of God waited in the days of Noah.‖ Also they read how for this cause was the Gospel preached to them that are dead that they might be judged as men are in the flesh, but live according to God in the spirit;** also the reasoning of Paul to the effect that if there was no resurrection of the dead, why, then, were the Saints baptized for the dead;†† also how the fathers without those of later generations cannot be made perfect.‡‡ All of which passages, however, have been regarded as among the mysteries of the word of God, incomprehensible, dark. But touched by the Prophet Elijah's hand, imparting to them their true import, how bright they glow with spiritual light and life! and what a sense of largeness and power is given to the Gospel of Jesus Christ when from this mission of Elijah's there comes the power to apply the principles and ordinances of salvation to all the children of men (save the sons of perdition; and these, thank God! are but few) in all ages of the world, and whether living or dead! How the horizon of things respecting the Gospel of Christ is pushed back from the walled-in limits of that pseudo-Christianity current among men, by this spirit and power of Elijah that has come into the

* Church History Vol. I p. 12, also Mal. iv: 5, 6.

† Isaiah xlii: 7.

‡ Ibid. xlix: 6-9.

§ Ibid. lxi: I.

‖ I Peter iii: 18-20.

** Ibid. iv: 6.

†† I. Cor. xv: 29

‡‡ Heb. xi.

world! The fact that such a spirit has come into the world is sustained
by palpable evidences. The truth of my statement will be recognized
when I say that within the last fifty years there has arisen throughout
the world an increased spirit of interest among men concerning their
ancestors that scarcely stops this side of the marvelous. In all lands
men are earnestly seeking for their genealogies, and many volumes are
issued from the press annually in which the pedigrees of men of all
sorts and conditions are given. Some may be said to be possessed almost of a mania, on this subject so ardent are they in seeking for a
knowledge of their fore-fathers, and this all quite apart from any direct
work that is being done along the same lines by the Latter-day Saints;
though the work of the Saints in the temples for their dead is greatly
helped by this outside circumstance to which I call attention. Why and
whence this spirit in the hearts of the children which turns the attention of men to the fathers of former generations, if it is not a consequence of the fulfillment of Elijah's predicted mission that before the
great and dreadful day of the Lord should come he [Elijah] would be
sent to turn the heart of the children to the fathers, and the heart of
the fathers to the children?*

Of the work done by the Latter-day Saints in consequence of the
restoration of these special keys of the Priesthood by the hand of Elijah
I need scarcely speak. That the spirit which came into the world by
reason of Elijah's special dispensation of authority to Joseph Smith is
working upon the hearts of the Latter-day Saints is evidenced by the
building of the beautiful temple at Nauvoo, and by the erection of the
world-famed temple in Salt Lake City; also by the erection of magnifi-
cent temples in Logan, Manti and St. George—all in Utah. These temples have all been erected in response to the diffusion of that spirit
that attended upon Elijah's mission; and are evidences in stone that
the Saints have partaken of that spirit which turns the hearts of the
children to the fathers. Another palpable evidence to the same great
truth is seen in the throngs which daily visit these temples to perform
the ordinances of salvation for the dead; not only baptism for the dead,
but also the confirmations, ordinations and sealings by which the
fathers shall be prepared for the kingdom of God, and all the families
of men be set in order, united together by bonds, covenants and established relations that shall be in harmony with that heavenly kingdom
which the redeemed of God shall inherit. The full importance of this
work—its height and depth—is not yet appreciated by the children of
men; but so great it is that the period of our Church History which
witnesses its beginning—even if it were the only achievement—must
ever be regarded as an important period.

* Mal. 4; 5, 6.

Calamitous Events.

As for the calamitous events of the Church during the Kirtland period, what shall we say of them? Are they to be accounted wholly deplorable, or as part of that experience of the Church which makes for advancement? Unquestionably every experience is of value to an individual or an organization. Some experiences may be sad, and accounted at the time as disastrous; but are they really so? The rough wind which shakes it helps the young and slow-growing oak; for by reason of this very shaking the tree takes firmer hold of the earth; wider spread the roots; deeper down into the soil are they thrust, until the sapling, once so easily shaken, becomes a monarch in the forest, mocks the howling tempest, until its height and frame become worthy of the land and atmosphere in which it grows a giant tree. So may grow a government—civil or ecclesiastical—so may grow the Church, helped by the adverse circumstances which shake it to the very foundations on which it rests. Profitable if not sweet are the uses of adversity. As the winter's wind when it bites and blows upon man's body is no flatterer, but feelingly persuades him what he is, so the adverse circumstances which overtake an organization, such as the Church of Christ, may be very profitable to it. Such rebellions and apostasies as occurred in this Kirtland period of the Church's history but test and exhibit the strength of the fabric. Such circumstances force a review of the work as far as accomplished. The whole is re-examined to see if in it there is any flaw or defect; if any worthless material is being worked into its structure. Hence periods usually considered calamitous are accompanied by corrections of what may be wrong; and the body religious is purified by the expulsion of those whose rebellion and apostasy but prove them unworthy of the Lord's work. Let me be rightly understood here. I am not contending that adverse circumstances, rebellions and apostasies are in themselves good. Whatever may be the over-ruled results to the body religious, rebellion and apostasy spell condemnation and the destruction of spiritual life for the individuals overtaken by such calamities. But so long as human nature is what it now is—weak and sinful—just so long as out of that intractable material the Church of Christ has the mission to prepare men for the Father's kingdom, just so long will there be occasional calamities periods in the history of the Church such as was the year 1837 at Kirtland. But what after all are such periods but times of purification, of cleansing? During the previous years of success in the ministry, there had been gathered into the Church all classes of men. As in former dispensations of the Gospel, so in this last dispensation; the kingdom of heaven is like unto a net cast into the sea, that gathers of every kind of fish; and when it is full, they draw it to shore, and sit down, and gather the good into vessels, and cast the bad away. The first step in the process of correcting human nature is to discover its defects. It may not always follow that when the defects are made known they will be corrected. But it is true that no correction will be made until the necessity of correction is manifest, until the defects are pointed out. Hence God has said: "If men will come unto me, I will show unto them their weaknesses." But, unhappily, it sometimes is the case that men resist God, they love their sins, they become hardened in their iniquity, they resist the Spirit, and prove themselves unworthy of the Father's kingdom. What then? Shall they pollute that kingdom, or shall they be cast out as material unfitted for the Master's use, and of their own volition choose to remain so? There can be but one reasonable answer to the question. They refuse to go peaceably, however. They are boisterous, they accuse the innocent, they justify their own course, they seek to wreck the Church, to bring to pass chaos; and in the midst of this disorder they are cast out; and although this may not always end their power to work mischief, or create annoyance for the body-religious—for the power to work evil is still with them—yet the Church is rid of them, and in no way can be regarded as responsible for their wickedness. It is our custom to enumerate such scenes as among the calamitous events of the Church; and they are so, in some aspects of the case. As already remarked it is a calamitous time for those who are cast out, for they are overcome of the evil one; and as the heavens wept when the Son of the Morning and his following were cast out of heaven, so it is to be expected that the Saints will be sad, and sorrow over those who are overcome of the adversary. But for the Church herself it is well that this intractable material is gotten rid of; that the body religious is purged of those who can only be a source of weakness and of shame to her. She is helped by the event; purified by it; strengthened; made more acceptable with God and pleasing to reasonable men. It is only in a modified sense, then, that this latter part of the Kirtland period of the Church's history can be regarded as a calamitous time. There is more adversity yet to follow in the experience of the Saints; much distress and many sore trials; and so shall there continue to be such times of trial as long as the Church remains the Church militant. Not until she becomes the Church triumphant, and is glorified by the presence of her Great Head, the Lord Jesus Christ, can the Saints hope for an absolute discontinuance of the occasional recurrence of what are generally considered trying or calamitous events.

HISTORY

OF THE

CHURCH OF JESUS CHRIST OF LATTER-DAY SAINTS

VOL. II.

HISTORY

OF THE

CHURCH OF JESUS CHRIST

——OF——

LATTER-DAY SAINTS.

PERIOD I.

HISTORY OF JOSEPH SMITH, THE PROPHET.

CHAPTER I.

THE YEAR EIGHTEEN HUNDRED AND THIRTY - FOUR—AFFAIRS IN ZION AND KIRTLAND.

January 1, 1834.—The scattered Saints in Missouri commenced the year eighteen hundred and thirty-four, with a conference, which they held in Clay county, on the first day of January, at which Bishop Partridge presided. After transacting much business relative to comforting and strengthening the scattered members of the Church, it was

Condition of the Saints in Missouri.

Resolved, That Lyman Wight and Parley P. Pratt be sent as special messengers, to represent the situation of the scattered brethren in Missouri, to the Presidency and Church in Kirtland, and ask their advice.

1 Vol II

On the evening of the 2nd of January, a Bishop's court
assembled in Kirtland to investigate the case
of Wesley Hurlburt, against whom charges
had been preferred by Harriet Howe and others
to the effect "that Hurlburt had denied the faith, spoken
reproachfully of the Church, did not believe Joseph was
a true Prophet," etc. Hurlburt was in the place, but did
not appear before the court, consequently was cut off.

Excommuni-
cation of Wes-
ley Hurlburt.

The threats of the mob about Kirtland through the fall
and winter had been such as to cause the
brethren to be constantly on the lookout, and
those who labored on the temple were engaged at night
watching to protect the walls they had laid during the
day, from threatened violence. On the morning of the
8th of January, about 1 o'clock, the inhabitants of Kirtland were alarmed by the firing of about thirteen rounds
of cannon, by the mob, on the hill about half a mile
northwest of the village.*

Mob Threats
at Kirtland.

On the evening of the 11th of January, Joseph Smith,
Jun., Frederick G. Williams, Newel K. Whitney, John Johnson, Oliver Cowdery, and
Orson Hyde united in prayer, and asked the Lord to grant
the following petitions:

A Prayer.

1.—That the Lord would grant that our lives might be
precious in His sight; that He would watch over our persons, and give His angels charge concerning us and our
families, that no evil nor unseen hand might be permitted
to harm us.

2.—That the Lord would also hold the lives of all the
United Order as sacred, and not suffer that any of them
should be taken.

---

* Of these days in Kirtland Elder Heber C. Kimball in his Journal says: "The
Church was in a state of poverty and distress, in consequence of which it appeared
almost impossible that the commandments could be fulfilled [relative to the Kirtland Temple]; at the same time our enemies were raging and threatening destruction upon us, and we had to guard ourselves night after night, and for weeks were
not permitted to take off our clothes, and were obliged to lay with our fire locks in
our arms."—*Times and Seasons*, vol. vi, p. 771.

3.—That the Lord would grant that Brother Joseph might prevail over his enemy, even Dr. Hurlburt, who has threatened his life, whom Joseph has caused to be taken with a precept; that the Lord would fill the heart of the court with a spirit to do justice, and cause that the law of the land may be magnified in bringing Hurlburt to justice.

4.—That the Lord in the order of His providence, would provide the Bishop of this Church [at Kirtland] with means sufficient to discharge every debt, in due season, that the Order owes, that the Church may not be brought into disrepute, and the Saints be afflicted by the hands of their enemies.

5.—That the Lord would protect our printing press from the hands of evil men, and give us means to send forth His record, even His Gospel, that the ears of all may hear it; and also that we may print His Scriptures; and also that He would give those who were appointed to conduct the press, wisdom sufficient that the cause may not be hindered, but that men's eyes may thereby be opened to see the truth.

6.—That the Lord would deliver Zion, and gather in His scattered people to possess it in peace; and also, while in their dispersion, that He would provide for them that they perish not from hunger or cold; and finally, that God, in the name of Jesus, would gather His elect speedily, and unveil His face, that His Saints might behold His glory, and dwell with Him.   Amen.

As soon as the Governor of Missouri intimated, or the news began to circulate, that the "Mormons" (as the people called the members of the Church), would be restored to their possessions in Jackson county (if they desired to be), the priests of all denominations, as the men behind the scene, with the mob, began to set their springs in motion, and by their secret councils, and false publications and insinuations, soured the public mind, and prevented the administration

Efforts of Sectarian Priests Against Restoration of Exiles.

of the laws, so that anything like a return to their houses
and lands, or recovery of damages for losses sustained,
seemed as distant as the day of judgment. The powers
of wickedness and darkness walked hand in hand together, and the Saints mourned.

January 16.—I visited Brother Jenkins Salisbury, and
spent the night. O Lord! keep us and my family safe,
until I return unto them; O my God, have mercy on my
brethren in Zion, for Christ's sake. Amen.

January 22.—The Presidency of the High Priesthood
wrote from Kirtland to the brethren in Christ Jesus,
scattered from Zion—scattered abroad from the land of
their inheritance:

THE ELDERS OF THE CHURCH IN KIRTLAND, TO THEIR
BRETHREN ABROAD.*

Dear Brethren in Christ, and Companions in Tribulation:

When we call to remembrance the ties with which we are bound
to those who embrace the everlasting covenant, and the fellowship
and love with which the hearts of the children of our Lord's kingdom should be united, we cherish a belief that you will bear with
us, when we take this course to communicate to you some of the many
thoughts which occupy our minds, and press with continued weight
upon our hearts, as we reflect upon the vast importance and responsi-

* The use of "abroad" here does not have reference to foreign lands, but means
those who were scattered from their homes in Missouri.

This communication of the Elders of the Church at Kirtland, to their brethren
scattered abroad, does not appear in the History of the Prophet, but is found in
the *Evening and Morning Star,* Vol. II, Nos. 17, 18, 19. The document is evidently dictated by the Prophet and is of such doctrinal importance that it is
thought proper to give it place in the body of the Church History. It treats of the
origin of law, human and divine, and man's relations thereto; the antiquity of the
Gospel; the virtue of the atonement of Christ; the importance of men in this
age being in communication with God through the means of revelation; the bitterness and fate of apostates. The document is a complete refutation of the charges
of bad motives behind the conduct of the Saints. No man, I believe, can read this
document and then believe that those who issued it were evil disposed men bent on
deceiving mankind.

The late President Daniel H. Wells was wont to say that some time previous to
his joining the Church he was satisfied that Joseph Smith was an inspired man
because of his intuitive knowledge of the fundamental principles of law—a view
that will be confirmed by a perusal of the parts of this communication which deal
with the origin, force, and relations of law.

bility of your callings, in the sight of the Master of the vineyard.
And though our communications to you may be frequent, yet we
believe they will be received on your part with brotherly feelings;
and that from us your unworthy brethren, you will suffer a word of
exhortation to have place in your hearts, as you see the great extent
of the power and dominion of the prince of darkness, and realize
how vast the numbers are who are crowding the road to death without ever giving heed to the cheering sound of the Gospel of our
Lord Jesus Christ.

Consider for a moment, brethren, the fulfillment of the words of
the prophet; for we behold that darkness covers the earth, and
gross darkness the minds of the inhabitants thereof—that crimes of
every description are increasing among men—vices of great enor-
mity are practiced—the rising generation growing up in the fullness
of pride and arrogance—the aged losing every sense of conviction,
and seemingly banishing every thought of a day of retribution—
intemperance, immorality, extravagance, pride, blindness of heart,
idolatry, the loss of natural affection; the love of this world, and
indifference toward the things of eternity increasing among those
who profess a belief in the religion of heaven, and infidelity spreading
itself in consequence of the same—men giving themselves up to
commit acts of the foulest kind, and deeds of the blackest dye,
blaspheming, defrauding, blasting the reputation of neighbors, stealing, robbing, murdering; advocating error and opposing the truth,
forsaking the covenant of heaven, and denying the faith of Jesus—
and in the midst of all this, the day of the Lord fast approaching
when none except those who have won the wedding garment will be
permitted to eat and drink in the presence of the Bridegroom, the
Prince of Peace!

Impressed with the truth of these facts what can be the feelings
of those who have been partakers of the heavenly gift and have
tasted the good word of God, and the powers of the world to come?
Who but those who can see the awful precipice upon which the world
of mankind stands in this generation, can labor in the vineyard of
the Lord without feeling a sense of the world's deplorable situation?
Who but those who have duly considered the condescension of the
Father of our spirits, in providing a sacrifice for His creatures, a
plan of redemption, a power of atonement, a scheme of salvation,
having as its great objects, the bringing of men back into the presence of the King of heaven, crowning them in the celestial glory,
and making them heirs with the Son to that inheritance which is
incorruptible, undefiled, and which fadeth not away—who but such
can realize the importance of a perfect walk before all men, and a

diligence in calling upon all men to partake of these blessings? How indescribably glorious are these things to mankind! Of a truth they may be considered tidings of great joy to all people; and tidings, too, that ought to fill the earth and cheer the hearts of every one when sounded in his ears. The reflection that everyone is to receive according to his own diligence and perseverance while in the vineyard, ought to inspire everyone who is called to be a minister of these glad tidings, to so improve his talent that he may gain other talents, that when the Master sits down to take an account of the conduct of His servants, it may be said, Well done, good and faithful servant: thou hast been faithful over a few things; I will now make thee ruler over many things: enter thou into the joy of thy Lord.

Some may pretend to say that the world in this age is fast increasing in righteousness; that the dark ages of superstition and blindness have passed, when the faith of Christ was known and held only by a few, when ecclesiastic power had an almost universal control over Christendom, and the consciences of men were bound by the strong chains of priestly power: but now, the gloomy cloud is burst, and the Gospel is shining with all the resplendent glory of an apostolic day; and that the kingdom of the Messiah is greatly spreading, that the Gospel of our Lord is carried to divers nations of the earth, the Scriptures translating into different tongues; the ministers of truth crossing the vast deep to proclaim to men in darkness a risen Savior, and to erect the standard of Emanuel where light has never shone; and that the idol is destroyed, the temple of images forsaken; and those who but a short time previous followed the traditions of their fathers and sacrificed their own flesh to appease the wrath of some imaginary god, are now raising their voices in the worship of the Most High, and are lifting their thoughts up to Him with the full expectation that one day they will meet with a joyful reception in His everlasting kingdom!

But a moment's candid reflection upon the principles of these systems, the manner in which they are conducted, the individuals employed, the apparent object held out as an inducement to cause them to act, we think, is sufficient for every candid man to draw a conclusion in his own mind whether this is the order of heaven or not. We deem it a just principle, and it is one the force of which we believe ought to be duly considered by every individual, that all men are created equal, and that all have the privilege of thinking for themselves upon all matters relative to conscience. Consequently, then, we are not disposed, had we the power, to deprive any one of exercising that free independence of mind which heaven has so graciously bestowed upon the human family as one of its choicest gifts; but we take the liberty (and this we have a right to do) of looking at this order of things a few moments, and contrasting it with the order of God as we find it in the sacred Scriptures. In this review, however, we shall present the points as we consider they were really designed by the great Giver to be understood, and the happy result arising from a performance of the requirements of heaven as revealed to every one who obeys them; and the consequence attending a false construction, a misrepresentation, or a forced meaning that was never designed in the mind of the Lord when He condescended to speak from the heavens to men for their salvation.

Previous to entering upon a subject of so great moment to the human family there is a prominent item which suggests itself to our minds, which, here, in few words, we wish to discuss: All regularly organized and well established governments have certain laws by which, more or less, the innocent are protected and the guilty punished. The fact admitted, that certain laws are good, equitable and just, ought to be binding upon the individual who admits this, and lead him to observe in the strictest manner an obedience to those laws. These laws when violated, or broken by the individual, must, in justice, convict his mind with a double force, if possible, of the extent and magnitude of his crime; because he could have no plea of ignorance to produce; and his act of transgression was openly committed against light and knowledge. But the individual who may be ignorant and imperceptibly transgresses or violates laws, though the voice of the country requires that he should suffer, yet he will never feel that remorse of conscience that the other will, and that keen, cutting reflection will never rise in his breast that otherwise would, had he done the deed, or committed the offense in full conviction that he was breaking the law of his country, and having previously acknowledged the same to be just. It is not our intention by these remarks, to attempt to place the law of man on a parallel with the law of heaven; because we do not consider that it is formed in the same wisdom and propriety; neither do we consider that it is sufficient in itself to bestow anything on man in comparison with the law of heaven, even should it promise it. The laws of men may guarantee to a people protection in the honorable pursuits of this life, and the temporal happiness arising from a protection against unjust insults and injuries: and when this is said, all is said, that can be in truth, of the power, extent, and influence of the laws of men, exclusive of the law of God. The law of heaven is presented to man, and as such guarantees to all who obey it a reward far beyond any earthly consideration; though it does not promise that the believer in every age should be exempt from the afflictions and troubles arising from different sources in consequence of the acts of wicked men on earth. Still in the midst of all this there is a promise predicated upon the fact that it is the law of heaven, which transcends the law of man, as far as eternal life the temporal; and as the blessings which God is able to give, are greater than those which can be given by man.   Then, certainly, if the law of man is binding upon man when acknowledged, how much more must the law of heaven be!   And as much as the law of heaven is more perfect than the law of man, so much greater must be the reward if obeyed. The law of man promises safety in temporal life; but the law of God promises that life which is eternal, even an inheritance at God's own right hand, secure from all the powers of the wicked one.

We consider that God has created man with a mind capable of instruction, and a faculty which may be enlarged in proportion to the heed and diligence given to the light communicated from heaven to the intellect; and that the nearer man approaches perfection, the clearer are his views, and the greater his enjoyments, till he has overcome the evils of his life and lost every desire for sin; and like the ancients, arrives at that point of faith where he is wrapped in the power and glory of his Maker, and is caught up to dwell with Him.   But we consider that this is a station to which no man ever arrived in a moment: he must have been instructed in the government and laws of that kingdom by proper degrees, until his mind is capable in some measure of comprehending the propriety, justice, equality, and consistency of the same.   For further instruction we refer you to Deut. xxxii, where the Lord says, that Jacob is the lot of his inheritance.   He found him in a desert land, and in the waste, howling wilderness; He led him about, He instructed him, He kept him as the apple of His eye, etc.; which will show the force of the last item advanced, that it is necessary for men to receive an understanding concerning the laws of the heavenly kingdom, before they are permitted to enter it: we mean the celestial glory.   So dissimilar are the governments of men, and so divers are their laws, from the government and laws of heaven, that a man, for instance, hearing that there was a country on this globe called the United States of North America, could take his journey to this place without first learning the laws of government; but the conditions of God's kingdom are such, that all who are made partakers of that glory, are under the necessity of learning something respecting it previous to their entering into it.   But the foreigner can come to this country without knowing a syllable of its laws, or even subscribing to obey them after he arrives.   Why?   Because the government of the United States does not require it: it only requires an obedience to its laws after the individual has arrived within its jurisdiction.

As we previously remarked, we do not attempt to place the law of man on a parallel with the law of heaven; but we will bring forward another item, to further urge the propriety of yielding obedience to the law of heaven, after the fact is admitted, that the laws of man are binding upon man. Were a king to extend his dominion over the habitable earth, and send forth his laws which were of the most perfect kind, and command his subjects one and all to yield obedience to the same, and add as a reward to those who obeyed them, that at a certain period they should be called to attend the marriage of his son, who in due time was to receive the kingdom, and they should be made equal with him in the same; and fix as a penalty for disobedience that every individual guilty of it should be cast out at the marriage feast, and have no part nor portion with his government, what rational mind could for a moment accuse the king with injustice for punishing such rebellious subjects? In the first place his laws were just, easy to be complied with, and perfect: nothing of a tyrannical nature was required of them; but the very construction of the laws was equity and beauty; and when obeyed would produce the happiest condition possible to all who adhered to them, beside the last great benefit of sitting down with a royal robe in the presence of the king at the great, grand marriage supper of his son, and be made equal with him in all the afiairs of the kingdom.

When these royal laws were issued, and promulgated throughout the vast dominion, every subject, when interrogated whether he believed them to be from his sovereign or not, answered, Yes; I know they are, I am acquainted with the signature, for it is as usual. *Thus saith the King!* This admitted, the subject is bound by every consideration of honor to his country, his king, and his own personal character, to observe in the strictest sense every requisition in the royal edict. Should any escape the search of the ambassadors of the king and never hear these last laws, giving his subjects such exalted privileges, an excuse might be urged in their behalf, and they escape the censure of the king. But for those who had heard, who had admitted, and who had promised obedience to these just laws no excuse could be urged; and when brought into the presence of the king, certainly, justice would require that they should suffer a penalty. Could that king be just in admitting these rebellious individuals into the full enjoyment and privileges with his son, and those who had been obedient to his commandments? Certainly not. Because they disregarded the voice of their lawful king; they had no regard for his virtuous laws, for his dignity, nor for the honor of his name; neither for the honor of their country, nor their private virtue. They regarded not his authority enough to obey him, neither did they regard the immediate advantages and blessings arising from these laws if kept, so destitute were they of virtue and goodness; and above all, they regarded so little the joy and satisfaction of a legal seat in the presence of the king's only son, and to be made equal with him in all the blessings, honors, comforts, and felicities of his kingdom, that they turned away from a participation in them, and considered that they were beneath their present notice though they had no doubt as to the real authenticity of the royal edict.

We ask, again, would the king be just in admitting these rebels to all the privileges of his kingdom, with those who had served him with the strictest integrity? We again answer, No. Such individuals would be dangerous characters in any government: good and wholesome laws they despise; just and perfect principles they trample under their feet as something beneath their notice; and the commands of their sovereign which they had once acknowledged to be equitable they entirely disregard. How could a government be conducted with harmony if its administrators were possessed with such different dispositions and different principles? Could it prosper? Could it flourish? Would harmony prevail? Would order be established, and could justice be executed in righteousness in all branches of its departments? No! In it were two classes of men as dissimilar as light and darkness, virtue and vice, justice and injustice, truth and falsehood, holiness and sin. One class were perfectly harmless and virtuous: they knew what virtue was for they had lived in the fullest enjoyment of it, and their fidelity to truth had been fairly tested by a series of years of faithful obedience to all its heavenly precepts. They knew what good order was, for they had been orderly and obedient to the laws imposed on them by their wise sovereign, and had experienced the benefits arising from a life spent in his government till he has now seen proper to make them equal with his son. Such individuals would indeed adorn any court where perfection was one of its main springs of action, and shine far more faire than the richest gem in the diadem of the prince.

The other class were a set of individuals who disregarded every principle of justice and equity; and this is demonstrated from the fact, that when just laws were issued by the king, which were perfectly equitable, they were so lost to a sense of righteousness that they disregarded those laws, notwithstanding an obedience to them would have produced at the time, as regards their own personal comfort and advantage, the happiest result possible. They were entirely destitute of harmony and virtue, so much so that virtuous laws they despised. They had proven themselves unworthy a place in the joys of the prince, because they had for a series of years lived in open violation of his government. Certainly, then, those two classes of men could not hold the reins of the same government at the same time in peace; for internal jars, broils, and discords would rack it to the center, were such a form of government to exist under such a system. The virtuous could not enjoy peace in the constant and unceasing schemes and evil plans of the wicked; neither could the wicked have enjoyment in the constant perseverance of the righteous to do justly. That there must be an agreement in this government, or it could not stand, must be admitted by all. Should the king convey the reins into the hands of the rebellious the government must soon fall; for every government, from the creation to the present, when it ceased to be virtuous, and failed to execute justice, sooner or later has been overthrown. And without virtuous principles to actuate a government all care for justice is soon lost, and the only motive which prompts it to act is ambition and selfishness. Should the king admit these rebels into his house to make them equal with the others, he would condescend beneath his dignity, because he once issued virtuous laws which were received by a part of his subjects, and the reward affixed was a seat at the marriage feast, and an adoption into his own family as lawful heirs. So that should he now offer any thing different he would destroy forever that government which he once so diligently labored to establish and preserve and which he once had wisdom to organize. Such indivinuals as the last named, would be a bane to a virtuous government, and would prove its overthrow if suffered to hold a part in conducting it.

We take the sacred writings into our hands, and admit that they were given by direct inspiration for the good of man. We believe that God condescended to speak from the heavens and declare His will concerning the human family, to give them just and holy laws, to regulate their conduct, and guide them in a direct way, that in due time He might take them to Himself, and make them joint heirs with His Son. But when this fact is admitted, that the immediate will of heaven is contained in the Scriptures, are we not bound as rational creatures to live in accordance to all its precepts? Will the mere admission, that this is the will of heaven ever benefit us if we do not comply with all its teachings? Do we not offer violence to the Supreme Intelligence of heaven, when we admit the truth of its teachings, and do not obey them? Do we not descend below our own knowledge, and the better wisdom which heaven has endowed us with, by such a course of conduct? For these reasons, if we have direct revelations given us from heaven, surely those revelations were never given to be trifled with, without the trifler's incurring displeasure and vengence upon his own head, if there is any justice in heaven; and that there is must be admitted by every individual who admits the truth and force of God's teachings, His blessings and cursings, as contained in the sacred volume.

Here, then, we have this part of our subject immediately before us for consideration: God has in reserve a time, or period appointed in His own bosom, when He will bring all His subjects, who have obeyed His voice and kept His commandments, into His celestial rest. This rest is of such perfection and glory, that man has need of a preparation before he can, according to the laws of that kingdom, enter it and enjoy its blessings. This being the fact, God has given certain laws to the human family, which, if observed, are sufficient to prepare them to inherit this rest. This, then, we conclude, was the purpose of God in giving His laws to us: if not, why, or for what were they given? If the whole family of man were as well off without them as they might be with them, for what purpose or intent were they ever given? Was it that God wanted to merely show that He could talk? It would be nonsense to suppose that He would condescend to talk in vain: for it would be in vain, and to no purpose whatever [if the law of God were of no benefit to man]: because, all the commandments contained in the law of the Lord, have the sure promise annexed of a reward to all who obey, predicated upon the fact that they are really the promises of a Being who cannot lie, One who is abundantly able to fulfill every tittle of His word: and if man were as well prepared, or could be as well prepared, to meet God without their ever having been given in the first instance, why were they ever given? for certainly, in that case they can now do him no good.

As we previously remarked, all well established and properly organized governments have certain fixed and prominent laws for the regulation and management of the same. If man has grown to wisdom and is capable of discerning the propriety of laws to govern nations, what less can be expected from the Ruler and Upholder of the universe? Can we suppose that He has a kingdom without laws? Or do we believe that it is composed of an innumerable company of beings who are entirely beyond all law? Consequently have need of nothing to govern or regulate them? Would not such ideas be a reproach to our Great Parent, and at variance with His glorious intelligence? Would it not be asserting that man had found out a secret beyond Deity? That he had learned that it was good to have laws, while God after existing from eternity and having power to create man, had not found out that it was proper to have laws for His government? We admit that God is the great source and fountain from whence proceeds all good; that He is perfect intelligence, and that His wisdom is alone sufficient to govern and regulate the mighty creations and worlds which shine and blaze with such magnificence and splendor over our heads, as though touched with His finger and moved by His Almighty word. And if so, it is done and regulated by law; for without law all must certainly fall into chaos. If, then, we admit that God is the source of all wisdom and understanding, we must admit that by His direct inspiration He has taught man that law is necessary in order to govern and regulate His own immediate interest and welfare: for this reason, that law is beneficial to promote peace and happiness among men. And as before remarked, God is the source from whence proceeds all good; and if man is benefitted by law, then certainly, law is good; and if law is good, then law, or the principle of it emanated from God; for God is the source of all good; consequently, then, he was the first Author of law, or the principle of it, to mankind.

We would remind you, brethren, of the fatigues, trials, privations, and persecutions, which the ancient saints endured for the sole purpose of persuading men of the excellency and propriety of the faith of Christ, were it in our opinion necessary, or if it would serve in any respect to stimulate you to labor in the vineyard of the Lord with any more diligence. But we have reason to believe (if you make the holy Scriptures a sufficient part of your studies), that their perseverance is known to you all; as also that they were willing to sacrifice the present honors and pleasures of this world, that they might obtain an assurance of a crown of life from the hand of our Lord; and their excellent example in labor, which manifests their zeal to us in the cause which they embraced, you are daily striving to pattern. And not only these examples of the Saints, but the commandments of our Lord, we hope are constantly revolving in your hearts, teaching you, not only His will in proclaiming His Gospel, but His meekness and perfect walk before all, even in those times of severe persecutions and abuse which were heaped upon Him by a wicked and adulterous generation. Remember, brethren, that He has called you unto holiness; and need we say, to be like Him in purity? How wise, how holy; how chaste, and how perfect, then, you ought to conduct yourselves in His sight; and remember, too, that His eyes are continually upon you. Viewing these facts in a proper light, you cannot be insensible, that without a strict observance of all His divine requirements, you may, at least, be found wanting; and if so, you will admit, that your lot will be cast among the unprofitable servants. We beseech you, therefore, brethren, to improve upon all things committed to your charge, that you lose not your reward.

No doubt, the course which we pursued in our last communication to you, is yet familiar to your minds; that we there endeavored to show, as far as possible, the propriety, in part, of adhering to the law of heaven; and also, the consistency in looking to heaven for a law or rule to serve us as a guide in this present state of existence, that we may be prepared to meet that which inevitably awaits us, as well as all mankind. There is an importance, perhaps, attached to this subject, which the world has not so fully examined as it requires. Think for a moment, of the greatness of the Being who created the Universe; and

ask, could He be so unconsistent with his own character, as to leave
man without a law or rule by which to regulate his conduct, after placing him here, where, according to the formation of his nature he must
in a short period sink into the dust? Is there nothing further; is there
no existence beyond this vail of death which is so suddenly to be cast
over all of us? If there is, why not that Being who had power to place
us here, inform us something of the hereafter? If we had power to
place ourselves in this present existence, why not have power to know
what shall follow when that dark vail is cast over our bodies? If in
this life we receive our all; if when we crumble back to dust we are no
more, from what source did we emanate, and what was the purpose of
our existence? If this life were all, we should be led to query, whether
or not there was really any substance in existence, and we might with
propriety say, "Let us eat, drink, and be merry, for to morrow we
die!" But if this life is all, then why this constant toiling, why this
continual warfare, and why this unceasing trouble? But this life is
not all, the voice of *reason*, the language of *inspiration*, and the Spirit
of the living God, our Creator, teaches us, as we hold the record of
truth in our hands, that this is not the case, that this is not so; for, the
heavens declare the glory of a God, and the firmament showeth His
handiwork; and a moment's reflection is sufficient to teach every man
of common intelligence, that all these are not the mere productions of
chance, nor could they be supported by any power less than an Almigthy
hand; and He that can mark the power of Omnipotence, inscribed
upon the heavens, can also see God's own handwriting in the sacred
volume: and he who reads it oftenest will like it best, and he who is
acquainted with it, will know the hand wherever he can see it; and
when once discovered, it will not only receive an acknowledgment, but
an obedience to all its heavenly precepts. For a moment reflect: what
could have been the purpose of our Father in giving to us a law? Was
it that it might be obeyed, or disobeyed? And think further, too, not
only of the propriety, but of the importance of attending to His laws
in every particular. If, then, there is an importance in this respect,
is there not a responsibility of great weight resting upon those who are
called to declare these truths to men? Were we capable of laying any
thing before you as a just comparison, we would cheerfully do it; but
in this our ability fails, and we are inclined to think that man is unable,
without assistance beyond what has been given to those before, of expressing in words the greatness of this important subject. We can
only say, that if an anticipation of the joys of the celestial glory, as
witnessed to the hearts of the humble is not sufficient, we will leave to
yourselves the result of your own diligence; for God ere long, will call

all His servants before Him, and there from His own hand they will receive a just recompense and a righteous reward for all their labors.

* * * * * * * * * * * * *

It is reasonable to suppose, that man departed from the first teachings, or instructions which he received from heaven in the first age, and refused by his disobedience to be governed by them. Consequently, he formed such laws as best suited his own mind, or as he supposed, were best adapted to his situation. But that God had influenced man more or less since that time in the formation of law for His benefit we have no hesitancy in believing; for, as before remarked, being the source of all good, every just and equitable law was in a greater or less degree influenced by Him. And though man in his own supposed wisdom would not admit the influence of a power superior to his own, yet for wise and great purposes, for the good and happiness of His creatures, God has instructed man to form wise and wholesome laws, since he had departed from Him and refused to be governed by those laws which God had given by His own voice from on high in the beginning. But notwithstanding the transgression, by which man had cut himself off from an immediate intercourse with his Maker without a Mediator, it appears that the great and glorious plan of His redemption was previously provided; the sacrifice prepared; the atonement wrought out in the mind and purpose of God, even in the person of the Son, through whom man was now to look for acceptance, and through whose merits he was now taught that he alone could find redemption, since the word had been pronounced, Unto dust thou shalt return.

But that man was not able himself to erect a system, or plan with power sufficient to free him from a destruction which awaited him, is evident from the fact that God, as before remarked, prepared a sacrifice in the gift of His own Son who should be sent in due time, to prepare a way, or open a door through which man might enter into the Lord's presence, whence he had been cast out for disobedience. From time to time these glad tidings were sounded in the ears of men in different ages of the world down to the time of Messiah's coming. By faith in this atonement or plan of redemption, Abel offered to God a sacrifice that was accepted, which was the firstlings of the flock. Cain offered of the fruit of the ground, and was not accepted, because he could not do it in faith, he could have no faith, or could not exercise faith contrary to the plan of heaven. It must be shedding the blood of the Only Begotten to atone for man; for this was the plan of redemption, and without the shedding of blood was no remission; and as the sacrifice was instituted for a type, by which man was to discern the great Sacrifice which God had prepared; to offer a sacrifice contrary to that, no faith could be exercised, because redemption was not purchased in that way, nor the power of atonement instituted after that order; consequently Cain could have no faith; and whatsoever is not of faith, is sin. But Abel offered an acceptable sacrifice, by which he obtained witness that he was righteous, God Himself testyfying of his gifts. Certainly, the shedding of the blood of a beast could be beneficial to no man, except it was done in imitation, or as a type, or explanation of what was to be offered through the gift of God Himself; and this performance done with an eye looking forward in faith on the power of that great Sacrifice for a remission of sins. But however various may have been, and may be at the present time, the opinions of men respecting the conduct of Abel, and the knowledge which he had on the subject of atonement, it is evident in our minds, that he was instructed more fully in the plan than what the Bible speaks of, for how could he offer a sacrifice in faith, looking to God for a remission of his sins in the power of the great atonement, without having been previouosly instructed in that plan? And further, if he was accepted of God, what were the ordinances performed further than the offering of the firstlings of the flock?

It is said by Paul in his letter to the Hebrew brethren, that Abel obtained witness that he was righteous, God testifying of his gifts. To whom did God testify of the gifts of Abel, was it to Paul? We have very little on this important subject in the forepart of the Bible. But it is said that Abel himself obtained witness that he was righteous. Then certainly God spoke to him: indeed, it is said that God talked with him: and if He did, would He not, seeing that Abel was righteous, deliver to him the whole plan of the Gospel. And is not the Gospel the news of the redemption? How could Abel offer a sacrifice and look forward with faith on the Son of God for a remission of his sins, and not understand the Gospel? The mere shedding of the blood of beasts or offering anything else in sacrifice, could not procure a remission of sins, except it were performed in faith of something to come; if it could, Cain's offering must have been as good as Abel's. And if Abel was taught of the coming of the Son of God, was he not taught also of His ordinances? We all admit that the Gospel has ordinances, and if so, had it not always ordinances, and were not its ordinances alwas the same? Perhaps our friends will say that the Gospel and its ordinances were not known till the days of John, the son of Zacharias, in the days of Herod, the king of Judea. But we will here look at this point: For our own part we cannot believe that the ancients in all ages were so ignorant of the system of heaven as many suppose, since all that were ever saved, were saved through the power of this great plan of redemption, as much before the coming of Christ as since; if not, God has had different plans in operation (if we may so express it), to bring men back to dwell with Himself; and this we cannot believe, since there has been no change in the constitution of man since he fell; and the ordinance or institution of offering blood in sacrifice, was only designed to be performed till Christ was offered up and shed His blood —as said before—that man might look forward in faith to that time. It will be noticed that, according to Paul, (see Gal. iii: 8) the Gospel was preached to Abraham. We would like to be informed in what name the Gospel was then preached, whether it was in the name of Christ or some other name. If in any other name, was it the Gospel? And if it was the Gospel, and that preached in the name of Christ, had it any ordinances? If not, was it the Gospel? And if it had ordinances what were they? Our friends may say, perhaps, that there were never any ordinances except those of offering sacrifices before the coming of Christ, and that it could not be possible for the Gospel to have been administered while the law of sacrifices of blood was in force. But we will recollect that Abraham offered sacrifice, and notwithstanding this, had the Gospel preached to him. That the offering of sacrifice was only to point the mind forward to Christ, we infer from these remarkable words of Jesus to the Jews: "Your Father Abraham rejoiced to see my day: and he saw it, and was glad" (John viii: 56.) So, then, because the ancients offered sacrifice it did not hinder their hearing the Gospel; but served, as we said before, to open their eyes, and enable them to look forward to the time of the coming of the Savior, and rejoice in His redemption. We find also, that when the Israelites came out of Egypt they had the Gospel preached to them, according to Paul in his letter to the Hebrews, which says: "For unto us was the Gospel preached, as well as unto them: but the word preached did not profit them, not being mixed with faith in them that heard it" (see Heb. iv:2). It is said again, in Gal. iii:19, that the law (of Moses. or the Levitical law) was "added" because of transgression. What, we ask, was this law added to, if it was not added to the Gospel? It must be plain that it was added to the Gospel, since we learn that they had the Gospel preached to them. From these few facts, we conclude that whenever the Lord revealed Himself to men in ancient days, and commanded them to offer sacrifice to Him, that it was done that they might look forward in faith to the time of His coming, and rely upon the power of that atonement for a remission of their sins. And this they have done, thousands who have gone before us, whose garments are spotless, and who are, like Job, waiting with an assurance like his, that they will see Him in the *latter day* upon the earth, even in their flesh.

We may conclude, that though there were different dispensations. yet all things which God communicated to His people were calculated to draw their minds to the great object, and to teach them to rely upon God alone as the author of their salvation, as contained in His law.

From what we can draw from the Scriptures relative to the teachings of heaven, we are induced to think that much instruction has been given to man since the beginning which we do not possess now. This may not agree with the opinions of some of our friends who are bold to say that we have everything written in the Bible which God ever spoke to man since the world began, and that if he had ever said anything more we should certainly have received it. But we ask, does it remain for a people who never had faith enough to call down one scrap of revelation from heaven, and for all they now are indebted to the faith of another people who lived hundreds and thousands of years before them, does it remain for them to say how much God has spoken and how much he has not spoken? We have what we have, and the Bible contains what it does contain: but to say that God never said anything more to man than is there recorded, would be saying at once that we have at last received a revelation; for it must require one to advance thus far, because it is nowhere said in that volume by the mouth of God, that He would not, after giving, what is there contained, speak again; and if any man has found out for a fact that the Bible contains all that God ever revealed to man he has ascertained it by an immediate revelation, other than has been previously written by the prophets and apostles. But through the kind providence of our Father a portion of His word which He delivered to His ancient saints, has fallen into our hands, is presented to us with a promise of a reward if obeyed, and with a penalty if disobeyed. That all are deeply interested in these laws or teachings, must be admitted by all who acknowledge their divine authenticity.

It may be proper for us to notice in this place a few of the many blessings held out in this law of heaven as a reward to those who obey its teachings. God has appointed a day in which He will judge the world, and this He has given an assurance of in that He raised up His Son Jesus Christ from the dead—the point on which the hope of all who believe the inspired record is founded for their future happiness and enjoyment; because, "If Christ be not risen," said Paul to the Corinthians, "your faith is vain; ye are yet in your sins. Then they also which are fallen asleep in Christ have perished" (see 1 Cor. xv). If the resurrection from the dead be not an important point, or item in our faith, we must confess that we know nothing about it; for if there be no resurrection from the dead, then Christ has not risen; and if Christ has not risen He was not the Son of God; and if He was not the Son of God, there is not nor cannot be a Son of God, if the present book called the Scriptures is true; because the time has gone by when, according to that book, He was to make His appearance. On this subject, however, we are reminded of the words of Peter to the Jewish Sanhedrim, when speaking of Christ, he says that God raised Him from the dead, and we (the apostles) are His witnesses of these things, and so is the Holy Ghost, whom God had given to them that obey Him (see Acts v). So that after the testimony of the Scriptures on this point, the assurance is given by the Holy Ghost, bearing witness to those who obey Him, that Christ Himself has assuredly risen from the dead; and if He has risen from the dead, He will, by His power, bring all men to stand before Him: for if He has risen from the dead the bands of the temporal death are broken that the grave has no victory, If then, the grave has no victory, those who keep the sayings of Jesus and obey His teachings have not only a promise of a resurrection from the dead, but an assurance of being admitted into His glorious kingdom; for, He Himself says, "Where I am there also shall my servant be" (see John xii).

In the 22nd chapter of Luke's account of the Messiah, we find the kingdom of heaven likened unto a king who made a marriage for his son. That this son was the Messiah will not be disputed, since it was the kingdom of heaven that was represented in the parable; and that the Saints, or those who are found faithful to the Lord, are the individuals who will be found worthy to inherit a seat at the marriage-supper, is evident from the sayings of John in the Revelation where he represents the sound which he heard in heaven to be like a great multitude, or like the voice of mighty thunderings, saying, the Lord God Omnipotent reigneth. Let us be glad and rejoice, and give honor to Him; for the marriage of the Lamb is come, and His wife hath made herself ready. And to her was granted that she should be arrayed in fine linen, clean and white: For the fine linen is the righteousness of Saints (Rev. xix).

That those who keep the commandments of the Lord and walk in His statutes to the end, are the only individuals permitted to sit at this glorious feast, is evident from the following items in Paul's last letter to Timothy, which was written just previous to his death,— he says: "I have fought a good fight, I have finished my course, I have kept the faith: henceforth there is laid up for me a crown of righteousness which the Lord, the righteous Judge shall give me at that day: and not to me only, but unto all them also that love His appearing." No one who believes the account, will doubt for a moment this assertion of Paul which was made, as he knew, just before he was to take his leave of this world. Though he once, according to his own word, persecuted the Church of God and wasted it, yet after embracing the faith, his labors were unceasing to spread the glorious news: and like a faithful soldier, when called to give his life in the cause which he had espoused, he laid it down, as he says, with an assurance of an eternal crown. Follow the labors of this Apostle from the time of his conversion to the time of his death, and you will have a fair sample of industry and patience in promulgating the Gospel of Christ. Derided, whipped, and stoned, the moment he escaped the hands of his persecutors he as zealously as ever proclaimed the doctrine of the Savior.   And all may know that he did not embrace the faith for honor in this life, nor for the gain of earthly goods.   What, then, could have induced him to undergo all this toil?   It was, as he said, that he might obtain the crown of righteousness from the hand of God.   No one, we presume, will doubt the faitnfulness of Paul to the end.   None will say that he did not keep the faith, that he did not fight the good fight, that he did not preach and persuade to the last.   And what was he to receive? A crown of righteousness.   And what shall others receive who do not labor faithfully, and continue to the end?   We leave such to search out their own promises if any they have; and if they have any they are welcome to them, on our part, for the Lord says that every man is to receive according to his works.   Reflect for a moment, brethren, and enquire, whether you would consider yourselves worthy a seat at the marriage feast with Paul and others like him, if you had been unfaithful? Had you not fought the good fight, and kept the faith, could you expect to receive?   Have you a promise of receiving a crown of righteousness from the hand of the Lord, with the Church of the First Born?   Here then, we understand, that Paul rested his hope in Christ, because he had kept the faith, and loved his appearing and from His hand he had a promise of receiving a crown of righteousness.   If the Saints are not to reign, for what purpose are they crowned?   In an exhortation of the Lord to a certain church in Asia, which was built up in the days of the Apostles, unto whom He communicated His word on that occasion by His servant John, He says, "Behold, I come quickly: hold that fast which thou hast, that no man take thy crown."   And again, "To him that over- cometh will I grant to sit with me in my throne, even as I also overcame, and am set down with my Father in His throne" (see Rev. iii).   And again, it is written, "Behold, now are we the sons of God, and it doth not yet appear what we shall be: but we know that, when He shall ap- pear, we shall be like Him; for we shall see Him as He is. And every man that hath this hope in him, purifieth himself, even as He is pure" (I John iii: 2, 3).   How is it that these old Apostles should say so much on the subject of the coming of Christ?   He certainly had once come; but Paul says, To all who love His appearing, shall be given the crown: and John says, When He shall appear, we shall be like Him; for we shall see Him as He is.   Can we mistake such language as this?   Do we not offer violence to our own good judgment when we deny the second coming of the Messiah?   When has He partaken of the fruit of the vine new with His ancient Apostles in His Father's kingdom, as He prom- ised He would just before He was crucified?   In Paul's epistle to the

Philippians, (iii: 20, 21), he says: "For our conversation is in heaven; from whence also we look for the Savior, the Lord Jesus Christ; who shall change our vile body, that it may be fashioned like unto His glorious body, according to the working whereby He is able even to subdue all things unto Himself." We find another promise to individuals living in the church at Sardis who had not defiled their garments: "And they shall walk with me in white: for they are worthy. He that overcometh, the same shall be clothed in white raiment; and I will not blot out his name out of the book of life, but I will confess his name before my Father, and before His angels." John represents the sound which he heard from heaven, as giving thanks and glory to God, saying that the Lamb was worthy to take the book and to open its seals; because He was slain, and had made them kings and priests unto God: and they should reign on the earth (see Rev. v). In the 20th chapter we find a length of time specified, during which Satan is to be confined in his own place, and the Saints reign in peace, all these promises and blessings we find contained in the law of the Lord, which the righteous are to enjoy; and we might enumerate many more places where the same or similar promises are made to the faithful, but we do not deem it of importance to rehearse them here, as this epistle is now lengthy; and our brethren, no doubt, are familiar with them all.

Most assuredly it is, however, that the ancients, though persecuted and afflicted by men, obtained from God promises of such weight and glory, that our hearts are often filled with gratitude that we are even permitted to look upon them while we contemplate that there is no respect of persons in His sight, and that in every nation, he that feareth God and worketh righteousness, is acceptable with Him. But from the few items previously quoted we can draw the conclusion that there is to be a day when all will be judged of their works, and rewarded according to the same; that those who have kept the faith will be crowned with a crown of righteousness; be clothed in white raiment; be admitted to the marriage feast; be free from every affliction, and reign with Christ on the earth, where, according to the ancient promise, they will partake of the fruit of the vine new in the glorious kingdom with Him; at least we find that such promises were made to the ancient Saints. And though we cannot claim these promises which were made to the ancients for they are not our property, merely because they were made to the ancient Saints, yet if we are the children of the Most High, and are called with the same calling with which they were called, and embrace the same covenant that they embraced, and are faithful to the testimony of our Lord as they were, we can approach the Father in the name of Christ as they approached Him, and for ourselves obtain the same promises. These promises, when obtained, if ever by us, will not be because Peter, John, and the other Apostles, with the churches at Sardis, Pergamos, Philadelphia, and elsewhere, walked in the fear of God and had power and faith to prevail and obtain them; but it will be because we, ourselves, have faith and approach God in the name of His Son Jesus Christ, even as they did; and when these promises are obtained, they will be promises directly to us, or they will do us no good. They will be communicated for our benefit, being our own property (through the gift of God), earned by our own diligence in keeping His commandments, and walking uprightly before Him. If not, to what end serves the Gospel of our Lord Jesus Christ, and why was it ever communicated to us?

Previous to commencing this letter we designed giving you some instruction upon the regulation of the Church; but that will be given hereafter.

In our own country, surrounded with blessings innumerable, to which thousands of our fellow men are strangers, enjoying unspeakable bene- fits and inexpressible comforts, when once our situation is compared with the ancient Saints, as followers of the Lamb of God who has taken away our sins by His own blood, we are bound to rejoice and give thanks to Him always. Since the organization of the Church of Christ, or the Church of the Latter-day Saints, on the 6th of April, 1830, we have had the satisfaction of witnessing the spread of the truth into various parts of our land, notwithstanding its enemies have exerted their unceasing diligence to stop its course and prevent its progress; though evil and designing men have combined to destroy the innocent, because their own craft was in danger; and these have been assisted in raising mobs and circulating falsehoods by a miserable set of apostates who have for wicked and unbecoming conduct been expelled from the body of which they were once members, yet the glorious Gospel in its fullness is spreading and daily gaining converts; and our prayer to God is, that it may continue, and numbers be added of such as shall be eternally saved.

The Messiah's kingdom on earth is of that kind of government, that there has always been numerous apostates, for the reason that it admits of no sins unrepented of without excluding the individual from its fellowship. Our Lord said, "Strive to enter in at the straight gate; for many, I say unto you, will seek to enter in, and shall not be able." And again, many are called, but few are chosen. Paul said to the elders of the Church at Ephesus, after he had labored three years with them, that he knew that some of their own number would turn away from the faith, and seek to lead away disciples after them. None, we presume, in this generation will pretend that he has the experience of Paul in building up the Church of Christ; and yet, after his departure from the

Church at Ephesus,many, even of the elders,turned away from the truth; and what is almost always the case, sought to lead away disciples after them. Strange as it may appear at first thought,yet it is no less strange than true, that notwithstanding all the professed determination to live godly, apostates after turning from the faith of Christ, unless they have speedily repented, have sooner or later fallen into the snares of the wicked one, and have been left destitute of the Spirit of God, to manifest their wickedness in the eyes of multitudes. From apostates the faithful have received the severest persecutions. Judas was rebuked and immediately betrayed his Lord into the hands of His enemies,because Satan entered into him. There is a superior intelligence bestowed upon such as obeyed the Gospel with full purpose of heart, which, if sinned against, the apostate is left naked and destitute of the Spirit of God, and he is, in truth, nigh unto cursing, and his end is to be burned. When once that light which was in them is taken from them they become as much darkened as they were previously enlightened, and then, no marvel, if all their power should be enlisted against the truth, and they, Judas like, seek the destruction of those who were their greatest benefactors. What nearer friend on earth, or in heaven, had Judas than the Savior? And his first object was to destroy Him. Who, among all the Saints in these last days, can consider himself as good as our Lord? Who is as perfect? Who is as pure? Who is as holy as He was? Are they to be found? He never transgressed or broke a commandment or law of heaven—no deceit was in His mouth, neither was guile found in His heart. And yet one that ate with Him,who had often drunk of the same cup, was the first to lift up his heel against Him. Where is one like Christ? He cannot be found on earth. Then why should His followers complain, if from those whom they once called brethren, and considered as standing in the nearest relation in the everlasting covenant they should receive persecution? From what source emanated the principle which has ever been manifested by apostates from the true Church to persecute with double diligence, and seek with double perseverance, to destroy those whom they once professed to love, with whom they once communed, and with whom they once covenanted to strive with every power in righteousness to obtain the rest of God? Perhaps our brethren will say the same that caused Satan to seek to overthrow the kingdom of God, because he himself was evil, and God's kingdom is holy.   *   *   *   *   *   *   *   *   *   *

The great plan of salvation is a theme which ought to occupy our strict attention, and be regarded as one of heaven's best gifts to mankind. No consideration whatever ought to deter us from showing ourselves approved in the sight of God, according to His divine requirement. Men not unfrequently forget that they are dependent upon heaven for every blessing which they are permitted to enjoy, and that for every opportunity granted them they are to give an account. You know, brethren, that when the Master in the Savior's parable of the stewards called his servants before him he gave them several talents to improve on while he should tarry abroad for a little season, and when he returned he called for an accounting. So it is now. Our Master is absent only for a little season, and at the end of it He will call each to render an account; and where the five talents were bestowed, ten will be required; and he that has made no improvement will be cast out as an unprofitable servant, while the faithful will enjoy everlasting honors. Therefore we earnestly implore the grace of our Father to rest upon you, through Jesus Christ His Son, that you may not faint in the hour of temptation, nor be overcome in the time of persecution.

On the evening of the 28th of January, Brothers Oliver Cowdery, Frederick G. Williams, and myself, being agreed, bowed before the Lord, and united in prayer, that God would continue to deliver me and my brethren from "Doctor" Hurlburt,[*] that he may not prevail against us in the law-suit that is pending; and also that God would soften the hearts of Eden Smith, —— Jones, —— Lowd, —— Lyman, and also Mr. Bardsley, that they might obey the Gospel; or if they would not repent, that the Lord would send faithful Saints to purchase their farms, that this Stake may be strengthened. and its borders enlarged. O Lord, grant it for Christ's sake. Amen.

Prayer of the First Presidency.

January 31.—It is my prayer to the Lord that three thousand subscribers may be added to the STAR in the time of three years.

February 1.—Every expedient preparation was making by the Church in Kirtland, and Clay county, to have those who have been driven from their possessions in Jackson county, returned.

Preparations for Returning Exiles to Zion.

February 9.—A conference of High Priests, Elders and officers of the Church of Christ in New Portage, Medina county, Ohio, was called at the house of Brother

* The case of Joseph Smith *vs.* "Doctor" Hurlburt did not come to trial until the 4th of April, 1834, when the "Doctor" was bound over to keep the peace.

Kirlins, which I attended. It had been suggested that Elder Rigdon might remove from Kirtland to New Portage; but after listening to the proceedings of a previous conference in Portage, from Brothers Palmer and Bosworth, it was decided that Elder Rigdon should not remove; and that the brethren in New Portage should assist all in their power to build the Lord's House in Kirtland; and that the brethren erect only a temporary or cheap place for meeting in Portage, as that was not to be established as a Stake of Zion at present; and that course would enable them to do more for the House in Kirtland.

Conference of High Priests and Elders at New Portage.

At a council of the High Priests and Elders, (Orson Hyde, clerk,) at my house in Kirtland, on the evening of the 12th of February, I remarked that I should endeavor to set before the council the dignity of the office which had been conferred on me by the ministering of the angel of God, by His own voice, and by the voice of this Church; that I had never set before any council in all the order in which it ought to be conducted, which, perhaps, has deprived the councils of some or many blessings.

And I continued and said, no man is capable of judging a matter, in council, unless his own heart is pure; and that we are frequently so filled with prejudice, or have a beam in our own eye, that we are not capable of passing right decisions.

But to return to the subject of order; in ancient days councils were conducted with such strict propriety, that no one was allowed to whisper, be weary, leave the room, or get uneasy in the least, until the voice of the Lord, by revelation, or the voice of the council by the Spirit, was obtained, which has not been observed in this Church to the present time. It was understood in ancient days, that if one man could stay in council, another could; and if the president could spend his time, the members could also; but in our councils, generally, one will be uneasy, another asleep; one praying,

Order in Ancient Councils.

another not; one's mind on the business of the council, and another thinking on something else.

Our acts are recorded, and at a future day they will be laid before us, and if we should fail to judge right and injure our fellow-beings, they may there, perhaps, condemn us; there they are of great consequence, and to me the consequence appears to be of force, beyond anything which I am able to express. Ask yourselves, brethren, how much you have exercised yourselves in prayer since you heard of this council; and if you are now prepared to sit in council upon the soul of your brother.

Responsibility of Those who sit in Judgment.

I then gave a relation of my situation at the time I obtained the record [Book of Mormon], the persecutions I met with, and prophesied that I would stand and shine like the sun in the firmament, when my enemies and the gainsayers of my testimony shall be put down and cut off, and their names blotted out from among men.

The Prophet's Predicted Triumph.

The council proceeded to investigate certain charges presented by Elder Rigdon against Martin Harris; one was, that he told A. C. Russell, Esq., that Joseph drank too much liquor when he was translating the Book of Mormon; and that he wrestled with many men and threw them; and that he (Harris) exalted himself above Joseph, in that he said, "Brother Joseph knew not the contents of the Book of Mormon, until it was translated, but that he himself knew all about it before it was translated."

Trial of Martin Harris.

Brother Harris did not tell Esq. Russell that Brother Joseph drank too much liquor while translating the Book of Mormon, but this thing occurred previous to the translating of the Book; he confessed that his mind was darkened, and that he had said many things inadvertently, calculated to wound the feelings of his brethren, and promised to do better. The council forgave him, with much good advice.

Brother Leonard Rich was called in question for transgressing the Word of Wisdom, and for selling the revelations at an extortionate price, while he was journeying east with Father Lyons, Brother Rich confessed, and the council forgave him upon his promising to do better and reform his life.

Trial of Leonard Rich.

CHAPTER II.

ORGANIZATION OF THE HIGH COUNCIL—FIRST CASES BEFORE
THE COUNCIL.

*Minutes of the Organization of the High Council of the Church of Christ
of Latter-day Saints, Kirtland, February 17, 1834.**

1. This day a general council of twenty-four High Priests assembled
at the house of Joseph Smith, Jun., by revelation, and proceeded to organize the High Council of the Church of Christ, which was to consist
of twelve High Priests, and one or three Presidents, as the case might
require.

2. The High Council was appointed by revelation for the purpose
of settling important difficulties which might arise in the Church, which
could not be settled by the Church or the Bishop's council to the satisfaction of the parties.

3. Joseph Smith, Jun., Sidney Rigdon, and Frederick G. Williams,
were acknowledged Presidents by the voice of the Council; and Joseph
Smith, Sen., John Smith, Joseph Coe, John Johnson, Martin Harris,
John S. Carter, Jared Carter, Oliver Cowdery, Samuel H.Smith, Orson
Hyde, Sylvester Smith, and Luke Johson, High Priests, were chosen
to be a standing Council for the Church, by the unanimous voice of the
Council.

4. The above-named Councilors were then asked whether they
accepted their appointments, and whether they would act in that office
according to the law of heaven: to which they all answered that they
accepted their appointments, and would fill their offices according to
the grace of God bestowed upon them.

5. The number composing the Council, who voted in the name and
for the Church, in appointing the above named Councilors were forty-
three, as follows:—Nine High Priests, seventeen Elders, four Priests,
and thirteen members.

5. Voted: that the High Council cannot have power to act without
seven of the above-named Councilors, or their regularly appointed suc-
cessors, are present.

7. These seven shall have power to appoint other High Priests,
whom they may consider worthy and capable to act in the place of
absent Councilors.

* Doctrine and Covenants, sec. cii.

8. Noted: that whenever any vacancy shall occur by the death, removal from office for transgression, or removal from the bounds of this Church government, of any one of the above-named Councilors, it shall be filled by the nomination of the President or Presidents, and sanctioned by the voice of a general council of High Priests, convened for that purpose, to act in the name of the Church.

9. The President of the Church, who is also the President of the Council, is appointed by revelation, and acknowledged in his administration, by the voice of the Church.

10. And it is according to the dignity of his office that he should preside over the Council of the Church; and it is his privilege to be assisted by two other Presidents, appointed after the same manner he himself was appointed;

11. And in case of the absence of one or both of those who are appointed to assist him, he has power to preside over the Council without an assistant: and in case he himself is absent, the other Presidents have power to preside in his stead, both, or either of them.

12. Whenever a High Council of the Church of Christ is regularly organized, according to the foregoing pattern, it shall be the duty of the twelve Councilors to cast lots by numbers, and thereby ascertain, who of the twelve shall speak first, commencing with number one, and so in succession to number twelve.

13. Whenever this Council convenes to act upon any case, the twelve Councilors shall consider whether it is a difficult one or not; if it is not, two only of the Councilors shall speak upon it, according to the form above written.

14. But if it is thought to be difficult, four shall be appointed; and if more difficult, six; but in no case shall more than six be appointed to speak.

15. The accused, in all cases, has a right to one half of the Council, to prevent insult or injustice;

16. And the Councilors appointed to speak before the Council, are to present the case after the evidence is examined, in its true light before the Council, and every man is to speak according to equity and justice.

17. Those Councilors who draw even numbers, that is 2, 4, 6, 8, 10, and 12, are the individuals who are to stand up in behalf of the accused, and prevent insult and injustice.

18. In all cases the accuser and accused shall have a privilege of speaking for themselves before the Council after the evidences are heard, and the Councilors who are appointed to speak on the case, have finished their remarks.

19. After the evidences are heard, the Councilor, accuser and accused have spoken, the President shall give a decision according to the

understanding which he shall have of the case, and call upon the twelve Councilors to sanction the same by their vote.

20. But should the remaining Councilors, who have not spoken, or any one of them, after hearing the evidences and pleadings impartially, discover an error in the decision of the President, they can manifest it, and the case shall have a re-hearing;

21. And if, after a careful re-hearing, any additional light is shown upon the case, the decision shall be altered accordingly;

22. But in case no additional light is given, the first decision shall stand, the majority of the Council having power to determine the same.

23. In case of difficulty, respecting doctrine or principle, (if there is not a sufficiency written to make the case clear to the minds of the Council,) the President may inquire and obtain the mind of the Lord by revelation.

24. The High Priests, when abroad, have power to call and organize a Council after the manner of the foregoing to settle difficulties when the parties, or either of them, shall request it;

25. And the said Council of High Priests shall have power to appoint one of their own number, to preside over such Council for the time being.

26. It shall be the duty of said Council to transmit immediately, a copy of their proceedings, with a full statement of the testimony accompanying their decision, to the High Council of the seat of the First Presidency of the Church,

27. Should the parties, or either of them be dissatisfied with the decision of said Council, they may appeal to the High Council of the seat of the First Presidency of the Church, and have a re-hearing, which case shall there be conducted, according to the former pattern written, as though no such decision had been made.

28. The Council of High Priests abroad, is only to be called on the most difficult cases of Church matters; and no common or ordinary case is to be sufficient to call such Council.

29. The traveling or located High Priests abroad, have power to say whether it is necessary to call such a Council or not.

30. There is a distinction between the High Council of traveling High Priests abroad, and the traveling High Council composed of the Twelve Apostles, in their decisions.

31. From the decision of the former there can be an appeal, but from the decision of the latter there cannot.

32. The latter can only be called in question by the general authorities of the Church in case of transgression.

33. Resolved, that the President or Presidents of the seat of the First Presidency of the Church, shall have power to determine whether any

such case, as may be appealed, is justly entitled to a re-hearing, after examining the appeal and the evidences and statements accompanying it.

34. The twelve Councilors then proceeded to cast lots or ballot, to ascertain who should speak first, and the following was the result, namely:—

1 OLIVER COWDERY,
2 JOSEPH COE,
3 SAMUEL H. SMITH,
4 LUKE JOHNSON,
5 JOHN S. CARTER,
6 SYLVESTER SMITH,
7 JOHN JOHNSON,
8 ORSON HYDE,
9 JARED CARTER,
10 JOSEPH SMITH, SEN.,
11 JOHN SMITH,
12 MARTIN HARRIS.

After prayer the conference adjourned.

OLIVER COWDERY, } Clerks.
ORSON HYDE,

On the 18th of January I reviewed and corrected the minutes of the organization of the High Council, and on the 19th of February, the Council assembled according to adjournment, from the 17th, (Oliver Cowdery and Orson Hyde, clerks,) when the revised minutes were presented and read to the Council. I urged the necessity of prayer, that the Spirit might be given, that the things of the Spirit might be judged thereby, because the carnal mind cannot discern the things of God. The minutes were read three times, and unanimously adopted and received for a form and constitution of the High Council of the Church of Christ hereafter; with this provision, that if the President should hereafter discover anything lacking in the same, he should be privileged to supply it.

Supplementary Proceedings in the Organization of the High Council.

The number present who received the above-named document, was twenty-six High Priests, eighteen Elders, three Priests, one Teacher, and fourteen private members, making in all sixty-two.

After giving such instruction as the Spirit dictated, I laid my hands upon the heads of the two assistant Presidents severally and blessed them, that they might have wisdom to magnify their office and power to prevail over the adversary.

I also laid my hands upon the twelve Councilors, and commanded a blessing to rest upon them, that they might have wisdom and power to counsel in righteousness, upon all subjects that might be laid before them. I also prayed that they might be delivered from those evils to which they were most exposed, and that their lives might be prolonged on the earth.

My father, Joseph, then laid his hands upon my head, and said,

Joseph, I lay my hands upon thy head, and pronounce the blessings of thy progenitors upon thee, that thou mayest hold the keys of the mysteries of the kingdom of heaven until the coming of the Lord. Amen.

He also laid his hands upon the head of his son Samuel, and said,

Samuel, I lay my hands upon thy head, and pronounce the blessings of thy progenitors upon thee, that thou mayest remain a Priest of the Most High God, and like Samuel of old, hear His voice, saying, Samuel, Samuel. Amen.

Father John Johnson, also, laid his hands upon the head of his son Luke, and said,

My Father in heaven, I ask Thee to bless this my son, according to the blessings of his forefathers; that he may be strengthened in his ministry, according to his holy calling. Amen.

I then gave the assistant Presidents a solemn charge to do their duty in righteousness, and in the fear of God; I also charged the twelve Councilors in a similar manner, all in the name of Jesus Christ.

We all raised our hands to heaven in token of the everlasting covenant, and the Lord blessed us with His Spirit. I then declared the council organized according to the ancient order, and also according to the mind of the Lord.

The following complaint was then presented before the Council, by Ezra Thayer, a High Priest: *First Case before the High Council.*

KIRTLAND, February 19, 1834.

1o the President of the High Council of the Church of Christ.

The following charges I prefer against Elder Curtis Hodges, Sen., of this Church: First, for an error in spirit; second, for an error in the manner of his address, which consisted in loud speaking, and a want of clearness in articulation, which was calculated to do injury to the cause of God; and also, for contending that that was a good and proper spirit that actuated him thus to speak—all of which I consider unbecoming in an Elder in this Church, and request a hearing before the High Concil.

(Signed)   EZRA THAYER.

Elder Hodges pleaded "not guilty" of the above charges.

Father Lions was called on to substantiate the above charges, and his testimony was pointed against Brother Hodges. Brother Story testified that Elder Hodges talked so loud at a prayer meeting that the neighbors came out to see if some one was hurt. At another meeting, he said that Elder Thayer rebuked him for his error, but he did not receive the rebuke; that he raised his voice so high, that he could not articulate so as to be understood; and that his teaching brought a damper upon the meet ng, and was not edifying. Brother Erastus Babbitt was then called upon, who testified that Elder Hodges was guilty of hollowing so loud that in a measure he lost his voice, and uttered but little else distinctly than "Glory to heaven's King." His testimony against Brother Hodges was pointed. Brother Truman Wait testified much to the same effect.

Councilor Oliver Cowdery stood up on the part of the accuser, and opened the case clearly.

Councilor Joseph Coe stood up on the part of the accused, but could say but a few words.

The accuser and the accused then spoke for themselves, after which the President arose and laid open the case still more plainly, and gave his decision, which was, that the charges in the declaration had been sustained by good witnesses; also, that Elder Hodges ought to have confessed when rebuked by Elder Thayer; also, if he had the Spirit of the Lord at the meetings, where he hollowed, he must have abused it, and grieved it away. All the Council agreed with the decision.

Elder Hodges then rose and said he now saw his error, but never saw it before; and appeared to feel thankful that he saw it. He said he had learned more during this trial than he had since he came into the Church; confessed freely his error, and said he would attend to the overcoming of that evil, the Lord being his helper.

The Council forgave him, and adjourned to the evening of the 20th.

February 20.—The High Council met this evening to determine concerning the Elders going out to preach.

Minutes of the High Council.

The president opened the Council by prayer.

At a church meeting, held in Pennsylvania, Erie county, and Springfield township, by Orson Pratt and Lyman E. Johnson, High Priests, some of the members of that church refused to partake of the Sacrament, because the Elder administering it did not observe the Word of Wisdom to obey it. Elder Johnson argued that they were justified in so doing, because the Elder was in transgression. Elder Pratt argued that the church was bound to receive the Supper under the administration of an Elder, so long as he retained his office or license. Voted that six Councilors should speak upon the subject.

The Council then proceeded to try the question, whether disobedience to the Word of Wisdom was a transgression sufficient to deprive an official member from holding office in the Church, after having it sufficiently taught him.

Councilors Samuel H. Smith, Luke S. Johnson, John S. Carter, Sylvester Smith, John Johnson and Orson Hyde, were called to speak upon the case then before the Council.   After the Councilors had spoken, the President proceeded to give the decision:

No official member in this Church is worthy to hold an office, after having the Word of Wisdom properly taught him, and he, the official member, neglecting to comply with or obey it; which decision the Council confirmed by vote.

The President then asked if there were any Elders present who would go to Canada, and preach the Gospel to that people; for they have written a number of letters for help.   And the whole Council felt as though the Spirit required the Elders to go there.   It was, therefore, decided by the Council, that Lyman E. Johnson and Milton Holmes should travel together into Canada; that Zebedee Coltrin and Henry Herriman travel together into Canada; and that Jared Carter and Phineas Young travel together, if they can so arrange their affairs at home as to be liberated.

It was also decided that Elder Oliver Granger should travel eastward as soon as his circumstances would permit, and that he could travel alone on account of his age; it was also decided that Elder Martin Harris should travel alone whenever he travels; that Elders John S. Carter and Jesse Smith travel east together as soon as they can; and that Elder Brigham Young should travel alone, it being his own choice; also that James Durfee and Edward Marvin should travel together eastward; that Sidney Rigdon and John P. Greene go to Strongville, that Orson Pratt and Harrison Sagers travel together for the time being; and that there should be a general conference held at Saco, in the state of Maine, on the 13th day of June, 1834.

It was furthermore voted that Elder Orson Hyde, accompanied by Elder Orson Pratt, go east to obtain donations for Zion, and means to redeem the farm on which the house of the Lord stands.

The Church and Council then prayed with uplifted hands, that they might be prospered in their mission.

                                   ORSON HYDE,   }
                                   OLIVER COWDERY,   } Clerks.

CHAPTER III.

THE CAUSE AND OBJECT OF THE JACKSON COUNTY PERSECUTION—THE PROPHET'S MISSION THROUGH WESTERN NEW YORK.

February 24.—I received the following:

*Revelation.**

1. Verily I say unto you, my friends, behold I will give unto you a revelation and commandment, that ye may know how to act in the discharge of your duties concerning the salvation and redemption of your brethren who have been scattered on the land of Zion;

2. Being driven and smitten by the hand of mine enemies, on whom I will pour out my wrath without measure in mine own time;

3. For I have suffered them thus far, that they might fill up the measure of their iniquities, that their cup might be full;

4. And that those who call themselves after my name might be chastened for a little season with a sore and grievous chastisement, because they did not hearken altogether unto the precepts and commandments which I gave unto them.

5. But verily I say unto you, that I have decreed a decree which my people shall realize, inasmuch as they hearken from this very hour, unto the counsel which I, the Lord their God, shall give unto them.

6. Behold they shall, for I have decreed it, begin to prevail against mine enemies from this very hour,

7. And by hearkening to observe all the words which I, the Lord their God, shall speak unto them, they shall never cease to prevail until the kingdoms of the world are subdued under my feet, and the earth is given unto the saints, to possess it for ever and ever.

8. But inasmuch as they keep not my commandments, and hearken not to observe all my words, the kingdoms of the world shall prevail against them,

9. For they were set to be a light unto the world, and to be saviors of men;

* Doctrine and Covenants, sec. ciii.

10. And inasmuch as they are not the saviors of men, they are as salt that has lost its savor, and is thenceforth good for nothing but to be cast out and trodden under foot of men.

11. But verily I say unto you, I have decreed that your brethren which have been scattered shall return to the lands of their inheritances, and shall build up the waste places of Zion.

12. For after much tribulation, as I have said unto you in a former commandment, cometh the blessing.

13. Behold, this is the blessing which I have promised after your tribulations, and the tribulations of your brethren: your redemption, and the redemption of your brethren, even their restoration to the land of Zion, to be established no more to be thrown down;

14. Nevertheless, if they pollute their inheritances they shall be thrown down, for I will not spare them if they pollute their inheritances.

15. Behold, I say unto you, the redemption of Zion must needs come by power;

16. Therefore, I will raise up unto my people a man, who shall lead them like as Moses led the children of Israel,

17. For ye are the children of Israel, and of the seed of Abraham, and ye must needs be led out of bondage by power, and with a stretched out arm:

18. And as your fathers were led at the first, even so shall the redemption of Zion be.

19. Therefore let not your hearts faint, for I say unto you as I said unto your fathers, mine angel shall go up before you, but not my presence;

20. But I say unto you, mine angels shall go up before you, and also my presence, and in time ye shall possess the goodly land.

21. Verily, verily I say unto you, that my servant Baurak Ale (Joseph Smith, Jun.,) is the man to whom I likened the servant to whom the Lord of the vineyard spake in the parable which I have given unto you.

22. Therefore let my servant Baurak Ale (Joseph Smith, Jun.,) say unto the strength of my house, my young men and the middle aged, gather yourselves together unto the land of Zion, upon the lands which I have bought with money that has been consecrated unto me:

23. And let all the churches send up wise men with their moneys, and purchase lands even as I have commanded them;

24. And inasmuch as mine enemies come against you to drive you from my goodly land, which I have consecrated to be the land of Zion: even from your own lands after these testimonies, which ye have brought before me against them, ye shall curse them;

25. And whomsoever ye curse, I will curse, and ye shall avenge me of mine enemies;

26. And my presence shall be with you even in avenging me of mine enemies, unto the third and fourth generation of them that hate me.

27. Let no man be afraid to lay down his life for my sake, for whoso layeth down his life for my sake shall find it again;

28. And whoso is not willing to lay down his life for my sake, is not my disciple.

29. It is my will that my servant Sidney Rigdon shall lift up his voice in the congregations in the eastern countries, in preparing the churches to keep the commandments which I have given unto them concerning the restoration and redemption of Zion.

30. It is my will that my servant Parley P. Pratt and my servant Lyman Wight should not return to the land of their brethren, until they have obtained companies to go up unto the land of Zion, by tens, or by twenties, or by fifties, or by an hundred, until they have obtained to the number of five hundred of the strength of my house.

31. Behold this is my will; ask and ye shall receive, but men do not always do my will;

32. Therefore, if you cannot obtain five hundred, seek diligently, that peradventure you may obtain three hundred;

33. And if you cannot obtain three hundred, seek diligently, that peradventure ye may obtain one hundred.

34. But verily I say unto you, a commandment I give unto you, that ye shall not go up unto the land of Zion, until you have obtained a hundred of the strength of my house, to go up with you unto the land of Zion.

35. Therefore as I said unto you, ask and ye shall receive; pray earnestly that peradventure my servant Baurak Ale (Joseph Smith, Jun.,) may go with you, and preside in the midst of my people, and organize my kingdom upon the consecrated land, and establish the children of Zion upon the laws and commandments which have been, and which shall be, given unto you.

36. All victory and glory is brought to pass unto you through your diligence, faithfulness and prayers of faith.

37. Let my servant Parley P. Pratt journey with my servant Joseph Smith, Jun.

38. Let my servant Lyman Wight journey with my servant Sidney Rigdon.

39. Let my servant Hyrum Smith journey with my servant Frederick G. Williams.

40. Let my servant Orson Hyde journey with my servant Orson Pratt,

whithersoever my servant Joseph Smith, Jun., shall counsel them, in obtaining the fulfillment of these commandments which I have given unto you, and leave the residue in my hands. Even so. Amen.

The High Council of the Church also met this day at my house for the purpose of giving an audience or hearing to Lyman Wight and Parley P. Pratt, delegates from the Church in Missouri, to represent to us the state of the Church in that place.

Arrival of Delegation from the Church in Missouri.

Minutes of Council Meeting.

President Joseph opened the Council by prayer. Two of the standing Councilors were absent, namely, Joseph Coe and John Smith. Hyrum Smith was chosen to act in the place of John Smith, and John P. Greene to act in the place of Joseph Coe. Thus the High Council was organized, and six Councilors were appointed to speak. Brothers Parley P. Pratt and Lyman Wight, messengers from Zion, arose, and laid their business before the Council, and delivered their message, the substance of which was: when, how and by what means Zion was to be redeemed from her enemies. They said that our brethren who had been driven away from their lands and scattered abroad, had found so much favor in the eyes of the people [of Clay county, Mo.,] that they could obtain food and raiment of them for their labor, insomuch that they were comfortable. But the idea of their being driven away from the land of Zion pained their very souls, and they desired of God, by earnest prayer, to return with songs of everlasting joy, as said Isaiah, the prophet.

They also said that none of their lands were sold into the hands of our enemies, except a piece of thirty acres owned by Brother William E. McLellin, which he sold into the hands of the enemy, and seven acres more which he would have sold to the enemy if a brother had not come forward and purchased it and paid him his money.

Brother Joseph then arose, and said that he was going to Zion, to assist in redeeming it. He called for the voice of the Council to sanction his going, which was given without a dissenting voice. He then called for volunteers to go with him, when some thirty or forty volunteered to go, who were present at the Council. It was a question whether the company should go by water or by land, and after a short investigation it was decided unanimously that they go by land. Joseph Smith, Jun., was nominated to be the commander-in-chief of the armies of Israel, and the leader of those who volunteered to go and assist in the redemption of Zion: the nomination was seconded and carried by the vote of all present. Council then adjourned by prayer and thanksgiving.

ORSON HYDE,   } Clerks.
OLIVER COWDERY,   }

February 26.—I started from home to obtain volunteers

The Prophet seeks Volunteers to Redeem Zion.
for Zion, in compliance with the foregoing revelation and action of the High Council; and on the 27th, stayed at Brother Roundy's.

To show the feelings of a certain portion of the public, at this period, I copy the following from the February number of the *Evening and Morning Star*, page 271:

We copy the following article from the *North Star*, headed "The Mormons," printed in Danville, Vermont, by E. Eaton:

"We have received the first number of the 'Mormon' *Morning and Evening Star* [the *Evening and Morning Star*], resuscitated in Kirtland, Ohio. *It is the same assuming, mysterious publication as its original.*"

While the press and many of the public were breathing

Cheering Words.
the spirit of bitterness against the work of God, I received letters from many of our friends, which gave us occasion for rejoicing: amongst them, I extract from Brother Moses Chapman Nickerson's letter of December 20, 1833:*

Your labors in Canada have been the beginning of a good work; there are thirty-four members attached to the Church at Mount Pleasant, all of whom appear to live up to their profession, five of whom have spoken in tongues, and three have sung in tongues; and we live at the top of the mountain.

Also from Saco, Maine:

January 20, 1834.

BRETHREN IN THE LORD,—I have baptized about fourty in this section, and there are more convinced of the truth, but are still lingering on the threshhold of the Church, and I think the Lord will gather some of them into His kingdom. Brother Evan M. Greene labored with me

---

* This Mount Pleasant branch of the Church, it will be remembered, was organized by the Prophet and Sidney Rigdon, in the October previous. See vol. I, chap. xxx.

from the 16th of January, 1833, till the October following; while we were together, we baptized about one hundred and thirty. Brethren, pray for me, that I may have words of wisdom, and a door of utterance to declare the whole counsel of God, and rightly divide the word of truth, giving to every man his portion in due season; for my determination is, with the stick of Joseph [the Book of Mormon] in one hand, and the stick of Judah [the Bible] in the other, to labor diligently in this world, that my skirts may be clear from the blood of all men, and I stand acquitted before the bar of God.

I am yours in Christ

(Signed)　　JOHN F. BOYNTON.

We continued our journey, and, on the 28th of February stayed at a stranger's, who entertained us very kindly; and on the first of March arrived at Brother Lewis', in Westfield.

Incidents in the Prophet's Journey through Western New York.

On the 2nd, which was the Sabbath, Brother Parley P. Pratt preached, and I spoke in the evening; we had a good meeting. There is a small church in this place, which seems strong in the faith. O may God keep them in the faith, and save them, and lead them to Zion.

March 3.—We intended to start on our journey east, but concluded to tarry another day. O may God bless us with the gift of utterance to accomplish the journey and errand on which we are sent, and return safe to the land of Kirtland, and find my family all well. O Lord, bless my little children with health and long life, to do good in their generation, for Christ's sake. Amen.

Since leaving Kirtland, we passed through Thompson, Springfield, Elk Creek, Erie, Livonia, Silver Creek, Perrysburgn, Collins, China, Warsaw, Geneseo, Centreville, Catlin and Spafford, before we arrived at Westfield.

On the 4th instant, we continued our journey from Westfield, accompanied by Elder Gould; and after a ride of thirty-three miles arrived at Villanova, and tarried all night with a Brother McBride.

The next morning, March 5th, we went to Brother Nickerson's, and found him and his household full of faith and of the Holy Spirit.

We called the church together, and related unto them what had happened to our brethren in Zion, and opened to them the prophecies and revelations concerning the order of the gathering to Zion, and the means of her redemption; and I prophesied to them, and the Spirit of the Lord came mightily upon me, and with all readiness the young and middle-aged volunteered for Zion. The same evening we held two meetings, three or four miles distant from each other.

March 6.—We held another meeting at Brother Nickerson's. The few unbelievers that attended were outrageous, and the meeting ended in complete confusion.

March 7.—We proceeded on our journey, accompanied by Brother Nickerson, leaving Brothers Gould and Matthews to prepare and gather up the companies in the churches in that region, and meet us in Ohio, ready to start for Zion on the first of May. We arrived after dark at Ellicotville, the county seat of Cataraugus, and tried for lodgings at every tavern in the place. It being court time we found no room; but were obliged to ride on in the dark, through mud and rain;. and, after traveling about one mile, we found shelter, for which we paid more than tavern fare.

On the 8th, we arrived at Palmersville, at the house of Elder McGown, where we were invited to go to Esquire Walker's to spend the evening. We found them very friendly and somewhat believing, and tarried all night.

Sunday, March 9.—We preached in a school house, and had great attention. We found a few disciples who were firm in the faith; and, after meeting found many believing and could hardly get away from them, and appointed a meeting in Freedom for Monday the 10th, and stayed at Mr. Warren A. Cowdery's, where we were blessed with a full enjoyment of temporal and spiritual blessings, even all we needed, or were worthy to receive.

Monday 10.—Met our appointment, and preached to a great congregation; and at evening again preached to an overflowing house. After meeting, I proposed if any wished to obey, and would make it manifest, we would stay to administer to another meeting. A young man of the Methodist order arose and testified his faith in the fullness of the Gospel and desired to be baptized. We appointed another meeting for the next day.

Tuesday 11.—Fulfilled our appointment and baptized Heman T. Hyde,* after which we rode nine miles, and put up at Steward's tavern.

Wednesday 12.—We arrived at Father Bosley's, after a ride of thirty-six miles.

Thursday 13.—I preached.

Friday 14.—At Father Beaman's.†

March 15.—While at Father Beaman's, Elders Rigdon and Wight arrived, much to the joy of their souls and the Saints in Livonia.

---

* Of this incident Elder Parley P. Pratt, who was the Prophet's traveling companion on this mission, says: "We baptized a young man named Heman Hyde; his parents were Presbyterians, and his mother, on account of the strength of her traditions, thought that we were wrong, and told me afterwards that she would much rather have followed him to an earthly grave than to have seen him baptized. Soon afterwards, however, herself, her husband, and the rest of the family, with some thirty or forty others, were all baptized and organized into a branch of the Church—called the Freedom branch—from which nucleus the light spread and souls were gathered into the fold in all the regions round. Thus mightily grew the word of God, or the seed sown by that extraordinary personage, the Prophet and Seer of the nineteenth century." (Autobiography of Parley P. Pratt, p. 117.)

Speaking of the pleasure of his companionship with the Prophet, Elder Pratt also says: "As we journeyed day after day, and generally lodged together, we had much sweet communion concerning the things of God and the mysteries of His kingdom, and I received many admonitions and instructions which I shall never forget." (Ibid., p. 117.)

† Speaking of "Father Beaman" and his interesting family, Elder Parley P. Pratt has the following interesting passage, which discloses the fact that "Father Beaman" was acquainted with the work during the time that the Book of Mormon was translating: "Among those whose hospitality we shared in that vicinity [Geneseo] was old Father Beaman and his amiable and interesting family. He was a good singer, and so were his three daughters; we were much edified and comforted in their society, and were deeply interested in hearing the old gentleman and Brother Joseph converse on their early acquaintance and history. He [Beaman] had been intimate with Joseph long before the first organization of the Church; had assisted him to preserve the plates of the Book of Mormon from the enemy, and had at one time had them concealed under his own hearth." (Ibid., pp. 117, 118.)

Sunday 16.—Elder Rigdon preached to a large congregation in Geneseo, Elder Pratt preached in the afternoon of Monday, the 17th.

There was also the same day, March 17, a conference of Elders at Avon, Livingston county, New York, at the house of Alvah Beaman, which I attended. There were present also Sidney Rigdon, Parley P. Pratt, Lyman Wight, John Murdock, Orson Pratt and Orson Hyde, High Priests; and six Elders. I stated that the object of the Conference was to obtain young and middle-aged men to go and assist in the redemption of Zion, according to the commandment; and for the Church to gather up their riches, and send them to purchase lands according to the commandment of the Lord; also to devise means, or obtain money for the relief of the brethren in Kirtland, say two thousand dollars, which sum would deliver the Church in Kirtland from debt; and also determine the course which the several companies shall pursue, or the manner they shall journey when they shall leave this place.

The Conference at Avon, Livingston County.

It was voted by the Council, that Fathers Bosley and Nickerson, Elder McWithey, and Brother Roger Orton, should exert themselves to obtain two thousand dollars, for the present relief of Kirtland. They all agreed to do what they could to obtain it, firmly believing that it could be accomplished by the first of April. It was also decided that Elder Orson Hyde should tarry and preach in the regions round about, till the money should be obtained, and then carry it with him to Kirtland. It was also voted that I should return to Kirtland, accompanied by Elders Sidney Rigdon and Lyman Wight. Elders John Murdock and Orson Pratt were appointed to journey to Kirtland, preaching by the way; and Elders Parley P. Pratt and Henry Brown to visit the churches in Black River country, and obtain all the means they could to help Zion.

Tuesday, March 18.—Tarried at Father Bosley's through the day. On the 19th commenced my journey for

Kirtland, and stayed that night at Brother McWithey's tavern.

March 20.—Continued our journey. Dined at Brother Joseph Holbrook's, and at night tried three times to procure lodgings in the names of disciples, but could not succeed. After night had commenced we found a man, in China, named Reuben Wilson, who would keep us for money; thus we learn there are more places for money than for the disciples of Jesus, the Lamb of God.

March 21.—We came to the house of a man named Starks, six miles east of Springville; and on the 22nd arrived at Brother Vinson Knight's in Perrysburgh, Cataraugus county. On the 23rd we arrived at Father Nickerson's, in Perrysburgh, where we held meeting. On the 24th, I was not able to start, but felt determined to go the next morning.

March 25.—Journeyed from Father Nickerson's to Father Lewis', in Westfield, accompanied by Father Nickerson. On the 26th, continued our journey to Elk Creek, and stayed with Elder Hunt. The 27th, I came to Springfield, where I found Elder Sidney Rigdon, who had come on by a different route; and we arrived that night within sixteen miles of Painesville. Arrived home at Kirtland on the 28th of March, finding my family all well. The Lord be praised for this blessing!

March 27.—Remained at home and had great joy with my family. Sunday, the 30th, was at home, except going to hear Elder Rigdon preach.

CHAPTER IV.

TRIAL AND CONVICTION OF HURLBURT—EFFORTS IN BEHALF
OF THE REDEMPTION OF ZION—DISSOLUTION OF THE UNITED
ORDER OF ZION AND KIRTLAND.

Monday, March 31.—This day, Ira J. Willis, a young
The Whipping man who had been in the Church for some
of Ira J. Willis. time, and who was driven from Jackson
county into Clay county, returned thither to look for a
stray cow, and while at the house of Esquire Manship, a
justice of the peace (where he had called with Brother
John Follet, to prove his title to the cow), was caught by
that unhung land pirate and inhuman monster, Moses
Wilson, and whipped in a most cruel and savage manner,
while surrounded by some half dozen of the old mobbers.
This was an unpardonable act; all that know Mr. Willis
can bear testimony that he is a young man, honest, peaceable and unoffending, working righteousness, and mo-
lesting no one, May God reward Moses Wilson according
to his works.

I went to Chardon today to attend the court in the case
of "Doctor" Philastus Hurlburt.

April 1.—This day at Brother Rider's in Chardon. The
The Trial of court has not brought forward Hurlburt's
"Doctor" trial yet, and we were engaged in issuing
Hurlburt for subpœnas for witnesses. My soul delighteth
the Prophet's in the law of the Lord, for He forgiveth my
Life. sins, and will confound mine enemies. The Lord shall
destroy him who has lifted his heel against me, even that
wicked man Dr. Philastus Hurlburt; He will deliver him
to the fowls of heaven, and his bones shall be cast to the
blasts of the wind, for he lifted his arm against the
Almighty, therefore the Lord shall destroy him.

Wednesday, April the 2nd, and Thursday, the 3rd, attended the court. Hurlburt was on trial for threatening my life. Friday morning I returned home, and in the evening attended Council, of which the following are the minutes:

Minutes of Council.

KIRTLAND, April 4, 1834.

This evening a Council of High Priests assembled at the house of President Joseph Smith, Jun., to reconsider the case of Brother George F. James. President Joseph Smith, Jun., presiding.

Brother George said that he had often promised to take up his cross and magnify his calling, but had failed, and ought to have written to the President ere this time and given him the information that his pecuniary affairs called his attention at home, which prevented his fulfilling the promise he made to President Joseph Smith, in going out to proclaim the Gospel; and he sincerely asked pardon of the Lord, and of his brethren, and particularly of Brother Joseph. He also said he was willing to ask the forgiveness of this Church. He said relative to certain charges, which were, that he "had not attended meetings, and had treated lightly some of the weak," etc.; that he had attended meetings generally; and as far as speaking or treating lightly any brother because of his weakness, that was foreign from his mind, and was that which he had never done, nor could he ever find such principles in his bosom.

President Joseph Smith said he had no hardness; he only wished Brother George to consider this as a chastisement, and that the Council were bound to take notice of his conduct heretofore; but now, if Brother George was willing to walk according to the new covenant, he should have his hand of fellowship. The Council then expressed their satisfaction at Brother George's confession.

(Signed)   OLIVER COWDERY, Clerk.

April 5 —I went to Chardon as a witness for Father Johnson, and returned in the evening. Mr. Russell, the state's attorney for Portage county, called on me. He approached me in a gentlemanly manner, and treated me with great respect.

April 7.—Bishop Whitney, Elder Frederick G. Williams, Oliver Cowdery, Heber C. Kimball, and myself, met in the council room, and bowed down before the Lord, and prayed that He would furnish the means to deliver the Firm from debt, that they might be set at liberty; also, that I might prevail

Special Prayer.

against that wicked man, Hurlburt, and that he might be put to shame.

The Presidency wrote Elder Orson Hyde, who yet remained in the state of New York, as follows:

KIRTLAND, April 7, 1834.

DEAR BROTHER ORSON:—We received yours of the 31st ultimo in due course of mail, and were much grieved on learning that you were not likely to succeed according to our expectations. Myself, Brothers Newel, Frederick and Oliver, retired to the translating room, where prayer was wont to be made, and unbosomed our feelings before God; and cannot but exercise faith yet that you, in the miraculous providences of God, will succeed in obtaining help. The fact is, unless we can obtain help, I myself cannot go to Zion, and if I do not go, it will be impossible to get my brethren in Kirtland, any of them, to go; and if we do not go, it is in vain for our eastern brethren to think of going up to better themselves by obtaining so goodly a land, (which now can be obtained for one dollar and one quarter per acre,) and stand against that wicked mob; for unless they do the will of God, God will not help them; and if God does not help them, all is vain.

Now the fact is, this is the head of the Church and the life of the body; and those able men, as members of the body, God has appointed to be hands to administer to the necessities of the body. Now if a man's hand refuses to administer to the necessities of his body, it must perish of hunger; and if the body perish, all the members perish with it; and if the head fail, the whole body is sickened, the heart faints, and the body dies, the spirit takes its exit, and the carcase remains to be devoured by worms.

Now, Brother Orson, if this Church, which is essaying to be the Church of Christ will not help us, when they can do it without sacrifice, with those blessings which God has bestowed upon them, I prophesy —I speak the truth, I lie not—God shall take away their talent, and give it to those who have no talent, and shall prevent them from ever obtaining a place of refuge, or an inheritance upon the land of Zion; therefore they may tarry, for they might as well be overtaken where they are, as to incur the displeasure of God, and fall under His wrath by the way side, as to fall into the hands of a merciless mob, where there is no God to deliver, as salt that has lost its savor, and is thenceforth good for nothing, but to be trodden under foot of men.

We therefore adjure you to beseech them, in the name of the Lord, by the Son of God, to lend us a helping hand; and if all this will not soften their hearts to administer to our necessity for Zion's sake, turn your back upon them, and return speedily to Kirtland; and the blood of

Zion be upon their heads, even as upon the heads of her enemies; and let their recompense be as the recompense of her enemies; for thus shall it come to pass, saith the Lord of Hosts, who has the cattle upon a thousand hills, who has put forth His Almighty hand to bring to pass His strange act; and what man shall put forth his hand to steady the ark of God, or be found turning a deaf ear to the voice of His servant? God shall speak in due time, and all will be declared. Amen.

> Your brethren in the New Covenant,
>
> JOSEPH SMITH, JUN.,
> FREDERICK G. WILLIAMS,
> OLIVER COWDERY.

April 9.—After an impartial trial, the court decided that Dr. Philastus Hurlburt be bound over, under two hundred dollar bonds, to keep the peace for six months, and pay the cost, which amounted to nearly three hundred dollars, all of which was in answer to our prayers, for which I thank my Heavenly Father.* _{Judgment Against Hurlburt.}

On the 10th, had a council of the United Order, in which it was agreed that the Order should be dissolved, and each one have his stewardship set off to him. _{Dissolution of the United Order in Kirtland.}

The same day the brethren in Clay county, Missouri, executed the following letters and petitions, according to the revelation.†

---

* The closing paragraph of the order of the court in the Hurlburt case is as follows: "Wherefore it is ordered and adjudged by the court that the said Doctor P. Hurlburt enter into a new recognizance, with good and sufficient security, in the sum of two hundred dollars, hereafter to keep the peace and be of good behavior to the citizens of the state of Ohio generally, and to the said Joseph Smith, Junior, in particular, for the period of six months; and it is further ordered, that the said Doctor P. Hurlburt pay the costs of this prosecution, taxed at the sum of one hundred and twelve dollars and fifty-nine cents. And thereupon came the said Doctor P. Hurlburt, with Charles A. Holmes and Elijah Smith as his sureties, in open court, entered into a recognizance in the penal sum of two hundred dollars each, conditioned that the said Doctor P. Hurlburt shall, for the period of six months from and after this day, keep the peace and be of good behavior to all the citizens of the state of Ohio generally, and to the said Joseph Smith, Jun., in particular.

(Signed)   "M. BIRCHARD, P. J."

† See vol. I., pp. 483-488. The papers alluded to include a second petition to the President of the United States; a letter from A. S. Gilbert *et al.* accompanying same; one from W. W. Phelps *et al.* to Governor Dunklin, informing him of the petition to the President; and one from W. W. Phelps to Senator Thomas H. Benton, informing him of the petition to the President, etc.

Friday, April 11.—I attended meeting, and Father Tyler was restored to the fellowship of the Church.

On the 12th, I went to a place near Lake Erie, and spent the day in fishing, and visiting the brethren.

Sunday, 13.—Was sick, and unable to attend meeting.

Monday, 14.—I purchased some hay and oats, and got them home.

Tuesday, 15.—Hauled a load of hay; and on Wednesday plowed and sowed oats for Brother Frederick G. Williams.

Thursday, April 17.—I attended a meeting agreeable to appointment, at which time the import-
Deliverance of Zion Considered. ant subjects of the deliverance of Zion and the building of the Lord's House in Kirtland were discussed by Elder Rigdon. After the lecture, I requested the brethren and sisters to contribute all the money they could for the deliverance of Zion; and received twenty-nine dollars and sixty-eight cents.

April 18.—In company with Elders Sidney Rigdon, Oliver Cowdery and Zebedee Coltrin, I left
An Assault Thwarted by the Spirit. Kirtland for New Portage, to attend a conference; dined at W. W. Williams', in Newburg, and continuing our journey, after dark, we were hailed by a man who desired to ride. We were checked by the Spirit, and refused. He professed to be sick, but in a few minutes was joined by two others, who followed us hard, cursing and swearing; but we were successful in escaping their hands, through the providence of the Lord, and stayed that night at a tavern, where we were treated with civility.

April 19.—Continuing our journey, dined at Brother Joseph Bosworth's, in Copley, Medina county.
An Occasion of Prayer and Blessing. Brother Bosworth was strong in the faith, and if faithful may do much good. We arrived the same day at Brother Jonathan Taylor's, in Norton, where we were received with kindness. We soon retired to the wilderness, where we united in prayer and supplication for the blessings of the Lord to be given unto His Church. We

called upon the Father in the name of Jesus, to go with the brethren who were going to the land of Zion; and that I might have strength, and wisdom, and understanding sufficient to lead the people of the Lord, and to gather and establish the Saints upon the land of their inheritances, and organize them according to the will of Heaven, that they may be no more cast down forever. We then united in the laying on of hands.

Elders Rigdon, Cowdery and Coltrin laid their hands on my head, and conferred upon me all the blessings necessary to qualify me to stand before the Lord, in my calling, and return again in peace and triumph, to enjoy the society of my brethren.

Those present then laid their hands upon the head of Elder Rigdon, and confirmed upon him the blessings of wisdom and knowledge to preside over the Church in my absence, also to have the Spirit to assist Elder Cowdery in conducting the *Star*, in arranging the Book of Covenants; and pronounced the blessings of old age and peace upon him, till Zion is built up, and Kirtland established, till all his enemies are under his feet, and he receive a crown of eternal life in the kindom of God with us.

Previous to blessing Elder Rigdon, we laid hands on Elder Oliver Cowdery, and confirmed upon him the blessings of wisdom and understanding sufficient for his station that he be qualified to assist Elder Rigdon in arranging the Church Book of Covenants, which is soon to be published, and have intelligence in all things to do the work of printing.

After blessing Elder Rigdon, we laid our hands upon Brother Zebedee Coltrin, and confirmed the blessings of wisdom to preach the Gospel, even till it spreads to the islands of the seas, and to be spared to see three score years and ten, and see Zion built up, and Kirtland established forever, and even at last to receive a crown of life. Our hearts rejoiced, and we were comforted with the Holy Spirit.

Sunday, April 20.—Elder Rigdon entertained a large congregation of Saints with an interesting discourse upon the Fullness of Times.

April 21.—I attended conference, and had a glorious time. Some few volunteered to go to Zion, and others donated sixty-six dollars and thirty-seven cents for the benefit of the scattered brethren in Zion. The following is an extract from the minutes of the conference:

Minutes of Conference.

NORTON, MEDINA COUNTY, OHIO, April 21, 1834.

This day a conference of Elders assembled at the dwelling house of Brother Carpenter. President Joseph Smith, Jun., read the second chapter of Joel's prophecy, prayed, and addressed the conference as follows:

"It is very difficult for us to communicate to the churches all that God has revealed to us, in consequence of tradition; for we are differently situated from any other people that ever existed upon this earth; consequently those former revelations cannot be suited to our conditions; they were given to other people, who were before us; but in the last days, God was to call a remnant, in which was to be deliverance, as well as in Jerusalem and Zion. Now if God should give no more revelations, where will we find Zion and this remnant? The time is near when desolation is to cover the earth, and then God will have a place of deliverance in His remnant, and in Zion."

The President then gave a relation of obtaining and translating the Book of Mormon, the revelation of the Priesthood of Aaron, the organization of the Church in 1830, the revelation of the High Priesthood, and the gift of the Holy Ghost poured out upon the Church; and said:

"Take away the Book of Mormon and the revelations, and where is our religion? We have none; for without Zion, and a place of deliverance, we must fall; because the time is near when the sun will be darkened, and the moon turn to blood, and the stars fall from heaven, and the earth reel to and fro. Then, if this is the case, and if we are not sanctified and gathered to the places God has appointed, with all our former professions and our great love for the Bible, we must fall; we cannot stand; we cannot be saved; for God will gather out His Saints from the Gentiles, and then comes desolation and destruction, and none can escape except the pure in heart who are gathered."

Elder Rigdon addressed the conference, and said:

"On two points hang all the revelations that have ever been given, and these are the two advents of the Messiah. The first is past, and the second is now just before us; and consequently those who desire a part in this era which the angels desired to look into, have to be assembled with the Saints; for if they are not gathered, they must wail because of His coming. There is no part of His creation which will not feel a shock at this grand display of His power, for the ancient Saints will reign with Christ a thousand years. The gathered Saints will dwell under that reign, and those who are not gathered may expect to endure His wrath that length of time; for the rest of the dead are not to live till the thousand years are ended.

"It is vain for men of this generation to think of laying up and providing inheritances for their children, except they lay it up in the place where deliverance is appointed by the voice of God; for these are the days of vengeance, as were the days of Jeremiah; because, before his eyes were closed in death, the Jews were led captive, and the land possessed by another people. And so in this day; while the father is laying up gold for his son, the destroyer may lay him lifeless at his feet, and where then is all his treasure? Therefore if we, the islands of the sea, and all the ends of the earth, desire an inheritance for ourselves and our children, and themselves and their children, it must be obtained where God has appointed the places of deliverance."

Elder Rigdon adverted to the former covenants to Abraham, Isaac, and Jacob, and others of the ancients, which were to be realized in the last days; and spoke at some length upon the deliverance of Zion, the endowment of the Elders with power from on high according to former promises, and the spreading of the word of the Lord to the four winds. He first referred to the situation of the brethren in Missouri, and urged the importance of those who could, giving heed to the revelations by going up to their assistance; and those who could not go, to help those who are going with means for their expenses.

Elder Cowdery gave a brief relation of the mobbing in Missouri, and called for a contribution.

Elders Ambrose Palmer and Salmon Warner followed on the same subject.

Brother Joseph Bosworth spoke on the deliverance of Zion, and said he had no property, but if necessary for her deliverance he would sell his clothes at auction, if he might have left him as good a garment as the Savior had in the manger.

Others also spoke on the deliverance of Zion.

President Joseph Smith, Jun., prophesied.

"If Zion is not delivered, the time is near when all of this Church, wherever they may be found, will be persecuted and destroyed in like manner."

Elder Rigdon gave an account of the endowment of the ancient apostles, and laid before the conference the dimensions of the House to be built in Kirtland, and rehearsed the promise to the Elders in the last days, which they were to realize after the House of the Lord was built.

Brother Bosworth then related a few items of a vision, as a testimony of those things contained in the revelation read by Elder Rigdon, and his remarks thereon.

President Smith explained the revelation concerning the building of the Lord's House.

Elder Rigdon then spoke on the spreading of the word of the Lord; followed by several of the brethren.

The conference voted that Thomas Tripp be excluded from the Church in consequence of his imprudent conduct, with the privilege of an appeal to the Bishop's Council in Kirtland.

President Smith then laid hands on certain children, and blessed them in the name of the Lord.

Elder Rigdon administered the Sacrament.

There were present seven High Priests, and thirteen Elders.

Adjourned to the Monday preceding the second Sunday in September.

Closed by singing "Now my remnant of days," etc.

(Signed)   OLIVER COWDERY.
Clerk of the Conference.

April 22.—I returned to Kirtland.

April 23.—Assembled in Council with Elders Sidney Rigdon, Frederick G. Williams, Newel K. Whitney, John Johnson, and Oliver Cowdery; and united in asking the Lord to give Elder Zebedee Coltrin influence over Brother Jacob Myres, to obtain the money which he has gone to borrow for us, or cause him to come to this place and bring it himself. I also received the following:

Return of the Prophet and Party to Kirtland.

*Revelation given April 23, 1834, to Enoch [Joseph Smith, Jun.,] concerning the Order of the Church for the benefit of the poor.**

1. Verily I say unto you, my friends, I give unto you counsel, and a commandment, concerning all the properties which belong to the order which I commanded to be organized and established, to be an

---

* Doctrine and Covenants, sec. civ.

united order, and an everlating order for the benefit of my Church, and for the salvation of men until I come,

2. With promise immutable and unchangeable, that inasmuch as those whom I commanded were faithful, they should be blessed with a multiplicity of blessings;

3. But inasmuch as they were not faithful, they were nigh unto cursing.

4. Therefore, inasmuch as some of my servants have not kept the commandment but have broken the covenant through covetousness, and with feigned words, I have cursed them with a very sore and grievous curse;

5. For I, the Lord, have decreed in my heart, that inasmuch as any man belonging to the order shall be found a transgressor, or, in other words, shall break the covenant with which ye are bound, he shall be cursed in his life, and shall be trodden down by whom I will,

6. For I, the Lord, am not to be mocked in these things;

7. And all this, that the innocent among you may not be condemned with the unjust, and that the guilty among you may not escape, because I, the Lord, have promised unto you a crown of glory at my right hand.

8. Therefore, inasmuch as you are found transgressors, ye cannot escape my wrath in your lives;

9. Inasmuch as ye are cut off for transgression, ye cannot escape the buffetings of Satan until the day of redemption.

10. And now I give unto you power from this very hour, that if any man among you, of the order, is found a transgressor, and repenteth not of the evil, that ye shall deliver him over unto the buffetings of Satan, and he shall not have power to bring evil upon you.

11. It is wisdom in me; therefore, a commandment I give unto you, that ye shall organize yourselves and appoint every man his stewardship,

12. That every man may give an account unto me of the stewardship which is appointed unto him;

13. For it is expedient that I, the Lord, should make every man accountable as a steward over earthly blessings, which I have made and prepared for my creatures.

14. I, the Lord, stretched out the heavens, and built the earth, my very handy-work, and all things therein are mine;

15. And it is my purpose to provide for my Saints, for all things are mine;

16. But it must needs be done in mine own way; and behold this is the way that I, the Lord, have decreed to provide for my Saints, that the poor shall be exalted, in that the rich are made low;

17. For the earth is full, and there is enough and to spare; yea, I prepared all things, and have given unto the children of men to be agents unto themselves.

18. Therefore, if any man shall take of the abundance which I have made, and impart not his portion, according to the law of my gospel, unto the poor and the needy, he shall, with the wicked, lift up his eyes in hell, being in torment.

19. And now, verily I say unto you, concerning the properties of the order.

20. Let my servant Pelagoram (Sidney Rigdon) have appointed unto him the place where he now resides, and the lot of Tahhanes (the tannery) for his stewardship, for his support while he is laboring in my vineyard, even as I will, when I shall command him;

21. And let all things be done according to the counsel of the order, and united consent or voice of the order, which dwell in the land of Shinehah (Kirtland).

22. And this stewardship and blessing I, the Lord, confer upon my servant Pelagoram (Sidney Rigdon), for a blessing upon him, and his seed after him;

23. And I will multiply blessings upon him, inasmuch as he will be humble before me.

24. And again, let my servant Mahemson (Martin Harris) have appointed unto him, for his stewardship, the lot of land which my servant Zombre (John Johnson) obtained in exchange for his former inheritance, for him and his seed after him.

25. And inasmuch as he is faithful, I will multiply blessings upon him and his seed after him.

26. And let my servant Mahemson (Martin Harris) devote his moneys for the proclaiming of my words, according as my servant Gazelam (Joseph Smith, Jun.,) shall direct.

27. And again, let my servant Shederlaomach (Frederick G. Williams) have the place upon which he now dwells.

28. And let my servant Olihah (Oliver Cowdery) have the lot which is set off joining the house, which is to be for the Laneshine-house (printting office), which is lot number one, and also the lot upon which his father resides.

29. And let my servants Shederlaomach (Frederick G. Williams) and Olihah (Oliver Cowdery) have the Laneshine-house (printing office), and all things that pertain unto it;

30. And this shall be their stewardship which shall be appointed unto them:

31. And inasmuch as they are faithful, behold I will bless, and multiply blessings upon them.

32. And this is the beginning of the stewardship which I have appointed them, for them and their seed after them;

33. And inasmuch as they are faithful, I will multiply blessings upon them, and their seed after them, even a multiplicity of blessings.

34. And again, let my servant Zombre (John Johnson) have the house in which he lives, and the inheritance—all, save the ground which has been reserved for the building of my houses, which pertains to that inheritance, and those lots which have been named for my servant Olihah (Oliver Cowdery).

35. And, inasmuch as he is faithful, I will multiply blessings upon him.

36. And it is my will that he should sell the lots that are laid off for the building up of the city of my Saints, inasmuch as it shall be made known to him by the voice of the Spirit, and according to the counsel of the order, and by the voice of the order.

37. And this is the beginning of the stewardship which I have appointed unto him, for a blessing unto him, and his seed after him;

38. And inasmuch as he is faithful, I will multiply a multiplicity of blessings upon him.

39. And let my servant Ahashdah (Newel K. Whitney) have appointed unto him the houses and lot where he now resides, and the lot and building on which the Ozondah (mercantile establishment) stands, and also the lot which is now on the corner south of the Ozondah (mercantile establishment), and also the lot upon which the Shule (ashery) is situated.

40. And all this I have appointed unto my servant Ahashdah (Newel K. Whitney) for his stewardship, for a blessing upon him and his seed after him, for the benefit of the Ozondah (mercantile establishment) of my order which I have established for my Stake in the land of Shinehah (Kirtland).

41. Yea, verily, this is the stewardship which I have appointed unto my servant Ahashdah (N. K. Whitney), even this whole Ozondah (mercantile establishment), him and his agent, and his seed after him;

42. And inasmuch as he is faithful in keeping my commandments which I have given unto him, I will multiply blessings upon him, and his seed after him, even a multiplicity of blessings.

43 And again, let my servant Gazelam (Joseph Smith, Jun.,) have appointed unto him the lot which is laid off for the building of my house, which is forty rods long, and twelve wide, and also the inheritance upon which his father now resides.

44. And this is the beginning of the stewardship which I have appointed unto him, for a blessing upon him, and upon his father.

45. For, behold, I have reserved an inheritance for his father, for his

support; therefore he shall be reckoned in the house of my servant Gazelam (Joseph Smith, Jun.)

46. And I will multiply blessings upon the house of my servant Gazelam (Joseph Smith, Jun.,) inasmuch as he is faithful, even a multiplicity of blessings.

47. And now, a commandment I give unto you concerning Zion, that you shall no longer be bound as an United Order to your brethren of Zion, only on this wise:

48. After you are organized, you shall be called the United Order of the Stake of Zion, the city of Shinehah (Kirtland). And your brethren, after they are organized, shall be called the United Order of the City of Zion.

49. And they shall be organized in their own names, and in their own name; and they shall do their business in their own name, and in their own names;

50. And you shall do business in your own name, and in your own names.

51. And this I have commanded to be done for your salvation, and also for their salvation, in consequence of their being driven out and that which is to come.

52. The covenants being broken through transgression, by covetousness and feigned words;

53. Therefore you are dissolved as a United Order with your brethren, that you are not bound only up to this hour unto them, only on this wise, as I said, by loan as shall be agreed by this order in council, as your circumstances will admit and the voice of the council direct.

54. And again a commandment I give unto you concerning your stewardships which I have appointed unto you.

55. Behold, all these properties are mine, or else your faith is vain, and ye are found hypocrites, and the covenants which ye have made unto me are broken;

56. And if the properties are mine, then ye are stewards, otherwise ye are no stewards.

57. But, verily I say unto you, I have appointed unto you to be stewards over mine house, even stewards indeed;

58. And for this purpose I have commanded you to organize yourselves, even to shinelah (print) my words, the fullness of my scriptures, the revelations which I have given unto you, and which I shall hereafter, from time to time, give unto you,

59. For the purpose of building up my Church and Kingdom on the earth, and to prepare my people for the time when I shall dwell with them, which is nigh at hand.

60. And ye shall prepare for yourselves a place for a treasury, and consecrate it unto my name;

61. And ye shall appoint one among you to keep the treasury, and he shall be ordained unto this blessing;

62. And there shall be a seal upon the treasury, and all the sacred things shall be delivered into the treasury, and no man among you shall call it his own, or any part of it, for it shall belong to you all with one accord;

63. And I give it unto you from this very hour; and now see to it, that ye go to and make use of the stewardship which I have appointed unto you, exclusive of the sacred things, for the purpose of shinelane (printing) these sacred things as I have said;

64. And the avails of the sacred things shall be had in the treasury, and a seal shall be upon it, and it shall not be used or taken out of the treasury by any one, neither shall the seal be loosed which shall be placed upon it, only by the voice of the order, or by commandment.

65. And thus shall ye preserve the avails of the sacred things in the treasury for sacred and holy purposes:

66. And this shall be called the sacred treasury of the Lord; and a seal shall be kept upon it that it may be holy and consecrated unto the Lord.

67. And again, there shall be another treasury prepared, and a treasurer appointed to keep the treasury, and a seal shall be placed upon it;

68. And all moneys that you receive in your stewardships, by improving upon the properties which I have appointed unto you, in houses, or in lands, or in cattle, or in all things save it be the holy and sacred writings, which I have reserved unto myself, for holy and sacred purposes, shall be cast into the treasury as fast as you receive moneys, by hundreds, or by fifties, or by twenties, or by tens, or by fives;

69. Or in other words, if any man among you obtain five talents (dollars), let him cast them into the treasury; or if he obtain ten, or twenty, or fifty, or an hundred, let him do likewise;

70. And let not any among you say that it is his own, for it shall not be called his, nor any part of it;

71. And there shall not any part of it be used, or taken out of the treasury, only by the voice and common consent of the order.

72. And this shall be the voice and common consent of the order; that any man among you say to the treasurer, I have need of this to help me in my stewardship;

73. If it be five talents (dollars), or if it be ten talents (dollars,) or twenty, or fifty, or a hundred, the treasurer shall give unto him the sum which he requires, to help him in his stewardship.

74. Until he be found a transgressor, and it is manifest before the council of the order plainly, that he is an unfaithful and an unwise steward;

75. But so long as he is in full fellowship, and is faithful, and wise in his stewardship, this shall be his token unto the treasurer, that the treasurer shall not withhold.

76. But in case of transgression, the treasurer shall be subject unto the council and voice of the order.

77. And in case the treasurer is found an unfaithful and an unwise steward, he shall be subject to the council and voice of the order, and shall be removed out of his place, and another shall be appointed in his stead.

78. And again, verily I say unto you, concerning your debts, behold it is my will that you shall pay all your debts;

79. And it is my will that you shall humble yourselves before me, and obtain this blessing by your diligence and humility, and the prayer of faith;

80. And inasmuch as you are diligent and humble, and exercise the prayer of faith, behold, I will soften the hearts of those to whom you are in debt, until I shall send means unto you for your deliverance.

81. Therefore write speedily to Cainhannoch (New York), and write according to that which shall be dictated by my Spirit, and I will soften the hearts of those to whom you are in debt, that it shall be taken away out of their minds to bring affliction upon you.

82. And inasmuch as ye are humble and faithful, and call upon my name, behold I will give you the victory.

83. I give unto you a promise, that you shall be delivered this once out of your bondage;

84. Inasmuch as you obtain a chance to loan money by hundreds, or thousands, even until you shall loan enough to deliver yourselves from bondage, it is your privilege:

85. And pledge the properties which I have put into your hands, this once, by giving your names by common consent or otherwise, as it shall seem good unto you

86. I give unto you this privilege, this once, and behold, if you proceed to do the things which I have laid before you, according to my commandments, all these things are mine, and ye are my stewards, and the master will not suffer his house to be broken up. Even so. Amen.

CHAPTER V.

ZION'S CAMP—ITS JOURNEY FROM KIRTLAND TO MISSOURI.

ABOUT the last of April I received, by letters from friends in the East, and of brethren in Kirtland, the sum of two hundred and fifty-one dollars and sixty cents, towards the deliverance of Zion.

Aid for the Redemption of Zion.

May 1.—More than twenty of the brethren left Kirtland for Missouri, according to previous appointment, accompanied by four baggage wagons. They traveled to New Portage, and there tarried with the church until the remainder of the Kirtland company, who were not in readiness to start with them, arrived.

Gathering of Zion's Camp at New Portage.

The following letter from Elder Phelps to us, clearly shows the necessity there was of the Saints in Missouri receiving assistance:

LIBERTY, May 1, 1834.

DEAR BRETHREN—There are great moves in the west. Last week an alarm was spread in Jackson county, the seat of iniquity and bloodshed, that the "Mormons" were crossing the Missouri, to take possession of their lands, and nearly all the county turned out, "prepared for war;" on Saturday and on Sunday took the field, near old McGee's, above Blue; but no "Mormons" came; neither did Arthur* go over to

---

* The circumstance here alluded to is that a Mr. Arthur, a respectable and wealthy planter of Clay county, sent one of his black servants into Jackson county with a large wagon load of whisky, flour and bacon. After the servant had crossed the river, a stranger came out of the woods and began to burst open the barrels and destroy the flour, threatening the life of the negro if he should ever come into that county again. Mr. Arthur, it is needless to say, was not a member of the Church of Latter-day Saints, nor a member of any other religious society. Whether he was taken for a "Mormon" or not does not appear. (See *Evening and Morning Star*, vol. ii, p. 319.)

see about his "spilt whisky," so that the scene closed by burning our houses, or many of them. Our people had about one hundred and seventy buildings in Jackson, and a bonfire of nearly all of them at once made a light large enough to glare on their dark deed and cup of iniquity running over at midnight.

The crisis has come; all who will not take up arms with the mob and prepare to fight the "Mormons," have to leave Jackson county. I understand some have left the county, because they refused to fight an innocent people. It is said the mob will hold a "general muster" this week, for the purpose of learning who is who. We have reason to believe that they begin to slip over the Missouri, and commit small depredations upon our brethren settled near the river.

It is said to be enough to shock the stoutest heart to witness the drinking, swearing and ravings of most of the mob; nothing but the power of God can stop them in their latter-day crusade against the Church of Christ.

Our brethren are very industrious in putting in spring crops; and they are generally in good health, and the faithful are in strong hope of a glorious hereafter.

I remain yours, etc.,

W. W. PHELPS.

May 3.—Kirtland.

Minutes of a Conference of the Elders of the Church of Christ, which Church was organized in the township of Fayette, Seneca county, New York, on the 6th of April, A.D. 1830. *

President Joseph Smith, Jun., was chosen moderator, and Frederick G. Williams and Oliver Cowdery were appointed clerks.

After prayer, the conference proceeded to discuss the subject of

---

* The minutes of this conference are to be found in the *Evening and Morning Star*, vol. ii, p. 352. It will be observed from the heading that the Elders assembled in the conference are called *the Elders of the Church of Christ*. This is pointed out in order that it may be seen that while the conference adopted the title "The Church of the Latter-day Saints," and the Church was for some years called by that name, it was not the intention to regard the Church as any other than the Church of Christ. In an editorial upon this subject in the May number of the *Star* [minutes of the conference, however, designating the above name of the Church were not published until the July number of the *Star* was issued] the following occurs as a comment upon the action of this conference: "It is now more than four years since this Church was organized in these last days, and though the conferences have always shown by their minutes that they took no other name than the name of Christ, the Church has, particularly abroad, been called 'Mormonite.' As the members of this Church profess a belief in the truth of the Book of Mormon, the

names and appellations, when a motion was made by Sidney Rigdon, and seconded by Newel K. Whitney, that this Church be known hereafter by the name of "The Church of the Latter-day Saints." Remarks were made by the members, after which the motion passed by unanimous vote.

"Resolved, that this conference recommend to the conferences and churches abroad, that in making out and transmitting minutes of their proceedings, such minutes and proceedings be made out under the above title.

"Resolved, that these minutes be signed by the moderator and clerks, and published in the *Evening and Morning Star.*

JOSEPH SMITH, JUN., Moderator.

FREDERICK G. WILLIAMS, } Clerks.
OLIVER COWDERY,

May 5.—Having gathered and prepared clothing and other necessaries to carry to our brethren and sisters, who had been robbed and plundered of nearly all their effects; and having provided for ourselves horses, and wagons, and firearms, and all sorts of munitions of war of the most portable kind for self-defense—as our enemies are thick on every hand—I started with the remainder of the company from Kirtland for Missouri. This day we went as far as the town of Streetsborough, twenty-seven miles from Kirtland. We stayed in Mr. Ford's barn, where Uncle John Smith and Brigham Young had been preaching three months before. This day Brothers Brigham and Joseph Young went to Israel Barlow's, about three-quarters of a mile, and tarried over night. Brother Barlow returned with them in the morning and joined the camp. Brother Brigham Young

Departure of the Prophet from Kirtland for Missouri.

world, either out of contempt and ridicule, or to distinguish us from others, have been very lavish in bestowing the title of 'Mormonite.' Others may call themselves by their own, or by other names, and have the privilege of wearing them without our changing them or attempting so to do; but *we* do not accept the above title [Mormonite], nor shall we wear it as *our* name, though it may be lavished upon us double to what it has heretofore been. And when the bitterness of feeling now cherished in the bosoms of those who profess to be the followers of Christ, against the Church of the Latter-day Saints, shall cease to exist, and when fabrications and desipient reports concerning this society are no longer considered a virtue, it will take its rank, at least with others, and these stigmas will forever sleep with their inventors." (*Evening and Morning Star*, vol. ii, p. 317.)

had taken the families of Solomon Angel and Lorenzo Booth into his house, that they might accompany us to Missouri.

On the 6th we arrived at New Portage, about fifty miles distance from Kirtland, and joined our brethren who had gone before.

My company from Kirtland consisted of about one hundred men, mostly young men, and nearly all Elders, Priests, Teachers or Deacons. As our wagons were nearly filled with baggage, we had mostly to travel on foot.

On the 7th we made preparations for traveling, gathered all the moneys of every individual of the company, and appointed Frederick G. Williams paymaster to disburse the funds thus collected; and Zerubbabel Snow was chosen commissary general. The whole company now consisted of more than one hundred and thirty men, accompanied by twenty baggage wagons. We left but few men in Kirtland, viz.: Elders Sidney Rigdon, Oliver Cowdery, a few working on the Temple, and the aged.

Through the remainder of this day I continued to organize the company, appoint such other offic-
Organization of Zion's Camp. ers as were required, and gave such instructions as were necessary for the discipline, order, comfort and safety of all concerned. I also divided the whole band into companies of twelve, leaving each company to elect its own captain, who assigned each man in his respective company his post and duty, generally in the following order: Two cooks, two firemen; two tent men, two watermen, one runner, two wagoners and horsemen, and one commissary. We purchased flour and meal, baked our own bread, and cooked our own food, generally, which was good, though sometimes scanty; and sometimes we had johnny-cake, or corn-dodger, instead of flour bread. Every night before retiring to rest, at the sound of the trumpet, we bowed before the Lord in the several tents, and presented our

thank-offerings with prayer and supplication; and at the sound of the morning trumpet, about four o'clock, every man was again on his knees before the Lord, imploring His blessing for the day.

On the 8th we recommenced our march towards Zion, and pitched our tents for the night in a beauti- *The March of Zion's Camp.* ful grove at Chippeway, twelve miles from New Portage.

On the morning of the 9th we completed our organization by companies and proceeded onward, and encamped near Wooster; and on Saturday the 10th, passing through Mansfield, encamped for the Sabbath in Richfield township. About one hour after we had encamped, Elders Lyman E. Johnson, Willard Snow and a number of others joined the camp from the north part of Vermont.

Sunday 11.—Elder Sylvester Smith preached, and the company received the Sacrament of bread and wine.

Here we were increased in number by eight brethren, in company of Elder Elias Benner, from Richland and Stark counties, most of whom were Germans.

Monday, May 12.—We left Richfield, traveled about thirty-five miles, passed the Bucyrus, and en- *Incidents in Zion's Camp.* camped on the Sandusky plains, at a short distance from the place where the Indians roasted General Crawford, and near the Indian settlements.

On the 13th we passed through a long range of beech woods, where the roads were very bad. In many instances we had to fasten ropes to the wagons to haul them out of the sloughs and mud holes. Brother Parley P. Pratt broke his harness; the brethren fastened their ropes to his wagon, and drew it about three miles to the place of encampment on the Scioto river, while he rode singing and whistling.

Wednesday, May 14.—We passed on to Belle Fontaine, where we discovered refractory feelings in Sylvester Smith, who expressed great dissatisfaction because we were short of bread, although we had used all diligence to procure a supply, and Captain Brigham Young had previously sent two men ahead to provide supplies for his company.

Thursday, May 15.—We forded Mad river, and passing through a beautiful country, encamped a little west of Springfield. This night Moses Martin fell asleep on sentry duty, and I went and took his sword, and left him asleep.

Friday, May 16.—About nine o'clock, while I was riding in a wagon with Brother Hyrum, Ezra Thayer and George A. Smith, we came into a piece of thick woods of recent growth, where I told them that I felt much depressed in spirit and lonesome, and that there had been a great deal of bloodshed in that place, remarking that whenever a man of God is in a place where many have been killed, he will feel lonesome and unpleasant, and his spirits will sink.

In about forty rods from where I made this observation we came through the woods, and saw a large farm, and there near the road on our left, was a mound sixty feet high, containing human bones. This mound was covered with apple trees, and surrounded with oat fields, the ground being level for some distance around.

At dinner time some of the brethren expressed considerable fear on account of milk sickness, with which the people were troubled along our route. Many were afraid to use milk or butter, and appealed to me to know if it was not dangerous. I told them to use all they could get, unless they were told it was "sick." Some expressed fears that it might be sold to us by our enemies for the purpose of doing us injury. I told them not to fear; that if they would follow my counsel, and use all they could get from friend or enemy, it should do them good, and none be sick in consequence of it; and although we passed through neighborhoods where many of the people and cattle were infected with the sickness, yet my words were fulfilled.

While passing through Dayton, Ohio, great curiosity was manifested, various reports of our numbers and designs having gone before us. Some of the inhabitants inquired of the company where they were from, when Captain Young replied: "From every place but this, and we will soon be from this." "Where are you going?" 'To the West." *

Some ten or a dozen gentlemen came over from Dayton to ascertain our numbers, which they reported to be at least six hundred. These gentlemen also inquired of almost every man in the camp where he was from and where he was going, and what was his business. They returned to Dayton and reported that every man in the company was a gentleman and gave a respectful answer to every question asked, but they could not ascertain where we were going, or what was our business.

Delegation from Dayton.

This evening a courtmartial was held in the camp for the trial of Moses Martin for falling asleep while on picket duty. Brother Martin pleaded his own case, say-

---

* The late President Wilford Woodruff, who was a member of Zion's Camp, speaking at the celebration of the thirty-third anniversary (July 24, 1880,) of the entrance of the Pioneers into Salt Lake valley, speaking of Zion's Camp, said:

"We were followed by spies hundreds of miles to find out the object of our mission. We had some boys in the camp. George A. Smith was among the youngest. When they could get him alone they would question him, thinking that he looked green enough for them to get what they wanted out of him. The following questions were frequently put and answered:

" 'My boy, where are you from?'

" 'From the East.'

" 'Where are you going?'

" 'To the West.'

" 'What for?'

" 'To see where we can get land cheapest and best.'

" 'Who leads the camp?'

" 'Sometimes one, sometimes another.'

" 'What name?'

" 'Captain Wallace, Major Bruce. Orson Hyde, James Allred,' etc.

"This was about the information the spies obtained from any of the camp that were questioned." ("The Utah Pioneers," p. 18.)

ing that he was overcome with fatigue, and so overpowered that he could not keep awake, etc. I decided that
he should be acquitted with a warning never to go to sleep
again on watch, which was sanctioned by the court, and
I took occasion from this circumstance to give the brethren much useful instruction.

We forded the Miami river with our baggage wagons,
The Camp most of the men wading through the water. On
Enters the 17th of May we crossed the state line of
Indiana. Ohio, and encamped for the Sabbath just within
the limits of Indiana, having traveled about forty miles
that day. Our feet were very sore and blistered, our
stockings wet with blood, the weather being very warm.
At night a spy attempted to get into our camp, but was
prevented by our guard. We had our sentinels posted
every night, on account of spies who were continually
striving to harass us, steal our horses, etc.

This evening there was a difficulty between some of the
Difficulties brethren and Sylvester Smith, on occasion of
Within the which I was called to decide in the matter.
Camp. Finding a rebellious spirit in Sylvester Smith,
and to some extent in others, I told them they would meet
with misfortunes, difficulties and hindrances, and said,
"and you will know it before you leave this place," exhorting them to humble themselves before the Lord and
become united, that they might not be scourged. A very
singular occurrence took place that night and the next
day, concerning our teams. On Sunday morning, when
we arose, we found almost every horse in the camp so
badly foundered that we could scarcely lead them a few
rods to the water. The brethren then deeply realized the
effects of discord. When I learned the fact, I exclaimed
to the brethren, that for a witness that God overruled and
had His eye upon them, all those who would humble
themselves before the Lord should know that the hand of
God was in this misfortune, and their horses should be
restored to health immediately; and by twelve o'clock the

same day the horses were as nimble as ever, with the exception of one of Sylvester Smith's, which soon afterwards died.

Sunday, May 18.—We had preaching as usual, and the administration of the Sacrament.

About this time the Saints in Clay county, Missouri, established an armory, where they commenced manufacturing swords, dirks, pistols, stocking rifles, and repairing arms in general for their own defense against mob violence; many arms were purchased; for the leading men in Clay county rendered every facility in their power, in order, as they said, "to help the 'Mormons' settle their own difficulties, and pay the Jackson mob in their own way."

Monday, May, 19.—We traveled thirty-one miles and encamped in Franklin township, Henry county, in the beech woods.

Tuesday, May 20.—We encamped near Greenfield, having traveled about twenty-five miles, some part of the way being so bad I walked over the tops of my boots in mud, helping to pull through the wagons with ropes.

While we were eating dinner three gentlemen came riding up on very fine looking horses and commenced their inquiries of various ones concerning our traveling in so large a body, asking where we were from, and where we were going. The reply was as usual—some from the state of Maine; another would say, "I am from York state;" some from Massachusetts; some from Ohio; and some replied, "we are from the East, and as soon as we have done eating dinner we shall be going to the West again." They then addressed themselves to Dr. Frederick G. Williams to see if they could find out who the leader of the camp was. The doctor replied, "We have no one in particular." They asked if we had not a general to take the lead of the company. The reply was, "No one in particular." "But," said they, "is there not some one among you

Spies from the West in the Camp.

whom you call your captain, or leader, or who is superior to the rest?'' He answered, ''Sometimes one and sometimes another takes charge of the company, so as not to throw the burden upon any one in particular.'' These spies, who had come from the west, passed us several times that same day and the next.

Although threatened by our enemies that we should not pass through Indianopolis, we passed through that city on the 21st unmolested. All the inhabitants were quiet. At night we encamped a few miles west of Indianopolis. There had previously been so many reports that we should never be permitted to pass through this place, and that the governor would have us dispersed, that some of the brethren were afraid that we might have difficulty there. But I had told them, in the name of the Lord, we should not be disturbed and that we would pass through Indianopolis without the people knowing it. When near the place many got into the wagons, and, separating some little distance, passed through the city, while others walked down different streets, leaving the inhabitants wondering ''when that big company would come along.''

Indianopolis Incident.

Since the 18th we had followed the national road where it was passable, but frequently we had to take by-roads which were miry and led through thick woods.

Thursday, May 22.—We encamped on a small stream of water in a grove near Belleville.

Friday, May 23.—We encamped about four miles from Greencastle, after a hard drive.

Saturday, May, 24.—We crossed the Wabash river at Clinton in ferry boats, in quick time, and pushed on to the state line, where we arrived late in the evening, and encamped in an oak opening in Edgar county, Illionois.

Sunday, May 25.—We had no meeting, but attended to washing, baking, and preparing to resume our journey. A man in disguise, having on an old sealskin cap, came into our camp. He swore

A Jackson County Spy in Camp.

we were going up to Jackson county, and that we would never get over the Mississippi river alive. It was evident he was a spy, and I recollected having seen him in Jackson county, Missouri.

Monday, May 26.—A very hot day. We traveled through Paris and across a sixteen mile prairie; at noon we stopped to bait at a slough, about six miles from the timber, having no water to drink but such as was filled with living animals commonly called wigglers, and as we did not like to swallow them we strained the water before using it. This was the first prairie of any extent that we had come to on our journey, and was a great curiosity to many of the brethren. It was so very level that the deer miles off appeared but a short distance away; some of the brethren started out in pursuit before they were apprised of their mistake as to the distance. We continued our march, pulling our wagons through a small creek with ropes, and came to the house of Mr. Wayne, the only settler in the vicinity, where we found a well of water, which was one of the greatest comforts we could have received, as we were almost famished, and it was a long time before we could, or dared to satisfy our thirst. We crossed the Embarras river and encamped on a small branch of the same about one mile west. In pitching my tent we found three massasaugas or prairie rattlesnakes, which the brethren were about to kill, but I said, "Let them alone—don't hurt them! How will the serpent ever lose his venom, while the servants of God possess the same disposition, and continue to make war upon it? Men must become harmless, before the brute creation; and when men lose their vicious dispositions and cease to destroy the animal race, the lion and the lamb can dwell together, and the sucking child can play with the serpent in safety." The brethren took the serpents carefully on sticks and carried them across the creek. I exhorted the brethren not to kill a serpent, bird, or an animal of any kind during our journey unless it

Precept vs. Example—a Lesson.

became necessary in order to preserve ourselves from hunger.

I had frequently spoken on this subject, when on a certain occasion I came up to the brethren who were watching a squirrel on a tree, and to prove them and to know if they would heed my counsel, I took one of their guns, shot the squirrel and passed on, leaving the squirrel on the ground. Brother Orson Hyde, who was just behind, picked up the squirrel, and said, "We will cook this, that nothing may be lost." I perceived that the brethren understood what I did it for, and in their practice gave more heed to my precept than to my example, which was right.

This evening Brother Parley P. Pratt and Amasa Lyman returned from the Eugene branch, Indiana (where I had sent them), with a company of about a dozen men.

The reports of mobs which were continually saluting our ears caused the brethren to be constantly alive to the subject, and about eleven o'clock this evening our picket guards reported that they saw the fires of the mob on the southeast of us. I instantly arose and discovered the mistake; but wishing the brethren to enjoy the scene as well as myself, immediately discharged my gun, which was a signal to call all men to arms. When the companies were all paraded and ready for battle, I pointed them to the reflection of the rising moon resting on points of timber in the east, which gave the appearance of the reflection of the light of a number of camp fires. The scenery was most delightful, and was well worth the trouble of any man rising from his couch to witness, who had never seen the like on the broad prairie before. This circumstance proved that nearly every man in the camp was ready for battle, except Dean Gould, who was not baptized, and Captain Jazeniah B. Smith, who was suddenly taken with the colic, and did not leave his tent. The whole incident was very amusing.

A Call to Arms.

Tuesday, May 27.—Notwithstanding our enemies were continually breathing threats of violence, we did not fear, neither did we hesitate to prosecute our journey, for God was with us, and His angels went before us, and the faith of our little band was unwavering. We know that angels were our companions, for we saw them.*

Angels Attend the Camp.

We arrived at the Okaw branch of the Kaskaskia, where we found log canoes, which we lashed together, and ferried our baggage across the stream. We then swam our horses and wagons, and when arrived at the opposite shore, the brethren fastened ropes to the wagon tongues and helped the teams out of the water and up the steep, miry banks. Some of the brethren felled a tall tree across the river, on which they passed over, and carried some of their baggage on their backs. While we were passing over, George A. Smith discovered a spring that with a little digging furnished us with an abundant supply of excellent water, which afterwards received the name of "the Mormon Spring." This afternoon, Elder Solomon Humphreys, an aged brother of the camp,

---

* On this point Elder Parley P. Pratt, in his Autobiography, relates a most interesting incident. Elder Pratt was chiefly engaged as a recruiting officer along the line of the camp's march, and would fall in with the camp from time to time, with additional men, arms, stores, money, etc., as opportunity afforded. And now his story:

"On one occasion, I had traveled all night to overtake the camp with some men and means, and having breakfasted with them and changed horses, I again started ahead on express to visit other branches and do business, to again overtake them. At noon I had turned my horse loose from the carriage to feed on the grass in the midst of a broad level plain. No habitation was near; stillness and repose reigned around me; I sank down overpowered in a deep sleep, and might have lain in a state of oblivion till the shades of night had gathered around me, so completely was I exhausted for want of sleep and rest; but I had only slept a few moments till the horse had grazed sufficiently, when a voice, more loud and shrill than I had ever before heard, fell on my ear and thrilled through every part of my system; it said: 'Parley, it is time to be up and on your journey.' In the twinkling of an eye I was perfectly aroused; I sprang to my feet so suddenly that I could not recollect where I was or what was before me to perform. I related the circumstance afterwards to Brother Joseph Smith, and he bore testimony that it was the angel of the Lord who went before the camp who found me overpowered with sleep, and thus awoke me." (Autobiography of Parley P. Pratt, pp. 122, 123.)

having become exceedingly weary, lay down on the prairie to rest himself and fell asleep. When he awoke he saw, coiled up within one foot of his head, a rattlesnake lying between him and his hat, which he had in his hand when he fell asleep. The brethren gathered around him, saying, "It is a rattlesnake, let us kill it;" but Brother Humphreys said, "No, I'll protect him; you shan't hurt him, for he and I had a good nap together."

Wednesday, May 28.—We passed on as usual, except suffering much from want of water and provisions; and arrived at Decatur township. We encamped on a small stream of water, and here one of Brother Tanner's horses died.

Thurday, May 29.—Having to buy a horse we were detained until near noon. There was some murmuring among the brethren, many wishing to go on and not tarry with the rest of the company for the day, and some were already started. I sent for them to return and collected the whole company together, and instructed them not to scatter. I told them if they went ahead of the camp in a scattered condition they would become weary, lie down on the ground when their blood was heated, and they would be liable to take diseases, such as fever and ague, which are prevalent in this climate. They would also be in danger of being killed by an enemy, and none of us be the wiser for it.

Camp Diversions.

I then proposed for a diversion that we divide the camp into three parts and have a sham battle, which was agreed to. Brother Roger Orton led one division, Frederick G. Williams another division, while I remained in the camp with the third division. They retired to the woods with their divisions, and soon attacked the camp, which we defended by various maneuvers for some time. Many of our captains showed considerable tact and more acquaintance with military matters than I had expected. Everything passed off with good feelings, although Captain Heber C. Kimball, in receiving a charge, grasped Captain Lewis Zobriski's sword, and in endeavoring to take it from him, had the skin cut from the palm of his hand. After the sham battle was over, I called the camp together and cautioned the men to be careful in the future and control their spirits in such circumstances so as never to injure each other.

We traveled across the prairie and encamped in a strip of timber. When we stopped to dine, I wrote a letter to the brethren in Missouri, dated "Camp of Israel," requesting some of them to meet us as soon as possible and give me information of the state of things in Upper Missouri, and sent the letter to Springfield post office by Dr. Frederick G. Williams.

At this place I discovered that a part of my company had been served with sour bread, while I had received good, sweet bread from the same cook. I reproved Brother Zebedee Coltrin for this partiality, for I wanted my brethren to fare as well as I did.

The same day (May 29th) the brethren in Clay county wrote the following letter to his Excellency Daniel Dunklin: *Proposition to Divide Jackson County between Saints and the Mob.*

LIBERTY, MISSOURI, May 29, 1834.

SIR—Your communication to us of May 2nd, containing or enclosing an order on Colonel S. D. Lucas for the arms which were forcibly taken from us last November, was received on the 15th instant, and the order forwarded to Colonel Lucas at Independence, on the 17th, giving him the privilege of returning our arms at one of the several ferries in this county. His reply to the order was, that he would write what he would do by the next mail, May 22nd. But as he has removed to Lexington without writing, we are at a loss to know whether he means to delay returning them for a season, or entirely to refuse to restore them.

At any rate, the excitement, or rather spite, of the mob, runs so high against our people, that we think best to request your Excellency to have said arms returned through the agency of Colonel Allen or Captain Atchison. Report says the arms will not be returned, and much exertion is making by the mob to prevent our return to our possessions in Jackson county. We also understand that the mob is employing certain influential gentlemen to write to your Excellency, to persuade us to compromise our matters in difference with the Jackson mob, and probably *divide Jackson county.* We ask for our rights and no more.

Respectfully, your Excellency's servants,

(Signed)   W. W. PHELPS,

ALGERNON S. GILBERT,

JOHN CORRILL,

EDWARD PARTRIDGE.

Friday, May 30.—Frederick G. Williams and Almon
W. Babbitt* went ahead of the camp into

Passage of
Camp through
Springfield,
Illinois.

Springfield in disguise, to learn the feeling of the people and procure some powder. We passed through Springfield; our appearance excited considerable curiosity, and a great many questions were asked. The spies who had followed us so long pursued us very closely, changing their dress and horses several times a day.

Brother Eleazer Miller with others joined the company with three horses about noon, a little east of Rochester. This reinforcement was very seasonable, as many of our horses were afflicted as they very frequently are in changing country, climate and food. Many of the horses after eating the dry corn and prairie grass would be seized with colic and bloat very badly. Brother Ezra Thayre administered medicine mixed in a quart stone bottle, prepared as follows: A threepenny paper of tobacco, half an ounce of copperas and two table-spoonsfull of cayenne pepper, and the bottle filled with water when he could not procure whisky. One-half of a bottle constituted a dose, and would almost invariably cure a sick horse in a few minutes, and is worthy of remembrance. Brother Thayre called his medicine "18 by 24."

We encamped about three miles from Springfield on Spring Creek. Frederick G. Williams and Almon W.

---

* Almon W. Babbitt was born October 1, 1813, in Berkshire county, Mass. He was the son of Ira and Nancy Babbitt.

Babbitt returned to the camp with two kegs of powder, and reported that the people were somewhat excited, more however from a curiosity to know where we were going than from a desire to hinder us. A brother came to see us with the news that my brother Hyrum had passed on west the day before with a company, about fifty miles north of us, saying, "he has a fine company, and they all look mighty *pert.*" I asked him to accompany us to Missouri, but he replied, "I cannot." He went and stayed at a tavern over night with the spies, who said they followed us three hundred miles on purpose to take some advantage of us.

Saturday, May 31.—In the morning this brother came to me and said: "I would be mighty glad to go with you, but my business is such I cannot. Will a hundred dollars do you any good?" I replied, "Yes, it will, for we are short of money." He immediately remounted his horse and rode to Springfield, and within an hour after the camp had started he returned and said to me: "I am mighty sorry I cannot go with you. Here is a hundred dollars, and if I had had a few days' notice I could have got more." Arrival at Jacksonville, Illinois.

At noon we halted for dinner. A man, apparently drunk, came to the camp and said he had a large farm and forty cows a little way ahead, and if we would go there, he would give us all we wanted to eat and drink, feed our horses, etc. But I soon discovered that he was more sober than drunk, and that he was probably a spy.

Near night we arrived at a small stream of water about one mile from Jacksonville, where we found a pawpaw bush in the road, which had been dropped by Dr. Frederick G. Williams as a signal for us to camp. I had sent Dr. Williams forward in the morning on horseback to select a camp ground and watch the movements of our enemies. We pitched our tents in the place he had selected.

Agreeable to my instructions, about sunset Brother Roger Orton proclaimed aloud that there would be

preaching under the trees within the camp at half-past
ten o'clock on the morrow.   There was only one stranger
in the camp to hear the appointment.   Dr. Williams
had gone on to Jacksonville with his pill bags to spend the
night.

Sunday, June 1.—We had preaching, and many of the
inhabitants of the town came to hear.   Elder
John Carter, who had formerly been a Baptist
preacher, spoke in the morning, and was followed by four other Elders in the course of the day, all
of whom had formerly been preachers for different denominations.   When the inhabitants heard these Elders
they appeared much interested, and were very desirous
to know who we were, and we told them one had been a
Baptist preacher, and one a Campbellite; one a Reformed
Methodist, and another a Restorationer.   During the day
many questions were asked, but none could learn our
names, professions, business, or destination; and, although they suspected we were "Mormons," they were
very civil.*

A Puzzling
Religious
Service.

* In addition to confirming tne above narrative of the services on June 1, Elder
Heber C. Kimball, in his journal, adds some very interesting details, as follows:
"On Sunday, June 1, we preached all day, and many of the inhabitants of the
town came out to hear. Brother John Carter preached in the morning. By this
time the inhabitants began to flock down in companies to hear preaching, as they
understood we were professors of religion and had had a meeting in the morning.
Brother Joseph then proposed that some of the brethren should set forth different
portions of the Gospel in their discourses, as held by the religious world. He called
upon Brother Joseph Young to preach upon the principle of free salvation. He then
called upon Brother Brigham Young to speak, who set forth baptism as essential to salvation. He was followed by Brother Orson Hyde, who proved by the scriptures that
baptism was for the remission of sins. He next called upon Brother Lyman E.
Johnson, who spoke at some length upon the necessity of men being upright in
their walk, and keeping the Sabbath day holy. He then called upon Brother Orson
Pratt, who delivered an excellent discourse on the principle of the final restoration of
all things. The services of the day were concluded by a powerful exhortation from
Eleazer Miller.   *   *   *   After the day's services were over at this
place, many strangers were in our camp making remarks upon the preaching which
they had heard: They said Brother Joseph Young, by his preaching, they should
judge was a Methodist. They thought Brother Brigham Young was a close communion Baptist. Brother Orson Hyde they supposed was a Campbellite or Reformed Baptist. Brother Lyman E. Johnson they supposed was a Presbyterian,
and Brother Orson Pratt a Restorationer. They inquired if we all bolonged to one

Our enemies had threatened that we should not cross the Illinois river, but on Monday the 2nd we were ferried over without any difficulty. The ferryman counted, and declared there were five hundred of us, yet our true number was only about one hundred and fifty. Our company had been increased since our departure from Kirtland by volunteers from different branches of the Church through which we had passed. We encamped on the bank of the river until Tuesday the 3rd.

During our travels we visited several of the mounds which had been thrown up by the ancient in- The Finding habitants of this country—Nephites, Laman- of Zelph. ites, etc., and this morning I went up on a high mound, near the river, accompanied by the brethren. From this mound we could overlook the tops of the trees and view the prairie on each side of the river as far as our vision could extend, and the scenery was truly delightful.

On the top of the mound were stones which presented the appearance of three altars having been erected one above the other, according to the ancient order; and the remains of bones were strewn over the surface of the ground. The brethren procured a shovel and a hoe, and removing the earth to the depth of about one foot, discovered the skeleton of a man, almost entire, and between his ribs the stone point of a Lamanitish arrow, which evidently produced his death. Elder Burr Riggs retained the arrow. The contemplation of the scenery around us produced peculiar sensations in our bosoms; and subsequently the visions of the past being opened to my understanding by the Spirit of the Almighty, I discovered that the person whose skeleton was before us was a white Lamanite, a large, thick-set man, and a man of God. His name was Zelph. He was a warrior and chieftain under the great prophet Onandagus, who was known from the Hill Cumorah, or eastern sea

denomination. The answer was, We *were* some of us Baptists, some Methodists, some Presbyterians, some Campbellites, and some Restorationers." (*Times and Seasons,* vol. vi, pp. 772-3.)

to the Rocky mountains. The curse was taken from Zelph, or, at least, in part—one of his thigh bones was broken by a stone flung from a sling, while in battle, years before his death. He was killed in battle by the arrow found among his ribs, during the last great struggle of the Lamanites and Nephites.*

While we were refreshing ourselves and teams about the middle of the day [June 3rd], I got up on a wagon wheel, called the people together,and said that I would deliver a prophecy. After giving the brethren much good advice, exhorting them to faithfulness and humility, I said the Lord had revealed to me that a scourge would come upon the camp in consequence of the fractious and unruly spirits that appeared among them, and they should die like sheep with the rot; still, if they would repent and humble themselves before the Lord, the scourge, in a great measure, might be turned away; but, as the Lord lives, the members of this camp will suffer for giving way to their unruly temper.†

When we arrived at Atlas, I had a conversation with Colonel Ross, a wealthy gentleman of the neighborhood, who gave us a flattering account of the country, and wished to employ one hundred men, for which he proposed to make ready payment. He wanted brickmakers, builders, etc.

Here our commissary purchased twenty-five gallons of honey at twenty-five cents per gallon, and a dozen Mis-

Marginal note: A Prophecy.

Marginal note: Proposition of Colonel Ross.

---

* According to Elder Kimball's journal, the facts concerning the person whose bones had been found in the mound were not revealed to the Prophet Joseph until the camp had departed from the mound. He says:

"While on our way we felt anxious to know who the person was who had been killed by the arrow. It was made known to Joseph that he had been an officer who fell in battle in the last destruction among the Lamanites, and his name was Zelph. This caused us to rejoice much, to think that God was so mindful of us as to show these things to His servant. Brother Joseph had inquired of the Lord, and it was made known in a vision." (*Times and Seasons*, vol. vi, p. 788.)

† Elder Heber C. Kimball corroborates this prediction of the 3rd of June, closing his reference to it in his journal in these words: "Which [predicted calamity] afterwards actually did take place, to the sorrow of the brethren." (*Times and Seasons*, vol. vi, p. 788.)

souri cured hams, which proved to have been a little injured on the outside. There not being enough to supply
one for every company, my company agreed to do without. Our supper consisted of mush and honey, as we had
been unable to procure flour on account of the scarcity of
mills. After the fatigues of the day it hardly satisfied
hunger; but when we had finished, some six of the hams
were brought to our tent door and thrown down in anger,
the remark being, "We don't eat stinking meat." I
called on Brother Zebedee Coltrin, our cook, and told
him to be quick and fry some ham, as I had not had my
hunger fairly allayed for forty-eight hours. He immediately commenced cooking the ham, and for once my
company feasted to their full satisfaction.

We had just retired to rest when the picket guard announced Luke S. Johnson. He came into our
camp and made his report. He had visited a
number of influential men, among the rest a
Baptist minister, who expressed great anxiety that our
company should be stopped, and went to a magistrate to
inquire if there was not some law or pretext for stopping
us. He, the priest, said to the magistrate, "That company march and have guns like an army. They pitch
their tents by the side of the road; they set out guards,
and let nobody pass into their camp in the night; and they
are Mormons, and I believe they are going to kill the
people up in Jackson county, Missouri, and retake their
lands." The magistrate replied, "If you were traveling,
and did not wish to put up at public houses, or there
were none in the country, would you not camp by the
road side in a tent? And if you were afraid that your
horses and property would be stolen in a strange country,
would you not watch and keep guards?" "Why, yes,"
said the priest; "but they are Mormons!" "Well, I
can't hear but they mind their own business, and if you
and this stranger [meaning Luke S. Johnson] will mind
your own business, everything will be right." This Bap

Report of
Luke S.
Johnson.

tist priest treated Brother Luke S. Johnson with great politeness. He gave him his dinner, his wife washed his stockings; he gave him letters of introduction to men in Jackson county, and delivered to his charge some letters which he had received from Jackson county, which Brother Luke brought into the camp. He also stated that he had seen a man that morning who informed him that four hundred men were in readiness on the Missouri side, with ten hours' notice, to use up all the camp, and he was on his way to give them the notice.

A little before midnight we heard several guns fired
A False   to the west of us, which appeared to be answered
Alarm.   by one directly east. There was no settlement west of us nearer than the state of Missouri. This appearing so much like a signal, in addition to the many threats of our being attacked on crossing the Mississippi, I considered sufficient cause of alarm to put out a double picket guard and put the camp in a state of defense, so that every man might be ready at a moment's notice. It however proved to be a false alarm.*

Continuing our journey on the 4th, we encamped on the banks of the Mississippi river. At this place we were somewhat afflicted, and our enemies strongly threatened that we should not cross over into Missouri. The river being a mile and a half wide, and having but one ferry boat, it took two days for us to pass over.† While some were ferrying, others were engaged in hunting, fishing,

---

* Of this incident about the firing of the guns on the 3rd, Elder Kimball, in his journal, says: "There was a great excitement in the country through which we had passed, and also ahead of us; the mob threatened to stop us. Guns were fired in almost all directions through the night. Brother Joseph did not sleep much, if any, but was through the camp pretty much during the night."

† This account, given under date of the 4th of June, really covers both the 4th and 5th, and the journey was made from Atlas to the Missouri side of the Mississippi during the two days, the 4th and 5th. While encamped on Snye island, the brethren manifested a disposition to scatter through the woods for hunting, "but I advised them to the contrary," said the prophet. He then continues: "Some of the brethren went on to the sand bar and got a quantity of turtles' eggs, as they supposed. I told them they were snakes' eggs, and they must not eat them; but some of them thought they knew more about it than I did, and still

etc. As we arrived, we encamped on the bank, within the limits of Missouri.

While at this place, Sylvester Smith rebelled against the order of the company, and gave vent to his feelings against myself in particular. This was the first outbreak of importance which had occurred to mar our peace since we commenced our journey.*

persisted they were turtles' eggs. I said they were snakes' eggs—eat snakes' eggs, will you? The man that eats them will be sorry for it; you will be sick. Notwithstanding all I said, several brethren ate them, and were sick all the day after it."

* Of Sylvester Smith's rebellion against the order of the camp, Elder Kimball, in his journal, relates the following interesting circumstances:

"When we had all got over [the Mississippi], we camped about one mile back from the little town of Louisiana, in a beautiful oak grove, which is immediately on the bank of the river. At this place there were some feelings of hostility manifested again by Sylvester Smith, in consequence of a dog growling at him while he was marching his company up to the camp, he being the last that came over the river. The next morning Brother Joseph told the camp that he would descend to the spirit that was manifested by some of the brethren, to let them see the folly of their wickedness. He rose up and commenced speaking by saying, 'If any man insults me, or abuses me, I will stand in my own defense at the expense of my life; and if a dog growls at me, I will let him know that I am his master.' At this moment Sylvester Smith, who had just returned from where he had turned out his horses to feed, came up, and hearing Brother Joseph make those remarks, said, 'If that dog bites me, I'll kill him.' Brother Joseph turned to Sylvester and said, 'If you kill that dog, I'll whip you,' and then went on to show the brethren how wicked and unchristianlike such conduct appeared before the eyes of truth and justice."

CHAPTER VI.

ZION'S CAMP IN MISSOURI—LETTERS OF GOVERNOR DUNKLIN
AND OTHERS.

THE Elders in Clay county wrote Governor Dunklin as
follows:

LIBERTY, June 5, 1834.

DEAR SIR—We think the time is just at hand when our society will
be glad to avail themselves of the protection of a military guard, that
they may return to Jackson county.   We do not now know the precise
day, but Mr. Reese gives his opinion, that there would be no impropriety in petitioning your Excellency for an order on the commanding officer, to be sent by return mail, that we might have it in our
hands to present when our people get ready to start.   If this should
meet your approbation, and the order sent by return mail, we think it
would be of great convenience to our society.

We would also be obliged to your Excellency for information concerning the necessary expenses of ferriage, etc.   Are our people bound
to pay the ferriage on their return?   As they have already sustained
heavy losses, and many of them have lost their all, a mitigation of expenses on their return at this time, where they could legally be reduced,
would afford great relief; not only ferriage across the Missouri river,
but other items of expense that could lawfully be reduced.

We remain, your Excellency's most obedient servants,

A. S. GILBERT,
W. W. PHELPS,
EDWARD PARTRIDGE.

*Copy of a letter from Daniel Dunklin, Governor of the State of Missouri,
to Colonel J. Thornton, dated—*

CITY OF JEFFERSON, June 6, 1834.

DEAR SIR—I was pleased at the receipt of your letter, concurred in
by Messrs. Reese, Atchison and Doniphan, on the subject of the Mormon difficulties.   I should be gratified indeed if the parties could com-

promise upon the terms you suggest, or, indeed, upon any other terms satisfactory to themselves. But I should travel out of the line of strict duty, as chief executive officer of the government, were I to take upon myself the task of effecting a compromise between the parties. Had I not supposed it possible, yes, probable, that I should, as executive of the state, have to act, I should, before now, have interfered individually in the way you suggest, or in some other way, in order if possible to effect a compromise. Uncommitted as I am to either party, I shall feel no embarrassment in doing my duty—though it may be done with the most extreme regret. My duty in the relation which I now stand to the parties, is plain and straightforward. By an official interposition I might embarrass my course, and urge a measure for the purpose of effecting a compromise, and [if] it should fail, and in the end, should I feel it my duty to act contrary to the advice I had given, it might be said, that I either advised wrong, or that I was partial to one side or the other, in giving advice that I would not as an officer follow.

A more clear and indisputable right does not exist, than that of the Mormon people, who were expelled from their homes in Jackson county, to return and live on their lands; and if they cannot be persuaded, as a matter of policy, to give up that right, or to qualify it, my course, as the chief executive of the state, is a plain one. The constitution of the United States declares "that the citizens of each state shall be entitled to all privileges and immunities of citizens in the several states." Then we cannot interdict any people, who have a political franchise in the United States, from immigrating to this state, nor from choosing what part of the state they will settle in, provided they do not trespass on the property or rights of others. Our state constitution declares that the people's "right to bear arms, in defense of themselves and of the state, cannot be questioned." Then it is their constitutional right to arm themselves. Indeed, our military law makes it the duty of every man, not exempted by law, between the ages of eighteen and forty-five, to arm himself with a musket, rifle, or some firelock, with a certain quantity of ammunition, etc.; and again, our constitution says, "that all men have a natural and indefeasible right to worship Almighty God according to the dictates of their own consciences."

I am fully persuaded that the eccentricity of the religious opinions and practices of the Mormons is at the bottom of the outrages committed against them. They have the right constitutionally guaranteed to them, and it is indefeasible, to worship Joe Smith as a man, an angel, or even as the only true and living God, and to call their habitation Zion, the Holy Land, or even heaven itself. Indeed, there is nothing so absurd or ridiculous that they have not a right to adopt as their religion, so that in its exercise they do not interfere with the rights of others.

It is not long since an impostor assumed the character of Jesus Christ and attempted to minister as such; but I never heard of any combination to deprive him of his rights.

I consider it the duty of every good citizen of Jackson county and the adjoining counties to exert himself to effect a compromise of these difficulties; and were I assured that I would not have to act in my official capacity in the affair, I would visit the parties in person and exert myself to the utmost to settle it. My first advice would be to the Mormons, to sell out their lands in Jackson county, and to settle somewhere else, where they could live in peace, if they could get a fair price for them, and reasonable damages for injuries received. If this failed, I would try the citizens, and advise them to meet and rescind their illegal resolves of last summer, and agree to conform to the laws in every particular, in respect to the Mormons. If both these failed, I would then advice the plan you have suggested, for each party to take separate territory, and confine their members within their respective limits with the exception of the public right of ingress and egress upon the highway. If all these failed, then the simple question of legal right would have to settle it. It is this last that I am afraid I shall have to conform my action to in the end, and hence the necessity of keeping myself in the best situation to do my duty impartially.

Rumor says that both parties are preparing themselves with cannon. That would be illegal: it is not necessary to self-defense, as guaranteed by the constitution, and as there are no artillery companies organized in this state, nor field pieces provided by the public, any preparation of that kind will be considered as without right, and, in the present state of things, would be understood to be with criminal intent, I am told that the people of Jackson county expect assistance from the adjoining counties, to oppose the Mormons in taking or keeping possession of their lands. I should regret it extremely if any should be so imprudent as to do so; it would give a different aspect to the affair.

The citizens of Jackson county have a right to arm themselves and parade for military duty in their own county independent of the commander-in-chief; but if citizens march there in arms from other counties without order from the commander-in-chief or some one authorized by him, it would produce a very different state of things. Indeed, the Mormons have no right to march to Jackson county in arms, unless by order or permission of the commander-in-chief; men must not "levy war" in taking possession of their rights, any more than others should in opposing them in taking possession.

As you have manifested a deep interest in a peaceable compromise of this important affair, I presume you will not be unwilling to be placed in a situation in which, perhaps, you can be more serviceable to these parties. I have therefore taken the liberty of appointing you an aid to the commander-in-chief, and I hope it will be agreeable to you to accept. In this situation you can give your propositions all the influence they would have were they to emanate from the executive, without committing yourself or the commander-in-chief, in the event of failure. I should be glad if you, or some of the other gentlemen who joined you in your communication, would keep in close correspondence with these parties, and by each mail write to me.

The character of the state has been injured in consequence of this unfortunate affair; and I sincerely hope it may not be disgraced by it in the end;

With high respect, your obedient servant,

(Signed) DANIEL DUNKLIN.

June 6.—We resumed our journey,* and on the evening of the 7th† encamped in a piece of woods, near a spring of water, at Salt River. Here was a branch of the Church.

Arrival of the Camp at Salt River.

Sunday, June 8.—We had preaching, and in the course of the day were joined by Brothers Hyrum Smith and Lyman Wight, with a company of volunteers which they had gathered in Michigan.‡ The whole company now consisted of two hundred and five men, and twenty-five baggage

Arrival of Hyrum Smith and Lyman Wight.

* A note in the "Addenda" of the manuscript History to the "We resumed our journey"—etc., adds: "The men who had previously followed us passed us several times during the day, and were in search of us this evening. The guard heard them say, 'They have turned aside, damn 'em, we can't find 'em.' Elders Seth Johnson and Almon W. Babbitt, who had been sent to the Bowling Green branch to gather recruits, returned to the camp on the morning of the 7th with a small company, two wagons and several horses."

† A note in the "Addenda" to the manuscript History adds this statement, under the events of the 7th: "One of the camp walked on ahead to procure some milk. A number of men armed with guns met him and said: 'Here's one damn Mormon alone—let's kill him' But at the same instant they discovered a number of others just coming over the hill, when they immediately rode off in great haste. In the evening encamped in a grove near a spring, in Monroe county. A branch of the Church, known as the Salt River branch, but frequently called the Allred Settlement, was located here. We remained at this place several days, washing our clothes, and preparing to pursue our journey."

‡ The following is given in the "Addenda" of the manuscript History as a fuller account of the events under the date of the 8th: "Sunday, 8th, we were joined by my brother Hyrum Smith and Lyman Wight, with another company, who started from

wagons with two or three horses each. We remained at
Salt River until the 12th, refreshing and reorganizing
the camp, which reorganizing was done by electing
Lyman Wight general of the camp.*   I chose twenty
men for my life guards, of whom my Brother Hyrum was
chosen captain, and George A. Smith was my armor
bearer. The remainder of the company was organized
according to the pattern at New Portage. While at Salt
River, General Wight marched the camp on the prairie,
inspected our firelocks, ordered a discharge of the same
at targets by platoons, drilled us half a day, and returned
to camp.

About this time I dispatched Elders Orson Hyde and
Parley P. Pratt to Jefferson City with a message to Governor Dunklin, to ascertain if he
was ready to fulfill the proposition which he
had previously made to the brethren to reinstate them on

Messengers Sent to Governor Dunklin.

Pontiac, Michigan Territory, May 5th, the same day we started from Kirtland
having passed through Ann Arbor, Jacksonsburgh, Spring Arbor, Constantine,
Elkhart, crossed the Illinois river one mile below Ottawa, Pleasant Grove, Pekin,
Quincy and Palmyra. Elijah Fordham was their historian; Lyman Wight, steward; Hyrum Smith and Samuel Bent, moderators. We had agreed to meet at this
point, and the first company that arrived was to wait for the other. Soon after the
arrival of Brother Hyrum and his company, I dispatched Brother Luke Johnson
and Almon W. Babbitt with messages to the brethren in Clay county, fearing that
the letter which I sent from Springfield had miscarried. James Allred, Sen.,
and ten others of this branch joined our camp, which now numbered two hundred
and five men, all armed and equipped as the law directs. It was delightful to see
the company, for they were all young men, except one company whom we called the
Silver Greys, and who ate at my table. We were all in good spirits, and were
taught the sword practice by Brother William Cherry (who was a native of Ireland),
an expert drill master, wno had been in the British dragoon service for upwards
of twenty years, and deserves much credit for his unwearied exertions in imparting
all he knew to the brethren. This was our first attempt at learning the sword exercise. Brothers Hiram Stratton and Nelson Tubbs procured a shop of Myres
Mobley and repaired every firelock that was out of order, and David Elliott shod
our horses. Here Brother James Foster was taken sick. I proposed to him to
remain behind. He said, 'Brother Joseph, let me go with you if I die on the road.'
I told him in the name of the Lord, that if that was his faith, to go on his bed in
the wagon, and he should get better every day until he recovered, which was
literally fulfilled."

* Joseph Smith, however, was the commander-in-chief. The following occurs in
the "Addenda" to the manuscript History: "We organized the camp. I was acknowledged commander-in-chief and Lyman Wight general."

their lands in Jackson county, and leave them there to defend themselves.*

On June 9th Governor Dunklin wrote to W. W. Phelps and others: mailed at—

CITY OF JEFFERSON, June 9, 1834.

Herewith you have a second order for the delivery of your arms now in the possession of the militia of Jackson county. Colonel Lucas has resigned his command, he informs me. If Lieut.-Colonel Pitcher should be arrested before you receive this, you will please hold up the order until I am informed who may be appointed to the command of the regiment.

Respectfully,
(Signed)   DANIEL DUNKLIN.

The foregoing letter enclosed the following order:

CITY OF JEFFERSON, June 4, 1834.

Thomas Pitcher, Lieut.-Colonel commandant of the Thirty-third Regiment.

SIR—On the 2nd day of last May I issued an order to Colonel Lucas to deliver the fifty-two guns and one pistol, which you received from the Mormons on the 4th day of November last, and reported to him on the 3rd day of the succeeding December—to W. W. Phelps, Edward Partridge, John Corrill, John Whitmer, and A. S. Gilbert, or their order. On the 24th ultimo, Colonel Lucas wrote and informed me that he had resigned his commission and left the county of Jackson. You, as commandant of said regiment, are therefore commanded to collect the said arms, if they are not already in your possession, and deliver them to the aforesaid gentlemen or their order.

Respectfully,
DANIEL DUNKLIN, Commander-in-Chief.

The day following Judge Ryland wrote the following:

RICHMOND, June 10, 1834.

Mr. A. S. Gilbert:

SIR—Deeply impressed with a desire to do all in my power to settle or allay the disturbances between the Mormons and the citizens of Jackson county, I have concluded that it might have some tendency to effectuate this object by having the Mormons called together at Liberty next Monday, and there explain to them my notions and views of their present situation, and of the circumstances attendant. I therefore request you, sir, to use all your influence with your brethren, to

* This paragraph is a note in the "Addenda" of manuscript History.

get them to meet me next Monday in Liberty. I much fear and dread the consequences that are yet to ensue, unless I should succeed in my wishes to restore peace. It is the duty of all good men to use all proper and laudable means to establish peace. I expect a deputation of some of the most respectable citizens of Jackson county will meet me on Monday next at Liberty. I call upon you, in the name of humanity, therefore, to leave no efforts untried to collect your brethren at Liberty as requested. Should my efforts to make peace fail of success, there can be no wrong, sir, in the attempt, and I shall enjoy the consolation of having done my duty as a man, as well as a Christian.

I hope, sir, you will duly appreciate the motive which prompts me to address this letter to you, and will aid me with all your influence with your brethren in the prosecution of an object so much to be desired by all good men and citizens.

Yours very respectfully,

JOHN F. RYLAND.

June 12.—We left Salt River and traveled about fourteen miles. The inhabitants of Salt River manifested a great respect for us, and many of them accompanied us some distance on our journey.

Departure of Camp from Salt River.

I instructed the camp in the morning that if a gun was fired it would be considered an alarm; but in the course of the day, while I was a little ahead, I shot a squirrel for Brother Foster, when several of the brethren came running up to see what was the matter. I told them Brother Foster was sick; "I want you to pray for him." *

Friday 13.—Elder Kimball's horses, through the negligence of the guards, got loose and went back ten miles with others. He pursued them and returned with them to camp. Frederick G.

Reproof of Williams and Orton.

Williams and Roger Orton received a very severe chastisement for neglect of orders in not taking care of the teams when in charge of the guard. The reproof given to Roger Orton was more particularly for suffering Elder Kimball to go back after the horses, and he was one of my life guards, and it belonged to Orton to see that the team

---

* This paragraph is from notes in the "Addenda" of the manuscript History.

was attended to. But as the team was Kimball's, and he had taken the care of it all through, Orton still threw the care on him. The Silver Grey company, numbering fourteen, were attached to my mess, making it twenty-eight in number.*

Saturday 14.—Brother Joseph Hancock and another of the brethren were chased a considerable por- Enemies
tion of the day by four suspicious fellows on Eluded.
horseback, armed with guns, whom they eluded by traveling in the brush and thickets where horsemen could not ride. It was late when they returned to the camp.*

At night we encamped in an unsafe and unpleasant situation in a ravine, the only place we could get water for some miles. The country was a wild and uncultivated region.

In answer to Judge Ryland, the Elders wrote as follows:

NEAR LIBERTY, June 14, 1834.

Hon. J. F. Ryland:

DEAR SIR—Your communication of the 9th instant from Richmond was duly received, and at a public meeting of our society this day its contents were made known. Our brethren unanimously tender their thanks for the laudable disposition manifested on your part to effect peace between our society and the inhabitants of Jackson county; and as many as conveniently can will be present on Monday next. Entertaining some fears that your honor, in your zeal for peace, might unwarily recommend a sale of our lands in Jackson county, we have thought it expedient to give you reasonable notice, that no such proposition could possibly be acceded to by our society.

We have not heard that it was the intention of your honor to urge any such measure, but our enemies in Jackson county have long been trying to effect this object. In a letter from the governor to us, he says: "I have been requested to advise the Mormons to sell out and move away; but believing that it would have no good effect, I have withheld my advice." We give this quotation from the governor's letter to disprove the statement made in the *Upper Missouri Enquirer* of last Wednesday, and conclude by adding that "home is home," and that we

* Paragraph is from notes in the "Addenda" of the manuscript History.

want possession of our homes—from which we have been wickedly expelled—and those rights which belong to us as native free-born citizens of the United States.

Very respectfully, your friends and servants,

JOHN CORRILL, Chairman.
A. S. GILBERT, Secretary.

The foregoing was enclosed in the following letter to their lawyers:

GENTLEMEN—Will you be so good as to read the enclosed, then seal and hand it to the judge? We have given him an early hint, fearing that he might be induced by the solicitations of our enemies to propose a sale of our lands, which you well know would be like selling our children into slavery; and the urging of such a measure would avail nothing unless to produce an excitement against us in this county. As requested last Thursday, we hope you will he present on Monday.*

Your friends and servants,

JOHN CORRILL,
A. S. GILBERT.

To Messrs. Doniphan and Atchison.

* The same day, June 14, Elder John Corrill wrote to the editor of the *Evening and Morning Star*, giving an account of affairs in Jackson county; and as his communication gives a description of things in Jackson county not found elsewhere, I quote so much of the letter as was published in the *Star*, vol. ii. pp. 333, 334:

"The leaders of the mob are yet striving to keep up the same spirit of opposition, by instilling falsehoods into the minds of the people. They tell them that the 'Mormons' are coming upon them, *mob like*, to kill their women and children. They raised an alarm a few days ago which set the whole county of Jackson in an uproar —men riding in different directions and proclaiming, 'the Mormons are coming— they are now crossing the river—they are coming to kill, destroy,' etc. Some women and children left their houses, and fled to the woods and elsewhere, while the men, two hundred or three hundred, gathered together to oppose the 'Mormons,' as they supposed, in their return. They repaired to the different ferries on the river, to guard them, and I have been credibly informed that they have since continued to guard the river at the different crossing places from one end of Jackson county to the other. And for fear that we would return and enjoy our dwellings again, they set fire to and burned them down, and then raised the report that the 'Mormons' went over and burnt their houses, and I am informed that they have burnt them all, except a very few which are occupied by other families; and I have been told that they have destroyed our fences and other property that remained. What was the cause of this great alarm among them, I know not; for we are at home attending to our own business, and had not thought of returning at that time. Neither have we any thoughts of ever returning in the night time, or in the mob like manner which they represent to the people; for as we design to be governed in all cases by the laws of the land, we shall therefore return under the protection of the governor, as he has promised us. We therefore have no need to return and take them on surprise. as they falsely represent to the people; for we mean only to act on the principles of self-defense in all cases. But they state falsehoods to the people, for the purpose, I suppose, of keeping their strength good to oppose our return, which, I understand, they are determined to do, even to the shedding of blood; and it is said by the mob, that the whole county is combined together. They are arming themselves, and they have distributed our guns among them. But it is easy to be seen, that fear and consternation prevail among them; some of their leaders have already cleared out. Colonel S.D.Lucas has taken his goods and gone down the river; both the Chiles [Henry and Joel F.] have lately gone to the south on a long visit. Lawyer Hicks says, if no compromise is made he shall seek a location somewhere else; and I have been told that L.Franklin is going away soon; some other families, I have heard, are leaving through fear. As nearly as I can learn, the number that is determined to stand and oppose our return, even unto bloodshed, is about one hundred and fifty, or two hundred, in that county, though it is said that many from other counties will come to their assistance.

"They are trying to excite the people of this county [Clay] to drive us from here, and for this purpose, it is said, they are circulating a paper, and have got some signers; but the authorities of this county do not countenance them in this thing, and I think they cannot succeed; but it is said they are lurking about and seeking a chance to do private injury, but the brethren are on the lookout, and are preparing themselves with arms for self-defense, and I think if we firmly continue and persevere, according to the laws of the land, that we shall be enabled shortly to overcome the mob and obtain our rights.

"Yours. etc.,

"JOHN CORRILL."

CHAPTER VII.

ZION'S CAMP IN MISSOURI—EFFORTS AT ARBITRATION—THE
WORD OF THE LORD.

Sunday, June 15.*—Traveled twelve miles. While on
the way Orson Hyde and Parley P. Pratt returned to us from
Jefferson City, and reported that Governor
Dunklin refused to fulfill his promise to reinstate
the brethren on their lands in Jackson county
on the ground of impracticability.†

Governor
Dunklin re-
fuses to Re-
instate the
Saints on
their lands.

* This paragraph is a note in the "Addenda" of the Ms. Church History, page 13,
Book A.

† This refusal of Governor Dunklin to reinstate the Saints on their lands in
Jackson county must have been a severe blow to the hopes of Zion's Camp and the
Saints scattered in Clay county. From the time of their expulsion from Jackson
county the governor repeatedly said that the exiles had a right to be reinstated upon
their lands, and had promised that he would call out the militia of the State to reinstate them whenever they were ready and willing to return. In his communication
to Messrs. W. W. Phelps, Morley, *et al.*, under date of Feb. 4, 1834 (see Ch. Hist. Vol. I,
p. 476) he said in answer to their petition to be reinstated: "One of your requests needs
no evidence to support the right to have it granted; it is that your people be put in
possession of their homes, from which they had been expelled. But what may be the
duty of the Executive after that, will depend upon contingencies." Even a few days
before his interview with Messrs. Hyde and Pratt, in his letter to Colonel J. Thornton,
under date of June 6th, he had said: "A more clear and indisputable right does not
exist, than that of the Mormon people, who were expelled from their homes in Jackson county, to return and live on their lands; and if they cannot be persuaded as a
matter of policy to give up that right, or to qualify it, my course, as the chief,
executive officer of the state, is a plain one. The constitution of the United States
declares, that the citizens of each state shall be entitled to all privileges and immunities of citizens in the several states. Then we cannot interdict any people, who
have a political franchise in the United States, from immigrating to this state, nor
from choosing what part of the state they will settle in, provided they do not trespass on the property or rights of others." (See p. 85.)

In the face of this and other utterances the position now assumed by Governor
Dunklin was a manifestation of weakness truly lamentable.

We crossed the Chariton river at its mouth and encamped on the west bank.   Bishop Partridge came into the camp from Clay county.   We received much infor-   Arrival of mation from him concerning the hostile feelings   Bishop Partridge in and prejudices that existed against us in Mis-   Camp. souri in all quarters, but it gave us great satisfaction to receive intelligence from him of the union and good feeling that prevailed among the brethren.   We were in perils and threatened all the while, we were much troubled to get provisions, and had to live principally on corn meal, and were glad to get that.   Here Dean Gould was baptized by Lyman Wight.

Monday, June 16.*—Traveled to Grand river, ferried over it, and encamped on its bank.   The ferryman intended charging seventeen dollars; the brethren   The Camp said they would not pay it, but would sooner   Crosses Grand make a raft and ferry themselves over.   He then   River. agreed to take them over for twelve dollars which offer we accepted.   This morning was excessively hot, no air stirring, and traveling in the thick woods, a thunder shower coming on, the brethren caught all the water they could on the brims of their hats, and not catching enough to satisfy their thirst, they drank out of the horse tracks.

Martin Harris having boasted to the brethren that he could handle snakes with perfect safety, while fooling with a black snake with his bare feet, he received a   Martin Harris bite on his left foot.   The fact was communi-   Trifles with cated to me, and I took occasion to reprove him,   a Promise   of God. and exhort the brethren never to trifle with the promises of God.   I told them it was presumption for any one to provoke a serpent to bite him, but if a man of God was accidentally bitten by a poisonous serpent, he might have faith, or his brethren might have faith for him, so that the Lord would hear his prayer and he might be healed; but when a man designedly provokes a serpent to bite him,

---

* This and the paragraph following concerning Martin Harris, are notes in "Addenda" of the Ms. History. p. 14, Book A.

the principle is the same as when a man drinks deadly poison knowing it to be such. In that case no man has any claim on the promises of God to be healed.*

On this day, June 16th, the citizens of Clay county, to the number of eight hundred or a thousand, among whom Important Meeting at Liberty Court House. were the brethren, assembled at the court house in Liberty, in accordance with the request of Judge Ryland, expressed in his letter of the 10th instant, a deputation from Jackson county also attended the meeting and presented the following: —

Propositions of the people of Jackson county to the Mormons.

The undersigned committee, being fully authorized by the people of Jackson county, hereby propose to the Mormons, that they will buy all the land that the said Mormons own in the county of Jackson, and also all the improvements which the said Mormons had on any of the public lands in said county of Jackson, as they existed before the first disturbance between the people of Jackson and the Mormons, and for such as they have made since. They further propose that the value of said land and improvements shall be ascertained by three disinterested arbitrators, to be chosen and agreed to by both parties. They further propose, that should the parties disagree in the choice of arbitrators, then ————————is to choose them. They further propose, that twelve of the Mormons shall be permitted to go along with the arbitrators to show them their land and improvements while valuing the same, and such others of the Mormons as the arbitrators shall wish to do so, to give them information; and the people of Jackson hereby guarantee their entire safety while doing so. They further propose, that when the arbitrators report the value of the land and improvements, as aforesaid, the people of Jackson will pay the valuation, with one hundred per cent, added thereon, to the Mormons, within thirty days thereafter. They further propose, that the Mormons are not to make any effort, ever

* How beautifully in harmony is this counsel with the words of the Savior to Lucifer when the latter took him up and stood him on a pinnacle of the temple, and said: "If thou be the Son of God, cast thyself down: for it is written, He shall give his angels charge concerning thee: and in their hands they shall bear thee up, lest at any time thou dash thy foot against a stone. Jesus said unto him, It is written again, Thou shalt not tempt the Lord thy God" (Matt. iv: 6, 7.] Moreover, in this last dispensation when the promise of the spiritual gifts was renewed to the Saints, including the promise that "the poison of a serpent should not have power to harm them"—yet, saith the Lord, "a commandment I give unto them, that they shall not boast themselves of these things, neither speak them before the world, for these things are given unto you for your profit and for salvation" (Doc. & Cov., Sec. lxxxiv: 73).

after, to settle, either collectively or individually, within the limits of Jackson county. The Mormons are to enter into bonds to insure the conveyance of their land in Jackson county, according to the above terms, when the payment shall be made; and the committee will enter into a like bond, with such security as may be deemed sufficient for the payment of the money, according to the above proposition. While the arbitrators are investigating and deciding upon the matters referred to them, the Mormons are not to attempt to enter Jackson county, or to settle there, except such as are by the foregoing propositions permitted to go there.

They further propose that the people of Jackson will sell all their lands and improvements on public lands, in Jackson county, to the Mormons, the valuation to be obtained in the same manner, the same per cent in addition to be paid, and the time the money is to be paid is the same as the above set forth in our propositions to buy: the Mormons to give good security for the payment of the money, and the undersigned will give security that the land will be conveyed to the Mormons. They further propose, that all parties are to remain as they are till the payment is made, at which time the people of Jackson will give possession.

(Signed)   SAMUEL C. OWENS,
RICHARD FRISTOE,
THOS. HAYTON, SEN.,
THOS. CAMPBELL,
JOHN DAVIS,
THOS. JEFFREYS,
SMALLWOOD NOLAND,
ROBERT RICKMAN,
ABRAHAM MCCLELLAN,
S. V. NOLAND.

On presentation of the foregoing, Samuel C. Owens made a flaming war-speech, and General Doniphan replied on the side of peace.

Stirring Incidents at the Liberty Meeting.

The Rev. Mr. Riley, a Baptist priest, made a hot speech against the "Mormons," and said, "The Mormons have lived long enough in Clay county; and they must either clear out, or be cleared out."

Mr. Turnham, the moderator of the meeting, answered in a masterly manner; saying, "Let us be republicans; let us honor our country, and not disgrace it like Jackson county. For God's sake don't disfranchise or drive away

the Mormons.   They are better citizens than many of the
old inhabitants."

General Doniphan exclaimed, "That's a fact, and as
the Mormons have armed themselves, if they don't fight
they are cowards.   I love to hear that they have brethren
coming to their assistance.   Greater love can no man
show, than he who lays down his life for his brethren."

At this critical instant, the cocking of pistols, and the
unsheathing of other implements of death, denoted
desperation.   One moved "adjournment," another cried
"go on," and in the midst of this awful crisis a person
bawled in at the door, "a man stabbed!" The mass instantly rushed out to the spot, in hopes, as some said, that "a
Mormon had got killed," but as good luck would have it,
only one Missourian had dirked another, (one Calbert,
a blacksmith, had stabbed one Males, who had previously
whipped one Mormon nearly to death. and boasted of
having whipped many more).   The wound was dangerous, but the incident appeared providential as it seemed
as though the occurrence was necessary to break up the
meeting without further bloodshed, and give the Saints a
chance to consult what would be the most advisable thing
to do in such a critical instant. They immediately penned
the following answer to the propositions from Jackson
county, presented by Mr. Owens *et al.*

Answer of the Mormons to the Proposition of the People of Jackson County.

GENTLEMEN—Your propositions for an adjustment of the difficulties
between the citizens of Jackson county and the Mormons, is before us;
and as explained to you in the court house this day, we are not
authorized to say to you that our brethren will submit to your proposals;
but we agree to spread general notice, and call a meeting of our people,
the present week, and lay before you an answer as soon as Saturday or
Monday next. We can say for ourselves, and in behalf of our brethren,
that peace is what we desire and what we are disposed to cultivate with
all men; and to effect peace, we feel disposed to use all our influence,
as far as it will be required at our hands as free-born citizens of these
United States; and as fears have been expressed, that we design
hostilities against the inhabitants of Jackson county, we hereby pledge

ourselves to them, and to the hospitable citizens of Clay county, that we will not, and neither have we designed, as a people, to commence hostilities against the aforesaid citizens of Jackson county, or any other people.

Our answer shall be handed to Judge Turnham, the chairman of the meeting, even earlier than the time before stated, if possible.

(Signed)   W. W. PHELPS,
WM. E. M'LELLIN,
A. S. GILBERT,
JOHN CORRILL,
ISAAC MORLEY.

N.B.—As we are informed that large numbers of our people are on their way removing to Jackson county, we agree to use our influence immediately to prevent said company from entering into Jackson county, until you shall receive an answer to the propositions aforenamed.

It may be thought, at first view, that the mob committee made a fair proposition to the Saints, in offering to buy their lands at a price fixed by disinterested arbitrators and one hundred per centum added thereto, payment to be made in thirty days, and offering theirs on the same terms; but when it is understood that the mob held possession of a much larger quantity of land than the Saints, and that they only offered thirty days for the payment, having previously robbed the Saints of nearly everything, it will be readily seen that they were only making a sham to cover their previous unlawful conduct.

Reflections on the Jackson County Proposition.

The tempest of an immediate conflict seemed to be checked, and the Jackson mob to the number of about fifteen, with Samuel C. Owens and James Campbell at their head, started for Independence, Jackson county, to raise an army sufficient to meet me, before I could get into Clay county. Campbell swore, as he adjusted his pistols in his holsters, "The eagles and turkey buzzards shall eat my flesh if I do not fix Joe Smith and his army so that their skins will not hold shucks, before two days are passed." They went to the ferry and undertook to cross the Missouri river

A Mobber's Threat and God's Vengeance.

after dusk, and the angel of God saw fit to sink the boat about the middle of the river, and seven out of twelve that attempted to cross, were drowned. Thus, suddenly and justly, went they to their own place. Campbell was among the missing. He floated down the river some four or five miles, and lodged upon a pile of drift wood, where the eagles, buzzards, ravens, crows, and wild animals ate his flesh from his bones, to fulfill his own words, and left him a horrible example of God's vengeance. He was discovered about three weeks after by one Mr. Purtle. Owens saved his life only, after floating four miles down the stream, where he lodged upon an island, "swam off naked about day light, borrowed a mantle to hide his shame, and slipped home rather shy of the vengeance of God."

Tuesday, June 17.—At noon we crossed the Wakenda;

Incidents of Insubordination in the Camp.

it being high, we had to be ferried over. We were informed here that a party of men were gathered together on the Missouri river with the intention of attacking us that night. The prairie ahead of us was twenty-three miles long without any timber or palatable, healthy water. Some of the brethren wished to stop near the timber, and were about making arrangements to pitch their tents. We had but little provisions. I proposed to get some wood and water to carry with us, and go on into the prairie eight or ten miles. My brother Hyrum said he knew, in the name of the Lord, that it was best to go on to the prairie; and as he was my elder brother, I thought best to heed his counsel, though some were murmuring in the camp. We accordingly started. When Lyman Wight crossed the river he disapproved of our moving on to the prairie, upon which Sylvester Smith placed himself in the road, turned back all that he could by saying, "Are you following your general, or some other man?" and twenty stayed behind with Lyman Wight. We drove about eight miles on the prairie and encamped out of sight of timber.

The sun apparently went down, and rose again next morning in the grass. Our company had filled a couple of empty powder kegs with water; it tasted so bad we could not drink it, and all the water that we had was out of a slough filled with red living animals, and was putrid. About eleven o'clock Lyman Wight arrived with the company that had remained with him. I called them together and reproved them for tarrying behind, and not obeying my counsel, and told Lyman Wight never to do so again. He promised that he would stand by me forever, and never forsake me again, let the consequence be what it would; but Sylvester Smith manifested very refractory feelings.*

Wednesday, June 18.—As Hyrum Stratton and his companion were taking up their blankets this morning, they discovered two prairie rattle-snakes quietly sleeping under them, which they carefully carried out of the camp. This day my health was so poor I left the affairs of the camp to the management of General Wight. Having no provisions, we traveled seventeen miles before breakfast, and I rode in Elder Kimball's wagon. We crossed a slough half a mile wide through which most of the brethren were obliged to wade waist deep in mud and water. General Lyman Wight, who had traveled from Kirtland without a stocking on his foot, carried Brother Joseph Young through on his back. Our breakfast consisted entirely of corn meal mush, or hasty pudding. We had not meal enough in our company to make the mush of the consistence of good starch.

The Prophet's Illness.

After our ten o'clock breakfast we passed on to within one mile of Richmond. We encamped in a very small prairie surrounded by a thicket of hazel brush. When I arrived where the camp had pitched their tents, and viewed our unsafe

The Prophet's Anxiety for the Safety of the Camp.

* This paragraph is a note in the "Addenda" of the Ms. History, Book A, p. 14.

location, considering the danger of an attack from our
enemies, I almost forgot my sickness, went some distance
in the brush, bowed down and prayed my Heavenly
Father to suffer no evil to come upon us, but keep us safe
through the night. I obtained an assurance that we
should be safe until morning, notwithstanding about fifty
of the Jackson county mob crossed the Lexington Ferry
that evening for the purpose of joining the Ray county
mob and of making an attack upon us. All was quiet
in the camp through the night. While the brethren
were making their bed in Captain Brigham Young's tent,
one of them discovered a very musical rattlesnake which
they were about to kill. Captain Young told them not
to hurt him but carry him out of the tent, whereupon
Brother Carpenter took him in his hands, carried him
beyond all danger, and left him to enjoy his liberty,
telling him not to return.*

Thursday, June 19.—At daybreak, feeling that we were

Threats of
the Mob.   in a very unsafe situation, I counseled the
camp to move forward without delay, and
continued a lively march for about nine miles, when we
stopped for breakfast. While passing through Richmond,
Brother Luke Johnson observed a black woman in a
gentleman's garden near the road. She beckoned to him
and said, ''Come here, Massa.'' She was evidently much
agitated in her feelings. He went up to the fence, and
she said to him, ''There is a company of men lying in
wait here, who are calculating to kill you this morning
as you pass through.'' We halted for breakfast on an
eminence near a farm house. The owner furnished us with
a large quantity of milk, which gave a great relish to our
bacon and corn dodger, which our commissary had procured
that morning. When we asked the price of his milk he replied: ''He is a mean man that will sell milk; I could have
let you have more, if I had known you had been coming.''

* This paragraph and the one preceding it, under same date, are notes in the
"Addenda" of the Ms. History, Book A, p. 14.

He further said: "You have many enemies about here, and you may meet with some trouble; and it is a damned shame that every man can't come up and enjoy his religion, and everything else without being molested." It was near noon when we finished our breakfast, and we passed on in fine spirits, determined to go through and meet the brethren in Clay county. We traveled but a short distance when one wagon broke down, and the wheels ran off from others; and there seemed to be many things to hinder our progress, although we strove with all diligence to speed our way forward. This night we camped on an elevated piece of land between Little Fishing and Big Fishing rivers, which streams were formed by seven small streams or branches.*

As we halted and were making preparations for the night, five men armed with guns rode into our camp, and told us we should "see hell before morning;" and their accompanying oaths partook of all the malice of demons. They told us that sixty men were coming from Richmond, Ray county, and seventy more from Clay county, to join the Jackson county mob, who had sworn our utter destruction.

During this day, the Jackson county mob, to the number of about two hundred, made arrangements to cross the Missouri river, above the mouth of Fishing river, at Williams' ferry, into Clay county, and be ready to meet the Richmond mob near Fishing river ford, for our utter destruction; but after the first scow load of about forty had been set over the river, the scow in returning was met by a squall, and had great difficulty in reaching the Jackson side by dark.

When these five men were in our camp, swearing vengeance, the wind, thunder, and rising cloud indicated an approaching storm, and in a short time after they left the rain and hail began to

A Timely Storm.

* This paragraph is a note in the "Addenda" of the Ms. History, Book A, p. 15.

fall.* The storm was tremendous; wind and rain, hail
and thunder met them in great wrath, and soon softened
their direful courage, and frustrated all their designs to
"kill Joe Smith and his army." Instead of continuing
a cannonading which they commenced when the sun was
about one hour high, they crawled under wagons, into
hollow trees, and filled one old shanty, till the storm was
over, when their ammunition was soaked, and the forty
in Clay county were extremely anxious in the morning to
return to Jackson, having experienced the pitiless pelting
of the storm all night; and as soon as arrangements
could be made, this "forlorn hope" took the "back
track" for Independence, to join the main body of the
mob, fully satisfied, as were those survivors of the company who were drowned, that when Jehovah fights
they would rather be absent. The gratification is too
terrible.

Very little hail fell in our camp, but from half a mile
to a mile around, the stones or lumps of ice cut down
the crops of corn and vegetation generally, even cutting
limbs from trees, while the trees, themselves were twisted
into withes by the wind. The lightning flashed incessantly.

* Wilford Woodruff says that when the five men entered the camp there was not
a cloud to be seen in the whole heavens, but as the men left the camp there was a
small cloud like a black spot appeared in the north west, and it began to unroll
itself like a scroll, and in a few minutes the whole heavens were covered with a
pall as black as ink. This indicated a sudden storm which soon broke upon us
with wind, rain, thunder and lightning and hail. Our beds were soon afloat and
our tents blown down over our heads. We all fled into a Baptist meetinghouse.
As the Prophet Joseph came in shaking the water from his hat and clothing he
said, "Boys, there is some meaning to this. God is in this storm." We sang
praises to God, and lay all night on benches under cover while our enemies were
in the pelting storm. It was reported that the mob cavalry who fled into the
schoolhouse had to hold their horses by the bridles between the logs, but when
the heavy hail storm struck them they broke away, skinning the fingers of those
who were holding them. The horses fled before the storm and were not found for
several days. It was reported that the captain of the company in the schoolhouse
said it was a strange thing that they could do nothing against the Mormons but
what there must be some hail storm or some other thing to hinder their doing anything, but they did not feel disposed to acknowledge that God was fighting
our battles. (Wilford Woodruff's note in Ms. History of the Church, Book A
p. 332.)

which caused it to be so light in our camp through the night, that we could discern the most minute objects; and the roaring of the thunder was tremendous. The earth trembled and quaked, the rain fell in torrents, and, united, it seemed as if the mandate of vengeance had gone forth from the God of battles, to protect His servants from the destruction of their enemies, for the hail fell on them and not on us, and we suffered no harm, except the blowing down of some of our tents, and getting wet; while our enemies had holes made in their hats, and otherwise received damage, even the breaking of their rifle stocks, and the fleeing of their horses through fear and pain.

Many of my little band sheltered in an old meetinghouse through this night, and in the morning the water in Big Fishing river was about forty feet deep, where, the previous evening, it was no more than to our ankles, and our enemies swore that the water rose thirty feet in thirty minutes in the Little Fishing river. They reported that one of their men was killed by lightning, and that another had his hand torn off by his horse drawing his hand between the logs of a corn crib while he was holding him on the inside. They declared that if that was the way God fought for the Mormons, they might as well go about their business.

Friday 20.—This morning I counseled the brethren to discharge all their firearms, when it was found we had nearly six hundred shots, very few of which missed fire, which shows how very careful the brethren had been in taking care of their arms during the storm.

Care of Arms During the Storms.

We drove five miles on to the prairie where we could procure food for ourselves and horses, and defend ourselves from the rage of our enemies. While camped here on Saturday the 21st, Colonel Sconce, with two other leading men from Ray county, came to see us, desiring to know what our

The Visit of Col. Sconce to the Camp.

intentions were; "for," said he, "I see that there is an
Almighty power that protects this people, for I started
from Richmond, Ray county, with a company of armed
men, having a fixed dertermination to destroy you, but
was kept back by the storm, and was not able to reach
you." When he entered our camp he was seized with
such a trembling that he was obliged to sit down to compose himself; and when he had made known the object of
their visit, I arose, and, addressing them, gave a relation
of the sufferings of the Saints in Jackson county, and
also our persecutions generally, and what we had suffered
by our enemies for our religion; and that we had come one
thousand miles to assist our brethren, to bring them clothing,
etc., and to reinstate them upon their own lands; and that
we had no intention to molest or injure any people, but only
to administer to the wants of our afflicted friends; and that
the evil reports circulated about us were false, and got up by
our enemies to procure our destruction. When I had closed
a lenghty speech, the spirit of which melted them into
compassion, they arose and offered me their hands, and
said they would use their influence to allay the excitement which everywhere prevailed against us; and they
wept when they heard of our afflictions and persecutions,
and learned that our intentions were good. Accordingly
they went forth among the people, and made unwearied
exertions to allay the excitement.*

Brother Ezra Thayre and Joseph Hancock are sick with
the cholera. Thomas Heyes was taken today.
Cholera
Breaks out in Previous to crossing the Mississippi river I had
the Camp.
called the camp together† and told them that
in consequence of the disobedience of some who had been
unwilling to listen to my words, but had rebelled, God

* It is said of the prophet Joseph that if he could but once get the attention
even of his bitterest enemies his native eloquence, inspired by the truth and the
pathos of his people's sufferings, usually overwhelmed them; and in no instance
was his triumph more marked than in the one just related.

† The prediction will be found at p. 80.

had decreed that sickness should come upon the camp, and if they did not repent and humble themselves before God they should die like sheep with the rot; that I was sorry, but could not help it.* The scourge must come; repentance and humility may mitigate the chastisement, but cannot altogether avert it. But there were some who would not give heed to my words.

The brethren in Clay county wrote the committee of the Jackson mob the same day as follows:—

CLAY COUNTY, June 21, 1834.

GENTLEMEN—Your propositions of Monday last have been generally made known to our people, and we are instructed to inform you that they cannot be acceded to.

Honorable propositions to you are now making on our part, and we think we shall be enabled to deliver the same to you the early part of next week. We are happy to have it in our power to give you assurances that our brethren here, together with those who have arrived from the east, are unanimously disposed to make every sacrifice for an honorable adjustment of our differences, that could be required of free citizens of the United States.

Negotiations at the camp are now going on between some gentlemen of this county, and our brethren, which are calculated to allay the great excitement in your county. We are informed that the citizens of Jackson entertain fears that our people intend to invade their territory in a hostile manner. We assure you that their fears are groundless, such is not and never was our intention.

(Signed)   W. W. PHELPS,
                           A. S. GILBERT,
                           W. E. M'LELLIN,
                           JOHN CORRILL,
                           ISAAC MORLEY.

To S. C. Owens, and others of the Jackson committee.

June 22.—Brother Lyman Smith received a wound from the accidental discharge of a horse-pistol, from which he recovered in about three days.

---

* When he [the Prophet Joseph] spoke these things it pierced me like a dart, having a testimony that so it would be. (Extracts from H. C. Kimball's journal, *Times and Seasons*, Vol. vi, p. 804.)

Cornelius Gillium, the sheriff of Clay county, came
to our camp to hold consultation with us.

Visit of Clay County Sheriff to the Camp.
I marched my company into a grove near by,
and formed in a circle, with Gillium in the
centre. Gillium commenced by saying that he had heard
that Joseph Smith was in the camp, and if so he would
like to see him. I arose and replied, "I am the man."
This was the first time that I had been discovered or made
known to my enemies since I left Kirtland. Gillium then
gave us instruction concerning the manners, customs,
and dispositions of the people, and what course we
ought to pursue to secure their favor and protection,
making certain inquiries, to which we replied, which were
afterwards published, and will appear under date of
publication.

I received the following:—

*Revelation given on Fishing River, Missouri, June 22, 1834.**

1. Verily I say unto you who have assembled yourselves together
that you may learn my will concerning the redemption of mine afflicted
people:

2. Behold, I say unto you, were it not for the transgressions of my
people, speaking concerning the Church and not individuals, they might
have been redeemed even now;

3. But behold, they have not learned to be obedient to the things
which I required at their hands, but are full of all manner of evil, and
do not impart of their substance as becometh saints, to the poor and
afflicted among them,

4. And are not united according to the union required by the law of
the celestial kingdom;

5. And Zion cannot be built up unless it is by the principles of the
law of the celestial kingdom, otherwise I cannot receive her unto
myself;

6. And my people must needs be chastened until they learn obedience, if it must needs be, by the things which they suffer.

7. I speak not concerning those who are appointed to lead my people,
who are the first Elders of my Church, for they are not all under this
condemnation;

* Doctrine and Covenants, sec. cv.

8. But I speak concerning my churches abroad—there are many who will say, Where is their God? Behold, He will deliver them in time of trouble, otherwise we will not go up unto Zion, and will keep our moneys.

9. Therefore, in consequence of the transgressions of my people, it is expedient in me that mine Elders should wait for a little season for the redemption of Zion,

10. That they themselves may be prepared, and that my people may be taught more perfectly, and have experience, and know more perfectly concerning their duty, and the things which I require at their hands.

11. And this cannot be brought to pass until mine Elders are endowed with power from on high;

12. For behold, I have pepared a great endowment and blessing to be poured out upon them, inasmuch as they are faithful and continue in humility before me;

13. Therefore it is expedient in me that mine Elders should wait for a little season, for the redemption of Zion;

14. For behold, I do not require at their hands to fight the battles of Zion; for, as I said in a former commandment, even so will I fulfill—I will fight your battles.

15. Behold the destroyer I have sent forth to destroy and lay waste mine enemies: and not many years hence they shall not be left to pollute mine heritage, and to blaspheme my name upon the lands which I have consecrated for the gathering together of my saints.

16. Behold, I have commanded my servant Baurak Ale (Joseph Smith, Jun.,) to say unto the strength of my house, my warriors, my young men, and middle-aged, to gather together for the redemption of my people, and throw down the towers of mine enemies and scatter their watchmen;

17. But the strength of mine house have not hearkened unto my words;

18. But inasmuch as there are those who have hearkened unto my words, I have prepared a blessing and an endowment for them, if they continue faithful.

19. I have heard their prayers, and will accept their offering: and it is expedient in me, that they should be brought thus far for a trial of their faith.

20. And now, verily I say unto you, a commandment I give unto you, that as many as have come hither, that can stay in the region round about, let them stay;

21. And those that cannot stay, who have families in the east, let them tarry for a little season, inasmuch as my servant Joseph shall appoint unto them;

22. For I will counsel him concerning this matter, and all things whatsoever he shall appoint unto them shall be fulfilled.

23. And let all my people who dwell in the regions round about be very faithful, and prayerful, and humble before me, and reveal not the things which I have revealed unto them, until it is wisdom in me that they should be revealed.

24. Talk not of judgments, neither boast of faith, nor of mighty works, but carefully gather together, as much in one region as can be consistently with the feelings of the people;

25. And behold, I will give unto you favor and grace in their eyes, that you may rest in peace and safety, while you are saying unto the people, Execute judgment and justice for us according to law, and redress us of our wrongs.

26. Now, behold, I say unto you, my friends, in this way you may find favor in the eyes of the people, until the army of Israel becomes very great;

27. And I will soften the hearts of the people, as I did the heart of Pharaoh, from time to time, until my servant Baurak Ale (Joseph Smith, Jun.,) and Baneemy (mine Elders), whom I have appointed, shall have time to gather up the strength of my house,

28. And to have sent wise men, to fulfill that which I have commanded concerning the purchasing of all the lands in Jackson county that can be purchased, and in the adjoining counties round about;

29. For it is my will that these lands should be purchased, and after they are purchased that my Saints should possess them according to the laws of consecration which I have given;

30. And after these lands are purchased, I will hold the armies of Israel guiltless in taking possession of their own lands, which they have previously purchased with their moneys, and of throwing down the towers of mine enemies that may be upon them, and scattering their watchmen, and avenging me of mine enemies unto the third and fourth generation of them that hate me.

31. But firstly, let my army become very great, and let it be sanctified before me, that it may become fair as the sun, and clear as the moon, and that her banners may be terrible unto all nations;

32. That the kingdoms of this world may be constrained to acknowledge, that the kingdom of Zion is in very deed the kingdom of our God and His Christ; therefore let us become subject unto her laws.

33. Verily I say unto you, it is expedient in me that the first Elders of my Church should receive their endowment from on high in my house, which I have commanded to be built unto my name in the land of Kirtland;

34. And let those commandments which I have given concerning Zion and her law be executed and fulfilled, after her redemption;

35. There has been a day of calling, but the time has come for a day of choosing, and let those be chosen that are worthy;

36. And it shall be manifest unto my servant, by the voice of the Spirit, those that are chosen, and they shall be sanctified;

37. And inasmuch as they follow the counsel which they receive, they shall have power after many days to accomplish all things pertaining to Zion.

38. And again I say unto you, sue for peace not only to the people that have smitten you, but also to all people;

39. And lift up an ensign of peace, and make a proclamation of peace unto the ends of the earth;

40. And make proposals for peace unto those who have smitten you, according to the voice of the Spirit which is in you, and all things shall work together for your good;

41. Therefore be faithful, and behold, and lo, I am with you even unto the end. Even so. Amen.

CHAPTER VIII.

ZION'S CAMP DISBANDED—AN APPEAL.

June 23.—We resumed our march for Liberty, Clay county, taking a circuitous course around the heads of Fishing river, to avoid the deep water. When within five or six miles of Liberty, we were met by General Atchison and other gentlemen, who desired us not to go to Liberty because the feelings of the people were so much enraged against us. At their solicitation we turned our course, wheeling to the left, and crossing the prairie and woodland, came to Brother Algernon Sidney Gilbert's residence, and encamped on the bank of Rush creek, in Brother Burket's* field.

A council of High Priests assembled in fulfillment of the revelation given the day previous, and the following individuals were called and chosen, as they were made manifest unto me by the voice of the Spirit and revelation, to receive their endowments:

Edward Partridge was called and chosen, to go to Kirtland and receive his endowment with power from on high, and also, to stand in his office as Bishop to purchase lands in the state of Missouri.

William W. Phelps was called and chosen, and it was appointed unto him to receive his endowment with power from on high, and help to carry on the printing establishment in Kirtland, until Zion is redeemed.

Isaac Morley and John Corrill were called and chosen, and it was appointed unto them to receive their endowment with power from on high in Kirtland, and assist in

* Also given "Burghart's" in some of the Church records.

gathering up the strength of the Lord's house, and preach the Gospel.

John Whitmer and David Whitmer were called and chosen, and appointed to receive their endowment in Kirtland, and continue in their offices.

Algernon Sidney Gilbert was called and chosen, and appointed to receive his endowment in Kirtland, and to assist in gathering up the strength of the Lord's house, and to proclaim the everlasting Gospel until Zion is redeemed. But he said he "could not do it."

Peter Whitmer, Jun., Simeon Carter, Newel Knight, Parley P. Pratt, Christian Whitmer and Solomon Hancock were called and chosen; and it was appointed unto them to receive their endowment in Kirtland, with power from on high; to assist in gathering up the strength of the Lord's house; and to preach the everlasting Gospel.

Thomas B. Marsh was called and chosen; and it was appointed unto him to receive his endowment in Kirtland, his office to be made known hereafter.

Lyman Wight was called and chosen; and it was appointed unto him to receive his endowment in Kirtland, with power from on high; and return to Zion and have his office appointed unto him hereafter.

The same day the Elders made the following reply, before referred to, to "Samuel C. Owens and others, committee" of the Jackson county mob:

We, the undersigned committee, having full power and authority to settle and adjust all matters and differences existing between our people or society and the inhabitants of Jackson county, upon honorable and constitutional principles; therefore, if the said inhabitants of Jackson county will not let us return to our lands in peace, we are willing to propose first: that twelve disinterested men, six to be chosen by our people, and six by the inhabitants of Jackson county; and these twelve men shall say what the lands of those men are worth in that county, who cannot consent to live with us, and they shall receive their money for the same in one year from the time the treaty is made, and none of our people shall enter the county to reside till the money is paid. The said twelve men shall have power also to say what the damages shall be for the injuries we have sustained in the destruction of property and in being driven from our possessions, which amount of damages shall be deducted from the amount for their lands. Our object is peace, and an early answer will be expected.

(Signed)   W. W. PHELPS,
EDWARD PARTRIDGE,
ISAAC MORLEY,
JOHN CORRILL,
JOHN WHITMER,
A. S. GILBERT.

June 24.—This night the cholera burst forth among us, and about midnight it was manifested in its most virulent

Cholera in the Camp.

form. Our ears were saluted with cries and moanings, and lamentations on every hand; even those on guard fell to the earth with their guns in their hands, so sudden and powerful was the attack of this terrible disease. At the commencement, I attempted to lay on hands for their recovery, but I quickly learned by painful experience, that when the great Jehovah decrees destruction upon any people, and makes known His determination, man must not attempt to stay His hand. The moment I attempted to rebuke the disease I was attacked, and had I not desisted in my attempt to save the life of a brother, I would have sacrificed my own. The disease seized upon me like the talons of a hawk, and I said to the brethren: "If my work were done, you would have to put me in the ground without a coffin."

Early on the morning of the 25th, the camp was

Zion's Camp Disbanded.

separated into small bands, and dispersed among the brethren living in the vicinity; and I wrote and sent by express, to "Messrs. Thornton, Doniphan, and Atchison," as follows:

RUSH CREEK, CLAY COUNTY, June 25, 1834.

GENTLEMEN—Our company of men advanced yesterday from their encampment beyond Fishing river to Rush Creek, where their tents are again pitched. But feeling disposed to adopt every pacific measure, without jeopardizing our lives, to quiet the prejudices and fears of some part of the citizens of this county, we have concluded that our company shall be immediately dispersed, and continue so till every effort for an adjustment of differences between us and the people of Jackson has been made on our part, that would in any wise be required of us by disinterested men of republican principles.

I am respectfully, your obedient servant,

JOSEPH SMITH, JUN.

N.B.—You are now corresponding with the governor, (as I am informed); will you do us the favor to acquaint him of our efforts for a compromise. This information we want conveyed to the governor, inasmuch as his ears are stuffed with reports from Jackson, of our hostile intentions.   J. S.

I left Rush Creek the same day in company with David Whitmer and two other brethren, for the western part of Clay county. While traveling, we called at the house of a Mr. Moss for a drink of water. *Fear of the Cholera.* The woman of the house shouted from the door, that they had "no water for Mormons," that they were "afraid of the cholera," etc., at the same time throwing out her arms as if defending herself from the cholera in the form of a personage. We turned and departed, according to the commandment, and before a week had passed, the cholera entered that house, and that woman and three others of the family were dead.

When the cholera made its appearance, Elder John S. Carter was the first man who stepped forward to rebuke it, and upon this, was instantly seized, and became the first victim in the camp. He died *First Victims of the Cholera.* about six o'clock in the afternoon; and Seth Hitchcock died in about thirty minutes afterwards. Erastus Rudd died about the same moment, although a half a mile distant. He was buried by Jesse Smith, George A. Smith and two or three others, and while burying him, Jesse Smith was attacked with the cholera. As it was impossible to obtain coffins, the brethren rolled the corpses in blankets, carried them on a horse-sled about half a mile, buried them on the bank of a small stream, which empties into Rush creek, all of which was accomplished by dark. When they had returned from the burial, the brethren unitedly covenanted and prayed, hoping the disease would be stayed; but in vain, for while thus covenanting, Eber Wilcox died; and while some were digging the grave, others stood sentry with their fire arms, watching their enemies.*

* Of these sorrowful scenes Elder Heber C. Kimball in his journal, gives the following description, which ought not to be lost to the reader of Church History:

"When the Cholera first broke out in the camp, Brother John S. Carter was the first who went forth to rebuke it, but [he] himself, was immedaitely seized by it, and as before stated, was the first who was slain. In about thirty minutes after his death, Seth Hitchcock followed him; and it appeared as though we must sink under the destroyer with them. We were not able to obtain boards to make coffins, [for those who died], but were under the necessity of rolling them up in their blankets, and burying them in that manner. So we placed them on a sled, which was drawn by a horse about half a mile, where we buried them in a little bluff by the side of a small stream that emptied into Rush creek. This we accomplished by dark, and returned. Our hopes were that no more would die, but while we were uniting in a covenant to pray once more with uplifted hands to God, we looked at our beloved brother, Elder Wilcox, and he was gasping his last. At this scene my feelings were beyond expression. Those only who witnessed it, can realize anything of the nature of our sufferings, and I felt to weep, and pray to the Lord that He would spare my life that I might behold my dear family again. I felt to covenant with my brethren, and I felt in my heart never to commit another sin while I lived. We felt to sit and weep over our brethren, and so great was our sorrow that we could have washed them with our tears, to realize that they had traveled one thousand miles through so much fatigue to lay down their lives for our brethren—and who hath greater love than he who is willing to lay down his life for his brethren? This increased our love to them. About 12 o'clock at night we placed Brother Wilcox on a small sled, which we drew to the place of interment, with one hand hold of the rope, and in the other we bore our firelocks for our defense. While one or two were digging the grave, the rest stood with their arms to defend them. This was our situation, the enemies around us, and the destroyer in our midst. Soon after we returned another brother was taken away from our little band; thus it continued until five out of ten [attacked] were taken away. It was truly affecting to see the love manifested among the brethren for one another, during the affliction; Brother Joseph, seeing the sufferings of his brethren, stepped forward to rebuke the destroyer, but was immediately seized with the disease himself; and I assisted him a short distance from the place, when it was with difficulty he could walk. All that kept our enemies from us was the fear of the destroyer which the Lord so sent among us. After burying these five brethren, or about this time, I was seized by the hand of the destroyer, as I had gone in the woods to pray. I was instantly struck blind, and saw no way whereby I could free myself from the disease, only to exert myself by jumping and thrashing myself about, until my sight returned to me, and my blood began to circulate in my veins. I started and ran some distance, and by this means, through the help of God, I was enabled to extricate myself from the grasp of death. This circumstance took place in a piece of woods just behind Brother Sidney Gilbert's house. * * * * * * Two other brethren died at Brother Gilbert's house about this same time. One of these was a cousin to Brother Joseph Smith, the Prophet."

June 26.—The Elders wrote Governor Dunklin as follows:

Sir—A company of our people, exceeding two hundred men, arrived in this county the 19th instant, and encamped about twelve miles from Liberty, where they were met by several gentlemen from this [Clay] and Ray county,who went by request of the people, to ascertain the motives and designs of our people in approaching this county; and as the deputation was composed of gentlemen who appeared to possess humane feelings and republican principles, our people were rejoiced at the opportunity of an interchange of feelings, and an open and frank avowal of all their views and intentions in emigrating to this country with their arms. A full explanation having been given in a public address by our brother, Joseph Smith, Jun., which produced great satisfaction, the same in substance was afterwards reduced to writing, and handed to the aforesaid gentlemen, that it might be made public. The shedding of blood is, and ever has been, foreign and revolting to our feelings; for this reason, we have patiently endured the grossest indignities that freemen of this republic have ever been called to suffer; and we still continue to bear with heart-rending feelings, a deprivation of our rights. We commenced negotiations with the inhabitants of Jackson county for a compromise, wherein proposals on our part have been made which have been acknowledged by every disinterested man to be highly honorable and liberal. An answer to our proposition has not yet been received from the people of Jackson county.

If we fail in this attempt, we intend to make another effort and go all lenghts that could be required by human or divine law. As our proposals and correspondence with the inhabitants of Jackson county will doubtless hereafter be published, we think it unnecessary to detail the same in this communication. Our right to our soil in Jackson county we shall for ever claim, but to obtain peaceful possession we are willing to make great sacrifices. To allay excitement in this county, the aforesaid company of emigrants have dispersed to await the final end of all negotiations that can be made with the said county of Jackson.

Within the last week, one of our men being near the ferry, was seized by some Jackson citizens, while in this county, threatened with death if be made resistance, and carried over the river, a prisoner, to Independence, where he was put under guard one day, and after hearing many threats, was liberated. The houses of several of our brethren in this county have been forcibly entered by some of the inhabitants of Jackson, and a number of guns and small arms taken therefrom. We have been informed and have no doubt of the fact that where the men were absent from their houses, loaded guns were presented to the females, and their lives threatened if they made resistance.

Your second order of the restoration of our arms, was received last mail; we have not yet done anything with it. Hoping that the influence of the inhabitants of Jackson county will materially lessen in the surrounding counties, and the people become more tranquil, we think it wisdom to defer petitioning for a guard, while there exists a hope of a compromise.

We believe that the President would render us assistance in obtaining possession of our lands, if aided by the executive of this state in a petition, and thereby put an end to serious evils that are growing out of the Jackson county outrage.

In a letter from your Excellency, of April 20th, we had a word on the subject of petitioning. We should be pleased to hear further, and would here observe that no communication from the executive, giving his opinion or advice, will be made public, if requested not to do so.

We are respectfully, and with great regard,

Your obedient servants,

A. S. GILBERT,
W. W, PHELPS,
JOHN CORRILL.

The drafting and signing of the above, was the last public act of the keeper of the Lord's storehouse Algernon Sidney Gilbert, for he was attacked with the cholera the same day, and died about the 29th. He had been called to preach the Gospel, but had been known to say that he "would rather die than go forth to preach the Gospel to the Gentiles." *

Death of Algernon Sidney Gilbert.

* Heber C. Kimball remarks: "The Lord took him at his word." Extracts from Kimball's journal, *Times and Seasons*, Vol. vi, p. 839.

The remarks in the body of the history, and this expression from Elder Kimball's journal are liable to create a misunderstanding concerning Brother Algernon Sidney Gilbert, than whom the Lord has had few more devoted servants in this dispensation. The place and date of his birth cannot now be ascertained. His father's family resided in Huntington, Connecticut. Besides himself, there was a younger brother who joined the Church, but he died of cholera in St. Louis, Missouri, the same year as his elder brother. Elder Gilbert for some years was a successful merchant in Painesville, Ohio; and subsequently, with Newel K. Whitney, he founded the successful mercantile firm of Gilbert and Whitney in Kirtland, Ohio, at which place the Gospel found him in the year 1830. Later, he was called to go to Missouri, and was appointed keeper of the Lord's storehouse, and upon him also devolved the responsibility of purchasing lands for the Saints. He was devoted to the interest of the Saints and the Church. In the persecutions which came upon the people in Jackson county

The following is from the chairman of the committee of the Jackson county mob, to our lawyer:

INDEPENDENCE, MISSOURI, JUNE 26, 1834.

Mr. Amos Reese:

DEAR SIR—Since my return from Liberty, I have been busily engaged in conversing with the most influential men of our county, endeavoring to find out, if possible, what kind of a compromise will suit with the Mormons on their part. The people here, *en masse*, I find out, will do nothing like acceding to their last proposition. We will have a meeting if possible, on Monday next, at which time the proposals of the Mormons will be answered. In the meantime, I would be glad that they, the Mormons, would cast an eye back of Clinton, and see if that is not a country calculated for them.

Yours respectfully,

S. C. OWENS.

The cholera continued its ravages for about four days, when a remedy for the purging, vomiting, and cramping, was discovered; viz., dipping the persons afflicted in cold water, or pouring it upon them, and giving them whisky thickened with flour to the consistency of starch. Whisky was the only kind of spirits that could be procured at this place. About

List of the Victims of Cholera.

he sacrificed all his goods, and was among the six who offered their own lives for the lives of their friends in the Jackson county trouble. As to his refusing to accept the appointment to go and preach the Gospel to the Gentiles, that refusal did not arise from any lack of faith in the truth of God's great work, but from a native diffidence and a lack of confidence in his own ability to preach. He was a man of rare good sense, conservative and of sound judgment. All of which appears in the many communications drawn up in Missouri by him during the troublous times through which the Church passed in those days. Much of the correspondence between the Missouri brethren and Governor Dunklin was the work of Elder Gilbert, and it bears witness to the truth of what is here said of him. Nor did he entirely refuse to bear witness of the truth of the Gospel to others. In a communication to the *Messenger and Advocate* from Huntington, Connecticut, under date of September 24, 1834, his aged father, Eli Gilbert, describing the visit of his son to that place some two years previous, says: "He continued with us about two weeks, and in that time was pressed by his friends and acquaintances to meet them and others, and inform them concerning the people, and the Book of Mormon. This he cheerfully did, as often as his low state of health would permit; and although threatened and abused by some of our pious persecutors, yet [he was] not much hurt nor interrupted. When a meeting was held, a goodly number were brought to serious inquiry concerning these things, and several would gladly have received baptism, as they afterwards told me. And, thank God, some retain that desire and determination yet.''

sixty-eight of the Saints suffered from this disease, of which number fourteen died, viz.: John S. Carter, Eber Wilcox, Seth Hitchcock, Erastus Rudd, Algernon Sidney Gilbert, Alfred Fisk, Edward Ives, Noah Johnson, Jesse B. Lawson, Robert McCord, Elial Strong, Jesse J. Smith, Warren Ingalls and Betsy Parrish.

Among the most active of those who were engaged in taking care of the sick at the camp, burying the dead, etc., were John D. Parker, John Tanner, Nathan Tanner, Joseph B. Noble, Brigham Young, Joseph Young, Heber C. Kimball, Luke S. Johnson and Eleazar Miller.

I sent Hiram Page with instructions to bring Jesse J. Smith and George A. Smith to me at all hazards to the west part of the county, having had intimations that they were sick. He found that Jesse had been severely racked with the cholera all day, George A. Smith had taken care of him for upwards of thirty hours. Dr. Frederick G. Williams decided that the cholera had left him, and he would recover if not moved. On the morning of the 28th, George A. Smith was attacked and was immediately mounted on a hard-riding horse, rode fifteen miles, and came to me.

The last days of June I spent with my old Jackson county friends, in the western part of Clay county.

On the 1st of July Jesse J. Smith died. I crossed the Missouri river, in company with a few friends, into Jackson county, to set my feet once more on the "goodly land;" and on the 2nd I went down near Liberty, and visited the brethren. A considerable number of the Camp met me at Lyman Wight's. I told them if they would humble themselves before the Lord and covenant to keep His commandments and obey my counsel, the plague should be stayed from that hour, and there should not be another case of the cholera among them. The brethren covenanted to that effect with uplifted hands, and the plague was stayed.

The Prophet in the Goodly Land.

This day the *Enquirer* published the correspodence between the sheriff, Cornelius Gillium, and Zion's Camp, of the 22nd of June, as follows:

Gillium's Communication.

Being a citizen of Clay county, and knowing that there is considerable excitement amongst the people thereof, and also knowing that different reports are arriving almost hourly; and being requested by the Hon. J. F. Ryland to meet the Mormons under arms, and obtain from the leaders thereof the correctness of the various reports in circulation, the true intent and meaning of their present movements, and their views generally regarding the difficulties existing between them and Jackson county,—I did, in company with other gentlemen, call upon the said leaders of the Mormons, at their camp in Clay county; and now give to the people of Clay county their written statement, containing the substance of what passed between us.

(Signed)   CORNELIUS GILLIUM.

"Propositions of the Mormons.

"Being called upon by the above-named gentlemen, at our camp in Clay county, to ascertain from the leaders of our men our intentions, views, and designs, in approaching this county in the manner we have, we therefore the more cheerfully comply with their request, because we are called upon by gentlemen of good feelings, and who are disposed for peace and an amicable adjustment of the difficulties existing between us and the people of Jackson county. The reports of our intentions are various, and have gone abroad in a light calculated to arouse the feelings of almost every man. For instance, one report is, that we intend to demolish the printing office in Liberty; another report is, that we intend crossing the Missouri river on Sunday next, and falling upon women and children, and slaying them; another is, that our men were employed to perform this expedition, being taken from manufacturing establishments in the east, that had closed business; also that we carried a flag, bearing 'Peace' on one side, and 'War or Blood' on the other; and various other reports too numerous to mention, all of which a plain declaration of our intentions, from under our own hands will show are not correct.

"In the first place, it is not our intention to commit hostilities against any man, or set of men; it is not our intention to injure any man's person or property, except in defending ourselves. Our flag has been exhibited to the above gentlemen, who will be able to describe it. Our men were not taken from any manufacturing establishment. It is our intention to go back upon our lands in Jackson county, by order of the executive of the state, if possible. We have brought our arms with us for the purpose of self defense, as it is well known to almost every man of the State, that we have every reason to put ourselves in an attitude of defense, considering the abuse we have suffered in Jackson county. We are anxious for a settlement of the difficulties existing between us, upon honorable and constitutional principles.

"We are willing for twelve disinterested men, six to be chosen by each party, and these men shall say what the possessions of those men are worth who cannot live with us in the county; and they shall have their money in one year; and none of the Mormons shall enter that county to reside until the money is paid. The damages that we have sustained in consequence of being driven away, shall also be left to the above twelve men; or they may all live in the county, if they choose, and we will never molest them if they let us alone, and permit us to enjoy our rights. We want to live in peace with all men; and equal rights is all we ask. We wish to become permanent citizens of this State; and wish to bear our proportion in support of the government, and to be protected by its laws. If the above propositions are complied with, we are willing to give security on our part; and we shall want the same of the people of Jackson county for the performance of this agreement. We do not wish to settle down in a body, except where we can purchase the land with money; for to take possession by conquest or the shedding of blood is entirely foreign to our feelings. The shedding of blood we shall not be guilty of, until all just and honorable means among men prove insufficient to restore peace."

(Signed)

> JOSEPH SMITH, JUN.,
> FREDERICK G. WILLIAMS,
> LYMAN WIGHT,
> ROGER ORTON,
> ORSON HYDE,
> JOHN S. CARTER.

June 21st.

To John Lincoln, John Sconce, George R. Morehead, Jas. H. Long, James Collins.

On the third of July, the High Priests of Zion assembled in the yard of Col. Arthurs, where Lyman Wight

Organization of the High Council in Missouri.

lived, in Clay county, and I proceeded to organize a High Council, agreeable to the revelation and pattern given at Kirtland, for the purpose of settling important business that might

come before them, which could not be settled by the
Bishop and his council. David Whitmer was elected
president, and William W. Phelps and John Whitmer
assistant presidents. The following High Priests, viz.:
Christian Whitmer, Newel Knight, Lyman Wight, Calvin
Beebe, Wm. E. M'Lellin, Solomon Hancock, Thomas B.
Marsh, Simeon Carter, Parley P. Pratt, Orson Pratt, John
Murdock, and Levi Jackman, were appointed councilors;
and the Council adjourned to Monday. Frederick G.
Williams was clerk of the meeting.

I authorized General Lyman Wight to give a discharge
to every man of the Camp who had proved
himself faithful, certifying that fact and giving
him leave to return home.*

Members of
the Camp
Discharged.

* This formal order to discharge every man of Zion's Camp and release him to
return home may be considered as the termination of Zion's Camp expedition for
the redemption of Zion. Had Governor Dunklin possessed the courage to enforce the
law of the State; had he called out the militia of Missouri to reinstate the exiles
in their homes as at one time he expressed a willingness to do, the history of
Zion's Camp might have had a different ending; for the exiles reinstated in their
lands, and reinforced by the two hundred brethren who constituted Zion's Camp,
might have been able to have maintained their inheritances on that land; but
Governor Dunklin when the crisis came, lacked the necessary courage to fulfill
his promise, and without the moral assistance which the reinstatement of the
Saints upon their lands by the military forces of the State would give, the exiles
and Zion's Camp were powerless. Perhaps also another view is admissible. Had
the members of Zion's Camp been more faithful, less contentious, more united;
had the Saints in the eastern branches had more faith—faith to send up to Zion
more men and more money with which to strengthen the hands of the Saints on
the land of Zion—the history of Zion's Camp might have been different: for
with a larger force they would doubtless have been able to hold their lands against
the mob, independent of the action of the State authorities. But thus it is: what
men and great movements might attain to is often defeated, sometimes by the
actions of enemies, sometimes by the lack of devotion and faith and energy on the
part of those into whose hands great enterprises are committed. While God's
general purposes will never ultimately be defeated by man, still upon each side
of the general purposes of God a margin somewhat wide seems to have been left
in which those both for and against those purposes may write what history they
please—one that will meet with the approval of God, or one that will meet only
with condemnation—herein is the agency of man. But in the exercise of that
agency God's purposes will not be thwarted, for man's agency will not extend so
far as that; if it did, it would interfere with God's agency and decrees. The
order above, I again remark, closed the history of this first march of Zion's Camp;
and the redemption of Zion has been left to other hands, and to other times.
But that its redemption will come no one doubts who believes in the firm decrees
of God.

From this time I continued to give instruction to the
members of the High Council, Elders, those
who had traveled in the Camp with me, and
such others as desired information, until the
7th, when the Council assembled according to adjournment at the house of Elder Lyman Wight; present, fifteen
High Priests, eight Elders, four Priests, eight Teachers,
three Deacons, and several members. After singing and
prayer, I gave the Council such instructions in relation
to their high calling, as would enable them to proceed
to minister in their office agreeable to the pattern heretofore given; read the revelation on the subject; and told
them that if I should now be taken away, I had accomplished the great work the Lord had laid before me, and
that which I had desired of the Lord; and that I had
done my duty in organizing the High Council, through
which council the will of the Lord might be known on
all important occasions, in the building up of Zion,
and establishing truth in the earth.

Instructions to the High Council.

It was voted that those who were appointed on the 3rd,
should be confirmed in their appointments.

I then ordained David Whitmer, president, and W. W.
Phelps and John Whitmer, assistants; and the
twelve councilors. The twelve councilors
then proceeded to cast lots, to know who
should speak first, and the order of speaking, which
resulted as follows, viz.:

The Missouri Presidency and High Council.

Simeon Carter,	1	Parley P. Pratt,	2
Wm. E. M'Lellin,	3	Calvin Beebe,	4
Levi Jackman,	5	Solomon Hancock,	6
Christian Whitmer,	7	Newel Knight,	8
Orson Pratt,	9	Lyman Wight,	10
Thomas B. Marsh,	11	John Murdock.	12

Father Peter Whitmer came forward and blessed his
three sons, David, John and Christian Whitmer,
in the name of the Lord. Also Father Knight
blessed his son Newel.

Blessings.

Bishop Partridge stated to the Council that a greater responsibility rested upon him than before their organization, as it was not his privilege to counsel with any of them, except the president, and his own counselors; and desired their prayers that he might be enabled to act in righteousness.

I next presented the case of William W. Phelps to the Council, to have their decision whether or not he should take his family to Kirtland, and if so, when he should start; as it had been deemed necessary for him to assist in the printing establishment.

Sundry Items Determined by the High Council.

It was moved and carried that four of the councilors speak on the subject, two on each side, viz., Simeon Carter and Wm. E. M'Lellin, for William W. Phelps; and Parley P. Pratt and Calvin Beebe, for the church. After hearing the pleas, the president decided that it was the duty of William W. Phelps to go to Kirtland to assist in printing, and that his family remain in the region where they are, and that he have an honorable discharge from his station in Zion for a season, (as soon as he can accomplish his business). Signed by the president and clerk.

It was then proposed by W. W. Phelps, that David Whitmer, the president of the church in Zion, should go to Kirtland, and assist in promoting the cause of Christ, as being one of the three witnesses. This case was argued by Levi Jackman and Christian Whitmer in behalf of David Whitmer; and by Solomon Hancock and Newel Knight for the church; after which it was decided, as before, that Brother David Whitmer go to the East and assist in the great work of the gathering, and be his own judge as to leaving his family or taking them with him.

It was also decided that John Whitmer and Wm. E. M'Lellin go east, as soon as convenient.

The High Priests, Elders, Priests, Teachers, Deacons and members present, then covenanted with hands uplifted to heaven, that they would uphold Brother David

Whitmer, as president in Zion, in my absence; and John Whitmer and William W. Phelps, as assistant presidents or counselors; and myself as First President of the Church; and to uphold one another by faith and prayer.

Previous to entering into this covenant, and in pursuance of the revelation to the Saints to sue for and proclaim peace to the ends of the earth, the following appeal was written, and sanctioned by the High Council and First Presidency of the Church, at the foregoing sitting.

President Whitmer closed the Council by prayer.

FREDERICK G. WILLIAMS, Clerk.

An Appeal.*

Whereas the Church of Christ, recently styled the Church of the Latter-day Saints, contumeliously called "Mormons," or "Mormonites," has suffered many privations, afflictions, persecutions and losses on account of the religious belief and faith of its members, which belief and faith are founded in the revealed Word of God, as recorded in the Holy Bible, or the Book of Mormon, the Revelations and Commandments of our Savior Jesus Christ; and whereas the said Church, through revelation, commenced removing to the western boundaries of the State of Missouri, where lands were purchased of the government, and where it was calculated to purchase of those who were unwilling to reside with the Church, as a society, all lands that could be bought, for the purpose of building up a holy city unto God, a New Jerusalem, a place which we were desirous to call Zion, a place of refuge from the scourges and plagues that are so often mentioned in the Bible by the

* The editor of the *Evening and Morning Star* (Oliver Cowdery) thus concluded an editorial which preceded this "Appeal," published in the number of the *Star* above quoted:

"With the most of individuals and societies who have been traduced, and their characters and designs misrepresented, their last appeal has been made to the world or nation at large; here they rested their claim, and here the matter, with them, was brought to a final close. If the community approved their course, they triumphed; if not, it sank forever; but this is not the last resort of a people whose interest is in heaven, and whose hope is built upon the everlasting word of Omnipotence. When earthly courts and tribunals fail, and when the voice of the people is not given in their favor, and a place on earth is denied them, and their helpless, innocent posterity, their last great refuge is Jehovah; and if, like the ancients, they are driven from the face of society, that even a lodging place is forbidden them, they can wander in obscurity, not 'accepting deliverance,' till their change comes, and they 'obtain a better resurrection.' " *Evening and Morning Star*, vol. ii, p. 361.

prophets and apostles, which should be poured out upon the earth in the
last days; and whereas the inhabitants of Jackson county, Missouri,
have leagued and combined themselves against said Church, and have
driven the Saints from their lands, and have taken their arms from
them, and burned down many of their houses without any provocation;
and whereas, we have petitioned the governor of this state and the President of the United States for the redress of wrongs—the law being put
to defiance in Jackson county—and for the redemption of rights, that
we might be legally repossessed of our lands and property; and
whereas the said inhabitants of Jackson county have not only bound
themselves to keep us out of that county, but have armed themselves *cap
a pie*, and even with cannon for war; and whereas, our people residing
in Upper Missouri, have recently armed themselves for military duty
and self-defense, seeing their arms taken from them by the inhabitants
of Jackson county, were purposely kept from them; and whereas, a
number of the members of the Church in the East have emigrated to this
region of country, to settle and join with their brethren, with arms to
answer the military law, which has created some excitement among
the inhabitants of the upper counties of this state; whereupon, to show
that our object was only the peaceable possession of our rights and
property, and to purchase more lands in the regions round about, we
met a committee from Jackson county for compromise, and our emigrating brethren met some gentlemen from Clay and other counties, to
satisfy them that their motives were good, and their object peace, which
they did; and whereas, the propositions of the Jackson county committee could not be accepted on our part, because they proposed to
"buy or sell," and to sell our land would amount to a denial of our
faith, as that land is the place where the Zion of God shall stand,
according to our faith and belief in the revelations of God, and upon
which Israel will be gathered, according to the prophets; and, secondly, the propositions were unfair, notwithstanding they offered
double price for our lands, in thirty days, or to sell theirs at the same
rate, for this plain reason, that the whole large county of Jackson
would be as thirty to one, or nearly so, in comparison with the matter
in question, and in supposition, for one thousand dollars, two thousand
dollars to our people was asking for three hundred thousand dollars,
the exorbitant sum of six hundred thousand dollars, taking the land,
rich and poor, within thirty days, with the reproachable, vicious, un-
American, and unconstitutional proviso, that the committee on our part
bind themselves "that no Mormons should ever settle in Jackson
county;" and whereas, our committee proposed to the said Jackson
committee (if they would not grant us our rights otherwise), that our
people would buy the land of those who were unwilling to live among

our people, in that county, and pay them in one year, they allowing
the damage we have sustained in the loss of a printing office, apparatus
and book-work, houses, property, etc., to come out of the purchase-
money, but no answer returned; and whereas, to show our honest
intentions, and awaken the friends of virtue, humanity, and equal
rights, it becomes our duty to lay our case before the world, to be
weighed in the balances of public opinion.

Now, therefore, as citizens of the United States and leading Elders in
the Church of the Latter-day Saints, residing in the State of Missouri,
in behalf of the Church, we, the undersigned, do make this solemn
appeal to the people and constitutional authorities of this nation, and
to the ends of the earth, for peace; that we may have the privilege of
enjoying our religious rights and immunities, and worship God according to the dictates of our own consciences, as guaranteed to every
citizen by the constitution of the national and state governments; that
although the laws have been broken, and are defied in Jackson county,
we may be enabled to regain and enjoy our rights and property, agreeable to law, in this boasted land of liberty.

Since the disgraceful combination of the inhabitants of Jackson county has set the law at defiance, and put all hope of criminal prosecution
against them, in that vicinage, beyond the reach of judge or jury, and
left us but a distant expectation of civil remuneration for the great
amount of damages we have sustained, necessity compels us to complain
to the world; and if our case and calamity are not sufficient to excite
the commiseration of the humane, and open the hearts of the generous,
and fire the spirits of the patriotic, then has sympathy lost herself in
the wilderness, and justice fled from power; then has the dignity of
the ermine shrunk at the gigantic front of a mob, and the sacred mantle
of freedom been caught up to heaven, where the weary are at rest and
the wicked cannot come.

To be obedient to the commandments of our Lord and Savior, some
of the leaders of the Church commenced purchasing lands in the
western boundaries of the State of Missouri, according to the revelation
of God, for the city of Zion; in doing which, no law was evaded no
rights infringed, and no principle of religion neglected; but the laudable
foundation of a glorious work was begun, for the salvation of mankind
in the last days, agreeable to our faith, and according to the promises
in the sacred Scriptures of God. We verily believed—knowing that the
national and state constitutions, and the statute laws of the land, and
the commandments of the Lord allowed all men to worship as they
please—that we should be protected, not only by the laws of a free
republic, but by every republican throughout the realms of freedom.

The holy prophets have declared, that "it shall come to pass in the

last days that the mountain of the Lord's house shall be established
in the top of the mountains, and shall be exalted above the hills; and
all nations shall flow unto it. And many people shall go and say,
Come ye, and let us go up to the mountain of the Lord, to the house of
the God of Jacob; and He will teach us of His ways, and we will walk in
His paths: for out of Zion shall go forth the law, and the word of the
Lord from Jerusalem." And again, it was said by Joel, seemingly to
strengthen the faith of the Latter-day Saints in the above, "that whosoever shall call on the name of the Lord shall be delivered: for in
Mount Zion and in Jerusalem shall be deliverance, as the Lord hath
said, and in the remnant whom the Lord shall call." The Book of
Mormon, which we hold equally sacred with the Bible, says, "that
a New Jerusalem should be built up upon this land, unto the remnant of
the seed of Joseph, for the which things there has been a type."

In fact, all the prophets, from Moses to John the Revelator, have
spoken concerning these things. And in all good faith, by direct revelation from the Lord, as in days of old, we commenced the glorious
work, that a holy city, a new Jerusalem, even Zion, might be built up,
and a temple reared in this generation, whereunto, as saith the Lord,
all nations shall be invited. First, the rich and the learned, the wise
and the noble, were to be invited; and after that cometh the day of
His power. But the inhabitants of Jackson county arrayed themselves
against us because of our faith and belief, and destroyed our printing establishment to prevent the spread of the work, and drove men,
women and children from their lands, houses, and homes, to perish in
the approaching winter. Every blast carried the wailing of women
and the shrieks of children across the widespread prairie, sufficiently
horrible to draw tears from the savage or melt a heart of stone.

Now, that the world may know that our faith in the work and word
of the Lord is firm and unshaken; and to show all nations, kindreds,
tongues and people, that our object is good, for the good of all, we
come before the great family of mankind for peace, and ask their
hospitality and assistance for our comfort, and the preservation of our
persons and property, and solicit their charity for the great cause of
God. We are well aware that many slanderous reports and ridiculous
stories are in circulation against our religion and society; but as wise
men will hear both sides and then judge, we sincerely hope and trust
that the still, small voice of truth will be heard, and our great revelations read and candidly compared with the prophecies of the Bible,
that the great cause of our Redeemer may be supported by a liberal
share of public opinion, as well as by the unseen power of God.

It will be seen by reference to the Book of Commandments, page
135, that the Lord has said to the Church—and we mean to live by His
9 Vol II

words: "Let no man break the laws of the land, for he that keepeth the laws of God hath no need to break the laws of the land."* Therefore, as the people of God, we come before the world, and claim protection by law of the common officers of justice in every neighborhood where our people may be. We claim the same at the hands of the governors of the several states, and of the President of the United States, and of the friends of humanity and justice in every clime and country on the globe.

By the desperate acts of the inhabitants of Jackson county, many hundreds of American citizens are deprived of their lands and rights. It is reported, we mean to regain our possessions, and even Jackson county, "by the shedding of blood;" but if any man will take the pains to read the 153rd page of the Book of Commandments he will find it there said:

"Wherefore the land of Zion shall not be obtained but by purchase or by blood; otherwise there is none inheritance for you. And if by purchase, behold you are blessed; and if by blood, *as you are forbidden to shed blood*, lo, your enemies are upon you, and you shall be scourged from city to city, and from synagogue to synagogue, and but few shall stand to receive an inheritance."†

So we declare that we have ever meant and now mean to purchase the land of our inheritance of the government, like all honest men, and of those who would rather sell their farms than live in our society; and, as thousand have done before us, we solicit the aid of the children of men, and of government, to help us to obtain our rights in Jackson county, and the land whereon the Zion of God, according to our faith, shall stand in the last days, for the salvation and gathering of Israel.

Let no man be alarmed because our society has commenced gathering to build a city and a house for the Lord, as a refuge from present evils and coming calamities. Our forefathers came to this goodly land of America to shun persecution and enjoy their religious opinions and rights, as they thought proper; and the Lord, after much tribulation, blessed them; and has said that we should continue to importune for redress and redemption by the hands of those who are placed as rulers and are in authority over us, according to the laws and constitution of the people, which he has suffered to be established, and should be maintained for the rights and protection of all flesh, according to just and holy principles; that every man may act in doctrine and in principle pertaining to futurity according to the moral agency which He has given unto him; that every man may be accountable for his own sins in that day of judgment; and for this purpose He has established the

* Doctrine and Covenants, sec. lviii: 21.
† Doctrine and Covenants, sec. lxiii: 29-31.

constitution of this land by the hands of wise men, whom He raised up unto this very purpose, and redeemed the land by the shedding of blood.*

Now we seek peace, and ask our rights, even redress and redemption, at the hands of the rulers of this nation; not only our lands and property in Jackson county, but for free trade with all men, and unmolested emigration to any part of the Union, and for our inherent right to worship God as we please. We ask the restoration of these rights, because they have been taken from us or abridged by the violence and usurpation of the inhabitants of Jackson county. As a people we hold ourselves amenable to the laws of the land; and while the government remains as it is, the right to emigrate from state to state, from territory to territory, from county to county, and from vicinity to vicinity, is open to all men of whatever trade or creed, without hindrance or molestation; and as long as we are justifiable and honest in the eyes of the law, we claim it—whether we remove by single families or in bodies of hundreds—with that of carrying the necessary arms and accoutrements for military duty; and we believe that all honest men, who love their country and their country's glory, and have a wish to see the law magnified and made honorable, will not only help to perpetuate the great legacy of freedom that came unimpaired from the hands of our venerable fathers to us, but they will also protect us from insult and injury, and aid the work of God, that they may reap a reward in the regions of bliss, when all men receive according to their works.

In relation to our distress from the want of our lands in Jackson county, and for the want of property destroyed by fire and waste, rather than do any act contrary to law, we solemnly appeal to the people with whom we tarry, for protection from insult and harm, and for the comforts of life, by labor or otherwise, while we seek peace and satisfaction of our enemies through every possible and honorable means which humanity can dictate, or philanthropy urge, or religion require. We are citizens of this republic, and we ask our rights as republicans, not merely in our restoration to our lands and property in Jackson county, Missouri, but in being considered honest in our faith; honest in our deal, and honest before God, till, by due course of law, we may be proved otherwise; reserving the right of every man's being held amenable to the proper authority for his own crimes and sins.

"Crowns won by blood, by blood must be maintained;" and to avoid blood and strife, and more fully satisfy the world that our object is peace and good will to all mankind, we hereby APPEAL for peace to the ends of the earth and ask the protection of all people. We shall use

* Doctrine and Covenants, sec. ci: 76-80.

every fair means in our power to obtain our rights and immunities without force; setting an example for all true believers that we will not yield our faith and principles for any earthly consideration, whereby a precedent might be established that a majority may crush any religious sect with impunity. If we give up our rights in Jackson county, farewell to society! farewell to religion! farewell to our rights! farewell to property! farewell to life! The fate of our Church now might become the fate of the Methodists next week, the Catholics next month, and the overthrow of all societies next year, leaving nation after nation a wide waste, where reason and friendship once were.

Another, and the great object which we mean to help to accomplish, is the salvation of the souls of men. To bring to pass this glorious work, like many other religious denominations in all ages, we shall license Elders to preach the everlasting Gospel to all nations, according to the great commandment of our Lord and Savior Jesus Christ, as recorded in Matthew: "Go ye therefore, and teach all nations, baptizing them in the name of the Father, and of the Son, and of the Holy Ghost: teaching them to observe all things whatsoever I have commanded you: and, lo, I am with you alway, even unto the end of the world."

Thus we shall send laborers into the Lord's vineyard, to gather the wheat, and prepare the earth against the day when desolations shall be poured out without measure; and as it now is and ever has been considered one of the most honorable and glorious employments of men to carry good tidings to the nations, so we shall expect the clemency of all men, while we go forth, for the last time, to gather Israel for the glory of God, that He may suddenly come to His temple; that all nations may come and worship in His presence, when there shall be none to molest or make afraid, but the earth shall be filled with His knowledge and glory.

We live in an age of fearful imagination; with all the sincerity that common men are endowed with, the Saints have labored without pay, to instruct the United States that the gathering had commenced in the western boundaries of Missouri, to build a holy city, where, as may be seen in the eighteenth chapter of Isaiah, the present should "be brought unto the Lord of Hosts of a people scattered and peeled, and from a people terrible from their beginning hitherto; a nation meted out and trodden under foot, whose land the rivers have spoiled, to the place of the name of the Lord of Hosts, the Mount Zion:" and how few have come forth rejoicing that the hour of redemption was nigh! And some that came have turned away, which may cause thousands to exclaim, amid the general confusion and fright of the times, "Remember Lot's wife."

It would be a work of supererogation to labor to show the truth of the gathering of the children of Israel in these last days; for the prophet told us long ago, that it should "no more be said, The Lord liveth, that brought the children of Israel out of the land of Egypt, but, The Lord liveth, that brought up the children of Israel from the land of the north, and from all the lands whither He had driven them," and so it must be for the honor and glory of God.

The faith and religion of the Latter-day Saints are founded upon the old Scriptures, the Book of Mormon, and direct revelation from God; and while every event that happens around us is evidence of the truth of them, and an indicator that the great and terrible day of the Lord is near, we entreat the philanthropist, the moralist, and the honorable men of all creeds and sects, to read our publications, to examine the Bible, the Book of Mormon, and the Commandments, and listen to the fullness of the Gospel, and judge whether we are entitled to the credit of the world for honest motives and pure principles.

A cloud of bad omen seems to hang over this generation; men start up at the impulse of the moment, and defy and outstrip all law, while the destroyer is also abroad in the earth, wasting flesh without measure, and none can stay his course. In the midst of such portentous times, we feel an anxious desire to prepare, and help others to prepare, for coming events; and we candidly believe that no honest man will put forth his hand to stop the work of the Lord or persecute the Saints. In the name of Jesus Christ, we intreat the people of this nation to pause before they reject the works of the Lord or His servants; these, like all flesh, may be imperfect, but God is pure; hear ye Him.

While we ask peace and protection for the Saints, wherever they may be, we also solicit the charity and benevolence of all the worthy of the earth, to purchase the righteous a holy home, a place of rest, and a land of peace; believing that no man who knows he has a soul will keep back his mite, but cast it in for the benefit of Zion; thus, when time is no longer, he, with all the ransomed of the Lord, may stand in the fullness of joy, and view the grand pillar of heaven, which was built by the faith and charity of the Saints, beginning at Adam, with his motto in the base, "Repent and live," surrounded with a beautiful circle sign, supported by a cross about midway up its lofty column, staring the world in letters of blood, "The Kingdom of Heaven is at hand;" and finished with a plain top towering up in the midst of the celestial world-around which is written by the finger of Jehovah, "Eternal Life is the greatest gift of God."

Although we may fail to show all men the truth of the fullness of the Gospel, yet we hope to be able to convince some that we are neither deluded nor fanatics; but, like other men, have a claim on the world for land and for a living, as good and as great as our venerable fathers had for independence and liberty; that though the world has been made to believe, by false reports and vague stories, that the Saints—called "Mormons"—were meaner than the savages, still God has been our help in time of trouble, and has provided for us in due season, and, to use the language of Pope, He has let the work "spread undivided" and "operate unspent."

For the honor of our beloved country, and the continuation of its free government, we appeal for peace, for an example of forbearance, and the diffusion of the everlasting Gospel; we appeal to the humanity of all nations, and for the glory of God, before whom we must all answer for the deeds done in life, and for the hope of holiness hereafter, we mean to remain faithful to the end, continuing to pray to the Lord to spare us and the people from whatever is evil and not calculated to humble us, and prepare us for His presence and glory; at the same time beseeching Him, in the name of Jesus, to extend His blessings to whom He will, and His mercy to all; till by righteousness, the kingdoms of this world become fair as the sun and clear as the moon.

(Signed)   W. W. PHELPS,
                DAVID WHITMER,
                JOHN WHITMER,
                EDWARD PARTRIDGE,
                JOHN CORRILL,
                ISAAC MORLEY,
                PARLEY P. PRATT,
                LYMAN WIGHT,
                NEWEL KNIGHT,
                THOMAS B. MARSH,
                SIMEON CERTER,
                CALVIN BEEBE.

Missouri, United States, July, 1834.

CHAPTER IX.

RETURN OF THE PROPHET TO KIRTLAND—SUNDRY EVENTS IN
MISSOURI.

ON the 8th of July I went to the eastern part of Clay
county, and held a meeting in the evening at the
house of Thomas B. Marsh. Those present were The Prophet Returns to Kirtland.
chiefly High Priests and Elders. On the 9th
I started for Kirtland, in company with my brother
Hyrum, Frederick G. Williams, William E. M'Lellin and
others, in a wagon.

July 10.—Elder Corrill wrote as follows:

Samuel C. Owens, Esq.:

SIR—The last time I saw you in Liberty you said that an answer to
our proposals, you thought, would be forwarded soon; but it has not
been done. We are anxiously waiting to have a compromise effected,
if possible. Respecting our wheat in Jackson county, can it be secured
so that we can receive the avails of it. or not, seeing that we are at
present prohibited the privilege [of harvesting it]?

JOHN CORRILL.

P. S.—Please hand the following to Colonel Pitcher.

J. C.

LIBERTY, July 10, 1834.

Colonel Thomas Pitcher:

SIR—The following is a true copy of an order from the governor for
our arms. Have the goodness to return an answer as soon as possible,
that we may know whether we can have the arms upon said order or
not; also, when. Send word when we can receive them, and we will
appoint an agent to receive and receipt the same. Be assured we do
not wish to obtain them from any hostile intentions, but merely because

the right of property is ours. If I remember right, there is one gun and a sword more than the order calls for.

JOHN CORRILL.

[Here followed a copy of the Governor's order of May 2, to Colonel Lucas.]*

On the 12th the High Council of Zion assembled in Clay county, and appointed Edward Partridge, Orson Pratt, Isaac Morley and Zebedee Coltrin to visit the scattered and afflicted brethren in that region, and teach them the ways of truth and holiness, and set them in order according as the Lord shall direct; but it was decided that it was not wisdom for the Elders generally to hold public meetings in that region.

Assembling of the High Council in Missouri.

It was also decided that Amasa Lyman assist Lyman Wight in his mission of gathering the strength of the Lord's house, to which labor I had appointed him.

July 31.—The High Council of Zion assembled, and heard the report of Edward Partridge, Orson Pratt, Zebedee Coltrin, and Isaac Morley, concerning the mission appointed them at the previous council.

President David Whitmer gave the council some good instructions, to the effect that it was their duty to transact all business in order, and when any case is brought forward for investigation, every member should be attentive and patient to what is passing in all cases, and avoid confusion and contention, which are offensive in the sight of the Lord. He also addressed the Elders, and said it was not pleasing in the sight of the Lord for any man to go forth and preach the Gospel of peace, unless he is qualified to set forth its principles in plainness to those whom he endeavors to instruct; and also he should be informed as to the rules and regulations of the Church of the Latter-day Saints; for just

The Counsel of David Whitmer.

* Vol. i, p. 491.

as a man is, and as he teaches and acts, so will his followers be, let them be ever so full of notions and whims. He also addressed the congregation, and told them it was not wisdom for the brethren to vote at the approaching election; and the council acquiesced in the instructions of the president.

William W. Phelps proposed to the council to appoint a certain number of Elders to hold public meetings in that section of country [Clay county], as often as should be deemed necessary, to teach the disciples how to escape the indignation of their enemies, and keep in favor with those who were friendly disposed. Simeon Carter, John Corrill, Parley P. Pratt and Orson Pratt were appointed by the unanimous voice of the council and congregation to fill the mission.

Proposition of W. W. Phelps.

Elder Nathan West preferred charges against Samuel Brown, High Priest, for teaching contrary to counsel, namely, encouraging the brethren in practicing gifts (speaking in tongues,) in ordaining Sylvester Hulet a High Priest (without counsel) in a clandestine manner; asserting that he had obtained a witness of the Lord, which was a command to perform the same on receiving the gift of tongues, which gift he had never before received, but afterwards said that he had been in possession of that gift for the space of a year; and in undervaluing the authority and righteousness of the H gh Council by charging Elder West not to say anything that would tend to prejudice their minds, lest they might not judge righteously.

Charges Against Samuel Brown.

The charges were sustained by the testimony of Leonard Rich, Charles English, Brother Bruce, Edward Partridge, Hiram Page, Roxa Slade, Caleb Baldwin, and Sylvester Hulet. President David Whitmer gave the following decision, which was sanctioned by the council:

"According to testimony and the voice of the Holy Spirit, which is in us, we say unto you, that God, in His infinite mercy, doth yet grant you a space for repentance; therefore, if you confess all the charges which have been alleged against you to be just, and in a spirit that we can receive it, then you [Samuel Brown] can stand as a private member in this Church, otherwise we have no fellowship for you; and also, that the ordination of Sylvester Hulet, by Samuel Brown, is illegal and not acknowledged by us to be of God, and therefore it is void.

Brother Brown confessed the charges, and gave up his license, but retained his membership.*

Council adjourned on the evening of the first of August; but previous to adjourning, the Council gave the following letter to the Elders appointed to visit the churches in Clay county:

Letter of Appointment to the Elders.

To the Latter-day Saints who have been driven from the land of their inheritance, and also those who are gathering in the regions round about, in the western boundaries of Missouri. The High Council established according to the pattern given by our blessed Savior Jesus Christ, send greeting:

DEAR BRETHREN—We have appointed our beloved brother and companion in tribulation, John Corrill, to meet you in the name of the Lord Jesus. He, in connection with others also duly appointed, will visit you alternately for the purpose of instructing you in the necessary qualifications of the Latter-day Saints; that they may be perfected, that the officers and members of the body of Christ may become very prayerful and very faithful, strictly keeping all the commandments, and walking in holiness before the Lord continually; that all that mean to have the destroyer pass over them, as the children of Israel, and not slay them, may live according to the "word of wisdom;" that the Saints, by industry, diligence, faithfulness, and the prayer of faith, may become purified, and enter upon their inheritance, to build up Zion, according to the word of the Lord.

We are sure if the Saints are very humble, very watchful, and very prayerful, that few will be deceived by those who have not authority to teach, or who have not the spirit to teach according to the power of the

---

* The closing words in the decision signed by David Whitmer and W. W. Phelps as moderators and John Whitmer, clerk, are: "Therefore Brother Brown stands as a private member in this Church—all this by the voice of the councilors." (Far West Record of High Council (Ms.), p. 57.)

Holy Ghost, and the scriptures. Lest any man's blood be required at your hands, we beseech you, as you value the salvation of souls, who are within, to set an example worthy to be followed by those who are without the kingdom of our God and His Christ, that peace by grace, and blessings by righteousness, may attend you, until you are sanctified and redeemed.

Dated, Clay county, August 1, 1834.

About this t me I arrived in Kirtland, after a tedious journey from the midst of enemies; mobs, cholera, and excessively hot weather, having parted from those whom I started with on the 9th ultimo, at different points of the journey.

Arrival of the Prophet in Kirtland.

August 4.—[Kirtland.] A council of Elders ordained Thomas Colburn, Elder; and resolved to send Elder Zerubbabel Snow to Canada, to labor in the ministry.

August 6.—The High Council of Zion assembled in Clay county, and resolved that Leonard Rich act in the place of Parley P. Pratt, who was absent, and Amasa Lyman in place of William E. M'Lellin, absent.

Charges Against the Hulet Branch.

The following charge was then preferred:

This may certify, that whereas, the brethren and sisters comprising that part of the Church known by the name of the Hulet Branch, have imbibed certain principles concerning the gifts that are not thought to be correct by the remainder of the Church; which principles seem to have a tendency to cause disunion in the Church.

I, therefore, as a well wisher in the cause of Christ, and for the peace, and love, and upholding of the great cause of God, do hereby pray that the High Council will take into consideration the above report, that we all may come to understanding and grow until we all come unto the perfect stature of men and women in Christ Jesus.

(Signed)   NATHAN WEST.

Charles English testified that tne Hulet Branch believed that they received the word of the Lord by the gift of tongues, and would not proceed to their temporal business without receiving the word of the Lord. Sylvester Hulet would speak, and

Testimony Against the Hulet Branch

Sally Crandall interpret. Said they would not receive the teachings of ordained members, even Brother Joseph Smith, Jun., himself, unless it agreed with their gifts. Said they received the word of the Lord while they were in Jackson county, that they were to be persecuted by their brethren in Clay county, and now it had come. Also said that the heads of the Church would have to come down and receive the gifts as they did. Said that they, the Hulet Branch, had come up to their privileges more than the rest of the Church. They thought they were right; but if they could be convinced that they were wrong, they would retract. Sister Crandall professed to know and see men's hearts.

Philo Dibble concurred in the foregoing testimony, and also testified that Sister Crandall saw the hearts of King Follett and Hiram Page, and they were not right.

Hiram Page testified that Lyman Leonard said, if it was necessary to lay aside the gifts for a season, they would receive a knowledge of it through the gifts.

Nathan West concurred in the foregoing testimony, also testified that Sally Crandall saw his heart, that it was full of eyes; also eyes in others' hearts, some few, some many eyes.

Daniel Stanton testified that Sally Crandall said she saw his heart and saw two books in it, and that there was a Nephite standing behind him to push him into his duty; also that Sylvester Hulet spoke in tongues in meeting, and Sally Crandall interpreted thus: Verily, verily, thus saith the Lord unto you, little band, ye must beware, for there are many who are seeking to pry into your privileges.

Absalom Crichfield testified that when he was in Jackson county last spring, the Hulet Branch said, in tongues, that they would be safe, during the night, from any interruption by the mob; but, before morning, Lyman Leonard and Josiah Sumner were whipped; they also said that they saw my heart, and three young women in it.

Brother Batson and Alpheus Gifford concurred in much

of the foregoing testimony, and also other similar circumstances in addition.

After an adjournment of three-quarters of an hour, the president instructed the speakers not to seek to excel, but speak according to truth and equity; and that they ought to chase darkness from their minds, and be exercised on the subject upon which they were to speak, in order that they might touch upon points of doctrine, bring hidden things to light, and make dark things, clear, etc.

After councilors had spoken, the president said: "As for the gift of tongues in the manner it was used in the Hulet Branch, the devil deceived them, and they obtained not the word of the Lord, as they supposed, but were deceived; and as for the gift of "seeing," as held by the Hulet Branch, it is of the devil, saith the Lord God."

Decision of the Council in the Hulet Branch Case.

The council were unanimous in sanctioning the decision, and appointed Amasa Lyman and Simeon Carter to go and labor with Brother Hulet and Sister Crandall, and others of like faith, and set the truth in order before them.

I have been thus particular in giving the history of this council, as the gift of tongues is so often made use of by Satan to deceive the Saints.

The council adjourned to the 7th, when about twenty Elders were sent forth to preach the Gospel to the world, but not in Jackson or Clay counties, or their vicinity.

Elders Sent Forth to Preach.

President David Whitmer testified to the council that William Batson was not capable of filling his office of Elder, because he had not discretion and understanding sufficient to act wisely in that capacity, whereupon the council voted unanimously, that his office and license be taken from him; to which he consented, and gave up his license.

The Case of William Batson.

Elias and Isaac Higbee, and Jesse Hitchcock, were ordained to the High Priesthood, and council adjourned to the 21st of August.

CHAPTER X.

CHARGES AGAINST THE PROPHET ON HIS RETURN FROM ZION'S
CAMP EXPEDITION—TRIAL OF ELDER SYLVESTER SMITH.

Minutes of a Council held at Kirtland, August 11, 1834.

This day a number of High Priests and Elders of the Church of the
Latter-day Saints, assembled in the new school house, for the purpose
of investigating a matter of difficulty growing out of certain reports,
or statements, made by Elder Sylvester Smith, one of the High
Councilors of this Church, accusing President Joseph Smith, Jun.,
with criminal conduct during his journey to and from Missouri this
spring and summer.

After calling the meeting to order, President Joseph Smith spoke at
considerable length upon the circumstances of their journey to and
from Missouri, and very minutely laid open the causes out of which
the jealousies of Brother Sylvester Smith and others had grown. He
made a satisfactory statement concerning his rebukes and chastisements
upon Sylvester Smith and others, and also concerning the distribution
of monies and other properties, calling on brethren present who
accompanied him, to attest the same, all of which was satisfactory to
the brethren present, as appeared by their own remarks afterwards.

After President Joseph Smith had closed his lengthy remarks, Brother
Sylvester Smith made some observations relative to the subject of
their difficulties, and began to make a partial confession for his
previous conduct, asking forgiveness for accusing Brother Joseph
publicly, on the Saturday previous, of prophesying lies in the name of
the Lord; and for abusing (as he had said) his (Sylvester's) character
before the brethren, while journeying to the west.

Elder Rigdon made some remarks, by way of reproof, upon the
conduct of Sylvester Smith.

Elder John P. Greene spoke: others also, followed by the clerk
[Oliver Cowdery]: after which, on motion of Elder Rigdon, the
assembly arranged itself into a council, Bishop Newel K. Whitney
presiding, and proceeded to discuss how this difficulty should be
disposed of.

Elder John Smith thought that for Brother Sylvester to make a public confession in the *Star*, would be the way to heal the wound.

Elder Cahoon followed with nearly the same remarks.

Elder Isaac Hill thought it ought to be quashed and go no further: followed with the same from Elder I. Bishop.

Samuel H. Smith said that it was his opinion that Brother Sylvester ought to make a more public confession· and send by letter, to those who are in the same transgression with himself, and inform them of this decision; and then, if necessary, make it public in the *Star*.

Elder Orson Hyde thought the confession ought to be as liberal as the accusation, or that it ought to be written and published.

Elder John P. Greene said, that if Brother Sylvester would view this thing in its proper light, he would be willing to make a public confession, and send it forth; and he advised him to do this for the salvation of the churches abroad.

Elder Isaac Story said, that it was his opinion, that the plaster ought to be as large as the wound; that a proper statement ought to be published abroad.

The clerk [Oliver Cowdery] then proposed that the council send a certificate or resolution, informing the churches abroad, that the conduct of President Joseph Smith has been investigated, and that he has acted in a proper manner, and in every respect has conducted himself to the satisfaction of the Church in Kirtland; and also let Brother Sylvester make a proper confession, following the same minutes.

Elders Amasa Lyman, Peter Shirts, Truman Wait, Roswell Evans, Alpheus Cutler, and Thomas Burdick, made remarks to the same effect.

Elder Sidney Rigdon made a few remarks upon the attitude in which Sylvester stood before the world, in endeavoring to preach the Gospel.

Elder Orson Hyde moved for a decision relative to the first question, viz., What is to be done to arrest the evil.

The moderator [Bishop Newel K. Whitney] then proceeded, after a few remarks, to give a decision according to a motion previously made, viz., that an article be published in the *Evening and Morning Star*, by the direction of the Council, that the Church in Kirtland has investigated the conduct of President Joseph Smith, Jun., while journeying to the west, and returning; and that we find that he has acted in every respect in an honorable and proper manner with all monies and other properties entrusted to his charge; after which a vote was taken and carried to the above effect.

A motion was then made by Orson Hyde, and seconded by Sidney Rigdon, that a committee of three be appointed to write the article for the *Star*, agreeable to the decision.

Oliver Cowdery, Thomas Burdick and Orson Hyde, were nominated and appointed a committee by unanimous vote.

Brother Sylvester then said that he was willing to publish a confession in the *Star*.

OLIVER COWDERY, Clerk.

I wrote to Lyman Wight, Edward Partridge, John

The Prophet Reports His Vindication to the Elders in Missouri.

Corrill, Isaac Morley, and others of the High Council of Zion, from Kirtland, August 16, 1834, as follows:

DEAR BRETHREN—After so long a time, I dictate a few lines to you, to let you know that I am in Kirtland, and that I found all well when I arrived, as pertaining to health; but our common adversary had taken the advantage of our Brother Sylvester Smith, and others, who gave a false coloring to almost every transaction, from the time we left Kirtland, until we returned, and thereby stirred up a great difficulty in the Church against me. Accordingly I was met in the face and eyes, as soon as I had got home, with a catalogue of charges as black as the author of lies himself; and the cry was Tyrant—Pope —King—Usurper—Abuser of men—Angel—False Prophet—Prophesying lies in the name of the Lord—Taking consecrated monies— and every other lie to fill up and complete the catalogue. Such experiences may be necessary to perfect the Church, and render our traducers mete for the devourer, and the shaft of the destroying angel. In consequence of having to combat all these, I have not been able to regulate my mind, so as to give you counsel, and the information that you needed; but that God who rules on high, and thunders judgments upon Israel when they transgress, has given me power from the time I was born into the kingdom to stand; and I have succeeded in putting all gainsayers and enemies to flight, unto the present time; and notwithstanding the adversary laid a plan, which was more subtle than all others, as you will see by the next *Star*, I now swim in good, clean water, with my head out.

I shall now proceed to give you such counsel as the Spirit of the Lord may dictate. You will recollect that your business must be done by your High Council. You will recollect that the first Elders are to receive their endowment in Kirtland, before the redemption of Zion. You will recollect that   Council will have power to say who of the first Elders among the children of Zion are accounted worthy; and you will also recollect that you have my testimony in behalf of certain ones, previous to my departure. You will recollect that the sooner these ambassadors of the Most High are dispatched to bear testimony, to lift up a warning voice, and proclaim the everlasting Gospel, and to use every convincing proof and faculty with this generation, while on their journey to Kirtland—the better it will be for them and for Zion. Inasmuch as the indignation of the people sleepeth for a while our time should be employed to the best advantage; although it is not the will of God, that these ambassadors should hold their peace after they have started upon their journey. They should arouse the sympathy of the people.

I would recommend to Brother Phelps, (if he be yet there,) to write a petition, such as will be approved by the High Council; and let every signer be obtained that can be, in the State of Missouri by them while they are on their journey to this place [Kirtland] that peradventure we may learn whether we have friends or not in these United States.

This petition is to be sent to the governor of Missouri, to solicit him to call on the President of the United States for a guard to protect our brethren in Jackson county, upon their own lands, from the insults and abuse of the mob.

And I would recommend to Brother Wight to enter complaint to the governor as often as he receives any insults or injury; and in case that they proceed to endeavor to take life, or tear down houses, and if the citizens of Clay county do not befriend us, to gather up the little army, and be set over immediately into Jackson county, and trust in God, and do the best he can in maintaining the ground. But, in case the excitement continues to be allayed, and peace prevails, use every effort to prevail on the churches to gather to those regions and locate themselves, to be in readiness to move into Jackson county in two years from the eleventh of September next, which is the appointed time for the redemption of Zion. If—verily I say unto you—if the Church with one united effort perform their duties; if they do this, the work shall be complete—if they do not this in all humility, making preparation from this time forth, like Joseph in Egypt, laying up store against the time of famine, every man having his tent, his horses, his chariots, his armory, his cattle, his family, and his whole substance in readiness against the time when it shall be said: To your tents, O Israel! Let not this be noised abroad; let every heart beat in silence, and every mouth be shut.

Now, my beloved brethren, you will learn by this we have a great work to do, and but little time to do it in; and if we do not exert ourselves to the utmost in gathering up the strength of the Lord's house that this thing may be accomplished, behold there remaineth a scourge for the Church, even that they shall be driven from city to city, and but few shall remain to receive an inheritance; if those things are not kept, there remaineth a scourge also; therefore, be wise this once, O ye children of Zion! and give heed to my counsel, saith the Lord.

I would inform Bishop Partridge that the bill I received from him was good, and when I can get our money changed for another, I will mail it to him.

The brethren, up to now, have generally arrived from Clay county in health, notwithstanding the warm season. I would also inform Bishop Partridge that I am not satisfied with Brother Hulet concerning the colt, and so long as unrighteous acts are suffered in the Church, it cannot be sanctified, neither can Zion be redeemed; and also that I was obliged to leave the consecrated horn in Illinois, also Brother William E. M'Lellin, who was sick. We expect when he recovers that he will come to Kirtland. He was very humble, and I entertain no doubt as to his standing while he continues so. We have a desire to hear concerning the cholera, and whether Sister Bunnel is yet alive. Inform us as to all deaths, and give the names and standing of all those who are called away.

The cholera is raging in Detroit, Cleveland, Fairport, Buffalo, and other places. We found it in Chariton as we came through and almost every other place. It is an awful and solemn day, but this is only the foreshadowing of what is to come.

The churches seem to be in a cold, languid and disconsolate state; and as the revolution of the earth is once in twenty-four hours, so we may look for frequent revolutions among this wicked and perverse generation, and also in the Church of Christ. When the head is sick, the whole body is faint; and when the Church lifts up the head, the angel will bring us good tidings. Even so. Amen.

JOSEPH SMITH, JUN.

August 21.—Doctor Frederick G. Williams returned from Cleveland and told us concerning the plague, and after much consultation, we agreed that Dr.

The Plague of Cholera in Cleveland.

Williams should go to Cleveland and commence administering to the sick, for the purpose of obtaining blessings for them, and for the glory of the Lord. Accordingly, we (Joseph, Frederick, and Oliver,) united in prayer before the Lord for this thing. Now, O Lord, grant us these blessings in the name of Jesus Christ. Amen.

The same day the High Council of Zion assembled at

the house of Lyman Wight, and Elders Simeon Carter and Amasa Lyman made a report concerning their mission to the Hulet branch. They found the church willing to receive the decision of the last council respecting the false spirits with which they had been troubled.

Affairs in Missouri—Hulet Branch Troubles.

John Corrill entered a complaint against Lyman Wight for teaching that "all disease in this Church is of the devil, and that medicine administered to the sick is of the devil; for the sick in the Church ought to live by faith."

Charge Against Lyman Wight.

Elder Wight acknowledged that he had taught the doctrine, and rather believed it to be correct.

The President decided that it was not lawful to teach the Church that all disease is of the devil, but if there is anyone who has this faith, let him have it to himself; and if there are any who believe that roots and herbs administered to the sick, and all wholesome vegetables which God has ordained for the use of man—and if any say that such things applied to the sick, in order that they may receive health, and this medicine is applied by any member of the Church—if there are any among you that teach that these things are of Satan, such teaching is not of God.

On the 23rd of August, a council convened for the purpose of hearing the resolutions designed for the *Star*, which were to be drawn up by Elders Oliver Cowdery, Thomas Burdick, and Orson Hyde, on the subject of the difficulty existing between President Joseph Smith, Jun., and Sylvester Smith.

Resolutions of Vindication.

Elder Reynolds Cahoon presided in consequence of the ill health of Bishop Whitney.

The following preamble and resolutions were read and adopted, to wit:—

Whereas a report having come to this place [Kirtland] censuring the conduct of President Joseph Smith, Jun., relative to his proceedings during his late journey to and from Missouri; and whereas said report was calculated to create an unfavorable influence as regards the moral character and honesty of our brother, it becomes necessary for us to investigate the matter, and report the same to our brethren abroad; Therefore,—

Resolved: That after hearing from the mouths of some that a suspicion rested upon their minds relative to the conduct of our President as regards his honesty and godly walk, we have investigated his whole proceedings by calling upon those who accompanied him to and from Missouri, and we are happy to have it in our power to say to our brethren abroad, one and all, that we are satisfied with his conduct, having learned from the clearest evidence, that he has acted in every respect worthy his high and responsible station in this Church, and has prudently and cautiously preserved the good of this society at large, and is still worthy of our esteem and fellowship, and that those reports could have originated in the minds of none except such as either from a natural misunderstanding, or a natural jealousy, are easily led to conceive of evils where none exists.

Resolved: That we say to our brethren that while we are surrounded by thousands eager to grasp at a shadow, if they have a hope of turning it into a falsehood for the injury of the Gospel, we exhort them to be steadfast and immovable in the truth, resting assured that while they continue to walk in the Holy Covenant they have confessed to embrace, that nothing can in the end operate against their good; and that while wickedness abounds, as in days of old, the characters of those seeking the greatest good for their fellow men will be shamefully traduced and every act of their lives misrepresented, and a false shade thrown over their worthy deeds, all this is calculated to create an evil prejudice in the minds of the community, to prevent, if possible, the increase of light, the better to effect evil purposes and keep man in error. We say, dear brethren, may peace and the blessings of our Lord Jesus Christ be multiplied unto you through the knowledge of truth, forever.

Resolved: That the minutes be signed by the moderator and clerk, and published to the churches in the *Evening and Morning Star.*

REYNOLDS CAHOON, Moderator.
OLIVER COWDERY, Clerk.

We, the undersigned, members of the above named Conference, for the satisfaction of our brethren abroad, feel it to be our duty to say to those with whom we have a personal acquaintance, that we were present during the foregoing investigation, and cheerfully concur in the spirit of the above minutes, and join in saying that we are perfectly satisfied that whatever impressions may have gone abroad, or whatever may remain with any in this vicinity, relative to the conduct of our President, Joseph Smith, Jun, we are certain (from evidence) that he conducted himself in all respects as set forth in the resolutions of this Conference. We are induced to make these statements that the innocent may not suffer wrongfully, and that the minds of our brethren and friends may be satisfied, that every appearance of evil is, in this place, searched out, and that nothing urbecoming a society of people professing godliness is suffered to exist among them.

IRA AMES, Benson, Vermont.
ASA LYMAN, Parishville, New York.
JOHN RUDD, Springfield, Erie county, Pennsylvania.
ISAAC STOREY, Warsaw, New York.
WILLIAM BURGESS, Bolton, New York.
JONAS PUTNAM, Bolton, New York.
J. B. BOSWORTH, from the church in Norton.
ROSWELL EVANS, Waterford, Vermont.
JOHN SMITH, Potsdam, New York.
ORSON JOHNSON, Bath, New Hampshire.
OLIVER HIGLEY, Jamestown.
ALMAN SHERMAN, Pomfret, New York.
JACOB BUMP, Silver Creek, New York.
ISAAC HILL, East Liverpool, Ohio.
LORENZO YOUNG, the same.

The undersigned members of this Conference, having accompanied President Joseph Smith, Jun., to and from Missouri, certify that the above is a correct statement concerning his character and conduct.

LYMAN E. JOHNSON.
HEBER C. KIMBALL.*

Brother Sylvester Smith objected to abiding by the decision of the former council, and proceeded to justify himself in his former conduct; and after much discussion, the following resolution was offered by the clerk, and passed by unanimous vote:—

Sylvester Smith Refuses to Accept the Decision of the Council.

Resolved: That in consequence of the stand our brother, Sylvester Smith, has taken against the former decision of this council, that we judge him guilty of a misdemeanor, unbecoming a man in his high sta-

* The foregoing resolutions to this point were all published in the *Evening and Morning Star*, Vol. II, No. 23, August, 1834.

tion, and except a humble confession be made to this council, he stands rebuked, and disqualified to act further in his office in the Church, until he make proper satisfaction, or till a trial before the Bishop, assisted by twelve High Priests can be had.

OLIVER COWDERY,
Clerk of Council.

August 28, 1834.—This day the High Council assembled according to the direction of Bishop Whitney, to try Brother Sylvester Smith, charged with a misdemeanor. The following is a copy of the complaint:—

Formal Trial of Sylvester Smith.

To Newel K. Whitney, Bishop of the Church of Latter-day Saints in Kirtland,

Sir, I prefer the following charges against Sylvester Smith, a High Priest of said Church:—

1st. He has refused to submit to the decision of a council of the High Priests and Elders of this Church, held in this place on the 11th of this month, given in a case of difficulty between said Sylvester Smith and Joseph Smith, Jun.

2nd. He continues to charge said Joseph Smith, contrary to the decision of the before mentioned council, with improper conduct in his proceedings as President of the Church of the Latter-day Saints, during his journey the past season to the State of Missouri.

As these things are exceedingly grievous to many of the Saints in Kirtland, and very prejudicial to the cause of truth in general, I therefore require that you summon the High Council of this Church to investigate this case, that a final decision may be had upon the same. I say the High Council because it is a case affecting the Presidency of said Church.*   SIDNEY RIGDON.

Kirtland, Ohio, August 23, 1834.

* This has reference to the special High Council of the Church authorized to try the President of the High Priesthood, who is also the President of the Church, should he be found in transgression. The Council consists of the Presiding Bishop of the Church, assisted by twelve High Priests, agreeable to the revelation which says: "And inasmuch as a President of the High Priesthood shall transgress, he shall be had in remembrance before the common Council of the Church, who shall be assisted by twelve counselors of the High Priesthood; and their decision upon his head shall be an end of controversy concerning him. Thus, none shall be exempt from the justice and the laws of God, that all things may be done in order and in solemnity before Him, according to truth and righteousness."—Doctrine and Covenants, Sec. cvii: 82-84.

As remarked by Elder Rigdon, inasmuch as this case was one involving charges against the Presidency of the Church, it was proper that it should be heard by this special council of the Church.

Bishop Whitney notifies Sylvester Smith of the Charge.

KIRTLAND, OHIO, August 27, 1834.

BROTHER SYLVESTER SMITH—Whereas complaint has been made to me by Counselor Sidney Rigdon, setting forth that you have been violating the laws of the Church of the Latter-day Saints, you are therefore, notified to appear before the High Council of High Priests, to be held in the Council House, in Kirtland, on the 28th day of August, at ten o'clock, a. m., to answer to said charges, agreeably to the laws of the Church.

N. K. WHITNEY, Bishop.

The presidents proceeded to nominate a High Priest to fill the vacancy in the council, occasioned by the death of Elder John C. Carter, viz.: Orson Johnson—which nomination was carried unanimously, and he was ordained High Councilor under the hands of Counselor Sidney Rigdon.

Councilor Luke S. Johnson said he wished to be excused from sitting in this council, because he had been previously tempted on some matters, and that he had sinned, and wished to make a more public confession than he could make here.

After some remarks from the councilors, it was decided that Elder Johnson continue his seat in the council.

Elder John P. Greene was appointed to act in the place of Sylvester Smith; also Elder Amos Durfee in the place of John Johnson, Sen., who was absent; also Lyman Johnson in the place of Martin Harris.

The council was organized and complaint read. It was agreed that six councilors speak on the case. The Bishop then charged the council in the name of the Lord, to act according to truth and righteousness.

Elder Reynolds Cahoon testified that the testimony given before a council, on the 11th instant, was, that President Joseph Smith, Jun., had conducted himself in a proper manner, while journeying to and from Missouri; and that the council considered that Sylvester Smith had accused President Joseph Smith wrongfully, and was entirely in the fault. He further considered that everything bearing on or relating to this affair had been brought before the council, and from this they gave their decision.

Elder John P. Greene concurred in the foregoing statements, and he supposed that Brother Sylvester, on the 11th instant, saw the affair in the same light in consequence of his [Sylvester's] saying at the time, that he was not previously aware of the spirit that possessed him at the time he made his charges againt President Joseph Smith.

Elder Alpheus Cutler said that he considered that the evidence given before the council on the 27th was sufficient to prove that President

Joseph Smith had conducted himself in an honorable manner during his late journey to and from Missouri, and that he considered that the evidence there given was such that it could not be invalidated.

Elder Jacob Bump said that previous to the council on the 11th his mind had been agitated, and it was in consequence, in part, of reports which had been put in ciculation respecting President Smith's conduct during his late journey to and from Missouri; but when he heard the case investigated before that council his mind was satisfied that he had been misinformed, and was fully satisfied that President Joseph Smith had not acted in any respect contrary to righteousness before the Lord.

Elder Asa Lyman said, that previous to the council his mind had been agitated also, but was satisfied at the council; and he verily believed from the evidence there given that President Joseph Smith had not acted contrary to justice.

Elder Jacob Bump said that his mind was excited still further after conversing with Brother Sylvester, previous to the 11th, which served in a degree to excite his mind further.

Elder Edmund Bosley said that he understood the case on the 11th in the same light as stated by Brothers Cahoon and Whitney.

Elders John Rudd, Ezekiel Rider and Samuel H. Smith viewed the case in the same light.

Elder Orson Hyde said that he considered that Brother Sylvester was to publish a confession in the *Evening and Morning Star*, and that he himself had been in the fault, and that President Smith had not committed fault, as he [Sylvester had] previously stated.

Elders Alpheus Cutler, J. P. Greene, Ezekiel Rider, Jacob Bump, Samuel H. Smith, John Rudd and Frederick G. Williams concurred.

Elder Oliver Cowdery said, that after listening to all the reports and evidences, from the beginning up to the decision on the 11th instant, he considered that Brother Sylvester was to acknowledge that all the charges previously preferred in public against President Joseph Smith were ungrounded, and that he [Sylvester] was the one, and the only one in fault, touching all circumstances occurring between himself and President Joseph Smith, and that the other charges indirectly preferred as grievances of others, were also without foundation.

Elder John Smith concurred in the above.

Elder C. Durfee said that he considered that President Smith was acquitted, as not being guilty of any misdemeanor before the council on the 11th.

Elder Orson Hyde said that he had accompanied President Smith to Missouri from Mansfield in Ohio, except leaving him for a short time to visit the governor of Missouri. He was present when Brother Sylvester reproved President Smith concerning a certain difficulty arising about a dog; that he considered President Smith's reproofs were just at the time, as he well recollects stating the same in substance to President Smith. He said he did not consider this reproof had any tendency to lessen the esteem of the brethren for President Smith; but if it had, in consequence of a confession in general terms from President Smith about that time, he thought that sufficient to heal any hard feeling then existing against him, or that might exist; and that during his journey to the west, he could not say that he had seen anything in President Smith's conduct contrary to the true principles of his profession as a man of God.

Elder Luke S. Johnson said that he fell in company with President Joseph Smith at Mansfield, Ohio, and accompanied him most of the way to Missouri; and that during the whole course of the journey he did not see anything in his conduct to lessen his esteem for him as a man of God. But he said he heard President Joseph Smith reprove Brother Sylvester concerning a certain matter respecting some bread; he did not hear the whole, and thought at the time the reproofs were rather severe, but had learned since they were not any more severe than just.

President Joseph Smith was then called upon to make a statement concerning the transactions as they happened at the time these reproofs were given. He said that Brother John S. Carter came to him to know whether Brother Sylvester had conducted himself right in the affairs between him [Sylvester] and Brother Parley P. Pratt, when Brother Pratt called upon Brother Sylvester for some bread for supper. He learned from Brother Pratt's mouth that Brother Sylvester had more bread than he needed at the time, yet directed him to some one else, who, he [Brother Sylvester] said, had sufficient. President Smith then went with Brothers Pratt and John S. Carter to Brother Sylvester's tent, where Brother Sylvester justified himself in not imparting a portion of his bread to Brother Pratt. He then rebuked Brother Sylvester for contending that he had done right in this case, because, if this was so, brethren might frequently retire to rest without food, and as long as he [Brother Sylvester] had bread he was bound to impart to those who had none; and that, under these circumstances, Brother Sylvester had conducted himself contrary to the principles of Christ; and that his [Sylvester's] mind was darkened in consequence of this covetous spirit.

The moderator then adjourned the council until nine o'clock, a. m., tomorrow, at this place.

Elder Hyrum Smith closed by prayer.

August 29th, nine o'clock, a. m., council being organized in due form, the testimony was continued as follows:

Elder Luke S. Johnson said, in relation to a circumstance that occurred on the twenty-five mile prairie in Missouri, that by a direction from the leader of the camp he had been back to inspect the crossing at a certain creek; that when he came up with the camp he found it moving, and as he was behind, he went on till he came up with Brother Wight's and Sylvester's company, and found them out of the road building a fire to cook supper. As the teams passed on Brother Sylvester called to the leaders of companies (those who were yet behind), and asked them whom they were following; whether General Wight or some other man. Some hesitated a little and went on. After taking supper he [Luke] went on with their company.

When he came up with the camp from the creek he found that the ensign or flag commonly carried ahead for the camp to follow,was then moving forward. He further said that he understood that Joseph was appointed to lead the camp; that he always, or generally, gave orders when the camp should move forward, and when it should stop; that when on his way to the creek the second time he met President Smith, who told him that he Joseph should order the camp to move into the prairie. When the camp came to order on the prairie in the evening, Brothers Wight and Sylvester were called upon to state why they had sought to divide the camp. They both acknowledged that they had been out of the way by so doing, and were reproved for their conduct. Relative to an assertion heretofore made, that President Smith did at the time throw a trumpet or horn at Brother Sylvester, he did not consider at the time that the President had any intention of throwing it at Brother Sylvester, because he might have hit him with it, being so near to him as he was; it only fell to the ground near to them (himself and Brother Sylvester), but supposed that he had had it in his hand, and only threw it down as usual. He further said that the reproofs given by President Smith at the time were no more severe than he had often heard him give previously; that he did not consider him angry, as he has been represented.

Elder Hyrum Smith said, that when the camp first came to the creek he and his brother Joseph were forward; that while the teams were crossing Brother Joseph asked whether it was advisable to move into the prairie to camp. After consultation it was first advised to camp in the bushes in the edge of the prairie. While making preparations to encamp they were informed that a mob intended to make an attack upon them that night. They further consulted upon their situation, and himself and Brother Thayer were requested by Brother Joseph to go on to the edge of the prairie, where they might encamp. They looked out a place, but it was near the bushes, and Brother Joseph gave an order to go forward on to the prairie. Some complained of the order because they could not find fuel with which to cook their supper. They were told that it would be advisable to carry wood for that pur- pose. Some further remarks were offered on the subject of a visit from a mob, and preparations were made with the guns, etc. Some fears were entertained for the teams and families yet crossing the creek, and it was thought advisable to send back a company, among whom was Luke S. Johnson, to guard and assist them over. He then took the flag or standard—as he had previously carried it—and gave the word to move forward, and the teams immediately began to follow. After the company had come upon the prairie, himself and Elder Roger Orton received an order to call on Lyman Wight to place a strong guard around the camp that night; but he [Wight] refused doing anything further, because he supposed that he [Hyrum] had ordered the camp on to the prairie without an order from the commander of the company. He was then informed by Brother Joseph that it was by his [Joseph's] order that the camp moved on to the prairie. He was pres- ent when Brother Joseph reproved Lyman Wight and Sylvester Smith, and saw the transactions concerning the trumpet or horn; and as to Brother Joseph's intention or design to throw it at Sylvester, he had no such thought at the time, nor could he have had such thought since; that at the time when Joseph had finished his remarks to Lyman Wight and Sylvester Smith he threw the horn on the ground, and Brother Wight told him the next day that he had had a jealousy existing in his mind against him [Hyrum] for some days, but now his mind was satisfied, and he now had no hardness or jealousy. He further said, that when he received the order for moving the camp on the prairie, Brothers Lyman and Sylvester were near by.

Adjourned to one o'clock p. m.

Council met according to adjournment. The clerk called the names of the councilors and parties, when business was resumed.

Elder Brigham Young said, that he was in company with President Joseph Smith, Jun., from about twenty-seven miles of this place [Kirt- land till they arrived in Clay county, Missouri; that at the time the difficulty occurred on the Twenty-five Mile Prairie, when the camp was divided, he concurred in what Brother Hyrum had said, and that he could not relate it any more circumstantially than he had done. He further said that he had not seen anything in President Smith's con- duct to justify the charge previously made by Brother Sylvester "that his heart was corrupt." So far from this, he had not seen the least shadow of anything of the kind. He had not seen anything in his [Joseph's] conduct, during his journey to the west, unbecoming his profession as a man of God.

Question by Sylvester Smith.—Did you not think that my character

was injured in the minds of the weaker part of the camp in consequence of those reproofs and chastisements which were given me by
Brother Joseph?

Answer.—I did not.

Elder Young further said in regard to a certain difficulty over a dog,
that on a certain evening after crossing the Mississippi river, Brother
Sylvester came up with the remaining part of the camp, when the dog
came out and barked at him; he knew not whether the dog bit him or
not. The next morning, after hearing considerable complaint and
murmuring concerning the dog, President Smith spoke to several
brethren present and said, "I will descend to that spirit that is in the
camp, to show you the spirit you are of, for I want to drive it from the
camp. *The man that kills that dog, (or my dog),I will whip him.*" He
thought that about this time Brother Sylvester came up, and said, "*If
that dog bites me I will kill him.*" Joseph replied, "If you do, I will
whip you." Sylvester said, "If you do, I shall defend myself the best
way that I can!" Brother Joseph then said that he "would do it in the
name of the Lord."

President Smith then asked the brethren if they were not ashamed
of such a spirit. Said he, "*I am.*"

He then proceeded to reprove them for condescending to that spirit;
that they ought to be above it; that it was the spirit of a dog; and
men ought never to place themselves on a level with the beasts; but be
possessed of a more noble disposition. He [Joseph] then said, he had
condescended to that spirit, in order to show the spirit which was
among them.

Elder Young further said, that this explanation gave general satisfaction, and the most of the brethren saw that he had only made these remarks for the purpose of instructing them, and warning them against
such a spirit or disposition.

Elders Lyman E. Johnson and Heber C. Kimball concurred.

Elder David Elliot said he was not present when those reproofs were
given in the morning; that the circumstances were related to him afterwards, which unfavorably affected his mind, and gave him some dis-
agreable feelings; that at noon he heard President Joseph give a further explanation, which perfectly satisfied him.

He further said, that during the forenoon he learned there were many
of the brethren dissatisfied with President Smith's remarks in the
morning concerning the dog, but that after the explanation at noon so
generally given, he thought that every one in the camp might have understood President Smith's purpose.

Elder Lorenzo Booth concurred in the statement of Elder Young;
though he was not present in the morning when the reproofs were given

concerning the dog; that he was with President Smith from twenty-seven miles from this place [Kirtland] to Missouri, and a part of the way home; that he did not see anything in President Smith's character derogatory to a man professing religion; that he was present during a certain transaction which occurred during their journey home, respecting certain articles of bedding: that he had heard since his return that President Smith and Ezra Thayer had fought; that he was present during the whole transaction, and there was no fighting.

He further said, in relation to a certain report which had come to his knowledge since his return from Missouri, that President Smith had taken a bed quilt which was not his property; that while at New Portage, Ohio, on their way to Missouri, one of the brethren gave him [Joseph] two bed quilts, which he [Booth] had charge of, as he was the individual who drove the team for President Smith, and had charge of the baggage; that before leaving Clay county, Missouri, he [Booth] took them to be washed, and after starting for home he put them on board of the wagon, the baggage of which he had the charge during their journey home; that he brought the same back with him, has seen them since, and knows that the one which was said to be the property of another individual, is the one which was given President Smith at Norton.

Counselor Frederick G. Williams said, while at Norton certain articles were handed him to mark, among which were two bed quilts, which he marked with common ink; has seen certain bed quilts since his return, and has no doubt but this one in question is the one he marked.

Elder Brigham Young further said relative to a difficulty about some bread, that Elder John S. Carter, on their journey to Missouri, on the line between Ohio and Indiana, said to President Smith, "Is this thing right?" "What thing?" "Concerning Parley P. Pratt's asking Brother Sylvester for some bread for supper."

He then learned that Brother Pratt had asked Brother Sylvester for some bread; that Sylvester had bread at the time, but directed Brother Pratt to some one else, who he [Sylvester] said had sufficient; that Elder Pratt called upon that individual, and could not obtain any; that he was present when President Smith told Brother Sylvester that he had not acted right in the matter, that he ought to impart when he had it instead of directing one where he was not certain he could obtain, that by so doing some might be deprived of food at times.

He further said, that Brother Sylvester contended he had been right, and justified his own conduct in the matter; that Joseph reasoned with Sylvester to convince him that he [Sylvester] was in fault; but he continued to justify his course till President Smith reproved him sharply.

He frequently heard the brethren speak of this circumstance, and all whom he had heard say anything on the subject, manifested a satisfaction with President Smith, and thought his observations correct, and the principles which he advanced, just.

Elder Lyman Sherman said that he concurred in Elder Young's statement concerning the bread; that he thought it was generally known that Elder Pratt, in consequence of Brother Sylvester's not furnishing him with bread, was deprived of bread that night; that at the time he [Joseph] told him [Sylvester] that Brother Parley did not obtain any bread in consequence of Brother Sylvester not supplying him with it.

Elder Jacob Bump said, that since the brethren's return from the west he had gone with Sylvester to Elder Rigdon to advise concerning the adjusting of certain complaints which were in circulation respecting President Joseph Smith's conduct on the journey to and from Missouri; that Brother Sylvester told Brother Rigdon that Elder Pratt did obtain bread of the individual to whom he sent him.

Elder Orson Hyde said, that he concurred in the statements of Elder Brigham Young concerning the circumstances which occurred at the time the difficulty arose about the bread.

Elders Lyman Johnson and Heber C. Kimball concurred in the same statement.

Elder Orson Hyde then exhibited an account current, taken from the receipts of monies and other property expended during their late journey to and from Missouri.

This account was taken from documents during the journey by Counselor Frederick G. Williams, who said that the account exhibited was correctly taken from his accounts, as he had the charge of the monies, and attended to paying them out, etc.

The case was then submitted to the council, and the councilors severally spoke in their turns, followed by the complainant and accused, as follows:—First, the councilors: Jared Carter commenced fifteen minutes before six o'clock, p.m., and spoke twenty-five minutes. Joseph Smith,Sen., commenced ten minutes past six o'clock and spoke five minutes. John Smith commenced fifteen minutes past six o'clock and spoke ten minutes. Lyman E. Johnson commenced twenty-five minutes past six o'clock and spoke one minute. Oliver Cowdery commenced twenty-eight minutes past six and spoke two hours and twelve minutes. Joseph Coe commenced twenty minutes before nine o'clock and spoke five minutes.

The accuser, Sidney Rigdon, commenced fifteen minutes before nine o'clock and spoke five minutes. Oliver Cowdery spoke seven minutes more.

The accused, Sylvester Smith, commenced eighteen minutes before ten o'clock and spoke one hour and eighteen minutes.

The Moderator then gave the following decision:

"That if Brother Sylvester Smith will acknowledge the following items of complaint before this council, and publish the same in print; that he can remain yet a member of this Church, otherwise he is expelled from the same, viz.:   First, he is to acknowledge that he has wickedly and maliciously accused our President, Joseph Smith, Jun., with prophesying lies in the name of the Lord, once on the line between Ohio and Indiana, and at another time after crossing the Mississippi river, and at another time, after leaving the Church in Missouri, at Florida; that he is to acknowledge, that in making these charges against President Joseph Smith, Jun., he has himself wilfully and maliciously lied; that he has maliciously told falsehoods in saying that President Joseph Smith, Jun., has abused him with insulting and abusive language, and also in injuring his character and standing before the brethren while journeying to Missouri; that he further cast out insinuations concerning President Joseph Smith's character, which was also an evil and malicious design to injure President Smith's standing in the Church; that he further acknowledge that he has abused the former councils which have sat upon this case, and wickedly and maliciously insulted their just and righteous decisions; that he has further tantalized this present council, in seeking to excuse himself contrary to the advice of the counselors, after acknowledging that it was organized by the direction of revelation; and further, that he has wilfully and maliciously lied, by saying that Brother Joseph Smith, Jun., had prohibited the liberty of speech on their journey to Missouri; that he also acknowledge that he has wickedly and maliciously lied by charging President Joseph Smith, Jun., of being possessed of a heart as corrupt as hell."

The councilors were then called upon to give their assent to the foregoing decision, and they concurred unanimously.

"I hereby certify that the foregoing charges or complaint are just and true, and hereby acknowledge the same, as set forth in the decisions of this council, by signing my own proper name to their minutes, with my own hand.

(Signed)   "SYLVESTER SMITH."

The above was signed for fear of punishment.*

* This remark assigning a "fear of punishment" as the reason why Sylvester Smith signed the above acquiescence in the decision of the council, may have been true at the time it was signed; but in justice to Sylvester Smith the fact ought to be known that after time to reflect upon his conduct and his accusation against the Prophet his mind underwent a very radical change: for in a communication to the *Messenger and Advocate*, under date of October 28, 1834, he

The council then proceeded to other business, President Joseph Smith presiding.

Council agreed that the Church in Kirtland be instructed in their particular duties, etc., on Sunday next, by President Joseph Smith, Jun. It was further decided that Elder Brigham Young be appointed to take the lead in singing in our meetings.

The council then closed, at fifteen minutes before three o'clock, a. m., on the 30th of August, 1834. Brother Reynolds Cahoon prayed.

OLIVER COWDERY,

ORSON HYDE,

Clerks.

volunteered a most complete vindication of the Prophet's course while on the Zion's Camp expedition, and made a most humble confession of his own shortcomings. Following is the communication referred to:

Dear Brother:

"Having heard that certain reports are circulating abroad, prejudicial to the character of Brother Joseph Smith, Jun., and that said reports purport to have come from me, I have thought proper to give the public a plain statement of the facts concerning this matter. It is true, that some difficulties arose between Brother Joseph Smith, Jun., and myself, in our travels the past summer to Missouri; and that on our return to this place I laid my grievances before a general council, where they were investigated in full, in an examination which lasted several days, and the result showed to the satisfaction of all present, I believe, but especially to myself, that in all things Brother Joseph Smith, Jun., had conducted worthily, and adorned his profession as a man of God, while journeying to and from Missouri. And it is no more than just that I should confess my faults by saying unto all people, so far as your valuable and instructive paper has circulation, that the things that I accused Brother Smith of were without foundation; as most clearly proven, by the evidence which was called, to my satisfaction. And in fact, I have not at any time withdrawn my confidence and fellowship from Brother Joseph Smith, Jun., but thought that he had inadvertently erred, being but flesh and blood, like the rest of Adam's family. But I am now perfectly satisfied that the errors of which I accused him before the council, did not exist, and were never committed by him; and my contrition has been and still continues to be deep, because I admitted thoughts into my heart which were not right concerning him; and because that I have been the means of giving rise to reports which have gone abroad, censuring the conduct of Brother Joseph Smith, Jun., which reports are without foundation. And I hope that this disclosure of the truth, written by my own hand, and sent abroad into the world, through the medium of the *Messenger and Advocate*, will put a final end to all evil reports and censurings which have sprung out of anything that I have said or done.

"I wish still further to state for the relief of my own feelings, which you must be sensible are deeply wounded in consequence of what has happened, that I know for myself, because I have received testimony from the heavens that the work of the Lord, brought forth by means of the Book of Mormon, in our day through the instrumentality of Brother Joseph Smith Jun., is eternal truth, and must stand, though the heavens and the earth pass away.

"Please give publication to the above, and oblige a lover of righteousness and truth.   Yours in the testimony of Jesus,

"SYLVESTER SMITH."

"To O. Cowdery, Kirtland, October 28, 1834."

CHAPTER XI.

A MOMENT'S PEACE—COUNCIL MEETINGS IN OHIO AND MISSOURI.

THE excitement of the people began to subside and the Saints, both in Missouri and Ohio, began to enjoy a little peace. The elders began to go forth, two and two, preaching the word to all that would hear, and many were added to the Church daily.* *Temporary Peace.*

September 1.—I continued to preside over the Church, and in forwarding the building of the house of the Lord in Kirtland. I acted as foreman in the Temple stone quarry, and when other duties would permit, labored with my own hands. *The Prophet as Foreman.*

September 2. — Conference wrote Brother William Cherry, by Orson Hyde, clerk, to correct a report to the effect that "he had been cut off from the Church;" and advising the brethren not to find fault with one another, after having returned from such an arduous journey as that to Missouri had been, and especially since their offerings had been accepted of the Lord; also encouraging Brother Cherry and others to move west. *Message to Wm. Cherry.*

On the 4th, Elder Edmund Bosley said that, if he could obtain the management of his property, in one year, he would consecrate it for the printing of the word of the Lord. *Covenant of Edmund Bosley.*

---

* End of manuscript "Record A."

Minutes of a Conference of Elders, at New Portage, Ohio,
held September 8, 1834.

After prayer, President Joseph Smith, Jun., and Oliver Cowdery united in anointing with oil and laying hands upon a sick sister. She said she was healed, but requested us to pray that her faith fail not, saying if she did not doubt she would not be afflicted any more.

President Joseph Smith then made remarks upon the subject of false spirits.

Elder Ambrose Palmer presented a case that had previously occasioned some difficulty in the Church, which was that Brother Carpenter had been tried for a fault before the Church, and the Church gave him a certain time to reflect whether he would acknowledge his error or not. Brother Gordon, at the time, spoke in tongues, and declared that Brother Carpenter should not be shown any lenity. Elder Palmer wished instruction on this point, whether they had proceeded right or not, as Brother Carpenter was dissatisfied.

President Joseph Smith then gave an explanation of the gift of tongues, that it was particularly instituted for the preaching of the Gospel to other nations and languages, but it was not given for the government of the Church.

He further said, if Brother Gordon introduced the gift of tongues as a testimony against Brother Carpenter, it was contrary to the rules and regulations of the Church, because in all our decisions we must judge from actual testimony.

Elder Gordon said the testimony was received and the decision given before the gift of tongues was manifested.

President Smith advised that we speak in our own language in all such matters, and then the adversary cannot lead our minds astray.

Elder Palmer stated that when he was presiding in a conference, several of the brethren spoke out of order, and Elder J. B. Bosworth refused to submit to order according to his request; and he wished instructions on this point, whether he or some one else should preside over this branch of the Church; and also whether such conduct could be approved in conferences.

Brother Gordon made some remarks on the same subject.

President Smith said, relative to the first question, that Brother Gordon's tongue in the end did operate as testimony, as, by his remarks in tongues, the former decision was set aside and his [given in tongues] taken; that it was his [President Smith's] decision that Brother Gordon's manifestation was incorrect, and from a suspicious mind. He approved the first decision, but discarded the second.

Brother Joseph Keeler acknowledged that in the former decision he had acted hastily himself in urging Brother Carpenter to make acknowledgment without having time to reflect; and asked forgiveness wherein he had erred.

Brother Gordon said he discovered that he was in error, and was satisfied with the counsel, and was willing to ask forgiveness of the brethren and of the Lord.

Decision was then given on the second question, that Elder Bosworth was out of his place in opposing Elder Palmer when the latter presided in the conference.

The two decisions were confirmed by unanimous vote of the conference.

A motion was then made and passed by unanimous vote that a letter be written to Brother J.B. Bosworth, informing him of the last decision —that he acted out of place in opposing Elder Palmer in a former conference when requested to take his seat that the business might proceed according to order—and that such letter be signed by the clerk of this conference.

The case of Elder Milton Stow was then presented. when it was proven that he had delivered prophecies at two different times that were not true; at one time in saying that Zion was already redeemed, and at another in saying that Brother Carpenter was cut off forever and also in saying that Sister Carpenter was dead.

It was decided by vote, that Brother Milton Stow be and by the decision of this conference is, suspended from the privileges of this Church of Latter-day Saints, and from acting in the authority of an Elder in said Church of the Latter-day Saints, till he appear before the Bishop's council in Kirtland and make proper satisfaction.

Conference closed by prayer.

OLIVER COWDERY, Clerk of Conference.

The following letter was written according to the instruction of the conference, as recorded in the foregoing minutes:—

NEW PORTAGE, OHIO, September 8, 1834.

To Joseph B. Bosworth, a High Priest in the Church of Latter-day Saints.

DEAR BROTHER:—By a decision of this conference I am directed to inform you that a difficulty has been presented to this body which arose in a former conference between yourself and Elder Ambrose Palmer, to the effect that in a former conference where Elder Palmer presided, according to the office of his appointment as president of this [New Portage] branch of the Church of the Latter-day Saints, you, when requested by him to be seated, refused to submit to his decision, and spoke disrespectfully to our brother while acting in his calling, which has occasioned offense to the conference. It is the decision, therefore, of this conference, that you come before the Church, (as you are not present to do it at this conference) and make the proper confession required in the law of the Lord. Why I say disrespectfully is because when you were requested to be seated and to desist from speaking, you said you had as much right to speak as Elder Palmer.

OLIVER COWDERY, Clerk of Conference.

Extracts from the minutes of the High Council of Zion, assembled in Clay County, September 10, 1834.

The following brethren were chosen to fill the places of absent members:—Zebedee Coltrin for Parley P. Pratt; Hazen Aldrich for Solomon Hancock; Elias Higbee for Newell Knight; Isaac Higbee for William E. M'Lellin; Peter Dustin for Orson Pratt.

Elisha H. Groves was ordained a High Priest.

A letter was read from President Joseph Smith to W. W. Phelps, dated 16th of August; also a petition written by W. W. Phelps to the governor of the state of Missouri was read and accepted.

Calvin Beebe and Levi Jackman were nominated as first Elders to go forth to Kirtland, preaching by the way, and if approved by President Joseph Smith, should be accounted worthy, and numbered as such.*

It was decided by the President, and sanctioned by the Council, that the first Elders go forth as soon as they can get ready, and preach by the way to Kirtland.

Voted, that those Elders that came up in the camp apply for a release from Lyman Wight,† and receive a recommandation to Bishop Partridge, to go forth to preach the Gospel.

THOMAS B. MARSH, Secretary pro tem.

* That is, they should be numbered among the Elders to receive their endowments in Kirtland, if approved by the Prophet, Seer, and Revelator, Joseph Smith, as provided by the revelation of June 22nd. (See p. 108.)

† Who, it will be remembered, was appointed "General of the Camp" (p.88); and n the absence of the "Commander-in-Chief," was first in command; hence the direction to apply to him for release.

Minutes of the High Council at Kirtland, September 24, 1834.

Joseph Smith, Jun., presiding, assisted by Sidney Rigdon and Frederick G. Williams, counselors.

Jared Carter and Martin Harris were absent.

After prayer, the president made some remarks; when the case of Sylvester Smith was called up to inquire whether or not, under existing circumstances, he can fill the office of High Councilor.

It was decided that four Councilors speak on the case, viz.: Samuel H. Smith and Orson Johnson, Luke Johnson and Orson Hyde.

The Councilors severally spoke in their course, followed by Brother Sylvester; after which the assistent-presidents spoke; when the president gave a decision, that Brother Sylvester stand no longer a High Councilor, but that he retain the office of High Priest, and continue to lift up his voice in the name of Jesus in preaching the Gospel—to which the council assented, and Brother Sylvester gave his assent with thankfulness.

The President nominated Hyrum Smith to fill the office vacated by Sylvester Smith. The nomination was seconded by the clerk. The Councilors and all present voted for the nomination.

The President led in prayer, and then he ordained Hyrum Smith to the office of High Councilor, pronouncing blessings upon him in the name of the Lord; after which Joseph Smith, Sen., blessed his son Hyrum in the name of the Lord, confirming the same blessings.

Elders John P. Greene and Brigham Young were then appointed to fill the vacancies occasioned by the absence of Councilors Jared Carter and Martin Harris.

The council then proceeded to appoint a commitee to arrange the items of the doctrine of Jesus Christ, for the government of the Church of Latter-day Saints, which Church was organized and commenced its rise on the 6th of April, 1830. These items are to be taken from the Bible, Book of Mormon, and the revelations which have been given to the Church up to this date, or that shall be given until such arrangements are made.

Councilor Samuel H. Smith nominated President Joseph Smith, Jun., Oliver Cowdery, Sidney Rigdon, and Frederick G. Williams to compose said committee, which was seconded by Councilor Hyrum Smith. The Councilors then gave their vote in the affirmative, which was also agreed to by the whole conference.

The council then decided that said committee, after arranging and publishing said Book of Covenants, have the avails of the same.

The council then decided that a notice be published to the churches and conferences abroad that High Priests be ordained hereafter, in the High Council at Kirtland, and receive licence signed by the clerk of the council.

The council decided that Bishop Whitney be privileged, considering his present embarrassed circumstances, to make such arrangements with his store as he shall deem most advisable.

Closed by prayer.

OLIVER COWDERY,
ORSON HYDE,
Clerks.

CHAPTER XII.

CHANGE IN CHURCH PERIODICALS—THE COVENANT OF TITH-
ING—CLOSE OF THE YEAR 1834.

October 1–15.—Great exertions were made to expedite the work of the Lord's house, and notwithstanding it was commenced almost with nothing, as to means, yet the way opened as we proceeded, and the Saints rejoiced. The former part of October was spent in arranging matters respecting the Lord's house and the printing office, for it had previously been published that the *Evening and Morning Star* would be discontinued, and a new paper issued in its place, entitled *The Latter-day Saints Messenger and Advocate.**

"Messenger and Advocate" Founded.

* The following is the explanation given in the *Evening and Morning Star* for this change in the name of the Church periodical: "As the *Evening and Morning Star* was designed to be published at Missouri, it was considered that another name would be more appropriate for a paper in this place [Kirtland], consequently, as the name of this Church has lately been entitled the Church of the Latter-day Saints, and since it is destined, at least for a season, to bear the reproach and stigma of this world, it is no more than just that a paper disseminating the doctrines believed by the same, and advocating its character and rights should be entitled *The Latter-day Saints Messenger and Advocate.*"

There was also a change announced in the form of the Church periodical. The *Evening and Morning Star* as first published was a quarto, but the *Messenger and Advocate* was to be published in octavo form for greater convenience in binding and preserving. It was also announced that the two volumes of the *Star* would be reprinted in octavo form; which, by the way, was done.

This first number of the *Messenger and Advocate* contained a summary of the most prominent points of doctrine believed in by the Church at that time, signed by Oliver Cowdery; and as the doctrine development in the Church is a prominent feature of this work, that summary is here appended:

"We believe in God, and His Son Jesus Christ. We believe that God, from the beginning, revealed Himself to man, and that whenever He has had a people on earth, He always has revealed Himself to them by the Holy Ghost, the ministering

Having accomplished all that could be done at present, on the 16th of the month, in company with my brother

The Prophet's
Labors in
Michigan. Hyrum Smith, and Elders David Whitmer, Frederick G. Williams, Oliver Cowdery, and Roger Orton, left Kirtland for the purpose of visiting some Saints in the state of Michigan, where, after a tolerably pleasant journey, we arrived at Pontiac on the 20th.

While on our way up the lake on board the steamer *Monroe*, Elder Cowdery had a short discussion with a man calling his name Ellmer. He said that he was "personally acquainted with Joe Smith, had heard him preach his lies,

of angels or His own voice. We do not believe that He ever had a church on earth without revealing Himself to that church; consequently there were apostles, prophets, evangelists, pastors, and teachers in the same.

"We believe that God is the same in all ages, and that it requires the same holiness, purity, and religion to save a man now as it did anciently; and that, as He is no respecter of persons, always has, and always will reveal Himself to men when they call upon Him.

"We believe that God has revealed Himself to men in this age, and commenced to raise up a church preparatory to His second advent, when He will come in the clouds of heaven with power and great glory.

"We believe that the popular religious theories of the day are incorrect; that they are without parallel in the revelations of God, as sanctioned by Him; and that however faithfully they may be adhered to, or however jealously or warmly they may be defended, they will never stand the strict scrutiny of the word of life.

"We believe that all men are born free and equal; that no man, combination of men, or government of men has power or authority to compel or force others to embrace any system of religion, or religious creed, or to use force or violence to prevent others from enjoying their own opinions, or practicing the same, so long as they do not molest or disturb others in a manner to deprive them of their privileges as free citizens, or of worshiping God as they choose, and that any attempt to do so is an assumption unwarrantable in the revelations of heaven, and strikes at the root of civil liberty, and is a subversion of all equitable principles between man and man.

"We believe that God has set His hand the second time to recover the remnant of His people, Israel; and that the time is near when He will bring them from the four winds with songs of everlasting joy, and reinstate them upon their own lands which He gave their fathers by covenant.

"And further, we believe in embracing good wherever it may be found; of proving all things, and holding fast to that which is righteous. This, in short, is our belief, and we stand ready to defend it upon its own foundation whenever it is assailed by men of character and respectability. And while we act upon these broad principles, we trust in God that we shall never be confounded.

"OLIVER COWDERY."

"Kirtland, Ohio, October, 1834."

and now, since he was dead, he was glad! He had heard Joe Smith preach in Bainbridge Chenango county, New York, five years since; he knew it to be him, that he [Joseph Smith] was a dark complexioned man," etc. Ellmer appeared to exult most in that "Joe" was dead, and made his observations in my presence. I concluded that he learned it from the popular priests of the day, who, through fear that their craft will be injured, if their systems are compared with the truth, seek to ridicule those who teach the truth, and thus I am suffering under the tongue of slander for Christ's sake, unceasingly. God have mercy on such, if they will quit their lying. I need not state my complexion to those that have seen me, and those who have read my history thus far, will recollect that five years ago I was not a preacher, as Ellmer represented; neither did I ever preach in Bainbridge.*

After preaching, and teaching the Saints in Michigan as long as our time would allow, we returned to Kirtland, greatly refreshed from our journey, and much pleased with our friends in that section of the Lord's vineyard.

It now being the last of the month, and the Elders beginning to come in, it was necessary to make preparations for the school for the Elders, wherein they might be more perfectly instructed in the great things of God, during the coming winter. A building for a printing office was nearly finished, and the lower story of this building was set apart for that pur-

Preparation of the School for the Elders.

---

* In a communication to the first number of the *Messenger and Advocate*, October, 1834, Elder Oliver Cowdery gives substantially the same account of this incident. After a somewhat lengthy statement of how he refuted Ellmer's assertion that the Savior had not been seen since His ascension, he continues:

"How far this conversation was, or will be, productive of good, I am unable to say; but by that means numbers heard, and no doubt felt an increased anxiety to learn something further relative to this 'strange work.' One individual purchased a Book of Mormon, notwithstanding Mr. Ellmer's bitter cry of 'Joe Smith' and 'false prophets,' and will thus have the privilege of hearing the truth, though he may be separated far from those who have authority to administer the ordinances of the everlasting Gospel. May heaven inspire his heart to seek diligently until he obtains a certain knowledge of the kingdom of our God in these last days."

pose, (the school) when it was completed. So the Lord opened the way according to our faith and works, and blessed be His name.

No month ever found me more busily engaged than November; but as my life consisted of activity and unyielding exertions, I made this my rule: *When*

Strenuous
Life of the
Prophet.
the Lord commands, do it. Among other matters, the following letter was sent to George James, Brownhelm, Ohio, by order of the High Council:

KIRTLAND, November 10, 1834.

DEAR BROTHER:—There having been serious complaints presented to us against you, we sincerely request you to come to Kirtland immediately, as it will be necessary that a proper notice be taken of the same. We do not write the above with a view to accuse you ourselves, but you know the great responsibility resting upon us and the propriety of noticing charges, especially when they are preferred against men in important and interesting stations in the Church of the Saints. We have truly written the above with feelings of deep interest for your own welfare and standing in the Church; and we do hope you will not fail to come down immediately, as the representations made to us will require immediate notice. It is necessary for us to inform you that until you appear and make the satisfaction requisite, you are suspended from acting in the authority of the office to which you have been previously ordained.

With feelings of respect we subscribe ourselves, your brethren in the New Covenant,

JOSEPH SMITH, JUN.
SIDNEY RIGDON.

OLIVER COWDERY,
Clerk of the High Council.

I continued my labors daily, preparing for the school, and received the following:

Revelation given November 25, 1834.[*]

1. It is my will that my servant Warren A. Cowdery should be appointed and ordained a presiding High Priest over my Church in the land of Freedom and the regions round about;

[*] Doctrine and Covenants, sec. civ

2. And should preach my everlasting Gospel, and lift up his voice and warn the people, not only in his own place, but in the adjoining counties.

3. And devote his whole time to this high and holy calling which I now give unto him, seeking diligently the kingdom of heaven and its righteousness, and all things necessary shall be added thereunto, for the laborer is worthy of his hire.

4. And again, verily I say unto you, the coming of the Lord draweth nigh, and it overtaketh the world as a thief in the night:

5. Therefore, gird up your loins that you may be the children of light, and that day shall not overtake you as a thief.

6. And again, verily I say unto you, there was joy in heaven when my servant Warren bowed to my sceptre, and separated himself from the crafts of men.

7. Therefore, blessed is my servant Warren, for I will have mercy on him, and notwithstanding the vanity of his heart, I will lift him up, inasmuch as he will humble himself before me;

8. And I will give him grace and assurance wherewith he may stand, and if he continue to be a faithful witness and a light unto the Church, I have prepared a crown for him in the mansions of my Father. Even so. Amen.

The same day, Hon. J. T. V. Thompson, Missouri state senator, wrote Elder Phelps, at Liberty, as follows:

JEFFERSON CITY, Nov. 25, 1834.

DEAR SIR:—I will say to you that your case with the Jackson people has been mentioned to the highest officer in the state, the governor. He speaks of it in his message, and so much of his message will be referred to a commitee. I am not able to say what will be their report, but I will write you again.

I have the honor, etc.,

J. T. V. THOMPSON.

The following is that portion of the governor's message referred to in the foregoing letter:

In July, 1833, a large portion of the citizens of Jackson county organized themselves and entered into resolutions to expel from that county a religious sect called Mormons, who had become obnoxious to them. In November following, they effected their object; not, however, without the loss of several lives.

In the judicial inquiry into these outrages, the civil authorities who had cognizance of them, deemed it proper to have a military guard for the purpose of giving protection during the progress of the trials. This was ordered, and the Attorney-General was requested to give his atten- tion during the investigation, both of which were performed, but all to no purpose. As yet none has been punished for these outrages, and it is believed that, under our present laws, conviction for any violence committed against a Mormon cannot be had in Jackson county. These unfortunate people are now forbidden to take possession of their homes, and the principal part of them, I am informed, are at this time living in an adjoining county, in a great measure upon the charity of its citizens. It is for you to determine what amendements the laws may require so as to guard against such acts of violence for the future.

Minutes of a Council held at Kirtland, November 28th.

A council convened this evening to transact business according to the regulations of the Church; Joseph Smith, Jun., Sidndy Rigdon and Frederick G. Williams presiding. Eight councilors present.

John Johnson and Hyrum Smith were appointed to speak.

A letter from the church in Lewis, Essex county, New York, was presented by Brothers John H. Tippits, and Joseph H. Tippits, and read by the clerk. Said letter contained an account of money and other property sent by the church in Lewis, in the care of said brethren, to carry to Missouri to purchase land. These Elders wished the advice of the council, whether they had better pursue their journey or not.

The two Councilors spoke on the case, followed by President Williams, Councilor Orson Hyde and the clerk; after which President Rigdon gave a decision that our brethren be advised to tarry in this place dur- ing the winter; in which the council concurred.

The two brethren then arose respectively and said they were perfectly satisfied with the decision of the council.

The amount donated by the church in Lewis is, according to their letter, in cash, $473.29. The amount in *Star* property is $375.11. Total, $848.40.

The council then decided that President Joseph Smith, Jun., take such amount of said money as those brethren can part with for the present, by giving sufficient security, to be paid with interest by the 15th of April, 1835.

It was ascertained by the council that Sister Caroline Tippits held $149.75 of the money mentioned in said letter, she was accordingly called into the council, and expressed a willingness to loan the same.

One note of $280 was drawn in favor of John H. Tippits, and another of $150, in favor of Caroline Tippits, each due April 15, 1835. Signed by Joseph Smith, Jun., Oliver Cowdery, and Frederick G. Williams.   OLIVER COWDERY, Clerk.

The following letter was presented by John H. Tippits, and formed the subject for consideration by the preceding council, written to President Joseph Smith, Jun., and the High Council in Kirtland, by Alvah L. Tippits, to be sent greeting:

President Smith will recollect the time I left Kirtland last winter in order to come to dispose of the property I had in possession, which I have been striving to do from that time till about the first of September last, but I have felt very uneasy while the commandment has gone forth for the eastern churches to flee unto the West.

The 1st, or about the 1st of September, with two of my brethren, I took the revelation concerning the redemption of Zion and read it, and then we agreed to ask God to enable us to obey the same. As we live in the eastern states, our minds were impressed with these important lines:

"Therefore, a commandment I give unto all the churches, that they shall continue to gather together unto the places which I have appointed; nevertheless as I have said unto you in a former commandment, let not your gathering be in haste, nor by flight; but let all things be prepared before you: and in order that all things be prepared before you, observe the commandment which I have given concerning these things, which saith, or teacheth, to purchase all the lands with money, which can be purchased or money, in the region round about the land which I have appointed to be the land of Zion, for the beginning of the gathering of my Saints; all the land which can be purchased in Jackson county and the counties round about, and leave the residue in mine hand. Now, verily I say unto you, let all the churches gather together all their monies; let these things be done in their time, but not in haste, and observe to have all things prepared before you. And let honorable men be appointed, even wise men, and send them to purchase these lands; and the churches in the eastern countries, when they are built up, if they will hearken unto this counsel, they may buy lands and gather together upon them; and in this way they may establish Zion."*

After further consideration and much prayer, we carried the case before the church in this place, which met the approbation of the same

* Doctrine and Covenants; sec. ci: 67-74.

Accordingly we strove to become of one heart and one mind, and appointed a day for fasting and prayer, and asked the Lord to enable us to collect all our monies; and appointed a day for the church to come together for counsel.

Accordingly we came together, and after conversation, chose a moderator and clerk to keep the records of the church; counseled concerning property owned by the church, and commenced to make sale and collect pay according to the voice of the church, in order to collect all monies owned by the church, and send by the hands of wise men, who were appointed by the voice of the church; one Elder and one Priest, according to the will of God.

ALVAH L. TIPPITS.

Lewis, County of Essex,
New York, October 20, 1834.

The members of a branch of the Church of the Latter-day Saints, agreeable to the requirement of heaven, have striven to unite their hearts and views, in order to be found spotless before the blazing throne of the Great Jehovah when He comes to make up His jewels, and for this end to send property by the hands of wise men, appointed by the voice of the church, agreeable to the revelation concerning the redemption of Zion, for the purpose of purchasing land in Jackson county, or counties round about, for the inheritance of the Church. Agreeable to this, we give our names with the affixed sums annexed:

	Cash	Property
Joseph H. Tippts	$98.67	$120.37
Alvah Tippits	34.63	80.00
John H. Tippits	171.05	51.93
Henry Adams	11.13	8.75
Zebulon Adams	1.75	
Caroline Tippits	151.06	107.00
David Bragg	5.00	1.06
Gustavus A. Perry		6.00

Total, $848.40; $100.00 for boots and shoes, to be left in Kirtland.

The wise men appointed are John H. Tippits and Joseph H. Tippits.

On the evening of the 29th of November, I united in prayer with Brother Oliver for the continuance of blessings. After giving thanks for the relief which the Lord had lately sent us by opening the hearts of the brethren from the east, to loan us $430; *The Covenant of Tithing.* after commencing and rejoicing before the Lord on this occasion, we agreed to enter into the following covenant with the Lord, viz.:

That if the Lord will prosper us in our business and open the way before us that we may obtain means to pay our debts; that we be not troubled nor brought into disrepute before the world, nor His people; after that, of all that He shall give unto us, we will give a tenth to be bestowed upon the poor in His Church, or as He shall command; and that we will be faithful over that which He has entrusted to our care, that we may obtain much; and that our children after us shall remember to observe this sacred and holy covenant; and that our children, and our children's children, may know of the same, we have subscribed our names with our own hands.

(Signed)   JOSEPH SMITH, JUN.
OLIVER COWDERY.

A Prayer.

And now, O Father, as Thou didst prosper our father Jacob, and bless him with protection and prosperity wherever he went, from the time he made a like covenant before and with Thee; as Thou didst even the same night, open the heavens unto him and manifest great mercy and power, and give him promises, wilt Thou do so with us his sons; and as his blessings prevailed above his progenitors unto the utmost bounds of the everlasting hills, even so may our blessings prevail like his; and may Thy servants be preserved from the power and influence of wicked and unrighteous men; may every weapon formed against us fall upon the head of him who shall form it; may we be blessed with a name and a place among Thy Saints here, and Thy sanctified when they shall rest. Amen.

November 30.—While reflecting on the goodness and mercy of God this evening, a prophecy was put into our hearts, that in a short time the *A Prophecy.* Lord would arrange His providences in a merciful manner and send us assistance to deliver us from debt and bondage.

December 1.—Our school for the Elders was now well

attended, and with the lectures on theology,* which were

School at
Kirtland for
the Elders.

regularly delivered, absorbed for the time being everything else of a temporal nature. The classes, being mostly Elders gave the most studious attention to the all-important object of qualifying themselves as messengers of Jesus Christ, to be ready to do His will in carrying glad tidings to all that would open their eyes, ears and hearts.

According to the direction of the Holy Spirit, on the evening of the 5th of December, while assembled with Sidney

Oliver Cowdery Ordained
an Assistant
President.

Rigdon, Frederick G. Williams, and Oliver Cowdery, conversing upon the welfare of the Church, I laid my hands on Brother Oliver Cowdery, and ordained him an assistant-president, saying these words: "In the name of Jesus Christ, who was crucified for the sins of the world, I lay my hands upon thee and ordain thee an assistant-president to the High and Holy Priesthood, in the Church of the Latter-day Saints."†

---

* These "Lectures on Theology" here referred to were afterwards prepared by the Prophet, (see page 180) and published in the Doctrine and Covenants under the title "Lectures on Faith." They are seven in number, and occupy the first seventy-five pages in the current editions of the Doctrine and Covenants. They are not to be regarded as of equal authority in matters of doctrine with the revelations of God in the Doctrine and Covenants, but as stated by Elder John Smith, who, when the book of Doctrine and Covenants was submitted to the several quorums of the Priesthood for acceptance, (August 17, 1835,) speaking in behalf of the Kirtland High Council, "bore record that the revelations in said book were true, and that the lectures judicially were written and compiled, and were profitable for doctrine." The distinction which Elder John Smith here makes should be observed as a marking the difference between the Lectures on Faith and the revelations of God in the Doctrine and Covenants.

† This meeting of the 5th of December was a most interesting occasion. The minutes of it are found in the hand writing of Oliver Cowdery in the back of Record A, Ms. It would appear, according to these minutes, that the express purpose of the meeting of the brethren named in the Prophet's history was to recognize Oliver Cowdery in his station as the second Elder in the Church, a position for which he was designated in the revelations of God, and to which he was ordained under the hand of the Prophet, (Doctrine and Covenants, sec. 20: 3,4). It is explained in the minutes that the reason why he had not been able to officiate in his calling as said second Elder in the Church was because of his necessary absence in Zion (Missouri) to assist W. W. Phelps in conducting the printing business of the Church, etc.; hence Sidney Rigdon and Frederick G. Williams had been ordained as assistant-presidents in the Church during this necessary absence of Elder Cowdery. Another

On the 11th, Elder Phelps wrote from Liberty, Clay county, to J. T. V. Thompson, Jefferson City, in reply to his letter of the 25th November, expressive of thankfulness to his Excellency, Governor Dunklin, for introducing the sufferings of the Saints in his message; also asking counsel "whether it would avail anything for the society to petition the legislature for an act to reinstate them in their rights," etc.; and requesting him to confer with his friends and his Excellency on the subject, and give an early answer.

Thanks to Governor Dunklin.

About the middle of the month, the message of Governor Dunklin, of Missouri, to the legislature, arrived at Kirtland. It was read with great interest, and revived the hopes of the Church for the scattered brethren of Jackson county.

Revived Hopes.

Elder Phelps wrote again to Esquire Thompson, on the 18th as follows:

DEAR SIR—By this mail I have forwarded to Captain Atchison, of the lower house, a petition and documents, on the subject of our rights in Jackson county. He will hand them to you for the senate, when they are through with them in the house. I shall be greatly obliged, if you will lay them before your honorable body; and any information

item of interest recorded in these minutes is the word of the Lord by way of reproof through the Spirit concerning the failure of the brethren and the Church in general to properly recognize each other by their official titles in the Church. This item appears in the minutes as follows: "After assembling we received a rebuke for our former uncultivated and disrespectful manner of communication and salutation with and unto each other by the voice of the Spirit, saying unto us: 'Verily, condemnation resteth upon you, who are appointed to lead my Church, and to be saviors of men; and also upon the Church; and there must needs be a repentance and a reformation among you, in all things, in your examples before the Church and before the world, in all your manners, habits and customs, and salutations one toward another; rendering unto every man the respect due the office, calling, and priesthood whereunto I, the Lord, have appointed and ordained you. Amen.'" "It is only necessary to say," continue the minutes, "relative to the foregoing reproof and instruction, that though it was given in sharpness, it occasioned gladness and joy, and we were willing to repent and reform in every particular, according to the instruction given. It is also proper to remark that after the reproof was given, we all confessed, voluntarily, that such had been the manifestation of the Spirit a long time since, in consequence of which, the rebuke came with great sharpness."

you may require, or even personal attendance, write, and you shall have it if it is in my power. As a people, all we ask is our rights.

With esteem, etc.,

W. W. Phelps.

On the 20th Messrs. Thompson and Atchison wrote Elder Phelps from the ''Senate Chamber,'' acknowledging the receipt of his letter, stating that the committee on the Governor's message had not reported, and recommending the Saints to get up a petition to the legislature, with as many signatures as possible, promising their assistance and influence to obtain redress of grievances. A petition was accordingly forwarded; but the year closed without bringing anything to pass for the relief of the Saints in Missouri.*

Thompson and Atchison Promise Assistance.

* The following letter from Governor Dunklin, in response to the petitions referred to in the text above, is found as an addenda in the manuscript history for 1835, Note A:

"To the petitions which we sent up to Missouri, Governor Dunklin replied as follows:

"City of Jefferson, January 22, 1836.

"To Messrs. W. W. Phelps and others,

"Gentlemen:—Your numerous petitions, post-marked 'Kirtland,' came safe to hand. It is unnecessary for me to repeat to you my feelings on the subject of your grievances; what they were you have been already apprised; and they have undergone no change. Your case was presented by me to the last General Assembly of this state. They did not legislate upon the subject. I am, however, persuaded that it was for want of a constitutional power to pass any law that could afford you a proper remedy prevented their acting upon the subject. Your feelings are very natural when such causes exist to produce them, but you misconceive your case, and consequently do not advert to the proper remedy; you cannot make a case of invasion or insurrection out of the outrages committed on your persons or property in Jackson county, and unless one of those could be made out, it would be idle to address the President of the United States. If such a case had been made out, as executive of this state, I should have immediately ordered out a military force to repel or suppress it. The mob in New York to which you cite me, is not in point. The military force was then resorted to for the purpose of quelling the mob. You wish this kind of force used to restore justice. However palpable and grievous the outrages have been upon you, your only remedy for injuries done, must be in and through the courts of justice. On a former occasion I informed you I was then in correspondence with the General Government for a depot of arms on the Missouri river, near our western boundary line. For reasons unknown to me, the Secretary of War has taken no steps during the last year towards the fulfillment of that object. I have renewed the subject through our delegation in Congress this winter. When this object shall be attained, it may furnish you a place of resort for protection, in case of emergency, should you think proper to risk yourselves on your lands in Jackson county again.

Respectfully,

DANIEL DUNKLIN.

CHAPTER XIII.

THE LECTURES ON FAITH—TWELVE APOSTLES CHOSEN AND
ORDAINED.

January, 1835.—During the month of January, I was
engaged in the school of the Elders, and in
preparing the lectures on theology for publication in the book of Doctrine and Covenants, which the committee appointed last September
were now compiling.

The Lectures
on Theology.

Certain brethren from Bolton, New York, came for
counsel, relative to their proceeding to the
West; and the High Council assembled on the
18th. After a long investigation I decided
that Elder Tanner assist with his might to
build up the cause by tarrying in Kirtland; which decision received the unanimous vote of the council.

Brethren
Moving West
Halted at
Kirtland.

The school of the Elders will continue, and arrangements were also made, according to the revelation of
June, 1829,* for choosing "the Twelve Apostles" to be
especial messengers to bear the Gospel among the nations.

On the Sabbath previous to the 14th of February, (February 8th) Brothers Joseph and Brigham Young came to
my house after meeting, and sung for me; the Spirit of
the Lord was poured out upon us, and I told them I
wanted to see those brethren together, who went up to
Zion in the camp, the previous summer, for I had a

* Doctrine and Covenants, sec. xviii.

blessing for them; and a meeting was appointed of which the following are the minutes:*

Minutes of the Meetings at which the Twelve Apostles were Chosen, Ordained and Instructed.

Kirtland, *February 14, 1835.*—This day, a meeting was called of those who journeyed last season to Zion for the purpose of laying the foundation of its redemption, together with as many other of the brethren and sisters as were disposed to attend.

President Joseph Smith, Jun., presiding, read the 15th chapter of John, and said: Let us endeavor to solemnize our minds that we may receive a blessing, by calling on the Lord. After an appropriate and

* Elder Joseph Young gives the following interesting account of the above meeting mentioned by the Prophet: "On the 8th day of February, in the year of our Lord 1835, the Prophet Joseph Smith called Elders Brigham and Joseph Young to the chamber of his residence, in Kirtland, Ohio, it being on the Sabbath day. After they were seated and he had made some preliminaries, he proceeded to relate a vision to these brethren, of the state and condition of those men who died in Zion's Camp, in Missouri. He said, 'Brethren, I have seen those men who died of the cholera in our camp; and the Lord knows, if I get a mansion as bright as theirs, I ask no more.' At this relation he wept, and for some time could not speak. When he had relieved himself of his feelings, in describing the vision, he resumed the conversation, and addressed himself to Brother Brigham Young. He said to him, 'I wish you to notify all the brethren living in the branches, within a reasonable distance from this place, to meet at a general conference on Saturday next. I shall then and there appoint twelve Special Witnesses, to open the door of the Gospel to foreign nations, and you,' said he (speaking to Brother Brigham), 'will be one of them.' He then proceeded to enlarge upon the duties of their calling. The interest that was taken on the occasion of this announcement, produced in the minds of the two Elders present a great sensation and many reflections; having previously notified Brother Brigham Young that he would be one of the Witnesses, but said nothing to Joseph, until he had exhausted much of his feelings in regard to the Twelve, which took up some little time. He then turned to Elder Joseph Young with quite an earnestness, as though the vision of his mind was extended still further, and addressing him. said, 'Brother Joseph, the Lord has made you President of the Seventies.' They had heard of Moses and seventy Elders of Israel, and of Jesus appointing 'other Seventies,' but had never heard of Twelve Apostles and of Seventies being called in this Church before. It was a strange saying, 'The Lord has made you President of the Seventies,' as though it had already taken place, and it caused these brethren to marvel. The Prophet did not say that any others would be called to be the bearers of this message abroad, but the inference might be clearly drawn, that this was his meaning, from the language he used at the time. Agreeable to his request to Elder Brigham Young, the branches were all notified, and a meeting of the brethren in general conference was held in Kirtland, in the new school house under the printing office, on the following Saturday, February 14th, when the Twelve were appointed and ordained, and the conference adjourned for two weeks."—"History of the organization of the Seventies," by Joseph Young, Sen. (1878) pp. 1, 2.

affecting prayer, the brethren who went to Zion [in Zion's camp] were requested to take their seats together in a part of the house by themselves.

President Smith then stated that the meeting had been called, because God had commanded it; and it was made known to him by vision* and by the Holy Spirit. He then gave a relation of some of the circumstances attending us while journeying to Zion—our trials, sufferings: and said God had not designed all this for nothing, but He had it in remembrance yet;† and it was the will of God that those who went to Zion, with a determination to lay down their lives, if necessary, should be ordained to the ministry, and go forth to prune the vineyard for the last time, or the coming of the Lord, which was nigh—even fifty-six years should wind up the scene.

The President also said many things; such as the weak things, even the smallest and weakest among us, shall be powerful and mighty, and great things shall be accomplished by you from this hour; and you shall begin to feel the whisperings of the Spirit of God; and the work of God shall begin to break forth from this time; and you shall be endowed with power from on high.

President then called up all those who went to Zion, if they were agreed with him in the statement which he had made, to arise; and they all arose and stood upon their feet.

He then called upon the remainder of the congregation, to know if they also sanctioned the move, and they all raised their right hand.

* This vision, in which the Prophet evidently saw the order of the Church organization, is several times alluded to by him. By reference to the note on page 181 it will be observed that President Smith there refers to the vision in such a manner as to lead one to believe that he saw that Brigham Young would be one of the Twelve, and Joseph Young President of the Seventies. He also refers to this vision in the revelation which appears in chapter xiv; (Doctrine and Covenants, sec. cvii, 93). Describing the order of the Seventies, he says: "And it is according to the *vision*, showing the order of the Seventies, that there shall be seven Presidents to preside over them, chosen out of the number of the Seventy." It was doubtless in this vision also that the Prophet saw the manner in which the Twelve should be chosen.

† Elder Joseph Young in his "History of the Organization of the Seventies," (page 14) says that the following sentiment was delivered by the Prophet Joseph Smith in an address to the Elders assembled in Kirtland soon after the Seventies were organized: "Brethren, some of you are angry with me, because you did not fight in Missouri; but let me tell you, God did not want you to fight. He could not organize His kingdom with twelve men to open the Gospel door to the nations of the earth, and with seventy men under their direction to follow in their tracks, unless He took them from a body of men who had offered their lives, and who had made as great a sacrifice as did Abraham. Now the Lord has got His Twelve and His Seventy, and there will be other quorums of Seventies called, who will make the sacrifice, and those who have not made their sacrifices and their offerings now, will make them hereafter."

The names of those who went to Zion in the camp are as follows:*

Hazen Aldrich,
Joseph S. Allen,
Isaac Allred,
James Allred,
Martin Allred,
Milo Andrus,
Solomon Angel,
Allen A. Avery,
Almon W. Babbitt,
Alexander Badlam,
Samuel Baker,
Nathan Bennett Baldwin,
Elam Barber,
Israel Barlow,
Lorenzo D. Barnes,
Edson Barney,
Royal Barney,
Henry Benner,
Samuel Bent,
Hiram Backman,
Lorenzo Booth,
George W. Brooks,
Albert Brown,
Harry Brown,
Samuel Brown,
John Brownell,
Peter Buchanan,
Alden Burdick,
Harrison Burgess,
David Byur,
William F. Cahoon,
John Carpenter,
John S. Carter,
Daniel Cathcart,
Solon Foster,
Jacob Gates,
Benjamin Gifford,

Alonzo Champlin,
Jacob Chapman,
William Cherry,
John M. Chidester,
Alden Childs,
Nathaniel Childs,
Stephen Childs,
Albert Clements,
Thomas Colborn,
Alanson Colby,
Zera S. Cole,
Zebedee Coltrin,
Libeus T. Coon,
Horace Cowan,
Lyman Curtis,
Mecham Curtis,
Solomon W. Denton,
Peter Doff,
David D. Dort,
John Duncan,
James Dunn,
Philemon Duzette,
Philip Ettleman,
Bradford W. Elliot,
David Elliot,
David Evans,
Asa Field,
Edmund Fisher,
Alfred Fisk,
Hezekiah Fisk,
Elijah Fordham,
George Fordham,
Frederick Forney,
John Fossett,
James Foster,
William S. Ivie,
William Jessop,

* A full list of those who went up to Zion, including women and children, is here published in place of the partial list heretofore published in the History of Joseph Smith in the *Millennial Star*, volume xv, page 205.

Levi Gifford,
Sherman Gilbert,
Tru Glidden,
Dean C. Gould,
Jedediah M. Grant,
Addison Green,
Michael Griffith,
Everett Griswold,
Elisha Groves,
Joseph Hancock,
Levi W. Hancock,
Joseph Harmon,
Henry Herriman,
Martin Harris,
Joseph Hartshorn,
Thomas Hayes,
Nelson Higgins,
Seth Hitchcock,
Amos Hogers,
Chandler Holbrook,
Joseph Holbrook,
Milton Holmes,
Osmon Houghton,
Marshal Hubbard,
Solomon Humphrey,
Joseph Huntsman,
John Hustin,
Elias Hutchins,
Heman T. Hyde,
Orson Hyde,
Warren S. Ingalls,
Edward Ivie,
James R. Ivie,
John A. Ivie;
David W. Patten,
William D. Pratt,
Leonard Rich,
Darwin Richardson,
Burr Riggs,
Harpin Riggs,
Nathaniel Riggs,
Milcher Riley,
Alanson Ripley,

Luke S. Johnson,
Lyman E. Johnson,
Noah Johnson,
Seth Johnson,
Isaac Jones,
Levi Jones,
Charles Kelley,
Heber C. Kimball,
Samuel Kingsley,
Dennis Lake,
Jesse B. Lawson,
L. S. Lewis,
Josiah Littlefield,
Lyman O. Littlefield,
Waldo Littlefield,
Amasa M. Lyman,
Moses Martin,
Edward W. Marvin,
Reuben McBride,
Robert McCord,
Eleazer Miller,
John Miller,
Justin Morse,
John Murdock,
Freeman Nickerson,
Levi S. Nickerson,
Uriah C. Nickerson,
Joseph Nicholas,
Joseph B. Noble,
Ur. North,
Roger Orton,
John D. Parker,
Warren Parrish,
Orson Pratt,
Parley P. Pratt,
Charles C. Rich,
Samuel Thompson,
Wm. P. Tippetts,
Tinney Thomas,
Nelson Tribbs,
Joel Vaughn,
Salmon Warner,
William Weden,

Lewis Robbins,
Erastus Rudd,
William Henry Sagers,
Wilkins Jenkins Salisbury,
Henry Sherman,
Lyman Sherman,
Henry Shibley,
Cyrus Smalling,
Avery Smith,
George A. Smith,
Hyrum Smith,
Jackson Smith,
Zechariah B. Smith,
Joseph Smith,
Lyman Smith,
Sylvester Smith,
William Smith,
Willard Snow,
Harvey Stanley,
Hyrum Stratton,
Zerubbabel Snow,
Daniel Stephens,
Elias Strong,
John Joshua Tanner,
Ezra Thayer,
Nathan Tanner,
James L. Thompson,
Elias Wells,
Alexander Whitesides,
Andrew W. Whitlock,
Lyman Wight,
Eber Wilcox,
Sylvester B. Wilkinson,
Frederick G. Williams.
Alonzo Winchester,
Benjamin Winchester,
Lupton Winchester,
Alvin Winegar,
Samuel Winegar,
Hiram Winter,
Henry Wissmiller,
Wilford Woodruff,
Brigham Young,
Joseph Young.

WOMEN IN ZION'S CAMP.

Charlotte Alvord,
Sophronia Curtis,
Mary Snow Gates,
Nancy Lambson Holbrook,
Betsy Parrish,
Ada Clements,
Mary Chidester,
Diana Drake,
Eunice Holbrook,
Mrs. Houghton,
——Ripley.

CHILDREN IN ZION'S CAMP.

Diana Holbrook, daughter of Chandler Holbrook,
Sarah Lucretia Holbrook, daughter of Joseph Holbrook,
Charlotte Holbrook, daughter of Joseph Holbrook,
—————————, daughter of Alvin Winegar,
Sarah Pulsipher, daughter of Zera Pulsipher,
John P. Chidester, son of John M. Chidester,
Eunice Chidester, daughter of John M. Chidester.

President Joseph Smith, Jun., after making many remarks on the subject of choosing the Twelve, wanted an expression from the brethren, if they would be satisfied to have the Spirit of the Lord dictate in the choice of the Elders to be Apostles; whereupon all the Elders present expressed their anxious desire to have it so.

A hymn was then sung, "Hark, listen to the trumpeters."* President Hyrum Smith prayed, and meeting was dismissed for one hour.

Assembled pursuant to adjournment, and commenced with prayer.

President Joseph Smith, Jun., said that the first business of the meeting was, for the Three Witnesses† of the Book of Mormon, to pray, each

---

* The hymn was peculiarly suited to the occasion. Some of the stanzas follow:

"Hark! listen to the trumpeters!
They sound for volunteers;
On Zion's bright and flowery mount
Behold the officers.

"Their horses white, their armor bright,
With courage bold they stand,
Enlisting soldiers for their king,
To march to Zion's land.

*   *   *

"We want no cowards in our bands,
Who will our colors fly:
We call for valiant-hearted men,
Who're not afraid to die.

"To see our armies on parade,
How martial they appear!
All armed and dressed in uniform,
They look like men of war.

"They follow their great General.
The great Eternal Lamb—
His garments stained in his own blood—
King Jesus is His name."

† It was made known to the Prophet and Oliver Cowdery as early as June, 1829, that there would be Twelve Apostles chosen in this dipensation. In that revelation (Doctrine and Covenants, sec. xviii: 37) the Lord, addressing Oliver Cowdery and David Whitmer, said: "And now, behold, I give unto you Oliver Cowdery, and also unto David Whitmer, that you shall search out the Twelve, who shall have the desires of which I have spoken." That is, desires to take upon them the name of Jesus Christ with full purpose of heart. It will be observed that in this revelation only two of the Three Witnesses are named, yet Martin Harris was associated with his fellow Witnesses in choosing and ordaining the Twelve Apostles. I think it was designed from the first that the Three Witnesses should choose the Twelve Special Witnesses of the name and mission of the Lord Jesus Christ—the Twelve Apostles; but at the time the revelation of June, 1829, was given, making known that Twelve Apostles would be called, and designating Oliver Cowdery and David Whitmer as the ones to choose them, Martin Harris was out of favor with the Lord, and I suggest that it was for that reason doubtless that his name was omitted at that time. The evidence that Martin Harris was wavering about that time in his adherence to the Prophet and the work of God is found in Doctrine and Covenants, sec. xix, given in the month of June, 1829; in which revelation Martin Harris is sharply reproved for such wavering; for his

one, and then proceed to choose twelve men from the Church, as Apostles, to go to all nations, kindreds, tongues, and people.

The Three Witnesses, viz., Oliver Cowdery, David Whitmer, and Martin Harris, united in prayer.

These Three Witnesses were then blessed by the laying on of the hands of the Presidency.

The Witnesses then, according to a former commandment, proceeded to make choice of the Twelve. Their names are as follows:

1.	Lyman E. Johnson,	7.	William E. M'Lellin,
2.	Brigham Young,	8.	John F. Boynton,
3.	Heber C. Kimball,	9.	Orson Pratt,
4.	Orson Hyde,	10.	William Smith,
5.	David W. Patten,	11.	Thomas P. Marsh,
6.	Luke S. Johnson,	12.	Parley P. Pratt,

Lyman E. Johnson, Brigham Young and Heber C. Kimball came forward; and the Three Witnesses laid their hands upon each one's head and prayed, separately.*

covetousness; for hesitating to dispose of his land to meet the obligations entered into with the printer. He is commanded to repent of all these things, which, happily he did; but evidently not before the revelation concerning the choosing of the Twelve (Doctrine and Covenants, sec. xviii) was given, for which reason doubtless his name is not there associated with those of his fellow Witnesses when they were designated to choose the Twelve Apostles. As already stated, however, in the vision in which the Prophet Joseph saw more perfectly the organization of the Church, and the manner in which the Twelve were to be chosen, he undoubtedly learned that it was in harmony with the order of things that the Three Witnesses should choose the Twelve Special Witnesses, and hence appointed Martin Harris to assist Oliver Cowdery and David Whitmer in choosing the Apostles.

A word, by the way, in relation to the appropriateness of the Three Witnesses choosing the Twelve. In the revelation defining the special calling of the Twelve Apostles it is written: "The Twelve traveling counselors are called to be the Twelve Apostles, or special witnesses of the name of Christ in all the world; thus differing from other officers in the Church in the duties of their calling. (Doctrine and Covenants, sec. cvii: 23). From this it appears that the *special* calling of the Twelve is to be Witnesses for the Lord Jesus Christ in all the world; hence it was preeminently proper that these Twelve Witnesses should be chosen by the Three very special Witnesses—witnesses of the Book of Mormon in particular, and of God's marvelous work in general.

* Much interest has been manifested in the Church concerning who was mouth in ordaining respectively the brethren of the first Twelve. Most likely the Three Witnesses who ordained the Apostles were mouth in the order in which they have always stood as Witnesses, viz., Oliver Cowdery first, David Whitmer second, and Martin Harris third. If they officiated in this order then Oliver Cowdery ordained Lyman E. Johnson; David Whitmer, Brigham Young; and Martin Harris, Heber C. Kimball. It has been suggested by some that the Prophet Joseph may have joined the Three Witnesses in ordaining the Twelve, and in that event would be mouth first, and therefore ordained Lyman E. Johnson, leaving Oliver Cowdery to ordain Brigham

The blessing of Lyman E. Johnson was, in the name of Jesus Christ, that he should bear the tidings of salvation to nations, tongues, and people, until the utmost corners of the earth shall hear the tidings; and that he shall be a witness of the things of God to nations and tongues, and that holy angels shall administer to him occasionally; and that no power of the enemy shall prevent him from going forth and doing the work of the Lord; and that he shall live until the gathering is accomplished, according to the holy prophets; and he shall be like unto Enoch; and his faith shall be like unto his; and he shall be called great among all the living; and Satan shall tremble before him; and he shall see the Savior come and stand upon the earth with power and great glory.

The blessing of Brigham Young was that he should be strong in body, that he might go forth and gather the elect, preparatory to the great day of the coming of the Lord; and that he might be strong and mighty, declaring the tidings to nations that know not God; that he may add ten talents; that he may come to Zion with many sheaves. He shall go forth from land to land and from sea to sea; and shall behold heavenly messengers going forth; and his life shall be prolonged; and the Holy

Young, David Whitmer, Heber C. Kimball. This, however, is not likely since but three of those who had been chosen were called up at the above meeting to be ordained, one for each Witness. Besides, the express language of the minutes of the proceedings is, "The Three Witnesses laid their hands upon each one's head and prayed separately; that is each ordained his man. The statement of Heber C. Kimball in the published extracts of his journal, also confirms this view of the matter. After giving the names of the Twelve men chosen he says: "After having expressed our feeling on this occasion, we were severally called into the stand, and there received our ordinations, *under the hands of Oliver Cowdery, David Whitmer, and Martin Harris. These brethren ordained us to the Apostleship,* and predicted many things which should come to pass, that we should have power to heal the sick, cast out devils, raise the dead, give sight to the blind, have power to remove mountains, and all things should be subject to us through the name of Jesus Christ, and angels should minister unto us, and many more things, too numerous to mention." He also adds the following interesting item with reference to the ordinations of that day: "After we [referring to the first three called up to receive ordination] had been thus ordained by these brethren, the First Presidency laid their hands on us and confirmed these blessings and ordinations, and likewise predicted many things which should come to pass." (*Times and Seasons,* vol. vi, p. 868). While these statements make it very clear that the Prophet Joseph did not join with the Three Witnesses in ordaining the Apostles—except in the way of confirming the ordination they received from the Witnesses, as described by Elder Kimball—the minutes of the meeting held February 21st, at which Parley P. Pratt was ordained, state that he was "ordained one of the Twelve by President Joseph Smith, Jun., David Whitmer, and Oliver Cowdery." Martin Harris must have been absent, and the Prophet evidently joined Oliver Cowdery and David Whitmer on that occasion because of the absence of Harris; but whether or not the Prophet was mouth on that occasion does not appear in the minutes or in Elder Pratt's autobiography.

Priesthood is conferred on him, that he may do wonders in the name of Jesus; that he may cast out devils, heal the sick, raise the dead, open the eyes of the blind, go forth from land to land and from sea to sea; and that heathen nations shall even call him God himself, if he do not rebuke them.

Heber C. Kimball's blessing was, in substance, that he shall be made like unto those who have been blessed before him; and be favored with the same blessing. That he might receive visions; the ministration of angels, and hear their voice; and even come into the presence of God; that many millions may be converted by his instrumentality; that angels may waft him from place to place, and that he may stand unto the coming of our Lord, and receive a crown in the Kingdom of our God; that he be made acquainted with the day when Christ shall come; that he shall be made perfect in faith; and that the deaf shall hear, the lame shall walk, the blind shall see, and greater things than these shall he do; that he shall have boldness of speech before the nations, and great power.

A hymn was then sung, "Glorious things of thee are spoken," etc.; and the congreagation was dismissed by President Joseph Smith, Jun.

Sunday, February 15.—The congregation again assembled.

President Cowdery made some observations upon the nature of the meeting, calling upon the Lord for his assistance; after which a number of certificates from brethren that had recently returned from Zion were read and accepted.

President Cowdery then called forward Orson Hyde, David W. Patten and Luke Johnson, and proceeded to their ordinations and blessings.

Orson Hyde's Blessing:—Oliver Cowdery called upon the Lord to smile upon him; that his faith be made perfect, and that the blessings pronounced may be realized; that he be made mighty, and be endued with powers from on high, and go forth to the nations of the earth to proclaim the Gospel, that he may escape all the pollutions of the world; that the angels shall uphold him; and that he shall go forth according to the commandment, both to Jew and Gentile, and to all nations, kingdoms and tongues; that all who hear his voice shall acknowledge him to be a servant of God; that he shall be equal with his brethren in holding the keys of the kingdom; that he may stand on the earth and bring souls till Christ comes. We know that he loves Thee, O, Lord, and may this Thy servant be able to walk through pestilence and not be harmed; and the powers of darkness have no ascendency over him; may he have power to smite the earth with pestilence; to divide waters, and lead through the Saints; may he go from land to land and from sea to sea, and may he be like one of the three Nephites.

David W. Patten's blessing:—O God, give this Thy servant, a knowledge of Thy will; may he be like one of old, who bore testimony of Jesus; may he be a new man from this day forth. He shall be equal with his brethren, the Twelve, and have the qualifications of the prophets before him. May his body be strong and never be weary; may he walk and not faint. May he have power over all diseases, and faith according to his desires; may the heavens be opened upon him speedily; that he may bear testimony from knowledge; that he may go to nations and isles afar off. May he have a knowledge of the things of the Kingdom, from the beginning, and be able to tear down priestcraft like a lion. May he have power to smite his enemies before him, with utter destruction. May he continue till the Lord comes. O Father, we seal these blessings upon him. Even so. Amen.

Luke S. Johnson's Blessing:—Our Father in heaven, look down in mercy upon us, and upon this Thy servant, whom we ordain to the ministry of the Twelve. He shall be prepared and preserved, and be like those we have blessed before him. The nations shall tremble before him. He shall hear the voice of God; he shall comfort the hearts of the Saints always. The angels shall bear him up till he shall finish his ministry. He shall be delivered, and come forth with Israel. He shall bear testimony to the kings of the earth, and hold communion with the Father, with the Son, and with the general assembly and Church of the first-born. If cast into prison, he shall be able to comfort the hearts of his comrades. His tongue shall be loosed, and he shall have power to lead many to Zion, and sit down with them; the Ancient of Days shall pronounce this blessing, that he has been faithful; he shall have strength, wisdom, and power; he shall go among the covenant people and speak all their tongues where he shall go. All these blessings we confirm upon him in the name of Jesus. Amen.

William E. M'Lellin's Blessing:—In the name of the Lord, wisdom and intelligence shall be poured out upon him, to enable him to perform the great work that is incumbent upon him; that he may be spared until the Saints are gathered; that he may stand before kings and rulers to bear testimony, and be upheld by holy angels; and the nations of the earth shall acknowledge that God has sent him; he shall have power to overcome his enemies; and his life shall be spared in the midst of pestilence and destruction, and in the midst of his enemies. He shall be a prince and savior to God's people. The tempter shall not overcome him, nor his enemies prevail against him; the heavens shall be opened unto him, as unto men in days of old. He shall be mighty in the hands of God, and shall convince thousands that God has sent him; and his days may be prolonged until the coming of the Son of Man. He shall be wafted as on eagles' wings, from country to country, and from people to people; and be able to do wonders in the midst of this generation. Even so. Amen.

John F. Boynton's Blessing:—Thou hast prevailed and thou shalt prevail, and thou shalt declare the Gospel unto many nations. Thou shalt be made mighty before God; and although thou shalt be cast out from the face of men, yet thou shalt have power to prevail. Thou shalt lead the elect triumphantly to the places of refuge; thou shalt be like the brethren who have been blessed before thee. Thou shalt stand in that day of calamity when the wicked shall be consumed, and present unto the Father, spotless, the fruits of thy labor. Thou shalt overcome all the evils that are in the world; thou shalt have wisdom to put to silence all the wisdom of the wise; and thou shalt see the face of thy Redeemer in the flesh. These blessings are pronounced and sealed upon thee. Even so. Amen.

William Smith's Blessing:—We pray that he may be purified in heart; that he may have communion with God; that he may be equal with his brethren in holding the keys of this ministry; that he may be kept and be instrumental in leading Israel forth, that he may be delivered from the hands of those who seek to destroy him; that he may be enabled to bear testimony to the nations that Jesus lives; that he may stand in the midst of pestilence and destruction. He shall be mighty in the hands of God, in bringing about the restoration of Israel. The nations shall rejoice at the greatness of the gifts which God has bestowed upon him: that his tongue shall be loosed; he shall have power to do great things in the name of Jesus. He shall be preserved and remain on the earth, until Christ shall come to take vengeance on the wicked. Adjourned.

Kirtland, February 21st, 1835: Pursuant to adjournment, a meeting of the Church was held, and after prayer by President David Whitmer, and a short address by President Oliver Cowdery to the congregation, Elder Parley P. Pratt was called to the stand, and ordained one of the Twelve, by President Joseph Smith, Jun., David Whitmer, and Oliver Cowdery. O Lord, smile from heaven upon this thy servant; forgive his sins, sanctify his heart, and prepare him to receive the blessing. Increase his love for Thee and for Thy cause; increase his intelligence; communicate to him all that wisdom, that prudence, and that understanding, which he needs as a minister of righteousness and to magnify

the Apostleship whereunto he is called.   May a double portion of that
Spirit which was communicated to the disciples of our Lord and Savior
to lead them unto all truth, rest down upon him, and go with him where
he goes, that nothing shall prevail against him, that he may be delivered
from prisons, from the power of his enemies, and from the adversary of
all righteousness.   May he be able to mount up on wings as an eagle,
to run and not be weary, to walk and not faint; may he have great wisdom and intelligence, and be able to lead thine elect through this thorny
maze.   Let sickness and death have no power over him; let him be
equal with his brethren in bringing many sons and daughters to glory,
and many nations to a knowledge of the truth.   Great blessings shall
rest upon thee; thy faith shall increase; thou shalt have great power to
prevail.   The vail of the heavens shall be rolled up; thou shalt be permitted to gaze within it, and receive instructions from on high.   No arm
that is formed and lifted against thee shall prosper; no power shall prevail; for thou shalt have power with God, and shalt proclaim His Gospel.
Thou wilt be afflicted, but thou shalt be delivered, and conquer all thy
foes.   Thine office shall never be taken from thee; thou shalt be called
great; angels shall carry thee from place to place.   Thy sins are forgiven, and thy name written in the Lamb's Book of Life.   Even so.
Amen.

Apostolic Charge given by Oliver Cowdery to Parley P. Pratt:

I am aware, dear Brother, that the mind naturally claims something new; but the same thing rehearsed frequently profits us.   You
will have the same difficulties to encounter in fulfilling this ministry,
that the ancient Apostle had.   You have enlisted in a cause that
requires your whole attention; you ought, therefore, to count
the cost; and to become a polished shaft, you must be sensible,
requires the labor of years; and your station requires a perfect
polish.   It is required of you not merely to travel a few miles
in the country, but in distant countries: you must endure much labor,
much toil, and many privations, to become perfectly polished.   Your
calling is not like that of the husbandman, to cultivate a stinted portion
of the planet on which we dwell, and when heaven has given the former
and the latter rain, and mellow autumn ripened his fruit, gathers it in,
and congratulates himself for a season in the intermission of his toils,
while he anticipates his winter evenings of relaxation and fire-side enjoyments.   But, dear Brother, it is far otherwise with you.   Your labor
must be incessant, and your toil great; you must go forth and labor
till the great work is done.   It will require a series of years to accomplish it; but you will have this pleasing consolation, that your heavenly
Father requires it; the field is His; the work is His; and He will not

only cheer you, animate you, and buoy you up in your pilgrimage, in your arduous toils; but when your work is done, and your labor over, He will take you unto Himself. But before this consummation of your felicity, bring your mind to bear upon what will be imperiously required of you to accomplish, viz., the great work that lies before you. Count well the cost. You have read of the persecutions and trials of ancient days. Has not bitter experience taught you that they are the same now? You will be dragged before the authorities for the religion you profess; and it were better not to set out, than to start and look back, or shrink when dangers thicken around you, or appalling death stares you in the face. I have spoken these things, dear brother, because I have seen them in visions. There are strong dungeons and gloomy prisons for you. These should not appal you. You must be called a good or a bad man. The ancients passed through the same experience. They had this testimony—that they had seen the Savior after He rose from the dead. You must bear the same testimony; or your mission, your labor, your toil, will be in vain. You must bear the same testimony, that there is but one God, one Mediator; he that hath seen Him, will know Him, and testify of Him. Beware of pride; beware of evil; shun the very appearance of it; for the time is coming when, if you do not give heed to these things, you will have a fall. Among your many afflictions, vou will have many blessings also; but you must pass through many afflictions, in order to receive the glory that is in reserve for you. You will meet thousands, who, when they first see you, will know nothing about salvation by Jesus Christ; you shall see a nation born in a day. A great work lies before you, and the time is near when you must bid farewell to your native land, cross the mighty deep, and sound the tocsin of alarm to other nations, kindreds, tongues, and people. Remember that all your hopes of deliverance from danger and from death, will rest upon your faithfulness to God; in His cause, you must necessarily serve Him with a perfect heart and a willing mind. Avoid strife and vain glory; think not yourself better than your brethren, but pray for them, as well as for yourself; and if you are faithful, great will be yoar blessings; but if you are not, your stewardship will be taken from you, and another appointed in your stead.

Elder Pratt gave his hand to President Oliver Cowdery, and said he had received ordination, and should fulfill the ministry according to the grace given him; to which the President replied, Go forth, and angels shall bear thee up; and thou shalt come forth at the last day, bringing many with thee.

Thomas B. Marsh and Orson Pratt were absent on a mission.

Elder Marsh returned to Kirtland on the 25th of April, and Elder Orson Pratt on the 26th, and received their ordinations and blessings, which are recorded in this place, in connection with the ordinations and blessings of their brethren.*

Thomas B. Marsh's Blessing by President Oliver Cowdery.—Dear Brother—You are to be a minister of righteousness, and to this ministry and apostleship you are now to be ordained; and may all temporal and spiritual blessings attend you. Your sins are forgiven you, and you are to go forth and preach the everlasting Gospel. You shall travel from kingdom to kingdom and from nation to nation. Angels shall bear thee up, and thou shalt be instrumental in bringing thousands of the redeemed of the Lord to Zion. Sealed by President David Whitmer. Even so. Amen.

Orson Pratt's Blessing.—Dear Brother—You are chosen and set apart, to be ordained to this apostleship and this ministry; you shall go forth and preach the Gospel, and do a mighty work. You shall be sustained; the Holy Spirit shall enlighten thy mind; thou shalt travel from nation to nation; the Lord God shall preserve thee, and return thee safe, with songs of everlasting joy upon thy head. Confirmed by President David Whitmer.

General Charge to the Twelve.

The following general charge was given to the Twelve by President Oliver Cowdery:—Dear Brethren—Previous to delivering the charge, I shall read a part of a revelation. It is known to you, that previous to the organization of this Church in 1830, the Lord gave revelations, or the Church could not have been organized. The people of this Church were weak in faith compared with the ancients. Those who embarked in this cause were desirous to know how the work was to be conducted.

* According to Heber C. Kimball's Journal, Orson Pratt's ordination took place on the 5th of April, 1835, under the following circumstances: "Sunday morning, April 5, 1835.—The Twelve had not all as yet been together, for the last three mentioned [Orson Pratt, Thomas B. Marsh and Parley P. Pratt] were not present at the time of choosing, and as the time drew near that we should travel to the east, we appointed this day to bear our testimony unto our brethren and friends. We were all assembled together, with the exception of Brother Orson Pratt, who had not yet been with us. At this time, while we were praying, and wishing for his arrival, while opening the meeting, he entered the house. We rejoiced at his presence, and thanked the Lord for it. He was then ordained and we proceeded to speak according to our ages, the eldest speaking first. This day Brother Thomas B. Marsh, Brigham Young, David W. Patten, and myself spake." (Times and Seasons, vol. vi, p. 869.) The incident is given as Elder Kimball relates it because of its interest, but he is in error as to the date of the occurrence, since Elder Pratt himself, as well as the Prophet, gives the date of the former's ordination 26th of April, 1835. Elder Pratt also makes this entry in his journal: "April 24—Took the stage, and arrived in Kirtland on the 26th, about ten o'clock in the forenoon; walked into the meeting and learned that they had been prophesying that I would arrive there, so as to attend that meeting, although not one of them knew where I was. I was much rejoiced at meeting with the Saints."

They read many things in the Book of Mormon concerning their duty, and the way the great work ought to be done; but the minds of men are so constructed that they will not believe, without a testimony of seeing or hearing. The Lord gave us a revelation that, in process of time, there should be twelve men chosen to preach His Gospel to Jew and Gentile. Our minds have been on a constant stretch, to find who these twelve were; when the time should come we could not tell; but we sought the Lord by fasting and prayer to have our lives prolonged to see this day, to see you, and to take a retrospect of the difficulties through which we have passed; but having seen the day, it becomes my duty to deliver to you a charge; and first, a few remarks respecting your ministry. You have many revelations put into your hands—revelations to make you acquainted with the nature of your mission; you will have difficulties by reason of your visiting all the nations of the world. You will need wisdom in a tenfold proportion to what you have ever had; you will have to combat all the prejudices of all nations.

He then read the revelation,* and said: Have you desired this ministry with all your hearts? If you have desired it you are called of God, not of man, to go into the world.

He then read again, from the revelation, what the Lord said unto the Twelve. Brethren, you have had your duty presented in this revelation. You have been ordained to this holy Priesthood, you have received it from those who have the power and authority from an angel; you are to preach the Gospel to every nation. Should you in the least degree come short of your duty, great will be your condemnation; for the greater the calling the greater the transgression. I therefore warn you to cultivate great humility; for I know the pride of the human heart. Beware, lest the flatterers of the world lift you up; beware, lest your affections be captivated by worldly objects. Let your ministry be first. Remember, the souls of men are committed to your charge; and if you mind your calling, you shall always prosper.

You have been indebted to other men, in the first instance, for evidence; on that you have acted; but it is necessary that you receive a testimony from heaven for yourselves; so that you can bear testimony to the truth of the Book of Mormon, and that you have seen the face of God. That is more than the testimony of an angel. When the proper time arrives, you shall be able to bear this testimony to the world. When you bear testimony that you have seen God, this testimony God will never suffer to fall, but will bear you out; although many will not give heed, yet others will. You will therefore see the necessity of getting this testimony from heaven.

Never cease striving until you have seen God face to face. Strengthen your faith; cast off your doubts, your sins, and all your unbelief; and

* Doctrine and Covenants, sec. xviii.

nothing can prevent you from coming to God. Your ordination is not full and complete till God has laid His hand upon you. We require as much to qualify us as did those who have gone before us; God is the same. If the Savior in former days laid His hands upon His disciples, why not in latter days?

With regard to superiority, I must make a few remarks. The ancient apostles sought to be great; but lest the seeds of discord be sown in this matter; understand particularly the voice of the Spirit on this occasion. God does not love you better or more than others. You are to contend for the faith once delivered to the saints. Jacob, you know, wrestled till he had obtained. It was by fervent prayer and diligent search that you have obtained the testimony you are now able to bear. You are as one; you are equal in bearing the keys of the Kingdom to all nations. You are called to preach the Gospel of the Son of God to the nations of the earth; it is the will of your heavenly Father, that you proclaim His Gospel to the ends of the earth and the islands of the sea.

Be zealous to save souls. The soul of one man is as precious as the soul of another. You are to bear this message to those who consider themselves wise; and such may persecute you—they may seek your life. The adversary has always sought the life of the servants of God; you are therefore to be prepared at all times to make a sacrifice of your lives, should God require them in the advancement and building up of His cause. Murmur not at God. Be always prayerful; be always watchful. You will bear with me while I relieve the feelings of my heart. We shall not see another day like this; the time has fully come—the voice of the Spirit has come—to set these men apart.

You will see the time when you will desire to see such a day as this, and you will not see it. Every heart wishes you peace and proserity, but the scene with you will inevitably change. Let no man take your bishopric, and beware that you lose not your crowns. It will require your whole souls, it will require courage like Enoch's.

The time is near when you will be in the midst of congregations who will gnash their teeth upon you. The Gospel must roll forth, and it will until it fills the whole earth. Did I say congregations would gnash their teeth at you? Yea, I say, nations will oppose you—you will be considered the worst of men. Be not discouraged at this. When God pours out His Spirit, the enemy will rage; but God. remember, is on your right hand, and on your left. A man, though he be considered the worst, has joy, who is conscious that he pleases God.

The lives of those who proclaim the true Gospel will be in danger; this has been the case ever since the days of righteous Abel. The same opposition has been manifest whenever man came forward to publish the Gospel. The time is coming when you will be considered the worst of men by many, and by some the best. The time is coming when you will be perfectly familiar with the things of God. This testimony will make those who do not believe your testimony, seek your lives; but there are whole nations who will receive your testimony. They will call you good men. Be not lifted up when ye are called good men. Remember you are young men, and ye shall be spared. I include the other three. Bear them in mind in your prayers—carry their cases to the throne of grace; although the, are not present, yet you and they are equal. This appointment is calculated to create for you an affection for each other, stronger than death. You will travel to other nations; bear each other in mind. If one or more be cast into prisons, let the others pray for them, and deliver them by their prayers. Your lives shall be in great jeopardy; but the promise of God is, that you shall be delivered.

Remember, you are not to go to other nations till you receive your endowments. Tarry at Kirtland until you are endowed with power from on high. You need a fountain of wisdom, knowledge and intelligence such as you never had. Relative to the endowment, I make a remark or two, that there may be no mistake. The world cannot receive the things of God. He can endow you without worldly pomp or great parade. He can give you that wisdom, that intelligence, and that power, which characterized the ancient saints, and now characterizes the inhabitants of the upper world.

The greatness of your commission consists in this: you are to hold the keys of this ministry; you are to go to the nations afar off—nations that sit in darkness. The day is coming when the work of God must be done. Israel shall be gathered: the seed of Jacob shall be gathered from their long dispersion. There will be a feast to Israel, the elect of God. It is a sorrowful tale, but the Gospel must be preached, and God's ministers rejected: but where can Israel be found and receive your testimony, and not rejoice? Nowhere! The prophecies are full of great things that are to take place in the last days. After the elect are gathered out, destructions shall come on the inhabitants of the earth; all nations shall feel the wrath of God, after they have been warned by the Saints of the Most High. If you will not warn them, others will, and you will lose your crowns.

You must prepare your minds to bid a long farewell to Kirtland, even till the great day come. You will see what you never expected to see; you will need the mind of Enoch or Elijah, and the faith of the brother of Jared; you must be prepared to walk by faith, however appalling the prospect to human view; you, and each of you, should feel the force of the imperious mandate, Son, go labor in my vineyard, and cheerfully receive what comes; but in the end you will stand while others will fall. You have read in the revelation concerning ordination: Beware how you ordain, for all nations are not like this nation; they will willingly receive the ordinances at your hands to put you out of the way. There will be times when nothing but the angels of God can deliver you out of their hands.

We appeal to your intelligence, we appeal to your understanding, that we have so far discharged our duty to you. We consider it one of the greatest condescensions of our heavenly Father, in pointing you out to us; you will be stewards over this ministry; you have a work to do that no other men can do; you must proclaim the Gospel in its simplicity and purity; and we commend you to God and the word of His grace. You have our best wishes, you have our most fervent prayers, that you may be able to bear this testimony, that you have seen the face of God. Therefore call upon Him in faith in mighty prayer till you prevail, for it is your duty and your privilege to bear such testimony for yourselves. We now exhort you to be faithful to fulfill your calling; there must be no lack here; you must fulfill in all things; and permit us to repeat, all nations have a claim on you; you are bound together as the Three Witnesses were; notwithstanding you can part and meet, and meet and part again, till your heads are silvered over with age.

He then took them separately by the hand, and said, "Do you with full purpose of heart take part in this ministry, to proclaim the Gospel with all diligence, with these your brethren, according to the tenor and intent of the charge you have received?" Each of them answered in the affirmative.*

Important Items of Instructions to the Twelve.

KIRTLAND, February 27.

This evening, nine of the Twelve, viz., Lyman Johnson, Brigham Young, Heber C. Kimball, Orson Hyde, David W. Patten, Luke Johnson, William E. M'Lellin, John F. Boynton, and William Smith, assembled at the house of President Joseph Smith, Jun., who was present, with Frederick G. Williams, Sidney Rigdon, Bishop Whitney, and three Elders. Parley P. Pratt had gone to New Partage, and Orson Pratt and Thomas B. Marsh had not yet arrived to receive their ordination.

After prayer by President Joseph Smith, Jun., he said, if we heard patiently, he could lay before the council an item which would be of importance. He had for himself, learned a fact by experience, which, on recollection, always gave him deep sorrow. It is a fact, if I now had in my possession, every decision which had been had upon impor-

---

* Elder Parley P. Pratt, in his autobiography (page 127) refers to this question put to each of the Twelve Apostles by Elder Cowdery as the "Oath and Covenant of the Apostleship."

tant items of doctrine and duties since the commencement of this work, I would not part with them for any sum of money; but we have neglected to take minutes of such things, thinking, perhaps, that they would never benefit us afterwards; which, if we had them now, would decide almost every point of doctrine which might be agitated. But this has been neglected, and now we cannot bear record to the Church and to the world, of the great and glorious manifestations which have been made to us with that degree of power and authority we otherwise could, if we now had these things to publish abroad.

Since the Twelve are now chosen, I wish to tell them a course which they may pursue, and be benefited thereafter, in a point of light of which they are not now aware. If they will, every time they assemble, appoint a person to preside over them during the meeting, and one or more to keep a record of their proceedings, and on the decision of every question or item, be it what it may, let such decision be written, and such decision will forever remain upon record, and appear an item of covenant or doctrine. An item thus decided may appear, at the time, of little or no worth, but should it be published, and one of you lay hands on it after, you will find it of infinite worth, not only to your brethren, but it will be a feast to your own souls.

Here is another important item. If you assemble from time to time, and proceed to discuss important questions, and pass decisions upon the same, and fail to note them down, by and by you will be driven to straits from which you will not be able to extricate yourselves, because you may be in a situation not to bring your faith to bear with sufficient perfection or power to obtain the desired information; or, perhaps, for neglecting to write these things when God had revealed them, not esteeming them of sufficient worth, the Spirit may withdraw and God may be angry; and there is, or was, a vast knowledge, of infinite importance, which is now lost. What was the cause of this? It came in consequence of slothfulness, or a neglect to appoint a man to occupy a few moments in writing all these decisions.

Here let me prophesy. The time will come, when, if you neglect to do this thing, you will fall by the hands of unrighteous men. Were you to be brought before the authorities, and be accused of any crime or misdemeanor, and be as innocent as the angels of God, unless you can prove yourselves to have been somewhere else, your enemies will prevail against you; but if you can bring twelve men to testify that you were in a certain place, at that time, you will escape their hand. Now, if you will be careful to keep minutes of these things, as I have said, it will be one of the most important records ever seen; for all such decisions will ever after remain as items of doctrine and covenants.

The council then expressed their approbation concerning the foregoing remarks of President Smith, and appointed Orson Hyde and William E. M'Lellin clerks of the meeting.

President Smith proposed the following question: What importance is there attached to the calling of these Twelve Apostles, different from the other callings or officers of the Church?

After the question was discussed by Councilors Patten, Young, Smith, and M'Lellin, President Joseph Smith, Jun., gave the following decision:

They are the Twelve Apostles, who are called to the office of the Traveling High Council, who are to preside over the churches of the Saints, among the Gentiles, where there is a presidency established; and they are to travel and preach among the Gentiles, until the Lord shall command them to go to the Jews. They are to hold the keys of this ministry, to unlock the door of the Kingdom of heaven unto all nations, and to preach the Gospel to every creature. This is the power, authority, and virtue of their apostleship.

OLIVER COWDERY, Clerk.

Report of the Kirtland School.

KIRTLAND, OHIO, February 27, 1835.

Having been requested by the trustees of the "Kirtland School" to give a sketch of the number of students who have attended the institution, and of their progress in the different sciences, I cheerfully comply with the request, having been an instructor therein from its commencement in December last.

The school has been conducted under the immediate care and inspection of Joseph Smith, Jun., Frederick G. Williams, Sidney Rigdon, and Oliver Cowdery, trustees. When the school first commenced, we received into it both large and small, but in about three weeks the classes became so large and the house so crowded, that it was thought advisable to dismiss all the small students, and continue those only who wished to study penmanship, arithmetic, English grammar, and geography. Before we dismissed the small pupils, there were in all about one hundred and thirty who attended; since that time there have been upon an average about one hundred; the most of whom have received lectures upon English grammar; and for the last four weeks about seventy have been studying geography one-half the day, and grammar and writing the other part. Burdick's Arithmetic, Kirkham's Grammar, and Olney's Geography have been used, and Noah Webster's Dictionary as standard. Since the year 1827, I have taught school in five different states, and visited many schools in which I was not engaged as teacher; in none, I can say, with certainty, I have seen students make more rapid progress than in this.

WILLIAM E. M'LELLIN.

CHAPTER XIII.

THE ORGANIZATION OF THE SEVENTIES—BLESSING OF THE FAITHFUL ELDERS AND SAINTS.

ON the 28th of February, the Church in council assembled, commenced selecting certain individuals to be Seventies,* from the number of those who went up to Zion with me in the camp; and the following are the names of those who were ordained

The Calling of Seventies.

---

* The organization of quorums of Seventy in the Church was regarded as a very strange thing in modern times, but that such an organization had existed in the Church of God, both in the days of Moses and also in the days of Messiah, is evident from the scriptures. The Lord said to Moses: "Come up unto the Lord, thou, and Aaron, Nadab, and Abihu, and seventy of the elders of Israel; and worship ye afar off. * * * Then went up Moses, and Aaron, Nadab, and Abihu, and seventy of the elders of Israel. * * * And upon the nobles of the children of Israel He laid not His hand: also they saw God, and did eat and drink" (Exodus xxiv: 1, 9, 11). And again, "And the Lord said unto Moses, Gather unto me seventy men of the elders of Israel, whom thou knowest to be the elders of the people, and officers over them; and bring them unto the tabernacle of the congregation, that they may stand there with thee. And I will come down and talk with thee there: and I will take of the spirit which is upon thee, and will put it upon them; and they shall bear the burden of the people with thee, that thou bear it not thyself alone.   * * * And Moses went out, and told the people the words of the Lord, and gathered the seventy men of the elders of the people, and set them round about the tabernacle. And the Lord came down in a cloud, and spake unto him, and took of the Spirit that was upon him, and gave it unto the seventy elders: and it came to pass, that, when the Spirit rested upon them, they prophesied, and did not cease" (Numbers xi: 16, 17, 24, 25).

It is not clear from the Old Testament just what the functions of the Seventy were in the Hebrew Priesthood, but they certainly were endowed with prophetic powers, and it is quite probable that the Sanhedrim (consisting of seventy-one members, inclusive of the president,) of later Jewish times had some relation to this earlier council of Seventy.

The organization of the Seventy by the Savior is alluded to in the tenth chapter

and blessed at that time, to begin the organization of the first quorum of Seventies, according to the visions* and revelations which I have received. The Seventies are to constitute traveling quorums, to go into all the earth, whithersoever the Twelve Apostles shall call them.†

of Luke as follows: "After these things the Lord appointed other seventy also, [from this it appears that quorums of seventy had been appointed previous to this] and sent them two and two before His face into every city and place,whither He Himself would come. Therefore said He unto them, The harvest truly is great, but the laborers are few: pray ye therefore the Lord of the harvest, that He would sent forth laborers into His harvest. Go your way: behold, I send you forth as lambs among wolves. Carry neither purse nor scrip, nor shoes: and salute no man by the way. And into whatsoever house ye enter, first say, Peace be to this house. And if the Son of peace be there, your peace shall rest upon it: if not, it shall turn to you again. And in the same house remain, eating and drinking such things as they give: for the laborer is worthy of his hire. Go not from house to house." That is, while these men were sent forth without purse and scrip, it was evidently not the intention of the Lord that they should beg from door to door. Continuing His instructions, the Master said: "And into whatsoever city ye enter, and they receive you, eat such things as are set before you: and heal the sick that are therein, and say unto them, The kingdom of God is come nigh unto you. But into whatsoever city ye enter,and they receive you not,go your ways out into the streets of the same, and say, Even the very dust of your city, which cleaveth on us, we do wipe off against you. notwithstanding be ye sure of this, that the kingdom of God is come nigh unto you But I say unto you, that it shall be more tolerable in that day for Sodom,than for that city. * * He that heareth you heareth me; and he that despiseth you despiseth me and he that despiseth me despiseth Him that sent me." The Seventy, it appears went forth under these instructions and were successful, for Luke continues: "And the seventy returned again with joy, saying, Lord, even the devils are subject unto us through Thy name." After this very plain allusion to this order of the Priesthood called the Seventy, these instructions, and the definitions given of their duties and callings, there can be no doubt as to their constituting an important factor in the Christian Church organization. The absence of such quorums of Priesthood in modern church establishments is but one among many other evidences that the Church of Christ had ceased from among men.

* See page 182 (note).

† The quorums of Seventy, in other words—in connection with the Twelve Apostles, under whose direction they labor—constitute the foreign ministry of the Church; and when the kind of labor they are expected to perform is taken into account, it will be found that their organization is admirably adopted for their work— the means are adequate to the end proposed. In all other quorums of the high Priesthood, excepting the Twelve, the presidency consists of a president and two counselors, but the presidency of the quorum of Seventy consists of seven presidents, equal in authority. For the sake of order, however, precedence is recognized in seniority of ordination; that is, the senior president by ordination—not of age— presides in the council, and over the quorum; and in the event of his absence, then the next senior president by ordination has the right of initiative and presides, and so on down the line of presidents. The order established in the Church for the work of the foreign ministry is for Elders to travel two and two. This doubtless for the reason that the Lord would establish His word by the mouths of two wit-

*Names of the Presidents and Members of the First Quorum of Seventies, Ordained Under the Hand of the Prophet Joseph Smith, with his two Counselors, Sidney Rigdon and Oliver Cowdery.**

PRESIDENTS.

Hazen Aldrich,
Joseph Young,
Levi W. Hancock,
Leonard Rich,
Zebedee Coltrin,
Lyman Sherman

Sylvester Smith.

MEMBERS.

Elias Hutchings,
Cyrus Smalling,
Levi Gifford,
Stephen Winchester,
Roger Orton,
Peter Buchannan,
John D. Parker,
David Elliot,
Samuel Brown,
Salmon Warner,
Jacob Chapman,
Charles Kelly,
Edmund Fisher,
Warren Parrish,
Joseph Hancock,
Alden Burdick,
Hiram Winters,

Harpin Riggs,
Edson Barney,
Joseph B. Noble,
Henry Benner,
David Evans,
Nathan B. Baldwin,
Burr Riggs,
Lewis Robbins,
Alexander Whitesides,
George W. Brooks,
Michael Griffith,
Royal Barney.
Libbeus T. Coons,
Willard Snow,
Jesse D. Harmon,
Heman T. Hyde,
Lorenzo D. Barnes.

nesses at least, to say nothing of the pleasure that would be derived from the companionship subsisting between two Elders while traveling among strangers, and even among enemies. A quorum of Seventy, if sent out into the world as a body, is capable of realizing all the advantages conceivable from organization. It can be broken up into just seven groups of ten members; with each group would be a president; these groups can be sub-divided into five pairs, who could scatter out into various neighborhoods, occasionally meet in conference with the group of ten to which the respective pairs belonged, and at greater intervals, the several groups could be called together for quorum conference. Thus a quorum of Seventy can be a veritable flying column, making proclamation of the Gospel, the like of which is to be found nowhere outside the Church of Christ.

* Instead of giving the forty names that here follow the statement of the Prophet in his history, I give the entire list of names that constituted the first quorum of Seventy, as written by the late President Joseph Young, in his "History of the Organization of the Seventies." All the brethren given in this list were not ordained on this 28th day of February, 1835, but all who were ordained on that date, of course, are included in this list. Of this organization of the quorum of Seventy, the statement of Elder Joseph Young, who became the senior president of the first council, has already been given at page 181.

Hiram Blackman,
William D. Pratt,
Zera S. Cole,
Jesse Huntsman,
Solomon Angel,
Henry Herriman,
Israel Barlow,
Wilkins Jenkins Salisbury
Nelson Higgins,
Harry Brown,
Jezeniah B. Smith,
Lorenzo Booth,
Alexander Badlam,
Zerubbabel Snow,

Hiram Stratton,
Moses Martin,
Lyman Smith,
Harvey Stanley,
Almon W. Babbitt,
William F. Cahoon,
Darwin Richardson,
Milo Andrus,
True Glidden,
Henry Shibley,
Harrison Burgess,
Jedediah M. Grant,
Daniel Stephens,
Amasa M. Lyman,

George A. Smith.

The council adjourned to the day following, March 1st, when, after attending the funeral of Seth Johnson, several who had recently been baptized, were confirmed, and the sacrament was administered to the Church. Previous to the administration, I spoke of the propriety of this institution in the Church, and urged the importance of doing it with acceptance before the Lord, and asked, How long do you suppose a man may partake of this ordinance unworthily, and the Lord not withdraw His Spirit from him? How long will he thus trifle with sacred things, and the Lord not give him over to the buffetings of Satan until the day of redemption! The Church should know if they are unworthy from time to time to partake, lest the servants of God be forbidden to administer it. Therefore our hearts ought to be humble, and we to repent of our sins, and put away evil from among us.

The Prophet's Remarks on the Sacrament.

After sacrament the council continued the ordination and blessing of those previously called; also John Murdock and S. W. Denton were ordained and blessed; Benjamin Winchester, Hyrum Smith, and Frederick G. Williams were blessed; and Joseph Young and Sylvester Smith were ordained presidents of Seventies.

More Ordinations.

*The Blessing of those who assisted in Building the House of the Lord
at Kirtland.*

March 7.—This day a meeting of the Church of Latter-day Saints
was called for the purpose of blessing, in the name of the Lord, those
who have heretofore assisted in building, by their labor and other means,
the House of the Lord in this place.

The morning was occupied by President Joseph Smith, Jun., in
teaching the Church the propriety and necessity of purifying itself.
In the afternoon, the names of those who had assisted to build the
house were taken, and further instructions received from President
Smith. He said that those who had distinguished themselves thus
far by consecrating to the upbuilding of the House of the Lord, as
well as laboring thereon, were to be remembered; that those who
build it should own it, and have the control of it.

After further remarks, those who performed the labor on the building voted unanimously that they would continue to labor thereon, till
the house should be completed.

President Sidney Rigdon was appointed to lay on hands and bestow
blessings in the name of the Lord.

The Presidents were blessed; and Reynolds Cahoon, Hyrum Smith,
and Jared Carter, the building committee, though the last two were not
present, yet their rights in the house were preserved.

The following are the names of those who were blessed in consequence of their labor on the house of the Lord in Kirtland, and those
who consecrated to its upbuilding:

Sidney Rigdon,	Maleum C. Davis,
Joseph Smith, Jun.,	Jaman Aldrich,
F. G. Williams,	John Young, Sen.,
Joseph Smith, Sen.,	Ezra Strong,
Oliver Cowdery,	Joel McWithy,
Newel K. Whitney,	Matthew Foy,
Reynolds Cahoon,	James Randall,
Hyrum Smith	John P. Greene,
Jared Carter,	Aaron E. Lyon,
Jacob Bump,	Thomas Burdick,
Artemus Millet,	Truman Wait,
Alpheus Cutler,	Edmund Bosley,
Asa Lyman,	William Bosley,
Josiah Butterfield,	William Perry,
Noah Packard,	Don Carlos Smith,
James Putnam,	Shadrach Roundy,
Isaac Hill,	Joel Johnson,

Edmund Durfee, Sen.,
Edmund Durfee, Jun.,
Gideon Ormsby,
Albert Miner,
Ira Ames,
Salmon Gee,
Peter Shirts,
Isaac Hubbard,
Horace Burgess,
Dexter Stillman,
Amos F. Herrick,
Mayhew Hillman,
William Carter,
William Burgess,
Giles Cook,
Almon Sherman,
Warren Smith,
Moses Bailey,
Sebe Ives,
Andrew H. Aldrich,
Ebenezar Jennings,
Oliver Granger,
Orson Johnson,
James Lake,
William Redfield,
Cyrus Lake,
Harvey Smith,
Isaac Cleveland,
William Barker,
Samuel S. Brannan,
John Wheeler,
Henry Baker,
William Fisk,
Henry Wilcox,
George Gee,
Lorenzo D. Young,
David Clough,
James Durfee,
Joseph Coe,
Thomas Gates,
Loren Babbitt,
Blake Baldwin,

Oliver Higley,
Evan M. Greene,
Levi Osgood,
Alpheus Harmon,
Joseph C. Kingsbury,
Ira Bond,
Z. H. Brewster,
Samuel Thomson,
John Ormsby,
Luman Carter,
John Smith,
Samuel H. Smith,
Thomas Fisher,
Starry Fisk,
Amos R. Orton,
Gad Yale,
John Johnson,
John Tanner,
Henry G. Sherwood,
Sidney Tanner,
Joseph Tippits,
Robert Quigley,
Erastus Babbitt,
Samuel Canfield,
Phineas H. Young,
Samuel Rolfe,
Calvin W. Stoddard,
Josiah Fuller,
Erastus Rudd,
Isaac G. Bishop,
Roswell Murray,
Benjamin Wells,
Nehemiah Harman,
Oliver Wetherby,
Thomas Hancock,
Josuah Grant,
William Draper,
Ransom Van Leuven,
Tunis Rappellee,
John Reed,
Samuel Wilcox,
Benjamin Johnson,

Joseph B. Bosworth.

The blessings and ordinations of particular individuals of the foregoing were as follows:—Reynolds Cahoon, Jacob Bump, and Artemus
Millet, were blessed with the blessings of heaven and a right in the
house of the Lord in Kirtland, agreeable to the labor they had performed thereon, and the means they had contributed.

Alpheus Cutler, Asa Lyman, Josiah Butterfield, Noah Packard,
Jonas Putnam, and Isaac Hill received the same blessing. The bless-
ing referred to was according to each man's labor or donation, and
in addition, Elder Packard was promised wisdom and ability to pro-
claim the Gospel. Edmund Durfee, Sen., Edmund Durfee, Jun., and
Gideon Ormsby received the same blessing, and Edmund Durfee, Jun.,
was ordained an Elder. Albert Miner, Ira Ames, Salmon Gee, Peter
Shirts, Isaac Hubbard, and Horace Burgess were blessed, and Peter
Shirts and Horace Burgess were ordained Elders. Dexter Stillman,
Amos F. Herrick, and Matthew Hillman were blessed. William Burgess, Jaman Aldrich, and John Young, Sen., were blessed. Giles
Cook, Jun., and M. C. Davis were blessed and ordained Elders. Wm.
Carter, who was blind, was promised a restoration of sight, if faithful. Ezra Strong, Joel McWithy, Matthew Foy, James Randall, and
Aaron C. Lyon were blessed. John P. Greene was ordained a missionary to the Lamanites, after others have unlocked the door, with
a promise of gathering many to Zion, and of returning with great
joy at the end of his mission, to enjoy the blessings of his family.
Thomas Burdick, Truman Wait and Edmund Bosley were blessed,
and Elder Bosley was told that God had a work for him, viz.: to
go and preach the Gospel to the sectarian priests of this age, to
call after them and hunt them up, wherever he could hear of them,
and preach the Gospel to them whether they will hear or forbear.
William Bosley and William Berry were blessed and ordained Elders.
Don Carlos Smith was blessed with a promise of wisdom to proclaim
the Gospel, and also to write in wisdom. Shadrach Roundy, Joel
Johnson, and Oliver Higbee were blessed.

Adjourned till tomorrow.

March 8th.—Met pursuant to adjournment. Evan M. Greene, Levi
Osgood, Alpheus Harmon, Joseph C. Kingsbury, Ira Bond, Z. H.
Brewster, Samuel Tompkins, John Ormsby, Luman Carter, John
Smith, Samuel H. Smith, Thomas Fisher, Starry Fisk, Amos R. Orton and Almon Sherman were blessed. Amos R. Orton was ordained
an Elder and a missionary to the Lamanites. Andrew H. Aldrich,
Thomas Bailey, Seba Ives, Ebenezer Jennings, Oliver Granger, Orson Johnson, Warren Smith, James Lake, and William Redfield were
blessed, and William Redfield was ordained an Elder. Cyrus Lake,

Harvey Smith, Isaac Cleveland, William Baker, Samuel S. Brannan, John Wheeler, Henry Baker, William Fisk, Henry Wilcox, George W. Gee, David Clough, and Lorenzo D. Young were blessed, and Elder Young was set apart as a missionary to the Lamanites. Jas. Durfee, Jos. Coe, Thos. Gates, Loren Babbitt, Blake Baldwin, and Jos. B. Baldwin were blessed. John Johnson, John Tanner and Gad Yale were blessed; and Gad Yale, being one who went to the relief of the brethren in Missouri, was blessed accordingly. Henry G. Sherwood, Sidney Tanner, Joseph H. Tippits, Robert Quigley, and Erastus Babbitt were blessed, and Samuel Canfield was blessed and ordained an Elder. Phineas H. Young, Samuel Rolfe, and Calvin H. Stoddard were blessed, and Elder Young was ordained a missionary to the Lamanites. Erastus Rudd, Josiah Fuller, Isaac H. Bishop, Roswell Murray, Benjamin Wells, Nehemiah Harman, Thomas Hancock, Oliver Wetherby, Joshua Grant, Jun., William Draper, Jun., Ransom Van Leuven, Tunis Rappellee, John Rudd, and Samuel Wilcox were blessed. Moses Martin, who went to Missouri, was set apart to be one of the Seventies, and blessed and warned as follows: "If thou art not purified, thou wilt not be able to execute thy commission. Thou wilt fall into the snares and into the hands of enemies who will take thy life; thou must begin to make a complete reformation in thyself."

OLIVER COWDERY,
Clerk.

The following belong to the Seventies, but the date of their ordinations is not definitely known: Milo Andrus, Joseph Winchester, Zerubbabel Snow, Heman T. Hyde, Henry Brown, Nelson Higgins, (Hezekiah Fisk was blessed, but was not one of the Seventies,) Henry Beaman, Jesse Huntsman, Royal Barney, Zebedee Coltrin, Henry Herriman, and Lorenzo D. Barnes. James L. Thompson was blessed, but not ordained.

CHAPTER XIV.

THE GREAT REVELATION ON PRIESTHOOD.

Minutes of Meetings of the Twelve.

KIRTLAND, March 12, 1835.—This evening the Twelve assembled, and the Council was opened by President Joseph Smith, Jun., and he proposed we take our first mission through the Eastern States, to the Atlantic Ocean, and hold conferences in the vicinity of the several branches of the Church for the purpose of regulating all things necessary for their welfare.

It was proposed that the Twelve leave Kirtland on the 4th day of May, which was unanimously agreed to.

It was then proposed that during their present mission, Elder Brigham Young should open the door of the Gospel to the remnants of Joseph, who dwell among the Gentiles, which was carried.

It was voted that the Twelve should hold their first conference in Kirtland, May 2nd; in Westfield, New York, May 9th; in Freedom, N.Y., May 22nd; in Lyonstown, N.Y., June 5th; at Pillow Point, June 10th; in West Loboro', Upper Canada, June 29th; in Johnsbury, Vermont, July 17th; in Bradford, Massachusetts, August 7th; in Dover, New Hampshire, September 4th; in Saco, Maine, September 18th; Farmington, Maine, October 2nd.

ORSON HYDE,
WM. E. M'LELLIN, Clerks.

KIRTLAND, March 28th.

This afternoon the Twelve met in council, and had a time of general confession. On reviewing our past course we are satisfied, and feel to confess also, that we have not realized the importance of our calling to that degree that we ought; we have been light-minded and vain, and in many things have done wrong. For all these things we have asked the forgiveness of our heavenly Father; and wherein we have grieved or wounded the feelings of the Presidency, we ask their forgiveness. The time when we are about to separate is near; and when we shall meet again, God only knows; we therefore feel to ask of him whom we have acknowledged to be our Prophet and Seer, that he inquire of God for us, and obtain a revelation, (if consistent) that we may look upon it when we are separated, that our hearts may be comforted. Our worthiness has not inspired us to make this request, but our unworthiness. We have unitedly asked God our heavenly Father to grant unto us through His Seer, a revelation of His mind and will concerning our duty the coming season, even a great revelation, that will enlarge our hearts, comfort us in adversity, and brighten our hopes amidst the powers of darkness.

Orson Hyde,
Wm. E. M'Lellin, Clerks.

To President Joseph Smith, Jun., Kirtland, Ohio.

In compliance with the above request,* I inquired of the Lord, and received for answer the following:

Revelation on Priesthood.†

1. There are in the Church two Priesthoods, namely, the Melchisedek and the Aaronic, including the Levitical Priesthood.

* At this point it may be well to note a singular thing with reference to nearly all the revelations that have been received in this dispensation; they came in response to enquiry, in response to prayer. "Ask and ye shall receive;" "Seek and ye shall find," seems to have been the principle on which the Lord has acted with reference to giving revelations. For instance, the Lord revealed Himself and His Son Jesus Christ to the Prophet Joseph in answer to the latter's earnest prayer to know the truth respecting the various religions; Moroni came three years later in response to the young Prophet's earnest prayer to know his standing before the Lord; nearly all the early revelations to individuals in the Church, to Joseph Smith, Sen., Hyrum Smith, Oliver Cowdery, Joseph Knight. David, Peter, John and Christian Whitmer were given in answer to the enquiry of these men to know their duty in respect of the work of the Lord then coming forth; the revelation on Church Organization and Government (Doc. and Cov. sec. 20), was given in response to Joseph and Oliver's prayers and enquiries concerning those things; so with reference to the revelations given to the Witnesses to the Book of Mormon; and in fact throughout the whole course of the work's development. This great revelation on Priesthood and the relations of the quorums to each other in the Church is also given in response to a most humble petition to the Prophet on the part of the Twelve; and, the Prophet says: *"I inquired of the Lord, and received for answer the following revelation,"* then follows the revelation.

† According to the explanatory note in the Doctrine and Covenants, sec. cvii, the fore part of this revelation, the first fifty-eight verses, was given March 28th, the same day the Twelve ask the Prophet to enquire of the Lord for them, the other items were revealed at sundry times.

2. Why the first is called the Melchisedek Priesthood, is because Melchisedek was such a great High Priest;

3. Before his day it was called *the Holy Priesthood after the Order of the Son of God.*

4. But out of respect or reverence to the name of the Supreme Being, to avoid the too frequent repetition of His name, they, the Church in ancient days, called that Priesthood after Melchisedek, or the Melchisedek Priesthood.

5. All other authorities or offices in the Church are appendages to this Priesthood;

6. But there are two divisions, or grand heads; one is the Melchisedek Priesthood, and the other is the Aaronic or Levitical Priesthood.

7. The office of an Elder comes under the Priesthood of Melchisedek.

8. The Melchisedek Priesthood holds the right of presidency, and has power and authority over all the offices in the Church, in all ages of the world, to administer in spiritual things.

9. The Presidency of the High Priesthood, after the Order of Melchisedek, have a right to officiate in all the offices in the Church.

10. High Priests after the Order of the Melchisedek Priesthood, have a right to officiate in their own standing, under the direction of the Presidency, in administering spiritual things, and also in the office of an Elder, Priest (of the Levitical order), Teacher, Deacon and member.

11. An Elder has a right to officiate in his stead, when the High Priest is not present.

12. The High Priest and Elder are to administer in spiritual things, agreeable to the covenants and commandments of the Church; and they have a right to officiate in all these offices of the Church, when there are no higher authorities present.

13. The second Priesthood is called the Priesthood of Aaron, because it was conferred upon Aaron and his seed, throughout all their generations.

14. Why it is called the lesser Priesthood, is because it is an appendage to the greater, or the Melchisedek Priesthood, and has power in administering outward ordinances.

15. The Bishopric is the Presidency of this Priesthood, and holds the keys or authority of the same.

16. No man has a legal right to this office, to hold the keys of this Priesthood, except he be a literal descendant of Aaron.

17. But as a High Priest of the Melchisedek Priesthood has authority to officiate in all the lesser offices, he may officiate in the office of Bishop, when no literal descendant of Aaron can be found, provided he is called,

and set apart, and ordained unto this power, by the hands of the Presidency of the Melchisedek Priesthood.

18. The power and authority of the higher, or Melchisedek Priesthood, is to hold the keys of all the spiritual blessings of the Church.

19. To have the privilege of receiving the mysteries of the kingdom of heaven, to have the heavens opened unto them, to commune with the general assembly and Church of the first-born, and to enjoy the communion and presence of God the Father, and Jesus, the Mediator of the New Covenant.

20. The power and authority of the lesser, or Aaronic Priesthood, is to hold the keys of the ministering of angels, and to administer in outward ordinances, the letter of the Gospel, the baptism of repentance for the remission of sins, agreeable to the covenants and commandments.

21. Of necessity there are Presidents, or presiding officers, growing out of, or appointed of, or from among those who are ordained to the several offices in these two Priesthoods.

22. Of the Melchisedek Priesthood three presiding High Priests, chosen by the body, appointed and ordained to that office, and upheld by the confidence, faith, and prayer of the Church, form a quorum of the Presidency of the Church.

23. The Twelve traveling councilors are called to be the Twelve Apostles, or especial witnesses of the name of Christ, in all the world, thus differing from other officers in the Church, in the duties of their calling;

24. And they form a quorum equal in authority and power to the three Presidents previously mentioned.

25. The Seventy are also called to preach the Gospel, and to be especial witnesses unto the Gentiles and in all the world; thus differing from other officers in the Church in the duties of their calling;

26. And they form a quorum equal in authority to that of the Twelve especial witnesses or Apostles, just named.

27. And every decision made by either of these quorums, must be by the unanimous voice of the same; that is, every member in each quorum must be agreed to its decisions, in order to make their decisions of the same power or validity one with the other.

28. (A majority may form a quorum when circumstances render it impossible to be otherwise.)

29. Unless this is the case, their decisions are not entitled to the same blessings which the decisions of a quorum of three Presidents were anciently, who were ordained after the order of Melchisedek, and were righteous and holy men.

30. The decisions of these quorums or either of them, are to be made in all righteousness, in holiness and lowliness of heart, meekness

and long-suffering, and in faith, and virtue, and knowledge, temperance, patience, godliness, brotherly kindness, and charity;

31. Because the promise is, if these things abound in them they shall not be unfruitful in the knowledge of the Lord.

32. And in case that any decision of these quorums is made in unrighteousness, it may be brought before a general assembly of the several quorums, which constitute the spiritual authorities of the Church, otherwise there can be no appeal from their decision.

33. The Twelve are a traveling, presiding High Council, to officiate in the name of the Lord, under the direction of the Presidency of the Church, agreeable to the institution of heaven, to build up the Church, and regulate all the affairs of the same, in all nations, first unto the Gentiles, and secondly unto the Jews.

34. The Seventy are to act in the name of the Lord, under the direction of the Twelve, or the Traveling High Council, in building up the Church, and regulating all the affairs of the same in all nations; first unto the Gentiles, and then to the Jews;

35. The Twelve being sent out, holding the keys to open the door by the proclamation of the Gospel of Jesus Christ, and first unto the Gentiles and then unto the Jews.

36. The standing High Councils at the Stakes of Zion form a quorum equal in authority, in the affairs of the Church, in all their decisions, to the quorum of the Presidency, or to the traveling High Council.

37. The High Council in Zion form a quorum equal in authority, in the affairs of the Church, in all their decisions, to the councils of the Twelve at the Stakes of Zion.

38. It is the duty of the traveling High Council, to call upon the Seventy, when they need assistance, to fill the several calls for preaching and administering the Gospel, instead of any others.

39. It is the duty of the Twelve, in all large branches of the Church, to ordain evangelical ministers, as they shall be designated unto them by revelation.

40. The order of this Priesthood was confirmed to be handed down from father to son, and rightly belongs to the literal descendants of the chosen seed, to whom the promises were made.

41. This order was instituted in the days of Adam, and came down by lineage in the following manner:

42. From Adam to Seth, who was ordained by Adam at the age of sixty-nine years, and was blessed by him three years previous to his (Adam's) death, and received the promise of God, by his father, that his posterity should be the chosen of the Lord, and that they should be preserved unto the end of the earth.

43. Because he (Seth) was a perfect man, and his likeness was the express likeness of his father insomuch that he seemed to be like unto his father in all things, and could be distinguished from him only by his age.

44. Enos was ordained at the age of an hundred and thirty-four years and four months, by the hand of Adam.

45. God called upon Cainan in the wilderness, in the fortieth year of his age, and he met Adam in journeying to the place Shedolamak; he was eighty-seven years old when he received his ordination.

46. Mahalaleel was four hundred and ninety-six years and seven days old, when he was ordained by the hand of Adam, who also blessed him.

47. Jared was two hundred years old when he was ordained under the hand of Adam, who also blessed him.

48. Enoch was twenty-five year old when he was ordained under the hand of Adam, and he was sixty-five when Adam blessed him.

49. And he saw the Lord, and he walked with Him, and was before His face continually; and he walked with God three hundred and sixty-five years, making him four hundred and thirty year old when he was translated.

50. Methuselah was one hundred years old when he was ordained under the hand of Adam.

51. Lamech was thirty-two years old when he was ordained under the hand of Seth.

52. Noah was ten years old when he was ordained under the hand of Methuselah.

53. Three years previous to the death of Adam, he called Seth, Enos, Cainan, Mahalaleel, Jared, Enoch, and Methuselah, who were all High Priests, with the residue of his posterity, who were righteous, into the valley of Adam-ondi Ahman, and there bestowed upon them his last blessing.

54. And the Lord appeared unto them, and they rose up and blessed Adam, and called him Michael the Prince, the Archangel.

55. And the Lord administered comfort unto Adam, and said unto him, I have set thee to be at the head; a multitude of nations shall come of thee; and thou art a prince over them for ever.

56. And Adam stood up in the midst of the congregation, and notwithstanding he was bowed down with age, being full of the Holy Ghost, predicted whatsoever should befall his posterity unto the latest generation.

57. These things were all written in the Book of Enoch, and are to be testified of in due time.

58. It is the duty of the Twelve, also, to ordain and set in

order all the other officers of the Church agreeable to the revelation which says:

59. To the Church of Christ in the land of Zion, in addition to the Church laws, respecting Church business.

60. Verily, I say unto you, saith the Lord of Hosts, there must needs be presiding Elders, to preside over those who are of the office of an Elder;

61. And also Priests to preside over those who are of the office of a Priest;

62. And also Teachers to preside over those who are of the office of a Teacher, in like manner; and also the Deacons;

63. Wherefore from Deacon to Teacher, and from Teacher to Priest, and from Priest to Elder, severally as they are appointed, according to the covenants and commandments of the Church;

64. Then comes the High Priesthood, which is the greatest of all.

65. Wherefore, it must needs be that one be appointed, of the High Priesthood, to preside over the Priesthood; and he shall be called President of the High Priesthood of the Church,

66. Or in other words, the presiding High Priest over the High Priesthood of the Church.

67. From the same comes the administering of ordinances, and blessings upon the Church, by the laying on of the hands.

68. Wherefore, the office of a Bishop is not equal unto it; for the office of a Bishop is in administering all temporal things;

69. Nevertheless, a Bishop must be chosen from the High Priesthood unless he is a literal descendant of Aaron;

70. For unless he is a literal descendant of Aaron he cannot hold the keys of that Priesthood;

71. Nevertheless, a High Priest, that is, after the order of Melchisedek, may be set apart unto the ministering of temporal things, having a knowledge of them by the Spirit of truth,

72. And also to be a judge in Israel, to do the business of the Church, to sit in judgment upon transgressors, upon testimony, as it shall be laid before him, according to the laws, by the assistance of his counselors, whom he has chosen, or will choose among the Elders of the Church;

73. This is the duty of a Bishop who is not a literal descendant of Aaron, but has been ordained to the High Priesthood after the order of Melchisedek.

74. Thus shall he be a judge, even a common judge among the inhabitants of Zion, or in a Stake of Zion, or in any branch of the Church where he shall be set apart unto this ministry, until the borders

of Zion are enlarged, and it becomes necessary to have other Bishops or judges in Zion, or elsewhere;

75. And inasmuch as there are other Bishops appointed, they shall act in the same office.

76. But a literal descendant of Aaron has a legal right to the Presidency of this Priesthood, to the keys of this ministry, to act in the office of Bishop independently, without counselors, except in a case where the President of the High Priesthood, after the order of Melchisedek, is tried; to sit as a judge in Israel:

77. And the decision of either of these councils, agreeable to the commandment, which says:

78. Again, verily I say unto you, the most important business of the Church, and the most difficult cases of the Church, inasmuch as there is not satisfaction upon the decision of the Bishop, or judges, it shall be handed over and carried up unto the Council of the Church, before the Presidency of the High Priesthood;

79. And the Presidency of the Council of the High Priesthood, shall have power to call other High Priests, even twelve, to assist as counselors; and thus the Presidency of the High Priesthood, and its counselors, shall have power to decide upon testimony, according to the laws of the Church;

80. And after this decision, it shall be had in remembrance no more before the Lord; for this is the highest Council of the Church of God; and a final decision upon controversies in spiritual matters.

81. There is not any person belonging to the Church who is exempt from this Council of the Church.

82. And inasmuch as a President of the High Priesthood shall transgress, he shall be had in remembrance before the common council of the Church, who shall be assisted by twelve counselors of the High Priesthood,

83. And their decision upon his head shall be an end of controversy concerning him.

84. Thus none shall be exempted from the justice and the laws of God; that all things may be done in order and in solemnity before him, according to truth and righteousness.

85. And again, verily I say unto you, the duty of a president over the office of a Deacon, is to preside over twelve Deacons, to sit in council with them, and to teach them their duty, edifying one another, as it is given according to the covenants.

86. And also the duty of the president over the office of the Teachers, is to preside over twenty-four of the Teachers, and to sit in council with them, teaching them the duties of their office as given in the covenants.

87. Also the duty of the president over the Priesthood of Aaron, is to preside over forty-eight Priests, and sit in council with them, to teach them the duties of their office, as it is given in the covenants;

88. This president is to be a Bishop; for this is one of the duties of this Priesthood.

89. Again, the duty of the president over the office of Elders, is to preside over ninety-six Elders, and to sit in council with them, and to teach them according to the covenants.

90. This presidency is a distinct one from that of the Seventy, and is designed for those who do not travel into all the world.

91. And again, the duty of the President of the office of the High Priesthood, is to preside over the whole Church, and to be like unto Moses.

92. Behold, here is wisdom; yea, to be a Seer, a Revelator, a Translator, and a Prophet, having all the gifts of God which He bestows upon the head of the Church.

93. And it is according to the vision showing the order of the Seventy, that they should have seven presidents to preside over them, chosen out of the number of the Seventy;

94. And the seventh president of these presidents is to preside over the six;

95. And these seven presidents are to choose other seventy beside the first seventy, to whom they belong; and are to preside over them;

96. And also other seventy, till seven times seventy, if the labor in the vineyard of necessity requires it;

97. And these seventy are to be traveling ministers unto the Gentiles first, and also unto the Jews;

98 Whereas other officers of the Church, who belong not unto the Twelve, neither to the Seventy, are not under the responsibility to travel among all nations, but are to travel as their circumstances shall allow; notwithstanding, they may hold as high and responsible offices in the Church.

99. Wherefore, now, let every man learn his duty, and to act in the office in which he is appointed, in all diligence.

100. He that is slothful shall not be counted worthy to stand, and he that learns not his duty and shows himself not approved, shall not be counted worthy to stand. Even so. Amen.

CHAPTER XV.

THE FIRST MISSION OF THE TWELVE.

THE school in Kirtland closed the last week in March, to give the Elders an opportunity to go forth and proclaim the Gospel, preparatory to the endowment.

Close of the Elders' School.

Sunday, March 29.—I preached about three hours, at Huntsburgh—where William E. M'Lellin had been holding a public discussion, on a challenge from J. M. Tracy, a Campbellite preacher, the two days previous, on the divinity of the Book of Mormon—at the close of which two were baptized; and, on Monday, four more came forward for baptism.

Public Discussion at Huntsburgh.

Minutes of Conference held at Freedom, N. Y.

April 3rd and 4th, a conference of the Saints was held at Freedom, New York, Sidney Rigdon presiding.

Fifteen branches of the Church were represented, five of which had not been previously represented at any conference, numbering about fifty members.

Elder Chester L. Heath, of Avon, was expelled from the Church, for breach of covenant, and not observing the Word of Wisdom.

WARREN A. COWDERY, Clerk.

Minutes of a Conference of the Twelve and the Seventies.

On the 26th of April the Twelve Apostles, and the Seventies who had been chosen, assembled in the temple (although unfinished), with a numerous concourse of people, to receive their charge and instructions from President Joseph Smith, Jun., relating to their mission and duties. The congregation being assembled, Elder Orson Pratt arrived from the south part of the state, making our number complete, Elder Thomas B. Marsh having arrived the day previous.

Meeting of the Twelve.

April 28.—The Twelve met this afternoon at the schoolroom, for the purpose of prayer and consultation. Elder David W. Patten opened the meeting by prayer.

Moved and carried, that when any member of the council wishes to speak, he shall arise and stand upon his feet.

Elder M'Lellin read the commandment given concerning the choosing of the Twelve; when it was voted that we each forgive one another every wrong that has existed among us, and that from henceforth each one of the Twelve love his brother as himself, in temporal as well as in spiritual things, always inquiring into each other's welfare.

Decided that the Twelve be ready and start on their mission from Elder Johnson's tavern on Monday, at two o'clock a. m., May 4th.

Elder Brigham Young then closed by prayer.

ORSON HYDE,

W. E. M'LELLIN,

Clerks.

Minutes of a General Council of the Priesthood.

May 2.—A grand council was held in Kirtland, composed of the following officers of the Church, viz: Presidents Joseph Smith, Jun., David Whitmer, Oliver Cowdery, Sidney Rigdon, Frederick G. Williams, Joseph Smith, Sen., and Hyrum Smith, with the council of the Twelve Apostles, Bishop Partridge and counselors, Bishop Whitney and counselors, and some of the Seventies, with their presidents, viz. Sylvester Smith, Leonard Rich, Lyman Sherman, Hazen Aldrich, Joseph Young, and Levi Hancock; and many Elders from different parts of the country. President Joseph Smith, Jun., presiding.

After the conference was opened, and the Twelve had taken their seats, President Joseph Smith, Jun., said that it would be the duty of the Twelve, when in council, to take their seats together according to age, the oldest to be seated at the head, and preside in the first council, the next oldest in the second, and so on until the youngest had presided; and then begin at the oldest again.*

---

* It should be observed here, that this arrangement has reference only to the first organization of the quorum of the Twelve. After this first arrangement, the brethren of that quorum held and now hold their place in it and preside according to seniority of ordination, not of age. Though it must be admitted, that this order was not always strictly observed; for instance, the late President Woodruff, for a number of years, ranked in the quorum of the Twelve before Elder John Taylorr; although the

The Twelve then took their seats according to age as follows: Thomas
B. Marsh, David W. Patten, Brigham Young, Heber C. Kimball, Or_
son Hyde, William E. M'Lellin, Parley P. Pratt, Luke S. Johnson
William Smith, Orson Pratt, John F. Boynton, and Lyman E. Johnson.

Items of Instruction to the Twelve and the Seventy.

President Joseph Smith then stated that the Twelve will have no
right to go into Zion, or any of its stakes, and there undertake to regulate the affairs thereof, where there is a standing high council; but it
is their duty to go abroad and regulate all matters relative to the different branches of the Church. When the Twelve are together, or a
quorum of them, in any church, they will have authority to act independently, and make decisions, and those decisions will be valid. But
where there is not a quorum, they will have to do business by the voice
of the Church. No standing High Council has authority to go into the
churches abroad, and regulate the matters thereof, for this belongs to
the Twelve. No standing High Council will ever be established only
in Zion, or one of her stakes.* When the Twelve pass a decision, it is
in the name of the Church, therefore it is valid.

No official member of the Church has authority to go into any branch
thereof, and ordain any minister for that Church, unless it is by the

latter was ordained first, and actually assisted in the ordination of President Woodruff at Far West in the spring of 1839. I think this case illustrates the inconsistency
of the idea that seniority of age should govern in fixing the standing of the members
in the quorum of the Twelve. Surely it would be nothing short of an absurdity
in order, for one just ordained to out-rank one that had taken part in his ordination.
The slight irregularity here noticed was corrected by President Brigham Young
some two years before his death, and President Taylor was accorded his place,
which gave him priority of standing in the quorum to Elder Woodruff. President
Taylor himself gives the following explanation of the matter: "Through some
inadvertency, or perhaps mixed up with the idea of seniority of age taking the
precedence, Wilford Woodruff's name was placed on the records at the time, and
for many years after, before that of John Taylor. This matter was investigated,
some time afterwards, by President Young and his council, sanctioned also by the
Twelve, whether [or not] John Taylor held the precedency and stood in gradation
prior to Brother Wilford Woodruff; and it was voted on and decided that his name
be placed before Wilford Woodruff's, although Wilford Woodruff was the older
man. The reason assigned for this change was, that although both were called at
the same time, John Taylor was ordained into the Twelve prior to Wilford Woodruff; and another prominent reason would be, that as John Taylor assisted in the
ordination of Elder Wilford Woodruff, he therefore must precede him in the council." (Succession in the Priesthood, a Discourse by President John Taylor—October,
1881—p. 16).

* But a *temporary* High Concil of High Priests abroad may be organized when
necessity requires it, the High Priests abroad (i. e., outside organized stakes of
Zion) having the power to determine when the organization of such High Council
is necessary. (See the revelation at page 30 this volume, verses 24-32).

voice of that branch. No Elder has authority to go into any branch of the Church, and appoint meetings, or attempt to regulate the affairs of the church, without the advice and consent of the presiding Elder of that branch.

If the first Seventy are all employed, and there is a call for more laborers, it will be the duty of the seven presidents of the first Seventy to call and ordain other Seventy and send them forth to labor in the vineyard, until, if needs be, they set apart seven times seventy, and even until there are one hundred and forty-four thousand thus set apart for the ministry.*

The Seventy are not to attend the conferences of the Twelve, unless they are called upon or requested so to do by the Twelve. The Twelve and the Seventy have particularly to depend upon their ministry for their support, and that of their families; and they have a right, by virtue of their offices, to call upon the churches to assist them.

Elder Henry Herriman was ordained one of the Seventy.

The circumstances of the presidents of the Seventy were severally considered, relative to their traveling in the vineyard: and it was unanimously agreed that they should hold themselves in readiness to go, at the call of the Twelve, when the Lord opens the way. Twenty-seven of the Seventy were also considered, and it was decided they should hold themselves in readiness to travel in the ministry, at the call of the president of the Seventy, as the Lord opens the way.

After an adjournment of one hour, the council re-assembled.

Ezra Thayre was suspended as an Elder and member, until investigation could be had before the bishop's court, complaint having been preferred against him by Oliver Granger.

Lorenzo D. Barnes was ordained one of the Seventy; also Henry Benner, Michael Griffiths, Royal Barney, and Lebbeus T. Coon, who, together with twenty others, were called upon to hold themselves in readiness to travel when circumstances might permit.

The Elders in Kirtland and its vicinity were then called upon, or their circumstances considered, and their names enrolled. President Joseph Smith, Jun., arose with the lists in his hand, and made

---

* In his notes on Church History, John Whitmer, who was the Church Historian at that time, says concerning the organization of the Seventy: "About the same time [i. e., that the quorum of the Twelve was organized] there were seventy High Priests chosen, who were called to be under the direction of the Twelve, and assist them according to their needs; and if seventy were not enough, call seventy more, until seventy times seventy." (Ms. p. 51.) John Whitmer, however, is mistaken in saying that they were High Priests that were chosen. They were chiefly chosen from among the Elders, and the few High Priests that were called into the quorum were afterwards requested to take their place with the High Priests again, and others were chosen to fill the vacancies thus created. (See "History of the Organization of the Seventies," Joseph Young, pp. 4, 5.)

some very appropriate remarks, relative to the deliverance of Zion; and, so much of the authority of the Church being present, moved that we never give up the struggle for Zion, even until death, or until Zion is redeemed.

The vote was unanimous, and given with deep feeling.

Voted, that all the Elders of the Church are bound to travel in the world to preach the Gospel, with all their might, mind, and strength, when their circumstances will admit of it; and that the door is now opened.

Voted, that Elders Brigham Young, John P, Greene, and Amos Orton be appointed to go and preach the Gospel to the remnants of Joseph, the door to be opened by Elder Brigham Young, and this will open the door to the whole house of Joseph.

Voted, that when another Seventy is required, the presidency of the first Seventy shall choose, ordain, and set them apart from among the most experienced of the Elders of the Church.

Voted, that whenever the labor of other Seventy is required, they are to be set apart and ordained to that office; those who are residing at Kirtland and the regions round about, who can come to Kirtland, to be set apart and ordained by the direction of the Presidency of the Church in Kirtland.

WM. E. M'LELLIN, Clerk.

The First Mission of the Twelve.

The Twelve left Kirtland this morning [May 4th],* and embarked on board the steamer *Sandusky*, at Fairport, and landed at Dunkirk, New York, 5 o'clock p. m., and after preaching in those regions a few days, met in conference at Westfield, May 9th, according to previous appointment; the church being present, and Thomas B. Marsh, the oldest of the quorum, presiding.

The following items were suggested for the consideration of the council:

Resolved, 1st: That the limits of this conference extend south and west to the line of Pennsylvania, north as far as Lake Erie, and east as far as Lodi, embracing the branches of Westfield, Silver Creek, Perrysburgh, and Lavona, to be called the "Westfield Conference."

* Presumably on the 4th of May, since that was the date fixed for starting on this mission by the Twelve at their meeting on the 28th of April preceding (see p. 219). John Whitmer, in his notes on Church History, however. fixes the date on the 5th of May. He says: "On the morning of the 5th of May, the Twelve took leave of their families and brethren, to fill their first mission under their commission, being commissioned to carry the Gospel to Gentile and also unto Jew, having the keys of the Gospel to unlock, and then call upon others to promulgate the same." (Whitmer's Ms., p. 50.)

2nd. Inquire into the standing of all the Elders within the bounds of this conference.

3rd. Inquire into the manner of their teaching, doctrines, etc.

4th. Inquire into the teaching, conduct, and faithfulness of all traveling Elders who have recently labored within the bounds of this conference.

5th. Hear a representation of the several branches of the Church.

On investigation, the standing and teaching of the Elders present met the approbation of the council, except the teaching of Elder Joseph Rose, which was, "that the Jewish church was the sun, and the Gentile church was the moon, etc.; when the Jewish church was scattered, then sun was darkened: and when the Gentile church is cut off, the moon will be turned to blood;" also some things relative to the apocalyptic beast with seven heads and ten horns.

He was shown his error, and willingly made a humble confession.

The faithfulness of all the traveling Elders was found to be good.

The members of the Westfield branch were represented as in good standing, but with a difficulty in the minds of some, relative to the baptism of Brother Lloyd L. Lewis, inasmuch as he was baptized by a traveling Elder without the church being called together to know if they would receive him to fellowship.

The council decided that if there was a fault, it was in the administrator, and not in the candidate. The branch numbered seventy-five.

The Lavona branch numbered twenty in good standing, but lacking in the enjoyment of the Spirit in consequence of a neglect to keep the Word of Wisdom.

After further instructions on general principles, the conference adjourned until 8 o'clock a. m., Monday, May 11.

Sunday, May 10.—Elders Marsh and Patten preached to an attentive congregation of about five hundred; after Sacrament, five persons desired baptism, which was attended to by Elder M'Lellin.

Monday, 11.—Conference met pursuant to adjournment.

Resolved unanimously—That this conference go to, immediately, and appoint their "wise men," and gather up their riches, and send them to Zion to purchase land, according to previous commandment, that all things be prepared before them in order to their gathering.

Much was said to the conference upon these important things; and the Saints covenanted before the Lord, that they would be strict to attend to our teaching.

After preaching by Elder Young at 3 o'clock p. m., and the farewell exhortation of the Twelve, seven individuals were baptized by Elder Orson Hyde, and they were confirmed in the evening.

After laying hands on many sick, who obtained relief, adjourned to the 22nd instant, to meet in Freedom, New York.

ORSON HYDE, Clerk.

The Conference at Freedom.

May 22.—The Twelve met in conference with the church in Freedom, New York, when, after an agreeable salutation and rejoicing in each other's prosperity, Elder David W. Patten being chairman, conference was opened by singing, and prayer by the President.

[Here let it be remarked, that it was the universal custom of the Twelve and the Presidency of the Church, to open and close all conferences and councils by prayer, and generally singing, so that this need not be named in this history hereafter.]

Resolved—That the limits of this conference extend from Lodi in the west, so far east as to include Avon, south to Pennsylvania, and north to Lake Ontario, called the "Freedom Conference," including the branches of Freedom, Rushford, Portage, Grove, Burns, Genesee, Avon, Java, Holland, Aurora, Greenwood, and Niagara.

The report concerning the labors and teachings of the Elders in the conference, and those who had recently traveled through the branches, was good.

The branch in Freedom numbered sixty-five; Rushford, twenty-eight; Burns, thirty; Holland, fifteen—represented by P. P. Pratt as having suffered much from false teachings by hypocrites and knaves: Aurora, four; Niagara, four; the numbers of the remaining branches not ascertained, but generally reported in good standing.

The council gave instruction concerning the "Word of Wisdom," the gift of tongues, prophesying, etc., and adjourned until tomorrow morning.

May 23.—Conference met to take into consideration the redemption of Zion.

After addresses by five of the council, the church expressed their determination to put into practice the teachings we had given, when the conference adjourned.

May 25.—The Twelve met in council to pray for one another until they should meet again; and,

Resolved—That we recommand and counsel Elders John Murdock and Lloyd Lewis to go to the churches at Chenango Point, New York, and Springville, Pennsylvania (among whom we understand there is some difficulty), and set in order the things that are wanting in those branches.

Resolved—That Elder Brigham Young go immediately from this place to an adjacent tribe of the remnants of Joseph, and open the door of salvation to that long dejected and afflicted people. The council, according to his request, laid their hands upon him, that he might have their faith and prayers, to fill, with humility and power, that very important mission.

They also laid hands on Elders John P. Greene and Amos Orton, for the same purpose, as they expected to accompany him.

ORSON HYDE, Clerk.

On the 5th of June, nine of the Twelve met in council at Rose, or Lyonstown, New York. There being so few of the brethren in that region, it was resolved that it was not necessary to establish a conference, after which council adjourned. After they had preached several sermons in the vicinity, Elders Brigham Young, Orson Hyde and William Smith returned to Kirtland, as witnesses in a certain case wherein President Joseph Smith, Jun., was concerned before the county court, in which he righteously triumphed over his enemies.*

ORSON HYDE, Clerk.

On the 19th of June, nine of the traveling High Council met with the church in conference at Pillow Point, New York, and resolved that the limits of the conference embrace all the northern part of the State, to be called the "Black River Conference." The Elders of the conference had been diligent in their callings. Their manner of teaching in some respects needed correction, which they gladly received.

The church at Pillow Point numbered twenty-one, but did not generally observe the Word of Wisdom. The church at Sackets Harbor numbered nineteen; Burville, seven; Champion, six; Ellesburg, thirty-three; Henderson, four; Alexandria, four· Lyme, four; and two in Orleans, three in Potsdam, and six in Stockholm.

After hearing the report of the churches, five of the council successively addressed the conference, upon the principles of church government, the nature and exercise of spiritual gifts, the Word of Wisdom, and the propriety of choosing wise men and sending them with moneys to purchase lands in Zion, so that they might not gather in confusion; and the conference unanimously acquiesced in the teachings of the council. Adjourned until the 20th, then met, and John Elmer was charged with holding very incorrect principles; such, for instance, that the Spirit of God sometimes took him and threw him down, and that he could die the death of the righteous, and of the wicked; and in order to show his power with God, he also stated that he had passed through a kind of death so as to become immortal, and would exist forever without any other death or

---

* What the case in question was cannot now be ascertained.

change, only growing brighter and brighter eternally. He persisted in these things, and would not receive teaching from the council, therefore was cut off. On Monday, five were baptized, and our public meeting closed.

ORSON HYDE, Clerk.

CHAPTER XVI.

PROGRESS OF AFFAIRS AT KIRTLAND—DISCOVERY OF THE BOOK OF ABRAHAM.

ABOUT the middle of May, W. W. Phelps and John Whitmer, Presidents of the Church in Missouri, arrived at Kirtland, and John Whitmer was appointed to take the place of President Oliver Cowdery, in conducting the *Messenger and Advocate.* *Change of Editors on the "Messenger and Advocate."*

Frederick G. Williams was appointed to edit the *Northern Times*, a weekly newspaper, which we had commenced in February last, in favor of Democracy; and W. W. Phelps (with his son Waterman) made his home with my family, and assisted the committee in compiling the Book of Doctrine and Covenants. *The "Northern Times."*

Minutes of Conference held at New Portage, June 6th.

The Elders and brethren assembled in conference, June 6th, at New Portage, Oliver Cowdery, presiding.

Elder David Matthews, who was suspended at a previous conference, for unchristian conduct, was present.

After hearing the testimony, the council unanimously agreed that there had been due contrition of spirit manifested by him, in his walk and conversation since his suspension; and Elder Matthews was restored.

Elder Barkdall preferred a claim against Elder Keeler, for services said to be rendered some eight or nine years since, and to have been awarded by a former council.

It appeared there had been a decision in favor of Elder Barkdall, but no testimony was produced by either of the parties to substantiate a claim, or prove a payment. It was, therefore, Resolved:—That both the accuser and the accused have manifested a bad spirit, and deserve the severe rebuke of this council.

Elder Milo Hays was tried for not obeying the Word of Wisdom, and for covenant breaking.

Both charges were sustained by testimony, and Elder Hays was excluded from the Church.

Several other cases of discipline were attended to, and conference adjourned at 12 o'clock at night.

Sunday morning, President Oliver Cowdery preached, after which four were baptized.

The council again organized in the evening, and ordained Jacob Myers an Elder.

The case of Elders Barkdall and Keeler was again called up; four councilors spoke on the subject, when it was decided that they have one week and no more to settle their differences with each other, and make confession to the Church, or lose their standing.

W. A. COWDERY, Clerk.

The Presidency, Bishop, and High Council of Zion, having removed to Kirtland, or gone forth in the vineyard,

Instructions of the Prophet to the Elders and Saints in Missouri.

I caused it to be published in the June number of the *Messenger and Advocate*, that according to the order of the kingdom begun in the last days, to prepare men for the rest of the Lord, the Elders in Zion or in her immediate region, have no authority or right to meddle with her spiritual affairs, to regulate her concerns, or hold councils for the expulsion of members, in her unorganized condition. The High Council has been expressly organized to administer in all her spiritual affairs; and the Bishop and his council are set over her temporal matters; so that the Elders' acts are null and void. *Now*, the Lord wants the wheat and tares to grow together; for Zion must be redeemed with judgment, and her converts with righteousness. Every Elder that can, after providing for his family (if he has any) and paying his debts, must go forth and clear his skirts from the blood of this generation. While they are in that region, [Missouri] instead of trying members for transgression, or offenses, let every one labor to prepare himself for the vineyard, sparing a little time to comfort the mourners, to bind up the broken-hearted, to reclaim the backslider, to bring back the wanderer, to re-invite into the kingdom such as have been cut off, by encouraging them to lay to while the day lasts, and work righteousness, and, with one heart and one mind, prepare to help to redeem Zion, that goodly land of promise, where the willing and obedient shall be blessed.*

* The whole article is so valuable that, notwithstanding to publish it entire leads to a repetition of part of the above, it is placed here in a foot note.

"TO THE SAINTS SCATTERED ABROAD.

"Dear Brethren:—It is a duty which every Saint ought to render to his brethren freely—to always love them, and ever succor them. To be justified before God we must love one another: we must overcome evil; we must visit the fatherless and the widow in their affliction, and we must keep ourselves unspotted from the world: for such virtues flow from the great fountain of pure religion. Strengthening our faith by adding every good quality that adorns the children of the blessed Jesus, we can pray in the season of prayer; we can love our neighbor as ourselves, and be faithful in tribulation, knowing that the reward of such is greater in the kingdom of heaven. What a consolation! What a joy! Let me live the life of the righteous, and let my reward be like this!

According to the order of the kingdom begun in the last days, to prepare men for the rest of the Lord, the Elders in Zion. or in her immediate region, have no authority or right to meddle with her spiritual affairs, to regulate her concerns, or hold councils for the expulsion of members in her unorganized condition. The High Council has been expressly organized to administer in all her spiritual affairs; and the Bishop and his council, are set over her temporal matters: so that the Elders' acts are null and void. Now the Lord wants the tares and wheat to grow together: for Zion must be redeemed with judgment, and her converts with righteousness. Every Elder that can, after providing for his family (if he has any) and paying his debts, must go forth and clear his skirts from the blood of this generation. While they are in that region instead of trying members for transgressions, or offenses, let every one labor to prepare himself for the vineyard, sparing a little time to comfort the mourners; to bind up the broken-hearted; to reclaim the backslider; to bring back the wanderer; to re invite into the kingdom such as have been cut off, by encouraging them to lay to while the day lasts, and work righteousness, and, with one heart and one mind, prepare to help redeem Zion, that goodly land of promise, where the willing and the obedient shall be blessed. Souls are as precious in the sight of God as they ever were; and the Elders were never called to drive any down to hell, but to persuade and invite all men everywhere to repent, that they may become the heirs of salvation. It is the acceptable year of the Lord: liberate the captives that they may sing hosanna. The Priests, too, should not be idle: their duties are plain, and unless they do them diligently, they cannot expect to be approved. Righteousness must be the aim of the Saints in all things, and when the covenants are published, they will learn that great things must be expected from them. Do good and work righteousness with an eye single to the glory of God, and you shall reap your reward when the Lord recompenses every one ac-

About this time, I received an introduction to Mr. Hewitt, a preacher who had come out from Europe, with his wife, to examine this work; he stated that he was delegated by his church for this purpose, and presented a letter of commendation, a copy of which follows:

The mission of Mr. Hewitt.

To the Saints of the Most High:

Dear Brethren in the Lord.—At a council of the pastors of our church, held March 28th, 1835, upon the propriety of Reverend John cording to his work. The Teachers and Deacons are the standing ministers of the Church, and in the absence of other officers, great things and holy walk are required of them. They must strengthen the members' faith; persuade such as are out of the way to repent, and turn to God and live; meekly persuade and urge every one to forgive one another all their trespasses, offenses and sins, that they may work out their own salvation with fear and trembling. Brethren, bear and forbear one with another, for so the Lord does with us. Pray for your enemies in the Church and curse not your foes without: for vengeance is mine, saith the Lord, and I will repay. To every ordained member, and to all, we say, b˜ merciful and you shall find mercy. Seek to help save souls, not to destroy them: for verily you know, that "there is more joy in heaven, over one sinner that repents, than there is over ninety and nine just persons that need no repentance." Strive not about the mysteries of the kingdom; cast not your pearls before swine, give not the bread of the children to dogs, lest you and the children should suffer, and you thereby offend your righteous Judge. Your brethren who leave their families, with whom they have enjoyed an earthly measure of peace and joy, to carry glad tidings around the world, expect great things of you, while you are privileged to enjoy the blessings of the Saints' society. They pray our heavenly Father that you may be very prayerful, very humble, and very charitable; working diligently, spiritually and temporally for the redemption of Zion, that the pure in heart may return with songs of everlasting joy to build up her waste places, and meet the Lord when He comes in His glory. Brethren, in the name of Jesus Christ. we entreat you to live worthy of the blessings that shall follow after much tribulation, to satiate the souls of them that hold out faithful to the end."—*Messenger and Advocate,* vol. 1, No. 8, pp. 137-8.

The substance of the foregoing article from the *Messenger and Advocate* is also contained, according to John Whitmer's history (manuscript page 52) in a letter to Hezekiah Peck, signed by Joseph Smith, Jun., Oliver Cowdery, Sidney Rigdon, Frederick G. Williams, W. W. Phelps and John Whitmer; the opening paragraph of which is as follows:

"The Presidency of Kirtland and Zion say that the Lord has manifested by revelation of His Spirit, that the High Priests, Teachers, Priests, and Deacons, or in other words, all the officers in the land of Clay County, Missouri, belonging to the Church, are more or less in transgression, because they have not enjoyed the Spirit of God sufficiently to be able to comprehend their duties respecting themselves and the welfare of Zion; thereby having been left to act in a manner that is detrimental to the interest, and also a hindrance to the redemption of Zion. Now if they will be wise, they will humble themselves in a peculiar manner that God may open the eyes of their understanding. It will be clearly manifested what the

Hewitt visiting you, it was resolved and approved that as he had an anxious desire to go to America to see things that are spoken of in one of your papers brought here by a merchant from New York, he should have, as he desired, the sanction of the council, and if it pleased the Lord, His approval.   The Lord hath seen our joy and gladness to hear that He was raising up a people for Himself in that part of the New World, as well as here.   O, may our faith increase that He may have Evangelists, Apostles, and Prophets, filled with the power of the Spirit, and performing His will in destroying the works of darkness.

The Reverend Mr. Hewitt was professor of mathematics in Rotherham Independent Seminary, and four years pastor of Barnsley Independent church.   He commenced preaching the doctrines we taught, about two years since, and was excommunicated.   Many of his flock followed him, so that he was eventually installed in the same church, and the Lord's work prospered.   As he is a living epistle, you will have, if all be well, a full explanation.   Many will follow, should he approve of the country, etc., who will help the cause, because the Lord hath favored them with this world's goods.   We had an utterance during our meeting, which caused us to sing for joy.   The Lord was pleased with our brother's holy determination to see you; and we understand that persecution had been great among you, or would be, but we were commanded not to fear, for He would be with us.   Praise the Lord.

The time is at hand when distance shall be no barrier between us; but when on the wings of love, Jehovah's messages shall be communicated by His Saints.   The Lord bless our brother, and may he prove a blessing to you.   Be not afraid of our enemies; they shall,

design and purposes of the Almighty are with regard to them, and the children of Zion, that they should let the High Council, which is appointed of God and ordained for that purpose, make and regulate all the affairs of Zion, and that it is the will of God that her children should stand still and see the salvation of redemption." Then follows the substance of the *Messenger and Advocate* article.   This letter has the following *post script* written personally by the Prophet, to Brother Peck, and is a gem which manifests the profound sympathy of the Prophet for the faithful in Israel:

"P. S.—Brother Hezekiah Peck: We remember your family with all the first families of the Church who first embraced the truth.   We remember your losses and sorrows; our first ties are not broken; we participate with you in the evil as well as the good, in the sorrows as well as the joys; our union, we trust, is stronger than death, and shall never be severed.   Remember us unto all who believe in the fullness of the Gospel of our Lord and Savior Jesus Christ.   We hereby authorize you, Hezekiah Peck, our beloved brother, to read this epistle and communicate it unto all the brotherhood in all that region of country.

"Dictated by me, your unworthy brother, and fellow laborer in the testimony of the Book of Mormon.   Signed by my own hand in the token of the everlasting covenant.   *Joseph Smith, Jun.*"

unless they repent, be cast down by the Lord of Hosts. The workers of iniquity have been used by the prince of darkness to play the counterfeit; but discernment has been given to us, that they were immediately put to shame, by being detected, so that the flock never suffered as yet by them.

Grace, mercy, and peace be unto you from God our Father, and from the Spirit, Jesus Christ our Lord. Amen.

I am, dear sir,
Your brother in the Gospel,
THOMAS SHAW.

Barnsley, April 21, 1835.*

The interview with Mr. Hewitt was brief, and he left with the understanding that he would call again and renew his investigations. As he did not return according to agreement, and hearing he was at Fairport, the council of the Presidency sent him the following letter:—

To the Reverend Mr. Hewitt:

Sir—In consequence of your not returning as we understood you would at your introduction to us, it was resolved and approved in council, on the evening of the 14th instant, that the bearer of this communication, Oliver Cowdery, one of the presiding Elders of our Church, should proceed to Fairport, and ascertain if possible, the cause of your delay; and this is done as one reason, that we feel an anxious desire for the salvation of the souls of men, and to satisfy your inquiries concerning the religion we profess. If at Fairport it is the sincere desire of the council, that Mr. Hewitt return, that we may satisfy him concerning our religion, and he satisfy us concerning his; for we feel as great a desire for the welfare of his people, as he can for ours.

With respect, etc.,
W. W. PHELPS, Clerk.

* This communication in the Prophet's history as published in the *Millennial Star* appears under the date of April 21st, 1835; but it was thought to be a better grouping of events to bring it down to this date—first half of June—where the whole incident may be disposed of in a single reference to it. Following is a remark of the Prophet's respecting the letter as published in the *Star*, but which under our present arrangement of the matter is not necessary in the text of the History: "One object, and only one, has induced us to lay the foregoing letter from England, before our readers; and that is, the good of the cause of God. It might have remained in our possession, perhaps for years, in silence, had it not been for circumstances, which we will briefly mention hereafter." These "circumstances" are those relating to the indifferent actions of Mr. Hewitt, as set forth in the text.

Elder Cowdery immediately repaired to Fairport, and on the day following reported to the Council that Mr. Hewitt was not in the place: that he left their letter with Mrs. Hewitt, who informed him that her "husband had frequently spoken of his wish to become further acquainted with the people whom he had come out from Europe to see." But the next we heard of the Reverend John Hewitt was that he had opened a school in Painsville, Ohio. *The indifference of Mr. Hewitt*

☐ Mr. Hewitt was an elder of the Irvingite* church, in Barn-

---

* This is not the name accepted by the church which Mr. Hewitt represented. The religious body usually called "Irvingites" object to any designation "which implies sectarianism" and therefore, they themselves use no other name than the "Catholic Apostolic Church," of which the congregation at Barnsley, England, was but a branch. Such was the prominence, however, for learning, social and ecclesiastical standing of Reverend Edward Irving that when he gave the influence of his name and standing to what was probably a really spiritual awakening among some of the people in western and southern Scotland, the movement received his name, hence "Irvingites." Mr. Irving was born in Annan, Dumfrieshire, August 15, 1792, and in his early ministry was associated with such men as Doctors Chalmers and Canning. He created no little stir in higher circles of religious society in London for a time; but his announcement of the near approach of the coming of the Son of Man, attended by the judgments of God, together with his strictures against the looseness of fashionable life, soon displeased the worldly who for a time flocked to hear him; and the people of fashion soon separated from his congregation. He taught the doctrine that the spiritual gifts of the Gospel were to continue forever in the church, together with the New Testament organization of the church. The Irvingite views of this New Testament organization are set forth in the following: "There are, as in the apostolic times, four ministeries: 1st, that of 'apostle;' 2nd, that of 'prophet;' 3rd, that of 'evangelist;' and 4th, that of 'pastor.' The apostles are invested with spiritual prerogatives; they alone can administer the Holy Ghost by laying on of hands; to them the mysteries of God are revealed and unfolded to the church; and they decide on matters of order and discipline. Nothing that transpires in any church in the way of 'prophetic utterance' can be authoritatively explained save by them; and the various 'angels of the churches' are bound to bring all such utterances under their cognizance, in order that they may be rightly interpreted. The function of the 'prophet' has been already indicated. The work of an 'evangelist' mainly consists in endeavoring to 'bring' in, those who are without. The 'angel' of the Catholic Apostolic Church, corresponds with the bishop of other Christian denominations. The ministers of each full congregation comprise an angel, with a four-fold ministry (consisting of elders, prophets, evangelists, and pastors;) and a ministry of deacons to take charge of temporal matters. This ministry is supported by tithes, the people giving a tenth of their income for the support of the priesthood. Church affairs were managed by a council of ministers of all classes, whose selection and arrangement are conceived to have been foreshadowed in the structure of the Mosaic tabernacle." The sympathy of the members of the Catholic Apostolic Church at Barnsley who believed in the spirit-

sley, England, and was sent as a delegate from that church, as expressed in the letter from Mr. Shaw, of April 21st, to visit the Saints in America, and ascertain their faith and principles; and if Mr. Hewitt found them as they expected, the Saints in America might expect help from them (the church in Barnsley) as they were rich in temporal things, and had received the gift of tongues in the church.

June 18.—Nine hundred and fifty dollars were subscribed for the temple, by the Saints in Kirt-
Subscriptions
for the Tem-   land. Great anxiety was manifested to roll on
ple.   the work.

The twenty-first, being Sunday, I preached in Kirtland on the Evangelical Order.*

Thursday, June 25.—There was a meeting in Kirtland to subscribe for the building of the Temple; and $6,232.50 was added to the list. Joseph Smith subscribed $500; Oliver Cowdery, $750; W. W. Phelps, $500; John Whitmer, $500; and Frederick G. Williams, $500; of the above, all of which they paid within one hour, and the people were astonished.

ual gifts of the Gospel, and what they understood to be the New Testament organization of the church, readily explains the interest they would naturally feel in
the Latter-day Saints in America, when they would come to hear of the things
which God had established among them; and it is regretted that they did not send a
more faithful representative than Mr. Hewitt to enquire into the work of the Lord
as developed in divine manifestations to the Prophet Joseph. "This Mr. Hewitt,"
says John Whitmer in his manuscript history of the Church, page 52, "did not
obey the Gospel; neither would he investigate the matter. Thus ended the mission
of Mr. Hewitt."

     * Of the evangelical or patriarchal order of Priesthood in the Church it is said in
the revelations of God: "The order of this Priesthood was confirmed to be handed
down from father to son, and rightly belongs to the literal descendants of the chosen
seed, to whom the promises were made. This order was instituted in the days of Adam,
and came down by lineage in the following manner." Then follow the names of
those who successively held the evangelical Priesthood in ancient times (Doctrine
and Covenants, sec. cvii). According to the word of the Lord, at the time this
order of Priesthood was conferred upon Hyrum Smith, brother of the Prophet, it is
said "The Patriarch holds the keys of the patriarchal blessings upon the heads of all
my people, that whoever he blesses shall be blessed, and whoever he curses shall
be cursed; that whatsoever he shall bind on earth shall be bound in heaven; and
whatsoever he shall loose on earth shall be loosed in heaven." (Doctrine and Covenants, cxxiv, 92, 93.) It was undoubtedly upon this order of priesthood that the
Prophet spoke in the meeting of the twenty-first of June.

June 29.—Six of the traveling High Council, viz.:—David W. Patten, Heber C. Kimball, Luke S. Johnson, Orson Pratt, John F. Boynton, and Lyman E. Johnson, assembled in conference with the church in Loborough, Upper Canada. The church in Loborough, composed of twenty-five members, were uninformed in many principles of the new covenant, not having had the same privilege of instruction as the churches in the United States.

Conference in Canada.

Brothers Henry and Jacob Wood, who had been suspended, had a rehearing, but were cut off. Elder Frederick M. Van Leuven, was appointed presiding Elder, and a number were added to the Church during their stay.

On the 3rd of July, Michael H. Chandler came to Kirtland to exhibit some Egyptian mummies. There were four human figures, together with some two or more rolls of papyrus covered with hieroglyphic figures and devices. As Mr.

Michael H. Chandler and the Egyptian Mummies.

Chandler had been told I could translate them, he brought me some of the characters, and I gave him the interpretation, and like a gentleman, he gave me the following certificate:

KIRTLAND, July 6, 1835.

This is to make known to all who may be desirous, concerning the knowledge of Mr. Joseph Smith, Jun., in deciphering the ancient Egyptian hieroglyphic characters in my possession, which I have, in many eminent cities, showed to the most learned; and, from the information that I could ever learn, or meet with, I find that of Mr. Joseph Smith, Jun., to correspond in the most minute matters.

MICHAEL H. CHANDLER,
Traveling with, and proprietor of, Egyptian mummies.*

Sunday 5.—I preached in the afternoon.

Michael H. Barton tried to get into the Church, but he was not willing to confess and forsake all his sins—and he was rejected.

The case of Michael H. Barton.

* Mr. Chandler is responsible for the English of the above certificate, and I do not feel at liberty to edit it.

Soon after this, some of the Saints at Kirtland purchased the mummies and papyrus, a description of which will appear hereafter, and with
W. W. Phelps and Oliver Cowdery as scribes,
I commenced the translation of some of the characters or
hieroglyphics, and much to our joy found that one of the
rolls contained the writings of Abraham, another the
writings of Joseph of Egypt, etc.,—a more full account of
which will appear in its place, as I proceed to examine or
unfold them.   Truly we can say, the Lord is beginning to
reveal the abundance of peace and truth.

The Writings of Abraham and Joseph.

On the 9th I rode to Cleveland, in company with Elder
Cowdery and others.   On the 14th a charge
was preferred against Elder Edmund Bosley,
to a council of the Presidency, for unchristian-like conduct, in breaking a certain sacred
covenant, made September 4, 1834.

Edmund Bosley Tried for Breaking Covenant.

I instructed the council on points of duty, such as
observing covenants, etc., and testified to the truth of the
above covenant.

President Oliver Cowdery testified that he himself
framed the covenant alluded to, and that at the time
when Bosley said that he had a witness that it was the
will of the Lord that he should consecrate the surplus of
his property over and above what would be needful for his
and his family's support.

Bishop Whitney stated that Elder Bosley agreed to let
the Presidency and others have money on loan, for the
printing of the Revelations, if he could control his property in one year, or, as soon as he obtained it.

Decided that Elder Bosley broke the covenant which he
made September 4, 1834—therefore he is not a member of
this Church, unless he make satisfaction to those whom
he injured.

Also Isaac H. Bishop was complained of as having
spoken evil of the High Council, by saying that "the
High Council had the wrong tree to bark up," which

was testified to by J. M. Corrill, President Rigdon and others.

It was decided that Isaac H. Bishop shall make public confession to the satisfaction of the injured, and walk as a Saint in all things.

The hand of the Lord shall be upon them, until they repent in sackcloth and ashes, and shall effect their temporal and spiritual interests unless they repent.

CHAPTER XVII.

SUNDRY COUNCIL MEETINGS IN VERMONT, OHIO, AND NEW YORK.

Minutes of the Vermont Conference.

July 17th.—The Twelve met in conference, agreeably to previous appointment, at St. Johnsbury, Vermont.

Resolved:—That this State be within the limits of this conference,and include the branches in Littleton, Dalton, and Landaff, in New Hampshire, to be called the Vermont Conference.

The St. Johnsbury branch numbered forty-one members; Danville, twenty-three; Charlton, twenty-one; Jay, eleven; Dalton, fifteen; Landaff, four; Littleton, ten; Andover, Vermont, fifteen; Beneeon, seven; and Lewis, New York, seventeen.

Six of the council addressed the conference on principles of faith and action.

Adjourned to the 18th, when the remaining six members of the council enforced the necessity of sending up wise men, and purchasing lands, according to the commandments—which the Saints readily agreed to do.

Sunday, 19th.—Our public meeting was attended by more than a thousand people, and during our conference nine were baptized.

ORSON HYDE,
WM. E. M'LELLIN,
Clerks.

The remainder of this month, I was continually engaged in translating an alphabet to the Book of Abraham, and **The Prophet at work on the Book of Abraham.** arranging a grammar of the Egyptian language as practiced by the ancients.

August 2nd, being the Sabbath, I preached a part of the day.

Minutes of the High Council at Kirtland.

Kirtland, August 4th, 1835, a High Council of the Church of Christ of Latter day Saints assembled in conference, consisting of Presidents Joseph Smith, Jun., Oliver Cowdery, Sidney Rigdon, Hyrum Smith, David Whitmer, John Whitmer, and W. W. Phelps, and others, to take into consideration certain items contained in letters from abroad— one from Warren A. Cowdery, Presiding Elder of the Freedom Conference, and one from Elder William E. M'Lellin. The first reads as follows:

"FREEDOM, July 29th, 1835.

"DEAR BROTHER:—Elder Jared Carter called on this church last Thursday, on his way east, soliciting donations and subscriptions for finishing the house in your place. Although the subject of such a mission, in connection with his name, had been mentioned in the *Messenger and Advocate*, still, as no other method had been taken to impress the subject on our minds, it had measurably passed out, or ceased to make any impression—therefore, we were in some degree taken on surprise. To the recollection of any of the church, neither the Twelve, the Bishop, nor any others clothed with authority have ever mentioned this subject to us, except incidentally. It surely was never made a subject of public instruction—as Brother Carter had just reasons to expect it had been, he felt an embarrassment peculiar to such a situation. He undertook to preach to us yesterday, but from the aforesaid embarrassment, or the deadness, or the covetousness of the church, he could get none of the Spirit of the Lord to assist him. I am free to say that I attributed more to the latter cause than the former; yet notwithstanding, we made out in donations and subscriptions which I trust will realize $341.37½. May the Lord bless and prosper him, and all His faithfull servants; and may they find favor in the sight of God and man, is the prayer of your unworthy brother,

"WARREN A. COWDERY.

"To Oliver Cowdery."

From this short letter we discover that the Elders failed in the outset to fill their great and important mission, as they know the Lord has commanded us to build a house, in which to receive an endowment, previous to the redemption of Zion; and that Zion could not be redeemed until this takes place. Knowing that the committee were to journey for the express purpose of soliciting donations, they have failed to hold them up and set forth this first important thing; and in consequence God has not blessed them as He otherwise would. We remind you of these things in the name of the Lord, and refer you to the Book of

Covenants, 2nd section, 2nd part, and 12th paragraph, and ask, did we not instruct you to remember first the house, secondly the cause of Zion, and then the publishing of the word to the nations?

The other item referred to is an extract from Elder William E. M'Lellin's letter to his wife, as follows:—

"You say that it will not be in your power to go to school this summer. I am glad that it is not, since Elder Hyde has returned and given me a description of the manner in which it is conducted; though we do not wish to cast any reflections."

This the Council considered to be a libel on the face of it. Elder M'Lellin says, "We do not wish to cast any reflections," when the highest insult and reflections are cast by it upon the Church, the Presidency, and those who are held in much higher estimation in the sight of God and this Church than themselves.

The vote of the Council was: We hereby inform Elders M'Lellin and Hyde that we withdraw our fellowship from them until they return and make satisfaction face to face.

We further inform the Twelve, that as far as we can learn from the churches through which we have traveled, you have set yourselves up as an independent council, subject to no authority of the Church, a kind of outlaws! This impression is wrong, and will, if persisted in, bring down the wrath and indignation of heaven upon your heads. The other ten are directed to proceed on and finish the conferences, and the two may act upon their own judgment whether to proceed or return.

President Joseph Smith, Jun., read to the Council a letter from Elder William Smith, which was approved, and filled our hearts with joy.

A letter was presented from Elder Thomas B. Marsh. The Council referred him to the commandment, which requires none to leave or bring his family without revelation or decision of the High Council.

We discover an error in Elder Marsh's letter—he says, "to the able preaching of William E. M'Lellin and Parley P. Pratt." We conclude that if it had been the preaching of the Lord, as it should have been, He would have had the honor, and not these men. To close, we add that unless this epistle is heeded in all its parts, in its full force, those who rebel against it shall be dealt with by the Lord accordingly, for we ask this, being agreed as touching this thing. We wish you to understand that your duty requires you to seek first the kingdom of heaven and its righteousness; that is, attend to the first things first, and then all things will be added, and that complaint about your families will be less frequent. Don't preach yourselves crucified for your wives' sake, but remember that Christ was crucified, and you are sent out to be special witnesses of this thing. Men do not wish to hear these little things, for there is no salvation in them, but there is in the other.

Let the hands of the ten be strengthened, and let them go forth in the name of the Lord, in the power of their mission, giving diligent heed to the direction of the Holy Spirit. We say, be strong in the Lord, and in the power of His might; for great things await you, and great blessings are in store for you. Let the power of the two be upon the Seventy until the two make full satisfaction; for the Seventy shall be blessed, and are blessed. The man who presumes to speak evil of the dignities which God has set in His Church, to his family, or to anybody else, shall be cursed in his generation. Remember the 109th Psalm. His bishopric shall be taken from him unless he speedily repents. Be it known that God is God, and when He speaks, let all the congregation say, Amen. We have evil insinuations enough in Kirtland to grapple with that are suggested by the father of lies, without having them from those who are sent out to put down insinuations. May God bless you to be more wise in the future. Amen.*

OLIVER COWDERY, Clerk.

Minutes of the Massachusetts Conference.

Bradford, Massachusetts, August 7th. Nine of the traveling High Council met and decided that the limits of the conference embrace the State of Massachusetts, to be called the Massachusetts Conference.

Elder Chase had his license and membership taken from him because of gambling for money, and then breaking bread to the Saints before he confessed his sins.

Elder Holmes' license was taken from him in consequence of a disagreement between him and his wife, which was of long standing. It was therefore considered that if a man cannot preserve peace in his own family, he is not qualified to rule the Church of God.

A letter of complaint was written to Kirtland by Elder Gibson Smith, of Norfolk, Connecticut, against Elder Gladden Bishop, upon which he was suspended, and referred to the conference at Bradford for trial. No one appeared to substantiate the complaint against Elder Bishop, who was, therefore, acquitted on that point; but upon further inquiry, it was proved that he had erred in spirit and in doctrine, and was considerably inclined to [excessive] enthusiasm, and much lifted up. The council therefore took his license from him, until he became more instructed, and also get his spirit and feelings more amalgamated with his brethren.

Elder James Patten of North Providence, Rhode Island, was excommunicated for improper conduct, and refusing to give up his license. This action was ordered to be published in the *Messenger and Advocate.*

* It appears that the minutes of this High Council at Kirtland were intended to be sent to the Twelve as a communication.

The people in this region were generally hard and unbelieving, and but little preaching called for, except by the Church.

The appointment for our conference at Dover, New Hampshire, was recalled on account of the small number of disciples in that place, and no business of importance to be transacted. Also the conferences at Saco and Farmington were altered so as to close at Farmington one month earlier than the former appointment, and notices accordingly were forwarded by mail.

ORSON HYDE, Clerk.

August 8th, a council was held in Kirtland, for the

Blessing the
"Sons of Zion."

purpose of laying hands on Father Duncan and others of the sons of Zion.

Minutes of the High Council.

The High Council of Kirtland assembled, August 10th, to hear complaint of President Joseph Smith, Jun., against Elder Reynolds Cahoon, in that the latter had failed to do his duty in correcting his children, and instructing them in the way of truth and righteousness; which was proved and decision given accordingly. Elder Cahoon confessed the correctness of the decision and promised to make public acknowledgment before the Church.

OLIVER COWDERY, Clerk.

CHAPTER XVIII.

THE BOOK OF DOCTRINE AND COVENANTS PRESENTED TO THE GENERAL ASSEMBLY OF THE PRIESTHOOD AND THE CHURCH.

A general assembly of the Church of Latter-day Saints was held at Kirtland on the 17th of August, 1835, to take into consideration the labors of a committee appointed by a general assembly of the Church on the 24th of September, 1834, for the purpose of arranging the items of the doctrine of Jesus Christ for the government of the Church. The names of the committee were: Joseph Smith, Jun., Sidney Rigdon, Oliver Cowdery and Frederick G. Williams, who, having finished said book according to the instructions given them, deem it necessary to call a general assembly of the Church to see whether the book be approved or not by the authorities of the Church: that it may, if approved, become a law and a rule of faith and practice to the Church. Wherefore, Oliver Cowdery and Sidney Rigdon, members of the First Presidency, (Presidents Joseph Smith, Jun., and Frederick G. Williams being absent on a visit to the Saints in Michigan,) appointed Thomas Burdick, Warren Parrish, and Sylvester Smith clerks, and proceeded to organize the whole assembly as follows:

They organized* the High Council of the church at Kirtland, and Presidents W. W. Phelps and John Whitmer organized the High Council of the church in Missouri.

Bishop Newel K. Whitney organized his counselors of the church in

---

* The use of the term "organized" here means merely that the various councils and quorums were arranged by their respective presidencies in the order proper for that assembly, not that they were then organized in the sense of bringing them into existence.

Kirtland, and acting Bishop John Corrill organized the counselors of the church in Missouri.

Presidents Leonard Rich, Levi W. Hancock, Sylvester Smith and Lyman Sherman organized the council of the Seventy. Elder John Gould, acting president, organized the Elders. Ira Ames, acting president, organized the Priests. Erastus Babbitt, acting president, organized the Teachers. William Burgess, acting president, organized the Deacons. And they also, as the assembly was large, appointed Thomas Gates, John Young, William Cowdery, Andrew H. Aldrich, Job L. Lewis and Oliver Higley assistant presidents of the day, to assist in preserving order in the whole assembly.

Elder Levi W. Hancock being appointed chorister, a hymn was sung, and the services for the day opened by the prayer of President Oliver Cowdery, and the solemnities of eternity rested upon the audience.

Another hymn was then sung. After transacting some business for the Church, such as ordaining Morris Phelps to the High Priesthood; Warren Parrish, to the First Seventy; Sherman Gilbert, an Elder; and blessing James Foster, Dean Gould, Berjamin Gifford, Elisha H. Groves and Joseph Hartshorn, the assembly adjourned for one hour.

Afternoon: A hymn was sung, when President Rigdon arose and rebuked some of the authorities for not being in their seats at the time appointed.

President Cowdery arose and introduced the "Book of Doctrine and Covenants of the Church of the Latter-day Saints," in behalf of the committee. He was followed by President Rigdon, who explained the manner by which they intended to obtain the voice of the assembly for or against said book.

According to said arrangement, W. W. Phelps bore record that the book presented to the assembly was true. President John Whitmer, also, rose and testified that it was true.

Elder John Smith, taking the lead of the High Council in Kirtland, bore record that the revelations in said book were true, and that the lectures were judiciously arranged and compiled, and were profitable for doctrine. Whereupon, the High Council of Kirtland accepted and acknowledged them as the doctrine and covenants of their faith by a unanimous vote.

Elder Levi Jackman, taking the lead for the High Council of the church in Missouri, bore testimony that the revelations in said book were true, and the said High Council of Missouri accepted and acknowledged them as the doctrine and covenants of their faith, by a unanimous vote.

President W. W. Phelps then read the written testimony of the Twelve, as follows:

TESTIMONY OF THE TWELVE APOSTLES TO THE TRUTH OF THE BOOK OF
DOCTRINE AND COVENANTS.

"*The testimony of the Witnesses to the Book of the Lord's Commandments, which commandments He gave to His Church through Joseph
Smith, Jun., who was appointed by the voice of the Church, for
this purpose.*

"We therefore feel willing to bear testimony to all the world of mankind, to every creature upon the face of all the earth, that the Lord has
borne record to our souls, through the Holy Ghost shed forth upon us,
that these Commandments were given by inspiration of God, and are
profitable for all men, and are verily true. We give this testimony
unto the world, the Lord being our helper; and it is through the grace
of God the Father, and His Son Jesus Christ, that we are permitted to
have this privilege of bearing this testimony unto the world, in the
which we rejoice exceedingly, praying the Lord always that the children
of men may be profited thereby.

(Signed)

"THOMAS B. MARSH,
"DAVID W. PATTEN,
"BRIGHAM YOUNG,
"HEBER C. KIMBALL,
"ORSON HYDE.
"WM. E. M'LELLIN,
"PARLEY P. PRATT,
"LUKE S. JOHNSON,
"WILLIAM SMITH,
"ORSON PRATT,
"JOHN F. BOYNTON,
"LYMAN E. JOHNSON."*

Elder Leonard Rich bore record of the truth of the book, and the
council of the Seventy accepted and acknowledged it as the doctrine
and covenants of their faith, by a unanimous vote.

Bishop Newel K. Whitney bore record of the truth of the book, and

* In this testimony of the Twelve to the Book of Doctrine and Covenants, as published in the History of Joseph Smith in the *Millennial Star*, the names of the
Apostles were not appended, but it is thought proper that they should be inserted
here in the order in which they stood in the quorum. The document was undoubtedly prepared before the departure of the Twelve for the east, as it was well known
that the work of the committee on selection and compilation would present the
Doctrine and Covenants to a general assembly before the Twelve would return.

with his counselors accepted and acknowledged it as the doctrine and covenants of their faith, by a unanimous vote.

Acting Bishop John Corrill bore record of the truth of the book, and with his counselors accepted and acknowledged it as the doctrine and covenants of their faith, by a unanimous vote.

Acting President John Gould gave his testimony in favor of the book, and with the Elders accepted and acknowledge it as the doctrine and covenants of their faith, by a unanimous vote.

Ira Ames, acting president of the Priests, gave his testimony in favor of the book, and with the Priests accepted and acknowledged it as the doctrine and covenants of their faith, by a unanimous vote.

Erastus Babbitt, acting president of the Teachers, gave his testimony in favor of the book, and they accepted and acknowledged it as the doctrine and covenants of their faith, by a unanimous vote.

William Burgess, acting president of the Deacons, bore record of the truth of the book, and they accepted and acknowledged it as the doctrine and covenants of their faith, by a unanimous vote.

The venerable assistant president, Thomas Gates, then bore record of the truth of the book, and with his five silver-haired assistants, and the whole congregation, accepted and acknowledged it as the doctrine and covenants of their faith, by a unanimous vote.

The several authorities and the general assembly, by a unanimous vote, accepted the labors of the committee.

President W. W. Phelps then read the following article on marriage,* which was accepted and adopted and ordered to be printed in said book, by a unanimous vote, namely:

Article on Marriage.

"According to the custom of all civilized nations, marriage is regulated by laws and ceremonies; therefore we believe that all marriages in this Church of Christ of Latter-day Saints should be solemnized in a public meeting or feast prepared for that purpose, and that the solemnization should be performed by a Presiding High Priest, High Priest, Bishop, Elder or Priest, not even prohibiting those persons who are desirous to get married, of being married by other authority. We believe that it

---

* It should be observed that this "Article on Marriage" presented by W. W. Phelps, and also the one on "Government and Laws in General," presented by Oliver Cowdery, were not presented as revelations and were not published as such at the time, but were expressions, of course, of the belief of the Saints at that period on those subjects. It should also be noted that these two articles were presented and acted upon in the absence of the Prophet who was at the time visiting Saints and preaching in Michigan.

is not right to prohibit members of this Church from marrying out of the Church, if it be their determination so to do; but such persons will be considered weak in the faith of our Lord Jesus Christ.

"Marriage should be celebrated with prayer and thanksgiving, and at the solemnization, the persons to be married, standing together, the man on the right and the woman on the left, shall be addressed by the person officiating as he shall be directed by the Holy Spirit, and if there be no legal objections, he shall say, calling each by name: 'You both mutually agree to be each other's companion, husband and wife, observing the legal rights belonging to this condition: that is, keeping yourselves wholly for each other, and from all others, during your lives?' And when they have both answered 'yes,' he shall pronounce them 'husband and wife,' in the name of the Lord Jesus Christ, and by virtue of the laws of the country and authority vested in him. 'May God add His blessings and keep you to fulfill your covenants from henceforth and forever. Amen.'

"The clerk of every church should keep a record of all marriages solemnized in his branch. All legal contracts of marriage made before a person is baptized into this Church should be held sacred and fulfilled. Inasmuch as this Church of Christ has been reproached with the crime of fornication and polygamy, we declare that we believe that one man should have one wife, and one woman but one husband, except in case of death, when either is at liberty to marry again. It is not right to persuade a woman to be baptized contrary to the will of her husband; neither is it lawful to influence her to leave her husband. All children are bound by law to obey their parents, and to influence them to embrace any religious faith, or be baptized, or leave their parents without their consent, is unlawful and unjust. We believe that husbands, parents, and masters, who exercise control over their wives, children and servants, and prevent them from embracing the truth, will have to answer for that sin."

President Oliver Cowdery then read the following article on "Governments and Laws in General," which was accepted and adopted and ordered to be printed in said book, by a unanimous vote:

Of Governments and Laws in General.

"That our belief with regard to earthly governments and laws in general may not be misinterpreted nor misunderstood, we have thought proper to present, at the close of this volume, our opinion concerning the same.

"We believe that governments were instituted of God for the benefit of man, and that he holds men accountable for their acts in relation to them, both in making laws and administering them for the good and safety of society.

"We believe that no government can exist in peace, except such laws are framed and held inviolate as will secure to each individual the free exercise of conscience, and the right and control of property, and the protection of life.

"We believe that all governments necessarily require civil officers and magistrates to enforce the laws of the same, and that such as will administer the law in equity and justice should be sought for, and upheld by the voice of the people (if a republic,) or the will of the sovereign.

"We believe that religion is instituted of God, and that men are amenable to Him, and to Him only, for the exercise of it, unless their religious opinions prompt them to infringe upon the rights and liberties of others; but we do not believe that human law has a right to interfere in prescribing rules of worship to bind the consciences of men, or dictate forms for public or private devotion; that the civil magistrate should restrain crime, but never control conscience; should punish guilt, but never suppress the freedom of the soul.

"We believe that all men are bound to sustain and uphold the respective governments in which they reside, while protected in their inherent and inalienable rights by the laws of such governments; and that sedition and rebellion are unbecoming every citizen thus protected, and should be punished accordingly; and that all governments have a right to enact such laws as in their own judgments are best calculated to secure the public interest; at the same time, however, holding sacred the freedom of conscience.

"We believe that every man should be honored in his station: ruler or magistrate as such—being placed for the protection of the innocent and the punishment of the guilty; and that to the laws all men owe respect and deference, as without them peace and harmony would be supplanted by anarchy and terror; human laws being instituted for the express purpose of regulating our interests as individuals and nations between man and man; and divine laws given of heaven prescribing rules on spiritual concerns, for faith and worship, both to be answered by man to his Maker.

"We believe that rulers, states, and governments have a right, and are bound to enact laws for the protection of all citizens in the free exercise of their religious belief; but we do not believe that they have a right, in justice, to deprive citizens of this privilege, or proscribe them in their opinions, so long as a regard and reverence are shown to the laws, and such religious opinions do not justify sedition or conspiracy.

"We believe that the commission of crime should be punished according to the nature of the offense, that murder, treason, robbery, theft, and the breach of the general peace, in all respects, should be punished according to their criminality, and their tendency to evil among men, by the laws of that government in which the offense is committed; and for the public peace and tranquility all men should step forward and use their ability in bringing offenders against good laws to punishment.

"We do not believe it just to mingle religious influence with civil government, whereby one religious society is fostered and another proscribed in its spiritual privileges, and the individual rights of its members, as citizens, denied.

"We believe that all religious societies have a right to deal with their members for disorderly conduct, according to the rules and regulations of such societies; provided that such dealings be for fellowship and good standing; but we do not believe that any religious society has authority to try men on the right of property or life, to take from them this world's goods, or to put them in jeopardy of either life or limb; or to inflict any physical punishment upon them; they can only excommunicate them from their society, and withdraw from them their fellowship.

"We believe that men should appeal to the civil law for redress of all wrongs and grievances where personal abuse is inflicted, or the right of property or character infringed, where such laws exist as will protect the same; but we believe that all men are justified in defending themselves, their friends and property, and the government from the unlawful assaults and encroachments of all persons in times of exigency when immediate appeal cannot be made to the laws, and relief afforded.

"We believe it just to preach the Gospel to the nations of the earth, and warn the righteous to save themselves from the corruption of the world; but we do not believe it right to interfere with bond servants; neither preach the Gospel to, nor baptize them contrary to the will and wish of their masters; nor to meddle with or influence them in the least to cause them to be dissatisfied with their situations in this life, thereby jeopardizing the lives of men; such interference we believe to be unlawful, and unjust, and dangerous to the peace of every government allowing human beings to be held in servitude."

A hymn was then sung. President Sidney Rigdon returned thanks;

after which the assembly was blessed by the Presidency with uplifted hands, and dismissed.

OLIVER COWDERY,

SIDNEY RIGDON,

Presidents.

THOMAS BURDICK,

WARREN PARRISH,

SYLVESTER SMITH,

Clerks.*

* Following is the title page and preface of the first edition of the Doctrine and Covenants.

DOCTRINE AND COVENANTS

OF

THE CHURCH OF THE LATTER-DAY SAINTS:

CAREFULLY SELECTED

FROM THE REVELATIONS OF GOD,

AND COMPILED BY

Joseph Smith, Junior,
Oliver Cowdery,
Sidney Rigdon,
Frederick G. Williams,
(Presiding Elders of the Church,)

PROPRIETORS.

———

KIRTLAND, OHIO,

PRINTED BY F. G. WILLIAMS & CO.,

For the Proprietors.

1835.

PREFACE.

———

To the Members of the Church of the Latter-day Saints,

DEAR BRETHREN:—We deem it to be unnecessary to entertain you with a lengthy preface to the following volume, but merely to say that it contains in short the leading items of the religion which we have professed to believe.

The first part of the book will be found to contain a series of lectures as delivered before a theological class in this place, and in consequence of their embracing the important doctrine of salvation, we have arranged them in the following work.

The second part contains items or principles for the regulation of the Church as taken from the revelations which have been given since its organization, as well as from former ones.

There may be an aversion in the minds of some against receiving anything purporting to be articles of religious faith, in consequence of there being so many now extant; but if men believe a system, and profess that it was given by inspiration, certainly the more intelligibly they can present it, the better. It does not make a principle untrue to print it, neither does it make it true not to print it.

The Church, viewing this subject to be of importance, appointed, through their servants and delegates the High Council, your servants to select and compile this work. Several reasons might be adduced in favor of this move of the Council, but we only add a few words. They knew that the Church was evil spoken of in many places, its faith and belief misrepresented, and the way of truth thus subverted. By some it was represented as disbelieving the Bible; by others as being an enemy to all good order and uprightness; and by others as being injurious to the peace of all governments, civil and political.

We have, therefore, endeavored to present, though in few words, our belief, and when we say this, humbly trust, the faith and principles of this society as a body.

We do not present this little volume with any other expectation than that we are to be called to answer to every principle advanced, in that day when the secrets of all hearts will be revealed, and the reward of every man's labor be given him.

With sentiments of esteem and sincere respect, we subscribe ourselves your brethren in the bonds of the Gospel of our Lord Jesus Christ,

> JOSEPH SMITH, JUN.,
> OLIVER COWDERY,
> SIDNEY RIGDON,
> FREDERICK G. WILLIAMS.

KIRTLAND, OHIO, February 17, 1835.

CHAPTER XIX.

THE PROPHET'S RETURN FROM MICHIGAN TO KIRTLAND—HIS ADDRESS TO THE ELDERS OF THE CHURCH.

Minutes of the High Council at Kirtland—Trial of Almon W. Babbitt.

On the 19th, a charge was preferred before a council of the Presidency, against Elder Almon W. Babbitt, for not keeping the Word of Wisdom; for stating the Book of Mormon was not essential to our salvation, and that we have no articles of faith except the Bible.

Elder J. B. Smith testified that Elder Babbitt had assumed the prerogative of dictating to him in his preaching; and that he was not keeping the Word of Wisdom.

Elder Babbitt said that he had taken the liberty to break the Word of Wisdom, from the example of President Joseph Smith, Jun., and others, but acknowledged that it was wrong; that he had taught the Book of Mormon and Commandments as he had thought to be wisdom, and for the good of the cause; that he had not intended to dictate to Elder J. B. Smith, but only to advise with him.

The council reproved Elder Babbitt, and instructed him to observe the Word of Wisdom, and commandments of the Lord in all things; also that it is not advisable for any Elder to take his wife with him on a mission to preach.

WARREN PARRISH, Clerk.

Conference at Saco, Maine.

Seven of the Twelve met in conference at Saco, Maine, August 21st.

The church in that place numbered fifty-seven; the Dover branch in New Hampshire, eight.

The council gave instructions on the redemption of Zion, the building of the Temple in Kirtland, and the printing of the word of God to the nations, etc., etc.; and some were added to the Church during their stay.

The church in Saco contributed seventy or eighty dollar, to assist the

Twelve to return home, which the Twelve recorded as a memento in their behalf, according to covenant.

Sunday, August 23.—I arrived at Kirtland from my visit to Michigan. Return of the Prophet to Kirtland.

On the 24th the High Council at Kirtland ordained Jonathan Stevens an Elder, and instructed him and his sons, Uzziel and Lyman, and his son-in-law, John E. Page,* Elders, to locate their families and then go forth and preach the Gospel; also that John E. Page. Joseph H. Tippits and J. W. Tippits go to Missouri this fall to purchase land for the church in Essex, New York, according to previous appointment by the voice of said church.

August 28.—This day I preached on the duty of wives.

The traveling High Council assembled in conference at Farmington, Maine, and resolved—that this be called the "Maine Conference." The The Conference at Farmington, Maine. church at Farmington numbered thirty-two; in Sitter B., twenyt-two; in Akwry, twenty-five; in Errol, New Hampshire, twenty; all in good standing.

September 1.—I wrote the following communication to John Whitmer, Esq., editor, which was published in the *Messenger and Advocate*, page The Prophet's Letter to the Elders. 179, *et seq.*:

TO THE ELDERS OF THE CHURCH OF LATTER-DAY SAINTS:†

After so long a time, and after so many things have been said, I feel it my duty to drop a few hints, that perhaps the Elders traveling through the world, to warn the inhabitants of the earth to flee the wrath to come, and save themselves from this untoward generation—

---

* John E. Page was born February 25, 1799, in Trenton Township, Oneida County, New York. He was baptized by the brother of Martin Harris—Emar Harris—in August, 1833, in Ohio, and ordained an Elder in September, 1833. He was now, on his removal to Kirtland, in his thirty-sixth year.

† This is a most important document, since in it the Prophet reviews the actions and motives of himself and associates in settling the Church in Missouri. It is a most just and conservative statement of the case, a statement in which the errors and overzeal of some of the Elders and Saints are admitted and deplored. It also admirably portrays the Prophet as the conservative force in the Church, and gives an insight into the greatness and inspiration of his mind.

may be aided in a measure, in doctrine, and in the way of their duty. I have been laboring in this cause for eight years, during which time I have traveled much, and have had much experience. I removed from Seneca County, New York, to Geauga County, Ohio, in February, 1831.

I received, by a heavenly vision, a commandment in June following, to take my journey to the western boundaries of the State of Missouri, and there designate the very spot which was to be the central place for the commencement of the gathering together of those who embrace the fullness of the everlasting Gospel. Accordingly I undertook the journey, with certain ones of my brethren, and after a long and tedious journey, suffering many privations and hardships, arrived in Jackson County, Missouri, and after viewing the country, seeking diligently at the hand of God, He manifested Himself unto us, and designated, to me and others, the very spot upon which He designed to commence the work of the gathering, and the upbuilding of an "holy city," which should be called Zion — Zion, because it is a place of righteousness, and all who build thereon are to worship the true and living God, and all believe in one doctrine, even the doctrine of our Lord and Savior Jesus Christ. "Thy watchmen shall lift up the voice; with the voice together shall they sing: for they shall see eye to eye, when the Lord shall bring again Zion" (Isaiah lii: 8).

Here we pause for a moment to make a few remarks upon the idea of gathering to this place. It is well known that there were lands belonging to the government, to be sold to individuals, and it was understood by all, at least we believed so, that we lived in a free country, a land of liberty and of laws, guaranteeing to every man, or any company of men, the right of purchasing lands, and settling and living upon them; therefore we thought no harm in advising the Latter-day Saints, or "Mormons," as they are reproachfully called, to gather to this place, inasmuch as it was their duty (and it was well understood so to be) to purchase with money, lands, and live upon them, not infringing upon the rights of any individual, or community of people; always keeping in view the saying, "Do unto others as you would wish others to do unto you;" following also the good injunction, "Deal justly, love mercy, and walk humbly with thy God."

These were our motives in teaching the people, or Latter-day Saints, to gather together, beginning at this place; and inasmuch as there are those who have had different views from this, we feel that it is a cause of deep regret. Be it known unto all men, that our principles concerning this thing have not been such as have been represented by those who, we have every reason to believe, are designing and wicked men, that have said that this was our doctrine: "To infringe upon the rights of a people who inhabit our civil and free country, such as to drive the inhabitants of Jackson County from their lands, and take possession thereof unlawfully." Far, yea, far be such a principle from our hearts. It never entered into our minds; and we only say, that God shall reward such in that day when He shall come to make up His jewels.

But to return to my subject. After having ascertained the very spot, and having the happiness of seeing quite a number of the families of my brethren comfortably situated upon the land, I took leave of them and journeyed back to Ohio, and used every influence and argument that lay in my power to get those who believed in the everlasting covenant, whose circumstances would admit, and whose families were willing to remove to the place which I had designated to be the land of Zion; and thus the sound of the gathering, and of the doctrine, went abroad into the world; and many, having a zeal not according to knowledge, and not understanding the pure principles of the doctrine of the Church, have, no doubt, in the heat of enthusiasm, taught and said many things which were derogatory to the genuine character and principles of the Church; and for these things we are heartily sorry, and would apologize, if apology would do any good.

But we pause here, and offer a remark upon the saying which we learn has gone abroad, and has been handled in a manner detrimental to the cause of truth, by saying, "that in preaching the doctrine of gathering,we break up families, and give license for men to leave their families,women their husbands, children their parents and slaves their masters,thereby deranging the order and breaking up the harmony and peace of society." We shall here show our faith, and thereby, as we humbly trust, put an end to these false and wicked misrepresentations, which have caused, we have every reason to believe, thousands to think they were doing God's service, when they were persecuting the children of God; whereas, if they could have enjoyed the true light, and had a just understanding of our principles, they would have embraced them with all their hearts, and been rejoicing in the love of the truth. And now to show our doctrine on this subject, we shall commence with the first principles of the Gospel, which are faith, repentance, and baptism for the remission of sins, and the gift of the Holy Ghost by the laying on of the hands. This we believe to be our duty—to teach to all mankind the doctrine of repentance,which we shall endeavor to show from the following quotations:

"Then opened He their understandings, that they might understand the scriptures, and said unto them, Thus it is written, and thus it behoved Christ to suffer, and to rise from the dead the third day: and that repentance and remission of sins should be preached in His name among all nations, beginning at Jerusalem" (Luke xxiv: 45, 46, 47).

By this we learn that it behoved Christ to suffer, and to be crucified, and rise again on the third day, for the express purpose that repentance and remission of sins should be preached to all nations.

"Then Peter said unto them, Repent, and be baptized every one of you in the name of Jesus Christ for the remission of sins, and ye shall receive the gift of the Holy Ghost. For the promise is unto you, and to your children, and to all that are afar off, even as many as the Lord our God shal call" (Acts ii: 38, 39).

By this we learn that the promise of the Holy Ghost is made unto as many as those to whom the doctrine of repentance was to be preached, which was unto all nations. And we discover also, that the promise was to extend by lineage; for Peter says, not only unto you, but "to your children, and to all that are afar off." From this we infer, that the promise was to continue unto their children's children, and even unto as many as the Lord their God should call. We discover here that we are blending two principles together in these quotations. The first is the principle of repentance, and the second is the principle of the remission of sins; and we learn from Peter that remission of sins is to be obtained by baptism in the name of the Lord Jesus Christ; and the gift of the Holy Ghost follows inevitably, for, says Peter, "you shall receive the Holy Ghost."

Therefore we believe in preaching the doctrine of repentance in all the world, both to old and young, rich and poor, bond and free, as we shall endeavor to show hereafter how, and in what manner, and how far, it is binding on the consciences of mankind, making proper distinctions between old and young, men, women, children and servants. But we discover, in order to be benefitted by the doctrine of repentance, we must believe in obtaining the remission of sins. And in order to obtain the remission of sins, we must believe in the doctrine of baptism in the name of the Lord Jesus Christ. And if we believe in baptism for the remission of sins, we may expect a fulfillment of the promise of the Holy Ghost, for the promise extends to all whom the Lord our God shall call; and hath He not surely said, as you will find in the last chapter of Revelation—"And the Spirit and the bride say, Come. And let him that heareth say, Come. And let him that is athirst come. And whosoever will, let him take the water of life freely" (Rev. xxii: 17).

Again, the Savior says, "Come unto me, all ye that labor, and are heavy laden, and I will give you rest. Take my yoke upon you, and learn of me; for I am meek and lowly in heart: and ye shall find rest unto your souls. For my yoke is easy, and my burden is light" (Matt. xi: 28, 29, 30).

Again, Isaiah says, "Look unto me, and be ye saved, all the ends of the earth: for I am God, and there is none else. I have sworne by myself, the word is gone out of my mouth in righteousness and shall not return, That unto me every knee shall bow, every tongue shall swear. Surely shall one say, in the Lord have I righteousness and strength: even to Him shall men come; and all that are incensed against Him shall be ashamed" (Isaiah xlv: 22-24).

And to show further connections in proof of the doctrine above named, we quote the following scriptures:

"Him hath God exalted with His right hand, to be a Prince and a Savior, for to give repentance to Israel, and forgiveness of sins. And we are His witnesses of these things; and so is also the Holy Ghost, whom God hath given to them that obey Him" (Acts v: 31, 32).

"But when they believed Philip, preaching the things concerning the Kingdom of God, and the name of Jesus Christ, they were baptized, both men and women. Then Simon, himself, believed also: and when he was baptized, he continued with Philip, and wondered, beholding the miracles and signs which were done. Now when the apostles which were at Jerusalem heard that Samaria had received the word of God, they sent unto them Peter and John: who, when they were come down, prayed for them, that they might receive the Holy Ghost: (for as yet he was fallen upon none of them, only they were baptized in the name of the Lord Jesus.) Then laid they their hands on them, and they received the Holy Ghost."

"And as they went on their way, they came unto a certain water, and the eunuch said, See, here is water, what doth hinder me to be baptized? And Philip said, If thou believest with all thine heart, thou mayest. And he answered and said, I believe that Jesus Christ is the Son of God. And he commanded the chariot to stand still, and they went down both into the water, both Philip and the eunuch, and he baptized him. And when they were come up out of the water, the Spirit of the Lord caught away Philip, and the eunuch saw him no more, and he went on his way rejoicing. But Philip was found at Azotus; and passing through, he preached in all the cities, till he came to Cesarea" (Acts viii: 12-17; 36-40).

"While Peter yet spake these words, the Holy Ghost fell on all them which heard the word. And they of the circumcision, which believed, were astonished, as many as came with Peter, because that on the Gentiles also was poured out the gift of the Holy Ghost, for they heard them speak with tongues and magnify God. Then answered Peter, Can any man forbid water, that these should not be baptized, which have received the Holy Ghost as well as we? And he commanded them to be baptized in the name of the Lord. Then prayed they him to tarry certain days" (Acts x: 44-48).

"And on the Sabbath, we went out of the city, by a river side where prayer was wont to be made; and we sat down and spake unto the women which resorted thither. And a certain woman, named Lydia, a seller of purple, of the city of Thyatira, which worshiped God, heard us; whose heart the Lord opened, that she attended unto the things spoken of by Paul. And when she was baptized, and her household, she besought us, saying, If ye have judged me to be faithfu to the Lord. come into my house, and abide there; and she constrained us" (Acts xvi: 13-15).

"And at midnight Paul and Silas prayed, and sang praises to God; and the prisoners heard them. And suddenly there was a great earthquake, so that the foundations of the prison were shaken; and immediately all the doors were opened, and every one's bands were loosed. And the keeper of the prison awaking out of his sleep, and seeing the prison doors open, he drew out his sword and would have killed himself, supposing the prisoners had been fled. But Paul cried with a loud voice, saying, Do thyself no harm, for we are all here. Then he called for a light, and sprang in, and came trembling and fell down before Paul and Silas, and brought them out, and said, Sirs, what must I do to be saved? And they said, Believe on the Lord Jesus Christ, and thou shalt be saved, and thy house. And they spoke unto him the word of the Lord, and to all that were in the house. And he took them the same hour of the night, and washed their stripes, and was baptized, he and all his straightway. And when he had brought them into his house, he set met before them, and rejoiced, believing in God, with all his house" (Acts xvi: 25-34).

"And it came to pass that while Apollos was at Corinth, Paul, having passed through the upper coasts, came to Ephesus, and finding certain disciples, he said unto them, Have ye received the Holy Ghost since ye believed? And they said unto him, we have not so much as heard whether there be any Holy Ghost. And he said unto them, Unto what then were ye baptized? And they said, Unto John's baptism. Then said Paul, John verily baptized with the baptism of repentance, saying unto the people, that they should believe on Him which should come after him, that is on Christ Jesus. When they heard this, they were baptized in the name of the Lord Jesus. And when Paul had laid his hands upon them, the Holy Ghost came on them, and they spake with tongues and prophesied" (Acts xix: 1-6).

"And one Ananias, a devout man according to the law, having a good report of all the Jews which dwelt there, came unto me, and stood and said unto me, Brother Saul, receive thy sight. And the same hour I looked upon him, and he said, The God of our fathers hath chosen thee that thou shouldst know His will, and see that Just One, and shouldst hear the word of His mouth. For thou shalt be his witness unto all men, of what thou hast seen and heard. And now, why tarriest thou? Arise and be baptized, and wash away thy sins, calling on the name of the Lord" (Acts xxii: 12-16).

"For when for the time ye ought to be teachers, ye have need that one teach you again which be the first principles of the oracles of God, and are become such as have need of milk and not of strong meat. For every one that useth milk is unskillful in the word of righteousness, for he is a babe. But strong meat belongeth to them that are of full age, even those who by reason of use, have their senses exercised to discern both good and evil" (Heb. v: 12-14).

"Therefore, leaving the principles of the doctrine of Christ, let us go on unto perfection; not laying again the foundation of repentance from dead works, and of faith toward God, and of the doctrine of baptisms, and of laying on of hands, of resurrection of the dead, and of eternal judgment. And this will we do, if God permit. For it is impossible for those who were once enlightened, and have tasted of the heavenly gift, and were made partakers of the Holy Ghost, and have tasted the good word of God, and the powers of the world to come, if they shall fall away, to renew them again unto repentance, seeing they crucify to themselves the Son of God afresh, and put Him to an open shame" (Heb. vi: 1-6).

These quotations are so plain, in proving the doctrine of repentance and baptism for the remission of sins, I deem it unnecessary to enlarge this letter with comments upon them; but I shall continue the subject in my next.

In the bonds of the new and everlasting covenant,

JOSEPH SMITH, JUN.

II.

TO THE ELDERS OF THE CHURCH OF THE LATTER-DAY SAINTS.*

At the close of my letter in the September number of the *Messenger and Advocate* I promised to continue the subject there commenced. I do so with a hope that it may be a benefit and a means of assistance in the labors of the Elders, while they are combating the prejudices of a crooked and preverse generation, by having in their possession the facts of my religious principles, which are misrepresented by almost all those whose crafts are in danger by the same; and also, to aid those who are anxiously inquiring, and have been excited to do so from rumor,

---

* It has been decided to let the several divisions of this communication to the Elders of the Church appear together in this one chapter. There were three separate communication of the Prophet, as they appear in the *Messenger and Advocate* for September, November and December, 1835, respectively; but as they constitute one continuous address, it is believed that it will in every way be better to have them appear together in one chapter.

to ascertain correctly what my principles are. I have been drawn into this course of proceeding by persecution, that is brought upon us from false rumors and misrepresentations concerning my sentiments.

But to proceed. In the letter alluded to, the principles of repentance and baptism for the remission of sins were not only set forth, but many passages of scripture were quoted, clearly elucidating the subject; let me add, I do positively rely upon the truth of those principles inculcated in the New Testament, and then pass on from the above named items, to the item or subject of the gathering, and show my views upon this point. It is a principle I esteem to be of the greatest importance to those who are looking for salvation in this generation, or in these, that may be called, "the latter times." All that the prophets that have written, from the days of righteous Abel, down to the last man that has left any testimony on record for our consideration, in speaking of the salvation of Israel in the last days, goes directly to show that it consists in the work of the gathering.

First, I shall begin by quoting from the prophecy of Enoch, speaking of the last days: "Righteousness will I sent down out of heaven, and truth will I send forth out of the earth, to bear testimony of mine Only Begotten, His resurrection from the dead (this resurrection I understand to be the corporeal body); yea, and also the resurrection of all men; righteousness and truth will I cause to sweep the earth as with a flood, to gather out mine own elect from the four quarters of the earth, unto a place which I shall prepare, a holy city, that my people may gird up their loins, and be looking forth for the time of my coming, for there shall be my tabernacle, and it shall be called Zion, a new Jerusalem" (Pearl of Great Price, ch. vii: 62, 1902 edition).

Now I understand by this quotation, that God clearly manifested to Enoch the redemption which He prepared, by offering the Messiah as a Lamb slain from before the foundation of the world; and by virtue of the same, the glorious resurrection of the Savior, and the resurrection of all the human family, even a resurrection of their corporeal bodies, is brought to pass; and also righteousness and truth are to sweep the earth as with a flood. And now, I ask, how righteousness and truth are going to sweep the earth as with a flood? I will answer. Men and angels are to be co-workers in bringing to pass this great work, and Zion is to be prepared, even a new Jerusalem, for the elect that are to be gathered from the four quarters of the earth, and to be established an holy city, for the tabernacle of the Lord shall be with them.

Now Enoch was in good company in his views upon this subject: "And I heard a great voice out of heaven, saying, Behold, the tabernacle of God is with men, and He will dwell with them, and they shall be His people and God Himself shall be with them, and be their God" (Revelation xxi: 3).

I discover by this quotation, that John upon the isle of Patmos, saw the same thing concerning the last days, which Enoch saw. But before the tabernacle can be with men, the elect must be gathered from the four quarters of the earth. And to show further upon this subject of the gathering, Moses, after having pronounced the blessing and cursing upon the children of Israel, for their obedience or disobedience, says thus:

"And it shall come to pass, when all these things are come upon thee, the blessing and the curse which I have set before thee, and thou shalt call them to mind, among all the nations whither the Lord thy God hath driven thee, and shalt return unto the Lord thy God, and shalt obey His voice, according to all that I command thee, this day, thou and thy children, with all thine heart, and with all thy soul, then the Lord thy God will turn thy captivity, and have compassion upon thee, and will return and gather thee from all the nations whither the Lord thy God hath scattered thee. If any of thine be driven out unto the outmost parts of heaven, from thence will the Lord thy God gather thee, and from thence will He fetch thee" (Deut. xxx: 1-4).

It has been said by many of the learned and wise men, or historians, that the Indians or aborigines of this continent, are of the scattered tribes of Israel. It has been conjectured by many others, that the aborigines of this continent are not of the tribes of Israel, but the ten tribes have been led away into some unknown regions of the north. Let this be as it may, the prophecy I have just quoted "will fetch them," in the last days, and place them in the land which their fathers possessed. And you will find in the 7th verse of the 30th chapter, quoted, "And the Lord thy God will put all these curses upon thine enemies, and on them that hate thee, which persecuted thee."

Many may say that this scripture is fulfilled, but let them mark carefully what the prophet says: "If any are driven out unto the utmost parts of heaven," (which must mean the breadth of the earth). Now this promise is good to any, if there should be such, that are driven out, even in the last days, therefore, the children of the fathers have claim unto this day. And if these curses are to be laid over on the heads of their enemies, wo be unto the Gentiles. (See Book of Mormon III Nephi, ch. xvi, current edition.) "Wo unto the unbelieving of the Gentiles, saith the Father." And again (see Book of Mormon, III Nephi xx: 22, current edition, which says), "Behold this people will I establish in this land, unto the fulfilling of the covenant which I made with your father Jacob, and it shall be a New Jerusalem." Now we learn from the Book of Mormon the very identical continent and spot of land upon which the New Jerusalem is to stand, and it must be caught up according to the vision of John upon the isle of Patmos.

Now many will feel disposed to say, that this New Jerusalem spoken of, is the Jerusalem that was built by the Jews on the eastern continent. But you will see, from Revelation xxi: 2, there was a New Jerusalem coming down from God out of heaven, adorned as a bride for her husband; that after this, the Revelator was caught away in the Spirit, to a great and high mountain, and saw the great and holy city descending out of heaven from God. Now there are two cities spoken of here. As everything cannot be had in so narrow a compass as a letter, I shall say with brevity, that there is a New Jerusalem to be establtshed on this continent, and also Jerusalem shall be rebuilt on the eastern continent (See Book of Mormon, Ether xiii: 1-12). "Behold, Ether saw the days of Christ, and he spake also concerning the house of Israel, and the Jerusalem from whence Lehi should come; after it should be destroyed, it should be build up again, a holy city unto the Lord, wherefore it could not be a New Jerusalem, for it nad been in a time of old." This may suffice, upon the subject of gathering, until my next.

I now proceed, at the close of my letter, to make a few remarks on the duty of Elders with regard to their teaching parents and children, husbands and wives, masters and slaves, or servants, as I said I would in my former letter.

And first, it becomes an Elder when he is traveling through the world, warning the inhabitants of the earth to gather together, that they may be built up an holy city unto the Lord, instead of commencing with chil-lren, or those who look up to parents or guardians to influence their minds, thereby drawing them from their duties, which they rightfully owe these legal guardians, they should commence their labors with parents, or guardians; and their teachings should be such as are calculated to turn the hearts of the fathers to the children, and the hearts of children to the fathers; and no influence should be used with children, contrary to the consent of their parents or guardians; but all such as can be persuaded in a lawful and righteous manner, and with common consent, we should feel it our duty to influence them to gather with the people of God. But otherwise let the responsibility rest upon the heads of parents or guardians, and all condemnation or consequences be upon their heads, according to the dispensation which he hath committed unto us; for God hath so ordained, that His work shall be cut short in righteousness, in the last days; therefore, first teach the parents, and then, with their consent, persuade the children to embrace the Gospel also. And if children embrace the Gospel, and their parents or guardians are unbelievers, teach them to stay at home and be obedient to their parents or guardians, if they require it; but if they consent to let them gather with the people of God, let them do so, and there shall be no wrong; and let all things be done carefully and righteously and God will extend to all such His guardian care.

And secondly, it is the duty of Elders, when they enter into any house, to let their labors and warning voice be unto the master of that house; and if he receive the Gospel, then he may extend his influence to his wife also, with consent, that peradventure she may receive the Gospel; but if a man receive not the Gospel, but gives his consent that his wife may receive it, and she believes, then let her receive it. But if a man forbid his wife, or his children, before they are of age, to receive the Gospel, then it should be the duty of the Elder to go his way, and use no influence against him, and let the responsibility be upon his head; shake off the dust of thy feet as a testimony against him, and thy skirts shall then be clear of their souls. Their sins are not to be answered upon such as God hath sent to warn them to flee the wrath to come, and save themselves from this untoward generation. The servants of God will not have gone over the nations of the Gentiles, with a warning voice, until the destroying angel will commence to waste the inhabitants of the earth, and as the prophet hath said. "It shall be a vexation to hear the report." I speak thus because I feel for my fellow men; I do it in the name of the Lord, being moved upon by the Holy Spirit. Oh, that I could snatch them from the vortex of misery, into which I behold them plunging themselves, by their sins; that I might be enabled by the warning voice, to be an instrument of bringing them to unfeigned repentance, that they might have faith to stand in the evil day!

Thirdly, it should be the duty of an Elder, when he enters into a house, to salute the master of that house, and if he gain his consent, then he may preach to all that are in that house; but if he gain not his consent, let him not go unto his slaves, or servants, but let the responsibility be upon the head of the master of that house, and the consequences thereof, and the guilt of that house is no longer upon his skirts, he is free; therefore, let him shake off the dust of his feet, and go his way. But if the master of that house give consent, the Elder may preach to his family, his wife, his children and his servants, his man-servants, or his maid-servants, or his slaves; then it should be the duty of the Elder to stand up boldly for the cause of Christ, and warn that people with one accord to repent and be baptized for the remission of sins, and for the Holy Ghost, always commanding them in the name of the Lord, in the spirit of meekness, to be kindly affectionate one toward another, that the fathers should be kind to their children, husbands to their wives, masters to their slaves or servants, children obedient to their parents, wives to their husbands, and slaves or servants to their masters.

"Wives submit yourselves unto your own husbands, as unto the Lord, for the husband is the head of the wife, even as Christ is the head of the Church; and He is the Savior of the body. Therefore, as the Church is subject unto Christ, so let the wives be to their own husbands, in everything. Husbands, love your wives, even as Christ also loved the Church and gave Himself for it, that He might sanctify and cleanse it with the washing of water by the Word, that He might present it to Himself a glorious Church, not having spot or wrinkle, or any such thing, but that it should be holy and without blemish, so ought men to love their own wives as their own bodies. He that loveth his wife, loveth himself, for no man ever yet hated his own flesh, but nourisheth and cherisheth it, even as the Lord the Church, for we are members of His body, of His flesh, and of His bones. For this cause shall a man leave his father and mother, and shall be joined unto his wife, and they two shall be one flesh" (Ephesians v: 22-31).

Wives, submit yourselves unto your own husbands, as it is fit in the Lord. Husbands, love your wives, and be not bitter against them. Children, obey your parents in all things, for this is well pleasing unto the Lord. Fathers, provoke not your children to anger, lest they be discouraged. Servants, obey in all things your masters, according to the flesh, not with eye-service, as men-pleasers, but in singleness of heart, fearing God (Colossians iii: 18-22).

But I must close this letter, and resume the subject in another number.

In the bonds of the New and Everlasting Covenant,

JOSEPH SMITH, JUN.

III.

TO THE ELDERS OF THE CHURCH OF LATTER-DAY SAINTS.

I have shown unto you, in my last, that there are two Jerusalems spoken of in holy writ, in a manner I think satisfactory to your minds; at any rate I have given my views upon the subject. I shall now proceed to make some remarks from the sayings of the Savior, recorded in the 13th chapter of His Gospel according to St. Matthew, which, in my mind, afford us as clear an understanding upon the important subject of the gathering, as anything recorded in the Bible. At the time the Savior spoke these beautiful sayings and parables contained in the chapter above quoted, we find Him seated in a ship on account of the multitude that pressed upon Him to hear His words; and He commenced teaching them, saying:

"Behold, a sower went forth to sow, and when he sowed, some seeds fell by the way side, and the fowls came and devoured them up: some fell upon stony places, where they had not much earth; and forthwith they sprang up because they had no deepness of earth: and when the sun was up they were scorched: and because they had no root they withered away. And some fell among thorns; and the thorns sprung up and choked them: but other fell in good ground, and brought forth fruit, some an hundred fold, some sixty fold, some thirty fold. Who hath ears to hear, let him hear.

"And the disciples came and said unto Him, Why speakest thou unto them in parables? [I would here remark, that the 'them' made use of in this interrogation, is a personal pronoun, and refers to the multitude.] He answered and said unto them, [that is unto the disciples,] because it is given unto *you* to know the mysteries of the Kingdom of Heaven, but to *them*, [that is, unbelievers,] it is not given; for whosoever hath, to him shall be given, and he shall have more abundance; but whosoever hath not, from him shall be taken away even that he hath."

We understand from this saying, that those who had been previously looking for a Messiah to come, according to the testimony of the Prophets, and were then, at that time looking for a Messiah, but had not sufficient light, on account of their unbelief, to discern Him to be their Savior; and He being the true Messiah, consequently they must be disappointed, and lose even all the knowledge, or have taken away from them all the light, understanding, and faith which they had upon this subject; therefore he that will not receive the greater light, must have taken away from him all the light which he hath; and if the light which is in you become darkness, behold, how great is that darkness! "Therefore," says the Savior, "speak I unto them in parables, because they, seeing, see not, and hearing, they hear not, neither do they understand: and in them is fulfilled the prophecy of Esaias which saith, "By hearing ye shall hear, and shall not understand; and seeing ye shall see, and not perceive."

Now we discover that the very reason assigned by this prophet, why they would not receive the Messiah, was, because they did not or would not understand; and seeing, they did not perceive; "for this people's heart is waxed gross, and their ears are dull of hearing, their eyes have closed, lest at any time they should see with their eyes, and hear with their ears, and understand with their heart, and should be converted, and I should heal them." But what saith He to His disciples? "Blessed are your eyes for they see, and your ears for they hear, for verily I say unto you, that many prophets and righteous men have desired to see those things which ye see, and have not seen them; and to hear those things which ye hear, and have not heard them.''

We again make remark here—for we find that the very principle upon which the disciples were accounted blessed, was because they were permitted to see with their eyes and hear with their ears—that the condemnation which rested upon the multitude that received not His saying, was because they were not willing to see with their eyes, and hear with their ears; not because they could not, and were not privileged to see and hear, but because their hearts were full of iniquity and abominations; "as your fathers did, so do ye." The prophet, foreseeing that they would thus harden their hearts, plainly declared it; and herein is the condemnation of the world; that light hath come into the world, and men choose darkness rather than light, because their deeds are evil. This is so plainly taught by the Savior, that a wayfaring man need not mistake it.

And again—hear ye the parable of the sower. Men are in the habit, when the truth is exhibited by the servants of God, of saying, All is mystery; they have spoken in parables, and, therefore, are not to be understood. It is true they have eyes to see, and see not, but none are so blind as those who will not see; and, although the Savior spoke this to such characters, yet unto His disciples he expounded it plainly; and we have reason to be truly humble before the God of our fathers, that He bath left these things on record for us, so plain, that notwithstanding the exertions and combined influence of the priests of Baal, they have not power to blind our eyes, and darken our understanding, if we will but open our eyes, and read with candor, for a moment.

But listen to the explanation of the parable of the Sower: "When any one heareth the word of the Kingdom, and understandeth it not, then cometh the wicked one, and catcheth away that which was sown in his heart." Now mark the expression—that which was sown in his heart. This is he which receiveth seed by the way side. Men who have no principle of righteousness in themselves, and whose hearts are full of iniquity, and have no desire for the principles of truth, do not understand the word of truth when they hear it. The devil taketh away the word of truth out of their hearts, because there is no desire for righteousness in them. "But he that receiveth seed in stony places, the same is he that heareth the word, and anon, with joy receiveth it; yet hath he not root in himself, but dureth for a while: for when tribulation or persecution ariseth because of the word, by and by, he is offended. He also that receiveth seed among the thorns, is he that heareth the word; and the care of this world, and the deceitfulness of riches choke the word, and he becometh unfruitful. But he that received seed into the good ground is he that heareth the word, and understandeth it, which also beareth fruit, and bringeth forth, some an hundred fold, some sixty, some thirty.'' Thus the Savior Himself explains unto His disciples the parable which He put forth, and left no mystery or darkness upon the minds of those who firmly believe on His words.

We draw the conclusion, then, that the very reason why the multitude, or the world, as they were designated by the Savior, did not receive an explanation upon His parables, was because of unbelief. To you. He says, (speaking to His disciples,) it is given to know the mysteries of the Kingdom of God. And why? Because of the faith and confidence they had in Him. This parable was spoken to demonstrate the effects that are produced by the preaching of the word; and we believe that it has an allusion directly, to the commencement, or the setting up of the Kingdom in that age; therefore we shall continue to trace His sayings concerning this Kingdom from that time forth, even unto the end of the world.

"Another parable put He forth unto them, saying, [which parable has an allusion to the setting up of the Kingdom, in that age of the world also.] The Kingdom of Heaven is likened unto a man which sowed good seed in his field, but while men slept, his enemy came and sowed tares among the wheat, and went his way. But when the blade was sprung up, and brought forth fruit, then appeared the tares also; so the servants of the householder came and said unto him, Sir, didst not thou sow good seed in thy field? From whence, then, hath it tares? He said unto them, An enemy hath done this. The servants said unto him, Wilt thou then that we go and gather them up? But he said, Nay; lest while ye gather up the tares, ye root up also the wheat with them. Let both grow together until the harvest: and in the time of harvest I will say to the reapers, Gather ye together first the tares, and bind them in bundles to burn them, but gather the wheat into my barn.''

Now we learn by this parable, not only the setting up of the Kingdom in the days of the Savior, which is represented by the good seed, which produced fruit, but also the corruptions of the Church, which are represented by the tares, which were sown by the enemy, which His disciples would fain have plucked up, or cleansed the Church of, if their views had been favored by the Savior. But He, knowing all things, says, Not so. As much as to say, your views are not correct, the Church is in its infancy, and if you take this rash step, you will destroy the wheat, or the Church, with the tares; therefore it is better to let them grow together until the harvest, or the end of the world, which means the destruction of the wicked, which is not yet fulfilled, as we shall show hereafter, in the Savior's explanation of the parable, which is so plain that there is no room left for dubiety upon the mind, notwithstanding the cry of the priests—"parables, parables! figures,

figures! mystery, mystery! all is mystery!" But we find no room for doubt here, as the parables were all plainly elucidated.

And again, another parable put He forth unto them, having an allusion to the Kingdom that should be set up, just previous to or at the time of the harvest, which reads as follows—"The Kingdom of Heaven is like a grain of mustard seed, which a man took and sowed in his field: which indeed is the least of all seeds: but, when it is grown, it is the greatest among herbs, and becometh a tree, so that the birds of the air come and lodge in the branches thereof." Now we can discover plainly that this figure is given to represent the Church as it shall come forth in the last days. Behold, the Kingdom of Heaven is likened unto it. Now, what is like unto it?

Let us take the Book of Mormon, which a man took and hid in his field, securing it by his faith, to spring up in the last days, or in due time; let us behold it coming forth out of the ground, which is indeed accounted the least of all seeds, but behold it branching forth, yea, even towering, with lofty branches, and God-like majesty, until it, like the mustard seed, becomes the greatest of all herbs. And it is truth, and it has sprouted and come forth out of the earth, and righteousness begins to look down from heaven, and God is sending down His powers, gifts and angels, to lodge in the branches thereof.

The Kingdom of heaven is like unto a mustard seed. Behold, then is not this the Kingdom of heaven that is raising its head in the last days in the majesty of its God, even the Church of the Latter-day Saints, like an impenetrable, immovable rock in the midst of the mighty deep, exposed to the storms and tempests of Satan, but has, thus far, remained steadfast, and is still braving the mountain waves of opposition, which are driven by the tempestuous winds of sinking crafts, which have [dashed] and are still dashing with tremendous foam across its triumphant brow; urged onward with redoubled fury by the enemy of righteousness, with his pitchfork of lies, as you will see fairly represented in a cut contained in Mr. Howe's *Mormonism Unveiled?* And we hope that this adversary of truth will continue to stir up the sink of iniquity, that the people may the more readily discern between the righteous and the wicked.

We also would notice one of the modern sons of Sceva, who would fain have made people believe that he could cast out devils, by a certain pamphlet, the *Millennial Harbinger*, that went the rounds through our country; who felt so fully authorized to brand "Jo" Smith with the appellation of Elymas the sorcerer, and to say with Paul, "O full of all subtlety, and all mischief, thou child of the devil, thou enemy of all righteousness, wilt thou not cease to pervert the right ways of the Lord?" We would reply to this gentleman, Paul we know, and Christ

we know, but who are ye? And with the best of feeling would say to
him, in the language of Paul to those who said they were John's disciples, but had not so much as heard there was a Holy Ghost—to repent
and be baptized for the remission of sins, by those who have legal authority, and under their hands you shall receive the Holy Ghost,
according to the Scriptures:*

"Then laid they *their* hands upon them, and they received the Holy
Ghost (Acts viii: 17.) "And when Paul had laid his hands upon them
the Holy Ghost came on them and they spake with tongues and prophesied" (Acts xix: 6). "Of the doctrine of baptism, and of laying on of
hands, and of resurrection of the dead and of eternal judgment" (Hebrews vi: 2). "How, then, shall they call on him in whom they have not
believed? And how shall they believe in him of whom they have not
heard? And how shall they hear without a preacher? And how shall
they preach, except they be sent? As it is written, How beautiful are
the feet of them that preach the Gospel of peace, and bring glad tidings
of good things" (Romans x: 14, 15). But if this man will not take our
admonition, but will persist in his wicked course, we hope that he will
continue trying to cast out devils, that we may have the clearer proof
that the kingdom of Satan is divided against itself, and consequently
cannot stand; for a kingdom divided against itself, speedily hath an end.

If we were disposed to take this gentleman upon his own ground, and
justly heap upon him that which he so readily and unjustly heaps upon
others, we might go farther—we might say that he has wickedly and
maliciously lied about, villified and traduced the characters of innocent
men. We might invite the gentleman to a public investigation of these
matters, yea, and we do challenge him to an investigation upon any or
all principles wherein he feels opposed to us, in public or in private.
We might farther say that we could introduce him to *Mormonism Unveiled*, also to the right honorable Dr. Philastus Hurlburt, who is the

* In this and several of the following paragraphs the Prophet alludes to Alexander Campbell, founder of the sect of the "Disciples;" and also to an article which
appeared in the *Millennial Harbinger*, Vol. 2 (1831), pages 86-96. The reference
to Elymas, to which the Prophet so strongly replies, stands thus in Campbell's
aritcle—which was afterwards circulated as a pamphlet: "I have never felt so
fully authorized to address mortal man in the style in which Paul addressed Elymas the sorcerer as I feel towards this atheist Smith." (*Millennial Harbinger*,
Vol. 2, p. 96). That is, "O full of all subtlety and all mischief, thou child of the
devil, thou enemy of all righteousness, wilt thou not cease to pervert the right
ways of the Lord" (Acts xiii: 10).

The paragraph dealing with the laying on of hands, and the passages of scripture quoted in support of that doctrine, will also be the better understood when
it is known that while Mr. Campbell and his associates taught faith in God, repentance and baptism for the remission of sins, they rejected wholly the doctrine of
the laying on of hands for the gift of the Holy Ghost, and the enjoyment of the
spiritual blessings which accompany the possession of that Spirit.

legitimate author of the same. who is not so much a doctor of physics as of falsehood, or doctor by name.

We could also give him an introduction to the Reverend Mr. Howe, the illegitimate author of *Mormonism Unveiled*, in order to give currency to the publication, as Mr. Hurlburt about this time was bound over to court for threatening life. He is also an associate of the celebrated Mr. Clapp, who has of late immortalized his name, by swearing that he would not believe a Mormon under oath; and by his polite attention to Hurlburt's wife, which cost him (as we are informed) a round sum. Also his son Matthew testified, that the Book of Mormon had been proved false an hundred times, by Howe's book; and also that he would not believe a Mormon under oath. And also we could mention the Rev. Mr. Bentley, who, we believe, has been actively engaged in injuring the character of his brother-in-law, viz., Elder Sidney Rigdon.

Now the above statements are according to our best information, and we believe them to be true, and this is as fair a sample of the doctrine of Campbellism as we ask, taking the statements of these gentlemen, and judging them by their fruits; and we might add many more to the black catalogue; even the ringleaders not of the Nazarenes, (for how can any good thing come out of Nazareth) but of the far-famed Mentor mob, all sons and legitimate heirs of the same spirit of Alexander Campbell, and *Mormonism Unveiled*, according to the representation of the cut spoken of above.

The above clouds of darkness have long been beating like mountain waves upon the immovable rock of the Church of the Latter-day Saints; and notwithstanding all this, the mustard seed is still towering its lofty branches, higher and higher, and extending itself wider and wider; and the chariot wheels of the Kingdom are still rolling on, impelled by the mighty arm of Jehovah; and in spite of all opposition, will still roll on, until His words are all fulfilled.

Our readers will excuse us for deviating from the subject, when they take into consideration the abuses that have been heaped upon us heretofore, which we have tamely submitted to, until forbearance is no longer required at our hands. Having frequently turned both the right and left cheek, we believe it our duty now to stand up in our own defense. With these remarks we shall proceed with the subject of the gathering.

"And another parable spake He unto them. The Kingdom of heaven is like unto leaven which a woman took and hid in three measures of meal till the whole was leavened." It may be understood that the Church of the Latter-day Saints has taken its rise from a little leaven that was put into three witnesses. Behold, how much this is like the parable! It is fast leavening the lump, and will soon leaven the whole. But let us pass on.

"All these things spake Jesus unto the multitude in parables; and without a parable spake He not unto them: that it might be fulfilled which was spoken by the prophet, saying, I will open my mouth in parables; I will utter things which have been kept secret from the foundation of the world. Then Jesus sent the multitude away, and went into the house: and His disciples came unto Him, saying, Declare unto us the parable of the tares of the field. He answered and said unto them, He that soweth the good seed is the Son of Man; the field is the world; the good seed are the children of the Kingdom; but the tares are the children of the wicked one." Now let our readers mark the expression—"the field is the world, the tares are the children of the wicked one, the enemy that sowed them is the devil, the harvest is the end of the world, [let them carefully mark this expression—*the end of the world*,] and the reapers are the angels."

Now men cannot have any possible grounds to say that this is figurative, or that it does not mean what it says; for he is now explaining what He has previously spoken in parables; and according to this language, the end of the world is the destruction of the wicked, the harvest and the end of the world have an allusion directly to the human family in the last days, instead of the earth, as many have imagined; and that which shall precede the coming of the Son of Man, and the restitution of all things spoken of by the mouth of all the holy prophets since the world began; and the angels are to have something to do in this great work, for they are the reapers. As, therefore, the tares are gathered and burned in the fire, so shall it be in the end of the world; that is, as the servants of God go forth warning the nations, both priests and people, and as they harden their hearts and reject the light of truth, these first being delivered over to the buffetings of Satan, and the law and the testimony being closed up, as it was in the case of the Jews, they are left in darkness, and delivered over unto the day of burning; thus being bound up by their creeds, and their bands being made strong by their priests, are prepared for the fulfillment of the saying of the Savior—"The Son of Man shall send forth His angels, and gather out of His Kingdom all things that offend, and them which do iniquity, and shall cast them into a furnace of fire, there shall be wailing and gnashing of teeth." We understand that the work of gathering together of the wheat into barns, or garners, is to take place while the tares are being bound over, and preparing for the day of burning; that after the day of burnings, the righteous shall shine forth like the sun, in the Kingdom of their Father. Who hath ears to hear, let him hear.

But to illustrate more clearly this gathering: We have another parable—"Again, the Kingdom of heaven is like a treasure hid in a field, the which, when a man hath found, he hideth, and for joy thereof, goeth and selleth all that he hath, and buyeth that field!" The Saints work after this pattern. See the Church of the Latter-day Saints, selling all that they have, and gathering themselves together unto a place that they may purchase for an inheritance, that they may be together and bear each other's afflictions in the day of calamity.

"Again, the Kingdom of heaven is like unto a merchantman seeking goodly pearls, who, when he had found one pearl of great price, went and sold all that he had, and bought it." The Saints again work after this example. See men traveling to find places for Zion and her stakes or remnants, who, when they find the place for Zion, or the pearl of great price, straightway sell that they have, and buy it.

"Again, the Kingdom of heaven is like unto a net that was cast into the sea, and gathered of every kind, which when it was full they drew to shore, and sat down, and gathered the good into vessels, but cast the bad away." For the work of this pattern, behold the seed of Joseph, spreading forth the Gospel net upon the face of the earth, gathering of every kind, that the good may be saved in vessels prepared for that purpose, and the angels will take care of the bad. So shall it be at the end of the world—the angels shall come forth and sever the wicked from among the just, and cast them into the furnace of fire, and there shall be wailing and gnashing of teeth.

"Jesus saith unto them, Have you understood all these things? They say unto Him, Yea, Lord." And we say, yea, Lord; and well might they say, yea, Lord; for these things are so plain and so glorious, that every Saint in the last days must respond with a hearty Amen to them.

"Then said He unto them, therefore every scribe which is instructed in the kingdom of heaven, is like unto a man that is an householder, which bringeth forth out of his treasure things that are new and old."

For the works of this example, see the Book of Mormon coming forth out of the treasure of the heart. Also the covenants given to the Latter-day Saints, also the translation of the Bible—thus bringing forth out of the heart things new and old, thus answering to three measures of meal undergoing the purifying touch by a revelation of. Jesus Christ, and the ministering of angels, who have already commenced this work in the last days, which will answer to the leaven which leavened the whole lump. Amen.

So I close, but shall continue the subject in another number.*

In the bonds of the New and Everlasting Covenant,

JOSEPH SMITH, JUN.

* Notwithstanding this promise of the Prophet, the subject was not again renewed by him. About this time he was so overwhelmed with work and a multitude of other subjects that he did not find time to complete the work he had outlined in these papers.

CHAPTER XX.

SUNDRY AFFAIRS AT KIRTLAND—THE PLEDGE TO REDEEM ZION.

I WENT to New Portage on the 2nd of September, in company with Oliver Cowdery and Sidney Rigdon, to attend a conference; and returned on the 8th. I was engaged in various spiritual and temporal matters for several days. *Conference at New Portage.*

September 14.—In a meeting of a High Council and the Presidency at Kirtland, it was decided that, as the laborer is worthy of his hire, whenever President Jossph Smith, Sen., is called upon to pronounce Patriarchal blessings upon the Church, *Provision Made for Remunerating the Patriarch.* he be paid for his services at the rate of ten dollars per week and his expenses. It was further decided that President Frederick G. Williams be appointed and hereafter serve as scribe, to attend blessing meetings, and that he receive for his services, at the same ratio, having his expenses borne also. It was further decided that President Oliver Cowdery be appointed, and that he act hereafter as Recorder for the Church. It was further decided that Sister *Oliver Cowdery Appointed Church Recorder.* Emma Smith proceed to make a selection of Sacred Hymns, according to the revelation;* and that President W. W. Phelps be appointed to revise and arrange them for printing.

September 16.—The Presidency of the Church assembled and appointed David Whitmer and Samuel H. Smith a committee and general agents to act in the name of, and for, the "Literary Firm." *Agents for the "Literary Firm" of the Church Appointed.*

* See Vol. I, p. 104. Doctrine and Covenants. sec. xxv

MINUTES OF A HIGH COUNCIL HELD IN KIRTLAND, SEPTEMBER 16th, 1835.

The Trial of Elder Henry Green—Sidney Rigdon, Oliver Cowdery and Frederick G. Williams presiding.

A complaint was preferred by President Joseph Smith, Jun., against Brother Henry Green, for accusing President Joseph Smith, Jun., "of rebuking Brother Aldridge wrongfully, and under the influence of an evil spirit."

Brother Green being absent, President Rigdon arose and said, that it was the decision of the Presidency, that the Council proceed to examine the charge preferred, because Brother Green had been regularly summoned by himself.

The Council appointed one to speak on each side; after which the following testimony was heard:

Elder Sylvester Smith testified that Brother Green, on Monday morning last, said that Brother Aldridge was justified in what he said, and that Presidents Joseph and Hyrum Smith were wrong in abusing the old man; and after Elder Smith explained the matter to him, said, that if any man should do so by him, he should call him a scoundrel; and that he should say that any man who would talk as Joseph did, must have the devil in him.

Elder Lorin Babbitt said he was present when the above conversation took place, and heard a considerable part of it, and fully concurred in the statement of Elder Smith; and he heard Brother Green say, previous to the above talk, that although they accused Brother Aldridge of having an evil spirit, yet, if the truth were known, the devil was in them, (namely, Presidents Joseph and Hyrum); for if any man should ask my opinion, and then abuse me in that way, I should call him a scoundrel or a knave.

President Cowdery stated to the Council, that Brother Aldridge was not called upon to give his opinion concerning the book, but said what he did without being called upon to speak; for the book was only handed to him and others to look at, that they might see the quality and goodness.

President Joseph Smith arose and stated that he knew that Brother Aldridge was under the influence of an evil spirit, and had been for a long time.

Councilor Orson Johnson also said that he knew that this was so, by what he had seen and learned, and that he had heard from credible authority, that the old gentleman had been in the habit, for a long time, of neglecting prayer and family worship.

Councilor Samuel H. Smith said, that President Joseph Smith was in the line of his duty when he reproved Brother Aldridge for his evil; and, consequently, Brother Green must have been wrong in opposing him, and saying he [Joseph] acted like a scoundrel, and that the devil was in him.

Councilor Levi Jackman said that Brother Green could not be justified in opposing the servant of the Lord, while in the actual discharge of his duty, and that it was evident that Satan hath sought to make divisions in the Church, and had taken advantage of the occasion of presenting the book, to do this.

The book referred to, was purchased for recording "The Patriarchal Blessings."

President Frederick G. Williams said, that the wickedness of Brother Green in condemning President Smith is evident from the testimony; and that Brother Aldridge also did act foolishly, and by the influence of a wrong spirit, in questioning the integrity of the head of the Church, in the purchase of the book, and that President Smith was and is justifiable in doing as he has done in the matter, and should not be censured, as he has been by Brother Green.

President Oliver Cowdery then arose, and showed, by a few plain remarks who Satan had sought, from the beginning, to destroy the Book of Mormon; and in order to do this, had been actually levelling his shafts against the servants of God, who were called to bring it forth and bear testimony of it to the world; and now had sought occasion against the servants of God, in tempting brethren to say they had equivocated in the price of the record book, which was presented last Sabbath; and that Brother Aldridge, and perhaps others, fell under this evil influence, and Brother Green justifies them in this thing, and condemns President Smith, and is not, and ought not to be justified in so doing.

President Cowdery went on to show that the book was purchased as cheap as it could be, and was actually worth what was given for it, namely, twelve dollars.

Elder Cahoon requested leave to interrupt President Cowdery a moment, to inform the Council that, a moment before, Brother Green passed the house, and when the speaker told him the Council was considering his case, and requested him to come in, he said he should go about his own business, so went on his way regardless of the Council.

President Cowdery resumed, showing that the design of Brother Aldridge, or at least of the spirit that was in him, was to destry the character of the heads of the Church, by charging that we intended to speculate out of the brethren, and extort from them more than the cost of the book; and now, instead of regarding our feelings, he disregards us altogether, and shows that he has no faith in the High Council.

Soon afterwards Brother Green came in, and said that he had been detained longer than he intended, having been to Chagrin on business, and had to deliver the horse and harness to the owner before he could attend the Council.

President Rigdon then arose and decided that Brother Green should not have been hindered from being here, by any other business; and if so, he should have notified the Council, and requested an adjournment.

President Cowdery then observed, that he thought the case sufficiently brought before the Council, and would say no more. And President Rigdon proceeded to give his decision—that Brother Green should have gone, if he were grieved with President Smith, and told him of his difficulty, and should not have said anything about it to his neighbor. And again, that Mr. Aldridge, as has been shown, has been guilty of neglecting his prayers before God, and therefore has not had the Spirit of God to preserve him from the temptations of Satan, and has fallen into evil, and actually did do wrong in raising objections to the price of the book presented last Sabbath, and was under the influence of an evil spirit.

Brother Green fellowships the evil spirit in Brother Aldridge, and says he is justified in what he has done, and therefore it is evident that an evil spirit is reigning in the breast of Brother Green. And it is also as evident, that President Joseph Smith, Jun., was justified in rebuking that evil spirit, and it was not only justifiable in President Smith to rebuke that evil spirit, but it was also his duty as President and First High Priest in the Church of Christ, appointed of God to lead the same in all righteousness.

The decision, then, of the Presidency of the High Council is, in short, that Brother Green be and is now, excluded from this Church, and shall be a member no more, until he comes in by the ordinance of baptism, as appointed by the Gospel, to be done in the Church.

This was agreed to by all the Councilors except Joseph Coe, who queried whether Mr. Green should not have the privilege of confessing his faults, and still be retained in the Church. He therefore thought that it was the privilege of Brother Green to have a re-organization of the Council, and a rehearing. This was about to be granted and the council to be adjourned till tomorrow, but Councilor Coe requested some explanation from the President, and was instructed as follows:—

"When a serious offense is committed, and indignity offered to the High Council, then it is the privilege of the Presidency of the High Council to stamp it with indignation under foot, and cut off the offender as in the case just decided."

Councilor Coe then withdrew his objection to the decision of the

Presidency, which was acknowledged by the whole house, and council adjourned.

SYLVESTER SMITH, Clerk.

Minutes of a High Council held in Kirtland, September 19, 1835. The trial of Elder Jared Carter. President Joseph Smith, Jun., Oliver Cowdery, David Whitmer, Frederick G. Williams, Sidney Rigdon, and W. W. Phelps, present.

COUNCILORS.

John Smith,	Joseph Smith, Sen.,
Orson Johnson,	Joseph Coe,
Newel Knight,	Hyrum Smith,
John Whitmer,	Levi Jackman,
Samuel H. Smith,	Noah Packard,
John Johnson,	Roger Orton,

The object of the Council was stated by President Joseph Smith, Jun., as follows: "Some weeks since Elder Jared Carter preached on the Sabbath in the Church, and some of the brethren found fault with his teachings; and this Council is called upon to decide this matter, and to see who was in fault."

Six were appointed to speak.

Elder Jared Carter proceeded to speak largely, and explain his designs in teaching as he did, saying he believed God directed him by His Spirit, and afterwards being rebuked by Presidents Cowdery, Rigdon and Phelps, he called upon the Lord, and received again a witness of the Spirit that he was right, and the Presidents were wrong. Elder Carter taught in his concluding remarks, that God had shown him by laying His hand upon him in judgment, and delivering him therefrom, that he was thus rebuked by heaven for his iniquity, and that he was made an example to the whole Church, and God would curse them if they did not hold up the committee,* for he was made an example in this thing.

President Rigdon arose and said that he attended the meeting in which Elder Carter spoke, and was certain, and is certain, that he did not have the spirit of wisdom to direct; and after he had sat down, and Elder Samuel H. Smith had occupied some half an hour, filled with the Spirit, he arose again and said, that if any man spoke against the committee, God would curse him, and set the committee away above the common brethren, and said that God would take care of the committee, and the brethren had nothing to do with them, for their

* This was the temple building committee.

station was appointed them of God, and not of man; therefore God will curse any man or woman in the Church who shall speak evil of the committee. He told Elder Carter at the time, in private, that he did wrong; and in company with other of the Presidents, advised him after he should fill a certain mission to the east, that he should make a confession to the Church, in order to satisfy many of the brethren who were aggrieved with him.

President Phelps then arose, and said President Rigdon had truly related the matter, as far as he had gone; but one thing more—Elder Carter commanded the brethren to pray for the committee, and demanded it in the name of the Lord, with an authoritative voice and gesticulation, which are not according to the meekness of the spirit of Jesus.

President Oliver Cowdery arose and said: I do not intend to occupy much time in speaking for those who have spoken have expressed pretty much my mind and feelings on the subject; that in the advice which he and the other two Presidents had given Elder Carter, in the talk they had with him, they did have the spirit of meekness, and only desired to do him good, and had no personal feelings against him, and did not express any, but to the contrary.

President John Whitmer concurred in the statements of the above brethren, and said that he did not believe that God had made an example of Elder Carter, for he was not before the Church as such; and God had not so revealed it to the Saints; and again, it is vain that Elder Carter should command the Saints to pray for the committee, for in so doing, if they did not fellowship him, they must pray for his removal, and so all his designs would be frustrated.

Several others were called upon, and all testified that these things which have been expressed above were true and as they understood them; and one thing further. Elder Carter did say that even the faults of the committee might be charged back upon the brethren if they neglected to pray for them.

After hearing the testimony, the six Councilors spoke, and the sum of their conviction upon the matter was as follows:

Councilor John Smith said he thought that Elder Carter did not express the feelings of his heart, so as to be understood, and perhaps his heart was not so hard as his words.

Father Joseph Smith said that Elder Carter was exalted, and did not receive the admonitions of the Presidents, and in consequence lost the true spirit, and so has erred since the time of his discourse, and needs admonishing.

Councilor Orson Johnson agreed with the above.

Councilor Joseph Coe said that Elder Carter had a small degree of the Spirit in his discourse, and a greater degree in his remarks afterwards, but was awkward in expressing his views, not having much of the Spirit, and that the feelings of his heart were not as expressed by his words.

An inquiry was made of the Court whether this Councilor [Joseph Coe] was correct in appealing to the feelings of men's hearts, and not to the words and actions, as they appeared.

The Court decided that the Council must be confined to facts, words, and actions; and not go into feelings and designs which were not expressed.

The other Councilors concurred in the above.

Councilor Hyrum Smith said that Elder Carter had been blessed of God, and by the prayer of faith the sick had been healed under his administration; yet he does not always have the gift of God and wisdom to direct; so in the case before the Council. Pride had engendered in Elder Carter's heart a desire to excel, and the spirit of meekness was withdrawn, and he was left to err, as has been shown by the testimony, because he is not yet perfect. But he erred in understanding, and his words were wrong; yet the spirit of his heart, or the integrity of the same, might be good in the main.

Elder Carter then arose and said that he was willing to acknowledge his faults, and that he lacked wisdom. He went on to explain how he had erred, and why—being seized with the cholera while at the east, he called upon God for deliverance, and finally received the Spirit of God which healed him, and he then thought it was the same spirit which he had when preaching in Kirtland.

When he was through, President Oliver Cowdery arose, and said that Presidents Rigdon and Phelps had requested him to speak, and they would say nothing as it was getting late, and the case was already plain before the Court. He showed that a man might be highly excited and yet neither have the Spirit of God nor the spirit of Satan; but it came by his own spirit and judgment: therefore some things may be of God, others of men, and others from the adversary; and Elder Carter had in his sermon some of the Spirit of God, but in his last remarks he had it not, but his own spirit of justification and pride, commanding in the name of Jesus, and not by the spirit of Jesus or of meekness, and was very wrong in this thing, also in exalting the committee above the brethren, as if they might not be touched by the brethren; and again, when Elder Carter was healed, it came in answer to his earnest prayer before God; but his impressions about being made an example to the Church were not an answer to prayer, and might be wrong.

President Frederick G. Williams gave his decision, that Brother Carter did err with his lips in speaking, and also erred in understanding the Presidents who labored with him for it, and misinterpreted their admonitions, which led him into what followed, and finally has brought him before this Council.

President David Whitmer said, that according to the testimony it is plain that Elder Carter has lacked in humility, and also in confidence in his brethren, and erred as expressed by President Williams.

President Joseph Smith, Jun., arose, and said, that the decision of his mind was, that Brother Jared Carter erred in judgment in not understanding what the brethren desired of him when they labored with him; and he erred in spirit when he taught in the Church the things testified of here; and that the hand of the destroyer was laid upon him because he had a rebellious spirit from the beginning; and the word of the Lord has been spoken by my mouth, that it should come upon him, and this Council should see it, and now that he has been seized by the destroyer comes in fulfillment of His [the Lord's] word; and God requires him to bear testimony of it before the Church, and warn them to be careful, and not to do as he had done. But instead of doing this, he said he would prove the Book of Mormon, and one thing or another, not being sufficiently humble to deliver just the message that was required, and so he stumbled and could not get the Spirit, and the brethren were not edified, and he did not do the thing that God required, but erred in choosing words to communicate his thoughts; such as commanding the prayers of the Church instead of soliciting them, and also of making himself an example for the Church, when it was only the things that he suffered which were to be as a check upon transgression.

His rebelling against the advice and counsel of the Presidents was the cause of his falling into the hands of the destroyer again, as he had done before when he rebelled against the counsel that had been given him by the authorities of the Church; and that in all this, Elder Carter has not designed to do wickedly, but he erred in judgment, and deserves reproof, and the decision is—that he shall acknowledge his errors on the morrow, before the congregation, and say, Brethren, I am fully convinced that I have erred in spirit, in my remarks before you, when I spoke here a few Sabbaths since; and now I ask your forgiveness. And if he do this in full faith, and is truly humble before God, God will bless him abundantly as He hath been wont to do.

Elder Carter arose, and justified the decision of the Court, and promised to comply.

SYLVESTER SMITH, Clerk.

I labored in obtaining blessings, which were written by
Oliver Cowdery. We were thronged with company, so that our labor in this thing was hindered; but we obtained many precious things,
and our souls were blessed. O Lord, may Thy Holy Spirit
be with Thy servants forever.   Amen.

The Prophet
Seeks for
Blessings.

September 23.—I was at home writing blessings for my
most beloved brethren, but was hindered by a multitude
of visitors.   The Lord has blessed our souls
this day, and may God grant to continue His
mercies unto my house this night, for Christ's
sake.   This day my soul has desired the salvation of
Brother Ezra Thayer.   Also Brother Noah Packard came
to my house and loaned the committee one thousand dollars to assist building the house of the Lord.   Oh! may
God bless him a hundred fold, even of the things of the
earth, for this righteous act.   My heart is full of desire
today, to be blessed of the God of Abraham with prosperity, until I shall be able to pay all my debts, for it is
the delight of my soul to be honest.   O Lord, that thou
knowest right well.   Help me, and I will give to the
poor.

Delight of the
Prophet in
Being Honest.

Brothers William, John and Joseph Tippits started for
Missouri, the place designated for Zion, or the Saints'
gathering place.   They came to bid us farewell. The brethren came in to pray with them,
and Brother David Whitmer acted as spokesman.   He prayed in the spirit, and a glorious
time succeeded his prayer; joy filled our hearts and we
blessed them and bid them God speed, and promised them
a safe journey, and took them by the hand and bid them
farewell for a season.   May God grant them long life and
good days.   These blessings I ask upon them for Christ's
sake.   Amen.

Rejoicing
with Brethren
Bound for
Zion.

The High Council met at my house on the 24th to take
into consideration the redemption of Zion.   And it was
the voice of the Spirit of the Lord that we petition the

Governor, that is, those who have been driven out, shall
petition to be set back on their own lands next

The Covenant
to Work for
the Redemp-
tion of Zion.

spring, and that we go next season, to live or
die on our own lands, which we have purchased in Jackson County, Missouri.   We
truly had a good time, and covenanted to struggle for
this thing, until death shall dissolve the union; and if one
falls, that the remainder be not discouraged, but pursue
this object until it be accomplished; which may God
grant unto us in the name of Jesus Christ our Lord.
Also, this day drew up a subscription for enrolling the
names of those who are willing to go up to Missouri
next spring and settle; and I ask God in the name of Jesus
that we may obtain eight hundred or one thousand emigrants.

I spent the 25th of September at home.

CHAPTER XXI.

INCIDENTS FROM THE PROPHET'S EXPERIENCE IN KIRTLAND AND VICINITY.

September 26.—This morning the Twelve returned from their mission to the East, and on the same day the Council of the Presidency of the Church, consisting of Joseph Smith, Jun., Sidney Rigdon, David Whitmer, W. W. Phelps, John Whitmer, Hyrum Smith and Oliver Cowdery, met to consider the case of the Twelve who had previousiy been reproved in consequence of certain letters and reports coming to the ears of the Council. First, the items contained in Warren A. Cowdery's letter, in connection with certain other reports, derogatory to the character and teaching of the Twelve, were considered; and from the testimony of several witnesses (the Twelve) it was proved before the Council that said complaints originated in the minds of persons who were darkened in consequence of covetousness, or some other cause, rather than the spirit of truth. Second, one item contained in Elder Wm. E. M'Lellin's letter to his wife, expressing dissatisfaction with President Rigdon's school. Elder Orson Hyde was also designated with him [M'Lellin] or blamed in the matter, in which they were found to be in the fault, which they frankly confessed, and were forgiven and all things were satisfactorily settled.

Sunday 27.—I attended meeting. Elders Thomas B. Marsh, David W. Patten, Brigham Young and Heber C. Kimball preached and broke bread. The Lord poured out His Spirit and my soul was edified.

Return of the Twelve.

Minutes of the High Council at Kirtland. *Trial of Gladden Bishop,*

The High Council met for the trial of Gladden Bishop, on a charge preferred by the Twelve, "for advancing heretical doctrines, which were derogatory to the character of the Church."

Elder William Smith testified that when Elder Bishop was conversing with a brother concerning the two witnesses mentioned by the Prophets [Rev. xi] he said that he [Bishop] might be one of them, and that he [the brother] might be one himself; that he [Bishop] intended to prophesy the night that an advertisement was put up by an enemy, saying that the Mormon Prophet and others were to be sold by auction in public, that he would not be surprised if the man who put up the advertisement should die at the time of sale.

Elder Brigham Young corroborated the foregoing, and said that Bishop was very erroneous in his tenets of faith.

Elder John Boynton concurred.

Elder Thomas B. Marsh said that Bishop frequently told of women falling in love with him, and observed frequently when passing people that they felt his spirit; also that he was so indolent his presence was oppressive.

Elder L. Johnson testified that on a former trial before the Twelve for error in doctrine, such as, that he might be one of the two witnesses, and that he ought not to travel and preach on account of the women so often falling in love with him, he was not humble when reproved, but justified himself, and preferred a charge against the Council for harsh treatment.

Elder William Smith said, that Bishop, after taking a stand against the Council, finally said it was all right, they had dealt with him in righteousness.

Elders Marsh and Young corroborated the above, that he yielded after being overcome, also that he was capable of magnifying his office if he would.

Elder Heber C. Kimball concurred in the above, also that Bishop said, after he saw his case was hopeless, that the Council had turned him wrong side out.

Elder John P. Greene concurred in full, and, in addition to the above, said that Bishop was so indolent that he would not help himself to a drink of water.

After the pleas of the Councilors and the case was submitted for decision, Brother Bishop arose and made a humble confession for his transgression, and asked forgiveness of the High Council and all the Church, saying that he intended to learn wisdom from the revelations that God had given, and submitted himself to the decision of the Court, being perfectly satisfied with the whole course of the trial.

After much instruction, the President decided that the counsel of the Twelve in this case was given in righteousness, also that Brother Bishop's confession be published in the *Messenger and Advocate*, and he be received in full fellowship, and receive his ordination and license as before; which the Council concurred in, and Brother Bishop was ordained by the Court an Elder.

WARREN PARRISH, Clerk.

An attempt was made in the foregoing Council to criminate the Twelve before the High Council for cutting off Gladden Bishop at their Bradford conference, but their attempt totally failed. I decided that the High Council had nothing to do with the Twelve, or the decisions of the Twelve. But if the Twelve erred they were accountable only to the General Council of the authorities of the whole Church, according to the revelations.

The Authority to which the Twelve are Amenable.

In the afternoon a charge of adultery was preferred against Lorenzo L. Lewis, on general report circulating among the brethren, to which he pleaded not guilty, and the charge was changed to "an illicit intercourse with a female." Lewis confessed that he had disgraced the girl, himself, and the Church, but [was] not guilty of the charge. After hearing the testimony of witnesses, Elders Marsh, M'Lellin, Patten and William Smith, and the pleadings, Elder Lewis confessed that he had done wickedly and had made all the reparation he could, in his confession in the early part of this trial and required his name to be tak'n off the Church records, or dispose of him according to the mind of the Spirit, and submitted to the decision of the Council. The Council decided that Brother Lorenzo L. Lewis be cut off from the Church, being satisfied that the charge preferred is substantiated by evidence, and the Spirit of the Lord; but if he repent, and humble himself to the satisfaction of the Church, he should be received into it again and receive his license. The Council adjourned till morning.

Trial of Lorenzo L. Lewis.

The High Council met on the 29th, and heard a charge against Elder Allen Avery, on an appeal case from an El-
Trial of Elder Allen Avery. ders' Court in Zion, which took away his license for rebelling against their decision. Brother Avery frankly and readily complied with the requisition of the Council, and the President decided that he be restored to fellowship, and receive his license.

In these cases I acted on the part of the defense for the accused, to plead for mercy. The Lord
The Prophet on the Part of the Accused. blessed my soul, and the Council was greatly blessed also, and much good will result from our labors.

I was at home on the 30th, and was visited by many who came to inquire after the work of the Lord.

October 1.—This afternoon I labored on the Egyptian alphabet, in company with Brothers Oliver
The Prophet Learns the Principles of Astronomy as Understood by Abraham. Cowdery and W. W. Phelps, and during the research, the principles of astronomy as understood by Father Abraham and the ancients unfolded to our understanding, the particulars of which will appear hereafter.

On the 2nd of October I wrote the following letter for publication in the *Messenger and Advocate*, (continued from the 1st of September.)*

October 3.—I attended the High Council to investigate charges preferred by Reynolds Cahoon against Elder John
Charges Against the Goulds. Gould "for making expressions calculated to injure the cause we have espoused, and manifesting a strong dissatisfaction with the teachings of the Presidency." Also against Dean Gould for speaking unadvisedly against Elder Rigdon and other Elders.

In the case of John Gould, the accuser and defendant agreed the matter should be talked over, by which all difference of feeling was allayed. Gould confessed and was forgiven.

---

* For this communication see Article II, Chapter XIX. (Note.)

Dean Gould acknowledged that he spoke unadvisedly against President Rigdon, and was forgiven.

In the afternoon I waited on most of the Twelve, at my house, and exhibited to them the ancient records, and gave explanations. This day passed off with the blessing of the Lord.

Sunday, 4.—I started early in the morning, with Brother John Corrill, to hold a meeting in Perry. When about a mile from home we discovered two deer playing in the field, which diverted our minds by giving an impetus to our thoughts upon the subject of the creation of God. We conversed on many topics. The day passed off very agreeably, and the Lord blessed our souls. When we arrived at Perry, we were disappointed of a meeting, through mis-arrangement, but conversed freely with Brother Corrill's relatives, which allayed much prejudice. May the Lord have mercy on their souls. *The Prophet's Journey with John Corrill.*

Monday, 5.—I returned home, being much fatigued from riding in the rain. Spent the remainder of the day in reading and meditation, and in the evening attended a Council of the Twelve Apostles; had a glorious time, and gave them much instruction concerning their duties for time to come; told them that it was the will of God they should take their families to Missouri next season; also this fall to attend the solemn assembly of the first Elders, for the organization of the School of the Prophets; and attend to the ordinance of the washing of feet; and to prepare their hearts in all humility for an endowment with power from on high; to which they all agreed with one accord, and seemed to be greatly rejoiced. May God spare the lives of the Twelve to a good old age, for Christ the Redeemer's sake. Amen. *The Prophet's Meeting With the Twelve.*

Tuesday, 6.—At home. Elder Stevens came to my house and loaned Frederick G. Williams and Co. six hundred dollars, which greatly relieved us of our present

difficulties. May God bless and preserve his soul forever.
A Timely   In the afternoon called to visit my father, who
Loan.   was very sick with a fever: somewhat better
towards evening. Spent the rest of the day in reading
and meditation.

Wednesday, 7.—Went to visit my father, found him
very low, administered some mild herbs,
Illness of
Joseph Smith, agreeably to the commandment. May God
Sen.   grant to restore him immediately to health for
Christ the Redeemer's sake. Amen.

Bishop Whitney and Brother Hyrum Smith started by
stage for Buffalo, New York, to purchase goods to replenish the committee's store. May God grant, in the name
of Jesus, that their lives may be spared, and they have a
safe journey, and no accident or sickness of the least
kind befall them, that they may return in health and in
safety to the bosom of their families.

Blessed of the Lord is Brother Whitney, even the
Bishop of the Church of Latter-day Saints, for the Bishopric shall never be taken away from him
The Prophet's
Blessing on   while he liveth. And the time cometh that
Bishop Whit-   he shall overcome all the narrow-mindedness
ney.
of his heart, and all his covetous desires
that so easily beset him; and he shall deal with a liberal
hand to the poor and the needy, the sick and afflicted, the
widow and the fatherless. And marvelously and miracu-
lously shall the Lord his God provide for him, even that
he shall be blessed with a fullness of the good things of
this earth, and his seed after him from generation to generation. And it shall come to pass, that according to the
measure that he meteth out with a liberal hand to the
poor, so shall it be measured to him again by the hand
of his God, even an hundred fold. Angels shall guard
his house, and shall guard the lives of his posterity, and
they shall become very great and very numerous on the
earth. Whomsoever he blesseth, they shall be blessed;
and whomsoever he curseth, they shall be cursed; and

when his enemies seek him unto his hurt and destruction, let him rise up and curse, and the hand of God shall be upon his enemies in judgment, they shall be utterly confounded and brought to desolation. Therefore he shall be preserved unto the utmost, and his life shall be precious in the sight of the Lord, he shall rise up and shake himself, as a lion riseth out of his lair and roareth until he shaketh the hills; and as a lion goeth forth among the lesser beasts, so shall the going forth of him be whom the Lord hath anointed to exalt the poor, and to humble the rich, therefore his name shall be on high, and his rest among the sanctified. This afternoon I re-commenced translating the ancient records. *Translation of the Writings of Abraham Begun.*

Thursday, 8.—At home. I attended on my *The Prophet's* father with great anxiety.

Friday, 9.—At home. Waited on my father.

Saturday, 10.—At home, and visited the house of my father, found him failing very fast.

Sunday, 11.—Waited on my father again, who was very sick. In secret prayer in the morning, the Lord said, "My servant, thy father shall live." I waited on him all this day with my heart raised to *The Prophet's Care of His Father.* God in the name of Jesus Christ, that He would restore him to health, that I might be blessed with his company and advice, esteeming it one of the greatest earthly blessings to be blessed with the society of parents, whose mature years and experience render them capable of administering the most wholesome advice. At evening Brother David Whitmer came in. We called on the Lord in mighty prayer in the name of Jesus Christ, and laid our hands on him, and rebuked the disease. And God heard and answered our prayers—to the great joy and satisfaction of our souls. Our aged father arose and dressed himself, shouted, and praised the Lord. Called Brother William Smith, who had retired to rest, that he might praise the Lord with us, by joining in songs of praise to the Most High.

Monday, 12.—Rode to Willoughby, in company with my wife, to purchase some goods at William Lyon's store. On our return we found a Mr. Bradley lying across the road. He had been thrown from his wagon, and was much injured by the fall.

Tuesday, 13 —Visited my father, who was very much recovered from his sickness, indeed, which caused us to marvel at the might, power, and condescension of our Heavenly Father, in answering our prayers in his behalf.

Wednesday, 14.—At home.

Thursday, 15.—Labored in father's orchard, gathering apples.

Friday, 16.—Was called into the printing office, to settle some difficulties in that department. In the evening I baptized Ebenezer Robinson.* The Lord poured out His Spirit upon us and we had a good time.

Baptism of Ebenezer Robinson.

Saturday, 17.—Called my family together and arranged my domestic concerns, and dismissed my boarders.

Sunday, 18.—Attended meeting in the chapel, confirmed several that had been baptized, and blessed several children with the blessings of the New and Everlasting Covenant. Elder Parley P. Pratt preached in the forenoon, and Elder John F. Boynton in the afternoon. We had an interesting time.

Monday, 19.—At home. Exhibited the records of antiquity to a number who called to see them.

The Book of Abraham.

---

* Ebenezer Robinson, afterwards somewhat prominent in the Church in Missouri and Illinois as editor. printer and publisher, was born in the town of Floyd, Oneida County, New York, May 25, 1816; and was the son of Nathan and Mary Robinson. He was already a printer of considerable experience when he came to Kirtland in May, 1835, and began work in the Church printing establishment, then running under the firm name of F. G. Williams & Co., though not a member of the Church. For six months he boarded in the families of Oliver Cowdery, F. G. Williams and the Prophet Joseph. "We found them all very pious, good Christian people," he remarks, "(who) asked a blessing at the table and all attended to family worship morning and evening." (The "Return," Vol. I, p. 58). Mr. Robinson did not become immediately converted to the Gospel, but conviction gradually dawned upon his mind, and he finally declared his faith and was baptized by the Prophet as stated in the text.

Tuesday, 20.—At home. Preached in the evening in the school house.

Wednesday, 21.—At home.

Thursday, 22.—At home, attending to my domestic concerns.

Friday 23.—At home. At four o'clock, afternoon, Oliver Cowdery, David Whitmer, Hyrum Smith, John Whitmer, Sidney Rigdon, Samuel H. Smith, Frederick G. Williams and W. W. Phelps assembled, and we united in prayer, with one voice, before the Lord, for the following blessings: That the Lord would give us means sufficient to deliver us from all our afflictions and difficulties wherein we are placed by reason of our debts; that He would open the way and deliver Zion in the appointed time, and that without the shedding of blood; that He would hold our lives precious, and grant that we may live to the common age of man, and never fall into the hands nor power of the mob in Missouri, nor in any other place; that He would also preserve our posterity, that none of them fall, even unto the end of time; that He would give us blessings of the earth sufficient to carry us to Zion, and that we may purchase inheritances in that land, even enough to carry on and accomplish the work unto which He has appointed us; and also that He would assist all others who desire, according to His commandments, to go up and purchase inheritances, and all this easily and without perplexity and trouble; and finally, that in the end He would save us in His celestial kingdom. Amen.

Prayer for Special Blessings.

Saturday, 24.—Mr. Goodrich and wife called to see the ancient [Egyptian] records, and also Dr. Frederick G. Williams to see the mummies. Brothers Hawkes and Carpenter, from Michigan, visited us and tarried over night.

Sunday, 25.—Attended meeting with Brothers Hawkes and Carpenter. President Rigdon preached in the fore

noon, Elder Lyman E. Johnson in the afternoon, after
Meetings in
Kirtland. which Elder Seymour Brunson joined Brother
William Perry and Sister Eliza Brown in mat-
rimony, and I blessed them with long life and prosperity
in the name of Jesus Christ.

In the evening I attended prayer meeting, opened it, and
exhorted the brethren and sisters about one hour. The
Lord poured out His Spirit, and some glorious things
were spoken in the gift of tongues and interpreted concerning the redemption of Zion.

Monday, 26.—Went to Chardon to attend the County
Court in company with my brothers Hyrum, Samuel H.,
and Don Carlos Smith. Brother Samuel was called in
Trial of Sam-
uel Smith for
Neglect of
Military Duty question before this Court for not doing military duty, and was fined because we had not
our conference minutes with us for testimony
to prove that Frederick G. Williams was clerk of the conference. This testimony we should have carried with us
had it not been for the neglect of our counsel or lawyer,
who did not put us in possession of this information [i. e.
that we would need such testimony]. This we felt was a
want of fidelity to his client, and we consider it a base
insult, practiced upon us on account of our faith, that
the ungodly might have unlawful power over us, and
trample us under their unhallowed feet. And in consequence of this neglect, a fine was imposed upon Brother
Samuel of twenty dollars, including costs, for which he
was obliged to sell his cow to defray the expenses of the
same. And I say, in the name of Jesus Christ, that the
money which they have thus unjustly taken shall be a testimony against them, and canker, and eat their flesh as fire.

Tuesday, 27.—In the morning I was called to visit at
Brother Samuel Smith's. His wife was confined and in a
A Prayer and
Promise. dangerous condition. Brother Carlos went to
Chardon after Dr. Williams. I went out into
the field and bowed before the Lord and called upon Him
in mighty prayer in her behalf. And the word of the

Lord came unto me, saying, "My servant Frederick shall come, and shall have wisdom given him to deal prudently, and my handmaid shall be delivered of a living child, and be spared." The doctor came in about one hour afterwards, and in the course of two hours she was delivered, and thus what God had manifested to me was fulfilled every whit. This evening I preached in the school house to a crowded congregation.

Wednesday, 28.—At home, attending to my family affairs.

Thursday, 29.—Brother Warren Parrish commenced writing for me, at fifteen dollars per month. I paid him sixteen dollars in advance out of the committee's store. Father and Mother Smith visited us. While we sat writing Bishop Partridge passed our window, just returned from the East.

Warren Parrish Becomes the Prophet's Scribe.

I was called to appear before the High Council, which was then sitting, to give my testimony in an action brought by Brother William Smith against Brother David Elliot, for whipping his daughter unreasonably. My testimony was in Brother Elliot's favor, from conversation with the parents and the girl at their house in Chagrin, I was satisfied that the girl was in the fault, and that the neighbors were trying to create a difficulty.

Trial of David Elliot.

Returned to our writing room, went to Dr. Williams' after my large journal; made some observations to my scribe concerning the plan of the city, which is to be built up hereafter on this ground consecrated for a Stake of Zion.

While at the doctor's, Bishop Edward Partridge came in in company with President Phelps. I was much rejoiced to see him. We examined the mummies, returned home, and my scribe commenced writing in my journal a history of my life; concluded President Cowdery's second letter to W. W. Phelps, which President Williams had begun.

Bishop Whitney and his wife, with his father and mother, called to visit us. His parents having lately arrived

The Visit of Bishop Whitney's Parents to the Prophet

here from the East, called to make inquiry concerning the coming forth of the Book of Mormon. Bishop Partridge and some others came in. I then sat down and related to them the history of the coming forth of the book, the administration of the angel to me, and taught them the rudiments of the Gospel of Christ. They appeared well satisfied, and I expect to baptize them in a few days, though they have made no request of the kind.*

Went to the Council. The Presidency arose and adjourned. On my return Elder Boynton observed that long

Of Debates in Council.

debates were bad. I replied that it was generally the case that too much altercation was indulged in on both sides, and their debates protracted to an unprofitable length.

We were called to supper. While seated at table we indulged in a free interchange of thought, and Bishop

Hopes for Zion's Redemption.

Whitney observed to Bishop Partridge that the thought had just occurred to his mind that perhaps in about one year from this time they might be seated together around a table on the land of Zion. My wife observed she hoped it might be the case, that not only they, but the rest of the company present, might be seated around her table on that land of promise. The same sentiment was reciprocated from the company around the table, and my heart responded, Amen. God grant it, I ask in the name of Jesus Christ.

After supper I went to the High Council in company with my wife and some others that belonged to my household.

Disorder in a Council Meeting.

I was solicited to take a seat with the Presidency and preside on a trial of Sister Elliot. I did so. My mother was called upon for testimony, and began to relate circumstances that had been brought before the Church and settled. I objected

* The expectation was realized on the last day of October, see p. 297.

to such testimony. The complainant, Brother William Smith, arose and accused me of invalidating or doubting my mother's testimony, which I had not done, nor did I desire to do so. I told him he was out of order, and asked him to sit down. He refused. I repeated my request. He became enraged. I finally ordered him to sit down. He said he would not, unless I knocked him down. I was agitated in my feelings on account of his stubbornness, and was about to leave the house, but my father requested me not to do so. I complied, and the house was brought to order after much debate on the subject, and we proceeded to business.

The decision of the Council in the case of Brother Elliot was, "that the complaint was not without foundation, yet the charge has not been fully sustained, but he has acted injudiciously and brought a disgrace upon himself, his daughter, and upon this Church, because he ought to have trained his child in a way that she would not have required the rod at the age of fifteen years." Brother Elliot made his confession and was forgiven. Sister Elliot confessed her wrong and promised to do better, consequently the Council forgave her. And they were both restored to fellowship.

Friday, 30.—At home. Mr. Franc.s Porter, from Jefferson County, New York, a member of the Methodist church, called to make some inquiry about lands in this place (Kirtland), whether there were any valuable farms for sale, and whether a member of our Church could move into this vicinity and purchase lands and enjoy his own possessions and property without making them common stock. He had been requested to make this inquiry by some brethren who live in the town of Leroy, New York. I replied that I had a valuable farm joining the Temple lot I would sell, and that there were other lands for sale in this place and that we had no common stock business among us; that every man enjoys his own property, or can, if he is disposed, conse-

A Methodist's Inquiry into Conditions at Kirtland.

crate liberally or illiberally to the support of the poor and needy, or the building up of Zion. He also inquired how many members there were in this Church. I told him there were about five or six hundred who communed at our chapel, and perhaps a thousand in this vicinity.

In the evening I was presented with a letter from Brother William Smith, the purport of which is, that he

William Smith's Self-justification.

is censured by the brethren on account of what took place at the Council last night, and wishes to have the matter settled to the understanding of all, that he may not be censured unjustly, considering that his cause was a just one and that he had been materially injured. I replied that I thought we parted with the best of feelings, that I was not to blame on account of the dissatisfaction of others. I invited him to call and talk with me, and that I would talk with him in the spirit of meekness and give him all the satisfaction I could. This reply was by letter.

Saturday, 31.—In the morning Brother Hyrum Smith came in and said he had been much troubled all night and

Hyrum Smith as Peace-maker.

had not slept any, that something was wrong. While talking, Brother William Smith came in, according to my request last night. Brother Hyrum said that he must go to the store. I invited him to stay. He said he would go and do his business and return. He did so. While he was gone Brother William introduced the subject of our difficulty at the Council. I told him I did not want to converse upon the subject until Hyrum returned. He soon came in. I then proposed to relate the occurrences of the Council before named, and wherein I had been out of the way I would confess it, and ask his forgiveness, and then he should relate his story, and make confession wherein he had done wrong, and then leave it to Brother Hyrum Smith and Brother Parrish to decide the matter between us, and I would agree to the decision and be satisfied therewith.

William observed that he had not done wrong, and that I was always determined to carry my points whether right or wrong, and therefore he would not stand an equal chance with me. This was an insult, but I did not reply to him in a harsh manner, knowing his excitable disposition, but tried to reason with him and show him the propriety of a compliance with my request. I finally succeeded with the assistance of Brother Hyrum, in obtaining his assent to the proposition that I had made. I then related my story, and wherein I had been wrong I confessed it, and asked his forgiveness. After I got through he made his statements, justifying himself throughout in transgressing the order of the Council, and treating the authority of the Presidency with contempt. After he had got through Brother Hyrum began to make some remarks in the spirit of meekness. He (William) became enraged. I joined Brother Hyrum in trying to calm his stormy feelings, but to no purpose, he insisted that we intended to add abuse to injury, his passion increased, he arose abruptly, declared that he wanted no more to do with us. He rushed out at the door. We tried to prevail on him to stop, but all to no purpose. He went away in a passion, and soon after sent his license to me. He went home and spread the leaven of iniquity among my brothers, and especially prejudiced the mind of Brother Samuel. I soon learned that he was in the street exclaiming against me, and no doubt our enemies rejoiced at it. And where the matter will end I know not, but I pray God to forgive him and them, and give them humility and repentance.

The feelings of my heart I cannot express on this occasion, I can only pray my Heavenly Father to open their eyes, that they may discover where they stand, that they may extricate themselves from the snare they have fallen into.

After dinner I rode out in company with my wife and

children, Brother Don Carlos and some others. We visited
Brother Roundy* and family, who live near Willoughby.

Visit to Shad-   We had an interesting visit. As soon as I re-
rach Roundy.   turned I was called upon to baptize Samuel
Whitney and his wife and daughter. After baptism we
returned to their house and offered our thanks in prayer.
I obtained a testimony that my brother William would
return to the Church, and repair the wrong he had done,

* This is Shadrach Roundy who afterwards became prominent in Church affairs.
He was born in Rockingham, Windham County, Vermont, January 1, 1789. At
twenty-five he married Betsy Quimby. He first heard of the Gospel on moving
from Vermont to Onondaga County, New York, and in the winter of 1830-1 sought
out the Prophet, then residing at Fayette, Seneca County, New York. After his
first interview he was baptized; and subsequently his wife and all his children of
sufficient age received the Gospel. He removed with the New York Saints to
Ohio, settling near Willoughby, where the Prophet frequently visited him.

CHAPTER XXII.

THE MINISTRY OF THE PROPHET IN KIRTLAND.

Sunday, November 1.—Verily thus said the Lord unto me, His servant, Joseph Smith, Jun.—

Reproof of Reynolds Cahoon.

Revelation.

Mine anger is kindled against my servant Reynolds Cahoon, because of his iniquities, his covetous and dishonest principles, in himself and family, and he doth not purge them away and set his house in order. Therefore, if he repent not, chastisement awaiteth him, even as it seemeth good in my sight, therefore go and declare unto him these words.

I went immediately and delivered this message according as the Lord commanded me. I called him in, and read what the Lord had said concerning him. He acknowledged that it was verily so, and expressed much humility. I then went to meeting. Elder John Corrill preached a fine discourse.

In the afternoon President Phelps continued the services of the day by reading the fifth chapter of Matthew, also the laws regulating the High Council, and made some remarks upon them, after which, Sacrament was administered. I then confirmed a number who had been baptized, and blessed a number of children, in the name of Jesus Christ, with the blessings of the New and Everlasting Covenant. Notice was then given that the Elders' school would commence on the morrow.

Monday, November 2.—I was engaged in regulating the affairs of the school, after which I had my team prepared, and Sidney Rigdon, Oliver Cowdery, Frederick G. Williams, my scribe, and a number of others, went to Willoughby to hear Dr. Piexotto deliver a lecture on the theory and practice of physics. Called at Mr. Cushman's, dined, attended the lecture. Was treated with great respect throughout, and returned home.

School for the Elders Opened.

Lyman Wight arrived from Zion, also George A. and Lyman Smith returned from a mission to the east, after an absence of five months. The question was agitated whether Frederick G. Williams or Oliver Cowdery should go to New York, to make arrangements respecting a book-bindery. They referred the matter to me for a decision. And thus came the word of the Lord to me, saying—

Revelation.

It is not my will that my servant Frederick should go to New York, inasmuch as he wishes to go and visit his relations, that he may warn them to flee the wrath to come, let him go and see them for that purpose, and let that be his only business, and behold, in this thing, he shall be blessed with power to overcome their prejudices, verily thus saith the Lord. Amen.

Tuesday, November 3.—Thus came the word of the Lord unto me concerning the Twelve, saying—

Revelation to the Twelve.

Behold they are under condemnation, because they have not been sufficiently humble in my sight, and in consequence of their covetous desires, in that they have not dealt equally with each other in the division of the monies which came into their hands, nevertheless, some of them dealt equally. therefore they shall be rewarded; but verily I say unto you, they must all humble themselves before me, before they will be accounted worthy to receive an endowment, to go forth in my name unto all nations.

As for my servant William, let the Eleven humble themselves in prayer and in faith, and wait on me in patience, and my servant William shall return, and I will yet make him a polished shaft in my quiver, in bringing down the wickedness and abominations of men; and there shall be none mightier than he, in his day and generation, nevertheless if he repent not speedily, he shall be brought low, and shall be chastened sorely for all his iniquities he has committed against me; nevertheless the sin which he has sinned against me is not even now more grievous than the sin with which my servant David W. Patten, and my servant Orson Hyde, and my servant William E. M'Lellin have sinned against me, and the residue are not sufficiently humble before me.

Behold the parable which I spake concerning a man having twelve sons: for what man among you, having twelve sons, and is no respecter of them, and they serve him obediently, and he saith unto one, Be thou clothed in robes, and sit thou here; and to the other, Be thou clothed in rags, and sit thou there, and looketh upon his sons, and saith, I am just? Ye will answer, and say, no man; and ye answer truly; therefore, verily thus saith the Lord your God, I appoint these Twelve that they should be equal in their ministry, and in their portion, and in their evangelical rights; wherefore they have sinned a very grievous sin, inasmuch as they have made themselves unequal, and have not hearkened unto my voice; therefore, let them repent speedily, and prepare their hearts for the solemn assembly, and for the great day which is to come, verily thus saith the Lord. Amen.

I then went to assist in organizing the Elders' school. I called it to order and made some remarks upon the object of this school, and the great necessity of our rightly improving our time and reining up our minds to the sense of the great object that lies before us, viz—the glorious endowment that God has in store for the faithful.

Object of the Elders' School.

I then dedicated the school in the name of the Lord Jesus Christ.

After the school was dismissed, I attended a patriarchal meeting at brother Samuel Smith's; his wife's parents were blessed, also his child, named Susannah.

In the evening I preached in the school house, to a crowded congregation.

Wednesday, November 4.—At home in the morning. Attended school during school hours, made rapid progress in our studies. In the evening lectured on grammar at home. King Follet arrived from Zion this day.

Thursday, November 5.—Attended school. Isaac Morley came in from the east.

This morning I was called to visit Thomas Burdick, who was sick. I took my scribe with me, and we prayed

for and laid our hands on him in the name of the Lord
Jesus Christ, and rebuked his affliction.

William E. M'Lellin and Orson Hyde came in and desired to hear the Revelation concerning the Twelve. My
Inquiries   scribe read it to them. They expressed some
About the   little dissatisfaction, but after examining their
Revelation to
the Twelve.   own hearts, they acknowledged it to be the
word of the Lord, and said they were satisfied. After
school, Brigham Young came in, and desired also to hear
it read; after hearing it, he appeared perfectly satisfied.

In the evening I lectured on grammar.

Friday, November 6.—At home. Attended school during school hours, returned and spent the evening at home.
Reflections on   I was this morning introduced to a man from
the Nature of   the east. After hearing my name, he re-
Prophets.   marked that I was nothing but a man, indicat-
ing by this expression, that he had supposed that a person to whom the Lord should see fit to reveal His will,
must be something more than a man. He seemed to have
forgotten the saying that fell from the lips of St. James,
that Elias was a man subject to like passions as we are,
yet he had such power with God, that He, in answer to
his prayers, shut the heavens that they gave no rain for
the space of three years and six months; and again, in
answer to his prayer, the heavens gave forth rain, and
the earth gave forth fruit. Indeed, such is the darkness
and ignorance of this generation, that they look upon it
as incredible that a man should have any intercourse with
his Maker.

Isaac Morley   *Saturday, November 7.*—Spent the day at
and Edward   home attending to my domestic concerns. The
Partridge
Commended.   word of the Lord came unto me saying—

Revelation.

Behold I am well pleased with my servant Isaac Morley, and my
servant Edward Partridge, because of the integrity of their hearts in
laboring in my vineyard, for the salvation of the souls of men. Verily
I say unto you, their sins are forgiven them; therefore say unto them.

in my name, that it is my will that they should tarry for a little season, and attend the school, and also the solemn assembly, for a wise purpose in me. Even so. Amen.

Sunday, November 8.—Went to meeting in the morning at the usual hour. Zerubbabel Snow preached a very interesting discourse; in the afternoon Joseph Young preached. After preaching, Isaac Hill came forward to make some remarks by way of confession. He had previously been excommunicated from the Church for lying, and for an attempt to seduce a female. His confession was not satisfactory to my mind, and John Smith arose and made some remarks respecting the doings of the High Council, in the case of said Hill; that is, that he should make a public confession of his crime, and have it published in the *Messenger and Advocate.* He proposed that Mr. Hill should now make his confession before the congregation, and then immediately observed that he had forgiven Mr. Hill, which was in contradiction to the sentiment he first advanced. This I attributed to an error in judgment, not in design.

The Case of Isaac Hill.

President Rigdon then arose, and very abruptly militated against the sentiment of Uncle John, which had a direct tendency to destroy his influence, and bring him into disrepute in the eyes of the Church, which was not right. He also misrepresented Mr. Hill's case, and spread darkness rather than light upon the subject.

A vote of the Church was then called on Brother Hill's case, and he was restored without any further confession, viz., that he should be received into the Church by baptism, which was administered accordingly.

After I returned home, I labored with Uncle John, and convinced him that he was wrong; and he made his confession, to my satisfaction. I then went and labored with President Rigdon, and succeeded in convincing him also of his error, which he confessed to my satisfaction.

Labors of the Prophet with the Erring.

The word of the Lord came unto me, saying, that President Phelps and President John Whitmer were under condemnation before the Lord for their errors. For which they made satisfaction the same day.

I also took up a labor with John Corrill, for not partaking of the Sacrament; he made his confession. Also my wife, for leaving the meeting before Sacrament; she made no reply, but manifested contrition by weeping.

Monday, November 9.—After breakfast, Mary Whitcher came in and wished to see me. I granted her request. Case of Mary Whitcher. She gave a relation of her grievances, which are unfathomable at present, and if true, sore indeed; and I pray my Heavenly Father, to bring the truth of the case to light, that the reward due to evil doers may be given them, and that the afflicted and oppressed may be delivered.

While sitting in my house, between ten and eleven this morning, a man came in and introduced himself to me by the name of "Joshua, the Jewish Minister." Joshua, the Jewish Minister. His appearance was something singular, having a beard about three inches in length, quite grey; also his hair was long and considerably silvered with age; I thought him about fifty or fifty-five years old; tall, straight, slender built, of thin visage, blue eyes, and fair complexion; wore a sea-green frock coat and pantaloons, black fur hat with narrow brim; and, while speaking, frequently shut his eyes, with a scowl on his countenance. I made some inquiry after his name, but received no definite answer. We soon commenced talking on the subject of religion, and, after I had made some remarks concerning the Bible, I commenced giving him a relation of the circumstances connected with the coming forth of the Book of Mormon, as recorded in the former part of this history.

While I was relating a brief history of the establishment of the Church of Christ in the last days, Joshua seemed to be highly entertained. When I had closed my narration,

I observed that the hour of worship and dinner had arrived, and invited him to tarry, to which he consented. After dinner, the conversation was resumed, and Joshua proceeded to make some remarks on the prophecies, as follows—he observed that he was aware that I could bear stronger meat than many others, therefore he should open his mind the more freely:

The Doctrines of "Joshua the Jewish Minister."

Daniel has told us that he is to stand in his proper lot, in the latter days; according to his vision he had a right to shut it up, and also to open it again after many days, or in latter times. Daniel's image, whose head was gold, and body, arms, legs and feet, were composed of the different materials described in his vision, represents different governments. The golden head was to represent Nebuchadnezzar, King of Babylon; the other parts, other kings and forms of governments which I shall not now mention in detail, but confine my remarks more particularly to the feet of the image. The policy of the wicked spirit is to separate what God has joined together, and unite what He has separated, which the devil has succeeded in doing to admiration in the present state of society, which is like unto iron and clay.

There is confusion in all things, both political and religious; and notwithstanding all the efforts that are made to bring about a union, society remains disunited, and all attempts to unite it are as fruitless as to attempt to unite iron and clay. The feet of the image are the government of these United States. Other nations and kingdoms are looking up to her for an example of union, freedom, and equal rights, and therefore worship her as Daniel saw in the vision; although they are beginning to lose confidence in her, seeing the broils and discord that rise on her political and religious horizon. This image is characteristic of all governments.

We should leave Babylon. Twenty-four hours of improvement now, are worth as much as a year a hundred years ago. The spirits of the fathers that were cut down, or those that were under the altar, are now rising; this is the first resurrection. The Elder that falls first will rise last. We should not form any opinion only for the present, and leave the result of futurity with God. I have risen up out of obscurity, but was looked up to in temporal things when but a youth. It is not necessary that God should give us all things in His first commission to us, but in His second. John saw the angel deliver the Gospel in the last days. The small lights that God has given are sufficient to lead us out of Babylon; when we get out, we shall have the greater light.

I told Joshua I did not understand his remarks on the

resurrection, and wished him to explain. He replied that he did not feel impressed by the Spirit to unfold it further at present, but perhaps he might at some future time.

I then withdrew to transact some business with a gentleman who had called to see me, when Joshua informed my

Additional Views of Joshua.

scribe that he was born in Cambridge, Washington County, New York. He says that all the railroads, canals, and other improvements are projected by the spirits of the resurrection. The silence spoken of by John the Revelator, which is to be in heaven for the space of half an hour, is between 1830 and 1851, during which time the judgments of God will be poured out, after that time there will be peace.

Curiosity to see a man that was reputed to be a Jew, caused many to call during the day, and more particularly in the evening.

Suspicions were entertained that the said Joshua was the noted Matthias of New York, spoken so much of in

Matthias not Joshua.

the public prints, on account of the trials he endured in that place, before a court of justice, for murder, man-slaughter, contempt of court, whipping his daughter, etc.; for the last two crimes he was imprisoned, and came out about four months since. After some equivocating, he confessed that he really was Matthias.

After supper I proposed that he should deliver a lecture to us. He did so, sitting in his chair.

He commenced by saying, God said, let there be light, and there was light, which he dwelt upon throughout his discourse. He made some very excellent remarks, but his mind was evidently filled with darkness.

After the congregation dispersed, he conversed freely upon the circumstances that occurred in New York. His name is Robert Matthias. He says that Joshua is his priestly name. During all this time I did not contradict his sentiments, wishing to draw out all that I could concerning his faith.

Mr. Beaman, of New York, came to ask advice of me

whether or not he had better purchase lands in this vicinity, as he could not arrange his business to go to Missouri next spring. I advised him to come here and settle until he could move to Zion.

Tuesday, November 10.—I resumed conversation with Matthias, and desired him to enlighten my mind more on his views respecting the resurrection.

Matthias Dismissed by the Prophet.

He said that he posessed the spirit of his fathers, that he was a literal descendant of Matthias, the Apostle, who was chosen in the place of Judas that fell; that his spirit was resurrected in him; and that this was the way or scheme of eternal life—this transmigration of soul or spirit from father to son.

I told him that his doctrine was of the devil, that he was in reality in possession of a wicked and depraved spirit, although he professed to be the Spirit of truth itself; and he said also that he possessed the soul of Christ.

He tarried until Wednesday, 11th, when, after breakfast, I told him, that my God told me, that his god was the devil, and I could not keep him any longer, and he must depart. And so I, for once, cast out the devil in bodily shape, and I believe a murderer.

Attended school during school hours. Spent the evening around my fireside, teaching my family grammar. It commenced snowing this afternoon; wind very heavy.

Thursday, November 12.—Attended school again during school hours; rain and snow still falling, about one inch in depth and wind very heavy; the weather extremely unpleasant. The laborers who were finishing the outside of the chapel, were obliged to break off from their business at the commencement of this storm, on the 11th instant.

The Prophet's Meeting with the Twelve.

This evening, at 6 o'clock, met with the Council of the Twelve, by their request. Nine of them were present. Council opened by singing and prayer. And I made some remarks as follows—

The Prophet's Remarks to the Twelve.

I am happy in the enjoyment of this opportunity of meeting with this Council on this occasion. I am satisfied that the Spirit of the Lord is here, and I am satisfied with all the brethren present; and I need not say that you have my utmost confidence, and that I intend to uphold you to the uttermost, for I am well aware that you have to sustain my character against the vile calumnies and reproaches of this ungodly generation, and that you delight in so doing.

Darkness prevail sat this time as it did at the time Jesus Christ was about to be crucified. The powers of darkness strove to obscure the glorious Sun of rightousness, that began to dawn upon the world, and was soon to burst in great blessings upon the heads of the faithful; and let me tell you, brethren, that great blessings await us at this time, and will soon be poured out upon us, if we are faithful in all things, for we are even entitled to greater spiritual blessings than they were, because they had Christ in person with them, to instruct them in the great plan of salvation. His personal presence we have not, therefore we have need of greater faith, on account of our peculiar circumstances; and I am determined to do all that I can to uphold you, although I may do many things inadvertently that are not right in the sight of God.

You want to know many things that are before you, that you may know how to prepare yourselves for the great things that God is about to bring to pass. But there is one great deficiency or obstruction in the way, that deprives us of the greater blessings; and in order to make the foundation of this Church complete and permanent, we must remove this obstruction, which is, to attend to certain duties that we have not as yet attended to. I supposed I had established this Church on a permanent foundation when I went to Missouri, and indeed I did so, for if I had been taken away, it would have been enough, but I yet live, and therefore God requires more at my hands. The item to which I wish the more particularly to call your attention to-night, is the ordinance of washing of feet. This we have not done as yet, but it is necessary now, as much as it was in the days of the Savior; and we must have a place prepared, that we may attend to this ordinance aside from the world.

We have not desired as much from the hand of the Lord through faith and obedience, as we ought to have done, yet we have enjoyed great blessings, and we are not so sensible of this as we should be. When or where has God suffered one of the witnesses or first Elders of this Church to fall? Never, and no where. Amidst all the calamities and judgments that have befallen the inhabitants of the earth, His almighty arm has sustained us, men and devils have raged and spent their malice in vain. We must have all things prepared, and call our solemn assembly as the Lord has commanded us, that we may be able to accomplish His great work, and it must be done in God's own way. The house of the Lord must be prepared, and the solemn assembly called and organized in it, according to the order of the house of God; and in it we must attend to the ordinance of washing of feet. It was never intended for any but official members. It is calculated to unite our hearts, that we may be one in feeling and sentiment, and that our faith may be strong, so that Satan cannot overthrow us, nor have any power over us here.

The endowment you are so anxious about, you cannot comprehend now, nor could Gabriel explain it to the understanding of your dark minds; but strive to be prepared in your hearts, be faithful in all things, that when we meet in the solemn assembly, that is, when such as God shall name out of all the official members shall meet, we must be clean every whit. Let us be faithful and silent, brethren, and if God gives you a manifestation, keep it to yourselves; be watchful and prayerful, and you shall have a prelude of those joys that God will pour out on that day. Do not watch for iniquity in each other, if you do you will not get an endowment, for God will not bestow it on such. But if we are faithful, and live by every word that proceeds forth from the mouth of God, I will venture to prophesy that we shall get a blessing that will be worth remembering, if we should live as long as John the Revelator; our blessings will be such as we have not realized before, nor received in this generation. The order of the house of God has been, and ever will be, the same, even after Christ comes; and after the termination of the thousand years it will be the same; and we shall finally enter into the celestial Kingdom of God, and enjoy it forever.

You need an endowment, brethren, in order that you may be prepared and able to overcome all things; and those that reject your testimony will be damned. The sick will be healed, the lame made to walk, the deaf to hear, and the blind to see, through your instrumentality. But let me tell you, that you will not have power, after the endowment to heal those that have not faith, nor to benefit them, for you might as well expect to benefit a devil in hell as such as are possessed of his spirit, and are willing to keep it; for they are habitations for devils, and only fit for his society. But when you are endowed and prepared to preach the Gospel to all nations, kindred, and tongues, in their own languages, you must faithfully warn all, and bind up the testimony, and seal up the law, and the destroying angel will follow close at your heels, and exercise his tremendous mission upon the children of disobedience; and destroy the workers of iniquity, while the Saints will be gathered out from among them, and stand in holy places ready to meet the Bridegroom when he comes.

I feel disposed to speak a few words more to you, my brethren, concerning the endowment: All who are prepared, and are sufficiently pure to abide the presence of the Savior, will see Him in the solemn assembly.

The brethren expressed their gratification for the instruction I had given them. We then closed by prayer, when I returned home and retired to rest.

CHAPTER XXIII.

THE MINISTRY OF THE PROPHET IN KIRTLAND.

Friday, November 13.—Attended school during school hours: after school, returned home. Mr. Messenger, a Universalist minister, of Bainbridge, Chenango county, New York, came in to make some inquiries about Hezekiah Peck's family. We entered into conversation upon religious subjects, and went to President Rigdon's and spent the evening in conversation. We preached the Gospel to him, and bore testimony of what we had seen and heard.

The visit of Mr. Messenger.

He attempted to raise some objections, but the force of truth bore him down, and he was silent, although unbelieving.

I returned home and retired to rest.

Saturday, 14.—Thus came the word of the Lord unto me, saying:

Revelation to Warren Parrish.

Verily thus saith the Lord unto my servant Joseph, concerning my servant Warren Parrish. Behold his sins are forgiven him, because of his desires to do the works of righteousness. Therefore, inasmuch as he will continue to hearken unto my voice, he shall be blessed with wisdom, and with a sound mind, even above his fellows. Behold, it shall come to pass in his day, that he shall see great things show forth themselves unto my people; he shall see much of my ancient records, and shall know of hidden things, and shall be endowed with a knowledge of hidden languages; and if he desire and shall seek it at my hands, he shall be privileged with writing much of my word, as a scribe unto me for the benefit of my people; therefore this shall be his calling until I shall order it otherwise in my wisdom, and it shall be said of him in time to come, Behold Warren, the Lord's scribe for the Lord's Seer, whom He hath appointed in Israel. Therefore, if he will keep my commandments, he shall be lifted up at the last day. Even so. Amen.

This afternoon, Erastus Holmes, of Newbury, Ohio,
called on me to inquire about the establish-
Inquiries by Erastus Holmes. ment of the Church, and to be instructed in
doctrine more perfectly.

I gave him a brief relation of my experience while in my juvenile years, say from six years old up to the time I received my first vision, which was when I was about fourteen years old; also the revelations that I received afterwards concerning the Book of Mormon, and a short account of the rise and progress of the Church up to this date.

He listened very attentively, and seemed highly gratified, and intends to unite with the Church.

On Sabbath morning, 15th, he went with me to meeting, which was held in the schoolhouse, as the plastering of the chapel was not yet finished.

President Rigdon preached on the subject of men being called to preach the Gospel, their qualifications, etc. We had a fine discourse, it was very interesting indeed. Mr. Holmes was well satisfied, and returned and dined with me. Said Holmes has been a member of the Methodist church, and was excommunicated for receiving the Elders of the Latter-day Saints into his house.

Went to meeting in the afternoon. Before partaking of the Sacrament, Isaac Hill's case was agitated again, and settled after much controversy. He was retained in the Church, by making a humble acknowledgement before the Church, and consenting to have his confession published in the *Messenger and Advocate;* after which the ordinance of the Lord's Supper was administered, and the meeting closed late. Returned home and spent the evening.

Monday 16.—At home. Dictated the following letter for publication in the *Messenger and Advocate.**

---

* This refers to the Prophet's second communication to the *Messenger and Advocate* and will be found at page 259 *et seq.*

The same day, I received a letter from Harvey Whitlock, of which the following is a copy—

Harvey Whitlock's Letter.

DEAR SIR.—Having a few leisure moments, I have at last concluded to do what my own judgment has long dictated would be right, but the allurements of many vices have long retarded the hand that would wield the pen to make intelligent the communication that I wish to send to you; and even now, that ambition, which is a prevailing and predominant principle among the great mass of natural men, forbids that plainness of sentiment with which I wish to write; for know assuredly, sir, to you I wish to unbosom my feelings, and unveil the secrets of my heart, as before the omniscient Judge of all the earth. Be not surprised, when I declare unto you, as the Spirit will bear record, that my faith is firm and unshaken in the things of the everlasting Gospel, as it is proclaimed by the servants of the Latter-day Saints.

Dear Brother Joseph, (if I may be allowed the expression,) when I consider the happy times, and peaceful moments, and pleasant seasons I have enjoyed with you and this people, contrasted with my now degraded state; together with the high and important station I have held before God, and the abyss into which I have fallen—it is a subject that swells my heart too big for utterance, and I am overwhelmed with feelings that language cannot express. As I desire to know the will of God concerning me, and believing it is my duty to make known unto you my real situation, I shall dispassionately proceed to give a true and untarnished relation.

I need not tell you that in former times I have preached the word, and endeavored to be instant in season, and out of season—to reprove, rebuke, exhort, and faithfully to discharge that trust reposed in me. But oh! with what grief, and lamentable sorrow, and anguish, do I have to relate that I have fallen from that princely station whereunto our God has called me. Reasons why are unnecessary, may the fact suffice, and believe me when I tell you, that I have sunk myself (since my last separation from this body) in crimes of the deepest dye. And that I may the better enable you to understand what my real sins are, I will mention (although pride forbids it) some that I am not guilty of. My hands have not been stained with innocent blood, neither have I lain couched around the cottages of my fellow men, to seize and carry off the booty; nor have I slandered my neighbor, nor borne false testimony, nor taken unlawful hire, nor oppressed the widow or fatherless, neither have I persecuted the Saints. But my hands are swift to do iniquity, and my feet are fast running in the paths of vice and folly, and my heart is quick to devise wicked imaginations; nevertheless, I am impressed with the sure thought that I am fast hastening into a world of disembodied beings, without God, and with but one hope in the world, which is to know that to err is human, but to forgive is divine.

Much I might say in relation to myself, and the original difficulties with the Church, but I will forbear; and inasmuch as I have been charged with things that I am not guilty of, I am now more than doubly guilty, and am now willing to forgive and forget, only let me know that I am within the reach of mercy. If I am not, I have no reflections to cast, but say that I have sealed my own doom, and pronounced my own sentence. If the day is passed by with me, may I here beg leave to entreat of those who are still toiling up the rugged ascent, to make their way to the realms of endless felicity and delight, to stop not for anchors here below, follow not my example, but steer their course onward in spite of all the combined powers of earth and hell, for know that one misstep here is only retrievable by a thousand groans and tears before God.

Dear Brother Joseph, let me entreat you, on the reception of this letter, as you regard the salvation of my soul, to inquire at the hand of the Lord, in my behalf; for I this day, in the presence of God, do covenant to abide the word that may be given, for I am willing to receive any chastisement that the Lord sees I deserve. Now hear my prayer, and suffer me to break forth in the agony of my soul. O ye angels! that surround the throne of God, princes of heaven that excel in strength, ye who are clothed with transcendent brightness, plead, O plead for one of the most wretched of the sons of men. O ye heavens! whose azure arches rise immensely high, and stretch immeasurably wide— grand amphitheatre of nature, throne of the Eternal God, bow to hear the prayer of a poor, wretched, bewildered, way-wanderer to eternity. O! Thou great omnipotent and omnipresent Jehovah! Thou who sittest upon the throne, before whom all things are present; Thou maker, moulder, and fashioner of all things visible and invisible, breathe, O breathe into the ears of Thy servant the Prophet, words suitably adapted to my case and situation. Speak once more, make known Thy will concerning me; which favors I ask in the name of the Son of God. Amen.

Yours respectfully,

HARVEY WHITLOCK.

To Joseph Smith.

N.B.—I hope you will not let any business prevent you from answering this letter in haste.

I answered as follows:

KIRTLAND, November 16, 1835.

BROTHER HARVEY WHITLOCK—I have received your letter of the 28th of September, 1835, and I have read it twice, and it gave me sensations that are better imagined than described, let it suffice that I say that the very flood gates of my heart were broken up—I could not refrain from weeping. I thank God that it has entered into your heart to try to return to the Lord, and to this people, if it so be that He will have mercy upon you. I have inquired of the Lord concerning your case; these words came to me:

Revelation to Harvey Whitlock.

"Verily, thus saith the Lord unto you—Let him who was my servant Harvey, return unto me, and unto the bosom of my Church, and forsake all the sins wherewith he has offended against me, and pursue from henceforth a virtuous and upright life, and remain under the direction of those whom I have appointed to be pillars and heads of my Church. And behold, saith the Lord your God, his sins shall be blotted out from under heaven, and shall be forgotten from among men, and shall not come up in mine ears, nor be recorded as a memorial against him, but I will lift him up, as out of deep mire, and he shall be exalted upon the high places, and shall be counted worthy to stand among princes, and shall yet be made a polished shaft in my quiver for bringing down the strongholds of wickedness among those who set themselves up on high, that they may take counsel against me, and against my anointed ones in the last days. Therefore, let him prepare himself speedily and come unto you, even to Kirtland. And inasmuch as he shall hearken unto all your counsel from henceforth, he shall be restored unto his former state, and shall be saved unto the uttermost, even as the Lord your God liveth. Amen."

Thus you see, my dear brother, the willingness of our heavenly Father to forgive sins, and restore to favor all those who are willing to humble themselves before Him, and confess their sins, and forsake them, and return to Him with full purpose of heart, acting no hypocrisy, to serve Him to the end.

Marvel not that the Lord has condescended to speak from the heavens, and give you instructions whereby you may learn your duty. He has heard your prayers and witnessed your humility, and holds forth the hand of paternal affection for your return; the angels rejoice over you, while the Saints are willing to receive you again into fellowship.

I hope, on the receipt of this, you will lose no time in coming to Kirtland, for if you get here in season, you will have the privilege of at_ tending the school of the Prophets, which has already commenced, and also receive instructions in doctrine and principle, from those whom God has appointed, whereby you may be qualified to go forth, and declare the true doctrines of the Kingdom, according to the mind and will of God; and when you come to Kirtland, it will be explained to you why God has condescended to give you a revelation according to your request.

Please give my respects to your family, and be assured I am yours in the bonds of the new and everlasting covenant,

JOSEPH SMITH, JUN.

In the courseof the day, Father Beaman, Elder Strong, and others, called to counsel with me. In the evening a council was called at my house to counsel with Alva Beaman on the subject of his moving to Missouri. I had previously told him that the Lord had said that he had better go to Missouri next spring; however, he wished a council called. The council met, and President David Whitmer arose and said, the Spirit manifested to him that it was Brother Beaman's duty to go. Others bore the same testimony.

Council Concerning Brethren Going to Missouri.

The same night, I received the word of the Lord on Mr. Holmes' case. He had desired that I would inquire at the hand of the Lord, whether it was his duty to be baptized here, or wait until he returned home. The word of the Lord came unto me, saying, Mr. Holmes had better not be baptized here; that he had better not return by water; also that there were three men seeking his destruction; he must beware of his enemies.

The Word of the Lord as to Mr. Holmes' Baptism.

Tuesday 17.—Exhibited the alphabet of the ancient records, to Mr. Holmes, and some others. Went with him to Fredrick G. Williams', to see the mummies. We then took the parting hand, and he started for home, being strong in the faith of the Gospel of Jesus Christ, and determined to obey its requirements. I returned home and spent the day in dictating and comparing letters. A fine, pleasant day, although cool.

This evening, at early candle light, I preached at the schoolhouse.

Wednesday, 18.—At home in the forenoon, until about

eleven o'clock. I then went to Preserved Harris', to preach his father's funeral sermon, by the request of his family. I preached on the subject of the resurrection. The congregation were very attentive. My wife, my mother, and my scribe, accompanied me to the funeral. Pleasant outing, but cool and cloudy on our return.

Minutes of a Council Meeting at New Portage.

This day a Council of High Priests and Elders of the Church of Latter-day Saints, was held at New Portage, to hear the complaint of Sister Clarissa Matthews, against Elder Reuben Keeler, for prosecuting in a court of law, and taking her property on execution, (notwithstanding he had received his pay, or the most part of it) and refusing to allow her for what she had paid to him; also forfeiting his word, as he had frequently stated to her that he would not take her property in such a manner; and also for oppressing her family in an unchristian-like manner.

Elder Keeler pleaded not guilty, but the Council decided that he was guilty of the first and last charges; and gave judgment accordingly; with which Elder Keeler refused to comply, and said he would appeal to the High Council at Kirtland.

AMBROSE PALMER, Presiding Elder.
JOSEPH B. BOSWORTH, Clerk.

In the evening, Bishop Whitney, his wife, father, mother, and sister-in-law, came and invited me and my wife to go with them and visit Father Smith and family. My wife was unwell, and could not go, but my scribe and I went. *Debate on the Question of Miracles.*

When we arrived, some of the young Elders were about engaging in a debate on the subject of miracles. The question—"Was it, or was it not, the design of Christ to establish His Gospel by miracles?" After an interesting debate of three hours or more, during which time much talent was displayed, it was decided, by the President of the debate, in the negative, which was a righteous decision.

I discovered in this debate, much warmth displayed, too much zeal for mastery, too much of that enthusiasm that characterizes a lawyer at the bar, who is determined to defend his cause, right or wrong. I therefore availed myself of this favorable opportunity to drop a few words upon this subject, by way of advice, that they might improve their minds and cultivate their powers of intellect in a proper manner, that they might not incur the displeasure of heaven; that they should handle sacred things very sacredly, and with due deference to the opinions of others, and with an eye single to the glory of God.

Thursday, 19.—Went, in company with Dr. Williams and my scribe, to see how the workmen prospered in finishing the House of the Lord. The masons in the inside had commenced putting on the finishing coat of plaster. On my return, I met Lloyd and Lorenzo Lewis, and conversed with them upon the subject of their being disaffected. I found that they were not so, as touching the faith of the Church, but were displeased with some of the members. I returned home and spent the day in translating the Egyptian records. A warm and pleasant day.

Friday, 20.—At home in the morning. Weather warm and rainy. We spent the day in translating, and made rapid progress.

In the evening, President Cowdery returned from New York, bringing with him a quantity of Hebrew books, for the benefit of the school. He presented me with a Hebrew Bible, Lexicon, and Grammar, also a Greek Lexicon, and Webster's English Dictionary. President Cowdery had a prosperous journey, according to the prayers of the Saints in Kirtland.

Saturday, 21.—Spent the day at home, in examining my books, and studying the Hebrew alphabet.

At evening, met with our Hebrew class, to make some arrangements about a teacher. It was decided, by the voice of the school, to send to New York, for a Jew to

[Sidenotes:]
Translating the Egyptian Records.

Return of Oliver Cowdery from New York.

Arrangement for Studying Hebrew.

teach us the language, if we could get released from the engagements we had made with Dr. Piexotto to teach us, having ascertained that he was not qualified to give us the knowledge we wished to acquire of the Hebrew.

Sunday, *22.*—Went to meeting at the usual hour. Simeon Carter preached from the 7th of Matthew. President Rigdon's brother-in-law and other relatives were at meeting.

In the afternoon the meeting was held in the school-house.

In the evening, a Council of High Priests and Elders was held in the presence of the members of the Church, when Mr. Andrew Jackson Squires, who had been an ordained Elder in the Church, and for a time had preached the Gospel successfully, but after a while sent his license to President Smith, in a letter, came before the Council, and confessed that he had been in temptation, and fallen into error, so much as to join the Methodists; yet said he had no faith in their doctrine. He desired to return to the fellowship of the Church, asked forgiveness of the brethren, and restoration of his license.

Case of Andrew Jackson Squires.

I spoke of the impropriety of turning away from the truth, and going after a people so destitute of the spirit of righteousness as the Methodists.

President Rigdon showed the folly of fellowshiping any doctrine or spirit aside from that of Christ.

Mr. Squires arose and said he felt firm in the determination of doing the will of God in all things, or as far as in him lies the power; was sorry for his faults, and, by the grace of God, would forsake them in future.

Council and Church voted to restore him to fellowship, and the office of Elder also, and that the clerk give him a license.

Monday, *23.*—Several brethren called to converse with me, and see the records. Received a letter from Jared

Carter. Spent the day in conversation, and in studying the Hebrew. A stormy day.

Tuesday, 24.—At home. Spent the forenoon instructing those that called to inquire concerning the things of God in the last days.

In the afternoon we translated some of the Egyptian records.

I had an invitation to attend a wedding at Brother Hyrum Smith's in the evening; also to solemnize the matrimonial ceremony between Newel Knight and Lydia Goldthwaite. My wife accompanied me. On our arrival a considerable company had collected. The bridegroom and bride came in, and took their seats, which gave me to understand that they were ready. After prayers, I requested them to rise, and join hands. I then remarked that marriage was an institution of heaven, instituted in the garden of Eden; that it was necessary it should be solemnized by the authority of the everlasting Priesthood. The ceremony was original with me, and in substance as follows—You covenant to be each other's companions through life, and discharge the duties of husband and wife in every respect; to which they assented. I then pronounced them husband and wife in the name of God, and also pronounced upon them the blessings that the Lord conferred upon Adam and Eve in the garden of Eden, that is, to multiply and replenish the earth, with the addition of long life and prosperity. Dismissed them and returned home. Freezing cold, some snow on the ground.

The Marriage of Newel Knight.

Wednesday, 25.—Spent the day in translating. Harvey Redfield and Jesse Hithcock arrived from Missouri. The latter says that he has no doubt but a dose of poison was administered to him, in a bowl of milk, but God delivered him.

Translating the Egyptian Records.

Thursday, 26.—Spent the day in translating Egyptian characters from the papyrus, though severely afflicted with a cold. Robert Rathbone and George Morey arrived from Zion.

Friday, 27.—Much afflicted with my cold, yet I am determined to overcome in the name of the Lord Jesus Christ. Spent the day at home, reading Hebrew. Brother Parrish, my scribe, being afflicted with a cold, asked me to lay my hands on him in the name of the Lord. I did so, and in return I asked him to lay his hands on me. We were both rel.eved.

Saturday, 28.—Spent the morning in comparing our Journal. Elder Josiah Clark, from the state of Kentucky, called on me. Considerably recovered from my cold. Cold and stormy, snow falling, and The case of Josiah Clark. winter seems fast to be closing in, all nature shrinks before the chilling blasts of rigid winter. Elder Clark, above mentioned, whose residence is about three miles from Cincinnati, was bitten by a mad dog some three or four years since; has doctored much, and received some benefit, but is much afflicted notwithstanding He came here that he might be benefitted by the prayers of the Church. Accordingly we prayed for him and laid hands on him in the name of the Lord Jesus Christ, and anointed him with oil, and rebuked his afflictions, praying our heavenly Father to hear and answer our prayers, according to our faith. Cold and snowy.

Sunday, 29.—Went to meeting at the usual hour. Elder Morley preached; and in the afternoon, Bishop Partridge. These discourses were well adapted to the times in which we live, and the circumstances Preaching of Morley and Partridge. under which we are placed. Their words were words of wisdom, like apples of gold in pictures of silver, spoken in the simple accents of a child, yet sublime as the voice of an angel. The Saints appeared to be much pleased with the beautiful discourses of these two fathers in Israel. After these services closed, three of the Zion brethren came forward and received their blessings, and Solon Foster was ordained an Elder. The Lord's Supper was administered. Spent the evening at home. Snow fell about one foot deep. Very cold.

Monday, 30.—The snow continues to fall—an uncommon storm for this country, and this season of the year. Spent the day in reviewing and copying the letter I dictated on the 16th, concerning the gathering, for the *Messenger and Advocate.* Henry Capron, an old acquaintance from Manchester, New York, called on me. I showed him the Egyptian records.

CHAPTER XXIV.

MISCELLANEOUS LABORS OF THE PROPHET IN KIRTLAND.

December 1.—At home. Spent the day in writing for the *Messenger and Advocate.* Fine sleighing, and the snow yet falling.

Wednesday, 2.—A fine morning. I started to ride to Painesville with my family and scribe. When we were passing through Mentor Street, we overtook a team, with two men in the sleigh; I politely asked them to let me pass. They granted my request, and as we passed them they bawled out, "Do you get any revelations lately?" with an addition of blackguard language that I did not understand. This is a fair sample of the character of Mentor Street inhabitants, who are ready to abuse and scandalize men who never laid a straw in their way; and, in fact, those whose faces they never saw, and [whom they] cannot bring an accusation against, either of a temporal or spiritual nature, except their firm belief in the fullness of the Gospel. I was led to marvel at the longsuffering and condescension of our heavenly Father in permitting these ungodly wretches to possess this goodly land, which is indeed as beautifully situated, and its soil is as fertile, as any in this region of country, and its inhabitants are wealthy even blessed above measure in temporal things; and fain would God bless them with spiritual blessings, even eternal life,

Insolent
Treatment of
the Prophet.

were it not for their evil hearts of unbelief. And we are led to mingle our prayers with those of the Saints that have suffered the like treatment before us, whose souls are under the altar, crying to the Lord for vengeance upon those that dwell upon the earth. And we rejoice that the time is at hand, when the wicked who will not repent will be swept from the earth as with a besom of destruction, and the earth become an inheritance of the poor and the meek.

When we arrived at Painesville, we called at Sister Harriet Howe's, and left my wife and family to visit her, while we rode into town to do some business. Called and visited H. Kingsbury. Dined with Sister Howe and returned home. Had a fine ride—sleighing good, weather pleasant.

Thursday, 3.—At home. Wrote a letter to David Dort, Rochester, Michigan; another to Almira Schoby, Liberty, Clay County, Missouri.

At evening, visited with my wife at Thomas Carrico's. A respectable company awaited our arrival. After singing and prayer I delivered an address on matrimony, and joined in marriage Warren Parrish and Martha H. Raymond. Closed by singing and prayer. After refreshments, returned home, having spent the evening very agreeably.

Marriage of Warren Parrish.

Friday, 4.—In company with Vinson Knight, drew three hundred and fifty dollars out of Painesville Bank, on three months' credit, for which we gave the names of Frederick G. Williams & Co., Newel K. Whitney, John Johnson and Vinson Knight. Settled with Brother Hyrum Smith and Vinson Knight, and paid Knight two hundred and forty-five dollars; also have it in my power to pay J. Lewis, for which blessing I feel heartily thankful to my heavenly Father, and ask Him, in the name of Jesus Christ, to enable us to extricate ourselves from all embarrassments whatever, that we may not be brought into disrepute, that our enemies may

Financial Transactions.

not have any power over us. Spent the day at home, a part of the day studying Hebrew. Warm, with some rain, snow fast melting.

This evening a Mr. John Hollister, of Portage County, Ohio, called to see me on the subject of religion, and I spent the evening conversing with him. He tarried over night with me, and acknowledged in the morning that, although he had thought he knew something about religion, he was now sensible that he knew but little; which was the greatest trait of wisdom I could discover in him.

Conversation on Religion.

Saturday, 5.—Weather cold and freezing, with a moderate fall of snow. In the forenoon studying Hebrew with Dr. Frederick G. Williams and President Cowdery. I am laboring under some indisposition of health. Slept awhile, and arose feeling tolerably well, through the mercy of God. I received a letter from Reuben McBride, Vilanovia, New York; also another from Parley P. Pratt's mother-in-law, Herkimer County, New York, of no consequence as to what it contained, but it cost me twenty-five cents for postage. I mention this, as it is a common occurrence, and I am subjected to a great deal of expense by those whom I know nothing about, only that they are destitute of good manners; for if people wish to be benefitted with information from me, common respect and good breeding would dictate them to pay the postage on their letters.

A Matter of Postage.

I addressed the following letter to the editor of the *Messenger and Advocate:*

DEAR BROTHER—I wish to inform my friends and all others abroad, that whenever they wish to address me through the postoffice, they will be kind enough to pay the postage on the same. My friends will excuse me in this matter, as I am willing to pay postage on letters to hear from them; but I am unwilling to pay for insults and menaces; consequently must refuse all unpaid.

Yours in the Gospel,

JOSEPH SMITH, JUN.

Sunday, *6.*—Went to meeting at the usual hour.

An Unruly Member. Gideon Carter preached a splendid discourse.
In the afternoon we had an exhortation and
communion service. Some two or three weeks since,
Brother Draper insisted on leaving the meeting before
communion, and could not be prevailed on to tarry a few
moments, although we invited him to do so, as we did not
wish to have the house thrown into confusion. He observed that he "would not," if we excluded him from
the Church. Today he attempted to make a confession,
but it was not satisfactory to me, and I was constrained
by the Spirit to deliver him over to the buffetings of Satan,
until he should humble himself and repent of his sins, and
make satisfactory confession before the Church.

Monday, *7.*—Received a letter from Milton Holmes,
and was much rejoiced to hear from him, and of his success in proclaiming the Gospel. Wrote him a letter requesting him to return to Kirtland. Spent the day in
reading Hebrew. Mr. John Hollister called to take the
parting hand with me, and remarked that he had been in
darkness all his days, but had now found the truth and
intended to obey it.

This evening a number of brethren called to see the
records, which I exhibited and explained. Fine sleighing.

Tuesday, *8.*—At home. Read Hebrew in company with

Kindness of the Saints to the Prophet. Dr. Williams, President Cowdery, Brother Hy-
rum Smith and Orson Pratt. In the evening,
preached at the school house as usual, had
great liberty in speaking, congregation attentive. After
the services closed, the brethren proposed to haul wood
for me.

Wednesday, *9.*—At home. Wind south, strong, and
chilly. Elder Packard came in this morning, and made
me a present of twelve dollars, which he held in a note
against me. May God bless him for his liberality. Also,
James Aldrich sent me my note by the hand of Jesse
Hitchcock, on which there was twelve dollars due. And

may God bless him for his kindness to me. Also the brethren whose names are written below opened their hearts in great liberality, and paid me, at the committee's store, the sums set opposite their respective names, to wit:

John Corrill	. . $5 00	Salmon Gee	. . .	$0 75
Levi Jackman	. . 3 25	Harvey Stanley	. .	1 00
Elijah Fordham	. 5 25	Zemira Draper	. .	1 00
James Emmet	. . 5 00	Emer Harris	. . .	1 00
Newel Knight	. . 2 00	Truman Jackson	. .	1 00
Truman O. Angell	3 00	Samuel Rolf	. . .	1 25
William Felshaw	. 3 00	Elias Higbee	. . .	1 00
Albert Brown	. . 3 00	George Morey	. . .	1 00
William F. Cahoon	1 00	John Rudd	. . . .	0 50
Harlow Crosier	. 0 50	Alex. Badlam	. .	1 00

$40 50

With the addition of the two notes above . . . 24 00

Total . . $64 50

My heart swells with gratitude inexpressible when I realize the great condescension of my heavenly Father, in opening the hearts of these my beloved brethren to administer so liberally to my wants. *Gratitude of the Prophet.* And I ask God, in the name of Jesus Christ, to multiply blessings without number upon their heads, and bless me with much wisdom and understanding, and dispose of me to the best advantage for my brethren, and the advancement of His cause and kingdom. And whether my days are many or few, whether in life or in death, I say in my heart, O Lord, let me enjoy the society of such brethren.

Elder Tanner brought me half of a fatted hog for the benefit of my family. A few days since, Elder Shadrach Roundy brought me a quarter of beef. And may all the blessings named above be poured upon their heads, for their kindness towards me.

Thursday, 10.—This morning a number of brethren called to see the records, [Egyptian] which I exhibited to their satisfaction. This day my brethren met according to previous arrangement to chop and haul wood for me. Beautiful morning, indeed, and fine sleighing.

This afternoon I was called, in company with President David Whitmer, to visit Angeline Works. We

Healing of
Angeline
Works.

found her very sick, and so much deranged that she did not recognize her friends and intimate acquaintances. We prayed for her and laid hands on her in the name of Jesus Christ, and commanded her in His name to receive her senses, which were immediately restored. We also prayed that she might be restored to health; and she said she was better.

The board kiln had taken fire, and on our return we

Fire in the
Kirtland
Board Kiln.

found the brethren engaged in extinguishing the flames. After laboring about one hour against this destructive element, we succeeded in conquering it, and probably saved about one-fourth part of the lumber. I do not know the amount of loss the committee have sustained, but it must have been considerable, as there was much lumber in the kiln. There were about two hundred brethren engaged on this occasion; they displayed much activity and interest, and deserve much credit. The brethren have also been very industrious, and supplied me with my winter's wood, for which I am sincerely grateful to each and every one of them, and shall remember, with warm emotions, this expression of their goodness to me. And in the name of Jesus Christ I invoke the rich benediction of heaven to rest upon them and their families; and I ask my heavenly Father to preserve their health, and that of their wives and children, that they may have strength of body to perform their labors in their several occupations in life, and the use and activity of their limbs, also powers of intellect and understanding hearts, that they may treasure up wisdom, understanding and intelligence above measure, and be preserved from plagues, pestilence, and famine, and from the power of the adversary, and the hands of evil-designing men, and have power over all their enemies, and the way be prepared for them that they may journey to the land of Zion, and be established on their inheritances, to enjoy undisturbed peace and happiness forever, and ultimately be crowned with everlasting life in the celestial Kingdom of God, which blessing I ask in the name of Jesus of Nazareth.   Amen.

I would remember Elder Leonard Rich, who was the first one that proposed to the brethren to assist me in obtaining wood for the use of my family, for which I pray my heavenly Father to bless him with all the blessings named above.

The Prophet's Blessing on Leonard Rich.

And I shall ever remember him with much gratitude, for this testimony of benevolence and respect, and thank the great I AM for putting into his heart to do me this kindness.   And I say in my heart, I will trust in Thy goodness and mercy forever, O Lord, for Thy wisdom and benevolence, are unbounded, and beyond the comprehension of men, and all of Thy ways cannot be found out.

The petitions of the people from all parts of the United States to the Governor of Missouri to restore the Saints to their possessions, were arranged and mailed at Kirtland, this day, for Missouri.   The petitions were numerous, and the package large, the postage thereon being five dollars.   It was directed to the governor.

Friday, 11.—A fire broke out in a shoemaker's shop, owned by Orson Johnson, but the flames were soon extinguished by the active exertions of the brethren.   A pleasant morning.   Spent the day in reading and instructing those who called for advice.

Saturday, 12.—Spent the forenoon in reading.   About twelve o'clock a number of young persons called to see the Egyptian records.   My scribe exhibited them.   One of the young ladies who had been examining them, was asked if they had the appearance of antiquity.   She observed, with an air

The Prophet Reproves a Young Lady.

of contempt, that they had not. On hearing this, I was surprised at the ignorance she displayed, and I observed to her, that she was an anomaly in creation, for all the wise and learned that had examined them, without hesitation pronounced them ancient. I further remarked, that it was downright wickedness, ignorance, bigotry and superstition had caused her to make the remark; and that I would put it on record. And I have done so, because it is a fair sample of the prevailing spirit of the times, showing that the victims of priestcraft and superstition would not believe though one should rise from the dead.

In the evening attended a debate at Brother William Smith's, on the following question—Was it necessary for God to reveal Himself to mankind in order for their happiness? I was on the affirmative, and the last to speak on that side of the question; but, while listening with interest to the ingenuity displayed on both sides, I was called away to visit Sister Angeline Works, who was supposed to be dangerously sick. Elder John Corrill and myself went and prayed for her and laid hands on her in the name of Jesus Christ; and leaving her apparently better, returned home.

Debate at William Smith's.

Sunday, 13.—At the usual hour, ten a. m., attended meeting at the school house on the flats. Elder Jesse Hickcock preached a very feeling discourse.

In the afternoon, Elder Peter Whitmer related his experience; after which, President Frederick G. Williams related his also. They both spoke of many things connected with the rise and progress of this Church, which were interesting. After this, the Sacrament of the Lord's Supper was administered under the superintendence of President David Whitmer, after which, I made some remarks respecting prayer meetings, and our meeting was closed by invoking the blessing of heaven. I returned home and ordered my horse, and myself and scribe

Experiences of Elders Whitmer and Williams.

rode to Mr. E. Jenning's, where I joined Ebenezer Robinson and Angeline Works in matrimony, according to previous engagements. Miss Works had so far recovered from her illness as to be able to sit in her easy chair while I pronounced the marriage ceremony.

We then rode to Mr. McWhithy's a distance of about three miles from town, where I had been solicited to attend another marriage. We found a large and respectable number of friends present. I had been requested to make some preliminary remarks on the subject of matrimony, touching the design of the Almighty in its institution, also the duties of husbands and wives towards each other. And after opening our interview with singing and prayer, I delivered a lecture of about forty minutes, in which all seemed interested, except one or two individuals, who manifested a spirit of groveling contempt, which I was constrained to reprove and rebuke sharply. After I had closed my remarks, I sealed the matrimonial engagement between Mr. E. Webb and Miss E. A. McWhithy, in the name of God, and pronouncing the blessings of heaven upon their heads, closed by returning thanks. A sumptuous feast was then spread, and the company invited to seat themselves at the table by pairs, male and female, commencing with the eldest. The festival was conducted with propriety and decorum, and cheerfulness prevailed. After spending the evening agreeable until nine o'clock, we pronounced a blessing upon the company and returned home. This day the board kiln took fire again.

Monday, 14.—A number of brethren from New York called to visit me and see the Egyptian records. Also Elder Harris returned from Palmyra, New York, and Brother Francis Eaton of the same place, and Sister Harriet Howe called to visit us.

After dinner, attended the funeral of Sylvester Smith's youngest child. And in the evening met, according to previous notice, to make arrangements to guard against

Marriages in Kirtland.

fire, and organize a company for this purpose; also counseled on other affairs of a temporal nature.
Samuel Barnum came to my house, much
afflicted with a swollen arm. As he had not
sufficient faith to be healed, my wife applied a poultice
of herbs, and he tarried over night. I spent the day at
home reading Hebrew, and visiting with friends who
called to see me.

Precautions
Against
Incendiaries.

CHAPTER XXV.

THE TROUBLES OF ORSON HYDE AND WILLIAM SMITH—THE BOOK OF ABRAHAM—CLOSE OF THE YEAR.

Tuesday, December 15.—At home, and, as usual, was blessed with much company. Samuel Barnum is very sick, his arm much inflamed.

This afternoon, Elder Orson Hyde handed me a letter, the purport of which was, that he was dissatisfied with the committee* in their dealings with him, in temporal affairs, that is, that they did not deal as liberal with him as they did with Elder William Smith; also requested me to reconcile the revelation given to the Twelve since their return from the east.† That unless these things and others named in the letter, could be reconciled to his mind, his honor would not stand united with them. This I believe is the amount of the contents of the letter, although much was written.

My feelings on this occasion were much lacerated, knowing that I had dealt in righteousness with him in all things, and endeavored to promote his happiness and well being as much as lay in my power. And I feel that

Complaints of Orson Hyde.

---

* This committee was the one having in charge the building of the Kirtland Temple. They were also managers of a store in Kirtland, through which much of the business connected with the construction of the temple was accomplished. The committee consisted of Hyrum Smith, Reynolds Cahoon and Jared Carter.

† That is, Elder Hyde desired that the Prophet would reconcile the conduct of the above named committee with some of the revelations which in Elder Hyde's opinion taught that the Twelve were to be equal in both temporal and spiritual things. See Elder Hyde's letter, page 335.

these reflections are ungrateful, and founded in jealousy, and that the adversary is striving with all his subtle devices and influence to destroy him, by causing a division among the Twelve whom God has chosen to open the Gospel kingdom to all nations. But I pray Thee, my heavenly Father, in the name of Jesus of Nazareth, that he may be delivered from the power of the destroyer, that his faith fail not in this hour of temptation, and prepare him, and all the Elders, to receive an endowment in Thy house, even according to Thine own order from time to time, as Thou seest them worthy to be called into Thy solemn assembly.

Wednesday, 16.—Weather extremely cold. I went to the Council room to lay before the Presidency, the letter that I received yesterday from Elder Orson Hyde; but when I arrived, I found that I had lost said letter, but I laid the substance of it, as far as I could recollect it, before the Council; but they had not time to attend to it on account of other business; accordingly adjourned until Monday evening, the 20th inst. Returned home.

Elders William E. M'Lellin, Brigham Young, and Jared Carter, called and paid me a visit with which I was much gratified. I exhibited and explained the Egyptian records to them, and explained many things concerning the dealing of God with the ancients, and the formation of the planetary system.

Visit of Elders M'Lellin, Young, and Carter With the Prophet.

This evening, according to adjournment, I went to Brother William Smith's to take part in the debate that was commenced Saturday evening last. After the debate was concluded, and a decision given in favor of the affirmative of the question, some altercation took place upon the propriety of continuing the school [debate] fearing that it would not result in good. Brother William Smith opposed these measures, and insisted on having another question proposed, and at length became much enraged,

The Prophet Assaulted by Wm. Smith.

particularly at me, and used violence upon my person, and also upon Elder Jared Carter, and some others, for which I am grieved beyond measure, and can only pray God to forgive him, inasmuch as he repents of his wickedness, and humbles himself before the Lord. *Thursday, 17.*—At home, quite unwell. Elder Orson Hyde called to see me, and presented me with a copy of the letter he handed me on Tuesday last, which I had lost. The following is the copy—

Orson Hyde's Letter of Complaint.

DECEMBER 15th, 1835.

President Smith: Sir—You may esteem it a novel circumstance to receive a written communication from me at this time. My reasons for writing are the following—I have some things which I wish to communicate to you, and feeling a greater liberty to do it by writing alone by myself, I take this method, and it is generally the case you are thronged with business, and not convenient to spend much time in conversing upon subjects of the following nature. Therefore let these excuses palliate the novelty of the circumstance, and patiently hear my recital.

After the committee received their stock of fall and winter goods, I went to Elder Cahoon and told him I was destitute of a cloak, and wanted him to trust me, until spring, for materials to make one. He told me that he would trust me until January, but must then have his pay, as the payment for the goods became due at that time. I told him I knew not from whence the money would come, and I could not promise it so soon. But, in a few weeks after, I unexpectedly obtained the money to buy a cloak, and applied immediately to Elder Cahoon for one, and told him that I had the cash to pay for it; but he said the materials for cloaks were all sold, and that he could not accommodate me; and I will here venture a guess, that he has not realized the cash for one cloak pattern.

A few weeks after this, I called on Elder Cahoon again, and told him that I wanted cloth for some shirts, to the amount of four or five dollars. I told him that I would pay him in the spring, and sooner if I could. He let me have it. Not long after, my school was established, and some of the hands who labored on the house, attended, and wished to pay me at the committee's store for their tuition. I called at the store to see if any negotiation could be made, and they take me off where I owed them; but no such negotiation could be made. These, with

some other circumstances of a like character, called forth the following
reflection:

In the first place, I gave the committee $275.00 in cash, besides some
more, and during the last season, have traveled through the Middle and
Eastern states to support and uphold the store; and in so doing, have
reduced myself to nothing, in a pecuniary point. Under these circumstances, this establishment refused to render me that accommodation
which a worldling's establishment gladly would have done; and one,
too, which never received a donation from me, or in whose favor I never
raised my voice, or exerted my influence. But after all this, thought I,
it may be right, and I will be still—until, not long since, I ascertained
that Elder William Smith could go to the store and get whatever he
pleased, and no one to say, why do ye so? until his account has amounted
to seven hundred dollars, or thereabouts, and that he was a silent
partner in the concern, but not acknowledged as such, fearing that his
creditors would make a haul upon the store.

While we [the Twelve] were abroad this last season, we strained every
nerve to obtain a little something for our families, and regularly divided
the monies equally for aught I know, not knowing that William had such
a fountain at home, from whence he drew his support. I then called to
mind the Revelation in which myself, M'Lellin, and Patten were
chastened, and also the quotation in that revelation of the parable of
the twelve sons, as if the original meaning referred directly to the
Twelve Apostles of the Church of Latter-day Saints. I would now ask
if each one of the Twelve has not an equal right to the same accommo-
dations from that store, provided they are alike faithful? If not, with
such a combination, mine honor be not thou united. If each one has
the same right, take the baskets from off our noses, and put one to
William's nose; or if this cannot be done, reconcile the parable of the
twelve sons, with the superior privileges that William has. Pardon me
if I speak in parables or parody.

A certain shepherd had twelve sons, and he sent them out one day
to go and gather his flock which was scattered upon the mountains and
in the valleys afar off. They were all obedient to their father's mandate, and at evening they returned with the flock, and one son received
wool enough to make him warm and comfortable, and also received of
the flesh and milk of the flock, the other eleven received not so much
as one kid to make merry with their friends.

These facts, with some others, have disqualified my mind for studying the Hebrew language, at present; and believing as I do, that I
must sink or swim, or in other words, take care of myself, I have
thought that I should take the most efficient means in my power to get

out of debt; and to this end I proposed taking the school; but if I am
not thought competent to take the charge of it, or worthy to be placed
in that station, I must devise some other means to help myself, although
having been ordained to that office under your own hand, with a promise that it should not be taken from me.

The conclusion of the whole matter is: I am willing to continue and
do all I can, provided we can share equal benefits, one with the other,
and upon no other principle whatever. If one has his support from
the "public crib," let them all have it; but if one is pinched, I am willing to be, provided we are all alike. If the principle of impartiality
and equity can be observed by all, I think that I will not peep again.
If I am damned, it will be for doing what I think is right. There have
been two applications made to me to go into business since I talked of
taking the school, but it is in the world, and I had rather remain in
Kirtland, if I can consistently. All I ask is right.

I am, sir, with respect,

Your obedient servant,

ORSON HYDE.

To President J. Smith, Jun.,
    Kirtland, &c.

Elder Orson Hyde read the foregoing copy himself, and
I explained the objections he had set forth in it, and satisfied his mind upon every point, perfectly.   Reconcilia-
And he observed, after I got through, that he   tion of Orson
                                                 Hyde with the
was more than satisfied, and would attend the   Prophet.
Hebrew school, and took the parting hand with me with
every expression of friendship that a gentleman and a
Christian could manifest; which I felt to reciprocate with
cheerfulness, and entertain the best of feeling for him,
and most cheerfully forgive him the ingratitude which
was manifested in his letter, knowing that it was for want
of correct information, that his mind was disturbed, as far
as his reflections related to me; but on the part of the committee he was not treated right in all things; however, all
things are settled amicably, and no hardness exists between us and them.

I told Elder Cahoon, of the Temple committee, that we
must sustain the Twelve, and not let them go down; if we

do not, they must go down, for the burden is on them and
Charge to   is coming on them heavier and heavier.   If
Elder Cahoon
to Sustain the   the Twele go down, we must go down, but
Twelve.   we must sustain them.

My father and mother called this evening to see me upon the subject of the difficulty that occurred at their
house, on Wednesday evening, between me and my brother
Sorrow of   William.   They were sorely afflicted in mind
Father and
Mother Smith   on account of that occurrence.   I conversed
over William
Smith's Diffi   with them and convinced them that I was not
culty.   to blame in taking the course I did, but had
acted in righteousness in all things on that occasion.   I invited them to come and live with me.   They consented to
do so as soon as it was practicable.

Friday, 18.—Brother Hyrum Smith called to see me,
and read a letter that he received from William, in which
he asked forgiveness for the abuse he offered to him
The Sym-   (Hyrum) at the debate.   He tarried most of
pathy Be-
tween the   the forenoon, and conversed freely with me
Prophet and
his Brother   upon the subject of the difficulty existing be-
Hyrum.   tween me and Brother William.   He said that
he was perfectly satisfied with the course I had taken in rebuking William in his wickedness, but he is wounded to the
very soul, because of the conduct of William; and although
he experiences the tender feelings of a brother towards him,
yet he can but look upon his conduct as an abomination in
the sight of God.   And I could pray in my heart that all
my brethren were like unto my beloved brother Hyrum,
who possesses the mildness of a lamb, and the integrity
of a Job, and in short, the meekness and humility of
Christ; and I love him with that love that is stronger
than death, for I never had occasion to rebuke him, nor
he me, which he declared when he left me to-day.

This day received the following letter from Brother
William Smith:

William Smith's Letter to the Prophet.

BROTHER JOSEPH—Though I do not know but I have forfeited all right and title to the word brother, in consequence of what I have done, (for I consider, myself, that I am unworthy to be called one,) after coming to myself, and considering what I have done, I feel as though it was a duty to make a humble confession to you, for what I have done, or what took place the other evening; but leave this part of the subject at present. I was called to an account, by the Twelve, yesterday, for my conduct; or they desired to know my mind or determination, and what I was going to do. I told them that on reflection upon the many difficulties that I had had with the Church, and the much disgrace I had brought upon myself in consequence of these things, and also that my health would not permit me to go to school to make any preparations for the endowment, and that my health was such that I was not able to travel, that it would be better for them to appoint one, in the office, that would be better able to fill it, and by doing this they would throw me into the hands of the Church, and leave me where I was before I was chosen, then I would not be in a situation to bring so much disgrace upon the cause, when I fall into temptation; and perhaps, by this I might obtain salvation. You know my passions and the danger of falling from so high a station; and thus by withdrawing from the office of the Apostleship, while there is salvation for me, and remaining a member of the Church—I feel afraid, if I don't do this, it will be worse for me some other day.

And again, my health is poor, and I am not able to travel and it is necessary the office should not be idle. And again, I say, you know my passions, and I am afraid it will be the worse for me by and by. Do so, if the Lord will have mercy on me, and let me remain as a member in the Church, and then I can travel and preach when I am able. Do not think I am your enemy for what I have done. Perhaps you may say or ask why I have not remembered the good that you have done to me. When I reflect upon the injury I have done you, I must confess that I do not know what I have been about. I feel sorry for what I have done, and humbly ask your forgiveness. I have not confidence as yet to come and see you, for I feel ashamed of what I have done; and as I feel now, I feel as though all the confessions that I could make, verbally or by writing, would not be sufficient to atone for the transgression. Be this as it may, I am willing to make all the restitution you shall require. If I can stay in the Church as a member, I will try to make all the satisfaction possible.

Yours with respect,

WILLIAM SMITH.

P.S.—Do not cast me off for what I have done, but strive to save me in the Church as a member. I do repent of what I have done to you and ask your forgiveness. I consider the transgression, the other evening, of no small magnitude; but it is done, and I cannot help it now. I know, Brother Joseph, you are always willing to forgive; but I sometimes think, when I reflect upon the many injuries I have done you, I feel as though confession was hardly sufficient. But have mercy on me this once, and I will try to do so no more.

The Twelve called a Council yesterday, and sent over after me, and I went over. This Council, remember, was called together by them-selves and not by me.   W. S.

To the foregoing I gave the following answer the same day.

Letter of the Prophet to his Brother William.

BROTHER WILLIAM—Having received your letter, I now proceed to answer it, and shall first proceed to give a brief narration of my feelings and motives since the night I first came to the knowledge of your having a debating school, which was at the time I happened in with Bishop Whitney, his father and mother, &c.; and from that time I took an interest in it, and was delighted with it, and formed a determination to attend the school, for the purpose of obtaining information, and with the idea of imparting the same, through the assistance of the Spirit of the Lord, if by any means I should have faith to do so. And with this intent, I went to the school on last Wednesday night, not with the idea of breaking up the school, neither did it enter into my heart that there was any wrangling or jealousies in your heart against me. Notwithstanding, previous to my leaving home, there were feelings of solemnity rolling across my breast, which were unaccountable to me; and also these feelings continued by spells to depress my spirits, and seemed to manifest that all was not right, even after the school commenced, and during the debate, yet I strove to believe that all would work together for good. I was pleased with the power of the arguments that were used, and did not feel to cast any reflections upon any one that had spoken; but I felt it was the duty of old men that sat as Presidents, to be as grave, at least, as young men, and that it was our duty to smile (not) at solid arguments and sound reasonings; and be impressed with solemnity, which should be manifested in our countenances, when folly which militates against truth and righteousness, rears its head.

Therefore, in the spirit of my calling, and in view of the authority of the Priesthood that has been conferred upon me, it would be my duty to reprove whatever I esteemed to be wrong, fondly hoping in my heart, that all parties would consider it right, and therefore humble themselves, that Satan might not take the advantage of us, and hinder the progress of our school.

Now, Brother William, I want you should bear with me, notwithstanding my plainness. I would say to you that my feelings were grieved at the interruption you made upon Elder M'Lellin. I thought you should consider your relationship with him in your Apostleship, and not manifest any division of sentiment between you and him, for a surrounding multitude to take advantage of you; therefore, by way of entreaty, on account of the anxiety I had for your influence and welfare, I said unto you: Do not have any feelings; or something to that amount. Why I am thus particular, is, that if you have misconstrued my feelings towards you, you may be corrected. But to proceed. After the school was closed, Brother Hyrum requested the privilege of speaking; you objected; however, you said if he would not abuse the school, he might speak, and that you would not allow any man to abuse the school in your house. Now, you had no reason to suspect that Hyrum would abuse the school; therefore, my feelings were mortified at these unnecessary observations. I undertook to reason with you, but you manifested an inconsiderate and stubborn spirit. I then despaired of benefitting you, on account of the spirit you manifested, which drew from me the expression that you were as ugly as the devil. Father then commanded silence, and I formed a determination to obey his mandate, and was about to leave the house, with the impression that you was under the influence of a wicked spirit: you replied that you would say what you pleased in your own house. Father said: Say what you please, but let the rest hold their tongues. Then a reflection rushed through my mind, of the anxiety and care I have had for you and your family, in doing what I did in finishing your house, and providing flour for your family, &c.; and also, father had possession* in the house as well as yourself; and when at any time have I transgressed the commandments of my father, or sold my birthright, that I should not have the privilege of speaking in my father's house, or in other words, in my father's family, or in your house, (for so we will call it, and so it shall be,) that I should not have the privilege of reproving a younger brother? Therefore I said, I will speak, for I built the house, and it is as much mine as yours; or something to that effect. I should have said, that I helped to finish the house. I said it merely to show that it could not be the right spirit that would rise up for trifling matters, and undertake to put me to silence. I saw that your indignation was kindled against me, and you made towards me. I was not then to be moved, and I thought to pull off my loose coat, lest it should tangle me, and you be left to hurt me, but not with the intention of hurting you. But you were too quick for me, and having once fallen into the hands of a mob, and been wounded in my side, and now into the hands

---

* That is, Father Smith had assisted in building the house, and was also at that time making his home with William.

of a brother, my side gave way. And after having been rescued from your grasp, I left your house with feelings indescribable—the scenery had changed, and all those expectations that I had cherished, when going to your house, and brotherly kindness, charity, forbearance, and natural affection, that in duty bind us not to make each other offenders for a word. But alas! abuse, anger, malice, hatred, and rage, with a lame side, with marks of violence heaped upon me by a brother, were the reflections of my disappointment; and with these I returned home, not able to sit down or rise up without help, but, through the blessing of God, I am now better.

I received your letter and perused it with care. I have not entertained a feeling of malice against you. I am older than you and have endured more suffering, having been marred by mobs. The labors of my calling, a series of persecutions and injuries continually heaped upon me—all serve to debilitate my body; and it may be that I cannot boast of being stronger than you. If I could or could not, would this be an honor or dishonor to me? If I could boast, like David, of slaying a Goliah, who defied the armies of the living God; or, like Paul, of contending with Peter, face to face, with sound arguments, it might be an honor; but to mangle the flesh, or seek revenge upon one who never did you any wrong, cannot be a source of sweet reflection to you nor to me, neither to an honorable father and mother, brothers and sisters. And when we reflect with what care, and with what unremitting diligence our parents have striven to watch over us, and how many hours of sorrow and anxiety they have spent, over our cradles and bed-sides, in times of sickness, how careful we ought to be of their feelings in their old age! It cannot be a source of sweet reflection to us, to say or do anything that will bring their gray hairs down with sorrow to the grave.

In your letter you ask my forgiveness, which I readily grant. But it seems to me, that you still retain an idea that I have given you reasons to be angry or disaffected with me. Grant me the privilege of saying then, that however hasty and harsh I may have spoken at any time to you, it has been done for the express purpose of endeavoring to warn, exhort, admonish, and recue you from falling into difficulties and sorrows, which I foresaw you plunging into, by giving way to that wicked spirit, which you call your passions, which you should curb and break down, and put under your feet; which if you do not, you never can be saved, in my view, in the Kingdom of God. God requires the will of His creatures to be swallowed up in His will.

You desire to remain in the Church, but forsake your Apostleship. This is the stratagem of the evil one; when he has gained one advantage, he lays a plan for another. But by maintaining your Apostleship, in rising up and making one tremendous effort, you may overcome your passions and please God. And by forsaking your Apostleship, is not to be willing to make that sacrifice that God requires at your hands, and is to incur His displeasure; and without pleasing God, we do not think it will be any better for you. When a man falls one step, he must regain that step again, or fall another; he has still more to gain, or eventually all is lost.

I desire, Brother William, that you will humble yourself. I freely forgive you, and you know my unshaken and unchangeable disposition; I know in whom I trust; I stand upon the rock; the floods cannot, no, they shall not, overthrow me. You know the doctrine I teach is true, you know that God has blessed me. I brought salvation to my father's house, as an instrument in the hands of God when they were in a miserable situation. You know that it is my duty to admonish you, when you do wrong. This liberty I shall always take, and you shall have the same privilege. I take the liberty to admonish you, because of my birthright; and I grant you the privilege, because it is my duty to be humble, and receive rebuke and instruction from a brother, or a friend.

As it regards what course you shall pursue hereafter, I do not pretend to say; I leave you in the hands of God and His Church. Make your own decision; I will do you good, although you mar me, or slay me. By so doing, my garments shall be clear of your sins. And if at any time you should consider me to be an imposter, for heaven's sake leave me in the hands of God, and not think to take vengeance on me yourself. Tyranny, usurpation, and to take men's rights, ever has been and ever shall be banished from my heart. David sought not to kill Saul, although he was guilty of crimes that never entered my heart.

And now may God have mercy upon my father's house; may God take away enmity from between me and thee; and may all blessings be restored, and the past be forgotten forever. May humble repentance bring us both to Thee, O God, and to Thy power and protection, and a crown, to enjoy the society of father, mother, Alvin, Hyrum, Sophronia, Samuel, Catherine, Carlos, Lucy, the Saints, and all the sanctified in peace, forever, is the prayer of your brother,

JOSEPH SMITH, JUN.

To William Smith.

Saturday, 19.—At home. Sent the above letter to Brother William Smith. I have had many solemn feelings this day concerning my brother William, and have prayed in my heart fervently, that the Lord will not cast him off, but that he

Desire of the Prophet for William's Salvation.

may return to the God of Jacob, and magnify his Apostleship and calling. May this be his happy lot, for the Lord of glory's sake. Amen.

Sunday, 20.—At home all day. Took solid comfort with my family. Had many serious reflections. Brothers

Sundry Prayers of the Prophet for the Welfare of Various Brethren. Palmer and Taylor called to see me. I showed them the sacred records to their joy and satisfaction. O! may God have mercy upon these men, and keep them in the way of everlasting life, in the name of Jesus. Amen.

Monday, 21.—Spent this day at home, endeavoring to treasure up knowledge for the benefit of my calling. The day passed off very pleasantly. I thank the Lord for His blessings to my soul, His great mercy over my family in sparing our lives. O continue Thy care over me and mine, for Christ's sake.

Tuesday, 22.—At home. Continued my studies. O may God give me learning, even language; and endue me with qualifications to magnify His name while I live.

I also delivered an address to the Church, this evening. The Lord blessed my soul. My scribe is unwell. O may God heal him. And for his kindness to me, O my soul, be thou grateful to him, and bless him. And he shall be blessed of God for ever, for I believe him to be a faithful friend to me, therefore my soul delighteth in him. Amen.

Wednesday, 23.—In the forenoon, at home, studying the Greek language. And also waited upon the brethren who came in, and exhibited to them the papyrus. Afternoon, visited Brother Leonard Rich, with the relatives of Brother Oliver Cowdery. Had not a very agreeable visit, for I found them filled with prejudice against the work of the Lord, and their minds blinded with superstition and ignorance.

Thursday, 24.—The forenoon, at home. In the afternoon, I assisted the commissioner appointed by the [county] court, in surveying a road across my farm.

Friday, 25.—Enjoyed myself at home with my family, all day, it being Christmas, the only time I have had this privilege so satisfactorily for a long period. The Prophet's Christmas at Brother Jonathan Crosby called this evening. Home.

Saturday, 26.—Commenced again studying the Hebrew language, in company with Brothers Parrish and Williams. In the meantime, Brother Lyman Sherman came in, and requested to have the word of the Lord through me; "for," said he, "I have been wrought upon to make known to you my feelings and desires, and was promised that I should have a revelation which should make known my duty."

The Prophet's Renewal of the Study of Hebrew.

Revelation given to Lyman Sherman, December 26, 1835.

Verily thus saith the Lord unto you, my servant Lyman, your sins are forgiven you, because you have obeyed my voice in coming up hither this morning to receive counsel of him whom I have appointed. Therefore, let your soul be at rest concerning your spiritual standing, and resist no more my voice; and arise up and be more careful henceforth, in observing your vows which you have made, and do make, and you shall be blessed with exceeding great blessings. Wait patiently until the solemn assembly shall be called of my servants, then you shall be remembered with the first of mine Elders, and receive right by ordination with the rest of mine Elders, whom I have chosen. Behold, this is the promise of the Father unto you if you continue faithful; and it shall be fulfilled upon you in that day that you shall have right to preach my Gospel wheresoever I shall send you, from henceforth from that time. Therefore, strengthen your brethren in all your conversation, in all your prayers, in all your exhortations, and in all your doings; and behold, and lo! I am with you to bless you, and deliver you forever. Amen.

Sunday, 27.—At the usual hour, attending meeting at the school house. President Cowdery delivered a very able and interesting discourse. Sunday Services.

In the afternoon, Brother Hyrum Smith and Bishop Partridge delivered each a short and interesting lecture, after which Sacrament was administered.

While chopping wood at my door, on the 25th instant,

two gentlemen called, and requested an interview with
Trifling
Visitors. the heads of the Church, which I agreed to
grant them this morning, but they did not
come, and I consider they were trifling characters.

Monday, 28.—Having previously preferred a charge
against Almon W. Babbitt, for traducing my character,
Arraignment
of Almon W.
Babbitt. he was this morning called before the High
Council, and I attended with my witnesses,
and substantiated the charge against him;
and he in part acknowledged his fault, but not satisfactorily to the Council; and after parleying with him a long
time, and granting him every indulgence that righteousness required, the Council adjourned without obtaining a
full confession from him.

This day the Council of the Seventy met to render an
account of their travels and ministry, since they were
First Report
of the Seven-
ties. ordained to that Apostleship. The meeting
was interesting indeed, and my heart was
made glad while listening to the relation of
those that had been laboring in the vineyard of the Lord,
with such marvelous success. And I pray God to bless
them with an increase of faith and power, and keep them
all, with the endurance of faith in the name of Jesus
Christ to the end.

Tuesday, 29.—The following charges were preferred:

To the Honorable Presidency of the Church of Christ of Latter-day Saints,
against Elder William Smith.

1st. Unchristianlike conduct in speaking disrespectfully of President
Joseph Smith, Jun., and the revelations and commandments given
through him.

2nd. For attempting to inflict personal violence on President Joseph
Smith, Jun.

ORSON JOHNSON.

I remained at home until about ten o'clock. I then at-
Patriarchal
Blessing
Meeting. tended a blessing meeting at Oliver Olney's, in
company with my wife, and father and moth-
er, who had come to live with me. Also

my scribe went with us. A large company assembled, when Father Smith made some appropriate remarks. A hymn was sung and father opened the meeting by prayer. About fifteen persons then received patriarchal blessings under his hands. The services were concluded as they commenced. A table was crowned with the bounties of nature; and after invoking the benediction of heaven upon the rich repast, we fared sumptuously; and suffice it to say that we had a glorious meeting throughout, and I was much pleased with the harmony that existed among the brethren and sisters. We returned home, and at early candle-light I preached at the school house to a crowded congregation, who listened with attention about three hours. I had liberty in speaking. Some Presbyterians were present, as I afterwards learned; and I expect that some of my sayings sat like a garment that was well fitted, as I exposed their abominations in the language of the scriptures; and I pray God that it may be like a nail in a sure place, driven by the master of assemblies.

Wednesday, 30.—Spent the day reading Hebrew at the council room, in company with my scribe, who is recovering his health, which gives me much satisfaction, for I delight in his company. Hebrew Studies.

Thursday, 31.—At home. After attending to the duties of my family, retired to the council room to pursue my studies. The Council of the Twelve convened in the upper room, in the printing office, directly over the room where we were assembled in our studies. They sent for me, and the Presidency, or a part of them, to receive counsel from us on the subject of the council which is to be held on Saturday next. Questions of the Twelve Concerning Trial of William Smith.

In the afternoon I attended at the chapel to give directions concerning the upper rooms, and more especially the west room, which I intend occupying for a translating room, which will be prepared this week.

The public mind has been excited of late, by reports which have been circulated concerning certain Egyptian mummies and ancient records, which were pur- chased by certain gentlemen of Kirtland, last July. It has been said that the purchasers of these antiquities pretend they have the bodies of Abraham, Abimelech, (the king of the Philistines,) Joseph, who was sold into Egypt, &c., &c., for the pur- pose of attracting the attention of the multitude, and gulling the unwary; which is utterly false. Who these ancient inhabitants of Egypt were, I do not at present say. Abraham was buried on his own possession "in the cave of Machpelah, in the field of Ephron, the son of Zohah, the Hittite, which is before Mamre," which he purchased of the sons of Heth. Abimelech lived in the same country, and for aught we know, died there; and the children of Israel carried Joseph's bones from Egypt, when they went out under Moses; consequently, these could not have been found in Egypt, in the nineteenth century. The record of Abraham and Joseph, found with the mnmmies, is beautifully written on papyrus, with black, and a small part red, ink or paint, in perfect preservation. The characters are such as you find upon the coffins of mummies—hieroglyphics, etc.; with many characters of letters like the present (though probably not quite so square) form of the Hebrew without points. The records were obtained from one of the catacombs in Egypt, near the place where once stood the renowned city of Thebes, by the celebrated French traveler, Antonio Sebolo, in the year 1831. He procured license from Mehemet Ali, then Viceroy of Egypt, under the protec- tion of Chevalier Drovetti, the French Consul, in the year 1828, and employed four hundred and thirty-three men, four months and two days (if I understand correctly)— Egyptian or Turkish soldies, at from four to six cents per diem, each man. He entered the catacomb June 7, 1831, and obtained eleven mummies. There were several hun-

An Account of the Book of Abraham.

dred mummies in the same catacomb; about one hundred embalmed after the first order, and placed in niches, and two or three hundred after the second and third orders, and laid upon the floor or bottom of the grand cavity. The two last orders of embalmed were so decayed, that they could not be removed, and only eleven of the first, found in the niches. On his way from Alexandria to Paris, he put in at Trieste, and, after ten days' illness, expired. This was in the year 1832. Previous to his decease, he made a will of the whole, to Mr. Michael H. Chandler, (then in Philadelphia, Pa.,) his nephew, whom he supposed to be in Ireland. Accordingly, the whole were sent to Dublin, and Mr. Chandler's friends ordered them to New York, where they were received at the Custom House, in the winter or spring of 1833. In April, of the same year, Mr. Chandler paid the duties and took possession of his mummies. Up to this time, they had not been taken out of the coffins, nor the coffins opened. On opening the coffins, he discovered that in connection with two of the bodies, was something rolled up with the same kind of linen, saturated with the same bitumen, which, when examined, proved to be two rolls of papyrus, previously mentioned. Two or three other small pieces of papyrus, with astronomical calculations, epitaphs, &c., were found with others of the mummies. When Mr. Chandler discovered that there was something with the mummies, he supposed or hoped it might be some diamonds or valuable metal, and was no little chagrined when he saw his disappointment. "He was immediately told, while yet in the custom house, that there was no man in that city who could translate his roll: but was referred, by the same gentleman, (a stranger,) to Mr. Joseph Smith, Jun., who, continued he, possesses some kind of power or gifts, by which he had previously translated similar characters." I was then unknown to Mr. Chandler, neither did he know that such a book or work as the record of the Nephites, had been brought before the public. From New York, he took his collection on to Philadelphia, where he obtained the certificate of the learned,* and from thence came on to Kirtland, as before related, in July. Thus I have given a brief history of the manner in which the writings of the fathers, Abraham

* The account here given of how the Prophet came into possession of the writings of Abraham, and of Joseph, the son of Jacob, was adapted from an article in the *Messenger and Advocate,* (Volume II, Number 3, pages 233, 236, bearing date of December, 1835) signed by Oliver Cowdery. The article is addressed to William Frye, Esq., of Gilead, Calhoun County, Ill. The certificate of the "learned" referred to, is in the body of the article. It seems that Michael H. Chandler, the owner of the Egyptian mummies and the papyrus, exhibited his treasures in Philadelphia, and, while there, obtained the following opinion of several prominent doctors:

"Having examined with considerable attention and deep interest, a number of mummies from the Catacombs, near Thebes, in Egypt, and now exhibiting in the Arcade, we beg leave to recommend them to the observation of the curious inquirer on subjects of a period so long elapsed; probably not less than three thousand years ago. The features of some of these mummies are in perfect expression. The papyrus covered with black or red ink, or paint, in excellent preservation, are very interesting. The undersigned, unsolicited by any person connected by interest with this exhibition, have voluntarily set their names hereunto, for the simple purpose of calling the attention of the public to an interesting collection, not sufficiently know in this city."

JOHN REDMAN COXE, M. D.,
RICHARD HARLAN, M. D.,
J. PANCOAST, M. D.,
WILLIAM P. C. BARTON, M. D.,
E. F. RIVINUS, M. D.,
SAMUEL G. MORGAN, M. D.

"I concur in the above sentiments, concerning the collection of mummies in the Philadelphia Arcade, and consider them highly deserving the attention of the curious.

"W. E. HORNER, M. D."

Another paragraph in the article explains how it came about that Mr. Chandler gave the Prophet a certificate, concerning his belief in the Prophet's ability to decipher the Egyptian hieroglyphics of the papyrus—which certificate will be found at page 235, of this volume, under the date of the purchase of the mummies and papyrus by certain persons in Kirtland. From the paragraph referred to, it appears that on the morning that Mr. Chandler first presented his papyrus to the Prophet Joseph Smith, he was shown by the latter, a number of characters which had been copied from the Nephite plates, and found that there were some points of resemblance between some of the Nephite characters and some of the characters on the Egyptian papyrus. Mr. Chandler then asked the Prophet's opinion concerning the antiquity of the Egyptian papyrus, and also requested him to give a translation of the characters. The Prophet gave Mr. Chandler a translation of some few of the Egyptian characters, which agreed with the interpretation given by learned men in other cities, where the mummies and papyrus had been exhibited, whereupon Mr. Chandler gave the Prophet a certificate, stating that fact.

and Joseph, have been preserved, and how I came in possession of the same—a correct translation of which I shall give in its proper place.

To show the spirit of the public journals, such as the *Philadelphia Saturday Courier*, *New York Daily Advertiser*, *Sunday Morning News*, and the press generally, the past year, towards me and the cause of God, which I have fearlessly espoused, I quote the following, as a specimen of the whole, from M. M. Noah's *New York Evening Star:*

Tone of the American Press Toward the Prophet.

HEATHEN TEMPLE ON LAKE ERIE.

That bold-faced imposter, Joe Smith, of Gold Bible and Mormon memory, has caused his poor fanatic followers to erect on the shores of Lake Erie, near Painesville, Ohio, a stone building, 58 by 78 feet, with dormer windows, denominating the same "The Temple of the Lord." We should think this work of iniquity extorted out of the pockets of his dupes, as it reflects its shadows over the blue Lake, would make the waters crimson with shame at the prostitution of its beautiful banks to such unhallowed purposes.

Thus much from M. M. Noah, a Jew, who had used all the influence in his power, to dupe his fellow Jews, and make them believe that the New Jerusalem for them, was to be built on Grand Island, whose banks are surrounded by the waters of the same Lake Erie. The Lord reward him according to his deeds.

CHAPTER XXVI.

OPENING OF THE YEAR 1836—THE AMERICAN INDIANS—SPECIAL
COUNCIL MEETINGS IN KIRTLAND.

Friday Morning, January 1, 1836.—This being the beginning of a new year, my heart is filled with gratitude
to God that He has preserved my life, and
the lives of my family, while another year has
passed away. We have been sustained and
upheld in the midst of a wicked and preverse generation, although exposed to all the afflictions, temptations,
and misery that are incident to human life; for this I feel
to humble myself in dust and ashes, as it were, before the
Lord. But notwithstanding the gratitude that fills my
heart on retrospecting the past year, and the multiplied
blessings that have crowned our heads, my heart is pained
within me, because of the difficulty that exists in my
father's family. The devil has made a violent attack on
my brother William and Calvin Stoddard, and the powers
of darkness seem to lower over their minds, and not only
over theirs, but they also cast a gloomy shade over the
minds of my brethren and sisters, which prevents them from
seeing things as they really are; and the powers of earth
and hell seem combined to overthrow us and the Church,
by causing a division in the family; and indeed the adversary is bringing into requisition all his subtlety to
prevent the Saints from being endowed, by causing a
division among the Twelve, also among the Seventy, and
bickering and jealousies among the Elders and the official
members of the Church; and so the leaven of iniquity

Reflections of the Prophet.

ferments and spreads among the members of the Church. But I am determined that nothing on my part shall be lacking to adjust and amicably dispose of and settle all family difficulties on this day, that the ensuing year and years, be they few or many, may be spent in righteousness before God. And I know that the cloud will burst, and Satan's kingdom be laid in ruins, with all his black designs; and that the Saints will come forth like gold seven times tried in the fire, being made perfect through sufferings and temptations, and that the blessings of heaven and earth will be multiplied upon their heads; which may God grant for Christ's sake. Amen.

Brothers William and Hyrum, and Uncle John Smith, came to my house, and we went into a room by ourselves, in company with father and Elder Martin Harris. Father Smith then opened our interview by prayer, after which he expressed himself on the occasion in a very feeling and *Reconciliation of the Prophet and his Brother William.* pathetic manner, even with all the sympathy of a father, whose feelings were deeply wounded on account of the difficulty that was existing in the family; and while he addressed us, the Spirit of God rested down upon us in mighty power, and our hearts were melted. Brother William made a humble confession and asked my forgiveness for the abuse he had offered me. And wherein I had been out of the way, I asked his forgiveness. And the spirit of confession and forgiveness was mutual among us all, and we covenanted with each other, in the sight of God, and the holy angels, and the brethren, to strive thenceforward to build each other up in righteousness in all things, and not listen to evil reports concerning each other; but, like brothers indeed, go to each other, with our grievances, in the spirit of meekness, and be reconciled, and thereby promote our happiness, and the happiness of the family, and, in short, the happiness and wellbeing of all. My wife and mother and my scribe were then called in, and we repeated the covenant to them that we had entered into; and while gratitude swelled our bosoms, tears flowed from our eyes. I was then requested to close our interview, which I did, with prayer; and it was truly a jubilee and time of rejoicing; after which we all unitedly administered, by laying on of hands, to my cousin George A.Smith, who was immediately healed of a severe rheumatic affection all over the body, which caused excruciating pain.

Saturday, January 2.—According to previous arrangement, I went to the Council at nine o'clock. This Council was called to sit in judgment on a com-

Settlement of
William
Smith's case
Before the
Council.

plaint preferred against Brother William Smith, by Orson Johnson, on the 29th of December.

The Council organized and proceeded to business, but before entering on trial, Brother William arose and humbly confessed the charges preferred against him, and asked the forgiveness of the Council and the whole congregation.

A vote was then called to know whether his confession was satisfactory, and whether the brethren would extend again to him the hand of fellowship. With cheerfulness the whole congregation raised their hands to receive him.

Elder Almon W. Babbitt also confessed the charges which I preferred against him in a previous Council; and was received into fellowship.

Council voted that Vinson Knight and Thomas Grover should be ordained Elders. And some other business was transacted in union and fellowship, and the best of feeling seemed to prevail among the brethren, and our hearts were made glad on the occasion, and there was joy in heaven, and my soul doth magnify the Lord, for His goodness and mercy endure forever.

Elijah Fordham, Hyrum Dayton, Samuel James and John Herrot were also appointed by Council to be ordained Elders under my hands.

Sunday, 3.—Went to meeting at the usual hour. President Rigdon delivered a fine lecture upon the subject of Revelation.

In the afternoon I confirmed ten or twelve persons who had been baptized, among whom was Malcham C. Davis, who was baptized during the intermission today. Brother William Smith made his confession to the Church to their satisfaction, and was cordially received into fellowship again. The Lord's Supper was administered, and Brother William gave out an appointment to preach in the evening at early candle-light, and preached a fine discourse; and this day has been a day of rejoicing to me. The cloud that has been hanging over us has burst with blessings on our heads, and Satan has been foiled in his attempts to destroy me and the Church, by causing jealousies to arise in the hearts of some of the brethren; and I thank my heavenly Father for the union and harmony which now prevail in the Church.

Monday, 4.—Met and organized our Hebrew school according to the arrangements that were made on Saturday last. We had engaged Doctor Piexotto to teach us in the Hebrew language, when we had our room prepared. We informed him that we were ready and our room was prepared. And he agreed to wait on us this day, and deliver his introductory lecture. Yesterday he sent us word that he could not come until Wednesday next. A vote was then called to know whether we would submit to such treatment or not; and carried in the negative; and Elder Sylvester Smith was appointed clerk to write him on the subject, and inform him that his services were not wanted; and Elders William E. M'Lellin and Orson Hyde despatched to Hudson Seminary to hire a teacher. They were appointed by the voice of the school to act in their behalf. However, we concluded to go on with our school and do the best we could until we obtained a teacher; and by the voice of the school I con-

Preparation for the Hebrew School.

sented to render them all the assistance I was able to for the time being.

We are occupying the translating room for the use of the school, until another room can be prepared. It is the west room in the upper part of the Temple, and was consecrated this morning by prayer, offered up by Father Smith. This is the first day we have occupied it. This is a rainy time, and the roads are extremely muddy.

Met this evening at the Temple, to make arrangements for a singing school. After some discussion, a judicious arrangement was made, a committee of six was chosen to take charge of the singing department.

Tuesday, 5.—Attended the Hebrew school, divided it into classes. Had some debate with Elder Orson Pratt concerning the pronunciation of a Hebrew letter. He manifested a stubborn spirit, at which I was much grieved.

Wednesday, 6.—Attended school and spent most of the forenoon in settling the unpleasant feelings that existed in the breast of Elder Orson Pratt. After much controversy, he confessed his fault for entering into any controversy concerning so small a matter as the sound of a Hebrew letter, and asked the forgiveness of the whole school, and was cheerfully forgiven by all.

A Difference Between the Prophet and Orson Pratt.

Elder M'Lellin returned from Hudson, and reported to the school that he had hired a teacher to teach us the term of seven weeks, for three hundred and twenty dollars; that is, forty scholars for that amount; to commence in about fifteen days. He is highly celebrated as a Hebrew scholar, and proposes to give us sufficient knowledge during the above term to start us in reading and translating the language.

A New Teacher in Hebrew Employed.

A High Council assembled at Kirtland for the purpose of filling the vacancies of the High Council of Zion. Presidents David Whitmer, John Whitmer and W. W. Phelps, and fifteen High

Vacancies in the High Council Filled.

Priests and Elders present.   President Phelps announced
the death of Christian Whitmer on the 27th of November,
1835.   Four councilors, namely Parley P. Pratt, Orson
Pratt, William E. M'Lellin and Thomas B. Marsh, had
been chosen Apostles, or especial witnesses; and Elisha
H. Groves was appointed to take the place of Parley P.
Pratt in the High Council of Zion, John Hitchcock in the
place of William E. M'Lellin, George M. Hinkle of Orson
Pratt, Elias Higbee of Thomas B. Marsh, and Peter Whitmer, Jun., of Christian Whitmer, deceased; who were
ordained at the time to their office as councilors.

Much has been said and done of late by the general
government in relation to the Indians (Lamanites) within
the territorial limits of the United States.   The Gathering
One of the most important points in the faith   of Israel and
the American
of the Church of the Latter-day Saints,   Indians.
through the fullness of the everlasting Gospel, is the
gathering of Israel (of whom the Lamanites constitute a
part)—that happy time when Jacob shall go up to the
house of the Lord, to worship Him in spirit and in truth,
to live in holiness; when the Lord will restore His judges
as at the first, and His counselors as at the beginning;
when every man may sit under his own vine and fig tree,
and there will be none to molest or make afraid; when
He will turn to them a pure language, and the earth will
be filled with sacred knowledge, as the waters cover the
great deep; when it shall no longer be said, the Lord
lives that brought up the children of Israel out of the land
of Egypt, but the Lord lives that brought up the children
of Israel from the land of the north, and from all the lands
whither He has driven them.   That day is one, all important to all men.

In view of its importance, together with all that the
prophets have said about it before us, we feel like dropping
a few ideas in connection with the official statements from
the government concerning the Indians.   In speaking of
the gathering, we mean to be understood as speaking of it

according to scripture, the gathering of the elect of the Lord out of every nation on earth, and bringing them to the place of the Lord of Hosts, when the city of right-eousness shall be built, and where the people shall be of one heart and one mind, when the Savior comes; yea, where the people shall walk with God like Enoch, and be free from sin. The word of the Lord is precious; and when we read that the vail spread over all nations will be destroyed, and the pure in heart see God, and reign with Him a thousand years on earth, we want all honest men to have a chance to gather and build up a city of right-eousness, where even upon the bells of the horses shall be written *Holiness to the Lord*.

The Book of Mormon has made known who Israel is, upon this continent. And while we behold the govern-

Policy of the Government of the United States Respecting the Indians.

ment of the United States gathering the Indians, and locating them upon lands to be their own, how sweet it is to think that they may one day be gathered by the Gospel! Our venerable President of these United States (Andrew Jackson) speaks of the Indians as follows:

President Andrew Jackson's Views on the Policy of the General Government with Reference to the Indians.

The plan of removing the aboriginal people who yet remain within the settled portions of the United States, to the country west of the Mississippi River, approaches its consummation. It was adopted on the most mature consideration of the condition of this race, and ought to be persisted in till the object is accomplished, and prosecuted with as much vigor as a just regard to their circumstances will permit, and as far as their consent can be obtained. All preceding experiments for the improvement of the Indians have failed. It seems now to be an established fact, that they cannot live in contact with a civilized commu-nity and prosper. Ages of fruitless endeavors have at length brought us to a knowledge of this principle of intercommunication with them. The past we cannot recall, but the future we can provide for,

Independently of the treaty stipulations into which we have entered with the various tribes for the usufructuary rights ceded to us, no one can doubt the moral duty of the government of the United States to

protect, and, if possible, to preserve and perpetuate the scattered remnants of this race which are left within our borders. In the discharge
of this duty, an extensive region in the west has been assigned for their
permanent residence. It has been divided into districts, and allotted
among them. Many have already removed, and others are preparing
to go; and, with the exception of two small bands, living in Ohio and
Indiana, not exceeding fifteen hundred persons, and of the Cherokees,
all the tribes on the east side of the Mississippi, and extendig from
Lake Michigan to Florida, have entered into engagements which will
lead to their transplantation.

The plan for their removal and re-establishment is founded upon the
knowledge we have gained of their character and habits, and has been
dictated by a spirit of enlarged liberality. A territory exceeding in
extent to that relinquished has been granted to each tribe. Of its
climate, fertility, and capability to support an Indian population, the
representations are highly favorable. To these districts the Indians are
removed at the expense of the United States, and with certain supplies
of clothing, arms, ammunition, and other indispensable articles; they
are also furnished gratuitously with provisions for the period of a year
after their arrival at their new homes. In that time, from the nature
of the country, and of the products raised by them, they can subsist
themselves by agricultural labor, if they choose to resort to that mode
of life. If they do not, they are on the skirts of·the great prairies,
where countless herds of buffalo roam, and a short time suffices to adapt
their own habits to the changes which a change of the animals destined
for their food may require.

Ample arrangements have also been made for the support of schools;
in some instances, council houses and churches are to be erected, dwellings to be constructed for the chiefs, and mills for cotton use. Funds
have been set apart for the maintenance of the poor, the most necessary mechanical arts have been introduced, and blacksmiths, gun-
smiths, wheelwrights, millwrights, etc., are supported among them·
Steel and iron, and sometime salt are purchased for them; and plows
and other farming utensils.

Domestic animals, looms, spinning wheels, cards, etc., are presented
to them; and besides these beneficial arrangements, annuities are in all
cases paid, amounting in some instances to more than thirty dollars for
each individual of the tribe, and in all cases sufficiently great, if justly
divided and prudently expended, to enable them, in addition to their
own exertions, to live comfortably. And as a stimulus for exertion, it
is now provided by law, that in all cases of the appointment of inter-
preters, or other persons employed for the benefit of the Indians, a
preference shall be given to persons of Indian descent, if such can

be found, who are properly qualified for the discharge of the duties.

Such are the arrangements for the physical comfort and for the moral improvement of the Indians. The necessary measures for their political advancement and for their separation from our citizens have not been neglected. The pledge of the United States has been given by Congress, that the country designated for the residence of this people shall be "forever secured and guaranteed to them." A country west of Missouri and Arkansas has been assigned to them, into which the white settlements are not to be pushed. No political communities can be formed in that extensive region, except those that are established by the Indians themselves, or by the United States for them and with their concurrence. A barrier has thus been raised for their protection against the encroachments of the citizens, and guarding the Indians as far as possible, from those evils which have brought them to their present condition.

Summary authority has been given by law, to destroy all ardent spirits found in their country without waiting the doubtful result and slow process of a legal seizure.

I consider the absolute and unconditional interdiction of this article, among these people, as the first great step in their amelioration. Half-way measures will answer no purpose. These cannot successfully contend against the cupidity of the seller and the overpowering appetite of the buyer; and the destructive effects of the traffic are marked in every page of the history of our Indian intercourse.

Some general legislation seems necessary for the regulation of the relations which will exist in this new state of things between the government and people of the United States and those transplanted Indian tribes, and for the establishment among the latter, with their own consent, some of the principles of intercommunication which their juxta-position will call for; that moral may be substituted for physical force; the authority of a few simple laws, for the tomahawk; and that an end may be put to those bloody wars, whose prosecution seems to have made a part of their social system.

After the further detail of the arrangements are completed, with a very general supervision over them, they ought to be left to the progress of events. These, I indulge the hope, will secure their prosperity and improvement; and a large portion of the moral debt we owe them will be paid.

In addition to the above, we extract the following from the report on Indian affairs, made to Congress at the present session. We add and arrange according to circumstances:

The United Nation—Chippewas, Ottowas and Pottawatamies —about 1,000 in number, removed since September, 1834—possess 5,000,000 of acres of land on the east side of the Missouri and lying north-west of the north-west corner of Missouri [All these tribes may be rated at about 7,000].............................. 1,000

The Choctaws, about 19,000, in humber, have 15,000,000 of acres, lying between the Red River and the Canadian.......... 19,000

A small band of Quapaws, 200 or 300, perhaps near 95,000 acres, between the western boundary of the State of Missouri and the eastern boundary of the Osages........ 300

The Creeks, about 3,000 or 4,000, have 13,140,000 acres on Arkansas and Canadian rivers...................................... 4,000

The Seminoles, and other Florida Indians, to the number of say 25,000, included as the owners of the above 13,140,000 acres........ 25,000

The Cherokees, amounting to say 16,000, have 13,000,000 of acres, near the 36th degree of north latitude...................... 16,000

The Kickapoos, something less than 1,000, have 160,000 acres north of Fort Leavenworth 1,000

The Delawares, nearly 1,000, have 200,000 acres west and south of the Kickapoos................ 1,000

The Shawnees, 1,200 or 1,400, have 1,600,000 acres south side of Kansas River.. 1,400

The Ottawas, about 200, have 30,000 acres south of the Shawnees 200

The Weas, Pinkeshaws, Peoria, and Kashaskias, say 500 in all, have 260,000 acres south of the Shawnees...................... 500

The Senecas and Shawnees, say 500, have 100,000 acres on the western boundaries of the State of Missouri..................... 500

Of the native tribes west of the Mississippi, the report is as follows:

Sioux..	27,000
Iowas...	1,200
Sacs of the Missouri.......................................	500
Omahas.........................	1,400
Ottoes and Missourias...............	1,600
Pawnees........	10,000
Camanches.......................	7,000
Mandans.........	15,000

Minatares	15,000
Assinaboins	8,000
Crees	3,000
Gros Ventres	3,000
Crows	4,500
Quapaws	450
Caddoes*	2,000
Poncas	800
Arickarees	3,000
Cheyennes	2,000
Blackfeet	30,000
Foxes	1,600
Anepahas, Kioways, etc	14,000
Osages	5,120
Kansas	1,471
Sacs	4,800

The joy that we shall feel, in common with every honest American, and the joy that will eventually fill their bosoms on account of nationalizing the Indians, will be reward enough when it is shown that gathering them to themselves, and *for themselves*, to be associated with themselves, is a wise measure, and it reflects the highest honor upon our government. May they all be gathered in peace, and form a happy union among themselves, to which thousands may shout, *Esto perpetua.*

Hopes of the Prophet in Behalf of the Indians.

Thursday, 7.—Attended a sumptuous feast at Bishop Newel K. Whitney's. This feast was after the order of the Son of God—the lame, the halt, and the blind were invited, according to the instructions of the Savior. Our meeting was opened by singing, and prayer by Father Smith; after which Bishop Whitney's father and mother, and a number of others, were blessed with a patriarchal blessing. We then received a bountiful refreshment, furnished by the liberality of the Bishop. The company was large, and before we partook we had some of the songs of Zion sung; and our hearts were made glad by a foretaste of those joys that will be

A Feast at Bishop Whitney's.

* The agent reported these Indians as upwards of 2,000.

poured upon the heads of the Saints when they are gathered together on Mount Zion, to enjoy one another's society for evermore, even all the blessings of heaven, when there will be none to molest or make us afraid. Returned home, and spent the evening.

Friday, 8.—Spent the day in the Hebrew school, and made rapid progress in our studies. The plastering and hard-finishing on the outside of the Lord's house was commenced on the 2nd of November, 1835, and finished this day. The job was let to Artemas Millet and Lorenzo Young, at one thousand dollars. Jacob Bump took the job of plastering the inside of the house throughout, at fifteen hundred dollars, and commenced the same on the 9th of November last. He is still continuing the work, notwithstanding the inclemency of the weather.

Progress of Work on Kirtland Temple.

Saturday, 9.—Attended school in the forenoon. About eleven o'clock received the following note:

Bishop Whitney's Unique Invitation to the Prophet.

Thus saith the voice of the Spirit to me—If thy brother Joseph Smith, Jun., will attend the feast at thy house, this day (at twelve o'clock), the poor and the lame will rejoice in his presence, and also think themselves honored.

Yours in friendship and love,
NEWEL K. WHITNEY.

January 9, 1836.

I dismissed the school to accept this polite invitation, with my wife, father and mother. A large congregation assembled, a number were blessed under the hands of Father Smith, and we had a good time. Spent the evening at home.

Sunday, 10.—Attended meeting at the usual hour. Elder Wilbur Denton and Wilkins J. Salisbury preached in the forenoon, and Brothers Samuel and Don Carlos Smith in the afternoon. They all did well, considering their youth. Administered the Sacrament during intermission. Elder Martin Harris baptized three. Spent the evening at home.

Monday, 11.—There being no school, I spent the day at home. Many brethren called to see me, among whom

Visit of Alva Beaman to the Prophet.

was Alva Beaman, from Genesee County, New York, who had come to attend the solemn assembly. I delight in the society of my brethren and friends, and pray that the blessings of heaven and earth may be multiplied upon their heads.

Tuesday, 12.—I called on the Presidency of the Church, and made arrangements to meet tomorrow at ten o'clock,

Preparations for the Solemn Assembly.

a. m. to take into consideration the subject of the solemn assembly. This afternoon, a young man called to see the Egyptian manuscripts, which I exhibited. Also Brother Joseph Rose introduced to me, Russel Weaver, a Christian or Unitarian preacher, so-called, from Cambray, New York. We had some little controversy on prejudice, but soon came to an understanding. He spoke of the Gospel, and said he believed it, adding that it was good tidings of great joy. I replied that it was one thing to proclaim good tidings, and another to tell what these tidings were. He waived the conversation and withdrew.

Wednesday, 13.—At ten o'clock I met in council with the Presidency of Kirtland and Zion, namely, Joseph Smith, Sen., Sidney Rigdon, Hyrum Smith, David Whitmer, John Whitmer, and W. W. Phelps; also the Twelve Apostles, the High Council of Zion, and the High Council of Kirtland, the Bishops of Zion and Kirtland, the Presidency of the Seventies, and many more of the Elders. Some of the Councilors, both of Zion and Kirtland, were absent.

The council came to order, sung Adam-ondi-Ahman,*

* Adam-ondi-Ahman was known to the Saints at this time as the place where the Lord appeared unto Adam our Father, three years previous to his death, and ministered unto the righteous among his posterity assembled at that place; on which occasion Adam was called "Michael," "the Prince," "the Archangel," and the Lord administered unto Adam and said unto him, "I have set thee at the head: a multitude of nations shall come of thee, and thou art a prince over them." It was

and opened by prayer offered up by Joseph Smith, Sen.; when I made some remarks, in my introductory lecture before the autorities of the Church, in general terms, laying before them the business of the day, which was to supply some deficiencies in the Bishop's Council in this place, also in the High Council.

After some consideration upon the most proper manner of proceeding, Elder Vinson Knight was nominated as a counselor in the Bishopric at Kirtland. The nomination was made by the Bishop and seconded by the Presidency. The vote was then called from the Presidency, and carried; next from the High Council of Zion, and carried; from the Twelve, and carried; from the Council of the Seventy, and carried; from the Bishop of Zion and his Council, and carried. And Elder Knight was received by the universal voice and consent of all the authorities of the Church.

Vinson Knight Ordained into Kirtland Bishopric.

Elder Knight was then ordained under the hands of Bishop Newel K. Whitney, to the office of High Priest

this knowledge that inspired the hymn sung on that occasion, composed by W. W Phelps, and here follows:

> This earth was once a garden place,
>   With all her glories common;
> And men did live a holy race,
> And worship Jesus face to face,
>   In Adam-ondi-Ahman.

> We read that Enoch walked with God,
>   Above the power of Mammon;
> While Zion spread herself abroad,
> And saints and angels sang aloud,
>   In Adam-ondi-Ahman.

> Her land was good and greatly blessed,
>   Beyond old Israel's Canaan;
> Her fame was known from east to west;
> Her peace was great and pure the rest
>   Of Adam-ondi-Ahman.

> Hosanna to such days to come—
>   The Savior's second coming,
> When all the earth in glorious bloom
> Affords the Saints a holy home,
>   Like Adam-ondi-Ahman.

(L. D. S. Hymn Book, p. 277.)

and Bishop's counselor, to fill the place of Elder Hyrum Smith, who had been ordained to the Presidency of the High Council of Kirtland.

Council adjourned for one hour, by singing, "Come let us rejoice," etc.

Council assembled again at one o'clock p. m.

John P. Greene was nominated and seconded by the Presidency, a member of the High Council of Kirtland, Vacancies in and carried by the unanimous voice of all the the Kirtland High Council authority of the Church, to supply the place Filled. of President Oliver Cowdery, who had been elected to the Presidency of the High Council of Kirtland.

Elder Thomas Grover was elected in like manner, a Councilor in the High Council, to fill the vacancy occasioned by Luke S. Johnson's having been ordained one of the Twelve Apostles.

Elder Noah Packard was elected a member of the High Council of Kirtland, to fill the place of Sylvester Smith, who had been ordained to the Presidency of the Seventy.

Elder John E. Page was nominated, but being absent, his name was dropped.

Elder Joseph Kingsbury was unanimously chosen a High Councilor in Kirtland, to fill the vacancy occasioned by Orson Hyde's being ordained one of the Twelve Apostles.

Elder Samuel James was unanimously chosen a member of the High Council of Kirtland, in place of Joseph Smith, Sen.

The newly elected Councilors were then called forward in order as they were elected, and ordained under the hands of Presidents Rigdon, Joseph Smith, Jun., and Hyrum Smith, to be High Priests, and Councilors in this Stake of Zion. Many great and glorious blessings were pronounced upon the heads of these Councilors, by President Rigdon, who was spokesman on the occasion.

The Council next proceeded to fill the vacancies in the

High Council of Zion, occasioned by the absence of Councilors John Murdock and Solomon Hancock. Vacancies Filled in the And Elders Alva Beaman and Isaac McWithy High Council were appointed to serve as Councilors in the of Zion. High Council of Zion, for the time being.

Elders Nathaniel Milliken and Thomas Carrico were appointed by unanimous vote to officiate as doorkeepers in the House of the Lord.

Presidents Joseph Smith, Jun., Sidney Rigdon, W. W. Phelps, David Whitmer and Hyrum Smith were appointed to draft rules and regulations to govern the House of the Lord.

By unanimous voice of the assembly, moved, seconded, and carried, that no whispering shall be allowed in our councils or assemblies, nor any one allowed (except he be called upon or asks permission) to speak aloud upon any consideration whatever; and no man shall be interrupted while speaking, unless he is speaking out of place; and every man shall be allowed to speak in his turn.

Elder Milliken objected to officiate in the House of the Lord as doorkeeper, on account of his health; and was released by the voice of the assembly.

The minutes of the Council were then read, and Council adjourned until Friday, the 15th instant, at nine a. m., to the west school room, in the upper part of the temple.

President Sidney Rigdon requested some of the Presidency to lay their hands upon him, and re- Sidney Rigbuke a severe affliction in the face, which trou- don's Ailbles him most at night. Elders Hyrum Smith ment. and David Whitmer, by request, laid hands upon him and prayed for him, and rebuked his disease in the name of the Lord Jesus Christ. The whole assembly responded, Amen.

Elder David W. Patten requested our prayers in behalf of his wife, that she might be healed. I offered up a prayer for her recovery, and the assembly responded, Amen.

President Rigdon arose and made some very appropriate remarks touching the endowment, and dismissed the assembly by prayer.

This has been one of the best days that I ever spent; there has been an entire union of feeling expressed in all our proceedings this day; and the spirit of the God of Israel has rested upon us in mighty power, and it has been good for us to be here in this heavenly place in Christ Jesus; and although much fatigued with the labors of the day, yet my spiritual reward has been very great indeed. Spent the evening at home.

The Prophet's Joy.

Thursday, 14.—Nine o'clock. Met the Hebrew class at the school room in the Temple, and made some arrangements about our anticipated teacher, Mr. Joshua Seixas, of Hudson, Ohio.

The Coming of Professor Seixas.

I then returned to the council room in the printing office, to meet my colleagues who were appointed with myself to draft rules and regulations to be observed in the "House of the Lord," in Kirtland, built by the Church of the Latter-day Saints, in the year of our Lord 1834, which rules are as follows:

Rules and Regulations to be Observed in the House of the Lord in Kirtland.

I. It is according to the rules and regulations of all regularly and legally organized bodies to have a president to keep order.

II. The bodies thus organized are under obligation to be in subjection to that authority.

III. When a congregation assembles in this house, it shall submit to the following rules, that due respect may be paid to the order of worship, viz.:

1st. No man shall be interrupted who is appointed to speak by the Presidency of the Church, by any disorderly person or persons in the congregation, by whispering, by laughing, by talking, by menacing gestures, by getting up and running out in a disorderly manner, or by offering indignity to the manner of worship, or the religion, or to any officer of said Church while officiating in his office, in anywise whatsoever, by any display of ill manners or ill breeding, from old or young, rich or poor, male or female, bond or free, black or white, believer or unbeliever. And if any of the above insults are offered, such measures will be taken as are lawful, to punish the aggressor or aggressors, and eject them from the house.

2nd. An insult offered to the presiding Elder of said Church shall be considered an insult to the whole body. Also, an insult offered to any of the officers of said Church, while officiating, shall be considered an insult to the whole body.

3rd. All persons are prohibited from going up the stairs in times of worship.

4th. All persons are prohibited from exploring the house, except waited upon by a person appointed for that purpose.

5th. All persons are prohibited from going into the several pulpits, except the officers who are appointed to officiate in the same.

6th. All persons are prohibited from cutting, marking or marring the inside or outside of the house with a knife, pencil, or any other instrument whatever, under pain of such penalty as the law shall inflict.

7th. All children are prohibited from assembling in the house, above or below, or any part of it, to play, or for recreation, at any time: and all parents, guardians, or masters, shall be amenable for all damage that shall accrue in consequence of their children's misconduct.

8th. All persons, whether believers or unbelievers, shall be treated with due respect by the authorities of the Church.

9th. No imposition shall be practiced upon any members of the Church, by depriving them of their rights in the house.

Council adjourned *sine die*.

Returned home and spent the afternoon. Towards evening President Cowdery returned from Columbus, the capital of the State. I could spend but little time with him, being under obligation to attend at Mrs. Wilcox's, to join Mr. John Webb and Mrs. Catherine Wilcox in matrimony: also Mr. Thomas Carrico and Miss Elizabeth Baker, at the same place; all of which I performed in the customary manner in the midst of a large assembly. We then partook of some refreshments, and our hearts were made glad with the fruit of the vine. This is according to the pattern set by our Savior Himself, and we feel disposed to patronize all the institutions of heaven.

Return of Oliver Cowdery from Columbus, Ohio.

Friday, 15.—At nine a. m., met in council agreeable to adjournment, at the Council room in the Temple, and seated the authorities of the Church agreeable to their respective offices. I then made some observations respecting the order of the day, and the great responsibility we were under to transact all our business in righteousness before God, inasmuch as our decisions will have a bearing upon all mankind, and upon all generations to come.

The Council Meeting in the Kirtland Temple.

Minutes of a Priesthood Meeting Held in Kirtland Temple, January 15, 1836.

Council opened in usual form, and proceeded to business by reading the rules and regulations to govern the house of the Lord, three times.

The vote of the Presidency was then called upon these rules, followed by the High Council of Kirtland, the High Council of Zion, the Twelve, the Seventy, the Bishops of Zion and Kirtland, with their Counselors, each in turn; and after a few queries, answers, and debates, the above rules passed the several quorums in their order, by the unanimous voice of the whole, and are therefore received and established as a law to govern the House of the Lord in Kirtland.

In the investigation of the subject, it was found that many who had deliberated upon it, were darkened in their minds, which drew forth some remarks from President Smith respecting the privileges of the authorities of the Church, that each should speak in his turn and in his place, and in his time and season, that there may be perfect order in all things; and that every man, before he makes an objection to any item that is brought before a council for consideration, should be sure that he can throw light upon the subject rather than spread darkness, and that his objection be founded in righteousness, which may be done by men applying themselves closely to study the mind and will of the Lord, whose Spirit always makes manifest and demonstrates the truth to the understanding of all who are in possession of the Spirit.

After one hour's adjournment of the Council, Elder Don Carlos Smith was nominated to be ordained to the High Priesthood, also to officiate as President, to preside over that body in Kirtland. The vote of the quorums was called for in their order, and their nomination passed through the whole house by unanimous voice.

Elder Alva Beaman was chosen in the same manner to preside over the Elders in Kirtland.

William Cowdery was nominated to officiate as President over the Priests of the Aaronic Priesthood in Kirtland.

The vote of the assembly was called, beginning at the Bishop's Council, and passing through the several authorities, until it came to the presidency of the High Council in Kirtland, and received their sanction, having been carried unanimously in all the departments below.

Oliver Olney was unanimously elected to preside over the Teachers in Kirtland.

Ira Bond was unanimously chosen to preside over the deacons in Kirtland.

Elders Don Carlos Smith and Alva Beaman were ordained to the offices to which they had been elected, under the hands of Presidents Joseph Smith, Jun., Sidney Rigdon, and Hyrum Smith, with many blessings.

Bishop Whitney, of Kirtland, then proceeded to ordain William Cowdery, Oliver Olney and Ira Bond, and pronounced many blessings upon them according to their offices and standing.

Moved, seconded, and carried, that all the several quorums take their turn in performing the office of doorkeeper in the House of the Lord; also, that Nathaniel Milliken, Thomas Carrico, Amos R. Orton, and Samuel Rolfe be appointed assistant doorkeepers.

Moved and carried, that the presidency of the High Council hold the keys of the House of the Lord, except the keys of one vestry, which is to be held by the Bishopric of the Aaronic Priesthood.

Moved, and carried unanimously, that John Corrill be appointed to take charge of the House of the Lord in Kirtland immediately, and that the laws regulating the House of the Lord go into effect from this time, and that Elder Corrill see that they are enforced, with the privilege of calling as many as he chooses to assist him.

Council adjourned *sine die*.

ORSON HYDE, Clerk

CHAPTER XXVII.

RECONCILIATION OF THE FIRST PRESIDENCY AND TWELVE
APOSTLES—PENTECOSTAL TIMES IN KIRTLAND.

Saturday, 16.—By request I met with the Council of the Twelve in company with my Counselors, Frederick G. Williams and Sidney Rigdon.

Special Council Meeting with the Twelve.

Council opened with singing, and prayer by Thomas B. Marsh, President of the Twelve. He arose and requested the privilege, in behalf of his colleagues, of each speaking in his turn without being interrupted; which was granted them.

Elder Marsh proceeded to unbosom his feelings touching the mission of the Twelve, and more particularly respecting a certain letter which they received from the Presidency of the High Council in Kirtland, while attending a conference in the state of Maine; also spoke of being placed, in the council on Friday last, below the Councils of Kirtland and Zion, having been previously placed next the Presidency in our assemblies; also observed that they were hurt on account of some remarks made by President Hyrum Smith, on the trial of Gladden Bishop, (who had been previously tried before the Council of the Twelve, while on their mission in the east,) who had by their request, thrown his case before the High Council in Kirtland, for investigation; and the Twelve considered that their proceedings with him, were in some degree discountenanced.

Elder Marsh then gave way to his brethren, and they arose and spoke in turn until they had all spoken, acquiescing in the observations of Elder Marsh, and made some additions to his remarks, which, in substance, were as follows: That the letter in question, which they received from the Presidency, in which two of their members were suspended, and the rest severely chastened, and that, too, upon testimony which was unwarranted; and particular stress was laid upon a certain letter which the Presidency had received from Dr. Warren E. Cowdery, of Freedom, New York, in which he preferred charges against them, which were false, and upon which the Presidency had acted in chastening them; and therefore the Twelve had concluded that the Presidency had lost confidence in them; and that whereas, the Church in this place had caressed them at the time of their appointment to the Apostleship, they now treated them coolly, and also appeared to have lost confidence in them.

They spoke of their having been in the work from the beginning almost, and had borne the burden in the heat of the day, and passed through many trials, and that the Presidency ought not to suspect their fidelity, nor lose confidence in them, neither ought they to have chastened them upon such testimony as was lying before them; also urged the necessity of an explanation upon the letter which they received from the Presidency, and the propriety of their having information respecting their duties, authority, etc., that they might come to an understanding in all things, that they might act in perfect unison and harmony before the Lord, and be prepared for the endowment; also that they had preferred a charge against Doctor Cowdery, for his unchristian conduct, which the Presidency had disregarded; also that President Oliver Cowdery, on a certain occasion, had made use of language to one of the Twelve that was unchristian and unbecoming any man; and that they would not submit to such treatment. The remarks of the Twelve were made in a very forcible and explicit manner, yet cool and deliberate.

President Smith observed that the Presidency had heard them patiently, and, in turn. should expect to be heard patiently also. And first, he remarked that it was necessary that the Twelve should state whether they were determined to persevere in the work of the Lord, whether the Presidency were able to satisfy them or not.

Vote called, and carried in the affirmative, unanimously.

President Smith then said to the Twelve that he had not lost confidence in them; they had no reason to suspect his confidence; and that he would be willing to be weighed in the scale of truth, today, in this matter, and risk it in the day of judgment. Respecting the chastening contained in the letter in question, which he acknowledged might have been expressed in too harsh language, which was not intentional, he asked their forgiveness, inasmuch as he had hurt their feelings; but nevertheless, the letter that Elder M'Lellin wrote back to Kirtland, while the Twelve were in the east, was harsh also, and he was willing to set the one against the other.

President Smith next proceeded to explain the duty of the Twelve, and their authority, which is next to the present Presidency, and that the arrangement of the assembly in this place, on the 15th instant, in placing the High Councils of Kirtland next the Presidency, was because the business to be transacted, was business relating to that body in particular, which was to fill the several quorums in Kirtland, not because they were first in office, and that the arrangements were the most judicious that could be made on the occasion; also the Twelve are not subject to any other than the first Presidency, viz., "myself," said the Prophet, "Sidney Rigdon, and Frederick G. Williams, who are now my Counselors; and where I am not, there is no First Presidency over the Twelve."

The Prophet also stated to the Twelve that he did not countenance the harsh language of President Cowdery to them, neither would he countenance it in himself nor in any other man, "although," said he, "I have sometimes spoken too harshly from the impulse of the moment, and inasmuch as I have wounded your feelings, brethren, I ask your forgiveness, for I love you and will hold you up with all my heart in all righteousness, before the Lord, and before all men; for be assured, brethren, I am willing to stem the torrent of all opposition, in storms and in tempests, in thunders and in lightnings, by sea and by land, in the wilderness or among false brethren, or mobs, or wherever God in His providence may call us. And I am determined that neither heights nor depths, principalities nor powers, things present or things to come, or any other creature, shall separate me from you. And I will now covenant with you before God, that I will not listen to or credit any derogatory report against any of you, nor condemn you upon any testimony beneath the heavens, short of that testimony which is infallible, until I can see you face to face, and know of a surety; and I do place unremitted confidence in your word, for I believe you to be men of truth. And I ask the same of you, when I tell you anything, that you place equal confidence in my word, for I will not tell you I know anything that I do not know. But I have already consumed more time than I intended when I commenced, and I will now give way to my colleagues."

President Rigdon arose next and acquiesced in what President Smith had said, and acknowledged to the Twelve that he had not done as he ought, in not citing Dr. Warren A. Cowdery to trial on the charges that were put into his hands by the Twelve; that he neglected his duty in this thing, for which he asked their forgiveness, and would now attend to it, if they desired him to do so;* and President Rigdon also observed

---

* Evidently this matter concerning Warren A. Cowdery was afterwards taken up and settled amicably, as the Doctor published the following note of explanation and acknowledgment in the February, 1836, number of the *Messenger and Advocate:*

"NOTICE.

"I hereby give to all whom it may concern, that Messrs. T. B. Marsh and others, denominated the 'Twelve,' while on their mission to the East, last season, received a letter from the Presidency of the Church in which they were censured for neglecting to teach the Church in Freedom, Cattaraugus County, N. Y., the neces-

to the Twelve, if he had spoken or reproved too harshly at any time, and had injured their feelings by so doing, he asked their forgiveness.

President Williams arose and acquiesced in the above sentiments, expressed by the Prophet and President Rigdon, in full, and said many good things.

The President of the Twelve then called a vote of that body, to know whether they were perfectly satisfied with the explanations given them, and whether they would enter into the covenant the Presidency had proposed to them, which was most readily manifested in the affirmative, by raising their hands to heaven in testimony of their willingness and desire to enter into this covenant, and their entire satisfaction with the explanation upon all tho difficulties that were on their minds. The brethren then took each other by the hand in confirmation of the covenant, and there was a perfect union of feeling on this occasion, and the hearts of all overflowed with blessings, which the brethren pronounced upon one another's heads as the Spirit gave them utterance.

In conclusion, the Prophet said: "My scribe is included in that covenant, and these blessings with us, for I love him for the truth and integrity that dwell in him. And may God enable us to perform our vows and covenants with each other, in all fidelity and righteousness before Him, that our influence may be felt among the nations of the earth, in mighty power, even to rend the kingdoms of darkness asunder, and triumph over priestcraft and spiritual wickedness in high places, and break in pieces all kingdoms that are opposed to the kingdom of Christ, and spread the light and truth of the everlasting Gospel from the rivers to the ends of the earth."

Elder Beaman came in for counsel, to know whether it was best for him to return before the solemn assembly or not. After consideration, the Council advised him to tarry.

Council dismissed by singing and prayer.

WARREN PARRISH, Clerk.

Sunday, 17.—Attended meeting at the school house at the usual hour; a large congregation assembled. I pro-sity of contributing of their earthly substance for the building of the House of the Lord in this place. The rebuke from the Presidency, (as the undersigned has been informed) was predicated upon a letter addressed by him, to the presidents or some one of them, stating that they, the Twelve, taught no such thing. The undersigned although actuated by the purest motives at the time he wrote believing he had stated nothing but the truth, has since become satisfied from the best of evidence, that that particular item in their instructions was not omitted as he had represented, he, therefore, most deeply regrets it, being sensible as he now is, that he was the cause (although innocent) of wounding the best of feelings, and depressing spirits buoyant with hope, while in the field of useful labor at a distance from home."—W. A. COWDERY.

ceeded to arrange the several quorums present, first the
Presidency, then the Twelve, and the Seventy
who were present, also the Councilors of Kirtland and Zion.

President Rigdon then arose and observed that instead
of preaching the time would be occupied by the Presidency and Twelve, in speaking each in his turn until
they had all spoken. The Lord poured out His Spirit upon us, and the brethren began to confess their faults one
to the other, and the congregation was soon overwhelmed
in tears, and some of our hearts were too big for utterance. The gift of tongues came on us also, like the rushing of a mighty wind, and my soul was filled with the
glory of God.

In the afternoon I joined three couple in matrimony,
in the public congregation, viz: William F. Cahoon and
Maranda Gibbs, Harvey Stanley and Larona
Cahoon, Tunis Rapley and Louisa Cutler.

We then administered the Sacrament, and dismissed the
congregation, which was so large that it was very unpleasant for all. We were then invited to a feast at
Elder Cahoon's which was prepared for the occasion, and
had a good time while partaking of the rich repast; and
I verily realized that it was good for brethren to dwell together in unity, like the dew upon the mountains of Israel,
where the Lord commanded blessings, even life forever-
more. Spent the evening at home.

Monday, 18.—Attended the Hebrew school. This day
the Elders' school was removed into the Temple, in the
room adjoining the Hebrew school.

Tuesday, 19.—Spent the day at school. The Lord
blessed us in our studies. This day we commenced reading in our Hebrew Bibles with
much success. It seems as if the Lord opens our

minds in a marvelous manner, to understand His word in
the original language; and my prayer is that God will
speedily endow us with a knowledge of all languages and

tongues, that His servants may go forth for the last time the better prepared to bind up the law, and seal up the testimony.

FORM OF MARRIAGE CERTIFICATE.

I hereby certify, that, agreeable to the rules and regulations of the Church of Jesus Christ of Latter-day Saints, on matrimony, Mr. William F. Cahoon and Miss Nancy M. Gibbs, both of this place, were joined in marriage, on Sabbath, the 17th, instant.

JOSEPH SMITH, JUN., { Presiding Elder of said Church.

Kirtland, Ohio, January 19th, 1836.

Wednesday, 20.—Attended school at the usual hour, and spent the day in reading and lecturing, and made some advancement in our studies.

In the evening I attended a matrimonial occasion with my family, at Mr. John Johnson's, having been invited to join Elder John F. Boynton and Miss Susan Lowell in marriage; a large and respectable company assembled, and were seated by Elders Orson Hyde and Warren Parrish, in the following order—The Presidency and their companions in the first seats, the Twelve Apostles in the second, the Seventy in the third, and the remainder of the congregation seated with their companions. Elder Boynton and lady, with their attendants, came in and were seated in front of the Presidency.

A hymn was sung, after which I addressed the throne of grace. I then arose and read aloud a license, (according to the law of the land) granting any minister of the Gospel the privilege of solemnizing the rights of matrimony, and after calling for objection, if any there were, against the anticipated alliance between Elder Boynton and Miss Lowell; after waiting a sufficient time and hearing no objection, I observed that all forever after this must hold their peace. I then invited them to join hands. I pronounced the ceremony, according to the rules and regulations of the Church of the Lat-

Marriage of J. F. Boynton.

ter-day Saints, in the name of God, and in the name of Jesus Christ. I pronounced upon them the blessings of Abraham, Isaac, and Jacob, and such other blessings as the Lord put into my heart; and being much under the influence of a cold, I then gave way, and President Rigdon arose and delivered a very forcible address, suited to the occasion, and closed the services of the evening by prayer.

Elders Orson Hyde, Luke S. Johnson, and Warren Parrish, then presented the Presidency with three servers of The Marriage glasses filled with wine, to bless. And it fell Feast. to my lot to attend to this duty, which I cheerfully discharged. It was then passed round in order, then the cake in the same order; and suffice it to say, our hearts were made glad while partaking of the bounty of earth which was presented, until we had taken our fill; and joy filled every bosom, and the countenances of old and young seemed to bloom alike with cheerfulness and smiles of youth; and an entire unison of feeling seemed to pervade the congregation, and indeed I doubt whether the pages of history can boast of a more splendid and innocent wedding and feast than this, for it was conducted after the order of heaven, which has a time for all things; and this being a time of rejoicing, we heartily embraced it and conducted ourselves accordingly. Took leave of the company and returned home.

Thursday, 21.—This morning, a minister from Connecticut, by the name of John W. Olived, called at my J. W. Olived house and inquired of my father: "Does the and the Prophet. Prophet live here?" My father replied he did not understand him. Mr. Olived asked the same question again and again, and received the same answer. He finally asked: "Does Mr. Smith live here?" Father replied: "O yes, sir, I understand you now." Father then stepped into my room and informed me that a gentleman had called to see me. I went into the room where he was, and the first question he asked me, after passing a compliment was: "How many members have you in your Church?" I replied that we had between fifteen hundred and two thousand in this branch. He then asked: "Wherein do you differ from other Christian denominations?" I replied, that we believe the Bible, and they do not. However, he affirmed that he believed the Bible. I told him then to be batized. He replied that he did not realize it to be his duty. But when I laid before him the principles of the Gospel, viz: faith and repentance; baptism, for the remission of sins; and the laying on of hands, for the reception of the Holy Ghost, he manifested much surprise. I observed that the hour for school had arrived, and I must attend. The man appeared astonished at our doctrine, but by no means hostile.

About three o'clock, p. m., I dismissed the school, and the Presidency retired to the attic story of the printing office, where we attended the ordinance of washing our bodies in pure water. We also perfumed our bodies and our heads, in the name of the Lord. *Washing and Anointings in Kirtland Temple.*

At early candle-light I met with the Presidency at the west school room, in the Temple, to attend to the ordinance of anointing our heads with holy oil; also the Councils of Kirtland and Zion met in the two adjoining rooms, and waited in prayer while we attended to the ordinance. I took the oil in my left hand, Father Smith being seated before me, and the remainder of the Presidency encircled him round about. We then stretched our right hands towards heaven, and blessed the oil, and consecrated it in the name of Jesus Christ.

We then laid our hands upon our aged Father Smith, and invoked the blessings of heaven. I then anointed his head with the consecrated oil, and sealed many blessings upon him. The Presidency then in turn laid their hands upon his head, beginning at the oldest, until they had all laid their hands upon him, and pronounced such blessings upon his head, *The Prophet Blessed to Lead Israel in the Last Days.*

as the Lord put into their hearts, all blessing him to be our Patriarch, to anoint our heads, and attend to all duties that pertain to that office. The Presidency then took the seat in their turn, according to their age, beginning at the oldest, and received their anointing and blessing under the hands of Father Smith. And in my turn, my father anointed my head, and sealed upon me the blessings of Moses, to lead Israel in the latter days, even as Moses led him in days of old; also the blessings of Abraham, Isaac and Jacob. All of the Presidency laid their hands upon me, and pronounced upon my head many prophecies and blessings, many of which I shall not notice at this time. But as Paul said, so say I, let us come to visions and revelations.

The heavens were opened upon us, and I beheld the celestial kingdom of God, and the glory thereof, whether
The Prophet's Vision of the Celestial Kingdom. in the body or out I cannot tell. I saw the transcendent beauty of the gate through which the heirs of that kingdom will enter, which was like unto circling flames of fire; also the blazing throne of God, whereon was seated the Father and the Son. I saw the beautiful streets of that kingdom, which had the appearance of being paved with gold. I saw Fathers Adam and Abraham, and my father and mother, my brother,
Alvin Smith. Alvin, that has long since slept, and marvelled how it was that he had obtained an inheritance in that kingdom, seeing that he had departed this life before the Lord had set His hand to gather Israel the second time, and had not been baptized for the remission of sins.

Thus came the voice of the Lord unto me, saying—

Revelation.

All who have died without a knowledge of this Gospel, who would have received it if they had been permitted to tarry, shall be heirs of the celestial kingdom of God; also all that shall die henceforth without a knowledge of it, who would have received it with all their hearts, shall be heirs of that kingdom, for I, the Lord, will judge all men according to their works, according to the desire of their hearts.

And I also beheld that all children who die before they arrive at the years of accountability, are saved in the celestial kingdom of heaven. I saw the The Salvation Twelve Apostles of the Lamb, who are now of Children. upon the earth, who hold the keys of this last ministry, in foreign lands, standing together in a circle, much fatigued, with their clothes tattered and feet swollen, with their eyes cast downward, and Jesus standing in their midst, and they did not behold Him. The Savior looked upon them and wept.

I also beheld Elder M'Lellin in the south, standing upon a hill, surrounded by a vast multitude, preaching to them, and a lame man standing before him The Prophet's supported by his crutches; he threw them down Vision of the Twelve. at his word and leaped as a hart, by the mighty power of God. Also, I saw Elder Brigham Young standing in a strange land, in the far south and west, in a desert place, upon a rock in the midst of about a dozen men of color, who appeared hostile. He was preaching to them in their own tongue, and the angel of God standing above his head, with a drawn sword in his hand, protecting him, but he did not see it. And I finally saw the Twelve in the celestial kingdom of God. I also beheld the redemption of Zion, and many things which the tongue of man cannot describe in full.

Many of my brethren who received the ordinance with me saw glorious visions also. Angels ministered unto them as well as to myself, and the power of Ministrations the Highest rested upon us, the house was of Angels. filled with the glory of God, and we shouted Hosanna to God and the Lamb. My scribe also received his anointing with us, and saw, in a vision, the armies of heaven protecting the Saints in their return to Zion, and many things which I saw.

The Bishop of Kirtland with his Counselors, and the Bishop of Zion with his Counselors, were present with us, and received their anointings under the hands of Father

Smith, and this was confirmed by the Presidency, and
the glories of heaven were unfolded to them also.

We then invited the High Councilors of Kirtland and
High Councils Zion into our room, and President Hyrum
of Zion and Smith anointed the head of the President of the
Kirtland
Anointed. Councilors in Kirtland, and President David
Wnitmer the head of the President of the Councilors of Zion.
The President of each quorum then anointed the heads
of his colleagues, each in his turn, beginning at the oldest.

The visions of heaven were opened to them also. Some
of them saw the face of the Savior, and others were ministered unto by holy angels, and the spirit of
Further Vis- prophecy and revelation was poured out in
ions and Rev-
elations. mighty power; and loud hosannas, and glory
to God in the highest, saluted the heavens, for we all
communed with the heavenly host. And I saw in my
vision all of the Presidency in the celestial kingdom of
God, and many others that were present. Our meeting
was opened by singing, and prayer was offered up by the
head of each quorum; and closed by singing, and invoking the benediction of heaven, with uplifted hands. Retired between one and two o'clock in the morning.

Friday 22.—Attended at the school room at the usual
hour, but instead of pursuing our studies, we spent the
time in rehearsing to each other the glorious scenes that
occurred on the preceding evening, while attending to the
ordinance of holy anointing.

In the evening we met at the same place, with the
Council of the Twelve, and the Presidency of
Anointing of the Seventy, who were to receive this ordi-
the Twelve
and Seventy. nance [of anointing and blessing]. The High
Councils of Kirtland and Zion were present also.

After calling to order and organizing, the Presidency
proceeded to consecrate the oil.

We then laid our hands upon Elder Thomas B. Marsh,
who is President of the Twelve, and ordained him to the
authority of anointing his brethren. I then poured the

consecrated oil upon his head, in the name of Jesus Christ, and sealed such blessings upon him as the Lord put into my heart. The rest of the Presidency then laid their hands upon him and blessed him, each in his turn, beginning at the oldest. He then anointed and blessed his brethren from the oldest to the youngest. I also laid my hands upon them, and pronounced many great and glorious things upon their heads. The heavens were opened, and angels ministered unto us.

The Twelve then proceeded to anoint and bless the Presidency of the Seventy, and seal upon their heads power and authority to anoint their brethren.

The heavens were opened unto Elder Sylvester Smith, and he, leaping up, exclaimed: "The horsemen of Israel and the chariots thereof."

Brother Don C. Smith was also anointed and blessed to preside over the High Priests' quorum.

President Rigdon arose to conclude the services of the evening by invoking the blessing of heaven upon the Lord's anointed, which he did in an eloquent manner; the congregation shouted a long hosanna: the gift of tongues fell upon us in mighty power, angels mingled their voices with ours, while their presence was in our midst, and unceasing praises swelled our bosoms for the space of half-an-hour.

Blessing of the Lord's Anointed.

I then observed to the brethren, that it was time to retire. We accordingly closed our interview and returned home at about two o'clock in the morning, and the Spirit and visions of God attended me through the night.

To the petitions which we sent up to Missouri, Governor Dunklin replied as follows: *

CITY OF JEFFERSON, Jan. 22nd, 1836.

To Messrs. W. W. Phelps and Others,

GENTLEMEN:—Your numerous petitions, post-marked "Kirtland,"

---

* The communication from Governor Dunklin, of Missouri, which follows, is found as "Note H," in the addenda of the manuscript History, Book "B." And is placed here in the Prophet's narrative, under the date on which it was written, *viz.* January 22, 1836.

came safe to hand. It is unnecessary for me to repeat to you my feelings on the subject of your grievances. What they were you have been already apprised, and, they have undergone no change. Your case was presented by me to the last General Assembly of the state. They did not legislate upon the subject. I am, however, persuaded, that it was for want of a constitutional power to pass any law that could afford you a proper remedy, prevented their acting upon the subject. Your feelings are very natural, when such causes exist to produce them; but you misconceive your case, and, consequently, do not advert to the proper remedy. You cannot make a case of *invasion* or *insurrection* of the outrages committed upon your persons or property in Jackson County. And, unless one of those could be made out, it would be idle to address the President of the United States. If such a case had been made out, as Executive of this state, I should have immediately ordered out a military force to repel or suppress it. The mob in New York, to which you cite me, is not in point. The military force was there resorted to, for the purpose of *quieting* the mob. You wish this kind of a force used to *restore* justice. However palpable and grievous the outrages have been upon you, your only remedy for injuries done must be in and through the courts of justice. On a former occasion I informed you I was then in correspondence with the General Government, for a depot of arms, on the Missouri river, near our western boundary line· For reasons unknown to me, the Secretary of War has taken no steps during the last year towards the fulfillment of the subject. I have renewed the subject through our delegation in Congress, this winter. When this object shall be attained, it may furnish you a place of resort, for protection, in case of emergency, should you think proper to risk yourselves on your lands, in Jackson County, again.

Respectfully,

[Signed]   DANL. DUNKLIN.

Saturday, 23.—Attended at the school room, as usual, and we came together filled with the Spirit, as on the past evening, and did not feel like studying, but commenced conversing upon heavenly things, and we spent the day agreeably and profitably. Elder Alva Beaman had been tempted to doubt the things which we received the evenings before, and he made an humble confession, and asked forgiveness of the school, which was joyfully accorded him, and he said he would try to resist Satan in the future.

Sunday, 24.—Met the several quorums in the room under the printing office, and, after organizing and opening by prayer, called upon the High Council of Kirtland to proceed and confess their sins, as they might be directed by the Spirit, and they occupied the first part of the day, and confessed and exhorted as the Spirit led.

Continuation of Spiritual Meetings.

In the afternoon, attended meeting again, and saw the bread and wine administered to the quorums and brethren who were present.

In the evening met the Presidency in the chamber over the printing room, and counseled on the subject of endowment, and the preparation for the solemn assembly, which is to be called when the house of the Lord is finished.

Monday, 25.—Received a line from my scribe, informing me of his ill health, as follows—

Illness of Warren Parrish.

BROTHER JOSEPH—My great desire is to be in your company and in the assembly of the Saints, where God opens the heavens, and exhibits the treasures of eternity. It is the only thing that has stimulated me, for a number of days past, to leave my house; for be assured, dear brother, my bodily affliction is severe. I have a violent cough, more especially at night, which deprives me of my appetite, and my strength fails, and writing has a particular tendency to injure my lungs, while I am under the influence of such a cough. I therefore, with reluctance, send your journal to you, until my health improves.

Yours in haste,

WARREN PARRISH.

P. S.—Brother Joseph, pray for me, and ask the prayers of the class on my account also.   W. P.

Appointed Elder Sylvester Smith, acting scribe, for the time being, or, till Elder Parrish shall recover his health. Spent the day at home, receiving visitors.

Tuesday, 26.—Mr. Seixas arrived from Hudson, to teach the Hebrew language, and I attended upon the organizing of the class, for the purpose of receiving lectures upon Hebrew grammar. His hours of instruction are from ten to eleven, a. m.; and from two to

Arrival of Prof. Seixas.

three, p. m. His instruction pleased me much.   I think he will be a help to the class in learning Hebrew.

Wednesday, *27.*—Attended school as usual, and also attended to other matters which came before me.

Thursday, *28.*—Attended school at the usual hour.

In the evening met the quorum of High Priests, in the west room of the upper loft of the Lord's house, and, in

Continuation of Ministrations and Visions.

company with my counselors, consecrated and anointed the counselors of the presidents of the High Priests' quorum, and, having instructed them and set the quorum in order, I left them to perform the holy anointing, and went to the quorum of Elders at the other end of the room. I assisted in anointing the counselors of the president of the Elders, and gave the instruction necessary for the occasion, and left the president and his counselors to anoint the Elders, while I should go to the adjoining room, and attend to organizing and instructing the quorum of the Seventy.

I found the Twelve Apostles assembled with this quorum, and I proceeded, with the quorum of the Presidency, to instruct them, and also the seven presidents of the Seventy Elders, to call upon God with up-lifted hands, to seal the blessings which had been promised to them by the holy anointing. As I organized this quorum, with the presidency in this room, President Sylvester Smith saw a pillar of fire rest down and abide upon the heads of the quorum, as we stood in the midst of the Twelve.

When the Twelve and the seven presidents were through with their sealing prayer, I called upon President Sidney Rigdon to seal them with uplifted hands; and when he had done this, and cried hosanna, that all the congregation should join him, and shout hosanna to God and the Lamb, and glory to God in the highest.   It was done so, and Elder Roger Orton saw a mighty angel riding upon a horse of fire, with a flaming sword in his hand, followed by five others, encircle the house, and protect the Saints, even the Lord's anointed, from the power of Satan and a host of evil spirits, which were striving to disturb the Saints.

President William Smith, one of the Twelve, saw the heavens opened, and the Lord's host protecting the Lord's anointed.

President Zebedee Coltrin, one of the seven presidents of the Seventy, saw the Savior extended before him, as upon the cross, and a little after, crowned with glory upon his head above the bsightness of the sun.

After these things were over, and a glorious vision, which I saw, had passed, I instructed the seven presidents to proceed and anoint the Seventy, and returned to the room of the High Priests and Elders, and attended to the sealing of what they had done, with up-lifted hands.

The Lord assisted my brother, Don Carlos, the president of the High Priests, to go forward with the anointing of the High Priests, so that he had performed it to the acceptance of the Lord, notwithstanding he was very young and inexperienced in such duties; and I felt to praise God with a loud hosanna, for His goodness to me and my father's family, and to all the children of men. Praise the Lord, all ye, His Saints, praise His holy name.

After these quorums were dismissed, I retired to my home, filled with the Spirit, and my soul cried hosanna to God and the Lamb, through the silent watches of the night; and while my eyes were closed in sleep, the visions of the Lord were sweet unto me, and His glory was round about me. Praise the Lord.

Friday, 29.—Attended school and read Hebrew. I received a line from the presidency of the Elders' quorum, they wishing to know whom they should receive into their quorum, I answered verbally.

Afternoon, I called in all my father's family and made a feast, and related my feelings towards them. My father pronounced patriarchal blessings on the heads of Henry Gannet, Charles H. Smith, Marietta Carter, Angeline Carter, Johanna Carter, and

The Prophet Feasts his Father's Family.

Nancy Carter. This was a good time to me, and all the family rejoiced together. We continued the meeting till about eight o'clock in the evening, and related the goodness of God to us, in opening our eyes to see the visions of heaven, and in sending His holy angels to minister unto us the word of life. We sang the praise of God in animated strains, and the power of union and love was felt and enjoyed.

Saturday, 30.—Attended school, as usual, and waited upon several visitors, and showed them the record of Abraham. Mr. Seixas, our Hebrew teacher, examined it with deep interest, and pronounced it to be original beyond all doubt. He is a man of excellent understanding, and has a knowledge of many languages which were spoken by the ancients, and he is an honorable man, so far as I can judge yet.

Resolutions.

At a conference of the Presidency of the Church, it was resolved that no one be ordained to an office in the Church in Kirtland, without the voice of the several quorums, when assembled for Church business.

Resolved—That Alva Beaman, president of the Elders, be directed to give to the Presidents of the Church a list of the names of the several Elders, comprising his quorum, and all other Elders in Kirtland, not belonging to any quorum now established.

Resolved—That Harvey Whitlock be restored to the Church, in full fellowship, on his being rebaptized, and after, be ordained to the High Priesthood.   OLIVER COWDERY, Clerk.

In the evening, went to the upper rooms of the Lord's house, and set the different quorums in order. Instructed

Anointing the the presidents of the Seventy concerning the
Seventy.   order of their anointing, and requested them
to proceed and anoint the Seventy. Having set all the quorums in order, I returned to my house, being weary with continual anxiety and labor, in putting all the authorities in order, and in striving to purify them for the solemn assembly, according to the commandment of the Lord.

Sunday, 31.—Attended divine service in the school house, arranged the several quorums of the authorities of the Church, appointed doorkeepers to keep order about the door, because of the crowd, and to prevent the house from being excessively crowded. The High Council of Zion occupied the first part of the day, in speaking as they were led, and relating experiences, trials, etc.

Afternoon. House came to order, as usual, and President Sidney Rigdon delivered a short discourse, and we attended to the breaking of bread.

In the evening, my father attended to the blessing of three brethren, at President Oliver Cowdery's. Spent the evening at home.

CHAPTER XXVIII.

THE PROPHET'S MINISTRY AND STUDIES IN KIRTLAND.

Monday, February 1, 1836.—Attended school as usual,
Further and in company with the other members of the
Arrangements committee organized another class of thirty,
for the Study
of Hebrew. to receive Mr. Seixas' lectures on the Hebrew.

In the evening, attended to the organizing of the
quorums of High Priests, Elders, Seventy, and Bishops,
in the upper rooms of the house of the Lord, and after
blessing each quorum in the name of the Lord, I returned
home. I had another interview with Mr. Seixas, our Hebrew teacher, and related to him some of the dealings of
God with me, and gave him some of the evidence of the
truth of the work of the latter days. He listened cordially
and did not oppose.

Tuesday 2.—Attended school as usual, and to various
other duties.

Went to the school house in the evening, and heard an
animated discourse delivered by President Rigdon. He
TheGathering touched on the outlines of our faith, showed
of Israel. the scattering and gathering of Israel, from
the Scriptures, and the stick of Joseph in the hands of
Ephraim, as also from the scriptures of Moses. It was
an interesting meeting, the Spirit bore record that the
Lord was well pleased.

Wednesday, 3.—Morning, attended our Hebrew lecture.

Afternoon, studied with Oliver Cowdery and Sylvester
Smith. Received many visitors, and showed them the

Records of Abraham. My father blessed three with a patriarchal blessing. President Alva Beaman handed in seventy of his quorum designed for another Seventy if God will. Names for the Second Quorum of Seventy.

Thursday, 4.—Attended school, and assisted in forming a class of twenty-two members to read at three o'clock, p. m. The other twenty-three read at eleven o'clock. The first class recites at a quarter Hebrew Class Arrangements before ten, a. m., and the second a quarter before two, p. m. We have a great want of books, but are determined to do the best we can. May the Lord help us to obtain this language, that we may read the Scriptures in the language in which they were given.

Friday, 5.—Attended school, and assisted the committee to make arrangements to supply the third and fourth classes with books; concluded to divide a Bible into several parts, for the benefit of said classes; continued my studies in the Hebrew; received several visitors, and attended various duties.

Saturday, 6.—Called the anointed together to receive the seal of all their blessings. The High Priests and Elders in the council room as usual, the Seventy with the Twelve in the second room, and the Bishops in the third. I labored with each of these quorums for some time to bring them to the Arrangements of Quorums to Receive Spiritual Blessings. order which God had shown to me, which is as follows: The first part to be spent in solemn prayer before God, without any talking or confusion; and the conclusion with a sealing prayer by President Rigdon, when all the quorums were to shout with one accord a solemn hosanna to God and the Lamb, with an Amen, Amen and Amen; and then all take seats and lift up their hearts in silent prayer to God, and if any obtain a prophecy or vision, to rise and speak that all may be edified and rejoice together.

I had considerable trouble to get all the quorums united in this order. I went from room to room repeatedly, and charged each separately, assuring them that it was according to the mind of God, yet, notwithstanding all my labor, while I was in the east room with the Bishops' quorum, I felt, by the Spirit, that something was wrong in the quorum of Elders in the west room, and I immediately requested Presidents Oliver Cowdery and Hyrum Smith to go in and see what was the matter. The quorum of Elders had not observed the order which I had given them, and were reminded of it by President Don Carlos Smith, and mildly requested to preserve order, and continue in prayer. Some of them replied that they had a teacher of their own, and did not wish to be troubled by others. This caused the Spirit of the Lord to withdraw; this interrupted the meeting, and this quorum lost their blessing in a great measure.

The other quorums were more careful, and the quorum of the Seventy enjoyed a great flow of the Holy Spirit. Many arose and spoke, testifying that they were filled with the Holy Ghost, which was like fire in their bones, so that they could not hold their peace, but were constrained to cry hosanna to God and the Lamb, and glory in the highest.

President William Smith, one of the Twelve, saw a
vision of the Twelve, and Seven in council to-

Visions in the
Kirtland
Temple.
gether, in old England, and prophesied that a great work would be done by them in the old countries, and God was already beginning to work in the hearts of the people.

President Zebedee Coltrin, one of the Seven, saw a vision of the Lord's host. And others were filled with the Spirit, and spake with tongues and prophesied. This was a time of rejoicing long to be remembered. Praise the Lord.

Sunday, 7.—Attended meeting at the usual hour. The quorums were seated according to their official standing in the Church. The Bishop of Zion and his counselors occupied the forenoon in confession and exhortation. The

Bishop of Kirtland and his counselors occupied the stand in the afternoon. The discourses of these two quorums were very interesting. A number of letters of commendation were presented and read, a vote was called, and all were received into the Church in Kirtland. Bread was broken and blessed, and while it was passing, President Rigdon commenced speaking from Acts ii, and continued about fifteen minutes. His reasoning was good. The wine was then blessed and passed, after which meeting dismissed.

In the evening, met with the Presidency in the loft of the printing office, in company with the presidency of the Seventy, to choose other Seventy also. Blessed one of the Zion brethren. Dismissed and retired.

Monday, 8.—Attended school at the usual hour.

In the afternoon, lectured in the upper room of the printing office with some of the brethren. At evening, visited Mr. Seixas, in company with Presidents Rigdon and Cowdery. He conversed freely; is an interesting man. Elder Parrish, my scribe, received my journal again. His health is so much improved, that he thinks he will be able, with the blessing of God, to perform his duty.

Warren Parrish Resumes his Duty as Scribe.

Tuesday, 9.—Spent the day in studying the Hebrew language. Fine weather and sleighing. Evening at home.

Wednesday, 10.—At ten o'clock, met at the school room to read Hebrew.

Afternoon, read in the upper room of the printing office.

At four o'clock, called at the school room in the Temple to make some arrangements concerning the classes. On my return, I was informed that Brother Hyrum Smith had cut himself. I immediately repaired to his house, and found him badly wounded in his left arm, he had fallen on his ax, which caused a wound about four or five inches in length. Doctor Williams sewed it up and dressed it, and I feel to thank God that it is no worse, and I ask my Heavenly Father in the name of Jesus Christ to heal my brother

Hyrum Smith Meets with an Accident.

Hyrum, and bless my father's family, one and all, with peace and plenty, and eternal life.

Thursday, 11.—Attended school, and read Hebrew with the morning class.

Spent the afternoon in reading, and in exhibiting the Egyptian records to those who called to see me, and heaven's blessings have attended me.

Friday, 12.—Spent the day in reading Hebrew, and attending to the duties of my family, and the duties of the Church.

I met in company with the several quorums in the school room in the temple, at evening, to take into consideration the subject of ordination. I made some remarks upon the subject of our meeting, which were as follows: Many are desiring to be ordained to the ministry, who are not called, consequently the Lord is displeased. Secondly, many already have been ordained, who ought not to hold official stations in the Church, because they dishonor themselves and the Church, and bring persecution swiftly upon us, in consequence of their zeal without knowledge. I requested the quorums to take some measures to regulate the same. I proposed some resolutions, and remarked to the brethren that the subject was now before them, and open for discussion.

Remarks of the Prophet on Those Unworthy of the Ministry.

The subject was discussed by Presidents Sidney Rigdon and Oliver Cowdery, and Elder Martin Harris, and others, and resolutions were drafted by my scribe (who served as clerk on the occasion), read, and rejected. It was then proposed that I should indite resolutions, which I did as follows:

The Prophet's Draft of Resolutions.

First. Resolved—That no one be ordained to any office in the Church in this stake of Zion, at Kirtland, without the unanimous voice of the several bodies that constitute this quorum, who are appointed to do Church business in the name of said Church, viz., the Presidency of the Church; the Twelve Apostles of the Lamb; the twelve High

Councilors of Kirtland; the twelve High Councilors of Zion; the Bishop of Kirtland and his counselors; the Bishop of Zion and his counselors; and the seven presidents of Seventies; until otherwise ordered by said quorums.

Second. And further Resolved—That no one be ordained in the branches of said Church abroad, unless they are recommended by the voice of the respective branches of the Church to which they belong, to a general conference appointed by the heads of the Church, and from that conference receive their ordination. The foregoing resolu· tions were concurred in by the presidents of the Seventies.

Saturday, 13.—Spent the day in reading Hebrew.

At noon I prepared a horse and sleigh for Professor Seixas to go to Hudson and see his family.

Action of the Twelve on the Resolutions Governing Ordinations.

At one o'clock p. m. the council of the Twelve Apostles met in the house of the Lord, and after prayer and consultation upon the nature and expediency of the preceding resolutions offered in council on the 12th instant, it was unanimously agreed to offer the following amendment to the second resolution, (perfectly acquiescing in the first) viz.: That none be ordained to any office in the branches to which they be. long; but to be recommended to a general conference appointed by those, or under the direction of those, who are designated in the book of Doctrine and Covenants, as having authority to ordain and set in order all the officers of the Church abroad, and from that conference receive their ordination.

THOMAS B. MARSH,
Chairman,
ORSON HYDE,
WM. E. M'LELLIN,
Clerks.

Sunday, 14.—Attended to the ordinance of baptism before meeting.

At the usual hour attended meeting. The presidents of the Seventy expressed their feelings on the occasion, and their faith in the Book of Mormon and the revelations, also their entire confidence in all the quorums that are organized in the Church of Latter-day Saints. A good time—the Spirit of God

The Faith and Confidence of Seventy.

rested upon the congregation. Administered the Sacrament, and confirmed a number that had been baptized, and then dismissed the meeting.

Monday 15.—Attended school at the usual hours.

Spent the afternoon in reading Hebrew and in receiving and waiting on visitors. On this day we commenced translating the Hebrew language, under the instruction of Professor Seixas, and he stated that we were the most forward of any class he ever instructed for the same length of time.

Progress in the Study of Hebrew.

Tuesday, 16.—Attended school at the usual hour. Resumed our translating, and made rapid progress. Many called to see the House of the Lord, and the Egyptian manuscript, and to visit me. Extremely cold weather, and fine sleighing.

Wednesday, 17.—Attended the school and read and translated with my class as usual. My soul delights in reading the word of the Lord in the original, and I am determined to pursue the study of the languages, until I shall become master of them, if I am permitted to live long enough. At any rate, so long as I do live, I am determined to make this my object; and with the blessing of God, I shall succeed to my satisfaction.

Elder Coe called to make some arrangements about the Egyptian mummies and records. He proposes to hire a room at John Johnson's Inn, and exhibit them there from day to day, at certain hours, that some benefit may be derived from them. I complied with his request, and only observed that they must be managed with prudence and care, especially the manuscripts.

Action of the Kirtland High Council on the Resolutions on Ordinations.

The High Council of Kirtland met in the House of the Lord at six o'clock, p. m., to discuss the subject of ordination, as laid before the Council on the 12th instant; and also the proposed amendment of the Twelve Apostles of the 13th. After discussing the resolutions drawn

by President Smith, it was voted unanimously that they should remain
entire, and the proposed amendment of the Twelve Apostles be rejected.

JOSEPH C. KINGSBURY, Clerk.

Thursday, 18.—Spent the day as usual in attending to
my family concerns, receiving and waiting upon those who
called for instructions, and attending to my studies.

Action of the High Council of Zion on the Resolution on Ordinations.

The High Council of Zion met in the upper room of the printing
offiice at seven o'clock p.m. to discuss the subject of ordination, as laid
before them in the council of the 12th instant, and also the amendment
of the Twelve Apostles.   After discussing the resolutions drawn up by
the President, it was voted unanimously that they should remain, and
that we perfectly acquiesce in said resolutions without any alteration
or amendment.

ELIAS HIGBEE, Clerk.

Friday, 19.—Attended with the morning class and
translated.   Professor Seixas handed me the names of a
few whom he had selected from the first class,
and requested us to meet together this after-   The Prophet's
noon and lecture, which we did, in the upper   Regard for
Prof. Seixas.
room of the printing office.   The names are as follows:
Presidents Sidney Rigdon, Oliver Cowdery, William W.
Phelps, Bishop Edward Partridge, Elders William E.
M'Lellin, Orson Hyde, Orson Pratt, Sylvester Smith, myself, and scribe.   These, and Prof. Seixas, to meet one hour
earlier on the following morning.

I conversed with Mr. Seixas on the subject of religion,
at my house this afternoon.   He listened with attention,
and appeared interested with my remarks.   And I believe
the Lord is striving with him, by His Holy Spirit, and
that he will eventually embrace the new and everlasting
covenant, for he is a chosen vessel unto the Lord to do
His people good; but I forbear lest I get to prophesying
upon his head.

This evening President Rigdon and myself called at Mr. Seixas' lodgings and conversed with him upon the subject of the school. Had a pleasant interview.

Saturday, 20.—At home attending to my domestic concerns.

At nine o'clock attended the school, and translated with the morning class.

Spent the afternoon with my class in the printing office and the evening at home.

Sunday, 21.—Spent the day at home in reading, meditation and prayer. I reviewed my lesson in Hebrew. Some three or four persons were baptized, and the powers of darkness seem to be giving way on all sides. Many who have been enemies to the work of the Lord, are beginning to enquire into the faith of the Latter-day Saints, and are friendly.

The Varied Activities of the Prophet.

Monday, 22.—Translated Hebrew with the first class in the morning. Returned home and made out my returns, to the county clerk on eleven marriages which I had solemnized within three months—eight by license from the clerk of the court of common pleas in Geauga County, Ohio, and three by publishment. Sent them to Chardon by Elijah Fuller. I baptized John O. Waterman.

Spent the afternoon translating with my scribe, Elder Warren Parrish, at his house.

At four o'clock met Professor Seixas and the school committee at the printing office, to make some arrangements for the advancement of the several classes.

Action of the First Presidency on the Resolutions on Ordinations.

The Presidency of the Church met and took in consideration the resolutions presented to the Twelve Apostles, (dated Feb. 12th), the presidents of Seventies, the High Councils of the Church for Zion and Kirtland. After due deliberation it was unanimously agreed that the original resolutions be adopted without amendments.

OLIVER COWDERY, Clerk of Council.

The lower room of the Temple is now prepared for painting. Elder Brigham Young was obliged to leave the Hebrew class and superintend the painting of the lower room until finished.*

This afternoon the sisters met to make the veil of the Temple. Father Smith presided over them, and gave them much good instruction. Closed by singing and prayer, which is customary at the commencement and close of all councils and meetings of the Church of Latter-day Saints, although not always mentioned in this record.

Tuesday, 23.—Read and translated Hebrew.

This afternoon the sisters met again at the Temple to work on the veil.†

Towards the close of the day I met with the Presidency and many of the brethren in the house of the Lord, and made some remarks from the pulpit upon the rise and progress of the Church of Christ of Latter-day Saints, and pronounced a blessing upon the sisters, for their liberality in giving their services so cheerfully, to make the veil for the Lord's House; also upon the congregation; and dismissed.

Wednesday, 24.—Attended to my studies as usual.

In the evening, met the quorums at the school room in the Temple to take into consideration the propriety or im-

---

* Elder Brigham Young, it should be remembered, in the town of Aurelius, Cayuga County, New York, had for twelve years followed the occupation of carpenter, joiner, painter and glazier. (See Life of Brigham Young, Tullidge, p. 77). Hence this appointment to supervise the work mentioned.

† "The Temple was so constructed that with white canvas curtains that could be dropped and raised at pleasure, the lower story was, whenever occasion reqnired, divided into four sections or compartments.   *   *   *   *   The two sets of pulpits, one on the east and the other to the west end of the building were intersected by the curtains extending from east to west, so as to leave half their lengths in each apartment, and they were occupied by the presiding officers who directed the services. Thus four separate meetings could be in session at the same time witbout in the least interfearing with each other, giving opportunity for four to exercise instead of one."—(Eliza R. Snow, Autobiography and Family Record of Lorenzo Snow, p. 12). It was upon these canvas curtains or "veils" tha the sisters were at work as stated in the text.

propriety of ordaining a large number of individuals who wish to be ordained to official stations in the Church. Each individual's name was presented and the voice of the assembly called; and William Wightman, Charles Wightman, David Cluff, Truman Jackson, Reuben Barton, Daniel Miles, and Moses Daily, were received, and nineteen were rejected. Their ordinations deferred until another time. Presidents Orson Hyde, Oliver Cowdery, and Sylvester Smith, were nominated to draft rules and regulations concerning licenses, and by vote of the assembly passed unanimously.

The Selection of Men for the Ministry.

Thomas Burdick was chosen by nomination to officiate as clerk, to record licenses, and is to receive pay for his services. Also voted that the Twelve and Seventy see that the calls for preaching in the region round about Kirtland be attended to, and filled by judicious Elders of this Church.

Thursday, 25.—Attended to my studies as usual, and made some advancement.

In the afternoon I was called upon by Elder Rigdon to go and see his wife, who was very sick. I did so in company with my scribe. We prayed for her and anointed her in the name of the Lord, and she began to recover from that very hour. Returned home and spent the evening there.

Friday, 26.—Read Hebrew with the first class in the morning.

Spent the afternoon in the printing office. Settled some misunderstanding between Brother William Smith and Professor Seixas.

Saturday 27.—Cold, and fine sleighing. I prepared my horse and sleigh for Mr. Seixas to ride to Hudson and visit his family, to return on Monday next. Attended with my class at the printing office, both in the forenoon and afternoon, lectured and also translated Hebrew.

Sunday, 28.—This morning two gentlemen, late from

Scotland, called to see me, to make inquiries about the work of the Lord in these last days. They treated me with respect, and the interview was pleasing to me, and I presume interesting to them. They attended our meeting with me, and expressed satisfaction at what they heard. They spoke of Irving,* the religious reformer, and his prophecies. After meeting I returned home and spent the after part of the day and evening in reading and translating the Hebrew.

Respectful Inquiries About the Work.

Monday, 29.—Spent the day in studying as usual. A man called to see the House of the Lord, in company with another gentleman. On entering the door they were politely invited, by the gentleman who had charge of the house, to take off their hats. One of them replied with the request unhesitatingly, while the other observed that he would not take off his hat nor bow to "Jo Smith," but that he had made "Jo" bow to him at a certain time. He was immediately informed by Elder Morey, the keeper of the house, that his first business was to leave, for when a man insulted Joseph Smith he, Brother Morey, was himself insulted. The man manifested much anger, but left the house. For this independence and resolution of Elder Morey, I respect him, and for the love he manifested towards me; and may Israel's God bless him, and give him an ascendency over all his enemies.

The Manliness of Elder Morey.

This afternoon Professor Seixas returned from Hudson and brought a few more Hebrew Bibles and one grammar of his second edition. Weather warm and sleighing failing fast.

Tuesday, March 1, 1836.—Attended school in the forenoon.

In the afternoon, at the printing office, and read and translated with my class until four o'clock. Returned home and attended to my domestic concerns. We have

---

* This is Mr. Edward Irving, the Scotch clergyman who founded the sect of the Irvingites. See pp. 233-4 this volume.

as yet fine sleighing, which is uncommon in this country at this season of the year.

Wednesday, *2*.—Pursued my studies as usual.

At seven o'clock in the evening the first class met, agreeable to the request of Mr. Seixas, at Elder Orson Hyde's, to spend one hour in translating. Returned at eight o'clock.

Thursday, *3*.—Attended to my studies in the Hebrew school. Some misunderstanding took place between Professor Seixas and some of his scholars respecting the sale of Bibles. His feelings were much hurt, apparently. He made some remarks concerning it to each class. At noon he called on the school committee, his feelings much depressed. We gave him all the satisfaction we could in righteousness, and his feelings were measurably allayed.

Misunder-
standing Over
Sale of Bibles.

This evening the several quorums met agreeable to adjournment, and were organized according to their official standing in the Church. I then arose and made some remarks on the object of our meeting, as follows:

First—To receive or reject certain resolutions that were drafted by a committee chosen for that purpose, at a preceding meeting, respecting licenses for Elders and other official members.

Second—To sanction, by the united voice of the quorums, certain resolutions respecting ordaining members that have passed through each quorum separately, without any alteration or amendment, excepting in the quorum of the Twelve.

After singing and prayer, President Oliver Cowdery, chairman of the committee appointed on the 24th ultimo, to draft resolutions respecting licenses, arose and made report in behalf of the committee, which was read three times by the chairman. The third time he read the resolutions he gave time and opportunity, after reading each article, for objections to be made, if any there were. No objections

Final Action
on Resolu-
tions on Ordi-
nations and
Licenses.

were raised, or alterations made, but an addition was
made to the sixth article extending the powers of the
chairman and clerk *pro tem.* to sign licenses, etc.

I then observed that these resolutions must needs pass
through each quorum separately, beginning at the presidency of each quorum, and consequently it must first be
thrown into the hands of the president of the Deacons and
his council, as equal rights and privileges is my motto;
and one man is as good as another, if he behaves as well;
and that all men should be esteemed alike, without regard
to distinctions of an official nature. The resolutions were
passed by the president of the Deacons and his council by
unanimous voice.

It was then presented before the presidents of the several quorums and their counselors in the following order,
and in the same manner as before, viz: the Teachers,
Priests, Bishop of Kirtland, Bishop of Zion, Elders, High
Priests, Seventy, High Council of Zion, High Council of
Kirtland, the Twelve, and, lastly, passed into the hands
of the Presidency of the Church, and all the quorums,
and received their unanimous sanction. The resolutions
are as follows:

Resolutions on Ordinations and Licenses.

Whereas, the records of the several conferences held by the Elders of
the Church, and the ordination of many of the official members of the
same, in many cases, have been imperfectly kept since its organization.
to avoid ever after any inconvenience, difficulty or injury, in consequence of such neglect, your committee recommend:

First—That all licenses hereafter granted by these autorities assembled as a quorum, or by general conference held for the purpose of
transacting the business of the Church, be recorded at full length by
a clerk appointed for that purpose, in a book to be kept in this
branch of the Church, until it shall be thought advisable by the heads
of the Church to order other books and appoint other clerks, to record
licenses as above; and that said recording clerk be required to indorse
a certificate under his own hand and signature, on the back of said
licenses, specifying the time when, and place where, such license was
recorded, and also a reference to the letter and page of the book containing the same.

Second—That this quorum appoint two persons to sign licenses given as aforesaid, one as chairman, and the other as clerk of conference; and that it shall be the duty of said persons appointed to sign licenses as clerk of conference immediately hereafter, to deliver the same into the hands of the recording clerk.

Third—That all general conferences abroad give each individual whom they ordain, a certificate, signed by the chairman and clerk of said conference, stating the time and place of such conference, and the office to which the individual has been ordained; and that when such certificate has been forwarded to the person hereafter authorized to sign licenses as clerk of conference, such person shall, together with chairman of conference, immediately sign a license; and said clerk of conference shall, after the same has been recorded, forward to the proper person.

Fourth—That all official members in good standing and fellowship in the various branches of this Church, be requested to forward their present licenses, accompanied by a certificate of their virtuous and faithful walk before the Lord, signed by the chairman and clerk of a general conference, or by the clerk of a branch of the Church in which such official member resides, by the advice and direction of such Church, to the clerk of conference, whose duty it shall be to fill a new license, as directed in the third article; and that all licenses, signed, recorded, and endorsed, as specified in the first article, shall be considered good, and valid to all intents and purposes, in the business and spiritual affairs of this Church, as a religious society, or before any court of record of this or any other country, wherein preachers of the Gospel are entitled to special privileges, answering in all respects as an original record, without the necessity of referring to any other document.

Fifth—That the recording clerk be required to publish quarterly, in paper published by some member or members of this Church, a list of the names of the several persons for whom he has recorded licenses within the last quarter of a year.

Sixth—That this quorum appoint two persons to sign licenses as chairman and clerk of conference *pro tem.* for the standing chairman and clerk, who shall be appointed as named in the second article, and also to act in their absence, in signing other licenses, as specified in the foregoing article.

President Joseph Smith, Jun., was nominated as chairman, Frederick G. Williams, as clerk, and Sidney Rigdon as chairman *pro tem.* and Oliver Cowdery as clerk *pro tem.* Vote from the several quorums called, in their order, and passed unanimously.

President Joseph Smith, Jun., made some remarks upon the resolution offered to the Council on the 12th of February. Followed by President Thomas B. Marsh, who called a vote of his quorum to ascertain whether they would repeal their amendment of the 13th of February. And nine of the Twelve voted in the affirmative, and three, viz., John F. Boynton, Lyman E. Johnson, and Orson Pratt, in the negative. And the original resolution of the 12th of February was passed.

Dismissed by prayer, half-past nine o'clock.

OLIVER COWDERY, Clerk.

Friday, 4.—Attended school as usual. The sleighing is failing fast, the icy chains of winter seem to be giving way under the influence of the returning sun, and spring will soon open to us with all its charms.

Saturday, 5.—Attended school. In the afternoon the board kiln took fire, and the lumber was princi- The Board pally consumed. To the best of my recollec- Kiln Again tion this is the fifth or sixth time it has burned Fired. this winter.

Sunday, 6.—Spent the day at home in the enjoyment of the society of my family, around the social fireside.

Monday, 7.—Spent the day in attending to my studies,

At the evening, met with my class at Professor Seixas' room and translated the 17th chapter of Genesis.

After the class was dismissed I was requested to tarry, with the rest of the committee, to make some arrangements about paying Mr. Seixas for his instruction, and to engage him for another quarter. We did not arrive at anything definite upon the point. However, Mr. Seixas has agreed to teach us three weeks longer, and perhaps a quarter, after having a vacation of two weeks, at the expiration of the present course.

Tuesday, 8.—Attended school and translated most of the 22nd chapter of Genesis. After my class was dismissed, retired to the printing office and translated ten verses of the 3rd of Exodus, which, with the first and second Psalms, are our next lesson.

Wednesday, 9.—Attended school as usual.

Thursday, 10.—Attended school in the morning Afternoon, read Hebrew in the office.

At evening went down to the Professor's room, to be instructed by him in the language. On account of the storm the class did not meet.

Friday, 11.—Met with the morning class at nine o'clock.

Further Arrangements of Hebrew Classes.

At ten, went into the office and made a division of our class for private studies, for our better accommodation and advancement in the language we are studying.

Presidents Rigdon, Phelps, and Cowdery, met at the printing office; Elders Orson Pratt, Sylvester Smith, and Bishop Partridge, at Luke S. Johnson's; Elders M'Lellin, Orson Hyde, and Warren Parrish, on the Flats.

This evening our class met at Mr. Seixas' room and spent an hour in our studies. Class dismissed and retired, except the school committee, who tarried and made some arrangements with Mr. Seixas about continuing longer with us and bringing his family to this place. This has been a very stormy day, and the snow is still falling fast, and the prospect is fair for another run of sleighing, which is uncommon for this country at this season of the year.

Saturday, 12.—Engaged a team to go to Hudson after Mr. Seixas' family and goods, also a horse

The Prophet's Reflection on Intemperance

and carriage for himself and wife. Cold weather and fine sleighing. I was informed today that a man by the name of Clark, who was under the influence of ardent spirits froze to death last night, near this place. How long, O Lord, will this monster intemperance find its victims on the earth! I fear until the earth is swept with the wrath and indignation of God, and Christ's kingdom becomes universal. O, come, Lord Jesus, and cut short Thy work in righteousness.

Elder Solomon Hancock received a letter from Missouri bearing the painful intelligence of the death of his wife. May the Lord bless him and comfort him in this hour of affliction.

Sunday, 13.—Met with the Presidency and some of

the Twelve, and counseled with them upon the subject of removing to Zion this spring. We conversed freely upon the importance of her redemption, and the necessity of the Presidency removing to that place, that their influence might be more effectually used in gathering the Saints to that country; and we finally resolved to emigrate on or before the 15th of May next, if kind Providence smiles upon us and opens the way before us.

Removal of the Presidency and Twelve to Zion Contemplated.

Monday, 14.—Attended school as usual. Professor Seixas returned from Hudson with his family.

Tuesday, 15.—At school in the forenoon.

In the afternoon met in the printing office. Received and waited upon those who called to see me, and attended to my domestic concerns.

In the evening met in the printing office and listened to a lecture on grammar.

Wednesday, 16.—Pursued my studies in the Hebrew language.

In the evening met the choir of singers in the Temple. They performed admirably considering the opportunities they have had.

The Temple Choir.

Thursday, 17.—At school in the morning; in the afternoon in the office.

In the evening met with the quorum in the west school room of the Lord's House to receive or reject certain individuals whose names were submitted for ordination, Erastus B. Whitman, Osmon M. Duel, Chapman Duncan, Joshua Bosley, and Heman Hyde, were received, and four were rejected by the united voice of the assembly.

Friday, 18.—Attended school with the morning class.

At ten o'clock went to the school house to attend the funeral of Susan Johnson, daughter of Ezekiel Johnson. She was a member of the Church of Latter-day Saints, and remained strong in the faith until her spirit took its departure from time into eternity. May God bless and comfort her afflicted parents, family,

Death of Susan Johnson.

connections and friends. President Rigdon delivered a
fine discourse on the occasion, and much solemnity prevailed.

Saturday, 19.—Read Hebrew with the morning class.
Spent the day in attending to my domestic concerns and
the affairs of the Church.

Withdrawal of Objections to the Resolutions on Ordinations.

Elders Orson Pratt, John F. Boynton, and Lyman E. Johnson, met
the Presidency of the Church and verbally withdrew all objections to
the second resolution presented to the quorums by the Presidency, on
the 12th of February, for the regulation of ordinations.

OLIVER COWDERY,
Clerk of Conference.

Sunday, 20.—Attended the house of worship. The
quorum of High Priests delivered short addresses to the
congregation, in a very feeling and impressive manner.
One individual was baptized during intermission.

In the afternoon administered the Lord's Supper, as
we are wont to do on every Sabbath, and the Lord blessed
our souls with the outpouring of His Spirit, and we were
made to rejoice in His goodness.

Monday, 21.—At school in the morning. After school
went to the printing office and prepared a
number of Elders' licenses, to send by Elder
Palmer to the court of Medina County, in
order to obtain licenses to marry, as the court
in this county will not grant us this privilege. Ten persons were baptized in this place.

Tuesday, 22.—Read Hebrew with the morning class.
Five young men were received into the Church by baptism
in this place today. This is a stormy day, the snow is
nearly a foot deep, an uncommon storm for this season of
the year.

Wednesday, 23.—Attended school. A pleasant day and
fine sleighing. Two were received into the Church by
baptism.

Thursday, *24.*—Attended school as usual.

In the evening met with my class at the printing office and listened to a lecture by Professor Seixas, upon the Hebrew language. After we were dismissed, we called at the school room to hear the choir of singers perform, which they did admirably. Five more were received into the Church by baptism this day.

Friday, *25.*—Attended school with the morning class, also at five o'clock p. m., and heard a lecture upon the Hebrew grammar. We have pleasant weather and good sleighing.

Saturday, *26.*—At home in the morning attending to my domestic concerns. After breakfast met with the Presidency to make arrangements for the solemn assembly; this business occupied the remainder of the day.

CHAPTER XXIX.

DEDICATION OF THE KIRTLAND TEMPLE—SPIRITUAL MANIFESTATIONS.

Sunday, March 27.—The congregation began to assemble at the Temple, at about seven o'clock, an hour earlier than the doors were to be opened. Many brethren had come in from the regions round about, to witness the dedication of the Lord's House and share in His blessings; and such was the anxiety on this occasion that some hundreds (probably five or six) assembled before the doors were opened. The presidents entered with the doorkeepers, and stationed the latter at the inner and outer doors; also placed our stewards to receive donations from those who should feel disposed to contribute something to defray the expense of building the House of the Lord. We also dedicated the pulpits, and consecrated them to the Lord.

The doors were then opened. Presidents Rigdon, Cowdery and myself seated the congregation as they came in, and, according to the best calculation we could make, we received between nine and ten hundred, which were as many as could be comfortably seated. We then informed the doorkeepers that we could receive no more, and a multitude were deprived of the benefits of the meeting on account of the house not being sufficiently capacious to receive them; and I felt to regret that any of my brethren and sisters should be deprived of the meeting, and I recom-

[Sidenote: Gathering of the Saints to the Dedication.]

[Sidenote: The Number at the First Meeting.]

mended them to repair to the schoolhouse and hold a meeting, which they did, and filled that house also, and yet many were left out.

The assembly was then organized in the following manner, viz.: west end of the house, Presidents Frederick G. Williams, Joseph Smith, Sen., and William W. Phelps occupying the first pulpit for the Melchisedek Priesthood; Presidents Joseph Smith, Jun., Hyrum Smith, and Sidney Rigdon, the second pulpit; Presidents David Whitmer, Oliver Cowdery, and John Whitmer, the third pulpit; the fourth was occupied by the President of the High Priests' quorum and his counselors, and two choristers. The Twelve Apostles on the right, in the three highest seats. The President of the Elders, his counselors and clerk, in the seat immediately below the Twelve. The High Council of Kirtland, consisting of twelve, on the left in the three first seats. The fourth seat, and next below the High Council, was occupied by Elders Warren A. Cowdery and Warren Parrish, who served as scribes. The pulpits in the east end of the house, for the Aaronic Priesthood, were occupied as follows: The Bishop of Kirtland and his counselors, in the first pulpit; the Bishop of Zion and his counselors, in the second pulpit; the president of the Priests and his counselors, in the third pulpit: the president of the Teachers and his counselors, and one chorister, in the fourth pulpit; the High Council of Zion, consisting of twelve counselors, on the right; the president of the Deacons and his counselors, in the seat below them; the seven presidents of Seventies, on the left. The choir of singers were seated in the four corners of the room, in seats prepared for that purpose.

Arrangement of the Assembly.

Received by contribution—nine hundred and sixty-three dollars.

At nine o'clock a. m. President Sidney Rigdon commenced the services of the day by reading the 96th and 24th Psalms.

An excellent choir of singers, led by M. C. Davis, sung the following hymn:

TUNE—*Sterling.*

Ere long the veil will rend in twain,
The King descend with all His train;
The earth shall shake with awful fright,
And all creation feel His might.

The angel's trumpet long shall sound,
And wake the nations under ground;
Throughout the vast domain of space
'Twill echo forth from place to place.

Lift up your heads, ye Saints, in peace,
The Savior comes for your release;
The day of the redeemed has come;
The Saints shall all be welcomed home.

Behold the church! it soars on high,
To meet the Saints amid the sky,
To hail the King in clouds of fire,
And strike and tune th' immortal lyre.

Hosanna! now the trump shall sound,
Proclaim the joys of heaven around,
When all the Saints together join
In songs of love, and all divine.

With Enoch here we all shall meet,
And worship at Messiah's feet,
Unite our hands and hearts in love,
And reign on thrones with Christ above.

The city that was seen of old,
Whose walls were jasper, streets were gold,
We'll now inherit, throned in might—
The Father and the Son's delight.

Celestial crowns we shall receive,
And glories great our God shall give;
While loud hosannas we'll proclaim,
And sound aloud our Savior's name.

Our hearts and tongues shall join in one,
To praise the Father and the Son;
While all the heavens shall shout again,
And all creation say, Amen.*

President Rigdon addressed the throne of grace in a devout and appropriate manner, and the following hymn was sung:

TUNE—*Weymouth.*

O happy souls, who pray
Where God appoints to hear!
O happy Saints, who pay
Their constant service there
 We'll praise Him still,
 And happy we
 Who love the way
 To Zion's hill.

No burning heats by day,
Nor blasts of evening air,
Shall take our health away,
If God be with us there.
 He is our sun,
 And He our shade
 To guard the head
 By night or noon.

God is the only Lord,
Our shield and our defense;
With gifts His hands are stored;
We draw our blessings thence.
 He will bestow
 On Jacob's race
 Peculiar grace,
 And glory too.†

President Rigdon then read the 18th, 19th and 20th verses of the 18th chapter of Matthew, and preached more particularly from the 20th verse: "Verily I say unto you, whatsoever ye shall bind on earth, shall be bound in heaven; and

Elder Rigdon's Discourse.

* Parley P. Pratt, author.
† W. W. Phelps, author.

whatsoever ye shall loose on earth, shall be loosed in heaven. Again I say unto you, that if two of you shall agree on earth as touching any thing that they shall ask, it shall be done for them of my Father which is in heaven. For where two or three are gathered together in my name, there am I in the midst of them." He spoke two hours and a half in his usual logical manner. His prayer and address were very forcible and sublime, and well adapted to the occasion. At one time, in the course of his remarks, he was rather pathetic, and drew tears from many eyes. He was then taking a retrospective view of the toils, privations, and anxieties of those who had labored upon the walls of the house to erect them; and added, there were those who had wet them with their tears, in the silent shades of night, while they were praying to the God of heaven to protect them, and stay the unhallowed hands of ruthless spoilers, who had uttered a prophecy, when the foundation was laid, that the walls would never be reared.

In reference to his main subject, he assumed as a postulate that in the days of the Savior there were synagogues where the Jews worshiped God, and in addition to them, the splendid temple at Jerusalem, yet, when on a certain occasion, one proposed to follow Christ, whithersoever He went, He, though heir of all things, cried out like one in the bitterness of His soul in abject poverty— "The foxes have holes, and the birds of the air have nests; but the Son of Man hath not where to lay His head." This, said the speaker, was evidence to his mind, that the Most High did not put His name there, and that He did not accept the worship of those who paid their vows and adorations there. This was evident from the fact that they would not receive Him, but thrust Him from them, saying: "Away with Him, crucify Him! crucify Him!" It was therefore abundantly evident that His Spirit did not dwell in them. They were the degenerate sons of noble sires, but they had long since slain the Prophets and Seers, through whom the Lord revealed Himself to the children of men. They were not led by revelation. *This*, said the speaker, was the grand difficulty among them—*their unbelief in present revelation*.

He further remarked, that their unbelief in present revelation, was the means of dividing that gen- Remarks on eration into the various sects and parties that Revelation. existed. They were zealous worshipers according to outward forms, but such worship was not required of them, nor was it acceptable to God. The Redeemer Himself, who knew the hearts of all men, called them a generation of vipers. It was proof positive to the speaker's mind, there being Pharisees, Sadducees, Herodians, and Essenes, all differing from one another, that they were led by the precepts and commandments of men. Each had something peculiar to himself, but all agreed in one thing, viz., to oppose the Savior; so that we discover He could, with the utmost propriety, exclaim, notwithstanding their synagogue and temple-worship: "The foxes have holes, and the birds of the air have nests, but the Son of Man hath not where to lay His head."

He took occasion here to remark that such diversity of sentiment ever had, and ever would obtain, The Consequence of Rewhen people were not led by present revela-jecting Prestion. This brought him to the inevitable con-ent Revelaclusion, that the various sects of the present tion. day, from their manifesting the same spirit, rested under the same condemnation, with those who were contemporary with the Savior. He admitted there were many houses, many sufficiently large, built for the worship of God, but not one except this, on the face of the whole earth, that was built by divine revelation; and were it not for this the dear Redeemer might, in this day of science, this day of intelligence, this day of religion, say to those who would follow Him: "The foxes have holes, the birds of the air have nests, but the Son of Man hath not where to lay His head."

After closing his discourse he called upon the several quorums, commencing with the Presidency, to manifest, by rising, their willingness to acknowledge me as a Prophet and Seer, and uphold me as such, by their prayers of faith.

Joseph Smith, Jun., Sustained as the Prophet and Seer of the Church.

All the quorums, in turn, cheerfully complied with this request.   He then called upon all the congregation of Saints, also, to give their assent by rising on their feet, which they did unanimously.

The following hymn was then sung:

TUNE—*Hosanna.*

Now let us rejoice in the day of salvation,
No longer as strangers on earth need we roam;
Good tidings are sounding to us and each nation,
And shortly the hour of redemption will come;
When all that was promised the Saints will be given,
And none will molest them from morn until even,
And earth will appear as the Garden of Eden,
And Jesus will say to all Israel, Come home.

We'll love one another, and never dissemble,
But cease to do evil, and ever be one;
And while the ungodly are fearing and tremble,
We'll watch for the day when the Savior will come:
When all that was promised the Saints will be given,
And none will molest them from morn until even,
And earth will appear as the Garden of Eden,
And Jesus will say to all Israel, Come home.

In faith we'll rely on the arm of Jehovah
To guide through these last days of trouble and gloom;
And, after the scourges and harvest are over,
We'll rise with the just when the Savior doth come.
Then all that was promised the Saints will be given,
And they will be crowned as the angels of heaven,
And earth will appear as the garden of Eden,
And Christ and His people will ever be one.*

After an intermission of twenty minutes, during which

* W. W. Phelps, author.

time the congregation kept their seats, the services of the day were resumed by singing "Adam-ondi-Ahman:"

> This earth was once a garden place,
>   With all her glories common;
> And men did live a holy race,
> And worship Jesus face to face,
>   In Adam-ondi-Ahman.
>
> We read that Enoch walked with God,
>   Above the power of Mammon;
> While Zion spread herself abroad,
> And Saints and angels sang aloud,
>   In Adam-ondi-Ahman.
>
> Her land was good and greatly blest,
>   Beyond old Israel's Canaan;
> Her fame was known from east to west;
> Her peace was great and pure the rest
>   Of Adam-ondi-Ahman.
>
> Hosanna to such days to come—
>   The Savior's second coming,
> When all the earth in glorious bloom
> Affords the Saints a holy home,
>   Like Adam-ondi-Ahman.[*]

I then made a short address, and called upon the several quorums, and all the congregation of Saints, to acknowledge the Presidency as Prophets and Seers, and uphold them by their prayers. They all covenanted to do so, by rising.

Presidency of Church and Twelve Apostles Sustained as Prophets, Seers and Revelators.

I then called upon the quorums and congregation of Saints to acknowledge the Twelve Apostles, who were present, as Prophets, Seers, Revelators, and special witnesses to all the nations of the earth, holding the keys of the kingdom, to unlock it, or cause it to be done, among them, and uphold them by their prayers, which they assented to by rising.

[*] W. W. Phelps, author.

I next called upon the quorums and congregation of

Saints to acknowledge the presidents of Seventies, who act as their representatives, as Apostles and special witnesses to the nations, to assist the Twelve in opening the Gospel kingdom among all people. and to uphold them by their prayers, which they did by rising.

I then called upon the quorums and congregation of

Saints to acknowledge the High Council of Kirtland, in all the authority of the Melchisedek Priesthood, and uphold them by their prayers, which they assented to by rising.

I then called upon the quorums and congregation of Saints to acknowledge, and uphold by their prayers, the Bishops of Kirtland and Zion, and their counselors, in all the authority of the Aaronic Priesthood, which they did by rising.

I next called upon the quorums and congregation of Saints to acknowledge the High Council of Zion, and uphold them by their prayers, in all the authority of the High Priesthood, which they did by rising.

I then called upon the quorums and all the Saints to

acknowledge the president of the Elders, and his counselors, and uphold them by their prayers, which they did by rising.

The quorums and congregation of Saints were then

The Presiden-
cies of the
Quorum of the
Lesser Priest-
hood Sus-
tained.
called upon to acknowledge, and uphold by their prayers, the presidents and counselors, of the Priests, Teachers and Deacons, which they did by rising.

The vote was unanimous in every instance, and I prophesied to all, that inasmuch as they would uphold

these men in their several stations, (alluding to the different quorums in the Church), the Lord would bless them; yea, in the name of Christ, the blessings of heaven should be theirs; and when the Lord's anointed go forth to proclaim the word, bearing

testimony to this generation, if they receive it they shall
be blessed; but if not, the judgments of God will follow
close upon them, until that city or that house which re
jects them, shall be left desolate.

The following hymn was then sung:

TUNE—*Dalston.*

How pleased and blessed was I
To hear the people cry:
"Come. let us seek our God today!"
Yes, with a cheerful zeal,
We'll haste to Zion's hill,
And there our vows and honors pay.

Zion, thrice happy place,
Adorned with wondrous grace,
And walls of strength embrace thee round,
In thee our tribes appear,
To praise and pray and hear
The sacred Gospel's joyful sound.

There, David's greater Son
Has fixed his royal throne;
He sits for grace and judgment there;
He bids the Saints be glad,
He makes the sinner sad,
And humble souls rejoice with fear.

May peace attend thy gate,
And joy within thee wait,
To bless the soul of every guest!
The man that seeks thy peace,
And wishes thine increase,
A thousand blessings on him rest.

My tongue repeats her vows,
"Peace to this sacred house!
For here my friends and kindred dwell;"
And since my glorious God
Makes thee His blest abode,
My soul shall ever love thee well.*

Watts, author.

The dedicatory prayer was then offered:

*The following Prayer was given by Revelation to Joseph, the Seer, and was Repeated in the Kirtland Temple at the time of its Dedication, March 27, 1836.**

PRAYER.

1. Thanks be to Thy name, O Lord God of Israel, who keepest covenant and shewest mercy unto Thy servants who walk uprightly before Thee, with all their hearts;

2. Thou who hast commanded Thy servants to build a house to Thy name in this place (Kirtland).

3. And now Thou beholdest, O Lord, that Thy servants have done according to Thy commandment,

4. And now we ask Thee, Holy Father, in the name of Jesus Christ, the Son of Thy bosom, in whose name alone, salvation can be administered to the children of men, we ask Thee, O Lord, to accept of this house, the workmanship of the hands of us, Thy servants, which Thou didst command us to build;

5. For Thou knowest that we have done this work through great tribulations; and out of our poverty we have given of our substance, to build a house to Thy name, that the Son of Man might have a place to manifest Himself to His people.

6. And as Thou hast said in a revelation, given to us, calling us Thy friends, saying, "Call your solemn assembly, as I have commanded you;

7. And as all have not faith, seek ye diligently, and teach one another words of wisdom; yea, seek ye out of the best books, words of wisdom, seek learning even by study, and also by faith.

8. Organize yourselves; prepare every needful thing, and establish a house, even a house of prayer, a house of fasting, a house of faith, a house of learning, a house of glory, a house of order, a house of God,

9. That your incomings may be in the name of the Lord, that your outgoings may be in the name of the Lord, that all your salutations may be in the name of the Lord, with uplifted hands unto the Most High."

10. And now, Holy Father, we ask Thee to assist us, Thy people, with Thy grace, in calling our solemn assembly, that it may be done to Thy honor, and to Thy divine acceptance,

11. And in a manner that we may be found worthy, in Thy sight, to secure a fulfillment of the promises which Thou hast made unto us, Thy people, in the revelations given unto us;

* Doctrine and Covenants, sec. cix.

12. That Thy glory may rest down upon Thy people, and upon this Thy house, which we now dedicate to Thee, that it may be sanctified and consecrated to be holy, and that Thy holy presence may be continually in this house,

13. And that all people who shall enter upon the threshold of the Lord's House, may feel Thy power, and feel constrained to acknowledge that Thou hast sanctified it, and that it is Thy house, a place of Thy holiness.

14. And do Thou grant, Holy Father, that all those who shall worship in this house, may be taught words of wisdom out of the best books, and that they may seek learning even by study, and also by faith, as Thou hast said;

15. And that they may grow up in Thee, and receive a fullness of the Holy Ghost, and be organized according to Thy laws, and be prepared to obtain every needful thing;

16. And that this house may be a house of prayer, a house of fasting, a house of faith, a house of glory and of God, even Thy house;

17. That all the incomings of Thy people, into this house, may be in the name of the Lord;

18. That all their outgoings from this house may be in the name of the Lord;

19. And that all their salutations may be in the name of the Lord, with holy hands, uplifted to the Most High;

20. And that no unclean thing shall be permitted to come into Thy house to pollute it;

21. And when Thy people transgress, any of them, they may speedily repent, and return unto Thee, and find favor in Thy sight, and be restored to the blessings which Thou hast ordained to be poured out upon those who shall reverence Thee in Thy house.

22. And we ask Thee, Holy Father, that Thy servants may go forth from this house, armed with Thy power, and that Thy name may be upon them, and Thy glory be round about them, and Thine angels have charge over them;

23. And from this place they may bear exceedingly great and glorious tidings, in truth, unto the ends of the earth, that they may know that this is Thy work, and that Thou hast put forth Thy hand, to fulfill that which Thou hast spoken by the mouths of the Prophets concerning the last days.

24. We ask Thee, Holy Father, to establish the people that shall worship, and honorably hold a name and standing in this Thy house to all generations, and for eternity,

25. That no weapon formed against them shall prosper; that he who diggeth a pit for them shall fall into the same himself.

26. That no combination of wickedness shall have power to rise up and prevail over Thy people upon whom Thy name shall be put in this house;

27. And if any people shall rise against this people, that Thine anger be kindled against them,

28. And if they shall smite this people, Thou wilt smite them, Thou wilt fight for Thy people as Thou didst in the day of battle, that they may be delivered from the hands of all their enemies.

29. We ask Thee, Holy Father, to confound, and astonish, and to bring to shame and confusion, all those who have spread lying reports, abroad, over the world, against Thy servant, or servants, if they will not repent, when the everlasting Gospel shall be proclaimed in their ears,

30. And that all their works may be brought to naught, and be swept away by the hail, and by the judgments which Thou wilt send upon them in Thine anger, that there may be an end to lyings and slanders against Thy people;

31. For Thou knowest, O Lord, that Thy servants have been innocent before Thee in bearing record of Thy name, for which they have suffered these things;

32. Therefore we plead before Thee for a full and complete deliverance from under this yoke;

33. Break it off, O Lord; break it off from the necks of Thy servants, by Thy power, that we may rise up in the midst of this generation and do Thy work.

34. Jehovah, have mercy upon this people, and as all men sin, forgive the transgressions of Thy people, and let them be blotted out forever.

35. Let the anointing of Thy ministers be sealed upon them with power from on high;

36. Let it be fulfilled upon them, as upon those on the day of Pentecost, let the gift of tongues be poured out upon Thy people, even cloven tongues as of fire, and the interpretation thereof,

37. And let Thy house be filled, as with a rushing mighty wind, with Thy glory.

38. Put upon Thy servants the testimony of the covenant, that when they go out and proclaim Thy word, they may seal up the law, and prepare the hearts of Thy Saints for all those judgments Thou art about to send, in Thy wrath, upon the inhabitants of the earth, because of their transgressions, that Thy people may not faint in the day of trouble.

39. And whatsoever city Thy servants shall enter, and the people of that city receive their testimony, let Thy peace and Thy salvation be

upon that city, that they may gather out of that city the righteous, that they may come forth to Zion, or to her stakes, the places of Thine appointment, with songs of everlasting joy,

40. And until this be accomplished, let not Thy judgments fall upon that city.

41. And whatsoever city Thy servants shall enter, and the people of that city receive not the testimony of Thy servants, and Thy servants warn them to save themselves from this untoward generation, let it be upon that city according to that which Thou hast spoken by the mouths of Thy Prophets;

42. But deliver Thou, O Jehovah we beseech Thee, Thy servants from their hands, and cleanse them from their blood.

43. O Lord, we delight not in the destruction of our fellow men; their souls are precious before Thee;

44. But Thy word must be fulfilled; help Thy servants to say, with Thy grace assisting them, Thy will be done, O Lord, and not ours.

45. We know that Thou hast spoken by the mouth of Thy Prophets terrible things concerning the wicked, in the last days—that Thou wilt pour out Thy judgments, without measure;

46. Therefore, O Lord, deliver Thy people from the calamity of the wicked; enable Thy servants to seal up the law, and bind up the testimony, that they may be prepared against the day of burning.

47. We ask Thee, Holy Father, to remember those who have been driven by the inhabitants of Jackson county, Missouri, from the lands of their inheritance, and break off, O Lord, this yoke of affliction that has been put upon them,

48. Thou knowest, O Lord, that they have been greatly oppressed and afflicted by wicked men, and our hearts flow out with sorrow, because of their grievous burdens.

49. O Lord, how long wilt Thou suffer this people to bear this affliction, and the cries of their innocent ones to ascend up in Thine ears, and their blood come up in testimony before Thee, and not make a display of Thy testimony in their behalf?

50. Have mercy, O Lord, upon the wicked mob, who have driven Thy people, that they may cease to spoil, that they may repent of their sins, if repentance is to be found;

51. But if they will not, make bare Thine arm, O Lord, and redeem that land which Thou didst appoint a Zion unto Thy people!

52. And if it cannot be otherwise, that the cause of Thy people may not fail before Thee, may Thine anger be kindled, and Thine indignation fall upon them, that they may be wasted away, both root and branch, from under heaven;

53. But inasmuch as they will repent, Thou art gracious and merci-

ful, and wilt turn away Thy wrath, when Thou lookest upon the face of Thine anointed.

54. Have mercy, O Lord, upon all the nations of the earth, have mercy upon the rulers of our land, may those principles which were so honorably and nobly defended, viz., the Constitution of our land, by our fathers, be established forever;

55. Remember the kings, princes, the nobles, and the great ones of the earth, and all people, and the churches, all the poor, the needy, and afflicted ones of the earth,

56. That their hearts may be softened, when Thy servants shall go out from Thy house, O Jehovah, to bear testimony of Thy name, that their prejudices may give way before the truth, and Thy people may obtain favor in the sight of all,

57. That all the ends of the earth may know that we Thy servants have heard Thy voice, and that Thou hast sent us,

58. That from among all these, Thy servants, the sons of Jacob, may gather out the righteous to build a holy city to Thy name, as Thou hast commanded them.

59. We ask Thee to appoint unto Zion other stakes, besides this one which Thou hast appointed, that the gathering of Thy people may roll on in great power and majesty, that Thy work may be cut short in righteousness.

60. Now these words, O Lord, we have spoken before Thee, concerning the revelations and commandments which Thou hast given unto us, who are identified with the Gentiles;

61. But Thou knowest that Thou hast a great love for the children of Jacob, who have been scattered upon the mountains, for a long time, in a cloudy and dark day;

62. We therefore ask Thee to have mercy upon the children of Jacob, that Jerusalem, from this hour, may begin to be redeemed,

63. And the yoke of bondage may begin to be broken off from the house of David.

64. And the children of Judah may begin to return to the lands which Thou didst give to Abraham, their father;

65. And cause that the remnants of Jacob, who have been cursed and smitten, because of their transgression, be converted from their wild and savage condition to the fullness of the everlasting Gospel,

66. That they may lay down their weapons of bloodshed, and cease their rebellions;

67. And may all the scattered remnants of Israel, who have been driven to the ends of the earth, come to a knowledge of the truth, believe in the Messiah, and be redeemed from oppression, and rejoice before Thee.

68. O Lord, remember Thy servant, Joseph Smith, Jun., and all his afflictions and persecutions—how he has covenanted with Jehovah, and vowed to Thee, O mighty God of Jacob—and the commandments which Thou hast given unto him, and that he hath sincerely striven to do Thy will.

69. Have mercy, O Lord, upon his wife and children, that they may be exalted in Thy presence, and preserved by Thy fostering hand;

70. Have mercy upon all their immediate connections, that their prejudices may be broken up, and swept away as with a flood, that they may be converted and redeemed with Israel, and know that Thou art God.

71. Remember, O Lord, the presidents, even all the presidents of Thy Church, that Thy right hand may exalt them, with all their families, and their immediate connections, that their names may be perpetuated, and had in everlasting remembrance, from generation to generation.

72. Remember all Thy Church, O Lord, with all their families, and all their immediate connections, with all their sick and afflicted ones, with all the poor and meek of the earth, that the kingdom which Thou hast set up without hands, may become a great mountain, and fill the whole earth;

73. That Thy Church may come forth out of the wilderness of darkness, and shine forth fair as the moon, clear as the sun, and terrible as an army with banners;

74. And be adorned as a bride for that day when Thou shalt unveil the heavens, and cause the mountains to flow down at Thy presence, and the valleys to be exalted, the rough places made smooth; that Thy glory may fill the earth,

75. That when the trump shall sound for the dead we shall be caught up in the clouds to meet Thee, that we may ever be with the Lord,

76. That our garments may be pure, that we may be clothed upon with robes of righteousness, with palms in our hands, and crowns of glory upon our heads, and reap eternal joy for all our sufferings.

77. O Lord God Almighty, hear us in these our petitions, and answer us from heaven, Thy holy habitation, where Thou sittest enthroned, with glory, honor, power, majesty, might, dominion, truth, justice, judgment, mercy, and an infinity of fullness, from everlasting to everlasting.

78. O hear, O hear, O hear us O Lord! and answer these petitions, and except the dedication of this house unto Thee, the work of our hands, which we have built unto Thy name.

79. And also this Church, to put upon it Thy name; and help us by the power of Thy Spirit, that we may mingle our voices with those

bright, shining seraphs around Thy throne, with acclamations of praise, singing hosanna to God and the Lamb;

80. And let these Thine anointed ones be clothed with salvation, and Thy Saints shout aloud for joy.   Amen and amen.

The choir then sang:

TUNE—*Hosanna.*

The Spirit of God like a fire is burning!
The latter-day glory begins to come forth;
The visions and blessings of old are returning,
The angels are coming to visit the earth.

CHORUS.

We'll sing and we'll shout with the armies of heaven—
Hosanna, hosanna to God and the Lamb!
Let glory to them in the highest be given,
Henceforth and forever: amen and amen.

The Lord is extending the Saints' understanding,
Restoring their judges and all as at first;
The knowledge and power of God are expanding;
The veil o'ver the earth is beginning to burst.
   We'll sing and we'll shou, etc.

We'll call in our solemn assemblies in spirit,
To spread forth the kingdom of heaven abroad,
That we through our faith may begin to inherit
The visions and blessings and glories ot God.
   We'll sing and we'll shout, etc.

We'll wash and be washed, and with oil be anointed,
Withal not omitting the washing of feet;
For he that receiveth his penny appointed
Must surely be clean at the harvest of wheat.
   We'll sing and we'll shout, etc.

Old Israel, that fled from the world for his freedom,
Must come with the cloud and the pillar amain;
And Moses and Aaron and Joshua lead him,
And feed him on manna from heaven again.
   We'll sing and we'll shout, etc.

How blessed the day when the lamb and the lion
Shall lie down together without any ire,
And Ephraim be crowned with his blessing in Zion,
As Jesus descends with His chariots of fire!

We'll sing and we'll shout with the armies of heaven—
Hosanna, hosanna to God and the Lamb!
Let glory to them in the highest be given,
Henceforth and forever: amen and amen!*

I then asked the several quorums separately, and then the congregation, if they accepted the dedication prayer, and acknowledged the house dedicated. The vote was unanimous in the affirmative, in every instance. Dedication of the Temple Accepted by the Priesthood and the Saints.

The Lord's Supper was then administered; President Don Carlos Smith blessed the bread and the wine, which was distributed by several Elders to the Church; after which I bore record of my mission, and of the ministration of angels. The Lord's Supper and Testimonies.

President Don Carlos Smith also bore testimony of the truth of the work of the Lord in which we were engaged.

President Oliver Cowdery testified of the truth of the Book of Mormon, and of the work of the Lord in these last days.

President Frederick G. Williams arose and testified that while President Rigdon was making his first prayer, an angel entered the window and took his seat between Father Smith and himself, and remained there during the prayer.

President David Whitmer also saw angels in the house.

President Hyrum Smith made some appropriate remarks congratulating those who had endured so many toils and privations to build the house.

President Rigdon then made a few appropriate closing remarks, and a short prayer, at the close of which we sealed the proceedings of the day by shouting hosanna,

* W. W. Phelps.

hosanna, hosanna to God and the Lamb, three times, sealing it each time with amen, amen, and amen.

President Brigham Young gave a short address in tongues, and David W. Patten interpreted, and gave a short exhortation in tongues himself, after which I blessed the congregation in the name of the Lord, and the assembly dispersed a little past four o'clock, having manifested the most quiet demeanor during the whole exercise.

I met the quorums in the evening and instructed them respecting the ordinance of washing of feet, which they were to attend to on Wednesday following;

Spiritual Manifestations in the Kirtland Temple.

and gave them instructions in relation to the spirit of prophecy, and called upon the congregation to speak, and not to fear to prophesy good concerning the Saints, for if you prophesy the falling of these hills and the rising of the valleys, the downfall of the enemies of Zion and the rising of the kingdom of God, it shall come to pass. Do not quench the Spirit, for the first one that opens his mouth shall receive the Spirit of prophecy.

Brother George A. Smith arose and began to prophesy, when a noise was heard like the sound of a rushing mighty wind, which filled the Temple, and all the congregation simultaneously arose, being moved upon by an invisible power; many began to speak in tongues and prophesy; others saw glorious visions; and I beheld the Temple was filled with angels, which fact I declared to the congregation. The people of the neighborhood came running together (hearing an unusual sound within, and seeing a bright light like a pillar of fire resting upon the Temple), and were astonished at what was taking place. This continued until the meeting closed at eleven p. m.

The number of official members present on this occasion was four hundred and sixteen, being a greater number than ever assembled on any former occasion.

CHAPTER XXX.

THE ORDINANCE OF WASHING OF FEET—VISIONS IN THE KIRT-
LAND TEMPLE—THE PROPHET ON ABOLITION.

Monday, March 28.—Attended school.   Very warm,
like spring.

Tuesday, 29.—Attended school, which was the last day
of our course of lectures in Hebrew, by Professor
Seixas.

At eleven o'clock, a.m., Presidents Joseph Smith, Jun.,
Frederick G. Williams, Sidney Rigdon, Hyrum Smith,
and Oliver Cowdery, met in the most holy place in the
Lord's House, and sought for a revelation from
Him concerning the authorities of the Church   *Seeking the Word and Will of the Lord.*
going to Zion, and other important matters.
After uniting in prayer, the voice of the Spirit
was that we should come into this place three times, and
also call the other presidents, the two Bishops and their
counselors, each to stand in his place, and fast through
the day and also the night, and that during this, if we
would humble ourselves, we should receive further communications from Him.   After this word was received we
immediately sent for the other brethren, who came.

The Presidency proceeded to ordain George Boosinger
to the High Priesthood, and anoint him.   This was in
consequence of his having administered unto us in temporal things in our distress, and also because he left the
place just previous to the dedication of the Lord's House,
to bring us the temporal means, previously named.   Soon

after this, the word of the Lord came, through President
Joseph Smith, Jun., that those who had entered the holy
place, must not leave the house until morning, but send
for such things as were necessary, and, also, during our
stay, we must cleanse our feet and partake of the Sacrament that we might be made holy before Him, and thereby be qualified to officiate in our calling, upon the morrow, in washing the feet of the Elders.

Accordingly we proceeded to cleanse our faces and our
feet, and then proceeded to wash one another's feet. Pres-
ident Sidney Rigdon first washed President
Joseph Smith, Junior's feet, and then, in turn,
was washed by him; after which President
Rigdon washed President Joseph Smith, Sen., and Hyrum
Smith. President Joseph Smith, Jun., washed President
Frederick G. Williams, and then President Hyrum Smith
washed President David Whitmer's and President Oliver
Cowdery's feet. Then President David Whitmer washed
President William W. Phelps' feet, and in tu:n President
Phelps washed President John Whitmer's feet. The
Bishops and their Counselors were then washed, after
which we partook of the bread and wine. The Holy Spirit
rested down upon us, and we continued in the Lord's
House all night, prephesying and giving glory to God.

The Washing of Feet.

Wednesday, 30.—At eight o'clock, according to appointment, the Presidency, the Twelve, the Seventies, the
High Council, the Bishops and their entire quorums, the
Elders and all the official members in this stake of Zion,
amounting to about three hundred, met in the
Temple of the Lord to attend to the ordinance
of washing of feet. I ascended the pulpit,
and remarked to the congregation that we
had passed through many trials and afflictions since the
organization of the Church, and that this is a year of
jubilee to us, and a time of rejoicing, and that it was expedient for us to prepare bread and wine sufficient to
make our hearts glad, as we should not, probably, leave

Continuance of the Ordi- nance of Feet Washing.

this house until morning; to this end we should call on the brethren to make a contribution. The stewards passed round and took up a liberal contribution, and messengers were despatched for bread and wine.

Tubs, water, and towels were prepared, and I called the house to order, and the Presidency proceeded to wash the feet of the Twelve, pronouncing many prophecies and blessings upon them in the name of the Lord Jesus; and then the Twelve proceeded to wash the feet of the Presidents of the several quorums. The brethren began to prophesy upon each other's heads, and upon the enemies of Christ, who inhabited Jackson county, Missouri; and continued prophesying, and blessing, and sealing them with hosanna and amen, until nearly seven o'clock in the evening.

The bread and the wine were then brought in, and I observed that we had fasted all the day, and lest we faint, as the Savior did so shall we do on this occasion; we shall bless the bread, and give it to the Twelve, and they to the multitude. While waiting, I made the following remarks: that the time that we were required to tarry in Kirtland to be endowed, would be fulfilled in a few days, and then the Elders would go forth, and each must stand for himself, *The Prophet's Instruction to the Elders Who Engage in the Ministry.* as it was not necessary for them to be sent out, two by two, as in former times, but to go in all meekness, in sobriety, and preach Jesus Christ and Him crucified; not to contend with others on account of their faith, or systems of religion, but pursue a steady course. This I delivered by way of commandment; and all who observe it not, will pull down persecution upon their heads, while those who do, shall always be filled with the Holy Ghost; this I pronounced as a prophecy, and sealed with hosanna and amen. Also that the Seventies are not called to serve tables, or preside over churches, to settle difficulties, but are to preach the Gospel and build them up, and set others, who do not belong to these quorums, to preside over them,

who are High Priests. The Twelve also are not to serve
tables, but to bear the keys of the Kingdom to all nations,
and unlock the door of the Gospel to them, and call upon
the Seventies to follow after them, and assist them. The
Twelve are at liberty to go wheresoever they will, and if
any one will say, I wish to go to such a place, let all the
rest say amen.

The Seventies are at liberty to go to Zion if they please,
or go wheresoever they will, and preach the Gospel; and
let the redemption of Zion be our object, and strive to
effect it by sending up all the strength of the Lord's House,
wherever we find them; and I want to enter into the
following covenant, that if any more of our brethren are
slain or driven from their lands in Missouri, by the mob,
we will give ourselves no rest, until we are avenged of our
enemies to the uttermost. This covenant was sealed
unanimously, with a hosanna and an amen.

I then observed to the quorums, that I had now completed the organization of the Church, and we had passed
through all the necessary ceremonies, that I had given
them all the instruction they needed, and that they now
were at liberty, after obtaining their licenses, to go forth
and build up the Kingdom of God, and that it was expedient for me and the Presidency to retire, having spent
the night previously in waiting upon the Lord in His
Temple, and having to attend another dedication on the
morrow, or conclude the one commenced on the last Sabbath, for the benefit of those of my brethren and sisters
who could not get into the house on the former occasion,
but that it was expedient for the brethren to tarry all night
and worship before the Lord in His house.

I left the meeting in the charge of the Twelve, and retired about nine o'clock in the evening. The
brethren continued exhorting, prophesying,
and speaking in tongues until five o'clock in
the morning. The Savior made His appearance to some,
while angels ministered to others, and it was a Pentecost

The Day—
March 30th—
A Pentecost.

and an endowment indeed, long to be remembered, for the sound shall go forth from this place into all the world, and the occurrences of this day shall be handed down upon the pages of sacred history, to all generations; as the day of Pentecost, so shall this day be numbered and celebrated as a year of jubilee, and time of rejoicing to the Saints of the Most High God.

Thursday, 31.—This day being set apart to perform again the ceremonies of the dedication, for the benefit of those who could not get into the house on the preceding Sabbath, I repaired to the Temple at eight, a. m., in company with the Presidency, and arranged our door keepers and stewards as on the former occasion. We then opened the doors, and a large congregation entered the house, and were comfortably seated. The authorities of the Church were seated in their respective places, and the services of the day were commenced, prosecuted and terminated in the same manner as at the former dedication, and the Spirit of God rested upon the congregation, and great solemnity prevailed.

The Second Day of Dedicatory Service.

Friday, April 1.—At home most of the day. Many brethren called to see me, some on temporal and some on spiritual business; among the number was Leman Copley, who testified against me in a suit I brought against Dr. Philastus Hurlburt for threatening my life. He confessed that he bore a false testimony against me in that suit, but verily thought, at the time, that he was right, but on calling to mind all the circumstances connected with the things that happened at that time, he was convinced that he was wrong, and humbly confessed it, and asked my forgiveness, which was readily granted. He also wished to be received into the Church again, by baptism, and was received according to his desire. He gave me his confession in writing.

Confession of Leman Copley to Bearing False Witness

Saturday, 2.—Transacted business of a temporal nature in the upper room in the printing office, in company with

Frederick G. Williams, Sidney Rigdon, Oliver Cowdery, William W. Phelps and John Whitmer, which was to have a bearing upon the redemption of Zion. After mature deliberation the council decided that Oliver Cowdery and myself should act as a board or committee to raise, in righteousness, all the money we could for a season, to send by, or to, certain wise men appointed to purchase lands in Zion in obedience to a revelation or commandment of the Lord, for the mutual benefit of the council.

The Prophet and Oliver Cowdery Appointed to Raise Money for the Redemption of Zion.

Also, it was agreed by the council that Sidney Rigdon and Frederick G. Williams exert themselves in devising ways and means with the stock on hand, the available outstanding claims of the company, and such other means as they shall deem most proper, to discharge the company's debts. It was also agreed that W. W. Phelps, John Whitmer, and David Whitmer have five hundred books of Doctrine and Covenants, when bound, and five hundred Hymn Books, together with the subscription list for the *Messenger and Advocate* and *Northern Times,** now due in Clay County, Missouri; and that Messrs. Phelps and John Whitmer be released from the responsibility of claims on them, or either of them, as joint partners in the firm.

As soon as the above plans were settled, I started with President Cowdery on our mission, and our success was such in one half day as to give us pleasing anticipations that we were doing the will of God, and assurance that His work prospered in our hands.

Sunday, 3.—Attended meeting in the Lord's House, and assisted the other Presidents of the Church in seating the congregation, and then became an attentive listener to the preaching from the stand. Thomas B. Marsh and David W. Patten spoke in the forenoon to an attentive

* This was the weekly newspaper which had been started in February, 1835, in support of Democracy; and which was edited by Frederick G. Williams.

audience of about one thousand persons. In the afternoon, I assisted the other Presidents in distributing the Lord's Supper to the Church, receiving it from the Twelve, whose privilege it was to officiate at the sacred desk this day. After having performed this service to my brethren, I retired to the pulpit, the veils being dropped, and bowed myself, with Oliver Cowdery, in solemn and silent prayer. After rising from prayer, the following vision was opened to both of us—

*Vision Manifested to Joseph the Seer and Oliver Cowdery.**

1. The veil was taken from our minds, and the eyes of our understanding were opened.

2. We saw the Lord standing upon the breastwork of the pulpit, before us, and under His feet was a paved work of pure gold in color like amber.

3. His eyes were as a flame of fire, the hair of His head was white like the pure snow, His countenance shone above the brightness of the sun, and His voice was as the sound of the rushing of great waters, even the voice of Jehovah, saying—

4. I am the first and the last, I am He who liveth, I am He who was slain, I am your advocate with the Father.

5. Behold, your sins are forgiven you, you are clean before me, therefore lift up your heads and rejoice.

6. Let the hearts of your brethren rejoice, and let the hearts of all my people rejoice, who have, with their might, built this house to my name.

7. For behold, I have accepted this house, and my name shall be here, and I will manifest myself to my people in mercy in this House.

8. Yea, I will appear unto my servants, and speak unto them with mine own voice, if my people will keep my commandments, and do not pollute this holy house.

9. Yea the hearts of thousands and tens of thousands shall greatly rejoice in consequence of the blessings which shall be poured out, and the endowment with which my servants have been endowed in this house;

10. And the fame of this house shall spread to foreign lands, and this is the beginning of the blessing which shall be poured out upon the heads of my people. Even so. Amen.

11. After this vision closed, the heavens were again opened unto us, and Moses appeared before us, and committed unto us the keys of the

_____
* Doctrine and Covenants, sec. cx.

gathering of Israel from the four parts of the earth, and the leading of the Ten Tribes from the land of the north.

12. After this, Elias appeared, and committed the dispensation of the Gospel of Abraham, saying, that in us, and our seed, all generations after us should be blessed.

13. After this vision had closed, another great and glorious vision burst upon us, for Elijah the Prophet, who was taken to heaven without tasting death, stood before us, and said—

14. Behold, the time has fully come, which was spoken of by the mouth of Malachi, testifying that he [Elijah] should be sent before the great and dreadful day of the Lord come.

15. To turn the hearts of the fathers to the children, and the children to the fathers, lest the whole earth be smitten with a curse.

16. Therefore the keys of this dispensation are committed into your hands, and by this ye may know that the great and dreadful day of the Lord is near, even at the doors.

Monday, 4.—The Elders began to spread abroad in all parts of the land, preaching the word.

Saturday, 9.—Myself and the principal heads of the Church, accompanied the wise men of Zion, namely, Bishop Partridge and his counselors, Isaac Morley and John Corrill, and President W. W. Phelps, on their way home, as far as Chardon; and after staying with them all night, blessed them in the morning, and returned to Kirtland.

Leading Elders Return to Zion— Missouri.

Soon after I wrote an article for the *Messenger and Advocate,* which was published in the April number as follows:—

The Prophet's Views on Abolition.

Brother Oliver Cowdery,

DEAR SIR:—This place [Kirtland] having recently been visited by a gentleman who advocated the principles or doctrines of those who are called Abolitionists, and his presence having created an interest in that subject, if you deem the following reflections of any service, or think they will have a tendency to correct the opinions of the Southern public, relative to the views and sentiments I entertain, as an individual, and which I am able to say from personal knowledge are the sentiments of others, you are at liberty to give them publicity in the columns of the *Advocate.* In one respect I am prompted to this course in consequence of many Elders having gone into the Southern States, besides there being now many in that country who have already embraced the fulness of the Gospel, as revealed through the Book of Mormon. I have learned by experience that the enemy of truth does not slumber, nor cease his exertions to bias the minds of communities against the servants of the Lord, by stirring up the indignation of men upon all matters of importance or interest; therefore I fear that the sound might go out, that "an Abolitionist" had held forth several times to this community, and that the public feeling was not aroused to create mobs or disturbances, leaving the impression that all he said was concurred in, and received as Gospel, and the word of salvation. I am happy to say that no violence, or breach of the public peace, was attempted; so far from this, all, except a very few, attended to their own vocations, and left the gentleman to hold forth his own arguments to nearly naked walls. I am aware that many, who profess to preach the Gospel, complain against their brethren of the same faith, who reside in the South, and are ready to withdraw the hand of fellowship, because they will not renounce the principle of slavery, and raise their voice against every thing of the kind. This must be a tender point, and one which should call forth the candid reflections of all men, and more especially before they advance in an opposition calculated to lay waste the fair states of the South, and let loose upon the world a community of people, who might, peradventure, overrun our country, and violate the most sacred principles of human society, chastity and virtue.

No one will pretend to say that the people of the free states are as capable of knowing the evils of slavery, as those who hold slaves. If slavery be an evil, who could we expect would first learn it: Would the people of the free states, or the people of the slave states? All must readily admit, that the latter would first learn this fact. If the fact were learned first by those immediately concerned, who would be more capable than they of prescribing a remedy? And besides, are not those who hold slaves, persons of ability, discernment and candor? Do they not expect to give an account at the bar of God for their conduct in this life? It may no doubt with propriety be said that many who hold slaves live without the fear of God before their eyes; but the same may be said of many in the free states. Then who is to be the judge in this matter? So long, then, as the people of the free states, are not interested in the freedom of the slaves, in any other way than upon the mere abstract principles of equal rights, and of the Gospel; and are ready to admit that there are men of piety, who reside in the South, who are immediately concerned, and until *they* complain and call for assistance, why not cease this clamor, and no further urge the slave to acts of murder, and the master to vigorous discipline, rendering both miserable, and unprepared to pursue that course which might otherwise lead them both to better their conditions? I do not believe that the people of the North have any more right to say that the South *shall not* hold slaves, than the South have to say the North shall.

And further, what benefit will it ever be to the slaves for persons to run over the free states, and excite indignation against their masters in the minds of thousands and tens of thousands, who understand nothing relative to their circumstances, or conditions? I mean particularly those who have never traveled in the South, and who in all their lives have scarcely ever seen a negro.

How any community can ever be excited with the chatter of such persons, boys and others, who are too indolent to obtain their living by honest industry, and are incapable of pursuing any occupation of a professional nature, is unaccountable to me; and when I see persons in the free states, signing documents against slavery, it is no less, in my mind, than an army of influence, and a declaration of hostilities, against the people of the South. What course can sooner divide our union?

After having expressed myself so freely upon this subject, I do not doubt, but those who have been forward in raising their voices against the South, will cry out against me as being uncharitable, unfeeling, unkind, and wholly unacquainted with the Gospel of Christ. It is my privilege then to name certain passages from the Bible, and examine the teachings of the ancients upon the matter as the fact is uncontrovertible that the first mention we have of slavery is found in the Holy Bible, pronounced by a man who was perfect in his generation, and walked with God. And so far from that prediction being averse to the mind of God, it remains as a lasting monument of the decree of Jehovah, to the shame and confusion of all who have cried out against the South, in consequence of their holding the sons of Ham in servitude. "And he said, Cursed be Canaan; a servant of servants shall he be unto his brethren." "Blessed be the Lord God of Shem; and Canaan shall be his servant" (Gen. ix: 25, 26).

Trace the history of the world from this notable event down to this day, and you will find the fulfillment of this singular prophecy. What could have been the design of the Almighty in this singular occurrence is not for me to say; but I can say, the curse is not yet taken off from the sons of Canaan, neither will be until it is affected by as great a power as caused it to come; and the people who interfere the least with the purposes of God in this matter, will come under the least condemnation before Him; and those who are determined to pursue a course, which shows an opposition, and a feverish restlessness against the decrees of the Lord, will learn, when perhaps it is too late for their own good, that God can do His own work, without the aid of those who are not dictated by His counsel.

I must not pass ever a notice of the history of Abraham, of whom so much is spoken in the Scripture. If we can credit the account, God conversed with him from time to time, and directed him in the way he should walk, saying, I am the Almighty; walk before me, and be thou perfect." Paul says the Gospel was preached to this man. And it is further said, that he had sheep and oxen, men-servants and maid-servants, etc. From this I conclude, that if the principle had been an evil one, in the midst of the communications made to this holy man, he would have been instructed to that effect, and if he was instructed against holding men servants and maid-servants, he never ceased to do it; consequently must have incurred the displeasure of the Lord, and thereby lost His blessings; which was not the fact.

Some may urge that the names man servant and maid-servant, only mean hired persons, who were at liberty to leave their masters or employers at any time. But we can easily settle this point, by turning to the history of Abraham's descendants, when governed by a law from the mouth of Jehovah Himself. I know that when an Israelite had been brought into servitude, in consequence of debt, or otherwise, at the seventh year he went from the task of his former master, or employer; but to no other people or nation was this granted in the law of Israel. And if after a man had served six years, he did not wish to be free, then the master was to bring him unto the judges—bore his ear with an awl, and that man was "to serve him forever." The conclusion I draw from this, is, that this people were led and governed by revelation, and if such a law was wrong, God only is to be blamed, and abolitionists are not responsible.

Now, before proceeding any farther, I wish to ask one or two questions: Were the Apostles men of God, and did they preach the Gospel? I have no doubt that those who believe the Bible, will admit that they were; and that they also knew the mind and will of God concerning what they wrote to the churches, which they were instrumental in building up. This being admitted, the matter can be put to rest without much argument, if we look at a few items in the New Testament. Paul says: "Servants be obedient to them that are your masters according to the flesh, with fear and trembling, in singleness of your heart, as unto Christ; not with eyeservice as men-pleasers; but as the servants of Christ, doing the will of God from the heart; with good will doing service, as to the Lord, and not to men: knowing that whatsoever good thing any man doeth, the same shall be received of the Lord, whether he be bond or free. And, ye masters, do the same things unto them, forbearing threatening: knowing that your Master also is in heaven: neither is there respect of persons with him" (Eph. vi: 5, 6, 7, 8, 9). Here is a lesson which might be profitable for all to learn; and the principle upon which the Church was anciently governed, is so plainly set forth, that an eye of truth might see and understand. Here certainly, are represented the master, and servant; and so far from instructions to the servant to leave his master, he is commanded to be in obedience, as unto the Lord; the master in turn, is required to treat him with kindness before God; understanding, at the same time, that he is to give an account. The hand of fellowship is not withdrawn from him in consequence of his having servants.

The same writer, in his first epistle to Timothy, the sixth chapter, and the first five verses, says,—"Let as many servants as are under the yoke count their own masters worthy of all honor, that the name of God and His doctrine be not blasphemed. And they that have believing masters, let them not despise them, because they are brethren; but rather do them service, because they are faithful and beloved, partakers of the benefit. These things teach and exhort. If any man teach otherwise, and consent not to wholesome words, even the words of our Lord Jesus Christ, and to the doctrine which is according to godliness; he is proud, knowing nothing, but doting about questions and strifes of words, whereof cometh envy, strife, railings, evil surmisings, perverse disputing of men of corrupt minds, and destitute of the truth, supposing that gain is godliness: from such withdraw thyself." This is so perfectly plain, that I see no need of comment. The Scripture stands for itself; and I believe that these men were better qualified to teach the will of God. than all the abolitionists in the world·

Before closing this communication, I beg leave to drop a word to the traveling Elders. You know, brethren, that great responsibility rests upon you; and that you are accountable to God, for all you teach the world. In my opinion, you will do well to search the Book of Covenants, in which you will see the belief of the Church, concerning masters and servants. All men are to be taught to repent; but we have no right to interfere with slaves, contrary to the mind and will of their masters. In fact it would be much better, and more prudent, not to preach at all to slaves, until after their masters are converted, and then teach the masters to use them with kindness; remembering that they are accountable to God, and the servants are bound to serve their masters with singleness of heart, without murmuring.

I do most sincerely hope that no one who is authorized from this Church to preach the Gospel, will so far depart from the Scriptures, as to be found stirring up strife and sedition against our brethren of the South. Having spoken frankly and freely, I leave all in the hands of God, who will direct all things for His glory, and the accomplishment of His work. Praying that God may spare you to do much good in this life, I subscribe myself your brother in the Lord,

JOSEPH SMITH, JUN.

CHAPTER XXXI.

PREDICTION OF THE PROPHET'S GRANDPARENTS—AGITATION
FOR THE REMOVAL OF THE SAINTS FROM CLAY COUNTY,
MISSOURI.

THE remainder of this month [April] and May also, was devoted to the spiritual interests of the brethren; and particularly in devising ways and means to build up Kirtland.

May 10.—Brother Heber C. Kimball came to me for counsel, to know whether he should go into the vineyard to proclaim the Gospel, or go to school. I told him he might do either that he should choose, for the Lord would bless him. He chose to go into the vineyard; and immediately went down through the State of New York, into Vermont, his native State. He stopped a short time, and then returned to the city of Ogdensburg, on the St. Lawrence river, where he built up a church of twenty members. When about leaving that place, my father, and uncle John Smith, came to him, and blessed the church with patriarchal blessings. When they came to Brother Kimball, they were very much depressed in spirits, for when they came through the town of Potsdam, their brother, Jesse Smith, having a spite against them in consequence of their religion, swore out an execution against my father, and levied upon his horse and wagon; and to settle the affair, and get out of his clutches, my uncle, Silas Smith, (who had returned to that place on private business) stepped forward and paid

Labors of Elder Heber C. Kimball.

fifty dollars, in order that they might pursue their journey home.

May, 16.—President Oliver Cowdery having preferred, to the High Council, a charge of unchristianlike conduct against Wilkins J. Salisbury, the Council assembled in the Lord's House, when it was proved that he had so conducted himself as to bring unnecessary persecution on me; that he had neglected his family, leaving them without wood, without provisions, or telling them where he was going, or when he would return; that he used strong drink and had been intimate with other women.

Dealing with Sundry Transgressors.

Elder Salisbury confessed his propensity for tale-bearing, and drinking strong liquor, but denied the other charges. The Council decided that he could no longer be an Elder or member in the Church until there was a thorough reformation.

Charges of unchristianlike conduct were also preferred against Sisters Hannah Brown, and L. Elliot. They confessed they had been guilty of telling falsehoods.

The Council reproved them, but permitted them to retain their standing in the Church.

The Council then withdrew fellowship from Elder Charles Kelly.*

My cousin, Elias Smith, arrived from St. Lawrence county, New York, with the information that his father and family, and Uncle Silas and family, were on their way to Kirtland, and that my grandmother [Mary Duty Smith, wife of Asael Smith] was at Fairport.

May 17.—I went in company with my brother Hyrum, in a carriage to Fairport, and brought home my grandmother, Mary Smith, aged ninety-theree years. She had not been baptized, on account of the opposition of Jesse Smith, her eldest son, who has always been an euemy to the work. She had

Arrival of the Prophet's Relatives in Kirtland.

---

* Charles Kelly was a member of Zion's Camp, also a member of the first quorum of Seventy. His offenses are named at page 444.

come five hundred miles to see her children, and knew all of us she had ever seen. She was much pleased at being introduced to her great grand-children, and expressed much pleasure and gratification on seeing me.

My grandfather, Asael Smith, long ago predicted that there would be a prophet raised up in his family, and my grandmother was fully satisfied that it was fulfilled in me. My grandfather Asael died in East Stockholm, St. Lawrence county, New York, after having received the Book of Mormon, and read it nearly through; and he declared that I was the very Prophet that he had long known would come in his family.

On the 18th, my uncle Silas Smith and family arrived from the east. My father, three of his brothers, and their mother, met the first time for many years. It was a happy day, for we had long prayed to see our grandmother and uncles in the Church.

On May 27, after a few days' visit with her children, which she enjoyed extremely well, my grandmother fell asleep without sickness, pain or regret. She breathed her last about sunset, and was buried in the burial ground near the Temple, after a funeral address had been delivered by Sidney Rigdon.* She had buried one daughter, Sarah; two Sons, Stephen and Samuel; and her husband, who died October 30, 1830, and left five sons and three daughters still living. At the death of my grandfather, who had kept a record, there were one hundred and ten children, grand children and great grand children. My uncle Stephen, and aunt Sarah, were buried side by side in the burial grounds in Royalton, Windsor county, Vermont. Stephen died July 25th, 1802, aged seventeen years, three months, and eleven days.

Death of the Prophet's Grandmother.

May 23.—The case of Elder Charles Kelly was again

---

* "She died firm in the faith of the Gospel, although she had never yielded obedience to any of its ordinances."—*Hist. of the Prophet Joseph, by Lucy Smith, ch. xii.*

brought before the High Council, then in session, and it
was proved that he left his family in a desti-
Case of
Chas. Kelley.   tute condition, about the time of the solemn
assembly, which, together with other unchristianlike conduct, led the Council to decide that he be
expelled from the Church.

Also Asael Perry was cut off from the Church for unchristianlike conduct.

Job L. Lewis was excommunicated, for treating the
Church with contempt.

May 17.—Died, in Kirtland, Miss Mary Smith, in
the thirty-fifth year of her age. The deceased was a
member of the Church of Latter-day Saints, and died in
the triumphs of faith.

June 2.—President Phelps wrote a letter from Liberty,
Missouri, to President Oliver Cowdery, from which I
make the following extracts:

Letter from W. W. Phelps to the Brethren in Kirtland.

Since I returned home to Missouri, I have been out on two expeditions, examining the regions of the "Far West." Soon after our
return, Bishop Partridge and myself passed from Liberty to the north-
west corner of Clay county, and examined the mills and streams, and
country around Mr. Smith's, generally denominated "Yankee Smith."
It is customary, you know, for the sake of *provincialism*, among nations,
kindreds and people, to nick-name [people] by their religion, or province
or ancestry; so that one can be distinguished by being an Israelite, a Ca-
naanite, a Christian, a "Mormon," a Methodist, or a Corn Cracker, or a
Mighty Hunter, &c., according to fancy or favor.

From Mr. Smith's, we proceeded north-easterly through some
timber and some prairie to Plattsburg, the county seat for Clinton
county, "a smart little town," containing from fifteen to twenty hewed
log cabins, and a two-story court house, thirty-two feet square. This
town is located on the west side of Horse and Smith's fork of the Little
Platte, contiguous to the timber on these streams, twenty-five miles
north of Liberty. The timber, mill, and water privileges may answer
a very small population, but for a large population they would be
nothing. There are now three stores, and soon will be four. Clinton
county is mostly prairie, with here and there a few fringes or spots of
timber on the creeks that run into the Little Platte and Grand River.

From this town we made the best course we could to the waters of Grand River. We had a "sort of road" towards Busby Fork, then we had to contend with naked prairie, patches of scrubby timber, deep banked creeks and branches, together with a rainy morning, and no compass; but with the blessing of the Lord, we came to "some house" in the afternoon, and passed into Ray county. On Shoal creek, where there is water, there are some tolerable mill sites; but the prairies— those "old clearings," peering one over another, as far as the eye can glance, flatten all common calculation as to timber for boards, rails, or future wants, for a thick population, according to the natural reasoning of men.

What the design of our heavenly Father was, or is, as to these vast prairies of the Far West, I know no further than we have revelation. The Book of Mormon terms them, the land of desolation; and when I get into a prairie so large that I am out of sight of timber, just as a seaman is "out of sight of land on the ocean," I have to exclaim— What are man and his works, compared with the Almighty and His creations? Who hath viewed His everlasting fields? Who hath counted His buffaloes? Who hath seen all His deer on a thousand prairies? The pinks variegate these wide-spread lawns, without the hand of man to aid them, and the bees of a thousand groves banquet on the flowers, unobserved, and sip the honey-dews of heaven. Nearly every skirt of timber to the state line on the north, I am informed, has some one in it. The back settlers are generally very honorable, and more hospitable than any people I ever saw, you are in most instances, welcome to the best they have.

W. W. PHELPS.

The High Council assembled in the Lord's house in Kirtland on the 16th of June, Presidents Sidney Rigdon, and Frederick G Williams presiding, to investigate the charges of "A want of benevolence to the poor, and charity to the Church," which I had previously preferred against Brother Preserved Harris and Elder Isaac McWithy. After a full and lengthy investigation, the Council decided that the charges were fully sustained against Preserved Harris, and that the hand of fellowship be withdrawn from him, until he shall see that the course he is pursuing is contrary to the Gospel of Jesus.

Case of Preserved Harris and Isaac McWithy.

In the pleas of the Councilors, in the case of Elder Mc

Withy, they decided that the charges had been fully sustained; after which, I spoke in my turn as accuser, and stated that I called on the accused, in company with President Oliver Cowdery, for money to send up to Zion, but could get none; afterwards saw him, and asked him if he would sell his farm. He at first seemed willing, and wished to build up Zion. He pleaded excuse in consequence of his liberality to the poor. We offered him three thousand dollars for his farm, would give him four or five hundred dollars to take him to Zion, and settle him there, and an obligation for the remainder, with good security and interest. He went and told Father Lyon that we demanded all his property, and so we lost four or five hundred dollars; because the accused told him [Lyon] such a story, [that] he calculated to keep it [the aforesaid four or five hundred dollars] himself.

The accused, Elder McWithy, arose and said it was the first time he had been called upon to clear himself before a High Council. He complained of being called contrary to the rules of the Gospel, before the Council. The president decided that as the case was now before the Council, this pl a could not now be urged, but should have been made in the beginning. Elder McWithy pleaded that he had relieved the wants of the poor, and did so many good things that he was astonished that he should hear such things as he had heard today, because he did not give all he had got to one man. If he had done wrong he asked forgiveness of God and the Church.

During the quarter ending the 3rd of June, 1836, two hundred and forty-four Elders', eleven Priests', three Teachers', and five Deacons' licenses were recorded in the license Records, in Kirtland, Ohio.

Departure
of the
Patriarch and
John Smith
on a Mission.

June 22.—My father and Uncle John Smith started on a mission to visit the branches of the Church in the Eastern States, to set them in order, and confer on the brethren their patriarchal blessings. I took my mother and Aunt Clarissa (my Uncle John's wife,) in a carriage, and accompanied them to Painsville, where we procured a bottle of wine, broke bread, ate and drank, and parted after the ancient order, with the blessings of God.

June 28.—Elder Warren Parrish wrote from Hickman county, Tennessee, stating that:—

Many citizens of the county of Benton, and some of Carroll had met in convention, headed by a Methodist priest, who was called to the chair, and the county clerk appointed secretary. They drew up resolutions to drive all the "Mormon preachers from their coast," signed by the sheriff and many who were sworn to be civil, peace-officers, also colonels, majors, &c. We enjoyed our meeting unmolested at Brother Utley's, on Saturday, the 19th instant. Hundreds had entered into the conspiracy. In the afternoon, a little before sunset, a company of some forty or fifty men made their appearance; some on foot, others mounted, two on a horse, with guns, sticks, clubs, &c. They were led by a sheriff, colonel, first and second major, other officers, and a Methodist priest, with a gun on his shoulder.

The sheriff informed us that he had states' warrant for David W. Patten, Warren Parrish, and Wilford Woodruff; issued on complaint of the Methodist priest, Matthew Williams, chairman as above; who swore that we had put forth the following false and pretended prophecy; viz.: that Christ would come the second time before this generation passes away; also that four individuals should receive the Holy Ghost within four and twenty hours. The company consisted, as we were informed, of Baptists, Methodists, Presbyterians, liars, drunkards, hog and horse thieves. So determined were they, to force us off at that late hour, that it was with much difficulty we could prevail on them to show us any lenity; however, they protracted the time of our appearance at court until Tuesday by giving our bond, with surety of two brethren, in the sum of one thousand dollars.

They intended to have led us into the woods, under the dark curtain of night with the pretension of taking us before the magistrate that they might the better execute their diabolical designs upon us.

On Tuesday, in company with about twenty brethren and warm friends, who were ready and willing to lay down their lives for us, we went before our rulers, and found about one hundred persons assembled, armed with guns, pistols, dirks, clubs, sticks, &c. At a late hour we prevailed on the sheriff to have the court called, which consisted of three magistrates, one of whom was rejected from the judgment-seat, because some of his family were members of our Church.

The sheriff, with leave of court, divested us of our arms, consisting of walking sticks and a pocket knife. A man by the name of Perkins, (who report says, had run his county for hog stealing, and also had been guilty of concealing a stolen horse, for which he had lost part of his nose,) was appointed by the court to act as states' attorney; or in other words mob solicitor-general, to abuse the innocent and screen the guilty.

After the conspirators had witnessed against us, the court refused to hear any testimony on our part, being controlled by the bandits. Perkins made a plea against us, but we were not permitted to reply. The verdict of the court was, that they concluded that the charges preferred against us had been sustained, and that we were bound over to court for trial. Our accusers did not attempt to prove that those who were promised the Holy Ghost did not receive it; and the candid can judge whether he who prophesies that Christ will come the second time in this generation, is a false prophet. Also our complainant testified that these crimes, were committed in 1834, and it is a well known fact that Elder Woodruff, whose name is on the warrant, (though not arrested,) was not in this state until 1835. So much for an oath from a Methodist priest.

While the court was preparing our bonds, another warrant was served on Elder Patten; the mob without, and the mob within, whose intoxicating zeal had arisen to its zenith, were threatening our lives, and seemed only to wait the dark shades of night, which were fast gathering round, to cover them, while they should wreak their hands in our blood; the influence of our friends, as instruments in the hands of our God, kept this gathering storm from bursting upon our heads. About this time the sheriff proposed to us that if we would leave the county in ten days, and pay the cost, they would set us at liberty; at the same time informing us it was the only way to escape the hands of the mob, who were hardly restrained from acts of violence. One of the brethren present offered to pay the cost, and all advised us to accept the offer; which, in itself, proved that we were innocent of any crime, although in its nature most insulting.

(Signed)   WARREN PARRISH.

Minutes of a Public Meeting at Liberty, Missouri.

On the 29th of June, a respectable number of the citizens being previously notified of the meeting, met at the court-house, in the town of Liberty, Missouri. On motion, John Bird was called to the chair, and John F. Doherty appointed secretary. The object of the meeting, was, by request of the chair, explained in a few appropriate remarks, by Colonel Wood; when on motion of Colonel William T. Wood, a committee of nine was appointed to draft resolutions expressive of the sense of this meeting; whereupon the following gentlemen were chosen—namely: John Thornton, Esq., Peter Rogers, Esq., Andrew Robertson, Esq., James T. V. Thompson, Colonel W. T. Wood, Doctor Woodson, J. Moss, James H. Hughes, Esq., David R. Atchison, Esq., and A. W. Doniphan, Esq., who retired and in a short time returned and made, through their chairman, Colonel John Thornton, the following unanimous report, which was read:

REPORT.

It is apparent to every reflecting mind that a crisis has arisen in this country, that requires the deep, cool, dispassionate consideration, and immediate action of every lover of peace, harmony and good order. We cannot conceal from ourselves the fact that at this moment the clouds of civil war are rolling up their fearful masses, and hanging over our devoted country. Solemn, dark and terrible. This painful state of things has been produced mainly by the rapid and increasing emigration of that people commonly called Mormons, during the last few months. It is known to all, that in November, 1833, these people were expelled from their homes in Jackson county, without money, without property, without the means of subsistence for themselves, their wives and their children, and like Noah's dove, without a resting place for their feet.

They came to our county thus friendless and penniless, (seeking as they said) but a temporary asylum from the storm of persecution by which they were then buffeted. Their destitute and miserable condition, at that inclement season of the year, excited the deep sympathies of the philanthropic and hospitable citizens of this county; and notwithstanding the thousand reports that were borne on the wings of the wind, charging them with almost every crime known to the laws of our country, yet our feelings of kindness and sympathy for human suffering prevailed over every obstacle, and they were received with friendship and treated with toleration, and often with remarks of peculiar kindness. They always declared that they looked not upon this county as their home, but as a temporary asylum; and that, whenever, a respectable portion of the citizens of this county should request it, they would promptly leave us in peace as they found us.

That period has now arrived. Duty to ourselves, to our families, and to the best interests of our country, requires at our hands, to demand the fulfillment of that pledge. They are charged by those who are opposed to them with an unfriendly determination to violate that pledge. Their rapid emigration, their large purchases, and offers to purchase lands, the remarks of the ignorant and imprudent portion of them, that this country is destined by heaven to be theirs are received and looked upon, by a large portion of this community, as strong and convincing proofs that they intend to make this county their permanent home, the centre and general rendezvous of their people.

These are some of the reasons why these people have become objects of the deepest hatred and detestation to many of our citizens. They are eastern men, whose manners, habits, customs, and even dialect, are essentially different from our own. They are *non*-slaveholders, and opposed to slavery, which in this peculiar period, when abolitionism has reared its deformed and haggard visage in our land, is well calculated to excite deep and abiding prejudices in any community where slavery is tolerated and protected.

In addition to all this, they are charged, as they have hitherto been, with keeping up a constant communication with our Indian tribes on our frontiers, with declaring, even from the pulpit, that the Indians are a part of God's chosen people, and are destined by heaven to inherit this land, in common with themselves. We do not vouch for the correctness of these statements; but whether they are true or false, their effect has been the same in exciting our community. In times of greater tranquility, such ridiculous remarks might well be regarded as the offspring of frenzied fanaticism; but at this time, our defenseless situation on the frontier, the bloody disasters of our fellow citizens in Florida, and other parts of the South, all tend to make a portion of our citizens regard such sentiments with horror, if not alarm. These and many other causes, have combined to raise a prejudice against them; and a feeling of hostility, that the first spark may, and we deeply fear will, ignite into all the horrors and desolations of a civil war, the worst evil that can befall any country.

We therefore feel it our duty to come forward, as mediators, and use every means in our power to prevent the occurrence of so great an evil. As the most efficacious means to arrest the evil, we urge on the Mormons to use every means to put an immediate stop to the emigration of their people to this county. We earnestly urge them to seek some other abiding place, where the manners, the habits, and customs of the people will be more consonant with their own.

For this purpose we would advise them to explore the territory of Wisconsin. This country is peculiarly suited to their conditions and their wants. It is almost entirely unsettled; they can there procure large bodies of land together, where there are no settlements, and none to interfere with them. It is a territory in which slavery is prohibited, and it is settled entirely with emigrants from the North and East.

The religious tenets of this people are so different from the present churches of the age, that they always have, and always will, excite deep prejudices against them in any populous country where they may locate. We, therefore, in a spirit of frank and friendly kindness, do advise them to seek a home where they may obtain large and separate bodies of land, and have a community of their own. We further say to them, if they regard their own safety and welfare, if they regard the welfare of their families, their wives and children, they will ponder with deep and solemn reflection on this friendly admonition.

If they have one spark of gratitude, they will not willingly plunge a people into civil war, who held out to them the friendly hand of assistance in that hour of dark distress, when there was few to say God save them. We can only say to them if they still persist in the blind course they have heretofore followed in flooding the country with their people, that we fear and firmly believe that an immediate civil war is the inevitable consequence. We know that there is not one among us who thirsts for the blood of that people.

We do not contend that we have the least right, under the Constitution and laws of the country, to expel them by force. But we would indeed be blind, if we did not foresee that the first blow that is struck, at this moment of deep excitement, must and will speedily involve every individual in a war, bearing ruin, woe, and desolation in its course. It matters but little how, where, or by whom, the war may begin, when the work of destruction commences, we must all be borne onward by the storm, or crushed beneath its fury. In a civil war, when our homes are the theatre on which it is fought, there can be no neutrals; let our opinions be what they may, we must fight in self-defense.

We want nothing, we ask nothing, we would have nothing from this people, we only ask them, for their own safety, and for ours, to take the least of the two evils. Most of them are destitute of land, have but little property, are late emigrants to this country, without relations, friends, or endearing ties to bind them to this land. At the risk of such imminent peril to them and to us, we request them to leave us, when their crops are gathered, their business settled, and they have made every suitable preparation to remove. Those who have forty acres of land, we are willing should remain until they can dispose of it without loss, if it should require years. But we urge, most strongly urge, that emigration cease, and cease immediately, as nothing else can or will allay for a moment, the deep excitement that is now unhappily agitating this community.

If the Mormons will comply with these friendly requisitions, we will use every exertion among our own citizens, to arrest this evil before it is forever too late; but if they are disregarded, we can promise neither them nor ourselves, a long continuation of the blessings of peace and harmony.

1st. Therefore be it Resolved by this meeting, that we view with feelings of the deepest regret the present unhappy situation of our country.

2nd. That it is the fixed and settled conviction of this meeting, that unless the people commonly called Mormons will agree to stop immediately the emigration of their people to this county, and take measures to remove themselves from it, a civil war is inevitable.

3rd. That a committee of ten be appointed to make known to the leaders of that people, the views of this meeting, and to urge upon them the propriety of acceding to these propositions.

4th. The said committee consisting of Andrew Robertson, Michael Arthur, Littlebury Sublet, John Baxter, James M. Hughes, W. J. Moss, John Bird, Peter Rogers, W. T. Wood and J. T. V. Thompson, who shall meet on the morrow at the house of Mr. Cowan, and confer with the Mormons, and report at this meeting, as soon thereafter as convenient, the reply of the Mormons to these requisitions.

5th. That if the Mormons agree to these propositions, we will use every means in our power to allay the excitement among our own citizens, and to get them to await the result of these things. That it is the opinion of this meeting that the recent emigrants among the Mormons should take measures to leave this county immediately, as they have no crops on hand, and nothing to lose by continuing their journey to some more friendly land. On motion of Wm. T. Wood, the preamble and resolutions were unanimously adopted. Be it resolved that this meeting adjourn until Saturday next.

JOHN BIRD, Chairman,
JOHN F. DOHERTY, Secretary.

Minutes of a Public Meeting of the Saints in Clay County, Missouri, Held to Consider the Proposition of the Citizens of Clay County that the Latter-day Saints Move into another Part of the State.

July 1, 1836. At a very large meeting of the Elders of the Church of Latter-day Saints, assembled in Clay county, Missouri, W. W. Phelps was called to the chair, and John Corrill appointed secretary. The preamble and resolutions from a meeting of citizens of the 29th ultimo, was read, and a committee of twelve, viz., Edward Partridge, Isaac Morley, Lyman Wight, Thomas B. Marsh, Elias Higby, Calvin Bebee, Isaac Hitchcock, Isaac Higby, Samuel Bent, Titus Billings, James Emmet, and R. Evans, were appointed, who retired, and after a short time reported the following preamble and resolutions:

Resolved, that we (the "Mormons," so called), are grateful for the kindness which has been shown to us by the citizens of Clay county since we have resided with them; and being desirous for peace, and wishing the good rather than the ill-will of mankind, we will use all honorable means to allay the excitement, and so far as we can, remove any foundation for jealousies against us as a people. We are aware that many rumors prejudicial to us as a society are afloat, and time only can prove their falsity to the world at large.

We deny having claim to this, or any other county, or country, further than we shall purchase the land with money, or more than the Constitution and laws allow us as free American citizens. We have taken no part for or against slavery; but are opposed to the abolitionists, and consider that men have a right to hold slaves or not, according to law.

We believe it just to preach the Gospel to the nations of the earth, and warn the righteous to save themselves from the corruptions of the world; but we do not believe it right to interfere with bond-servants, nor preach the Gospel to them, nor meddle with nor influence them in the least to cause them to be dissatisfied with their situation in this life; thereby jeopardizing the lives of men. Such interference we believe to be unlawful and unjust, and dangerous to the peace of every government allowing human beings to be held in servitude.

We deny holding any communications with the Indians; and mean to hold ourselves as ready to defend our country against their barbarous ravages, as any other people. We believe that all men are bound to sustain and uphold the respective governments in which they reside, while protected in their inherent and inalienable rights by the laws of such governments; and that sedition and rebellion are unbecoming every citizen thus protected, and should be punished accordingly. It is needless to enter into any further detail of our faith, or mention our sufferings; therefore—

First. Resolved: For the sake of friendship, and to be in a covenant of peace with the citizens of Clay county, and they to be in a covenant of peace with us, notwithstanding the necessary loss of property, and expense we incur in moving, we comply with the requisitions of their resolutions in leaving Clay county, as explained by the preamble accompanying the same; and that we will use our exertions to have the Church do the same; and that we will also exert ourselves to stop the tide of emigration of our people to this county.

Second. Resolved: That we accept the friendly offer verbally tendered to us by the committee yesterday, to assist us in selecting a location, and removing to it.

Third. Resolved, unanimously: That this meeting accept and adopt the above preamble and resolutions, which are here presented by the committee.

Fourth. Resolved: That Thomas B. Marsh, Lyman Wight, and Samuel Bent, be a committee to carry the minutes of these proceedings to the meeting of the citizens of Clay county, to be held tomorrow at Liberty.   The foregoing resolutions were unanimously adopted by the meeting.

W. W. PHELPS, Chairman,
JOHN CORRILL, Secretary.

Mtnutes of the Second Meeting of the Citizens of Clay County.

The citizens of Clay county met pursuant to adjournment. The chairman and secretary resumed their stations, when the committee appointed by the pulic meeting of the citizens at the court house, in Liberty, on the 29th ultimo, reported through their chairman, W. J. Moss, the foregoing preamble and resolutions of the Elders of the Church of Latter-day Saints, on the 1st instant, whereupon it was

Resolved, That this meeting do accept and receive the reply of the Mormons to the resolution passed on Wednesday, the 29th of June, as perfectly satisfactory.

Be it further *Resolved* by this meeting, that we will use our utmost endeavors to carry into effect the object contained in the preamble and resolutions passed on Wednesday, the 29th, as agreed to by the Mormons.

Be it further *Resolved*, That we urge it on our fellow citizens to keep the peace towards the Mormons, as good faith, justice, morality and religion require.

Be it further *Resolved*, That a committee of ten persons, two in each township, be appointed to raise money by subscription to aid those of the Mormons who may from necessity require it, to leave this county.

Resolved, That Samuel Tillery Jeremiah Minger and Abraham Shafer be appointed a committee to receive the pecuniary aid by subscription for the purpose of aiding the poor persons that may belong to the Mormons in removing from this county to their place of abode, and that the Elders of the Church be requested to report the above-named persons to the aforesaid committee, who will judge of the proofs and facts entitling the Mormons to pecuniary aid, and appropriate the funds accordingly.

Resolved, That the said committee be authorized to employ some suitable person to accompany those that may wish to examine a new country. It is also understood that if the money which may be received by the committee is not appropriated for the purpose above named, it shall be refunded back in proportion to the amount subscribed.

Resolved, That the chair appoint five persons in each township to carry the object of the above resolutions into effect.

The following gentlemen were then appointed in the different townships: For Liberty township, John Thornton, Joel Turnham, Peter

Rogers, John Bird, David R. Atchison; for Fishing River township, Elisha Cameron, E. Price, G. Withers, M. Welton, James Kazey; for Platte township, T. C. Gordon, S. Harris, W. Owen, L. Rollins, I. Marsh; for Washington township, B. Riley, S. Crawford, T. Findley, G. McIlvaine, P. Y. G. Bartee; for Gallatin township, D. Dale, N. Nash, William Todd, B. Ricketts, R. Forboin.

Be it further *Resolved*, That this meeting recommend the Mormons to the good treatment of the citizens of the adjoining counties. We also recommend the inhabitants of the neighboring counties to assist the Mormons in selecting some abiding place for their people where they will be, in a measure, the only occupants; and where none will be anxious to molest them.

Resolved, That the proceedings of this meeting be handed over to the publishers of the *Far West* with a request that it be printed, which was severally read and unanimously adopted, and meeting adjourned.

JOHN BIRD, Chairman,

JOHN F. DOHERTY, Secretary.

LIBERTY, July 2nd, 1836.

Letter from the Brethren at Kirtland to the Brethren in Missouri.

KIRTLAND, July 25th, 1836.

To W. W. Phelps and Others:

DEAR BRETHREN:—Yours of the first inst., accompanying the proceedings of a public meeting held by the people of Clay county, was duly received. We are sorry that this disturbance has broken out, but we do not consider it our fault. You are better acquainted with circumstances than we are, and, of course, have been directed by wisdom in your moves relative to leaving the county.

We forward you our letter to Mr. Thornton and others that you may know all that we have said. We advise that you be not the first aggressors. Give no occasion, and if the people will let you, dispose of your property, settle your affairs, and go in peace. You have thus far had an asylum, and now seek another, as God may direct.

Relative to your going to Wisconsin, we cannot say, we should think if you could stop short, in peace, you had better do so. You know our feelings relative to not giving the first offense, and also of protecting your wives and little ones in case a mob should seek their lives. We shall publish the proceedings of the public meeting, with your answer, as well as our letter. We mean that the world shall know all things as they transpire. If we are persecuted and driven men shall know it.

Be wise; let prudence dictate all your counsels; preserve peace with all men, if possible; stand by the Constitution of your country; observe its principles; and above all, show yourselves men of God, worthy citizens, and we doubt not, the community, ere long,will do you justice, and rise in indignation against those who are the instigators of your sufferings and afflictions.

In the bonds of brotherly love we subscribe ourselves, as ever,

> JOSEPH SMITH, JUN.,
> SIDNEY RIGDON,
> OLIVER COWDERY,
> F. G. WILLIAMS,
> HYRUM SMITH.

The letter to Mr. Thornton referred to above was as follows:

KIRTLAND, GEAUGA COUNTY, OHIO,

July 25, 1836.

To John Thornton, Esq., Peter Rogers, Esq., Andrew Robertson, Esq., James T. V. Thompson, Esq., Colonel William T. Wood, Doctor Woodson, I. Moss, James H. Hughes, Esq., David R. Atchison, Esq., and A. W. Doniphan, Esq.:

GENTLEMEN:—We have just perused, with feelings of deep interest, an article in the *Far West*, printed at Liberty, Clay county, Missouri, containing the proceeding of a public meeting of the citizens of said county on the subject of an excitement now prevailing among you, occasioned either from false reports against the Church of Latter-day Saints, or from the fact that said Church is considered dangerous to the welfare of your country; and will, if suffered among you under existing circumstances, cause the ties of peace and friendship, so desirable among all men, to be burst asunder, and bring war and desolation upon your own pleasant homes.

While rumor is afloat with her accustomed cunning, and while public opinion is fast rising, like a flood tide against the members of the Church, we cannot but admire the candor with which your preambles and resolutions were clothed, as presented to the citizens of Clay county on the 29th of June last; though, as you expressed in your report to said meeting, "We do not contend that we have the least right, under the Constitution and laws of the country, to expel them by force," yet communities may be at times unexpectedly thrown into a situation when wisdom, prudence, and that first item in nature's law, self defense, would dictate that the responsible and influential part [of a community] should step forward and guide the public mind in a course to save difficulty, preserve rights and spare the innocent blood from staining that soil so dearly purchased with the lives and fortunes of our fathers. As you have come forward as "mediators" to prevent the effusion of blood and save disasters consequent upon civil war, we take this opportunity to present to you, though strangers, and through you, if you wish, to the people of Clay county, our heart-felt gratitude for every kindness rendered our friends in affliction, when driven from their peaceful homes; and to yourselves, also, for the prudent course in the present excited state of your community; but in doing this, justice to ourselves, as communicants of that Church to which our friends belong, and duty towards them as acquaintances and former fellow citizens, require us to say something to exonerate them from the foul charges brought against them, to deprive them of their constitutional privileges and drive them from the face of society.

They have been charged, in consequence of the whims and vain notions of some few uninformed [persons], with claiming that upper country, [north-western Missouri], and that ere long they were to possess it at all hazards and in defiance of all consequences. This is unjust and far from having a foundation in truth; a thing not expected or looked for—not desired by this society as a people, and where the idea could have originated is unknown to us. We do not, neither did we ever, insinuate a thing of this kind, or hear it from the leading men of the society now in your country. There is nothing in all our religious faith to warrant it, but on the contrary, the most strict injunctions to live in obedience to the laws and follow peace with all men; and we doubt not but a recurrence to the Jackson county difficulties with our friends will fully satisfy you, that at least heretofore such has been the course followed by them, that instead of fighting for their own rights they have sacrificed them for a season to wait the redress guaranteed in the law and so anxiously looked for at a time distant from this.

We have been, and are still, clearly under the conviction that had our friends been disposed they might have maintained their possessions in Jackson county. They might have resorted to the same barbarous means with their neighbors, throwing down dwellings, threatening lives, driving innocent women and children from their homes, and thereby have annoyed their enemies equally at least; but to their credit—and it must ever remain upon the page of time to their honor—this they did not do. They had possessions, they had homes, they had sacred rights, and more still, they had helpless, harmless innocence, with an approving conscience that they had violated no law of their country or their God to urge them forword; but to show to all that they were willing to forego these for the peace of their country they tamely submitted, and have since been wanderers among strangers (though hospitable) without homes. We think these sufficient reasons to show to your patriotic minds that our friends, instead of having a wish to expel a community by force of arms, would suffer their rights to be taken from them before shedding blood.

Another charge brought against our friends is that of being dangerous in societies "where slavery is tolerated and practiced." Without occupying time here we refer you to the April (1836) number of the *Latter-day Saints' Messenger and Advocate*, printed at this place, a copy of which we forward to each of you. From the length of time which has elapsed since its publication, you can easily see it was put forth for no other reason than to correct the public mind generally, without a reference or expectation of any excitement of the nature of the one now in your county. Why we refer you particularly to this publication is because many of our friends who are now in the West were in this place when this paper made its appearance, and from personal observation gave it their decided approbation, and declared those sentiments to be their own in the fullest particular.

Another charge of great magnitude is brought against our friends in the West, that of "keeping up a constant communication with the Indian tribes on the frontier; with declaring even from the pulpit that the Indians are a part of God's chosen people, and are destined by heaven to inherit this land, in common with themselves." We know of nothing under the present aspect of our Indian relations calculated to arouse the fears of the people of the Upper Missouri more than a combination or influence of this nature; and we cannot look upon it as being other than one of the most subtle purposes of those whose feelings are embittered against our friends to turn the eye of suspicion upon them from every man who is acquainted with the barbarous cruelty of rude savages. Since a rumor was afloat that the western Indians were showing signs of war we have received frequent private letters from our friends who have not only expressed fears for their own safety, in case the Indians should break out, but a decided determination to be among the first to repel any invasion and defend the frontier from all hostilities. We mention the last fact because it was wholly uncalled for on our part and came previous to any excitement on the part of the people of Clay county against our friends and must definitely show that this charge is also untrue.

Another charge against our friends and one that is urged as a reason why they must immediately leave Clay county, is, that they are making, or are likely to make the same "their permanent home, the center and general rendezvous of their people." We have never understood such to be the purpose, wish, or design of this society; but on the contrary, have ever supposed that those who resided in Clay county only designed it as a temporary residence until the law and authority of our country should put them in the quiet possession of their homes in Jackson county; and such as had not possessions there could purchase to the entire satisfaction and interest of the people of Jackson county.

Having partially mentioned the leading objections urged against our friends, we would here add, that it has not been done with a view, on our part, to dissuade you from acting in strict conformity with your preamble and resolutions offered to the people of Clay county on the 29th ult., but from a sense of duty to a people embarrassed, persecuted and afflicted; for you are aware, gentlemen, that in times of excitement virtues are transformed into vices; acts, which in other cases and other circumstances would be considered upright and honorable, are interpreted contrary to their real intent and made objectionable and criminal; and from whom could we look for forbearance and compassion, with confidence and assurance, more than from those whose bosoms are warmed with those pure principles of patriotism with which you have been guided in the present instance, to secure the peace of your county and save a persecuted people from further violence and destruction?

It is said that our friends are poor; that they have but little or nothing to bind their feelings or wishes to Clay county, and that in consequence they have a less claim upon that county. We do not deny the fact that our friends are poor; but their persecutions have helped to render them so. While other men were peacefully following their vocations and extending their interests they have been deprived of the right of citizenship, prevented from enjoying their own, charged with violating the sacred principles of our Constitution and laws, made to feel the keenest aspersions of the tongue of slander, waded through all but death, and are now suffering under calumnies calculated to excite the indignation and hatred of every people among whom they dwell, thereby exposing them to destruction and inevitable ruin.

If a people, a community, or a society can accumulate wealth, increase in worldly fortune, improve in science and arts, rise to eminence in the eyes of the public, surmount these difficulties, so much as to bid defiance to poverty and wretchedness, it must be a new creation, a race of beings superhuman. But in all their poverty and wants we have yet to learn for the first time that our friends are not industrious and temperate; and wherein they have not always been the last to retaliate or resent an injury, and the first to overlook and forgive. We do not urge that there are no exceptions to be found; all communities, all societies and associations are cumbered with disorderly and less virtuous members—members who violate in a greater or less degree, the principles of the same; but this can be no just criterion by which to judge a whole society; and further still where a people are laboring under constant fear of being dispossessed; very little inducement is held out to excite them to be industrious.

We think, gentlemen, that we have pursued the subject far enough, and we here express to you, as we have in a letter accompanying this to our friends, our decided disapprobation to the idea of shedding blood, if any other course can be followed to avoid it; in which case, and which alone, we have urged upon our friends to desist, only in extreme cases of self defense; and in this case not to give the offense or provoke their fellow men to acts of violence, which we have no doubt they will observe as they ever have done; for you may rest assured, gentlemen, that we would be the last to advise our friends to shed the blood of men or commit one act to endanger the public peace. We have no doubt but our friends will leave your county, sooner or later; they have not only signified the same to us, but we have advised them so to do as fast as they can without incurring too much loss. It may be said that they have but little to lose if they lose the whole. But if they have but little that little is their all, and the necessities of the helpless urge them to make a prudent disposal of the same. We are highly pleased with a proposition in your preamble, suffering them to remain peaceably until a disposition can be made of their land, etc., which, if suffered, our fears are at once hushed, and we have every reason to believe that during the remaining part of the residence of our friends in your county the same feelings of friendship and kindness will continue to exist that have heretofore, and that when they leave you, you will have no reflection of sorrow that they have been sojourners among you.

To what distance or place they will remove we are unable to say; in that they must be dictated by judgment and prudence. They may explore the territory of Wisconsin, they may remove there, or they may stop on the other side, of this we are unable to say; but be they where they will we have this gratifying reflection, that they have never been the first, in an unjust manner, to violate the laws, injure their fellow men, or disturb the tranquility and peace under which any part of our country has heretofore reposed; and we cannot but believe that ere long, the public mind must undergo a change, when it will appear to the satisfaction of all that this people have been illy treated and abused without cause, and when as justice would demand, those who have been the instigators of their sufferings will be regarded as their true characters demand.

Our religious principles are before the world ready for the investigation of all men, yet we are aware that all the persecution against our friends has arisen in consequence of calumnies and misconstructions without foundation in truth and righteousness. This we have endured in common with all other religious societies at their first commencement. Should Providence order that we rise not as others before us to respectability and esteem, but be trodden down by the ruthless force of extermination, posterity will do us justice when our persecutors are equally low in the dust with ourselves, to hand down to succeeding generations the virtuous acts and forbearance of a people who sacrificed their reputation for their religion; and their earthly fortunes and happiness to preserve peace and save this land from being further drenched in blood.

We have no doubt but your very seasonable mediation in the time of so great an excitement will accomplish your most sanguine desires in preventing further disorder; and we hope, gentlemen, that while you reflect upon the fact that the citizens of Clay county are urgent for our friends to leave you, that you will also bear in mind that by their complying with your request to leave they are surrendering some of the dearest rights guaranteed in the Constitution of our country; and that human nature can be driven to a certain extent when it will yield no further. Therefore, while our friends suffer so much and forego so many sacred rights, we sincerely hope, and we have every reason to expect it, that a suitable forbearance may be shown by the people of Clay county; which, if done, the cloud which has been obscuring your horizon will disperse and you be left to enjoy peace, harmony and prosperity.

With sentiments of esteem and profound respect, we are, gentlemen, your obedient servants,

JOSEPH SMITH, JUN.,
SIDNEY RIGDON,
OLIVER COWDERY,
FREDERICK G. WILLIAMS,
HYRUM SMITH.

The following letter was received at Liberty, Clay county, Missouri, on the 28th of July:

Letter from Daniel Dunklin to the Saints in Missouri.

CITY OF JEFFERSON, July 18th, 1836.

Messrs. W. W. Phelps and Others:

GENTLEMEN:—The treatment your people have received, and are now receiving, is of an extraordinary character, such as is seldom experienced in any country by any people. As an individual I sympathize with you, and as the executive of the state, deeply deplore such a state of things. Your appeal to the executive is a natural one; but a proper understanding of our institutions will show you that yours is a case not for the special cognizance of the executive. It is a case, or, I may say, they are cases of individual wrongs. These, as I have before told you, are subjects for judicial interference; and there are cases sometimes of individual outrage which may be so popular as to render the action of courts of justice nugatory, in endeavoring to afford a remedy. I would refer you to the charge of Judge Lawless, made to the grand jury of St. Louis. Public sentiment may become paramount law; and when one man or society of men become so obnoxious to that sentiment as to determine the people to be rid of him or them, it is useless to run counter to it.

The time was when the people (except those in Jackson county) were divided, and the major part in your favor; that does not now seem to be the case. Why is this so? Does your conduct merit such censures as exist against you? It is not necessary for me to give my opinion. Your neighbors accuse your people of holding illicit communication with the Indians, and of being opposed to slavery. You deny. Whether the charge or the denial is true I cannot tell. The fact exists and your neighbors seem to believe it true; and whether true or false, the consequences will be the same (if your opponents are not merely gasconading), unless you can, by your conduct and arguments, convince them of your innocence. If you cannot do this, all I can say to you is that in this Republic the *vox populi* is the *vox Dei*.

Yours repectfully,

DANIEL DUNKLIN.

CHAPTER XXXII.

THE PROPHET'S MISSION—LABORS IN MASSACHUSETTS—THE
ORGANIZATION OF THE KIRTLAND SAFETY SOCIETY.

ON Monday afternoon, July 25th, in company with Sidney
Rigdon, Brother Hyrum Smith, and Oliver   Departure of
Cowdery, I left Kirtland, and at seven o'clock   the Prophet
the same evening, we took passage on board   from Kirtland
the steamer *Charles Townsend*, S. Fox, master, at Fairport, and the next evening, about ten o'clock we arrived
at Buffalo, New York, and took lodgings at the "Farmer's
Hotel." Here we met with Elders Orson Hyde and
Moses C. Nickerson, the former on his way to Canada,
and the latter from that province.

To avoid the crowding, fisting, fighting, racing and
rioting of the packets, we took passages on a line boat for
Utica, where we arrived about eight o'clock a. m. of the
29th, just in time to take the railroad car for Schenectady,
the first passenger car on the new road.* We were
more than six hours traveling eighty miles. The loco-
motive had hardly stopped before the cry was, "Albany
baggage: the cars start in five minutes." Amid a scene

* This was the Albany & Schenectady Railway, the first railroad contracted for in
New York; it began to operate in September, 1831. It was at that time called the
Mohawk & Hudson railroad and ran from Albany to Schenectady. Its charter was
issued in 1826 and is generally regarded as the earliest charter given in the United
States for the construction of a railroad.

of confusion, bustle, and crowding, we succeeded, after a good share of scuffling and pulling, in getting our trunks on board the luggage car for Albany where we arrived the same evening.

On the 30th, at seven o'clock a. m., we went on board
A Steamboat
Race. the steamer *John Mason*, which took us to the *Erie*, lying over the bar. While the passengers were stepping off the *John Mason*, the steamer *Rochester* passed us: "Now for a race," was the cry from different parts, and a race trial of speed it was; however, as fate or steam power of engine would have it, the *Erie*, after touching at Catskill and West Point, where the *Rochester* did not, went into New York a few minutes "ahead." By such undue pressure of steam the lives of thousands have been sacrificed, and I thanked God that myself and friends were safely landed.

While in New York I visited the burnt district—the part
The Great
Fire in New
York City. of the city where it was estimated fifteen millions of property was consumed by fire on the 16th of December, 1835,* according to the prediction of the ancient Prophets, that there should be "fire and vapor of smoke" in the last days.

From New York we continued our journey to Providence, on board a steamer; from thence to Boston, by
Arrival of the
Prophet's
Party in Sa-
lem, Mass. steam cars, and arrived in Salem, Massachusetts, early in August, where we hired a house, and occupied the same during the month, teaching the people from house to house, and preaching publicly, as opportunity presented; visiting occasionally, sections of the surrounding country, which are rich in the history of the Pilgrim Fathers of New England, in Indian warfare, religious superstition, bigotry, persecution, and learned ignorance.

The early settlers of Boston (the Emporium of New

* The fire here alluded to broke out on the night of the 16th of December, 1835, and in fourteen hours there was consumed over seventeen million dollars' worth of property. The burnt district covered several acres of ground in the most prominent business part of the city.

England), who had fled from their mother country to avoid persecution and death, soon became so Reflections of the Prophet on Religious Intolerance. lost to principles of justice and religious liberty as to whip and hang the Baptist and the Quaker, who like themselves, had fled from tyranny to a land of freedom; and the fathers of Salem from 1692 to 1693, whipped, imprisoned, tortured, and hung many of their citizens for supposed witchcraft; and quite recently,—while boasting of her light and knowledge, of her laws and religion, as surpassed by none on earth,— has New England been guilty of burning a Catholic convent in the vicinity of Charleston, and of scattering the inmates to the four winds; yes, in sight of the very spot where the fire of American Independence was first kindled, where a monument is now erecting in memory of the battle of Bunker Hill, and the fate of the immortal Warren, who bled, who died, on those sacred heights, to purchase religious liberty for his country— in sight of this very spot, have the religionists of the nineteenth century, demolished a noble brick edifice, hurling its inhabitants forth upon a cold, unfeeling world for protection and subsistence.

Well did the Savior say concerning such, "by their fruits you shall know them." And if the wicked mob who destroyed the Charleston convent, and the cool, calculating religious lookers on, who inspired their hearts with deeds of infamy, do not arise, and redress the wrong, and restore the injured four-fold, they in turn, will receive of the measure they have meted out till the just indignation of a righteous God is satisfied. When will man cease to war with man, and wrest from him his sacred rights of worshiping his God according as his conscience dictates? Holy Father, hasten the day.

I received the following:

*Revelation given in Salem, Massachusetts, August 6th, 1836.**

1. I, the Lord your God, am not displeased with your coming this journey, notwithstanding your follies;

* See Doctrine and Covenants sec. cxi.

2. I have much treasure in this city for you, for the benefit of Zion; and many people in this city whom I will gather out in due time for the benefit of Zion, through your instrumentality.

3. Therefore it is expedient that you should form acquaintance with men in this city, as you shall be led, and as it shall be given you;

4. And it shall come to pass in due time, that I will give this city into your hands; that you shall have power over it, insomuch that they shall not discover your secret parts; and its wealth pertaining to gold and silver shall be yours.

5. Concern not yourselves about your debts, for I will give you power to pay them.

6. Concern not yourselves about Zion, for I will deal mercifully with her.

7. Tarry in this place, and in the regions round about;

8. And the place where it is my will that you should tarry, for the main, shall be signalized unto you by the peace and power of my Spirit, that shall flow unto you.

9. This place you may obtain by hire, etc. And inquire diligently concerning the more ancient inhabitants and founders of this city;

10. For there are more treasures than one for you in this city;

11. Therefore be ye as wise as serpents and yet without sin, and I will order all things for your good, as fast as ye are able to receive them. Amen.

While here [at Salem] Brothers Brigham Young and Lyman E. Johnson arrived. Brother Young had been through New York, Vermont, and Massachusetts, in company with his brother Joseph Young. They visited their relations in this country, and baptized a good number into the Church; they remained in Boston two or three weeks, and baptized seventeen persons. We had a good visit with the brethren, for which I feel very thankful.

Thus I continued in Salem and vicinity until I returned to Kirtland, some time in the month of September. During this month the Church in Clay county, Missouri, commenced removing to their newly selected location on Shoal Creek, in the territory attached to Ray County.

During the quarter ending September 3rd, fifty-two Elders', six Priests', three Teachers', and two Deacons' licenses were recorded in the license records, in Kirtland, Ohio, by Thomas Burdick. The intelligence from the Elders abroad was interest-

Success of the Ministry.

ing. Elder Parley P. Pratt still continued his labors in Upper Canada, Toronto, and vicinity, with good success. Elder Lyman E. Johnson had been laboring in New Brunswick, and other places on the sea-board; and on the 12th, 13th, and 14th of August a conference was held by Elders Brigham Young and Lyman E. Johnson, at Newry, Maine, where seventeen branches were represented, numbering in all three hundred and seventeen members.

October 2nd, 1836.—My father and Uncle John Smith returned to Kirtland from their mission to the Eastern States, having traveled about two thousand four hundred miles, and visited Labors of the Patriarch Joseph Smith, Sen. nearly all the branches of the Church in New York, Vermont, New Hampshire, and Pennsylvania. During this mission they baptized many, conferred blessings upon many hundreds, and preached the Gospel to many thousands. They also visited their friends and relatives in the land of their nativity. My cousin, George A. Smith, returned the same day from his mission to Richland County, Ohio. Brother Heber C. Kimball returned to Kirtland, having been absent nearly five months, during which time he baptized thirty persons into the Church of the Latter-day Saints, this being in fulfillment of a blessing that I had conferred upon his head before he started on his mission.

Through the month of October the Saints continued to gather at Shoal Creek, Missouri, and my attention was particularly directed to the building up of Kirtland, and the spiritual interests of the Church. Movements of the Saints in Missouri.

On the 2nd of November the brethren at Kirtland drew up certain articles of agreement, preparatory to the organization of a banking institution, to be called the "Kirtland Safety Society." * Organization of Kirtland Safety Society President Oliver Cowdery was delegated to Philadelphia

---

* "Kirtland Safety Society Bank" was the full title of the proposed institution, and Oliver Cowdery had the plates on which bank notes were to be printed so engraved.

to procure plates for the institution; and Elder Orson Hyde to repair to Columbus with a petition to the legislature of Ohio, for an act of incorporation, which was presented at an early period of their session, but because we were "Mormons" the legislature raised some frivolous excuse on which they refused to grant us those banking privileges they so freely granted to others. Thus Elder Hyde was compelled to return without accomplishing the object of his mission, while Elder Cowdery succeeded at a great expense in procuring the plates, and bringing them to Kirtland.

Forty-four Elders' licenses were recorded in the license records at Kirtland during the quarter ending December 1st; also five Priests' and one Teachers' license, by Thomas Burdick.

Licenses.

The Saints having gathered in considerable numbers on Shoal Creek, Missouri, petitioned for an act of incorporation for a new county, which was granted about the middle of December, under the name of Caldwell County, from which time a fresh impetus was given to the gathering, and the county grew like Jonah's gourd.

Organization of Caldwell County.

Minutes of a Conference held in the House of the Lord at Kirtland on the 22nd of December, 1836.

The authorities of the Church being present, viz.: The First Presidency, the High Council of Kirtland, the quorum of the Twelve, the presidents of the Seventies, the president of the Elders and his counselors, and many other official members, such as Priests, Teachers, Deacons etc., the house was called to order, and the following motions were made and carried by the unanimous voice of the assembly:

First—That it has been the case that a very improper and unchristianlike course of conduct has been pursued by the Elders of this Church, and the churches abroad, in sending their poor from among them to this place, without the necessary means of subsistence. Whereas the Church in this place being poor from the beginning, having had to pay an extraordinate price for their lands, provisions, etc ; and having a serious burthen imposed upon them by comers and goers, from most parts of the world, and in assisting traveling Elder and theirs the families, while they themselves have been laboring in the vineyard of the Lord, to preach the Gospel; and also having suffered great loss in endeavoring to benefit Zion, it (the thing complained of) has become a serious matter which ought to be considered by us.

Therefore, after deliberate discussion upon the subject, it was moved seconded, and unanimously carried, that we have borne our part of this burden, and that it becomes the duty, henceforth, of all the churches abroad to provide for those who are objects of charity, that are not able to provide for themselves; and not send them from their midst, to burden the Church in this place, unless they come and prepare a place for them, and provide means for their support.

Second—That there be a stop put to churches or families gathering or moving to this place, without their first coming or sending their wise men to prepare a place for them, as our houses are all full, and our lands mostly occupied, except those houses that do not belong to the Church, which cannot be obtained without great sacrifice, especially when brethren with their families are crowding in upon us, and are compelled to purchase at any rate, and consequently are thrown into the hands of speculators, and extortioners, with which course the Lord is not well pleased. Also that the churches abroad be required to do according to the revelation contained in the book of Doctrine and Covenants, commencing at section 101: 72-74, which is as follows:

"Now verily I say unto you, let all the churches gather together all their monies; let these things be done in their time, be not in haste; and observe to have all things prepared before you, and let honorable men be appointed, even wise men, and send them to purchase these lands; and all branches of the Church in the eastern countries when they are built up, if they will harken unto this counsel, they may buy lands and gather together upon them, and in this way they may establish Zion."   JOSEPH SMITH, Chairman,
                                              WARREN PARRISH, Clerk.

On the 31st of December, at the setting of the sun, Dr. Willard Richards was baptized at Kirt-land, under the hands of President Brigham Young, in the presence of Heber C. Kimball and others, who had spent the afternoon in cutting the ice to prepare for the baptism.*

Baptism of Doctor Richards.

* Dr. Willard Richards was born at Hopkinton, Middlesex County, Massachusetts, June 24, 1804, and from the religious teachings of his parents (Joseph and Rhoda Richards), he was the subject of religious impressions from his earliest moments, although careless and indifferent in his external deportment. At the

*Minutes of a Meeting of the Members of the "Kirtland Safety Society,"
held on the 2nd day of January, 1837.*

At a special meeting of the "Kirtland Safety Society," two-thirds of
the members being present, Sidney Rigdon was called to the chair, and
Warren Parrish chosen secretary.

The house was called to order, and the object of the meeting explained by the chairman; which was—1st, to annul the old constitution,
which was adopted by the society, on the second day of November,
1836; which was, on motion by the unanimous voice of the meeting,
annulled. 2nd, to adopt articles of agreement, by which the "Kirtland Safety Society" is to be governed.

After much discussion and investigation, the following preamble and
articles of agreement were adopted by the unanimous voice of the
meeting:

We, the undersigned subscribers, for the promotion of our temporal
interests, and for the better management of our different occupations,

age of ten years he removed with his father's family to Richmond, in the same
state, where he witnessed several sectarian "revivals," and offered himself to the
Congregational church in that place, at the age of seventeen, having previously
passed the painful ordeal of conviction and conversion, according to that order,
even to the belief that he had committed the unpardonable sin; but the total disregard of that church to his request for admission, led him to a more thorough investigation of the principles of religion, when he became convinced that the sects
were all wrong, and that God had no church on earth, but that He would soon have
a church whose creed would be the truth, the whole truth, and nothing
but the truth, and from that time kept himself aloof from sectarian influence, boldly declaring his belief to all who wished to learn his views;
until the summer of 1835, while in the practice of medicine near Boston,
the Book of Mormon, which President Brigham Young had left with his cousin
Lucius Parker, at Southborough, accidentally or providentially fell in his way,
which was the first he had seen or heard of the Latter-day Saints, except the
scurrilous reports of the public prints, which amounted to nothing more than that
"a boy named Jo Smith, somewhere out west, had found a gold Bible." He
opened the book without regard to place, and totally ignorant of its design or
contents, and before reading half a page, declared "God or the Devil has had a
hand in that book, for man never wrote it." He read it twice through in about
ten days, and so firm was his conviction of the truth, that he immediately commenced settling his accounts, selling his medicine, and freeing himself from every
incumbrance, that he might go to Kirtland, seven hundred miles west, the nearest
point he could hear of a Saint, and give the work a thorough investigation;
firmly believing that if the doctrine was true, God had some greater work for
him to do than to peddle pills. But no sooner did he commence a settlement
than he was smitten with palsy, from which he suffered exceedingly, and was
prevented executing his design until October, 1836, when he arrived at Kirtland,
in company with his brother (Doctor Levi Richards, who attended him as phy-
sician), where he was most cordially and hospitably received and entertained by
his cousin, President Brigham Young, with whom he tarried, and gave the work
an unceasing and untiring investigation until the day of his baptism.

which consist in agriculture, mechanical arts, and merchandising, do hereby form ourselves into a firm or company for the before-mentioned objects, by the name of the "Kirtland Safety Society Anti-Banking Company," for the proper management of said firm, we individually and jointly enter into and adopt the following articles of agreement:

Article 1st. The capital stock of said society or firm shall not be less than four millions of dollars; to be divided into shares of fifty dollars each; and may be increased to any amount, at the discretion of the managers.

Art. 2nd. The management of said company shall be under the superintendence of thirty-two managers, to be chosen annually, by, and from among, the members of the same; each member being entitled to one vote for each share, which he, she, or they, may hold in said company; and said votes may be given by proxy or in *propria persona*.

Art. 3rd. It shall be the duty of said managers, when chosen, to elect from their number, a treasurer and secretary. It shall be the further duty of said managers to meet in the upper room of the office of said company, on the first Mondays of November and May, of each year, at 9 o'clock a. m., to inspect the books of said company, and transact such other business as may be deemed necessary.

Art. 4th. It shall be the duty of said managers to choose from among their number, seven men, who shall meet in the upper room of said office on Tuesday of each week, at 4 o'clock p. m., to inquire into and assist in all matters pertaining to said company.

Art. 5th. Each manager shall receive from the company one dollar per day for his services when called together at the annual and semi-annual meetings. The treasurer and secretary and the seven the committee of the managers, shall receive a compensation for their services as shall be agreed by the managers at their semi-annual meetings.

Art. 6th. The first election of managers, as set forth in the second article, shall take place at the meeting of the members to adopt this agreement, who shall hold their offices until the first Monday of November, 1837, unless removed by death or misdemeanor, and until others are duly elected. Every annual election of managers shall take place on the first Monday of November in each year. It shall be the duty of the treasurer and secretary of said company to receive the votes of the members by ballot, and declare the election.

Art. 7th. The books of the company shall be always open for the inspection of the members.

Art. 8th. It shall be the duty of the managers of the company to declare a divided once in six months; which dividend shall be apportioned among the members, according to the installments by them paid in.

Art. 9th. All persons subscribing stock in said firm shall pay their first installment at the time of subscribing, and other installments from time to time, as shall be required by the managers.

Art. 10th. The managers shall give thirty days notice in some public paper, printed in this county, previous to an installment being paid in. All subscribers residing out of the state, shall be required to pay in half the amount of their subscriptions at the time of subscribing; and the remainder, or such part thereof as shall be required at any time by the managers, after thirty days notice.

Art. 11th. The treasurer shall be empowered to call special meetings of the managers whenever he shall deem it necessary, separate and aside from the annual and semi-annual meetings.

Art. 12th. Two-thirds of the managers shall form a quorum to act at the semi-annual meetings, and any number of the seven, the committee of the managers, with the treasurer and secretary, or either of them, may form a quorum to transact business at the weekly meetings, and in case none of the seven is present at the weekly meetings, the treasurer and secretary must transact the business.

Art. 13th. The managers shall have power to enact such by-laws as they may deem necessary from time to time, provided they do not infringe upon these articles of agreement.

Art. 14th. All notes given by said society shall be signed by the treasurer and secretary thereof, and we, the individual members of said firm, hereby hold ourselves bound for the redemption of all such notes.

Art. 15th. The notes given for the benefit of said society shall be given to the treasurer in the following form: "Ninety days after date, we jointly, and severally, promise to pay A. B. or order,———dollars and———cents, value received." A record of which shall be made in the books at the time, of the amount, and by whom given, and when due, and deposited with the files and papers of said society.

Art. 16th. Any article in this agreement may be altered at any time, annulled, added unto, or expunged by the vote of two-thirds of the members of said society, except the 14th article, that shall remain unaltered during the existence of said company. For the true and faithful fulfillment of the above covenant and agreement, we individually bind ourselves to each other, under the penal sum of one hundred thousand dollars. In witness whereof we have hereunto set our hands and seals, the day and date first above written.

In connection with the above articles of agreement of the "Kirtland Safety Society," I published the following remarks to all who were preparing themselves, and appointing their wise men, for the purpose of building up Zion and

The Prophet's Remarks on the Kirtland Safety Society

her stakes in the January number of the *Messenger and Advocate:*

It is wisdom and according to the mind of the Holy Spirit, that you should call at Kirtland, and receive counsel and instruction upon those principles that are necessary to further the great work of the Lord, and to establish the children of the kingdom, according to the oracles of God; as they are had among us: and further, we invite the brethren from abroad, to call on us, and take stock in our Safety Society; and we would remind them also of the sayings of Isaiah, contained in the 60th chapter and more particularly the 9th and 17th verses, which are as follows: "Surely the isles shall wait for me, and the ships of Tarshish first, to bring thy sons from far, their silver and their gold [not their bank notes] with them, unto the name of the Lord thy God, and to the Holy One of Israel, because He hath glorified thee. * * * For brass I will bring gold, and for iron I will bring silver, and for wood, brass, and for stone, iron: I will also make thy officers peace, and thine exactors righteousness." Also 62nd chapter, 1st verse: "For Zion's sake will I not hold my peace, and for Jerusalem's sake I will not rest, until the righteousness thereof go forth as brightness, and the salvation thereof as a lamp that burneth."

JOSEPH SMITH, JUN.

CHAPTER XXXIII.

MEETINGS OF THE QUORUMS OF PRIESTHOOD IN THE KIRTLAND
TEMPLE—THE PROPHET'S INSTRUCTIONS ON PRIESTHOOD.

DURING the winter, the House of the Lord at Kirtland
was filled to overflowing with attentive hearers, mostly
communicants; and in the evenings the singers met under the direction of Elders Luman
Carter and Jonathan Crosby, Jun., who gave
instruction in the principles of vocal music.

The Arrangements for Classes and Meetings in Kirtland Temple.

On Monday evenings the quorum of High Priests meet in
the west room of the attic story, where they transact the
business of their particular quorum. On Tuesday evenings the Seventies occupy the same room. On Wednesday evenings the rooms are occupied by the quorum of
Elders. And on Thursday evening a prayer meeting is
held in the lower part of the house, free to all, though
generally conducted by Patriarch Joseph Smith, Sen.
The Twelve, the High Council and other quorums, generally meet each week to transact business, and during
the week the "Kirtland High School is taught in the
attic story, by H. M. Hawes, Esq., professor of the Greek
and Latin languages. The school numbers from one hundred and thirty-five to one hundred and forty students,
divided into three departments—the classic, where the
languages only are taught; the English department, where
mathematics, common arithmetic, geography, English
grammar, writing, and reading are taught; and the juve

nile department, the last two having each an assistant instructor. The school commenced in November, and on the first Wednesday in January the several classes passed a public examination in presence of the trustees of the school, parents and guardians, and their progress in study was found of the highest order.

Owing to the multiplicity of letters with which I was crowded from almost every quarter, I was compelled to decline all not postpaid, and gave notice of the same in the *Messenger and Advocate.*

The brethren in Missouri were very busy in gathering into Caldwell county, entering United States land, building houses, and preparing to put in crops in the spring.

Gathering of the Saints in Missouri.

On the first of February, 1837, the firm of Oliver Cowdery & Co. was dissolved by mutual consent, and the entire establishment was transferred to Joseph Smith, Jun., and Sidney Rigdon; and Warren A. Cowdery acted as their agent in the printing office and bookbindery, and editor of the *Messenger and Advocate.*

Firm of Cowdery & Co. Dissolved.

During the quarter ending March the 3rd, thirty-two Elders', seven Priests', three Teachers', and two Deacons' licenses were recorded in the license records in Kirtland, by Thomas Burdick.

Licenses.

A brief notice only was given, that a solemn assembly would be called, of the official members of the Church, on the 6th of April, for the purpose of washing, anointing, washing of feet, receiving instructions, and the further organization of the ministry. Meetings were held by the different quorums on Monday, 3rd, Tuesday, 4th, and Wednesday, 5th, to anoint such of their respective members as had not been washed and anointed, that all might be prepared for the meeting on the 6th.

Notice of a Solemn Assembly.

At an early hour on Thursday, the 6th of April, the official members asssembled in the House of the Lord,

when the time for the first two or three hours was spent
Washing of Feet. by the different quorums in washing of feet, singing, praying, and preparing to receive instructions from the Presidency. The Presidents, together with the Seventies and their presidents, repaired to the west room in the attic story, where, for want of time the preceding evening, it became necessary to seal the anointing of those who had recently been anointed and not sealed.

Another subject of vital importance to the Church, was
Regulation of the Seventies. the establishing of the grades of the different quorums. It was ascertained that all but one or two of the presidents of the Seventies were High Priests, and when they had ordained and set apart any from the quorums of Elders, into the quorum of Seventies, they had conferred upon them the High Priesthood, also.* This was declared to be wrong, and not according to the order of heaven. New Presidents of the Seventies were accordingly ordained to fill the places of such of them as were High Priests,† and the *ex-officio* presidents, and such of the Seventies as had been legally ordained to be High Priests, were directed to unite with the High Priests' quorum. All the quorums then assembled in the lower room of the Lord's House, where they were addressed by the presidents from the stand. The following, in substance, is what was said:

---

* That is they ordained them High Priests. Since they were Elders, however, they already possessed the High Priesthood, and hence it was only necessary to ordain them to the office of Seventy in that Priesthood; but the brethen who had immediate charge of ordaining Seventies (the first presidents of Seventies) seemed to have thought it necessary to ordain them High Priests in order for them to hold the High Priesthood, hence the correction made by the Prophet.

† In the selection and ordination of the council composed of the first seven presidents of Seventy, it had been overlooked, evidently, that the revelation on Priesthood, given March 28, 1835. specifically stated: "And it is according to the vision, showing the order of the Seventy, that they should have seven presidents to preside over them, *chosen out of the number of the Seventy.*"—(Doc. and Cov., sec. 107, verse 93). Five of those chosen to make up the first council were High Priests; therefore to make the action of the Church conform to the word of God, these High Priests were invited by the Prophet to take their place in the High Priests' quorum, that the first council might be made up of men "chosen out of the number of the Seventy" as provided by the law of God.

President Joseph Smith, Jun., addressed the assembly and said, the Melchizedek High Priesthood was no other than the Priesthood of the Son of God; that there are certain ordinances which belong to the Priesthood, from which flow certain results; *The Prophet on the Subject of Priesthood.* and the Presidents or Presidency are over the Church; and revelations of the mind and will of God to the Church, are to come through the Presidency. This is the order of heaven, and the power and privilege of this Priesthood. It is also the privilege of any officer in this Church to obtain revelations, so far as relates to his particular calling and duty in the Church. All are bound by the principles of virtue and happiness, but one great privilege of the Priesthood is to obtain revelations of the mind and will of God. It is also the privilege of the Melchizedek Priesthood, to reprove, rebuke, and admonish, as well as to receive revelation. If the Church knew all the commandments, one half they would condemn through prejudice and ignorance.

A High Priest, is a member of the same Melchizedek Priesthood with the Presidency, but not of the same power or authority in the Church. *The High Priests.* The Seventies are also members of the same Priesthood, [i. e. the High Priesthood], are a sort of traveling council or Priesthood, and may preside over a church or churches, until a High Priest can be had. The Seventies are to be taken from the quorum of Elders, and are not to be High Priests. They are subject to the direction and dictation of the Twelve, who have the keys of the ministry. All are to preach the Gospel, by the power and influence of the Holy Ghost; and no man can preach the Gospel without the Holy Ghost.

The Bishop is a High Priest, and necessarily so, because he is to preside over that particular branch of Church affairs, that is denominated *Bishops.* the Lesser Priesthood, and because we have no direct lineal descendant of Aaron, to whom it would of right belong. This is the same, or a branch of the same, Priesthood, which may be illustrated by the figure of the human body, which has different members, which have different offices to perform; all are necessary in their place, and the body is not complete without all the members.

From a retrospect of the requirements of the servants of God to preach the Gospel, we find few qualified even to be Priests, and if a Priest understands his duty, his calling, and ministry, and preaches by the Holy Ghost, his enjoyment is as great as if he were one of the Presidency; and his services are necessary in the body, as are also those of Teachers and Deacons. Therefore, in viewing the Church as a whole, we may strictly denominate it one Priesthood. President Smith also said:

The Dignity of the Lesser Officers.

"I frequently rebuke and admonish my brethren, and that because I love them, not because I wish to incur their displeasure, or mar their happiness. Such a course of conduct is not calculated to gain the good will of all, but rather the ill will of many; therefore, the situation in which I stand is an important one; so, you see, brethren, the higher the authority, the greater the difficulty of the station; but these rebukes and admonitions become necessary, from the perverseness of the brethren, for their temporal as well as spiritual welfare. They actually constitute a part of the duties of my station and calling. Others have other duties to perform, that are important, and far more enviable, and may be just as good, like the feet and hands, in their relation to the human body— neither can claim priority, or say to the other, I have no need of you. After all that has been said, the greatest and most important duty is to preach the Gospel.

Necessity for Occasional Reproofs.

"There are many causes of embarrassment, of a pecuniary nature now pressing upon the heads of the Church. They began poor; were needy, destitute, and were truly

afflicted by their enemies; yet the Lord commanded them
to go forth and preach the Gospel, to sacrifice Pecuniary
their time, their talents, their good name, and Embarrass-
                                                 ments of the
jeopardize their lives; and in addition to this, Presidency.
they were to build a house for the Lord, and prepare for
the gathering of the Saints. Thus it is easy to see this
must [have] involved them [in financial difficulties].
They had no temporal means in the beginning commen-
surate with such an undertaking; but this work must be
done; this place [Kirtland] had to be built up. Large
contracts have been entered into for lands on all sides,
where our enemies have signed away their rights. We
are indebted to them, but our brethren from abroad have
only to come with their money, take these contracts, relieve
their brethren from the pecuniary embarrassments under
which they now labor, and procure for themselves a
peaceable place of rest among us. This place must and
will be built up, and every brother that will take hold
and help secure and discharge those contracts that have
been made, shall be rich."

At 4 p. m. President Hyrum Smith addressed the assembly, principally in relation to the temporal affairs of
the Church, and censured those who counseled Remarks of
                                               Hyrum Smith
such brethren as moved to this place, when
they were not authorized to give advice. He also alluded,
in terms of disapprobation, to the practice of some individuals, in getting money from brethren that come in,
when it ought to be appropriated to the discharge of
heavy debts that are now hanging over the heads of the
Church, or for the payments of the land contracts which
had been made for the benefit of the Saints in this
place.

Twenty-five minutes before five, President Oliver Cowdery spoke, opposing the idea of Elders at- Oliver Cow-
tempting to preach or teach that which they dery.
did not know, etc.

President Sidney Rigdon rose a little before 5 p.m., and

after referring to the gathering, and the preaching of the

Sidney Rig-
don's Re-
marks on
ChurchDebts. Gospel, as the first things, alluded to the debt which had been contracted for building the Lord's House, and other purposes, and stated three principal items that constituted nearly the aggregate of debt that now remained unliquidated.

First a charge of six thousand dollars which was appropriated and expended in consequence of the brethren being driven by a lawless mob from their possessions in Jackson county. The second was the building of the Lord's House, the unliquidated debt of which was rising of thirteen thousand dollars. The third item of debt was for the purchase of land, that there might be a place of rest, a place of safety, a place that the Saints might lawfully call their own. All this is to lay a foundation for the gathering of Israel, and when the Elders go abroad they can speak understandingly, and urge the necessty and propriety of the gathering, from the fact that we have·a place for them, and it is the will of God they should come. Prey not one upon another, brethren, and for the time being say not, Pay me what thou owest; but contribute all in your power to discharge the great debts that now hang over the Church.

At half-past five, bread and water* were distributed

The Sacra-
ment—Use of
Water. liberally among the quorums, and it was truly a refreshing season to spirit and body. Many brethren and sisters assembled in the evening for prayer and exhortation, and some tarried nearly all night.

---

* In the revelation given in August 1830 (Sec. 27) the Lord said "it mattereth not what ye shall eat or what ye shall drink when ye partake of the Sacrament, if it so be that ye do it with an eye single to my glory," etc. This is the first occasion on record where water was used instead of wine, but it is possible that water may have been used in the Sacrament before this time.

CHAPTER XXXIV.

AFFAIRS IN ZION—APOSTASY AT KIRTLAND—APPOINTMENT OF THE BRITISH MISSION—ITS DEPARTURE FOR ENGLAND.

Minutes of the High Council at Far West.

FAR WEST, MO., April 7th.

At a meeting of the Presidency of the Church in Missouri, the High Council, Bishop and counselors, it was resolved that the city plat of Far West retain its present form; and that the alleys be opened by a majority of the owners of each square, or block, when they shall desire it; that the price and sale of the town lots be left to W. W. Phelps, John Whitmer, Edward Partridge, Isaac Morley, and John Corrill; that Jacob Whitmer, Elisha H. Groves, and George M. Hinkle be a building committee of the House of the Lord in this city (Far West); that Jacob Whitmer be received as High Councilor until the arrival of President David Whitmer; also that President David Whitmer, John Whitmer, and W. W. Phelps, superintend the building of the Lord's House, in this city, and receive revelations, visions, etc. concerning said house.

JOHN CORRILL, Clerk.

Charge Against Lyman Wight.

David W. Patten preferred a charge against Lyman Wight, for teaching erroneous doctrines, which was investigated by the High Council at Far West, April 24, 1837.

Seymour Brunson, George P. Dykes, and others, testified that Lyman Wight said that we (the Church) were under a telestial law, because God does not whip under a celestial law, therefore He took us (the Church) out of doors to whip us, as a parent took his children out of doors to chastise them; and that the book of Doctrine and Covenants was a telestial law; and the Book of Commandments (a part of the revelations printed in Jackson county) was a celestial law.

The Presidency decided, with the approbation of the Council, that Lyman Wight had taught erroneous doctrine, and that he be required to make an acknowledgment to the Council; also that he go and acknowledge to the churches where he had preached such abominable doctrine.

NATHAN WEST, Clerk.

Complaint against J. M. Patten.

Joshua Fairchild, David Pettigrew, Benjamin Johnson, and Sheffield Daniels entered a complaint against John Patten, for not fulfilling his contracts, or covenants, in consequence of which they were materially injured; which was proved by Lyman Wight and Abigail Daniels, before the High Council at Far West, May 22nd, 1837.

After a long investigation by the Councilors and parties, the Presidency, W. W. Phelps and John Whitmer, [it was decided] that both accuser and accused should be disfellowshiped, if they did not settle their difficulties. Jesse Hitchcock was then cut off from the High Council.

James Emmet, who had previously been disfellowshiped, made satisfaction, and was restored to fellowship; and John Corrill was appointed agent to the Church, and keeper of the Lord's Store House.

HARVEY GREEN, Clerk.

On the 28th of May a charge was preferred by John Corrill and others against John Patten, for not complying with his agreement, which charge being sustained by testimony, the High Council decided that John Patten be disfellowshiped until he make satisfaction.

Case of John Patten.

About this time the Presidency of the Church at Far West called a general meeting of the Church, at which were present the High Council, two of the Twelve Apostles, ten of the Seventies, the Bishop, and one counselor, when it was resolved that we withdraw fellowship from James Emmet, for unwise conduct, until he returns and makes satisfaction.

James Emmet Disfellowshiped.

Resolved unanimously, that we will not fellowship any ordained member who will not, or does not, observe the Word of Wisdom according to its literal reading.

Action in Relation to the Word of Wisdom.

Resolved unanimously, that we sanction the Literary Firm, and give them our voice and prayers, to manage all the affairs of the same, as far as it concerns this place, according to the revelation in book

Literary Firm Sustained.

of Doctrine and Covenants, first edition, published at
Kirtland, Ohio, page 152, section 26th, given November,
1831, (current edition, section 70).*

* A short time previous to the above recorded actions, viz., in the early part of
April preceding, an important meeting of the High Council of Zion was convened
and before it Presidents W. W. Phelps and John Whitmer (David Whitmer, the
President of Zion being absent) were arraigned for some irregularity in their conduct; and as the action of that Council will have an important bearing upon facts
which will later appear in the body of this history, I here give *in extenso* the
minutes of that Council meeting, which continued from the third to the seventh
of April.

Minutes of the High Council at Far West.

At a meeting of the High Council in Far West, April 3, 1837, seven of the
standing councilors were present. John Murdock was appointed moderator, and
Elias Higbee clerk.

Resolved, That the Council request the Presidents W. W. Phelps and John
Whitmer to give explanation of the following items:

First—By what authority was this place [Far West] pointed out as a city and [a
place for a] house of the Lord, and by whom?

Second—By what authority was a committee appointed and ordained to superintend the building of the House of the Lord?

Third—By what authority was Jacob Whitmer ordained to the High Priesthood?

Fourth—Have two presidents authority to lay out a city, and build a House of
God; independent of the counsel of the High Council?

Fifth—By what authority was one of the High Councilors disfellowshiped in the
name of the High Council without their knowledge?

Sixth—Has any individual or individuals a right to prefer a charge to the Presidency in Kirtland against any High Councilor, [of this Council] without the knowledge of the Council or [the] individual?

Seventh—Should not the High Council and Bishop of Zion, who are appointed to
do business for Zion, receive their inheritance in the care of that city in preference
to one who is not particularly called to labor for Zion, or an unbeliever?

Eight—Shall any intelligence relative to the building up of Zion be withheld
from the Council of Zion?

Ninth—Are the two presidents entitled to the profits arising from the sale of
land, on which the city is to be built in this place, independent of the authorities who have been appointed to labor with them for Zion and have suffered like
tribulations with them?

The Council then agreed to invite Presidents W. W. Phelps and John Whitmer,
also the Bishop, Edward Partridge, and his counselors; also the two Apostles, viz.,
Thomas B. Marsh and David W. Patten, to meet with them on the 5th, inst, that
the above named presidents might explain [answer] the foregoing questions and
that the subject might be investigated. The Concil then adjourned to the 5th at
ten o'clock.

FAR WEST, April 5th, 1837.

The Council convened agreeable to adjournment with the aforementioned Presidents, the Bishops and counselors; also the two Apostles. The Council opened by
prayer; but previous to proceeding to business the said presidents proposed that
the Bishop and his counselors, with the above named Apostles leave the Council;
which was objected to by the Council, the Bishop and Apostles. The presidents
still insisted on having a private council in the absence of the Bishop and his

Minutes of a High Council held in the Lord's House, in Kirtland, Monday, May 29, 1837, ten o'clock a. m.

Isaac Rogers, Artemas Millet, Abel Lamb, and Harlow Redfield, appeared as complainants against Presidents Frederick G. Williams and David Whitmer, and Elders Parley P. Pratt, Lyman Johnson, and Warren Parrish.

Sidney Rigdon presiding.

COUNCILORS.

John Smith,	John Johnson,
Jared Carter,	John P. Greene,
Noah Packard,	Oliver Granger,
Joseph Kingsbury,	Samuel H. Smith,
Joseph Coe,	Martin Harris,
Gideon Carter,	Willard Woodstock.

President Rigdon then read the following complaint:

"To the Presidency of the Church of Latter-day Saints:

"We, the undersigned, feeling ourselves aggrieved with the conduct counselors and the Apostles. All opposed the two presidents. The Bishops and the two Apostles gave them to understand that they had a right to remain, and that they therefore should remain. President Phelps then said he would dissolve the Council, upon which Thomas B. Marsh declared that if the Council should be dissolved he would prepare a charge against the two presidents, before the Bishop and twelve High Priests. The presidents then said they were willing to let all present remain in the house. The Council then proceeded to the investigation of the above named questions. They were not generally satisfactorily answered, which led the Council and others to strongly rebuke the late improper proceedings of the presidents. David W. Patten spoke against them with apparent indignation; stating that their proceedings had been iniquitous and fraudulent in the extreme, in unrighteously appropriating Church funds to their own enrichment, which had been plainly proven. April 6th was occupied in like discussions. April 7th, Council convened agreeable to appointment. The Bishop and counselors present, also the two Apostles. The above named presidents agreed to give up the town plat of Far West with four eighties on the commons to be disposed of by the High Council, the Bishop and his counselors and the said Apostles. After which, on motion, the Council adjourned. The Council met in Far West to take into consideration the affairs relative to the town plat; at which the council resolved, (it being agreed by all parties) to make over or that W. W. Phelps and John Whitmer make over, or transfer the town plat with four eighties, which are on the commons, into the hands of the Bishop of Zion; and that the avails arising from the sale of said lands should be appropriated to the benefit and upbuilding of "Poor, Bleeding Zion." In the above resolution, W. W. Phelps and John Whitmer acquiesced. Also resolved that whereas W. W. Phelps and John Whitmer had subscribed $1,000 each to the House of the Lord to be built in this place—which they were before intending to pay out of the avails of the town plat—be considered exempt from paying that subscription."—*Far West Record* [Ms.] pp. 72, 73.

of Presidents David Whitmer and Frederick G.Williams, and also with Elders Lyman E. Johnson, Parley P. Pratt, and Warren Parrish, believing that their course for some time past has been injurious to the Church of God, in which they are high officers, we therefore desire that the High Council should be assembled, and we should have an investigation of their behavior, believing it to be unworthy of their high calling—all of which we respectfully submit.

"ABEL LAMB,
"NATHAN HASKINS,
"HARLOW REDFIELD,
"ARTEMAS MILLET,
"ISAAC ROGERS.

"KIRTLAND, MAY, 1837."

Elder Warren Parrish then stated that the declaration just read was not in accordance with the copy which they [the accused] received of the charges preferred against them.

The resolution was then offered and carried, that three speak on a side.

The Council was then opened by prayer, by President Rigdon.

After a short address to the Councilors, by President Rigdon, President Frederick G.Williams arose, and wished to know by what authority he was called before the present Council; that according to the Book of Covenants, he ought to be tried before the Bishop's court.

After some discussion between Presidents Rigdon and Williams, President Rigdon gave his decision that President Williams should be tried before the present Council.

President David Whitmer also objected to being tried before the present Council.

President Williams then expressed a willingness to be tried for his conduct, and if this was the proper tribunal, he would be tried before it, but still thought it was not.

President David Whitmer objected to being tried before the present Council, stating that he thought the instructions in the Book of Covenants showed that this was not the proper authority to try him.

Councilor Greene gave it as his opinion that the present Council was not the proper authority to try Presidents Williams and Whitmer.

President Rigdon then submitted the case to the Councilors.

Councilor John Smith then put the question to the Council for decision, in substance as follows: Have the present Council authority, from the Book of Covenants, to try Presidents Williams and Whitmer? A majority of the Council decided that they could not conscientiously proceed to try Presidents Williams and Whitmer, and they were accordingly discharged.

After one hour's adjournment, the Council sat again at one o'clock p. m. Sidney Rigdon and Oliver Cowdery presiding.

Councilor John Smith stated that he had selected three High Priests to sit in the Council to fill vacancies, and asked the Council if they accepted the selection he had made. Council decided in the affirmative.

On motion of Warren Parrish, the Councilors were directed to sit as they were originally chosen, or according to the form in the book of Doctrine and Covenants as far as possible.

Resolved, that three speak on each side.

Councilor Martin Harris moved that President Frederick G. Williams take a seat with the presidents.

After much discussion as to the propriety of his sitting, motion carried, and President Williams took his seat.

Elder Parley P. Pratt then arose and objected to being tried by President Rigdon or Joseph Smith, Jun., in consequence of their having previously expressed their opinion against him, stating also that he could bring evidence to prove what he then said.

President Rigdon then stated that he had previously expressed his mind repecting the conduct of Elder Pratt, and that he had felt and said that Elder Pratt had done wrong, and he still thought so, and left it with the Council to decide whether, under such circumstances, he should proceed to try the case.

After much discussion between the councilors and parties, President Rigdon said that, under the present circumstances, he could not conscientiously proceed to try the case, and after a few remarks left the stand.

President Oliver Cowdery then said that although he might not be called upon to preside, yet if he should be, he should also be unfit to judge in the case, as he had previously expressed his opinion respecting the conduct of Elder Parley P. Pratt and others, and left the stand.

President Williams then arose and said, that as he had been implicated with the accused, he should be unwillig to preside in the case, and left the stand.

The Council and assembly then dispersed in confusion.

F. W. COWDERY, Clerk.

Some time this month, the *Messenger and Advocate* office and contents were transferred to William Marks,* of Portage, Allegheny County, New York, and Joseph Smith and Sidney Rigdon continued the office, by power of attorney from said Marks.

Transfer of the *Messenger and Advocate.*

* William Marks was born November 15, 1792, in Rutland, Rutland County, Vermont. This is the first mention of his name in the Prophet's narrative, and nothing can be learned of his career previous to this time.

At this time the spirit of speculation in lands and property of all kinds, which was so prevalent throughout the whole nation,* was taking deep root in the Church. As the fruits of this spirit, evil surmisings, fault-finding, disunion, dissension, and apostasy followed in quick succession, and it seemed as though all the powers of earth and hell were combining their influence in an especial manner to overthrow the Church at once, and make a final end.† Other banking

Conditions in Kirtland.

---

* As additional evidence that this financial maelstrom in which the "Kirtland Safety Society" met disaster was national and not merely local, I quote here the description of the wide-spread financial panic of 1837, as given in the History of the United States by Alexander H. Stephens: "Soon after Mr. Van Buren became President occurred a great commercial crisis. This was in April, 1837, and was occasioned by a reckless spirit of speculation, which had, for two or three preceding years, been fostered and encouraged by excessive banking, and the consequent expansion of paper currency beyond all the legitimate wants of the country. During the months of March and April of this year the failures in New York City alone amounted to over $100,000,000. The state of affairs became so distressing that petitions were sent to the President from several quarters, and a deputation of merchants and bankers of New York waited upon him in person, and solicited him to defer the immediate collection of duties, for which bonds had been given, and to rescind the treasury orders which had been issued under Jackson's administration, requiring dues to the government to be paid in specie. They also asked that an extra session of Congress should be called to adopt measures of relief. He granted their request so far only as to suspend suits on bonds, which had been given for the collection of duties. In a few days after his response to this deputation was made known in New York, all the banks in that city stopped specie payments, and their example was soon followed by nearly all the banks in all the states. In this emergency, Mr. Van Buren was compelled to convene an extra session of Congress, to provide for meeting demands on the treasury with legal currency. He accordingly summoned the Twenty-fifth Congress to meet at the capitol on the 4th day of September, 1837. The session lasted five or six weeks. In his message to Congress, Mr. Van Buren assigned as the causes of the unhappy condition of the country, the excessive issues of bank paper; the great fire in New York, in December, 1835; the large investments that had been made in unproductive lands, and other speculative enterprises. To meet the exigencies of the treasury, as well as to provide for the public relief, as far as to them seemed proper, Congress passed an act authorizing the issue of treasury notes to the amount of '10,-000,000' "—(History of the United States, by Alexander H. Stephens, p. 460).

† Of the condition of affairs in Kirtland at this time Eliza R. Snow, in her Biography of her brother, the late President Lorenzo Snow, says: "A spirit of specu-lation had crept into the hearts of some of the Twelve, and nearly, if not every quorum was more or less infected. Most of the Saints were poor, and now prosperity was dawning upon them—the Temple was completed, and in it they had been recipients of marvelous blessings, and many who had been humble and faithful to the performance of every duty—ready to go and come at every call of the Priesthood, were getting haughty in their spirits, and lifted up in the pride of

institutions refused the "Kirtland Safety Society's" notes.
The enemy abroad, and apostates in our midst, united
in their schemes, flour and provisions were turned towards
other markets, and many became disaffected toward me
as though I were the sole cause of those very evils I was
most strenuously striving against, and which were actually
brought upon us by the brethren not giving heed to my
counsel.

No quorum in the Church was entirely exempt from the
influence of those false spirits who are striving against me
for the mastery; even some of the Twelve were so far
lost to their high and responsible calling, as to begin to
take sides, secretly, with the enemy.*

their hearts. As the Saints drank in the love and spirit of the world, the Spirit of
the Lord withdrew from their hearts, and they were filled with pride and hatred
toward those who maintained their integrity. They linked themselves together in
an opposing party—pretended that they constituted the Church, and claimed that
the Temple belonged to them, and even attempted to hold it."

* Among those who were embittered against the Prophet at this time was Elder
Parley P. Pratt, and of this incident in his experience he says: About this time,
(summer of 1837) after I had returned from Canada, there were jarrings and discords in the Church at Kirtland, and many fell away and became enemies and
apostates. There were also envyings, lyings, strifes and divisions, which caused
much trouble and sorrow. By such spirits I was also accused, misrepresented and
abused. And at one time, I also was overcome by the same spirit in a great measure, and it seemed as if the very powers of darkness which war against the Saints
were let loose upon me. But the Lord knew my faith, my zeal, my integrity of
purpose, and He gave me the victory. I went to Brother Joseph Smith in tears,
and, with a broken heart and contrite spirit. confessed wherein I had erred in
spirit, murmured, or done or said amiss. He frankly forgave me, prayed for me
and blessed me. Thus, by experienc, I learned more fully to discern and to con-
trast the two spirits, and to resist the one and cleave to the other. And, being
tempted in all points, even as others, I learned how to bear with, and excuse, and
succor those who are tempted."—(Autobiography of Parley P. Pratt, pp. 183-4).

In the midst of these troubles there were reputations made as well as some lost.
Among those who were developed rather than destroyed by the troubles and temptations of these times was the late President John Taylor. Referring to a visit
which Elder Taylor made to Kirtland in the spring of 1837 his Biography states:
"At that time there was a bitter spirit of apostasy rife in Kirtland. A number in
the quorum of the Twelve were disaffected toward the Prophet, and the Church
seemed on the point of disintegration. Among others, Parley P. Pratt was floun-
dering in darkness, and coming to Elder Taylor told him of some things wherein he
considered the Prophet Joseph in error. To his remarks Elder Taylor replied: 'I am
surprised to hear you speak so, Brother Parley. Before you left Canada you bore a
strong testimony to Joseph Smith being a Prophet of God, and to the truth of the
work he has inaugurated; and you said you knew these things by revelation, and
the gift of the Holy Ghost. You gave to me a strict charge to the effect that though

In this state of things, and but a few weeks before the
Twelve were expecting to meet in full quorum,
(some of them having been absent for some
time), God revealed to me that something
new must be done for the salvation of His Church. And
on or about the first of June, 1837, Heber C. Kimball,
one of the Twelve, was set apart by the spirit of prophecy and revelation, prayer and laying on of hands, of the
First Presidency, to preside over a mission to England,
to be the first foreign mission of the Church of Christ in
the last days.* While we were about ordaining him, Orson

The British Mission Projected.

you or an angel from heaven was to declare anything else I was not to believe it.
Now Brother Parley, it is not man that I am following, but the Lord.   The principles you taught me led me to Him, and I now have the same testimony that you
then rejoiced in.   If the work was true six months ago, it is true today; if Joseph
was then a Prophet, he is now a Prophet.'   To the honor of Elder Pratt, be it said,
he sought no further to lead Elder Taylor astray; nor did he use much argument
in the first place.   'He and many others,' says Elder Taylor, 'were passing under
a dark cloud; he soon made all right with the Prophet Joseph, and was restored to
full fellowship.'   It was about this time that Elder Taylor first came prominently
before the Church.   The apostates met frequently in the Temple, and on one of
these occasions, on a Sunday—the Prophet Joseph was absent—Warren Parrish
made a violent attack upon the character of the Prophet, in which he was warmly
sustained by many of those present.   Towards the close of the meeting, Elder
Taylor asked the privilege of speaking.   It was granted him.   He referred, in
opening his remarks, to the ancient Israelites, and to their murmurings against
God and Moses, and then asked: 'From whence do we get our intelligence, and
knowledge of the laws, ordinances and doctrines of the kingdom of God? Who
understood even the first principles of the doctrines of Christ? Who in the Christian world taught them? If we, with our learning and intelligence, could not find
out the first principles, which was the case with myself and millions of others,
how can we find out the mysteries of the kingdom? It was Joseph Smith, under
the Almighty, who developed the first principles, and to him we must look for
further instructions.   If the spirit which he manifests does not bring blessings,
I am very much afraid that the one manifested by those who have spoken, will
not be very likely to secure them.   The children of Israel, formerly, after seeing
the power of God manifested in their midst, fell into rebellion and idolatry, and
there is certainly very great danger of our doing the same thing.'   While the apostates were neither convinced nor silenced by the remarks of Elder Taylor, the faithful Saints were strengthened, and saw in that fearless defender of the Prophet, a
champion of innocence and truth.   While on his part, in commenting on this circumstance, Elder Taylor remarks: 'I was pained on the one hand to witness the
hard feelings and severe expressions of apostates; while on the other, I rejoiced to
see the firmness, faith, integrity and joy of the faithful.' "—(Life of John Taylor,
pp. 39, 40, 41.)

   * Of this call of Heber C. Kimball to the Presidency of the British mission his
biographer (Bishop O. F. Whitney, his grandson) gives the following account:

Hyde, another of the Twelve, came in, and upon listening to what was passing, his heart melted within him, (for he had begun to drink of the cup filled with the overflowings of speculation), he acknowledged all his faults, asked forgiveness, and offered to accompany President Kimball on his mission to England. His offer was accepted, and he was set apart for that purpose.*

Thirty-five Elders', three Priests', two Teachers', and two Deacons' licenses were recorded in the license records in Kirtland, during the quarter ending June 3rd, by Thomas Burdick.

Licenses.

On the 10th of June, 1837, a conference of the Church

"On Sunday, the 4th day of June, 1837," says Heber C. Kimball, "the Prophet Joseph came to me, while I was seated in front of the stand, above the sacrament table, on the Melchisedek side of the Temple, in Kirtland, and whispering to me, said, 'Brother Heber, the Spirit of the Lord has whispered to me: Let my servant Heber go to England and proclaim my Gospel, and open the door of salvation to that nation.'" The thought was overpowering. He had been surprised at his call to the Apostleship; now he was overwhelmed. Like Jeremiah he staggered under the weight of his own weakness, exclaiming in self-humiliation: "O, Lord, I am a man of stammering tongue, and altogether unfit for such a work; how can I go to preach in that land, which is so famed throughout Christendom for learning, knowledge and piety; the nursery of religion; and to a people whose intelligence is proverbial! Feeling my weekness to go upon such an errand. I asked the Prophet if Brother Brigham might go with me. He replied that he wanted Brother Brigham to stay with him, for he had something else for him to do. The idea of such a mission was almost more than I could bear up under. I was almost ready to sink under the burden which was placed upon me. However, all these considerations did not deter me from the path of duty; the moment I understood the will of my heavenly Father, I felt a determination to go at all hazards, believing that He would support me by His almighty power, and endow me with every qualification that I needed; and although my family was dear to me, and I should have to leave them almost destitute, I felt that the cause of truth, the Gospel of Christ, outweighed every other consideration."—(Life of Heber C. Kimball, by O. F. Whitney, pp. 116, 117).

* The British mission was really an outgrowth of the work in Canada. "Several of the Saints in Canada," says Parley P. Pratt, in speaking of his labors there in the early spring of 1837, "were English, who had friends in England. Letters had already been sent to them with information of the rise of the Church, and of its principles. Several of the Canadian Elders felt a desire to go on a mission to their friends in that country. At length, Joseph Fielding, Isaac Russell, John Goodson and John Snider, of the Canadian Elders, were selected for a mission to England. Elders Heber C. Kimball and Orson Hyde, of the Quorum of the Twelve, were selected to go at the head of the mission, and Elder Willard Richards was appointed to accompany them."—(Autobiography of Parley P. Pratt, p. 183.)

was held at Portland, district of Johnstown, upper Canada, at which Elder John E. Page presided. There were present thirteen Elders, five Priests, eight Teachers, and six Deacons; and there were seven Elders, nine Priests, eleven Teachers and five Deacons ordained. West Bastard, Bedford, Bathurst, North Bathurst, East Bastard, Williamsburg, Leeds, and South Crosby branches were represented at the conference, comprising three hundred members in good standing, and five baptized at conference, total three hundred and five, being the fruits of the labors of Elder John E. Page in the last thirteen months.

Church Conference in Upper Canada.

Minutes of a High Council Meeting in Missouri.

At a meeting of the High Council, at the Committee Store, Far West, June 11, 1837, John Whitmer and W. W. Phelps presiding, Resolved by the Council and all present that the building committee be upheld in the mercantile business, by our prayers; that Lyman Wight, Simeon Carter and Elias Higbee be upheld in conducting a leather store; that John Corrill, Isaac Morley, and Calvin Bebee engage in the mercantile business if they choose; that the right of no man shall be infringed upon, to do as he choose according to the law of God and man; and that the above named men shall be upheld in purchasing goods as other men.

It was reported that certain individuals, not of the Church, were desirious, or were about to establish themselves as grocers, retailers of spirituous liquors, and so forth, in Far West, whereupon it was resolved that we will not uphold any man or men to take a partner out of the Church to trade or traffic in this line of business, or sell for any man or men out of the Church, in his name, or on commission.

David W. Patten requested that the Church pay his debts, and take him for security, that he might go forth and preach the Gospel.

Resolved that Elder Patten's request be granted, and that David W. Patten and Thomas B. Marsh, receive each a lot in the town of Far West, free of charge, and that the Bishop, if he approve, give a title.

JOHN CORRILL, Clerk.

The same evening, [11th of June] while I was engaged

in giving some special instructions to Elders Kimball and
The Prophet's Instructions to the British Missionaries. Hyde, and Priest Joseph Fielding,* concerning their mission to England, President Brigham Young came into my house, where we were sitting, accompanied by Dr. Willard Richards, who had just returned from a special business mission to New York, Boston, and other eastern cities, on which he started with President Young on the 14th of March—Dr. Richards having been previously ordained an Elder, viz., on the 6th of March, and President Young having returned from the mission a few days previous. My instructions to the brethren were, when they arrived in England, to adhere closely to the first principles of the Gospel, and remain silent concerning the gathering, the vision, and the Book of Doctrine and Covenants, until such time as the work was fully established, and it should be clearly made manifest by the Spirit to do otherwise.

Monday, June 12.—I was taken sick, and kept my room, unable to attend to business.

Elder Willard Richards, having reported his mission, requested the privilege of fulfilling a covenant which he
Willard Richards Added to the British Mission. made with President Kimball in January, which was, that he should, agreeable to his desire, accompany the Twelve on their first foreign mission. President Hyrum Smith and Sidney Rigdon granted his petition, laid their hands upon his head, and set him apart for the English mission.

Tuesday, 13.—My afflictions continued to increase, and were very severe, insomuch that I was unable to raise my
Illness of the Prophet. head from my pillow when the brethren called to bid me farewell; and at nine o'clock a. m. Elders Heber C. Kimball, Orson Hyde, Will-

* Joseph Fielding was born in Honeydon, Bradfordshire, England, and was the son of John and Rachel Fielding. He emigrated from England and located in Upper Canada, near Toronto, in 1832. Together with his two sisters, Mary and Rachel, he received the Gospel under the ministry of Elder Parley P. Pratt in May, 1832, and soon after was ordained a Priest and joined the mission to England as recorded in the text of the history above.

ard Richards, and Joseph Fielding, a Priest, a native of Honeydon, England, left Kirtland in company with President Brigham Young and several
of the Kirtland brethren and sisters, who continued
with them as far as Fairport, on Lake Erie, where the
missionaries took a steamer for Buffalo, directing their
course for New York City.

Wednesday, 14.—I continued to grow worse and worse
until my sufferings were excruciating, and
although in the midst of it all I felt to
rejoice in the salvation of Israel's God, yet
I found it expedient to call to my assistance
those means which a kind Providence had provided for the restoration of the sick, in connection with
the ordinances; and Dr. Levi Richards, at my request,
administered to me herbs and mild food, and nursed me
with all tenderness and attention; and my heavenly
Father blessed his administrations to the easing and comforting of my system, for I began to amend in a short
time, and in a few days I was able to resume my usual
labors.

This is one of the many instances in which I have suddenly been brought from a state of health, to the borders
of the grave, and as suddenly restored, for which my heart
swells with gratitude to my heavenly Father, and I feel
renewedly to dedicate myself and all my powers to His
service.

While I was thus afflicted, the enemy of all righteousness was suggesting, apostates reporting, and
the doubtful believing that my afflictions were
sent upon me, because I was in transgression,
and had taught the Church things contrary to godliness;
but of this the Lord judge between me and them, while I
pray my Father to forgive them the wrong they do.

The brethren appointed to the mission to England, landed
at Buffalo, and went down the canal. While walking
on its bank, President Kimball found an iron ring, about

Marginal notes:
Employment of Supplementary Means for Healing the Sick.

Dastardly Suggestions of Apostates.

one and one-fourth inch diameter, which he presented to
Elder Richards, saying, "I will make you a
present of this, keep it in remembrance
of me, for our friendship shall be as endless as this ring."

Progress of the British Mission.

The brethren having been disappointed in not receiving
funds from Canada, while at Buffalo, Elder Richards left
the company at Albany, and in company
with President Kimball visited his friends in
Richmond, Massachusetts, where they obtained means sufficient to continue their journey; and arrived in New
York on the eve of the 22nd of June, where they found
Elder Hyde and Brother Fielding, also three brethren
from Canada, viz., John Goodson,* one of the Seventies,
Elder Isaac Russell,† and John Snyder,‡ a Priest, who
had gone forward to join the mission; and on the 23rd
they engaged passage to Liverpool in the second cabin of
the merchant ship *Garrick*.

Arrival of British Mission in New York.

The brethren found but one member of the Church in
the City of New York, viz., Elder Elijah Fordham, who
was very attentive, and rendered them assistance ac-

* Concerning the place and time of the birth of John Goodson nothing can be
learned. He was, however, among those whom Elder Parley P. Pratt converted
in Upper Canada during his memorable mission in that land.

† Isaac Russell was born April 13, 1807, in Windy Hall, Cumberland County, England. His father's name was William Russell, and Isaac was the youngest of
thirteen children. The family emigrated to America about 1817, settling in Upper
Canada. In June, 1829, he married Mary Walton and made his home in Toronto,
where he received the Gospel under the ministry of Elder Parley P. Pratt. He
was ordained an Elder and engaged in missionary work in Upper Canada until he
joined the British mission under the leadership of Elder Heber C. Kimball, as stated
in the text.

‡ John Snyder was born in New Brunswick, Nova Scotia, November 11, 1800. He
removed with his father's family to Upper Canada, near Toronto. His father died
while John was yet a youth, but under the influence of his mother, a woman of
strong character and upright life, young Snyder grew to manhood with strong religious sentiments. In 1833, he joined, with the late President John Taylor, an
association of students of the Scriptures who were seeking for a profounder
knowledge of the truth. It was to this association that Elder Parley P. Pratt was
directed in 1836 and to whom he so frequently preached the Gospel that quite a
number of them united with the Church, John Snyder among them. Soon after
John Snyder was ordained to the Priesthood and joined the British mission as
stated in the text.

cording to his means, but they, being short of funds to pay their passage, etc., removed from their lodgings at Mrs. Fordham's (Elder Fordham's sister-in-law), on the 24th, and, hiring a room in an unfurnished store house of Elder Fordham's father, took lodgings on the floor, and ate their bread and drank their water, until they went on shipboard.

Sunday, 25.—The brethren remained in their lodgings fasting, praying and counciling for the success of the mission, and had a joyful time. In the afternoon two sectarian priests came in to talk and find fault, but they were soon confounded, and left. On the 28th the brethren deposited one of Orson Hyde's "Timely Warnings," in the New York postoffice, for each of the sectarian priests in the city, amounting to some hundreds. They went on board the *Garrick* on the 29th, and left the dock; on the 30th, lay at anchor in East River; and at 7:30 a. m., on the first of July, were towed out of harbor by a steamer, hoisted sail, and were out of sight of land at 4:30 p. m.

CHAPTER XXXV.

FINANCIAL CONDITION IN VARIOUS NATIONS—PROGRESS OF
THE BRITISH MISSION—CONFERENCES AT FAR WEST AND
KIRTLAND.

The following is an extract from a letter to the brethren
in Kirtland, written at—

FAR WEST, MISSOURI, July 7, 1837.

Monday, the 3rd of July, was a great and glorious day in Far West,
more than fifteen hundred Saints assembled at this place, and at half-
past eight in the morning, after prayer, singing, and an address, they proceeded to break the ground for the Lord's House. The day was beautiful; the Spirit of the Lord was with us. An excavation for this great
edifice, one hundred and ten feet long by eighty feet broad was nearly
finished. Tuesday, the 4th, we had a large meeting, and several of the
Missourians were baptized; our meetings, held in the open prairie, were
larger than they were in Kirtland, when I was there. We have more
or less to bless, confirm, and baptize, every Sabbath. This same day,
our school section was sold at auction, and although entirely a prairie,
it brought, on a year's credit, from $3.50 to $10.20 per acre, making
our first school fund five thousand and seventy dollars. Land cannot
be had around town now much less than ten dollars per acre.

Our numbers increase daily, and notwithstanding the season has been
cold and backward no one has lacked a meal or went hungry. Provisions
have risen in price, but not as high as accounts say they were abroad.
Public notice has been given by the mob in Daviess county, north of
us, for the Mormons to leave that county by the first of August and go
into Caldwell: our enemies will not slumber till Satan knows how vain
is his plotting. Our town gains some, we have about one hundred
buildings, eight of which are stores. If the brethren abroad are wise
and will come on with means and help enter the land and populate the
county and build the Lord's House, we shall soon have one of the most

precious spots on the globe; God grant that it may be so. Of late we receive little news from you, and we think much of that is exaggerated.

As ever,
W. W. PHELPS.

N. B.—Please say in your *Messenger and Advocate* "A postoffice has been established at Far West, Caldwell county, Missouri."

The same day (July 7th), the *Garrick* passed the banks of Newfoundland.

Some time previous to this I resigned my office in the "Kirtland Safety Society," disposed of my interest therein, and withdrew from the institution; being fully aware, after so long an experiment, that no institution of the kind, established upon just and righteous principles for a blessing not only to the Church but the whole nation, would be suffered to continue its operations in such an age of darkness, speculation and wickedness. Almost all banks throughout the country, one after the other, have suspended specie payment, and gold and silver have risen in value in direct ratio with the depreciation of paper currency. The great pressure of the money market is felt in England as well as America, and bread stuffs are everywhere high. The season has been cool, wet and backward.

The Prophet Resigns his Office in the "Safety Society."

Mexico, unwilling to acknowledge the independence of Texas, considers her inhabitants as rebellious subjects. Spain is divided against herself, wasting her blood and treasure in her own destruction. Portugal is rapidly exhausting her resources in princely luxuries. Poland has lost her rank among the nations to gratify the ambition of Nicholas, the Russian autocrat. The government of Buenos Ayres has declared war against Peru, and nearly all the republics of South America are mingled in the strife, while the Indians continue their depredations on the inhabitants of Florida. Trouble and distress are the grand topics of conversation amongst politicians, merchants, mechanics and dema gogues; and crimes, misdemeanors, and casualties, occupy a large space in the public journals.

Status of Various Nations.

Sunday, July 16.—Elder Hyde preached on the quarter-deck of the *Garrick* concerning the prophecies; the cabin passengers listened with attention, and were particularly affected during prayer, also a little child belonging to some of the steerage passengers, that was sick until it was considered hopeless, was healed by the power of God, President Kimball laying his hands upon it secretly.

On the 18th the *Garrick* entered St. George's Channel, in sight of Cape Clear.

On Thursday morning, July 20th, the *Garrick* anchored in the River Mersey, opposite Liverpool, and while the cable chains were yet rattling the merchant ship *South America*, which left New York at the same time with the *Garrick*, under a bet, it is said, of $10,000, as to which would be in Liverpool first, came alongside, having kept in sight daily during the voyage but never getting ahead of the *Garrick;* and in all the different stages from Kirtland to Liverpool, no vessel was permitted to go past the mission.

While the passengers were going on board a steamer Elders Kimball, Hyde, Richards, and Goodson jumped into a small boat and were rowed toward shore. When within leaping distance Elder Kimball sprang from the boat as if impelled by some superior power and alighted on the steps of the dock, followed instantly by Elders Hyde and Richards, all three of whom had not one farthing on earth at their command, while Elder Goodson, having a heavy purse of silver in his hand, waited until the vessel touched shore.

The Landing.

On the brethren went to Preston, about thirty miles from Liverpool, and as they alighted from the coach a large flag was unfurled nearly over their heads, with this inscription, in letters of gold, "Truth will Prevail," it being election day for members of Parliament. King William the Fourth had recently died and Queen Victoria was about to organize her cabinet. Taking lodgings in Wilford street, some of

"Truth will Prevail."

the Elders had an interview that evening with the Rev. James Fielding, brother of Joseph Fielding, who had a chapel in that place, where all the seven brethren went to hear him preach on Sunday, 23rd. After his sermon in the morning Mr. Fielding gave notice to his congregation that there were present some ministers from America, and they would occupy his pulpit in the afternoon. This unexpected offer was unsolicited but joyfully received, and in the afternoon President Kimball gave a brief relation of the history of the Church from the commencement, followed by Elder Hyde, who bore testimony to the same; thus was the key turned and the door of salvation opened to the inhabitants of England. At the close of the meeting Mr. Fielding offered his pulpit for the evening, when Elder Goodson preached and Brother Fielding bore testimony.

Kindness of Rev. James Fielding.

The same day that the Gospel was first preached in England I received the following

Revelation given at Kirtland, Ohio, July, 23rd, 1837. The word of the Lord unto Thomas B. Marsh, concerning the Twelve Apostles of the Lamb.*

1. Verily thus saith the Lord unto you, my servant Thomas, I have heard thy prayers, and thine alms have come up as a memorial before me, in behalf of those thy brethren who were chosen to bear testimony of my name, and to send it abroad among all nations, kindreds, tongues, and people, and ordained through the instrumentality of my servants.

2. Verily I say unto you, there have been some few things in thine heart and with thee with which I, the Lord, was not well pleased;

3. Nevertheless, inasmuch as thou hast abased thyself thou shalt be exalted, therefore all thy sins are forgiven thee.

4. Let thy heart be of good cheer before my face, and thou shalt bear record of my name, not only unto the Gentiles but also unto the Jews; and thou shalt send forth my word unto the ends of the earth.

5. Contend thou therefore morning by morning, and day after day let thy warning voice go forth, and when the night cometh, let not the inhabitants of the earth slumber because of thy speech.

6. Let thy habitation be known in Zion, and remove not thy house.

* Doctrine and Covenants, sec. cxii

for I, the Lord, have a great work for thee to do, in publishing my name among the children of men;

7. Therefore gird up thy loins for the work. Let thy feet be shod, also, for thou art chosen, and thy path lieth among the mountains, and among many nations;

8. And by thy word many high ones shall be brought low, and by thy word many low ones shall be exalted.

9. Thy voice shall be a rebuke unto the transgressor, and at thy rebuke let the tongue of the slanderer cease its perverseness.

10. Be thou humble, and the Lord thy God shall lead thee by the hand, and give thee answer to thy prayers.

11. I know thy heart, and have heard thy prayers concerning thy brethren. Be not partial toward them in love above many others; but let thy love be for them as for thyself, and let thy love abound unto all men, and unto all who love my name.

12. And pray for thy brethren of the Twelve. Admonish them sharply for my name's sake, and let them be admonished for all their sins, and be ye faithful before me unto my name.

13. And after their temptations and much tribulation, behold, I, the Lord, will feel after them, and if they harden not their hearts, and stiffen not their necks against me, they shall be converted and I will heal them.

14. Now, I say unto you, and what I say unto you I say unto all the Twelve, Arise and gird up your loins, take up your cross, follow me, and feed my sheep.

15. Exalt not yourselves; rebel not against my servant Joseph, for verily I say unto you, I am with him, and my hand shall be over him; and the keys which I have given unto him, and also to youward, shall not be taken from him till I come.

16. Verily I say unto you my servant Thomas, thou art the man whom I have chosen to hold the keys of my kingdom (as pertaining to the Twelve) abroad among all nations,

17. That thou mayest be my servant to unlock the door of the kingdom in all places where my servant Joseph, and my servant Sidney, and my servant Hyrum cannot come;

18. For on them have I laid the burden of all the churches for a little season;

19. Wherefore whithersoever they shall send you, go ye, and I will be with you; and in whatsoever place ye shall proclaim my name, an effectual door shall be opened unto you that they may receive my word;

20. Whosoever receiveth my word receiveth me, and whosoever receiveth me receiveth those (the First Presidency) whom I have sent, whom I have made counselors for my name's sake unto you.

21. And again, I say unto you, that whomsoever ye shall send in my name, by the voice of your brethren the Twelve, duly recommended and authorized by you, shall have power to open the door of my kingdom unto any nation, whithersoever ye shall send them,

22. Inasmuch as they shall humble themselves before me, and abide in my word, and harken to the voice of my Spirit.

23. Verily, verily I say unto you, darkness covereth the earth, and gross darkness the minds of the people, and all flesh has become corrupt before my face.

24. Behold, vengeance cometh speedily upon the inhabitants of the earth, a day of wrath, a day of burning, a day of desolation, of weeping, of mourning, and of lamentation, and as a whirlwind it shall come upon all the face of the earth, saith the Lord.

25. And upon my house shall it begin, and from my house shall it go forth, saith the Lord.

26. First among those among you, saith the Lord, who have professed to know my name, and have not known me, and have blasphemed against me in the midst of my house, saith the Lord.

27. Therfore see to it that you trouble not yourselves concerning the affairs of my Church in this place, saith the Lord;

28. But purify your hearts before me, and then go ye into all the world, and preach my Gospel unto every creature who has not received it,

29. And he that believeth and is baptized shall be saved, and he that believeth not and is not baptized, shall be damned.

30. For unto you (the Twelve) and those (the First Presidency) who are appointed with you, to be your counselors and your leaders, is the power of this Priesthood given, for the last days and for the last time, in the which is the dispensation of the fullness of times.

31. Which power you hold in connection with all those who have received a dispensation at any time from the beginning of the creation;

32. For verily I say unto you, the keys of the dispensation which ye have received have come down from the fathers, and last of all being sent down from heaven unto you.

33. Verily I say unto you, behold, how great is your calling. Cleanse your hearts and your garments, lest the blood of this generation be required at your hands.

34. Be faithful until I come, for I come quickly, and my reward is with me to recompense every man according as his work shall be. I am Alpha and Omega. Amen.

Albert P. Rockwood,* of Holliston, Massachusetts,

* Albert P. Rockwood was born June 5, 1805, in Holliston, Middlesex county, Massachusetts.

having heard of the Saints, through Elders Young and
Richards, came to Kirtland to investigate,
Baptism of
Albert P.   and was baptized on the 25th of July, by
Rockwood.   President Brigham Young.

Wednesday, 26.—Elder Hyde preached in the evening
in Mr. Fielding's chapel, and Elder Richards bore testimony. Much feeling was manifested by the
Progress of
the British   congregation, and many were convinced of
Mission.   the truth; but Mr. Fielding, fearing for the
loss of his society, more than the displeasure of heaven,
closed his doors against the brethren from that time, and
opposed the work with all his power. Invitations were
given to the Elders to preach in private houses in different parts of Preston, which opportunities were improved
daily, after the close of the factories.

Thursday, 27.—I started from Kirtland in company
with Elders Rigdon and Marsh for the purpose of visiting
the Saints in Canada. Brother Rockwood on
Vexatious
Law Suits at   his return home, Elder Brigham Young on a
Painesville.   mission to the eastern cities, started with us.
When we arrived at Painsville we were detained all day
by malicious and vexatious law suits. About sun-set I
got into my carriage to return home to Kirtland; at this
moment the sheriff sprang into the carriage, seized my
lines, and served another writ on me, which was sworn out
by a man who had a few weeks previously brought a new
fashioned cooking stove to Kirtland, and prevailed on me
to put it up in my kitchen, saying it would give credit to
his stove, wishing to have it tested by our people; and
now he thought would be a good time to get pay for it. I
gave my watch to the officer for security and we all returned home.

The following day I remained at home until evening,
when we set out again in Brother S. B. Stoddard's wagon
Second Start   to Ashtabula, a distance of thirty miles and
for Canada.   arrived there a little after daybreak and stayed
till afternoon and enjoyed ourselves very much in walking

on the beach and bathing in the beautiful, clear water of the lake. At four p. m. we took a deck passage on board the steamer for Buffalo. At night we all lay down to rest on the upper deck of the boat, and for pillows some took their boots, others their valises, and had a comfortable night's repose. We arrived at Buffalo the next morning in safety. Here* we separated from Brothers Brigham Young and Albert P. Rockwood, they going to the Eastern States; and myself, Brothers Sidney Rigdon and Thomas B. Marsh started for Toronto, Upper Canada.

About daybreak Sunday, July 30th, Elder Isaac Russell, who had been appointed to preach on the Obelisk in Preston market-place that day, and who slept in the second story of their *The British Mission—Attacked by Evil Spirits.* lodgings in Wilford street, went up to the third loft where Elders Hyde and Kimball were sleeping, and called upon them to pray for him, that he might be delivered from the evil spirits that were tormenting him to such a degree that he felt he could not live long unless he obtained relief. They immediately arose and laid hands on him and prayed that the Lord would have mercy on His servant and rebuke the devil. While thus engaged Elder Kimball was struck with great force by some invisible power and fell senseless on the floor; and the first thing Elder Kimball recollected was being supported by Elders Hyde and Russell beseeching the throne of grace in his behalf. They then laid him on the bed but his agony was so great he could not endure it, and arose, fell on his knees and prayed; then he arose and sat upon the bed while the brethren distinctly saw the evil spirits, who foamed and gnashed upon them with their teeth, by legions for the space of some minutes; Elder Richards was present the latter part of the time. About ten o'clock in the morning the brethren repaired to the river Ribble, according to previous appointment, and, in the midst of a large collection of people, baptized nine individuals, one of whom was George D. Watt, the first man baptized in England in this dispensation.

On Monday, the 31st of July, the Elders held a council and appointed Elders Goodson and Richards a mission to Bedford, and Elders Russell and Snyder to Alton, Cumberland county, continuing in prayer until morning, August 1st, when they took their departure for their several stations.

Spread of the Work in England.

The same day (August 1st) a general meeting of the Presidency, High Council, Bishop, and counselors and the Saints assembled at Far West. The High Council elected Thomas Grover a High Councilor in place of Jesse Hitchcock; and George Morey in place of Peter Whitmer, Jun., deceased; and Titus Billings was elected Bishop's counselor in place of John Corrill. Voted unanimously by the whole assembly that in the absence of the Presidency, Councilors, Bishop and counselors at Kirtland, the Elders in Missouri had no authority [to act as a Council for the Church], consequently their acts in that capacity during that space of time are considered null and void; and that every president of High Priests and Elders be ordained by some higher authority; and the president of any quorum having counselors may ordain them himself.

Affairs at Far West.

Elders Goodson and Richards arrived in Bedford on the 2nd and were joyfully received by the Rev. Timothy R. Matthews, to whom they had letters of introduction from his brother-in-law, Joseph Fielding, and were invited to preach in his chapel in the evening to his congregation.

Opening of the Work in Bedford.

Friday, 4.—Elder Kimball baptized Jennetta Richards* at Preston, daughter of the Rev. John Richards, of Walkerfold, Chaidgley, fifteen miles from Preston, and confirmed her at the water side. This was the first confirmation in England. Sister Richards returned home the day following, Saturday, 5th, and

First Confirmation in England.

* Jennetta Richards was born August 21, 1817, in Lancashire, England, and was the daughter of John and Ellen Richards.

persuaded her father to write to Elder Kimball to come and preach in his chapel.

The same day, August 5th, the Presidency, High Council, and all the authorities of the Church in Missouri, assembled in council at Far West, and unanimously resolved to go on moderately and build a house unto the name of the Lord in Far West, as they had means, and appointed Edward Partridge treasurer, to receive all the donations and subscriptions for the erection of the House of the Lord; Isaac Morley to be his secretary. Also voted that the committee, viz., Jacob Whitmer, Elisha H. Groves, and George M. Hinkle stand [as the building committee of the Lord's House at Far West]* until President David Whitmer goes to and returns from Kirtland; also, that the building committee of the House of the Lord have no store connected with building the house, but that every firm or individual that embarks in that business have, own, and claim such property as their own private individual property and stewardship.

Affairs in Far West— Building the Lord's House.

The Elders at Bedford continued to lecture in the basement of Mr. Matthews' chapel from evening to evening, with the most flattering prospects until this evening, when Elder Goodson, contrary to the most positive instructions of President Kimball, and without advising with any one, read publicly the vision from the Doctrine and Covenants, which turned the current of feeling generally, and nearly closed the door in all that region. Mr. Matthews wished the meetings to be removed from his house, but continued to attend the meetings occasionally and investigated the subject to considerable extent.

Goodson's Violation of Instructions.

In the August number of the *Messenger and Advocate* was published a prospectus for a new paper, to be published at Kirtland, Ohio, called the *Elders' Journal* of the Church of Latter-day Saints, to commence in October, edited by Joseph Smith, Jun.

The Elders' Journal.

* See page 481.

Elders Kimball and Hyde and Brother Fielding having
continued their labors in Preston, Elder Hyde preached
Confirmations   to a great multitude in the market place Sun-
at Preston.   day, the 6th of August, opposed by one Reverend gentleman who was quickly confounded by the
spirit of truth; and in the evening they met at the house
of Sister Ann Dawson and confirmed between forty and
fifty who had been baptized, most of whom had been
members of Mr. James Fielding's church, so mightily
grew the word, this being only the third Sabbath of the
brethren in Preston.   Mr. Fielding persecuted and called
the Elders "thieves, sheep stealers," etc., acknowledging
them good judges, having "stolen all the best of his flock."
Sister Dawson (a widown) kindly received the Elders into
her house and lodged them, which was a great blessing to the
brethren, as they were quite destitute, most of the people
extremely poor, and lodgings scarce; while they went
from house to house as invited, to procure their daily
meals.

Elder Kimball, having received a letter from Mr. John
Richards, inviting him to preach in his chapel, repaired
The Work in   to Walkerfold, where he was most hospitably
Walkerfold.   received, and the day following preached
three times in Mr. Richards' pulpit.

Elders Goodson and Richards baptized five at Bedford,
among whom, and the first, was Mrs. Ann Braddock, a
Baptisms at   widow, who was obliged to support her family
Bedford.   by her industry, yet she received the Elders
and lodged them.

Timothy R. Matthews, having investigated the work,
acknowledged the truth, and having previously borne testi-
The Failure of   mony of the same to his church in public, and
Mr. Matthews.   urged them to go forward, agreed with Elders
Goodson and Richards to meet them on the bank of the
river Ouse one hour before sunset and be baptized.   The
hour and the Elders arrived, but Mr. Matthews was not
there, he had gone out into the country to preach.

Elder Kimball preached on Monday and Wednesday evenings in Mr. Richards' chapel at Walkerfold, and on Thursday baptized six individuals. Mr. Matthews baptized himself in the river, and then went to baptizing his people, denouncing the Elders as false teachers and the doctrines of the Latter-day Saints as having come from hell, while he went to preaching the same doctrine, baptizing all, even infants, and laid on hands for confirmation.

Tuesday, _15._—The quorum of High Priests organized at Far West, Missouri, this day. Charles C. Rich* was ordained President of the High Priests' quorum in Missouri; and Henry Green president of the Elders in Caldwell county, August 20th.

Charles C. Rich Made President of High Priests in Missouri.

The same day Elders Wilford W. Woodruff and Jonathan H. Hale landed at Vinalhaven, on North Fox Island,† and commenced preaching.

Opening in the Fox Islands.

In the August number of the _Messenger and Advocate_ I published the following

CAUTION.

To the brethren and friends of the Church of the Latter-day Saints: I am disposed to say a word relative to the bills of the "Kirtland Safety Society Bank." I hereby warn them to beware of speculators, renegades, and gamblers, who are duping the unwary and unsuspecting, by palming upon them those bills, which are of no worth here. I discountenance and disapprove of any and all such practices. I know

---

* Charles C. Rich was born August 21, 1809, in Campbell county, Kentucky; and was the son of Joseph Rich and Nancy O. Neal. He was baptized by Ira M. Hinckley in Tazewell county, Illinois, on the first of April, 1832, and later was ordained an Elder by Zebedee Coltrin. He removed with his father to Far West, Missouri, in 1836. February 11, 1837, he married Sarah D. Pea.

† Fox Islands are off the south coast of Maine, directly east of Rockland. The principal town is Vinalhaven. The population of the islands at the time of Elder Woodruff's first visit is given at eighteen hundred, and the following is his description of the people and islands: "The inhabitants are generally wealthy, intelligent, industrious, generous and hospitable to strangers. North Island is nine miles long and two wide, population eight hundred; South Island is ten miles long and five wide, population one thousand." Elder Woodruff met with great success in his labors in this island and soon had a flourishing branch organized.

them to be detrimental to the best interests of society, as well as to the principles of religion.

[Signed]   JOSEPH SMITH, JUN.

In this month Elder Isaac Russell succeeded in establishing a small branch in Alston, England.

The Alston Branch.

At this time I was engaged in visiting the churches in Canada, preaching, baptizing, blessing the Saints and strengthening the branches.

The Prophet's Work in Canada.

I returned to Kirtland about the last of August and wrote the following letter, which I sent by the hand of Thomas B. Marsh:

KIRTLAND, GEAUGA, COUNTY, OHIO,
September 4, 1837.

Joseph Smith, Jun., President of the Church of Christ of the Latter-day Saints in all the world, to John Corrill and the whole Church in Zion, sendeth greeting.

Blessed be the God and Father of our Lord Jesus Christ who has blessed you with many blessings in Christ, and who has delivered you many times from the hands of your enemies, and planted you many times in a heavenly or holy place. My respects and love to you all, and my blessings upon all the faithful and true hearted in the New and Everlasting Covenant. Forasmuch as I have desired for a long time to see your faces and converse with you and instruct you in those things which have been revealed to me pertaining to the kingdom of God in the last days, I now write unto you offering as an apology my being bound with cords of affliction by the workers of iniquity, and also by the labors of the Church, endeavoring in all things to do the will of God for the salvation of the Church, both in temporal as well as spiritual things.

Brethren, we have waded through affliction and sorrow thus far for the will of God, that language is inadequate to describe. Pray ye therefore with more earnestness for our redemption. You have undoubtedly been informed by letter and otherwise of our difficulties in Kirtland, which are now about being settled; and that you may have a knowledge of the same, I inclose you the following minutes of the committee of the whole Church in Kirtland, the authorities, etc., referring you to my brother Hyrum and Brother Thomas B. Marsh for further particulars; also that you may know how to proceed to set in order and regulate the affairs of the Church in Zion whenever they become disorganized.

Minutes of a Conference Assembled in Committee of the whole Church at Kirtland on Sunday, the 3rd of September, 1837.

At nine o'clock in the morning George W. Robinson was called upon to take minutes of the conference. Sidney Rigdon then presented Joseph Smith, Jun., to the Church to know if they still looked upon and would still receive and uphold him as the President of the whole Church, and the vote was unanimous in the affirmative.

President Smith then presented Sidney Rigdon and Frederick G. Williams as his counselors, and to constitute with himself the three first Presidents of the Church. Voted unanimously in the affirmative, except for Frederick G. Williams, which was not carried unanimously.

President Smith then introduced Oliver Cowdery, Joseph Smith, Sen., Hyrum Smith, and John Smith for assistant counselors. These last four, together with the first three, are to be considered the heads of the Church. Carried unanimously.

Voted, that Newel K. Whitney hold his office as Bishop and continue to act as such in Kirtland, and that Reynolds Cahoon and Vinson Knight continue to act as counselors to the Bishop.

The Twelve Apostles were then presented one by one, when Thomas B. Marsh, David W. Patten, Brigham Young, Heber C. Kimball, Orson Hyde, Parley P. Pratt, Orson Pratt, William Smith, and William E. M'Lellin were received unanimously in their Apostleship, Luke S. Johnson, Lyman E. Johnson, and John F. Boynton were rejected and disfellowshiped, though privileged with confessing and making satisfaction.

Elder Boynton (who was the only one of the three present at the time) arose and endeavored to confess, justifying himself in his former conduct by reason of the failure of the bank.

His conduct was strongly protested against by Elder Brigham Young in a plain and energetic manner, stating various reasons why he could not receive him into fellowship until a hearty repentance and confession were manifested.

Elder Young was followed by Elder Marsh, who acquiesced in testimony and resolutions.

President Rigdon then addressed the assembly, showing the cause of the difficulty with Elders Boynton and Johnson in leaving their calling to attend to other occupations.

Elder Boynton again rose and still attributed his difficulties to the failure of the bank, stating that he understood the bank was instituted by the will of God, and he had been told that it should never fail, let men do what they would.

President Smith then arose and stated that if this had been declared no one had authority from him for so doing, for he had always said that unless the institution was conducted on righteous principles it would not stand.

A vote was then taken to know if the congregation was satisfied with Elder Boynton's confession; carried in the negative.

Conference adjourned for one hour.

Conference reassembled at two o'clock in the afternoon; opened by reading, singing, and prayer.

The President then arose and said he would call upon the Church to know if they were satisfied with their High Council, and should proceed to name them individually.

John Johnson, Joseph Coe, Joseph C. Kingsbury, and Martin Harris were objected to, also John P. Greene, but his case went over until he should be present.

Noah Packard, Jared Carter, Samuel H. Smith, were sustained.

Oliver Granger, Henry G. Sherwood, William Marks, Mayhew Hillman, Harlow Redfield, Asahel Smith, Phinehas Richards, and David Dort, were chosen to fill the places of those objected to, (and Thomas Grover having moved west) John Smith, chosen one of the presidents of the Church, all having belonged to the High Council.

The President then called upon the congregation to know if the recently appointed presidents of the Seventies should stand in their calling.

Voted that John Gaylord, James Forster, Salmon Gee, Daniel S. Miles, Joseph Young, Josiah Butterfield, and Levi W. Hancock, should reatain their offices as presidents of Seventies; John Gould was objected to.

The President then arose and made some remarks concerning the former presidents of the Seventies, the calling and authority of their Priesthood, etc.

Voted that the old presidents of the Seventies [who were High Priests] be referred to the quorum of High Priests; and also, that if any members of the quorum of the Seventies should be dissatisfied and would not submit to the present order and receive these last presidents, the latter should have power to demand their licenses, and the former should no longer be considered members of the Church.

Conference closed by prayer by the President.

JOSEPH SMITH, JUN., President,
GEORGE W. ROBINSON, Clerk.

Announcement concerning Oliver Cowdery.

DEAR BRETHREN—Oliver Cowdery has been in transgression, but as he is now chosen as one of the presidents or counselors, I trust that he will yet humble himself and magnify his calling, but if he should not, the Church will soon be under the necessity of raising their hands against him; therefore pray for him.

David Whitmer, Leonard Rich, and others have been in transgression, but we hope that they may be humble and ere long make satisfaction to the Church, otherwise they cannot retain their standing; therefore we say unto you, beware of all disaffected characters, for they come not to build up, but to destroy and scatter abroad. Though we or an angel from heaven preach any other Gospel, or introduce an order of things other than those things which ye have received, and are authorized to receive from the First Presidency, let him be accursed.

May God Almighty bless you all and keep you unto the coming and kingdom of our Lord and Savior Jesus Christ.

Yours in the bond of the New Covenant,

JOSEPH SMITH, JUN.

I received the following:

Revelation given at Kirtland, Ohio, September 4, 1837, making known the transgression of John Whitmer and William W. Phelps.

Verily thus saith the Lord unto you my servant Joseph—my servants John Whitmer and William W. Phelps have done those things which are not pleasing in my sight, therefore if they repent not they shall be removed out of their places. Amen.

September 9.—The High Council of Kirtland met in the Lord's House and organized by electing Jared Carter, president, and Phinehas Richards, clerk. The members elected on the 3rd were ordained and drew for their numbers, and the whole were arranged as follows: John P. Greene, No. 1; Asahel Smith, No. 2; Samuel H. Smith, 3; Mayhew Hillman, 4; William Marks, 5; Noah Packard, 6; Oliver Granger, 7; David Dort, 8; Jared Carter, 9; Phinehas Richards, 10; Henry G. Sherwood, 11; and Harlow Redfield, 12.

The High Council of Kirtland withdrew the hand of fellowship from Uriah and Lydia Ann Hawkins for unlawful matrimony, deceiving, and unchristianlike conduct.

Minutes of a Meeting in the Kirtland Temple.

Sunday, September 10th, 2 o'clock, afternoon, in an assembly of the Church in the Lord's House, Kirtland, President Rigdon read the rules and regulations of the House of the Lord, as passed by the different quorums on the 18th of January, 1836, when the Church voted to receive the same, and be governed by them.

The minutes of the High Council of the 9th instant were read, after which those of the Twelve who were disfellowshiped the previous Sabbath had opportunity to speak; and Luke S. Johnson, Lyman E. Johnson, and John F. Boynton made their confessions and were received into fellowship by vote of the Church, also to retain their apostleship.

President Smith read a letter from Elder Thomas B. Marsh to the Church, stating that before he started from Missouri he had received satisfaction from these Elders. Elder Young also stated the same.

High Councilor John P. Greene made some confessions to the Church, stating wherein he had been wrong for a short time past; and the Church voted that he be received into fellowship and retain his office.

President Rigdon made some observations on the business transacted last Sabbath, reproving some for the conjectures they had respecting President Smith and himself conniving together to remove certain individuals from office, etc., or at least to use their influence to do so. This he informed them was a mistake, for not one word had passed between them on the subject, neither had he a premiditated thought upon the subject.

President Smith then corrected some mistakes of certain individuals which had been circulated by them concerning what he had said on the last Sabbath.

The Lord's Supper was administered by Elders Luke S. and Lyman E. Johnson, and John F. Boynton.

GEORGE W. ROBINSON, Clerk.

When a lying spirit is abroad it is difficult for truth to be understood.

CHAPTER XXXVI.

THE GATHERING SAINTS — INCREASE IN THE NUMBER OF
STAKES CONTEMPLATED—COUNCILS IN ZION AND KIRT-
LAND—CLOSE OF THE VOLUME.

AT a conference of the authorities of the Church and
the Saints in the House of the Lord at Kirtland, September 17th, Bishop Newel K. Whitney said the
time had arrived when it became necessary
for him to travel, and necessarily he must
have an agent to act in his absence agreeable to the provisions made in the revelations. He nominated William
Marks, who was elected agent to the Bishop by unanimous vote.

Bishop's Agent Appointed.

George W. Robinson was unanimously elected general
Church recorder in place of Oliver Cowdery,
who had removed to Missouri.

The Church Recorder.

After taking into consideration the situation of Zion
and the Church in general, the conference decided that it
was of great importance to the cause of truth
in general, and the prosperity of the work,
that the Bishop and his counselors send abroad their
memorial to all the Saints throughout the land, as well as
to all well-wishers to the cause of Zion, and that their appeal go forth in the name and by the authority of the
Church to all the Saints scattered abroad.

The Bishop's Memorial.

The same evening the Elders assembled in conference
in the House of the Lord when I addressed
them on the subject of the gathering of the
Saints in the last days, and the duties of the different
quorums in relation thereto.

The Prophet on the Gathering.

It appeared manifest to the conference that the places appointed for the gathering of the Saints were at this time crowded to overflowing, and that it was necessary that there be more stakes of Zion appointed in order that the poor might have a place to gather to, "wherefore it was moved, seconded and voted unanimously that President Joseph Smith, Jun., and Sidney Rigdon be requested by this conference to go and appoint other stakes, or places of gathering, and that they receive a certificate of their appointment, signed by the clerk of the Church."

Other Stakes of Zion to be Appointed.

Elder William Marks, who had previously been appointed agent to the Bishop, being called upon arose and said that he would comply with the request of the Church, and the Lord being his helper he would discharge the duties of his office to the best of his ability. After which the Elders present who were in a situation to travel were called upon to number themselves, and there were numbered one hundred and nine, and they were divided into eight companies in the following order—number one to thirteen, called the first company, were appointed to travel east; No. 14 to 26, were to travel southeast; No, 27 to 39, south; No. 40 to 52, southwest; No. 53 to 65, west; No. 66 to 78, northwest; No. 79 to 91, north; No. 92 to 104, northeast. Five being left after this division, No. 105 was appointed to travel with the company going southeast; No. 106, with the company northwest; 107, south; 108, east; 109, with the north company. It was further appointed that those who might desire to travel a different course from the one which was appointed to the division to which they belonged, might have the privilege of changing with those of another division. And lastly it was appointed that the different divisions hold their own meetings, to make such arrangements as they should think proper in relation to their journeying.

Arrangements for Preaching the Gospel.

Agreeable to the vote of the conference on the 17th,

Bishop Whitney and counselors issued the memorial as follows:

KIRTLAND, OHIO, September 18th, 1837.

To the Saints Scattered Abroad, the Bishop of Kirtland and his Counselors send Greeting:

Whereas the Church in Kirtland has taken into consideration the affairs of the Latter-day Saints in general, having opportunities of making themselves acquainted with the situation of the Saints throughout the continent, and the very flattering prospects of the prosperity of the cause of God in our land, and also of the peculiar condition of the city of Kirtland, which is a kind of first fruits of the cities which the Lord has begun to build unto Himself in these last days, it has been deemed of great importance to the prosperity of the cause of truth in general, that the Bishop and his counselors send abroad this their memorial to all the Saints throughout the land, as well as to all well wishers to the cause of Zion in this our most happy country.

It is a fact well known that the Saints in the city of Kirtland have been called to endure great affliction for the truth's sake, and to bear a heavy burden in order that the foundation of the kingdom of God might be laid on a sure and certain basis, so that the prophetic vision of Daniel might most certainly be fulfilled, that this kingdom might break in pieces all other kingdoms and stand for ever.   The exertions of the enemy to prevent this have been very great; and through their great exertions they have given to the Saints great trouble, and caused them much expense.   In addition to this, they have had to publish the word of the Lord, which has been attended with great expense.   These things, together with building the House of the Lord, have embarrassed them very much; for when subscriptions failed they went on and accomplished the work of building the house themselves, plighting all that they had, property, credit, and reputation, and by these means accomplished this great work which is the wonder and admiration of the world.   This they have done in faith, believing that, as the multitude of Saints increased, their liberality would abound towards those who, regarding nothing but the salvation of the world, have thus exposed themselver to financial ruin in order that the work of the gathering might not fail.   And besides all this there have been a large number of poor who have had to receive assistance from the donations of the Church, which have tended to increase its embarrassments; and now so numerous are the Saints grown that it is impracticable for them all to gather to the places which are now appointed for this purpose.

The Church at Kirtland has, therefore, required at the hand of our beloved brethren, Joseph Smith, Jun., and Sidney Rigdon, men who have not thought their lives dear unto them in order that the cause of God might be established, presidents whom God has appointed to preside over the whole Church, and the persons to whom this work belongs, that they should go forth and lay off other stakes of Zion, or places of gathering, so that the poor may have a place of refuge, or places of refuge, in the day of tribulation which is coming swiftly on the earth. All these things will be attended with expense. Feeling ourselves under great responsibility by virtue of our office and calling in the Church of God, we present this our memorial to all the Saints, making a most solemn appeal to the feelings, benevolence and philanthropy of all the Saints into whose hands this our memorial comes, in faith and confidence that this appeal will not be made in vain.

It is the fixed purpose of our God, and has been so from the beginning, as appears by the testimony of the ancient Prophets, that the great work of the last days was to be accomplished by the tithing of His Saints. The Saints were required to bring their tithes into the store house, and after that, not before, they were to look for a blessing that there should not be room enough to receive it. (See Malachi 3rd chapter, 10th verse). Our appeal, then, to the Saints is founded on the best of testimony, that which no Saint will feel to gainsay, but rejoice to obey. The Saints of God will rejoice in all that the Lord does, and in doing all that the Lord requires. The sacrifice of righteousness which the Lord requires will be offered with a willing heart and ready mind, and with great joy, because they are accounted worthy to offer up sacrifice for His name.

In making this appeal to the benevolence of the Saints of God we do not only take into consideration the situation of the poor, the embarrassments of the stake of Kirtland, but also their own interests, for every Saint has an equal interest in building up the Zion of our God, for it is after the Lord has built up Zion that He will appear in His glory (Psalm cii: 16). We all look for the appearing of the great God and our Savior Jesus Christ, but we shall look in vain until Zion is built, for Zion is to be the dwelling place of our God when He comes (Joel iii: 21). Anyone who will read this chapter with attention will see that it treats of the last days, and of the Zion of the last days. How, then, is the Lord to dwell in Zion if Zion be not built up? This question we leave the Saints to answer. The salvation of the Saints one and all depends on the building up of Zion, for without this there is no salvation, for deliverance in the last days is found in Zion and in Jerusalem, and in the remnant whom the Lord our God shall call, or in other words, in the -stakes which He shall appoint (Joel ii: 32)

It is in Zion where the Lord is to create upon every dwelling place and upon her assemblies a cloud of smoke by day and the shining of a flaming fire by night. It is upon the glory of Zion that there will be a defense. It is in Zion that there shall be a tabernacle for a shadow in the day time from the heat, and for a place of refuge and for a covert from storm and from rain (Isaiah iv: 5, 6). It is upon the walls of Zion where the watchmen shall see eye to eye (Isaiah lii: 8).

Whatever is glorious, whatever is desirable, whatever pertains to salvation, either temporal or spiritual, our hopes, our expectations, our glory, and our reward, all depend on our building up Zion according to the testimony of the Prophets, for unless Zion is built our hopes perish, our expectations fail, our prospects are blasted, our salvation withers, and God will come and smite the whole earth with a curse. Hear, then, O ye Saints of the last days! And let this our appeal have a favorable reception among you. Let every Saint consider well the nature of his calling in the last days, and the great responsibility which rests upon him or her, as one to whom God has revealed His will; and make haste not only to the relief of Kirtland, but also to the building up of Zion. Let every man and every woman give heed the very instant that they embrace the Gospel, and exert themselves with energy to send on means to build up Zion, for our God bids us to hasten the building of the city, saying the time has come when the city must be pushed forward with unceasing exertions, for behold, the day of calamity draweth nigh, and unless the Saints hasten the building of the city they will not escape.

Be admonished, then, O ye Saints! And let not covetousness, which is idolatry, nor worldly ambition hinder you; but gather up your gold and your silver and all the means you have and send on to the Saints who are engaged in this great work of building the Zion of God, that there may be a place of refuge for you and for your children in the day of God's vengeance, when He shall come down on Idumea, or the world, in His fury and stamp them down in His wrath, and none shall escape but the inhabitants of Zion. What we say unto one we say unto all, haste, haste, and delay not! for the hour of desolation does not linger, and with all the power that the Saints have, and with all the diligence they can use they will scarcely escape.

The time is not far distant when some of those who now deride and mock the Saints for devoting their all to build up the Zion of God, will bless their name for having provided a city of refuge for them and their children, regardless of the ravings of ungodly priests, and the mockings of a stupid and ignorant people. In the confidence which we have in the good sense and righteous principles of the multitude of the

Saints, we send this our memorial in the name of our Master, Jesus, believing that this appeal will be received with great kindness, and will be attended to with untiring perseverance until the object for which it has been sent shall be accomplished.   And may the God of all grace pour out His richest blessings on your heads, and crown you with abundance, that the Zion of our God may flourish and cease not until the righteousness thereof shall go forth as the light and the salvation thereof as a lamp which burneth, is the prayer of your brethren in Christ Jesus.

NEWEL K. WHITNEY,
REYNOLDS CAHOON,
VINSON KNIGHT.

About this time Elder Parley P. Pratt, who was labor-

The Voice of Warning.

ing in New York, published his Voice of Warning, consisting of 216 pages.*

I started from Kirtland on the 27th of September, in company with Brother Sidney Rigdon, to fulfill the mis-

The Prophet's Departure for Missouri.

sion appointed us on the 18th of September by a conference of Elders, in establishing places of gathering for the Saints; Brothers William Smith and Vinson Knight accompanying us.

October 1.—Elder Lyman Sherman was elected High Councilor at Kirtland in place of Jared Carter, removed to Far West.

October 2.—Samuel H. Smith was elected president of the High Council, and council voted that if a councilor

* The above named publication, "A Voice of Warning and Instruction to all People," is the first argumentative and doctrinal work published by any of the Elders; and it is no disparagement of other works to say that this pioneer book of its class is not only the first in the matter of time when issued, but first also in excellence. It has been a most successful missionary; and thousands have been brought to a conviction of the truth through reading its pages. The first edition—three thousand copies—sold in about two years. A second edition—two thousand five hundred copies—was issued; and such was the increase in the demand for it that by 1846, the author could congratulate himself upon having seen it pass through five editions. During more than half a century since then "The Voice of Warning" has passed through many editions in English, and has been translated into seven foreign languages, and in a number of these several editions have been issued. The author, of honored memory, is to be congratulated upon the attainment of his fondest hopes respecting this work, as so prophetically expressed in the preface of the first European edition: "And should the author be called to sacrifice his life for the *Truth*, he will have the consolation that it will be said of him, as it was of Abel—'*He being dead, yet speaketh.*' "

absented himself from their meetings without a reasonable excuse, he should be reported to the Church as a delinquent. The High Council at Kirtland voted that the clerk grant licenses President of High Council Elected. to the members of the council (who wished to travel), signed by the president and clerk.

We arrived at Terre Haute, Indiana, on the 12th, about midway from Kirtland to Far West.

My brother Hyrum's wife, Jerusha Barden Smith, died on the 13th of October while I was at Terre Haute, and her husband at Far West. She left five small children and numerous relatives Death of Hyrum Smith's Wife. to mourn her loss; her demise was severely felt by all. She said to one of her tender offspring when on her dying bed, "Tell your father when he comes that the Lord has taken your mother home and left you for him to take care of." She died in full assurance of a part in the first resurrection.

October 15.—The High Priests' quorum at Kirtland decided to take Doctor Sampson Avard's license until he returns and make satisfaction; and the High Council concurred.

Minutes of High Council.

October 18.—The High Council and presidents of the different quorums met in the Lord's House, Samuel H. Smith presiding, and after a lengthy discussion concerning existing evils, agreed that it was time to commence the work of reform, and voted unanimously to meet again in the Lord's House on Monday evening next, and invite the different quorums to meet at the same time, and commence pruning the vine of God in Kirtland, and thus continue the work evening after evening until it shall be wisdom to stay their hands.

PHINEHAS RICHARDS, Clerk of the High Council.

Sunday 22.—The Church in Kirtland disfellowshiped twenty-two brethren and sisters until they make satisfaction for uniting with the world Twenty-two Disfellowshiped. in a dance the Thursday previous.

Minutes of High Council.

October 23.—The High Council of Kirtland appointed Luke S. Johnson, Reynolds Cahoon, and John Gould a committee to visit John Johnson, Jun., and see if he would desist from selling spirituous liquors to those who were in the habit of getting intoxicated, and report to the authorities of the Church those members who might drink spirits at his house.   Also voted that the Church see that all difficulties and differences be settled as speedily as possible; and that unruly children be reported to their parents, and if they neglect to take suitable notice of it, then the parents shall be reported to the authorities of the Church and dealt with accordingly.

Voted that we discountenance the use of ardent spirits in any way to sell or to be brought into this place for sale or use.

PHINEHAS RICHARDS, Clerk.

Sunday, October 29.—Nine more of the brethren and sisters were reported to the Church as having been en-

Confessions. gaged in the recreations of the 19th instant and eleven of the thirty-one that had been reported made confession.

On the 30th of October, Brothers Norris, Brewster, and others, presented to the High Council a plan for the better

Norris Brewster. organization of the Church in temporal affairs, stating that Moroni had appeared to Collins

Brewster. The council decided that it was a trick of the devil.

Most of those who were complained of for participating in the recreation on the 19th and had not confessed, ac-

More Confessions. knowledged their fault to the High Council on the first of November, and the remainder were required so to do or be cut off from the Church.

November 2.—The High Council voted that loungers

Action Against Loungers. about the streets should be labored with, and appointed a committee of three for that purpose.

The Church in Kirtland voted to sanction the appoint-

The Egyptian Records. ment of Brother Phinehas Richards and Reuben Hedlock, by the Presidency, to transact business for the Church in procuring means to translate and print the records taken from the Catacombs of Egypt, then in the Temple.

I arrived at Far West some time in the latter part of October or first of November. A meeting of some of the Church was called on the sixth to counsel on certain affairs of the Church,

Arrival of the Prophet at Far West.

which I attended with Brothers Rigdon and Hyrum Smith. There were present also Elders Thomas B. Marsh, William E. M'Lellin, Lyman E. Johnson, William Smith, and Vinson Knight, from Ohio, the High Council of the Church of Far West, and some other Elders. Prayer by W. W. Phelps. Several topics were discussed, when it was unanimously voted that it be recommended to the proprietors of the corporation of Far West to petition the trustees of said corporation to alter the streets or lessen them so as to make each block contain four acres of ground, and each block to be divided into four lots. Also voted unanimously that it is the opinion of this council that there is sufficient room in this country for the churches to continue gathering from abroad; also that the building of the House of the Lord be postponed until the Lord shall reveal it to be His will to have it commenced.

Adjourned until early candle light, and met accordingly, when remarks were made by many of the authorities present upon the previous disposition of the town plat, the purchase of land, etc.; and all difficulties were satisfactorily settled except a

The Settlement of Difficulties.

matter between Oliver Cowdery, Thomas B. Mash, and myself, which was referred to us with the agreement that our settlement of the affair would be sufficient for the council.

W. W. Phelps presided at this meeting, and Oliver Cowdery acted as clerk.

Minutes of a High Council at Kirtland.

The High Council and Bishop of Kirtland met in the Lord's House on Tuesday evening, November 7th to discuss the question, "Who presides when the presidents are absent?" but upon discussion were not able to come to any conclusion.

Thomas Burdick was appointed High Councilor in the place and absence of Phinehas Richards; and Harlow Redfield clerk for the time being.

President Joseph Smith, Sen., proposed that Brother Phinehas Richards be ordained under the hands of President John Smith and Bishop Whitney, and he was accordingly blessed for his mission.

PHINEHAS RICHARDS, Clerk.

Minutes of a Conference at Far West, Missouri, November 7th, 1837.

At a general assembly of the Church of Latter-day Saints, assembled at Far West to take into consideration and transact the business of said Church, Elder Thomas B. Marsh was chosen as moderator and Oliver Cowdery clerk.

After singing the moderator addressed the throne of grace in prayer, after which President Sidney Rigdon explained the object of the meeting, giving a relation of the recent reorganization of the Church in Kirtland. The minutes of said meeting at Kirtland were read by the moderator who also nominated Joseph Smith, Jun., the first President of the whole Church, to preside over the same.

All were requested (male and female) to vote; and he was unanimously chosen.

President Smith then made a few remarks accepting the appointment, requesting the prayers of the Church in his behalf. He also nominated President Sidney Rigdon to be one of his counselors, and he was unanimously chosen.

He then nominated Frederick G. Williams to be his second counselor, but he was objected to by Elder Lyman Wight in a few remarks referring to a certain letter written to this place by the said Frederick G. Williams.

Also Elder Marsh objected to President Williams.

Elder James Emmet also objected to President Williams.

Bishop Edward Partridge said he seconded President Williams' nomination and should vote for him; and as to said letter, he had heard it and saw nothing so criminal in it.

President David Whitmer also made a few remarks in President Williams' favor.

Elder Marsh made further remarks.

Elder Thomas Grover also objected to President Williams.

President Sidney Rigdon then nominated President Hyrum Smith to take President Williams' place.

The moderator called for a vote in favor of President Williams, but he was rejected.

He then called for a vote in favor of President Hyrum Smith, which was carried unanimously.

Some few remarks were made by Presidents David Whitmer and Sidney Rigdon.

David Whitmer was nominated as the President of this branch of the Church, but was objected to by Elder Marsh.

Bishop Edward Partridge said he should vote for President Whitmer.

Elder William E. M'Lellin made a few marks.

Elder George M. Hinkle and Elder King Follet made a few remarks in favor of President Whitmer.

Elders Caleb Baldwin and Seymour Brunson spoke against President Whitmer.

Elder Elisha H. Groves spoke in favor of President Whitmer.

Further remarks from Elder M'Lellin, by request of President Whitmer, gave general satisfaction.

Remarks were also made by President Joseph Smith, Jun., who called for an expression, which was carried by almost a unanimous vote in favor of President Whitmer.

President Joseph Smith, Jun., then nominated John Whitmer for an assistant president, who was objected to, and Elder Marsh spoke in opposition to him, and read a list of charges from a written document against him and President Phelps.

President John Whitmer then spoke a few words by way of confession, and was followed by Elder Isaac Morley.

The vote sustaining him was called, and carried unanimously.

The meeting adjourned for one hour.

Meeting convened according to adjournment, a hymn was sung and prayer offered by the moderator.

W. W. Phelps was nominated for an assistant president for this branch of the Church by President Joseph Smith, Jun.

Brother Phelps rose and made certain remarks on the subject of the charges referred to above by way of confession, whereupon the vote was put by President Rigdon and passed unanimously.

Elders John Murdock, Solomon Hancock, Elias Higbee, Calvin Bebee, John M. Hinkle, Thomas Grover, and Simeon Carter were unanimously chosen High Councilors.

Lyman Wight was nominated a member of the High Council but was objected to by John Anderson; they went aside to converse.

Newel Knight was unanimously chosen. George M. Hinkle was nominated, and objected to by Elder James Emmet, because he was too noisy; by King Follet because of his military office; and by James Durfee because he was a merchant.

Elder Hinkle made a few remarks.

The vote was called and was unanimous in Elder Hinkle's favor.

Levi Jackman and Elisha H. Groves were unanimously chosen.

John Anderson then took the stand and made his objections to Lyman Wight; after which Elder Wight also spoke.

The vote was called and Elder Wight was unanimously chosen.

The Twelve Apostles were then called, namely, Thomas B. Marsh, David W. Patten, Brigham Young, Heber C. Kimball, Orson Hyde, William E. M'Lellin, Parley P. Pratt, William Smith, Luke Johnson, Orson Pratt, John F. Boynton, and Lyman E. Johnson, and were unanimously sustained.

Bishop Edward Partridge was nominated to still act as Bishop, and was unanimously chosen; he then nominated Isaac Morley and Titus Billings for his counselers, who were also unanimously chosen.

Elder Isaac Morley was unanimously appointed Patriarch of this branch of the Church.

Elder John Corrill was chosen to be keeper of the Lord's Store House.

Elder Isaac Morley was then ordained to the office of Patriarch under the hands of Presidents Joseph Smith, Jun., Sidney Rigdon and Hyrum Smith.

The congregation, after a few remarks from Sidney Rigdon, unanimously voted not to support stores and shops selling spirituous liquors, tea, coffee, or tobacco.

A vote was called on the subject of the presidents of the Seventies; and those who have recently been appointed to that office, were unanimously received.

The congregation then united with President Sidney Rigdon, who, in the closing prayer, called upon their Lord to dedicate this land for the gathering of the Saints, and their inheritances.

THOMAS B. MARSH, Moderator,
OLIVER COWDERY, Clerk.

FAR WEST, MISSOURI, November 10, 1837.

At a general meeting of the ordained members of the Church in this place Elder Thomas B. Marsh opened the meeting by prayer, and President Sidney Rigdon read the memorial of the Bishop of Kirtland and his counselors, of September 18th, 1837, to the churches abroad. He then laid before the meeting the subject of laying off cities, of consecrating lands for public purposes, and for remunerating those who lay them off. It was unanimously voted that all city plats hereafter laid off, after remunerating those for their labor who may be engaged in appointing and laying off the same shall be consecrated for the public benefit of the Church, for building houses for public worship, or such other purposes as the Church shall say.

President Rigdon then read the prospectus of the *Elders' Journal,* which was unanimously received.

It was then unanimously voted that the persons present use their exertions to support said paper.

It was then voted that the town of Far West be enlarged so that it contain four sections, that is, two miles square.

Voted that Bishop Partridge and his counselors be appointed a committee to appraise the land adjacent to the present town plat and see that it is enlarged according to the above vote, provided the present holders of those lands will take such a price for the same as the above appraisers think them to be worth; and that the same be then disposed of as voted above.

A call was then made for those whose circumstances were such as to permit them to go out to preach to present themselves.   There were twenty-three who arose.

Sylvester H. Earl, Henry Jackman, Harrison Sagers, and John W. Clark were ordained Elders, and William J. Levans was ordained a Priest.

President Rigdon then closed the meeting by prayer.

THOMAS B. MARSH, Moderator,
OLIVER COWDERY, Clerk.

About this time I left Far West on my return to Kirtland.

Minutes of a High Council at Kirtland.

Kirtland, November 20th.   The High Council met in the Lord's House, John Smith presiding.

Reuben Hedlock preferred the following charge against Zenos H. Brewster, Jane Brewster, Collins Brewster, D. H. Dustin and wife, Moses R. Norris and wife, Eliza Norris, Samuel Barnet, Jemima Butler, Osman M. Duel, ———Butler, and Roxanna Repsher, for giving heed to revelations said to be translated from the Book of Moroni by Collins Brewster, and for entering into a written covenant different from the articles and covenants of the Church of Latter-day Saints, and following a vain and delusive spirit.

Two were appointed to speak on each side.

The writings and revelations kept and received by the accused were presented, and read by the clerk of the Council.

The accused pleaded not guilty.

Brother Felshaw was called forward by the plaintiff, who stated that he had visited the accused and labored with them according to the law of the Church; that the accused justified themselves, seeing the Church had not lived according to the former revelations, and they considered the High Council and others were in transgression; and that most of the accused appeared to be determined to pursue their own way, whether right or wrong.

Brother Allen said the accused appeared to manifest a hard spirit against the Presidents of the Church and the High Council.

Brother Dunn concurred.

Brother Sawyer stated that he heard Brother Norris say that those in authority were against him and if he could not establish an order of things here to his mind he would go out among the Gentiles and do it.

Brother Knight confirmed the foregoing testimony.

The accused called Brother Freeman, who stated that he had attended a number of the meetings of the accused and saw nothing out of the way.

Brother E. Strong confirmed Brother Freeman's statement, but did not know when he attended the meetings at which they received revelations for themselves.

Brother J. Foster agreed with the last two witnesses.

Brother Preston was called by the accuser, who testified that the accused refused to admit him into their meetings and that others were rejected.

Several witnesses testified that they attended their meetings and saw nothing wrong.

Others testified they had heard them speak against the heads of the Church and that Brother Joseph had many things to repent of, and one of them said he thought some put too much stress on the Priesthood, and that he was informed that Brother Norris laid his hands on Collins Brewster and ordained him a prophet, and that one of the accused said he was determined to pursue his own course whether it suited the High Council or not.

After the pleas of his councilors the accused spoke in justification of their course generally, when the Council decided that the charge had been fully sustained and withdrew fellowship from those who persisted in their course of conduct as before mentioned.

HARLOW REDFIELD, Clerk.

At a conference of Elders, consisting of all the authorities of the Church in Kirtland, November 27th, Elder Reuben Hedlock was chosen President of the Elders' quorum, in place of Elder Beaman, deceased.

Reuben Hedlock Chosen President of Elders.

November 30.—Daniel S. Miles presented a complaint

against Roger Orton "for abusing Elder Brigham Young, and for a general course of unchristianlike conduct." The accused having been notified to appear and answer for his conduct, and having refused, the High Council decided that he be cut off, for showing contempt to the authorities of the Church.

Excommunication of Rodger Orton.

Far West, December 6th.—The High Council and Bishop and counselors appointed Elias Higbee, Simeon Carter, and Elisha H. Groves, a committee to consider the propriety of proposing to the Church to pay the High Council for their time while engaged in council. Bishop Partridge, John Corrill, and Isaac Morley were appointed a committee to report upon the subject of raising a revenue to defray the expenses of the Church.

A Question of Compensation

David Whitmer was appointed to sign Elders' licenses, as chairman of the Council, and W. W. Phelps, as clerk; and Frederick G. Williams, to sign licenses as chairman *pro tempore*, in the absence of President Whitmer; and John Whitmer, as clerk *pro tempore;* and Oliver Cowdery, recording clerk, standing clerk of the Council, and recorder of patriarchal blessings at Far West.

Various Appointments

The committee on pay for the Council reported:

It is our united opinion that the Presidency, High Council, Bishop and conselors, clerk of the council, Patriarch and agents of the Church, (also any others who may be employed in Church business), receive per day, each, one dollar and fifty cents.

[Signed]

SIMEON CARTER,
ELIAS HIGBEE,
ELISHA H. GROVES.

Bishop Partridge reported to the Council that he had paid six hundred dollars to the lawyers to carry on suits against the Jackson mob, and three hundred dollars costs in carrying on said suits for which he had involved himself, and was paying ten per cent interest on the same; and petitioned the Council for leave to liquidate the debt out of the properties consecrated

Bishop Partridge's Report

for the benefit of the Church, and charge the Church for the same. The Council granted the petition.

Voted that the recorder of licenses and patriarchal blessings receive, for each one hundred words, ten cents.

Council adjourned to December 7th.

Council assembled on the 7th, according to adjournment, and heard the report of their Committee on raising a revenue to pay the officers of the Church for their services, and after much discussion and adjournment from time to time, dismissed the subject as being anti-scriptural.

I returned to Kirtland on or about the 10th of December. During my absence in Missouri Warren Parrish, John F. Boynton, Luke S. Johnson, Joseph Coe, and some others united together for the overthrow of the Church. Soon after my return this dissenting band openly and publicly renounced the Church of Christ of Latter-day Saints and claimed themselves to be the old standard, calling themselves the Church of Christ, excluding the word "Saints," and set me at naught, and the whole Church, denouncing us as heretics, not considering that the Saints shall possess the kingdom according to the Prophet Daniel.

Apostasy in Kirtland.

The *Elders' Journal* No. 2 for November was the last paper printed at Kirtland. Our printing establishment was attached to satisfy an unjust judgment of the county court, and soon after the whole printing apparatus and office were burned to the ground.

Last Paper Printed in Kirtland.

The work began to spread in England with great rapidity. On the 12th of September Elder Goodson left Bedford for Preston, and about the 1st of October sailed for America, in company with Brother Snyder, taking with him two hundred Books of Mormon, which the Elders in vain tried to persuade him to leave. Branches were established in Eccleston, Wrightington, Heskin, Euxton Bath, Daubers Lane, Chorley, Whittle, Leyland Moss, Ribchester, Thornley, Clithero, Wadding-

The Work in England.

ton, Downham, and other places round about Preston, where the brethren hired the "Cock Pit," a large and convenient building for preaching, but, being disturbed by some Methodist priests, were obliged to have the house licensed by the civil courts, according to the statutes of the realm, which, with the aid of two constables who voluntarily proffered their services, restored peace and order. And on Christmas day, December 25th, Elders Kimball and Hyde, and Joseph Fielding (who had previously been ordained an Elder) assembled in the "Cock Pit" with about three hundred Saints, several of whom were ordained to the lesser Priesthood, fourteen were confirmed, and about one hundred children were blessed by the Elders. This was the first public conference of the Church in England, and at this conference the Word of Wisdom was first publicly taught in that country.

While the work was thus rapidly progressing in Lancashire it continued gradually to progress at Bedford, also a branch was established at Bassynburn, and another at Peter's Green, by Elder Richards. *Progress of the British Mission.*

On the morning of the 22nd of December, 1837, Brother Brigham Young left Kirtland in consequence of the fury of the mob spirit that prevailed in the apostates who had threatened to destroy *Flight of Brigham Young from Kirtland* him because he would proclaim publicly and privately that he knew by the power of the Holy Ghost that I was a Prophet of the Most High God, that I had not transgressed and fallen as the apostates declared.

Apostasy, persecution, confusion, and mobocracy strove hard to bear rule at Kirtland, and thus closed the year 1837. *Close of the Year 1837.*

END OF VOL. II.

INDEX TO VOLUME II.